Faces of Anthropology

Faces of Anthropology

A READER FOR THE 21ST CENTURY

Sixth Edition

Edited by

Kevin A. Rafferty, Ph.D.

Dorothy Chinwe Ukaegbu, Ph.D.

COLLEGE OF SOUTHERN NEVADA

Prentice Hall

Boston   Columbus   Indianapolis   New York   San Francisco   Upper Saddle River
Amsterdam   Cape Town   Dubai   London   Madrid   Milan   Munich   Paris   Montréal   Toronto
Delhi   Mexico City   São Paulo   Sydney   Hong Kong   Seoul   Singapore   Taipei   Tokyo

VP, Editorial Director: Craig Campanella
Editor in Chief: Dickson Musslewhite
Publisher: Nancy Roberts
Editorial Assistant: Nart Varoqua
Director of Marketing: Brandy Dawson
Senior Marketing Manager: Laura Lee Manley
Marketing Assistant: Pat Walsh
Managing Editor: Maureen Richardson
Project Manager: Renata Butera
Operations Specialist: Renata Butera
Creative Art Director: Jayne Conte
Cover Designer: Suzanne Duda
Cover Art: Archeologists—thumb/Sutterstock images; Chukchi man—Konstantin Shevtsov/Sutterstock images
Full-Service Project Management: Saraswathi Muralidhar/PreMediaGlobal
Composition: PreMediaGlobal
Printer/Binder: Edwards Brothers
Cover Printer: Lehigh-Phoenix/Hagerstown

Permission to use copyrighted material gratefully acknowledged with the relevant article.

Library of Congress Cataloging-in-Publication Data

Faces of anthropology : a reader for the 21st century / edited by Kevin A. Rafferty,
    Dorothy Chinwe Ukaegbu.—6th ed.
        p. cm.
    Includes bibliographical references.
    ISBN-13: 978-0-205-64532-9
    ISBN-10: 0-205-64532-1
1. Anthropology.   I. Rafferty, Kevin A.   II. Ukaegbu, Dorothy Chinwe,
GN316.F34 2010
301—dc22

                                                              2010028373
10 9 8 7 6 5 4 3 2 1

Prentice Hall
is an imprint of

www.pearsonhighered.com

ISBN 10:   0-205-64532-1
ISBN 13: 978-0-205-64532-9

In loving memory of my mother, Imelda C. Ukaegbu, who in my early years encouraged me to appreciate the natural sciences by teaching me daily at home after school, but supported my detour to the social sciences in later years. To my beloved father, Ishmael C. Ukaegbu, a wonderful father and caring statesman; your memory lives on in the hearts of Biafran children refugees at Ogwa during the war. And to the memory of my dear brother, Guy Onyewuchi O. Ukaegbu, my intellectual companion and ardent critic.

—Dorothy Chinwe Ukaegbu

To my wife, Rhonda, who gave me the greatest gifts of all, her love and faith in my abilities. To my children, Jessica, Melissa, and Matthew, and my grandson Kevin, for filling my life with connections and events that are much more important than work ever could be. Finally, to my students who over the years have challenged, perplexed, and inspired me. I hope that I have returned their gifts in kind.

—Kevin A. Rafferty

Contents

SECTION FOUR: Family, Marriage, and Kinship   149

SECTION FIVE: Realities of Gender   181

SECTION SIX: Politics: Who Gets What, When, and How   219

Preface

The mission of *Faces of Anthropology* is to capture the entire realm of anthropology as reflected in the title. The many faces of anthropology are the ways and methods by which the field has focused on the human condition and changing social and cultural phenomena. The articles featured in this reader run the gamut of concepts employed by anthropology since its inception.

Anthropology began its study of human beings by searching for human origins. Since then, anthropologists have explored human diversity and emerging theoretical approaches for the understanding of human behavior. From its early beginnings in the nineteenth century, anthropology has amassed a vast body of knowledge about distant and various kinds of societies around the globe, in the process illustrating the similarities and differences among the world's cultures.

The twenty-first century global society, with its unprecedented problems, has presented new challenges that have altered the face of anthropology. As a result, anthropology has sought new ways of tackling problems with new methodologies and theories, employing new modes of analysis while modifying old ones, seeking new theories, and reexamining old issues in the light of new realities. Hence, this reader contains articles from both the old and new scholarships of anthropology.

This edition organizes its topics into ten sections for a broad overview of the field of anthropology within the context of traditional and recent approaches to anthropological study. The topics are the subfields of anthropology; fieldwork; subsistence and economics; family, marriage, and kinship; gender; politics; religion; symbolic expression; globalization; and the use of anthropology in solving human problems. A collection of articles are compiled for each topic. Each article features a segment or several aspects of anthropological problematics. Collectively, the articles in each section represent the range of traditional and recent foci of anthropology.

Each section of this reader begins with the "State of the Art," an overview of the trends in the particular area of anthropology, followed by an introduction to each of the articles for that area of anthropology. The article introductions are then followed by a new section we call "For Further Research." This section points the student to additional resources they can access, linked to an online research engine developed by Pearson called *MySearchLab*. This is intended to assist students in writing research papers or delving more deeply into the topic covered by the reader articles.

This reader is intended to support main introductory texts in anthropology. We hope the reader will find the book's mission truly reflected in the articles presented.

WHAT'S NEW IN THIS EDITION

Introductory Material Substantial revisions have been made to most sections of the "State of the Art" to reflect some new ideas and concepts in the field. A synopsis of trends in the anthropological studies of topical areas that were not included in the 5th edition, are added to this edition. Section ten, "State of the Art" bears a subtitle, "Applied Anthropology in Focus"—a recapitulation of its history, the basis for ethical principles, and current utility. In each "About the Articles" section material discussing deleted articles has been removed and material reflecting the new articles has been added. An entirely new segment has been added to each section introduction, entitled "For Further Research." This section, linked to an online research engine developed by Pearson called *MySearchLab*, is intended to assist students in writing research papers or delving more deeply into the topic covered by the reader articles (see the following).

New and Deleted Articles Fifteen articles from the previous edition have been removed and eleven new articles have been added. One of the new articles is considered a "classic" in the field to give students some historical perspective. The other added articles deal with modern human issues that anthropology is at the forefront in examining. These include the cultural and political issues surrounding Tibet, modern patterns of inheritance, different patterns of marriage and family relationships, and the personal impact of globalization in different cultures.

MYSEARCHLAB

mysearchlab The most ubiquitous and familiar resource for students is the Internet. Unfortunately one can spend hours searching the Web and getting lost in a maze of information that is undirected and unfocused. The publisher of this reader, Pearson/Prentice Hall, has developed a focused way for anthropology students to do research. It is called *MySearchLab* and is designed to help students (and some of us faculty) to find resources in an efficient and a rapid manner. When you go to the Website (www.MySearchLab.com), you are presented with several options that at first may seem confusing. On the home page are two resources that are pertinent to anthropology students. The first is *EBSCO's Content Select* that allows you to research by key word in an anthropology journal database. For example, if you are looking for information on Neanderthals, when you type in the key word "Neanderthal," you will have access to seventy-nine articles that have the word *Neanderthal* in the body of the article. From there you can narrow down your search.

The second resource on the home page is *Google Scholar*. Like any search engine, it can be somewhat indiscriminate. Typing in "Neanderthal" yields 21,900 references. There is an advanced search function that allows you to narrow down the sea of data. This allows the student to look for material containing exact phrases, by specific authors, in specific publications, by dates, or in generalized academic fields.

At the top of the *MySearchLab* home page is a link called "Search." Clicking on this link brings students to several additional resources that they can employ. The first is the *EBSCO Content Select*. There are also several other links that I recommend. The first is a section entitled *Additional Resources* which explains how students can access information in other ways: through interviews with people, using the Internet, television, and radio, and even how to use an actual physical library. This is how research was conducted prior to the Internet, and these are still invaluable sources of information that can be tapped.

The second link is called *My Libraries*. Pertinent for you is *MyAnthroLibrary* which contains articles culled from other Pearson resources such as ethnographies, case studies, and original articles. If you have a generalized research topic, and wish to know more about the subject matter before delving into more research, this material can help clarify in your mind what you want to research. The material can be accessed by topic, subdiscipline, genre, geography, author, or title. It is a fine way to clear the fog of confusion and overcome the panicky feeling that many students have when embarking on their first research endeavors.

Changing Faces of Anthropology: The Subfields

STATE OF THE ART: THE SUBFIELDS

The traditional division of anthropology into four main subfields—physical anthropology, archaeology, linguistics, and cultural anthropology—has been changing. There has been an increased tendency toward further diversification within each subfield. Some anthropologists even recommend the designation of applied anthropology as a recognized "fifth subfield" (Baba 1994). This call for change does not require the elimination of the subfield categories. Rather it argues that the specializations, with the exception of applied anthropology, contradict the "holistic mission" of anthropology that they purport to represent, and therefore the call seeks more collaboration among them (Borofsky 2002, Caleagno 2003, G.E. Marcus & M. Pisarro 2008, Faudree 2009). To live up to its name—"the holistic discipline"—anthropological research is expected to contain more than one subdivisional perspective. The articles in Section One reflect the original, traditional classifications, and they deal with theoretical and substantive issues within each subfield. The all-encompassing "applied anthropology" occupies Section Ten.

Physical Anthropology

In the nineteenth century people were seeking scientific explanations for the origin of the species. Scientists were concerned with biological changes in human beings over time. Charles Darwin's theory of evolution in 1859 provided the answer for this question. Following Darwin, *paleoanthropology* (the study of the chronology, physical structure, archaeological remains, and habitats of early hominids through an interdisciplinary approach) was utilized as a means of explaining the processes of human evolution. Shifts in emphasis led to the more detailed study of biology as scientists made advances in the field of physical anthropology. Skin color and physical variations constituted a source of interest in the human evolutionary spiral, as a way to identify the evolutionary factors that affect adaptation. Scientists thus looked at human genetics as an indispensable part of physical anthropology. They wanted to understand how the evolutionary spiral impacted patterns of hereditary traits as well as evolutionary distances between nonhuman primates. This led to the interest in *primatology*—the study of nonhuman primates—and thus to the examination of primate fossils. *Primate paleontology*—a branch of primatology that studies the fossil record of all primates, both human and nonhuman—focuses on the relationship between hominids (early humans) and the other primates such as monkeys and apes (Jurmain, Kilgore, Trevathan, & Nelson 2003; Haviland 2002).

Osteology, the study of skeletal remains, is another area of study that grew out of the study of evolution. Stature and growth patterns in the fossil population were seen as necessary to an understanding of primate evolution. *Paleopathology* is a branch of osteology that looks at such things as skeletal trauma and nutritional deficiencies and diseases of a particular population as a way to understand evolutionary patterns. *Anatomical studies* (the study of bone and dental structures) have expanded as a

1

result of a new ability to understand the linkage of limbs and skeletal tissue (Jurmain, Kilgore, Trevathan, & Nelson 2003). Osteology thus led to the rise of forensic anthropology.

Physical anthropology has a wide area of applied study in which information on human remains is made relevant to contemporary concerns or used to solve current problems. *Forensic anthropology* is a good example of that. It is used to identify victims of crimes such as murder or, in the international realm, victims of mass murder or genocide. The applied focus of anthropology penetrates into many medical and biological fields. For example, even conservation initiatives to protect seriously endangered species, thereby ensuring their survival, have benefited from the work of physical anthropologists.

Physical anthropology employs the scientific method, which involves problem identification, formulation of hypotheses, data collection and the testing of hypotheses, and theory formation (Jurmain, Kilgore, Trevathan, & Nelson 2003). The goal of physical anthropology, in conjunction with the general goal of anthropology, is to foster a better understanding of nonhuman primates as a means of understanding the behavior of contemporary human beings.

The theory of evolution continues to dominate physical anthropology as it focuses on various life forms, including modern ones. Current application of evolutionary theory continues to emphasize the indispensable role of natural selection in evolutionary change. However, contemporary theoretical arguments emphasize theories of *human evolutionary replacement,* with three main areas of debate. The first area of debate is the *out-of-Africa hypothesis* whereby human beings first migrated from Africa to other parts of the world. The second is the *multiregional argument* whereby human beings originated in several different places at the same time. The third argument is the *gene flow replacement model,* a combination of the previous two, which theorizes that human beings interbred in several different places (Jurmain, Kilgore, Trevathan, & Nelson 2003). *Punctuated equilibrium,* the view advanced by paleontologist Stephen Jay Gould, assumes that evolution can happen rapidly due to environmental factors. According to Jolly (2009), studies of human evolution in the past fifty years have resulted in more questions being asked of the "process" itself—the nature of the hominin (previously called hominid) pathway to modern humanity. Among the questions asked are: Is there a single phase of development or sequence of phases? Are there "shifts" in the direction of phases that resulted in different hominin lineages or branches that pursued their own line of evolution? Also, the exact identity of specimens as to which hominin lineage to assign them (taxonomy) has remained a puzzle. Awaiting definite assignment are "the trio of candidates"—Orrorrin, Sahelanthropos and the latest find, ardipithecus. Harvati, Frost & McNutty (2004) reconsidered neanderthal taxonomy and supported the theory that they are an extinct human specie, quite distinct in fact, and played no significant role in the evolution of modern humans. Regarding neanderthal origins debate, Hublin (2009) notes that fossil records reveal a migratory group of hominins of African origin (possibly neanderthals) who resettled in Western Eurasia, and brought the Acheulian technology. Hublin's view supports the "out of Africa hypothesis."

Archaeology

Archaeology began by using the material remains of past life to answer questions about the past. The goal of reconstructing the past has continued to characterize archaeology, although the field has expanded to include modern-day issues and their link to the past. The focus is not just on the archaeology of the "dead" but of the "living" as well. For example, in Iraq, archaeologists are exuming remains of 300,000 people discovered in mass graves of those executed during the reign of Sadam Hussein. They also played a major role in examining the debris of the World Trade Center identifying victims of terrorism (disaster archaeology). On a larger scale, archaeologists are dealing with modern social issues that were previously the concerns of cultural anthropology and other social sciences. There is a new interest in landfills and whatever data they may contain that would shed light on the activities of the present. Excavation has been the primary mode of archaeology since its inception, although numerous techniques and approaches have appeared and contributed to a more accurate description of the past. For example, archaeologists have come up with a range of dating techniques, the most popular being tree-ring dating, radio carbon dating, and thermoluminescence dating (Thomas 1999), Argon-Argon dating, pipestem dating, mean ceramic dates, trapped charge dating, and a host of others increasing annually (Kelly & Thomas 2010).

In their goal of reclaiming the past, archaeologists sought to reconstruct past lifeways in various aspects of human behavior, such as kinship, religion, art, technology, economy, ritual, settlement patterns, organization of domestic life, and population density. This has been the domain of *descriptive archaeology*. In contrast, *processual archaeology* was the method used in seeking answers to modern social issues, employing the scientific method to make broad generalizations of the human past, and in seeking to understand the evolution of modern society. The processual agenda embraces ecological, scientific, and evolutionary approaches in the study of archaeology. Thus, processual archaeology has served as an alternative to the descriptive mode of study which was in vogue in the 1950s. Processual archaeology sees culture from an outsider point of view and examines culture in a systematic way.

The changing world scene, including the demise of colonialism and the modern postwar eras, paved the way for a critique of the processual approach and the rise of postmodernism—a new way of thinking about archaeology. Postmodernism is a series of approaches that disregard the scientific method and allow for a more disconnected series of results by rejecting the causal viewpoints that are central to the scientific method. Postmodernism's central concerns have come to dominate some areas of archaeology, including such topics as power, ideology, gender, text, structure of community, discourse, structure, history, and the individual's role in society.

Many archaeologists still subscribe to the processual agenda. Contemporary Americanist archaeologists seek a middle ground that combines processual and postprocessual approaches. Today, archaeology is beginning to emphasize the delicate relationship between archaeologists and the people under study—the living descendants who extend a watchful eye over the study of their ancient past.

New areas of archaeology have emerged and continue to widen the scope of the field. Cognitive archaeology, for example, is concerned with the development of human consciousness, religion and ritual, symbolism, and iconography. Feminist archaeology is changing our perception of gender in the past. Applied anthropology is emphasizing the role of the archaeologist in managing resources of culture and heritage. Under the umbrella of applied anthropology, conservation archaeology is preserving antiquities and other remains from the remote and less-remote past. Other new developments include doing archaeology at the molecular level and analysis of ancient DNA from fossil remains to reconstruct human diets. Grassroots archeology focuses on local initiatives with an emphasis on working as partners with communities with the goal of uncovering their past. An example is the Kodiak area native association bingo funds to help students with research (Kelly & Thomas 2010). Archaeology is increasingly employing sophisticated technologies to locate sites, determine their content, and articulate sites without disturbing them (Thomas 1999). Presently archaeologists are rediscovering the utility of ancient technologies that are no longer in use, harnessing them to serve the needs of modern populations.

Linguistics

The search for human origins includes the search for language origins. Unlike earlier linguists who started out with written languages, anthropological linguists began by giving attention in their fieldwork to non-written languages. These non-written languages included archaic languages, knowledge of which must be gained through historical reconstructions of past cultures. This meant a partnership with other branches of anthropology, especially physical anthropology, in the search for human origins and evolutionary processes. The anthropological linguist was interested in how language evolved through evolutionary changes from nonhuman primates to human primates. This led to a greater interest in the biology of language, how the vocal tract, the brain and the pharynx, the tongue, oral cavity, windpipe, and other parts of the human body lead to speech. To understand the origin of the languages, anthropological linguists had to explore these parts of the body.

The search for the origin of language revealed a basic difference in communication between nonhuman primates and human beings. The features of productivity, displacement, traditional transmission, and duality of patterning are identified as uniquely human as is the ability for speech.

Productivity is the ability to formulate new messages. *Displacement* is the ability to refer to something that is not present. *Traditional transmission* is what links language with culture in the sense that language is something taught and learned and is transmitted from one generation to the next as part of tradition. *Duality of patterning* is the ability of languages to discriminate from few stimuli to a broader pattern of stimuli; that is, when a number of meaningless sounds can be combined in regularly patterned ways to produce a large number of meaningful phrases (Hickerson 2000, pp. 33–35). Non-human primates lack these attributes.

As linguistic anthropology developed, linguistic anthropologists continued to emphasize the biological denominators of language, as well as gestures, signs, cultural symbols, and the relationship between language and culture. They began to look for more detailed answers regarding language change—changes in words and sentences, and how changes in ideas translate into language change—by comparing modern, recent, and archaic languages. This comparative approach inevitably revealed universal features present in all known languages, including those of the past. Later on, as linguists looked for new ways of studying language, attention was given to language acquisition and socialization; how infants learn language in their cultural settings became a focus of study. In addition, linguists focused on the descriptive study of languages, consisting of *phonology*, the study of the sound system of a language; *morphology*, the structure of words; *syntax*, the rules governing the structure of sentences; and *grammar*, the complete description of all aspects of language. These were found to be universal among all languages.

Linguistic study has sought relationships between language and history with emphasis on language families. This has led to the identification of ancient (proto) and modern languages of Indo-European origins, uncovering proto-Algonqian roots (a Native American stock) and to an understanding of the spread of Bantu languages (an African stock). Some linguists prefer to focus on an in-depth exploration of the nature of the relationship between language and culture—the effects of cultural ideologies and worldviews in the use of language—and on linguistic change. In this context they focus on *metaphoric language* and the *production of added meaning*. They also study *language taxonomies*—how language is used to classify things in the world (ethnosemantics)—and the *kinship terms* used by language groups. Linguistic anthropologists also study the relationship between language and cognition—how different people use language to organize their experiences (Hickerson 2000; Rosman & Rubel 2004).

How other aspects of culture affect language is also an anthropological linguistic concern. A major branch of linguistic study is *sociolinguistics*, the study of how the members of a culture and subculture speak in various social settings. The focus of this area of study has included the relationship between language and gender, exemplified in gender styles in speech; the origins of contact languages; dialects; the relationship between class and language use; ethnic ways of speaking; and the relationship between language and nationalism as ethnic groups demand a share of the national heritage (Hickerson 2000).

All of these features continue to dominate the field of linguistics, including ongoing research into language families, geography and language boundaries, the spread of the languages of the superpowers, especially since the advent of colonialism, and how these languages are linked to the power structures of the receiving society (Rosman & Rubel 2004). There is renewed interest in preserving the linguistic forms of indigenous languages that are facing extinction. The impact of globalization on contemporary life is an on-going study. General anthropological theories continue to be relevant in anthropological linguistic studies. Presently, "performance theory" (see Section Five), and concepts like "interdiscursivity" (the relationship a discourse has to other discourses, such as the meaning of an utterance to other utterances), and "intertextuality" (the meaning of a 'text' is shaped by that of another text, forged in a medium of mutual communication. A 'text' refers to a system of 'signs' that is inclusive of, rather than separate from verbal and written forms), are popular. In 2008, a number of "stylistic studies" that linked the concerns of social and cultural anthropology to the analysis of "semiotic processes" (human representational practices such as stories, linguistic signs, signals, symbols, gestures, expressions etc,) appeared. Racist speech, (the reproduction of racism through language), gender styles and class-based speech patterns, and the use of language ideologies to understand linguistic change are among the main foci of research (Faudree 2009). New techniques of fieldwork, such as those outlined in Section Two of this reader, are being employed by anthropological linguistic fieldworkers as well.

Cultural Anthropology

After cultural anthropology, a subdivision of anthropology, gave birth to linguistics and archaeology, the latter split off to become distinct subfields of their own. Since then cultural anthropology has expanded tremendously into all aspects of culture, including the context of culture itself, and theories of culture, fieldwork, and social and cultural institutions like the family, marriage, kinship, religion, political systems, economic systems and their subsistence patterns, symbolic systems, and other types of social institutions. Currently, cultural anthropologists are dealing with the new phenomenon of globalization, which defies strict geographic boundaries. The progress made in these topical areas constitutes the contents of this reader, introduced with a summary of the trends for each area. The trends, or "State of the Art," show how cultural anthropology has broadened and developed over the years.

Cultural anthropology would be nonexistent without fieldwork, because fieldwork informs most of the knowledge about the human condition. The changes made in fieldwork, summarized in Section Two, are part and parcel of the developments in cultural anthropology. In the development of cultural anthropology, theories were proposed with a view to how best to study culture. From physical anthropology, ideas of biological evolution were borrowed to create the idea of a *cultural evolution* in terms of stages of behavioral development from "primitive" to "civilized." Cultural evolution was criticized and replaced with an anti-evolutionary theory of *cultural relativism* (equal validity of all cultures). Evolutionism later reappeared as *neo-evolutionism*, looking at causes and factors that promote the process of cultural evolution. *Functionalism* came afterward, stressing concepts of "function" and "structure" with regard to how each component of structure operated or functioned. Other anthropologists stressed the importance of structure alone and encouraged the search for more cultural institutions in a society. *Structuralism*, an alternative culture theory of the French school, likens the elements of culture to the elements of language. It looks for the underlying structure of a culture in a similar relationship as exists in language. A subsequent development, *historical anthropology* traces the history of cultures and how they are affected by macro changes.

In the past four decades, cultural anthropology has made the jump to an *interpretive approach*, without abandoning those previous theoretical schools of thought (Ember & Ember 2004; Rosman & Rubel 2004). The interpretive approach views culture as a system of symbols whose meanings must be deciphered. This approach fits in with the period of *deconstruction*—a method of trying to understand how meaning is constructed by ethnographers writing about the people they study, about the explicit and implicit meanings that a text contains, and about how readers read meaning into texts. Deconstruction led to disarray in anthropology, with multiple perspectives springing up in all directions and paving the way for the postmodernist critique and reexamination of anthropological methods. The *postmodernist perspective* has forced the field of anthropology to question sources and methods of constructing anthropological knowledge and to reexamine the nature of fieldwork. These developments are discussed in Section Two of this reader.

Cultural anthropology has journeyed through this developmental terrain and grappled with the issues of *writing culture* in the form of ethnography (Clifford & Marcus 1986), overhauling old ways of writing ethnography that seemed to distance the ethnographer from the text and removed from the text the voices of the people studied. More recent developments have attempted to reconcile postmodernist techniques in conducting ethnographic research and traditional ethnographic methods of data collection in anthropology (Aunger 1995; Roscoe 1995). Positivism contends that the only admissible form of knowledge is that derived from our sensory perceptions—observation or experience. The proposed reconciliation sought a marriage between *positivism/objectivism* (impersonal research involving the suppression of one's feelings and thoughts while focusing on external reality) and *subjectivism* (the product of the researchers' backgrounds, feelings, and thoughts). According to McGee and Warms (2004, pp. 609, 610) postmodernism of the 1980s and 1990s sought to "dissolve the distinction between the objective and subjective" by arguing that "objectivity is impossible to achieve because ethnographic writing reflects the background of the author." Thus "all observations are necessarily subjective."

Postmodernist critics such as Roy D'Andrade (1995) see no reconciliation between objectivism and subjectivism. He opposed post modernism on the grounds that "subjective judgments have an objective foundation that can be exposed to empirical examination." He reduced objectivity to "the degree to which an account gives information about the object being described" (McGee & Warms 2004, pp. 610, 611). Contrary to this definition is the idea that *matters of degree* are often controlled by the subjective. From D'Andrade's standpoint, anthropological research should either derive from objectivism or from a "moral model"—a concern with what is good or bad about the manner of conducting research and with the research itself, and who was at fault if something went wrong.

Postmodernists continue to put pressure on cultural anthropologists/ethnographers to yield to the "subtle forms of power and authority which are inherent in knowledge" (Lewellen 2003). Ethnographers must consider power in all its forms and sources, as power exists in both local (native's) knowledge and the ethnographer's knowledge, so long as it has impact on the doing of fieldwork and on the people under study. The crux is power sharing at all levels.

Nonetheless, traditional anthropology is not dead. Many cultural anthropologists prefer to study bounded cultures, while the nontraditionalists prefer to leave them open and admit external factors from a global perspective that impact on the group under study. This presents an increasing demand on the type of analysis that cultural anthropologists have to apply in research—analysis that must take into account the multiple forms of power that bear on the subject of research.

In the twenty-first century, cultural anthropologists will continue to look for culture in large and small things, in big and small places outside traditional settings, but traditional settings—among this or that cultural group—will always be the mainstay of cultural anthropology.

ABOUT THE ARTICLES

Both the Kunzig and Diamond articles examine hot-button issues facing the field of physical anthropology. Kunzig discusses the excavation of a burial of a four-year-old, seemingly endowed with physical features of both Neanderthals and anatomically modern human beings. This burial highlights a major controversy in human evolution. Were Neanderthals evolutionary "dead ends" and thus not direct ancestors of modern human beings, or were they sufficiently genetically similar to modern human beings to both interbreed with them and perhaps serve as our direct ancestors? Diamond's article deals with an evolutionary issue fraught with social and political significance in the present: What does the term *race* actually mean? His article demonstrates the falseness of our modern vernacular view of race as being a real category by showing the various ways "races" can be defined using criteria other than the traditional categories of skin color and body morphology.

The field of archaeology is represented by articles that present two levels of archaeological research and interpretation. Site-specific work is dealt with in Kennedy's article on excavations in Honolulu. He notes how data from a specific location can be used to elucidate larger regional issues of prehistoric human occupation and adaptation in the Hawaiian Islands. Mann's article deals with regional issues and controversies that drive and inform modern political and social thought and behavior. Incorporating data from throughout the Americas, Mann deals with several broad issues. One issue is the impact of European diseases on proto-historic Native American populations and its influence on the European colonization of the Americas. A second deals with the modern environmental movement and its view that the Americas were once "pristine" continents uncorrupted by cultures that lived in harmony with nature. Mann presents evidence that much of the environment of the Americas first encountered by Europeans was actually engineered over millennia by Native Americans, especially the grasslands of the North American Great Plains and the Amazonian rain forest. If this evidence is accurate, what does it mean to our current environmental ideas?

The linguistics subfield is represented by an article that deals with issues of linguistic loss and cultural survival. Smith discusses the concept of linguistic change and cultural loss from the viewpoint of Arabic speakers in the Turkish province of Hatay. At issue is an important question: How are language use and cultural identity linked?

The last subfield, cultural anthropology, is ably represented by the final articles in the section. The Kluckhohn article discusses the central concept of anthropology, *culture*. He explains what culture is, how it is different from but still affected by biological imperatives, and how it serves as a "map" created by individuals and groups. Aran discusses the *idea* of Tibet as it has evolved in the twentieth century. It is an illuminating and cautionary example about how the reality of a culture can be obscured by an idealized version promulgated by the political and cultural elite of a nation. Students may want to ask themselves how the idealized version of their own culture taught to them by schools and the media differs from the reality around them. The results are enlightening and represent cultural anthropological research at its best.

References

Aunger, R. "Ethnography: Storytelling or Science?" *Current Anthropology* 36, no. 1 (1995): 97–127.

Baba, M. L., "The Fifth Subdiscipline: Anthropological Practice and the Future of Anthropology,"*Human Organization* 53 (1994): 173–185.

Borofsky, R., "The Four Subfields: Anthropologists as Mythmakers," *American Anthropologist* 104, no. 2 (2002): 463–480.

Caleagno, J. "Keeping Biological Anthropology in Anthropology and Anthropology in Biology," *American Anthropologist* 105, no. 1 (2003): 6–15.

Clifford, J., & Marcus, G. E. *Writing Culture: The Poetics & Politics of Ethnography*, Berkeley: University of California Press, 1986.

D'Andrade, R., "Moral Models in Anthropology," in *Anthropological Theory: An Introductory History*, 3rd ed., McGee, John R. & Richard L. Warms, eds., pp. 609–626. New York, McGraw-Hill, 2004.

Ember, C., & Ember, M. *Cultural Anthropology*, 11th ed. Upper Saddle River, NJ: Pearson/Prentice Hall, 2004.

Faudree, P. "Linguistic Anthropology in 2008: An Election-Cycle Guide," *American Anthropologist*, 111, no. 2 (2009): 153–161.

Harvati, K., Frost, S., McNutty, K. P. *"Neanderthal Taxonomy Reconsidered: Implications of 3D Primate Models of Intra- and Interspecific Differences."* PNAS 1, no. 5 (2004): 1147–1152.

Haviland, W. *Cultural Anthropology*, 10th ed. Belmont, CA: Wadsworth, 2002.

Hublin, J. J. *"The Origins of Neanderthals,"* PNAS 106, no. 38 (2009): 16022–16027.

Hickerson, N. P. *Linguistic Anthropology,* 2nd ed. Belmont, CA: Thomson/Wadsworth, 2000.

Jurmain, R., Kilgore, L., Trevathan, W., & Nelson, H. *Introduction to Physical Anthropology,* 9th ed. Belmont, CA: Thomson/Wadsworth, 2003.

Kelly, R., & Thomas, D.H. Archaeology, 5th ed. Belmont, CA: Cengage Learning, 2010.

Lewellen, T. C. *Political Anthropology: An Introduction.* 3rd ed. Westport, CT: Praeger, 2003.

Marcus, G. E., & Pisarro, M. "The End(s) of Ethnography: Social/Cultural Anthropology's Signature Form of Producing Knowledge in Transition." *Cultural Anthropology* 23, no. 1 (Feb., 2008): 1–14.

McGee, J. R., & Warms, R. L. *Anthropological Theory: An Introductory History*, 3rd ed. New York: McGraw-Hill, 2004.

Roscoe, P. B. "The Perils of 'Positivism' in Cultural Anthropology." *American Anthropologist* 97, no. 3 (1995): 492–504.

Rosman, A., & Rubel, P. *The Tapestry of Culture: An Introduction to Cultural Anthropology*, 8th ed. New York: McGraw-Hill, 2004.

Thomas, D. H. *Archeology: Down to Earth,* 2nd ed. New York: Harcourt Brace, 1999.

For Further Research

For additional information on researching the topics discussed in the "State of the Art" section, please visit www.mysearchlab. com. In addition the following references should prove useful. These suggestions are not meant to be exhaustive but are designed to provide avenues that will assist the student in acquiring further information.

For cultural anthropology, there are two journals, among many, that are generally considered to be the venues for cutting-edge research. One is *American Anthropologist*. The other is *Current Anthropology*, featuring short commentaries on published articles that illuminate different sides of a research topic or theoretical issue. A good textbook is *Anthropology: The Human Challenge* (12th edition) by Haviland, Prins, Walrath, and McBride (2007, Wadsworth Publishing). For insight into the anthropological perspective, there is *Thinking Anthropologically: A Practical Guide for Students* by Salzman and Rice (2004, Pearson/Prentice Hall).

In archaeology, *American Antiquity* is a primary refereed journal. Another is the *Journal of Archaeological Science* which deals with scientific advances in the field. A good solid overview textbook is *In the Beginning* (12th edition) by Fagan and Corso (2009, Prentice Hall).

Three very solid journals can be recommended for biological/physical anthropology: *The Journal of Human Evolution*, *American Journal of Physical Anthropology*, and *Evolutionary Anthropology*. There are also many good textbooks on the subject. The one that is used extensively at our college is *Biological Anthropology: The Natural History of Mankind* (2nd edition) by Stanford, Allen, and Anton (2009, Pearson/Prentice Hall).

For anthropological linguistics journals, two of the best include the *Journal of Linguistic Anthropology* and *Anthropological Linguistics*. Two texts that the student will find useful are *Linguistics for Non-Linguists: A Primer with Exercises* by Frank and Riley (2000, Allyn & Bacon) and *Linguistic Anthropology* (2nd edition) by Parrott (2000, Thomson/Wadsworth).

Learning to Love Neanderthals

Robert Kunzig

What you want, when you hold a pendant fashioned 35,000 years ago by a Neanderthal—a fox's tooth with a tiny hole for a leather string—what you want is something only the movies can give. A close-up, in the lab's neon light, on the mottled canine between your fingers, the focus so tight you can see the scratches made by the stone tool. The picture fades, and next you see the same tooth in different hands, stronger ones with beefy fingers: the hands of the craftsman. He is piercing the tooth with a sharpened piece of flint. Behind him squats a rough tent of hides stretched over mammoth tusks; behind that the dark mouth of a cave. Before and below him a river meanders lazily between birches and willows. Reindeer graze on the far bank. On an early morning in spring, in northern Burgundy during the Ice Age, the light coming in low over the far bluff catches the craftsman's pale, weathered face. It is a human face. The eyes, under the jutting brow, are human eyes, alive with concentration, with memories of other seasons at this place, with intelligence and hope.

No, hold it: Maybe those Neanderthal eyes are blank as a cat's, all surface, with nothing behind them but dumb instinct and a bit of animal cunning—no memories, no plan, no clue.

Back to spring 1999 and the lab, at a modern campus of the University of Paris. An archeologist named Dominique Baffier holds the tooth. For the past few days newspapers the world over have been reporting the discovery in Portugal of the skeleton of a 4-year-old child, dead for 25,000 years. The discoverers, led by Portuguese archeologist João Zilhão, are making a groundbreaking claim, that the skeleton shows traces of both Neanderthal and modern human ancestry, evidence that modern humans did not simply extinguish the Neanderthals, as many researchers had come to think. Instead the two kinds of human were so alike that in Portugal, at least, they intermingled—and made love—for thousands of years.

The claim is controversial. So, too, and for similar reasons, is the fox tooth Baffier is holding. A collection of such ornaments is arrayed on the table in front of her, along with delicate bone tools—awls for punching through animal hides, needles for sewing or perhaps for pinning up hair. All these artifacts were dug from the mouth of a limestone cave four decades ago at Arcy-sur-Cure, a hundred miles southeast of Paris. Just in the past year, though, the Arcy artifacts have become the subject of heated debate. Zilhão, Baffier, and several French colleagues claim the artifacts show that Neanderthals were not inferior to our ancestors, the Cro-Magnons. Independently, they underwent the same leap into modernity, the same emergence of symbolic thought that millennia later allowed Cro-Magnons to paint on cave walls.

A fox-tooth pendant is not a cave painting, as Baffier well knows, for she studies those paintings too. But it is a symbolic statement. "Oh, it's beautiful," she says quietly, turning the Neanderthal pendant in her fingers, peering at it over her glasses. "It's beautiful and it's moving. A 35,000-year-old bijou—isn't that moving?"

João Zilhão, director of the Portuguese Institute of Archeology, got the call from his wife and fellow archeologist, Cristina Araújo, while he was at a conference in Japan. She had heard from João Maurício and Pedro Souto, coworkers at a Neanderthal cave site. They had heard from a student named Pedro Ferreira, who had gone looking for rock art in the Lapedo Valley, about 90 miles north of Lisbon, and had found some small paintings.

Source: Reprinted from *Discover*, November 1994, with permission of the author.

Last November 28, Maurício and Souto went to the Lapedo Valley—which is really a small, steep ravine, a bit over a mile long and a stone's-throw wide. Olive groves and wildflowers, vegetable fields and villages sprawl up to the lip of the canyon, but its cool, lush depths are a world apart. The small stream at the bottom, the Caranguejeira, is hidden by reeds and bushes; the canyon walls themselves are practically hidden by a riot of diverse greenery.

Ferreira showed Maurício and Souto his rock art, and they confirmed that it looked man-made and old (Copper Age, it turned out). Then they looked across the ravine to the south side. Above the treetops they could see a limestone wall leaning out over the canyon. Prehistoric humans liked to take shelter under overhanging rocks like that. Maurício and Souto decided to have a look.

They found a mess, construction debris strewn along the base of the cliff, including an abandoned trailer, an old tractor hood, and a giant section of concrete drainpipe. In a fissure in the wall, just above eye level, Maurício and Souto saw sediments laced with stone tools, lots of animal bones, and black flecks of charcoal—the remains of Paleolithic campfires. But all along the wall they could also see the white gouge marks left by the teeth of a steam shovel. To build a road, the owner of the area had created a flat terrace where before there had been a tall slope of sediment—sediment that had washed off the top of the cliff and collected at the base over tens of millennia. He had used a stream shovel to dig the dirt from the cliff.

In retrospect the demolition man did archeology a big favor. Otherwise, what is now the base of the cliff at Lapedo would still be buried. Maurício saw a rabbit burrow disappearing under the rock. He reached his hand in and pulled out a radius and an ulna—the bones of a human forearm, though he wasn't sure of that at the time.

When the news reached Zilhão, he called Cidália Duarte, a physical anthropologist at the Portuguese Institute of Architectural Heritage. They and Araújo went up to Lapedo the next weekend. While Zilhão examined the stone tools embedded in the cliff face seven feet up. Maurício took the bone lady to the bones in the burrow. "I looked at them," Duarte recalls, "and I said,

'Ooh—this is human! This is a kid!'" Meanwhile, Zilhão was looking at the stratigraphic sequence. He began to add it up: "If the kid is down there, and this up here is Solutrean ..."

Solutrean is the third of four successive cultures—Aurignacian, Gravetian, Solutrean, Magdalenian—of the Upper Paleolithic or Late Stone Age. The Solutrean happened around 20,000 years ago. If the Lapedo Valley kid was seven feet below Solutrean sediments, that suggested he died thousands of years before the Solutrean. Zilhão looked at the bones: They were stained reddish with ochre. Red ochre is one of the things Upper Paleolithic moderns painted caves with, but they also buried their dead with it; the color seems to have had symbolic significance.

"So I immediately recognized that something big was there," says Zilhão. "The question was whether the bulldozing had completely destroyed the burial, and all we had to do was collect the fragments, or if something was still there intact."

The next day, Monday, they went back to their day jobs in Lisbon. The following Friday evening they were back at Lapedo, with Duarte and Araújo digging. "By Sunday evening we were really upset, because all we could find were bits and pieces, fragments of bone, and they didn't even have this reddish color," Duarte recalls. With night falling and spirits crumbling, they started tidying up the dig. Those final offhand brushstrokes did it: The red began to appear. Soon, as Araújo and Duarte gently swept away more dirt, they saw a patch of sediment as red as wine and as large as ... a small child.

Now they faced a paleontological emergency: The skeleton was almost at the surface, exposed to the elements, which in this case included Boy Scouts. A troop had walked by during the weekend and regarded the diggers with ominous curiosity. That week Durate signed up for an unscheduled vacation. Zilhão quietly abandoned his airy director's office and his paperwork at the archeological institute. "I just went away without telling anybody," he says, "so as not to run the risk of a leak."

They started digging in earnest. Right away they realized how lucky they had been: In removing tens of feet of dirt, the steam shovel had missed by just a few inches the body of the child. Unfortunately it had not missed the skull—Duarte could only find fragments of that. One of the first, though, was a beauty: the left half of the lower jaw, including teeth. It had a sharply pointed chin, which is just what you would expect from a Cro-Magnon; Neanderthals had weak chins.

The child was lying on its back, with its head and torso tilted a bit to its left, toward the cliff, and its right hand on its pelvis. Its right side was crushed, but the left side was intact. Ribs, vertebrae, pelvis, fingers, toes, the long bones of the arms and legs—all were there. Duarte and Araújo worked steadily through the Christmas holidays, hiding their work every night under the old tractor hood. Soon they had a new problem: up to 500 visitors a day. Zilhão's desire to keep the excavation secret had run into his desire to have it documented. He had asked Portuguese public television to videotape it, which the TV folk were happy to do—provided they could also run the story. On Christmas Day it opened the evening news: "A Child is Born."

On Christmas Day itself, Duarte was at the site alone. "I wasn't going to leave it there all exposed," she says. The work that day, on the rib cage, was particularly delicate. She was digging with a syringe, squirting acetone around the bones to dissolve the dirt—acetone evaporates quickly, so it doesn't soak the bone—and then removing it with a paintbrush and a plastic spoon. She was squatting, kneeling, and sometimes lying on her side next to the Kid. Earlier, near the clavicle, she had found a tiny seashell, covered with red ochre, with a minute hole. The Kid had worn it as a pendant.

At first Zilhão and Duarte guessed they had excavated a boy. The arms and legs looked robust. But then Erik Trinkaus, a paleoanthropologist at Washington University in St. Louis, had a look at them. He decided the Kid was robust not because he was male, but because he had Neanderthal blood.

Trinkaus is a leading authority on both Neanderthal and early modern human anatomy. When the excavation started, Zilhão let him know right away. "João went out and got a digital camera and started e-mailing me images," Trinkaus says. He got excited too: While Upper

Paleolithic skeletons in general are rare, there are no reasonably complete children's skeletons at all. Right after New Year's, while Duarte was still excavating, Trinkaus hopped a plane to Portugal.

He measured all the bones he could, especially the limbs—his specialty. In 1981, Trinkaus published a paper on limb evolution that is still cited. In it he documented a geographic pattern in people today: They get shorter the farther they are from the tropics and the closer they are to the poles. More precisely, their extremities get shorter. Inuits and Lapps have shorter forearms relative to their upper arms and shorter shinbones relative to their thighbones than do the Masai of East Africa. There is a simple explanation: Shorter, stockier bodies fare better in cold climates because they have less surface area to radiate heat. By measuring fossil limbs, Trinkaus showed that Neanderthals, denizens of Ice Age Europe, were hyperarctic—they had an even smaller shinbone-thighbone ratio than do Lapps. Early moderns from the Near East and Europe, on the other hand, were decidedly tropical in their legginess, like Africans today.

This was some of the earliest evidence for a theory of human origins that had not even been formulated then, but has since become orthodoxy. The out-of-Africa theory holds that humans today are descended from a small population of (long-legged) early moderns that walked out of Africa around 100,000 years ago. As they spread all over the world, they replaced whatever archaic humans they met, which in Europe were the Neanderthals. In this view, Neanderthals are a distinct population and maybe even a distinct species that went extinct at the hands of our ancestors, leaving no legacy at all.

Two years ago, when a team led by Svante Pääbo, now of the Max Planck Institute for Evolutionary Anthropology in Leipzig, isolated DNA from a Neanderthal bone, many people thought the case had been clinched. The Neanderthal DNA was different enough that there seemed to be no trace of it in modern DNA; it suggested that Neanderthal and modern humans had evolved separately for half a million years and were unlikely to have interbred. Trinkaus was not moved: "There's a general impression that if something comes out of a million-dollar machine, then it's truth, whereas if something comes out of a bunch of dirty old bones that we clean with paintbrushes, then it's vague and ambiguous."

Based on his analysis of dirty bones from the Czech Republic and Croatia, Trinkaus has long favored a sort of watered-down out of Africa, in which the gene pool of modern humans migrating into Europe was seasoned by interbreeding with Neanderthals. The amount of interbreeding would have varied from place to place. One place Trinkaus didn't expect to see much, though, was on the Iberian peninsula, the last refuge of the Neanderthals.

Cro-Magnons reached northern Spain nearly 40,000 years ago, but for some reason they didn't spread south for another 10,000 years. By the time they crossed the Ebro frontier, as Zilhão has dubbed it after the large river in northern Spain, their kind had already executed striking cave paintings. South of the Ebro they encountered Neanderthals who were still making stone tools in the Middle Paleolithic fashion and not making ornaments at all. The better-armed modern invaders would have been almost as tall as the Masai and maybe as black; the indigenes would have been short and as pale as Lapps. It would be easy to picture the former simply wiping out the latter. But it is from this clash of cultures and anatomies, Trinkaus argues, that the Kid was born.

The sharp point of the Kid's chin screamed Cro-Magnon. So did the relatively small front teeth: Neanderthal front teeth were large compared with their molars. So did the red ochre burial style. And so, finally, did the radiocarbon date: At 24,500 years old, it was much younger than the last signs of Neanderthals.

But when Trinkaus measured the angle between the horizontal tooth line and the vertical line from the frontmost tooth down to the chin, the symphyseal angle, he got a clue that this was a strange Cro-Magnon. Instead of jutting forward of the teeth, the chin retreated a shade behind them. Cro-Magnon chins didn't do that, Trinkaus says, but Neanderthal chins did.

Even more significant, he thinks, are the limb proportions. Trinkaus measured the shinbone and the thighbone and found that the ratio fell way over at the Neanderthal end of the curve. He compared the circumference of the bones with

their length, and found that the child had leg bones strong enough to support a stocky Neanderthal body. The limb proportions along with the receding chin are enough, Trinkaus says, to prove the child had Neanderthal ancestors as well as Cro-Magnon ones. "It only takes one feature," he says. "We've got two."

But many of his peers are skeptical. Arctic limb proportions don't prove a Neanderthal influence, some argue, since Lapps have them too; maybe the Kid was just an ordinary Cro-Magnon who had adapted to the Ice Age. And the mere fact that the skeleton is that of a child—whose features were still changing, and for whom no good Cro-Magnon comparisons exist—makes some researchers uneasy. "If an adult skeleton had been found, nice and complete, I'm sure we would still have fierce discussions," says Jean-Jacques Hublin of the French National Center for Scientific Research. "But interpreting the remains of a child, of which almost none of the skull is left—that's really a perilous exercise."

This summer, as the dig progresses, Duarte will be looking for more pieces of the child's skull. Finding its two front teeth would be nice (Neanderthals had big ones), or the occipital bone in the rear of the skull (it bulged out in Neanderthals), or even the tiny labyrinth of the inner ear. Hublin has used that feature, and that feature alone, to diagnose a Neanderthal bone at Arcy-sur-Cure.

Duarte also hopes to find the Kid's parents; Upper Paleolithic burials often come in groups. But Trinkaus does not expect she will find a Neanderthal mom and a Cro-Magnon dad. Zilhão's archeological evidence suggests the Kid was born at least two millennia after Neanderthals and Cro-Magnons first met in Portugal. The Kid, Trinkaus argues, must be the product of interbreeding over that entire period, not a one-time hybrid produced by star-crossed lovers. "This is not just two individuals who happened to meet in the bushes," he says.

There is likely to be fierce discussion about that conclusion too. The out-of-Africa model can readily tolerate a little hanky-panky between Neanderthals and Cro-Magnons. "In fact I expect it," says Hublin. A few hybrids would even disprove the view that Neanderthals were a different species. Animals of closely related species can sometimes interbreed, and sometimes the offspring are even fertile.

But if whole populations of Neanderthals and Cro-Magnons were blending, the notion that Neanderthals were replaced by immigrant moderns begins to lose meaning. To out-of-Africa proponents, such blending would conflict with the genetic and fossil evidence, and with the simple observation that people today look like Cro-Magnons and not like Neanderthals. To paleontologists who don't believe the out-of-Africa model, however—who think modern humans evolved all over the world from interbreeding populations of archaic humans including Neanderthals—Trinkaus's Lapedo kid is welcome news.

Trinkaus himself has never taken sides in this bitter debate. He sees it now moving onto his middle ground: A migration out of Africa happened, sure, but the migrants also interbred to varying degrees with the people they met along the way. Neanderthals are not us, but neither are they an evolutionary dead end—the Kid, if he is right, puts the truth in the middle. "Trinkaus is in the stratosphere," says Zilhão. "He has believed this for a long time. I couldn't care less— they could just as well be different species as far as I'm concerned. This just comes in handy."

It comes in handy as ammunition in a separate fight that is Zilhão's own. That debate concerns how smart Neanderthals were, and it is centered on the cave digs at Arcy. When French archeologists excavated there in the 1950s, they found dozens of animal-tooth pendants, bone tools, and 40 pounds of red ochre spread over the floor. At other sites, such artifacts have been attributed to modern humans. A few years ago, though, after Hublin CT-scanned a skull fragment found alongside the artifacts, and revealed the inner ear, he convinced most people that the bone was that of a Neanderthal, and so were the artifacts.

The conventional explanation is that the Neanderthal craftsmen at Arcy must have been imitating our ancestors. Modern humans were invading western Europe at around the time— 35,000 to 45,000 years ago—when the Neanderthals were at Arcy. And whereas the few dozen ornaments found there are practically the only ones attributed to Neanderthals, thousands have been found at Cro-Magnon sites. Many researchers say it is common sense to assume that Neanderthals were "acculturated" by Cro-Magnons. Some even argue that the Neanderthals didn't really understand what they were doing. They copied such modern behaviors as wearing pendants, but they couldn't appreciate the symbolic meaning.

Lurking under all this is the question of why we survived and the Neanderthals didn't: Was it because their brains were inferior? That idea drives Zilhão up the wall. "What's involved here is not the wiring of the brain cells, it's the wiring of the brains into what we call culture," he says. "Forty thousand years ago, people couldn't read or write—are we saying they didn't have the intelligence?"

In a controversial paper published last year with Francesco d'Errico of the University of Bordeaux, and Dominique Baffier, Michèle Julien, and Jacques Pelegrin of the University of Paris, Zilhão tried to show that the Neanderthals were intelligent enough to make the Arcy artifacts—and thus the transition to Upper Paleolithic modernity—all by themselves. The Arcy Neanderthals, the researchers argued, made their tools and ornaments using techniques quite unlike those of the moderns—punching a clean hole through a fox tooth, for instance, whereas modern humans did a cruder job of gouging. Zilhão and d'Errico also claim to have proved, through a technical reanalysis of the highly uncertain dates attributed to nearly every relevant site in western Europe, that the Neanderthals couldn't have imitated Cro-Magnons—because they were acting modern thousands of years before any Cro-Magnons were around.

The Lapedo Valley kid drops into the murky waters of this debate like a cannonball. Some researchers say it makes no difference at all if the Kid is a hybrid. But if Trinkaus and Zilhão can prove that modern humans and Neanderthals mixed extensively in Portugal, it would surely affect our view of Neanderthals—by giving us an inkling of the view our ancestors held. Would they really have fraternized with beings who were too dim to understand the purpose of a necklace?

"If you have two populations of huntergatherers that are totally different species, that are doing things in very different ways, have different capabilities—they're not going to blend together," Trinkaus says. "They're going to remain separate. So the implication from Portugal is that when these people met, they viewed each other as people. One group may have looked a little funny to the other one—but beyond that they saw each other as human beings. And treated each other as such."

CRITICAL THINKING QUESTIONS

1. Recent physical anthropological theory suggests that modern humans had at least a role in the extinction of the Neanderthals. What new theory do the bones of the four-year-old child excavated in Portugal suggest?

2. What problems did Zilhão and his team face during the excavation of the child?

3. What physical attributes did the child's skeleton exhibit to suggest he may have been a Neanderthal/modern human hybrid?

4. What evidence is being debated regarding the intellectual capacities of the Neanderthals? What significance does this debate have to understanding our own humanity?

Race without Color

Jared Diamond

Science often violates simple common sense. Our eyes tell us that the Earth is flat, that the sun revolves around the Earth, and that we humans are not animals. But we now ignore that evidence of our senses. We have learned that our planet is in fact round and revolves around the sun, and that humans are slightly modified chimpanzees. The reality of human races is another commonsense "truth" destined to follow the flat Earth into oblivion. The commonsense view of races goes somewhat as follows. All native Swedes differ from all native Nigerians in appearance: there is no Swede whom you would mistake for a Nigerian, and vice versa. Swedes have lighter skin than Nigerians do. They also generally have blond or light brown hair, while Nigerians have very dark hair. Nigerians usually have more tightly coiled hair than Swedes do, dark eyes as opposed to eyes that are blue or gray, and fuller lips and broader noses.

In addition, other Europeans look much more like Swedes than like Nigerians, while other peoples of sub-Saharan Africa—except perhaps the Khoisan peoples of southern Africa—look much more like Nigerians than like Swedes. Yes, skin color does get darker in Europe toward the Mediterranean, but it is still lighter than the skin of sub-Saharan Africans. In Europe, very dark or curly hair becomes more common outside Scandinavia, but European hair is still not as tightly coiled as in Africa. Since it's easy then to distinguish almost any native European from any native sub-Saharan African, we recognize Europeans and sub-Saharan Africans as distinct races, which we name for their skin colors: whites and blacks, respectively.

WHAT COULD BE MORE OBJECTIVE?

As it turns out, this seemingly unassailable reasoning is not objective. There are many different, equally valid procedures for defining races, and those different procedures yield very different classifications. One such procedure would group Italians and Greeks with most African blacks. It would classify Xhosas—the South African "black" group to which President Nelson Mandela belongs—with Swedes rather than Nigerians. Another equally valid procedure would place Swedes with Fulani (a Nigerian "black" group) and not with Italians, who would again be grouped with most other African blacks. Still another procedure would keep Swedes and Italians separate from all African blacks but would throw the Swedes and Italians into the same race as New Guineans and American Indians. Faced with such differing classifications, many anthropologists today conclude that one cannot recognize any human races at all.

If we were just arguing about races of nonhuman animals, essentially the same uncertainties of classification would arise. But the debates would remain polite and would never attract attention outside the halls of academia. Classification of humans is different "only" in that it shapes our views of other peoples, fosters our subconscious differentiation between "us" and "them," and is invoked to justify political and socioeconomic discrimination. On this basis, many anthropologists therefore argue that even if one *could* classify humans into races, one should not.

Source: Reprinted from *Discover*, August 1999, with permission of the author.

To understand how such uncertainties in classification arise, let's steer clear of humans for a moment and instead focus on warblers and lions, about which we can easily remain dispassionate. Biologists begin by classifying living creatures into species. A species is a group of populations whose individual members would, if given the opportunity, interbreed with individuals of other populations of that group. But they would not interbreed with individuals of other species that are similarly defined. Thus all human populations, no matter how different they look, belong to the same species because they do interbreed and have interbred whenever they have encountered each other. Gorillas and humans, however, belong to two different species because—to the best of our knowledge—they have never interbred despite their coexisting in close proximity for millions of years.

We know that different populations classified together in the human species are visibly different. The same proves true for most other animal and plant species as well, whenever biologists look carefully. For example, consider one of the most familiar species of bird in North America, the yellow-rumped warbler. Breeding males of eastern and western North America can be distinguished at a glance by their throat color: white in the east, yellow in the west. Hence they are classified into two different races, or subspecies (alternative words with identical meanings), termed the myrtle and Audubon races, respectively. The white-throated eastern birds differ from the yellow-throated western birds in other characteristics as well, such as in voice and habitat preference. But where the two races meet, in western Canada, white-throated birds do indeed interbreed with yellow-throated birds. That's why we consider myrtle warblers and Audubon warblers as races of the same species rather than different species.

Racial classification of these birds is easy. Throat color, voice, and habitat preference all vary geographically in yellow-rumped warblers, but the variation of those three traits is "concordant"—that is, voice differences or habitat differences lead to the same racial classification as differences in throat color because the same populations that differ in throat color also differ in voice and habitat.

Racial classification of many other species, though, presents problems of concordance. For instance, a Pacific island bird species called the golden whistler varies from one island to the next. Some populations consist of big birds, some of small birds; some have black-winged males, others green-winged males; some have yellow-breasted females, others gray-breasted females; many other characteristics vary as well. But, unfortunately for humans like me who study these birds, those characteristics don't vary concordantly. Islands with green-winged males can have either yellow-breasted or gray-breasted females, and green-winged males are big on some islands but small on other islands. As a result, if you classified golden whistlers into races based on single traits, you would get entirely different classifications depending on which trait you chose.

Classification of these birds also presents problems of "hierarchy." Some of the golden whistler races recognized by ornithologists are wildly different from all the other races, but some are very similar to one another. They can therefore be grouped into a hierarchy of distinctness. You start by establishing the most distinct population as a race separate from all other populations. You then separate the most distinct of the remaining populations, and separating distinct populations or groups of populations as races or groups of races. The problem is that the extent to which you continue the racial classification is arbitrary, and it's a decision about which taxonomists disagree passionately. Some taxonomists, the "splitters," like to recognize many different races, partly for the egotistical motive of getting credit for having named a race. Other taxonomists, the "lumpers," prefer to recognize few races. Which type of taxonomist you are is a matter of personal preference.

How does that variability of traits by which we classify races come about in the first place? Some traits vary because of natural selection: that is, one form of the trait is advantageous for survival in one area, another form in a different area. For example, northern hares and weasels develop white fur in the winter, but southern ones retain brown fur year-round. The white winter fur is selected in the north for camouflage against the snow, while any animal unfortunate enough to turn white in the snowless southern states would stand out from afar against the brown ground and would be picked off by predators.

Other traits vary geographically because of *sexual* selection, meaning that those traits serve as arbitrary signals by which individuals of one sex attract mates of the opposite sex while intimidating rivals. Adult male lions, for instance, have a mane, but lionesses and young males don't. The adult male's mane signals to lionesses that he is sexually mature, and signals to young male rivals that he is a dangerous and experienced adversary. The length and color of a lion's mane vary among populations, being shorter and blacker in Indian lions than in African lions. Indian lions and lionesses evidently find short black manes sexy or intimidating; African lions don't.

Finally, some geographically variable traits have *no* known effect on survival and are invisible to rivals and to prospective sex partners. They merely reflect mutations that happened to arise and spread in one area. They could equally well have arisen and spread elsewhere—they just didn't.

Nothing that I've said about geographic variation in animals is likely to get me branded a racist. We don't attribute higher IQ or social status to black-winged whistlers than to green-winged whistlers. But now let's consider geographic variation in humans. We'll start with invisible traits, about which it's easy to remain dispassionate.

Many geographically variable human traits evolved by natural selection to adapt humans to particular climates or environments—just as the winter color of a hare or weasel did. Good examples are the mutations that people in tropical parts of the Old World evolved to help them survive malaria, the leading infectious disease of the old-world tropics. One such mutation is the sickle-cell gene, so-called because the red blood cells of people with that mutation tend to assume a sickle shape. People bearing the gene are more resistant to malaria than people without it. Not surprisingly, the gene is absent from northern Europe, where malaria is nonexistent, but it's common in tropical Africa, where malaria is widespread. Up to 40 percent of Africans in such areas carry the sickle-cell gene. It's also common in the malaria-ridden Arabian Peninsula and southern India, and rare or absent in the southernmost parts of South Africa, among the Xhosas, who live mostly beyond the tropical geographic range of malaria.

The geographic range of human malaria is much wider than the range of the sickle-cell gene. As it happens, other antimalarial genes take over the protective function of the sickle-cell gene in malarial Southeast Asia and New Guinea and in Italy, Greece, and other warm parts of the Mediterranean basin. Thus human races, if defined by antimalarial genes, would be very different from human races as traditionally defined by traits such as skin color. As classified by antimalarial genes (or their absence), Swedes are grouped with Xhosas but not with Italians or Greeks. Most other peoples usually viewed as African blacks are grouped with Arabia's "whites" and are kept separate from the "black" Xhosas.

Antimalarial genes exemplify the many features of our body chemistry that vary geographically under the influence of natural selection. Another such feature is the enzyme lactase, which enables us to digest the milk sugar lactose. Infant humans, like infants of almost all other mammal species, possess lactase and drink milk. Until about 6,000 years ago most humans, like all other mammal species, lost the lactase enzyme on reaching the age of weaning. The obvious reason is that it was unnecessary—no human or other mammal drank milk as an adult. Beginning around 4000 B.C., however, fresh milk obtained from domestic mammals became a major food for adults of a few human populations. Natural selection caused individuals in these populations to retain lactase into adulthood. Among such peoples are northern and central Europeans, Arabians, north Indians, and several milk-drinking black African peoples, such as the Fulani of West Africa. Adult lactase is much less common in southern European populations and in most other African black populations, as well as in all populations of east Asians, aboriginal Australians, and American Indians.

Once again races defined by body chemistry don't match races defined by skin color. Swedes belong with Fulani in the "lactase-positive race," while most African "blacks," Japanese, and American Indians belong in the "lactase-negative race."

Not all the effects of natural selection are as invisible as lactase and sickle cells. Environmental pressures have also produced more noticeable differences among peoples, particularly in body shapes. Among the tallest and most long-limbed peoples in the world are the Nilotic peoples, such as the Dinkas, who live in the hot, dry area of East Africa. At the opposite extreme in body shape are the Inuit, or Eskimo, who have compact bodies and relatively short arms and legs. The reasons have to do with heat loss. The greater the surface area of a warm body, the more body heat that's lost, since heat loss is directly proportional to surface area. For people of a given weight, a long-limbed, tall shape maximizes surface area, while a compact, short-limbed shape minimizes it. Dinkas and Inuit have opposite problems of heat balance: the former usually need desperately to get rid of body heat, while the latter need desperately to conserve it. Thus natural selection molded their body shapes oppositely, based on their contrasting climates.

(In modern times, such considerations of body shape have become important to athletic performance as well as to heat loss. Tall basketball players, for example, have an obvious advantage over short ones, and slender, long-limbed tall players have an advantage over stout, short-limbed tall players. In the United States, it's a familiar observation that African Americans are disproportionately represented among professional basketball players. Of course, a contributing reason has to do with their lack of socioeconomic opportunities. But part of the reason probably has to do with the prevalent body shapes of some black African groups as well. However, this example also illustrates the dangers in facile racial stereotyping. One can't make the sweeping generalization that "whites can't jump," or that "black's anatomy makes them better basketball players." Only certain African peoples are notably tall and long-limbed; even those exceptional peoples are tall and long-limbed only on the average and vary individually.)

Other visible traits that vary geographically among humans evolved by means of sexual selection. We all know that we find some individuals of the opposite sex more attractive than other individuals. We also know that in sizing up sex appeal, we pay more attention to certain parts of a prospective sex partner's body than to other parts. Men tend to be inordinately interested in women's breasts and much less concerned with women's toenails. Women, in turn, tend to be turned on by the shape of a man's buttocks or the details of a man's beard and body hair, if any, but not by the size of his feet.

But all those determinants of sex appeal vary geographically. Khoisan and Andaman Island women tend to have much larger buttocks than most other women. Nipple color and breast shape and size also vary geographically among women. European men are rather hairy by world standards, while Southeast Asian men tend to have very sparse beards and body hair.

What's the function of these traits that differ so markedly between men and women? They certainly don't aid survival: it's not the case that orange nipples help Khoisan women escape lions, while darker nipples help European women survive cold winters. Instead, these varying traits play a crucial role in sexual selection. Women with very large buttocks are a turn-on, or at least acceptable, to Khoisan and Andaman men but look freakish to many men from other parts of the world. Bearded and hairy men readily find mates in Europe but fare worse in Southeast Asia. The geographic variation of these traits, however, is as arbitrary as the geographic variation in the color of a lion's mane.

There is a third possible explanation for the function of geographically variable human traits, besides survival or sexual selection—namely, no function at all. A good example is provided by fingerprints, whose complex pattern of arches, loops, and whorls is determined genetically. Fingerprints also vary geographically: for example, Europeans' fingerprints tend to have many loops, while aboriginal Australians' fingerprints tend to have many whorls.

If we classify human populations by their fingerprints, most Europeans and black Africans would sort out together in one race, Jews and some Indonesians in another, and aboriginal Australians in still another. But those geographic variations in fingerprint patterns possess no known function whatsoever. They play no role in survival: whorls aren't especially suitable for grabbing kangaroos, nor do loops help bar mitzvah candidates hold on to the pointer for the Torah. They also play no role in sexual selection: while you've undoubtedly noticed whether your mate is bearded or has brown nipples, you surely haven't the faintest idea whether his or her fingerprints have more loops than whorls. Instead it's purely a matter of chance that whorls became common in aboriginal Australians, and loops among Jews. Our rhesus factor blood groups and numerous other human traits fall into the same category of genetic characteristics whose geographic variation serves no function.

You've probably been wondering when I was going to get back to skin color, eye color, and hair color and form. After all, those are the traits by which all of us members of the lay public, as well as traditional anthropologists, classify races. Does geographic variation in those traits function in survival, in sexual selection, or in nothing?

The usual view is that skin color varies geographically to enhance survival. Supposedly, people in sunny, tropical climates around the world have genetically dark skin, which is supposedly analogous to the temporary skin darkening of European whites in the summer. The supposed function of dark skin in sunny climates is for protection against skin cancer. Variations in eye color are also supposed to enhance survival under particular conditions, though no one has ever proposed a plausible hypothesis for how those variations might actually enhance survival.

Alas, the evidence for natural selection of skin color dissolves under scrutiny. Among tropical peoples, anthropologists love to stress the dark skins of African blacks, people of the southern Indian peninsula, and New Guineans and love to forget the pale skins of Amazonian Indians and Southeast Asians living at the same latitudes. To wriggle out of those paradoxes, anthropologists then plead the excuse that Amazonian Indians and Southeast Asians may not have been living in their present locations long enough to evolve dark skins. However, the ancestors of fair-skinned Swedes arrived even more recently in Scandinavia, and aboriginal Tasmanians were black-skinned despite their ancestors' having lived for at least the last 10,000 years at the latitude of Vladivostok.

Besides, when one takes into account cloud cover, peoples of equatorial West Africa and the New Guinea mountains actually receive no more ultraviolet radiation or hours of sunshine each year than do the Swiss. Compared with infectious diseases and other selective agents, skin cancer has been utterly trivial as a cause of death in human history, even for modern white settlers in the tropics. This objection is so obvious to believers in natural selection of skin color that they have proposed at least seven other supposed survival functions of skin color, without reaching agreement. Those other supposed functions include protection against rickets, frostbite, folic acid deficiency, beryllium poisoning, overheating, and overcooling. The diversity of these contradictory theories makes clear how far we are from understanding the survival value (if any) of skin color.

It wouldn't surprise me if dark skins do eventually prove to offer some advantage in tropical climates, but I expect the advantage to turn out to be a slight one that is easily overridden. But there's an overwhelming importance to skin, eye, and hair color that is obvious to all of us—sexual selection. Before we can reach a condition of intimacy permitting us to assess the beauty of a prospective sex partner's hidden physical attractions, we first have to pass muster for skin, eyes, and hair.

We all know how those highly visible "beauty traits" guide our choice of sex partners. Even the briefest personal ad in a newspaper mentions the advertiser's skin color, and the color of skin that he or she seeks in a partner. Skin color, of course, is also of overwhelming importance in our social prejudices. If you're a black African American trying to raise your children in white U.S. society, rickets and overheating are the least of the problems that might be solved by your skin color. Eye color and hair form and color, while not so overwhelmingly important as skin color, also play an obvious role in our sexual and social preferences. Just ask yourself why hair dyes, hair curlers, and hair straighteners enjoy such wide sales. You can bet that it's not to improve our chances of surviving grizzly bear attacks and other risks endemic to the North American continent.

Nearly 125 years ago, Charles Darwin himself, the discoverer of natural selection, dismissed its role as an explanation of geographic variation in human beauty traits. Everything that we have learned since then only reinforces Darwin's view.

We can now return to our original questions: Are human racial classifications that are based on different traits concordant with one another? What is the hierarchical relation among recognized races? What is the function of racially variable traits? What, really, are the traditional human races?

Regarding concordance, we *could* have classified races based on any number of geographically variable traits. The resulting classifications would not be at all concordant. Depending on whether we classified ourselves by antimalarial genes, lactase, fingerprints, or skin color, we could place Swedes in the same race as either Xhosas, Fulani, and Ainu of Japan, or Italians.

Regarding hierarchy, traditional classifications that emphasize skin color face unresolvable ambiguities. Anthropology textbooks often recognize five major races: "whites," "African blacks," "Mongoloids," "aboriginal Australians," and "Khoisans," each in turn divided into various numbers of sub-races. But there is no agreement on the number and delineation of the sub-races, or even of the major races. Are all five of the major races equally distinctive? Are Nigerians really less different from Xhosas than aboriginal Australians are from both? Should we recognize 3 or 15 sub-races of Mongoloids? These questions have remained unresolved because skin color and other traditional racial criteria are difficult to formulate mathematically.

A method that could in principle overcome these problems is to base racial classification on a combination of as many geographically variable genes as possible. Within the past decade, some biologists have shown renewed interest in developing a hierarchical classification of human populations—hierarchical not in the sense that it identifies superior and inferior races but in the sense of grouping and separating populations based on mathematical measures of genetic distinctness. While the biologists still haven't reached agreement, some of their studies suggest that human genetic diversity may be greatest in Africa. If so, the primary races of humanity may consist of several African races, plus one race to encompass all peoples of all other continents. Swedes, New Guineans, Japanese, and Navajo would then belong to the same primary race; the Khoisans of southern Africa would constitute another primary race by themselves; and African "blacks" and Pygmies would be divided among several other primary races.

As regards the function of all those traits that are useful for classifying human races, some serve to enhance survival, some to enhance sexual selection, while some serve no function at all. The traits we traditionally use are ones subject to sexual selection, which is not really surprising. These traits are not only visible at a distance but also highly variable; that's why they became the ones used throughout recorded history to make quick judgments about people. Racial classification didn't come from science but from the body's signals for differentiating attractive from unattractive sex partners, and for differentiating friend from foe.

Such snap judgments didn't threaten our existence back when people were armed only with spears and surrounded by others who looked mostly like themselves. In the modern world, though, we are armed with guns and plutonium, and we live our lives surrounded by people who are much more varied in appearance. The last thing we need now is to continue codifying all those different appearances into an arbitrary system of racial classification.

CRITICAL THINKING QUESTIONS

1. Define *race,* providing both the vernacular and scientific meanings of the word.
2. Why do humans classify the world, including other human groups?
3. What reasons does Diamond suggest cause human physical variation between groups? What are some of these variations?
4. Diamond suggests that race can be defined in a number of ways. What are some of the criteria that could be used, and how can these create what would seem to be unusual combinations?
5. How do "commonsense" classifications and knowledge contribute to modern human problems surrounding race in this country and around the world?

Digging Beneath Honolulu's Chinatown

Joseph Kennedy

In 1992 the city fathers of Honolulu elected to condemn and raze an old building in Chinatown in order to create room for needed low-income housing. The target for demolition was a two-story, L-shaped affair known as the H.Y. Wong building. Built in 1906, it was the last remaining wood-frame structure in the downtown area. Before any construction could begin, however, state and federal historic preservation mandates had to be satisfied, and my firm was hired to carry out an archaeological investigation of the site. A check of land records showed that the twenty-thousand-square-foot lot upon which the H.Y. Wong building stood had encompassed open space, grass houses, and later buildings without foundations or basements that would have disturbed underground deposits. It was therefore a rare opportunity for archaeological exploration in a modern urban setting. An 1852 document with a simple map even showed a prehistoric fishpond on the site. This must have been filled in by 1879, when another map showed two European-type structures on the same piece of real estate.

After examining historical documents and maps, five of us had the unsettling experience of inspecting the premises, which now served mainly as a haven for drug users. The abandoned street-level storefronts on the property were infested with rats and cockroaches. Conditions in the forsaken upstairs apartments were not much better, although there was still a hint of what they must have looked like in the 1920s and 1930s, when ordinary working people lived there, and in the period between 1940 and 1980, when this neighborhood gained a reputation as Honolulu's premier red-light district. Soon after our visit the building was razed, and our archaeological work began.

Most of what is now downtown Honolulu sits atop a geologically recent reef formation. In most places this rock lies no more than three feet below the surface, imposing a limit on archaeological investigation. Here, however, the soils proved to be about twelve feet deep. This was thanks to the action of Nuuanu Stream, a meandering watercourse that discharges into the harbor. The stream had interfered with reef formation and worn away established corals within its reach, creating a swampy estuary where soils accumulated. The site was not only a favored habitation of the early Polynesian settlers of Oahu—who arrived more than a thousand years ago—but was also, in 1792, the landing place of the first Westerners on the island.

The task of excavation fell to a team that worked very hard in what had become a rather unsavory urban location. Artifacts found in the soil ranged from bone fishhooks and stone adzes in the lowest layers to pocket calculators and hypodermic needles near the surface. In between, the excavators gathered thousands of pieces of decorated pottery, hundreds of nineteenth-century bottles, and clumps of glass that had been fused and commingled with other items, no doubt during the firestorms associated with major Chinatown blazes in 1886 and 1900. Sticky, compacted, clayey soil confirmed the presence of the former fishpond.

The earliest excavated layers dated to a time before human occupation, roughly between 3,400 and 2,200 years ago, when the site was a shallow, saltwater-to-somewhat-brackish lagoon, the result of a five-foot rise in sea level that had occurred two thousand years earlier. By about 200 B.C., the sea had fallen to its present level and the shore as we now know it began to take shape. Pollen samples trapped by the emergent land

Source: Reprinted from *Natural History,* June 1999, pp. 64–67; copyright © Natural History Magazine, Inc., 1999.

show that an open forest of loulu palms and other dry-to-moist forest species dominated this section of the island.

The earliest evidence of human occupation at our site was a thin layer of clay loam that was deposited in standing water. This layer represented the base level of the fishpond, a low, spring-fed area that had been partly enclosed with a two-and-a-half-foot-high wall made of basalt. Fishponds such as this were created by Hawaii's Polynesian settlers and their descendants so that they could continue the practice of fish-farming. Extending into the ocean—or built inland, sometimes next to streams—the ponds provided a substitute for the familiar lagoons and fringing reefs of their ancestral homelands.

Carbon dating indicated the wall was constructed about A.D. 890, which would make this the earliest known fishpond in Hawaii. By the time the pond was built, the loulu palm forest had disappeared, and the native shorebirds of the area were in their last days. Apparently this was a result of the human colonization of the Hawaiian Islands, which had probably begun at least three or four centuries earlier. Although native Hawaiians recognized a spiritual tie between humans and their environment, and protected certain plants and animals by imposing seasonal restrictions on their exploitation, archaeological excavations and historical accounts show that they also dramatically altered floral and faunal habitats by causing runaway fires, and they may have eaten some bird species to extinction. And the Polynesian rat—a stowaway on the great voyaging canoes—may well have done even more damage.

The lower levels of the pond sediment contained several traditional Hawaiian items, the most numerous being stones used in a game called maika. These crafted rock disks were rolled down long grass or dirt lanes. We also found a wooden handle with a small hole in its center, which we thought at first might be the grip portion of a meat hook. Subsequent research revealed its more grisly purpose. A very similar item archived in Honolulu's Bishop Museum is identified as a piece that secures one end of a strangulation cord. A prerogative of the indigenous ruling class was to carry out executions and sacrifices, and asphyxiation was one of the favored methods.

Following Western contact in the late eighteenth century, the archaeological record begins to reflect trends detailed in the history books, as objects of European and American manufacture began to replace native Hawaiian artifacts. Chinese goods joined the mix after 1852 and Japanese products arrived after 1868, with the first waves of contract laborers from East Asia. Then, as we already knew from documents, sometime between 1852 and 1879 the pond was filled in, probably in a single, planned effort. The pond fill, about five feet deep, yielded tens of thousands of artifacts representing the ethnic diversity of Hawaii's early historic period. Among these was a sword handle of the type used by British artillery officers, a gold finger ring with the Chinese characters for "rare deer" inscribed on the inside, American-made shoes, Russian coins, Japanese buttons, and trade beads from around the world.

Certain common artifacts helped us pinpoint the date the pond was actually filled in. Tobacco pipes from America, Scotland, England, and Germany, for example, had distinguishing names embossed on their bowls (Tom Thumb, Bent Harp, Cutty) that could be matched to archival records to establish their dates of manufacture. The nineteenth century was also a period of many well-documented technological advances in glass bottle making, and this allowed a rather precise dating of the nearly fifteen hundred excavated pieces of bottles for wine, spirits, sauces, medicines, and toiletries. The absence of pipes made later than 1867, and of bottles made earlier than 1864, pretty well narrowed down the time of the filling-in to a four-year period between 1864 and 1867. The capturing of this time window is significant because, according to property records, this land was owned by Hawaiians when the pond was filled. Contrary to a common assumption, these native people participated in the urbanization of early Honolulu.

Midway through the project, a rather remarkable event occurred. Seeds that had been buried in soils undisturbed since the mid-1800s began to germinate in the piles of earth dumped to the sides of the excavation. By the end of our fieldwork, an appreciative crew was marking the progress of a developing tobacco plant and, in a case of truly being nourished by the past, enjoying the taste of small, fresh tomatoes at lunch.

For visitor information write: Hawaii Visitors and Convention Bureau, Suite 801, 2270 Kalakaua Avenue, Honolulu, HI 96815 (808) 923-1811 www.gohawaii.com

Joseph Kennedy is senior archaeologist for Archaeological Consultants of the Pacific, Haleiwa, Hawaii.

CRITICAL THINKING QUESTIONS

1. What did a background check of records concerning the H.Y. Wong building reveal that encouraged excavation at the location?
2. What did the earliest excavation levels at the site reveal about the initial occupation of the Hawaiian Islands?
3. How was the impact of Western contact and colonization revealed in the younger excavation levels at the site?

1491

Charles C. Mann

Before it became the New World, the Western Hemisphere was vastly more populous and sophisticated than has been thought—an altogether more salubrious place to live at the time than, say, Europe. New evidence of both the extent of the population and its agricultural advancement leads to a remarkable conjecture: the Amazon rain forest may be largely a human artifact.

The plane took off in weather that was surprisingly cool for north-central Bolivia and flew east, toward the Brazilian border. In a few minutes the roads and houses disappeared, and the only evidence of human settlement was the cattle scattered over the savannah like jimmies on ice cream. Then they, too, disappeared. By that time the archaeologists had their cameras out and were clicking away in delight.

Below us was the Beni, a Bolivian province about the size of Illinois and Indiana put together, and nearly as flat. For almost half the year rain and snowmelt from the mountains to the south and west cover the land with an irregular, slowly moving skin of water that eventually ends up in the province's northern rivers, which are sub-subtributaries of the Amazon. The rest of the year the water dries up and the bright-green vastness turns into something that resembles a desert. This peculiar, remote, watery plain was what had drawn the researchers' attention, and not just because it was one of the few places on earth inhabited by people who might never have seen Westerners with cameras.

Clark Erickson and William Balée, the archaeologists, sat up front. Erickson is based at the University of Pennsylvania; he works in concert with a Bolivian archaeologist, whose seat in the plane I usurped that day. Balée is at Tulane University, in New Orleans. He is actually an anthropologist, but as native peoples have vanished, the distinction between anthropologists and archaeologists has blurred. The two men differ in build, temperament, and scholarly proclivity, but they pressed their faces to the windows with identical enthusiasm.

Dappled across the grasslands below was an archipelago of forest islands, many of them startingly round and hundreds of acres across. Each island rose ten or thirty or sixty feet above the floodplain, allowing trees to grow that would otherwise never survive the water. The forests were linked by raised berms, as straight as a rifle shot and up to three miles long. It is Erickson's belief that this entire landscape—30,000 square miles of forest mounds surrounded by raised fields and linked by causeways—was constructed by a complex, populous society more than 2,000 years ago. Balée, newer to the Beni, leaned toward this view but was not yet ready to commit himself.

Erickson and Balée belong to a cohort of scholars that has radically challenged conventional notions of what the Western Hemisphere was like before Columbus. When I went to high school, in the 1970s, I was taught that Indians came to the Americas across the Bering Strait about 12,000 years ago, that they lived for the most part in small, isolated groups, and that they had so little impact on their environment that even after millennia of habitation it remained mostly wilderness. My son picked up the same ideas at his schools. One way to summarize the views of people like Erickson and Balée would be to say that in their opinion this picture of Indian life is wrong in almost every aspect. Indians were here far longer than previously thought, these

Source: From the Atlantic Monthly, vol. 289, no. 3, pp. 41-53 (March 2002), reprinted by permission of the author.

researchers believe, and in much greater numbers. And they were so successful at imposing their will on the landscape that in 1492 Columbus set foot in a hemisphere thoroughly dominated by humankind.

Given the charged relations between white societies and native peoples, inquiry into Indian culture and history is inevitably contentious. But the recent scholarship is especially controversial. To begin with, some researchers—many but not all from an older generation—deride the new theories as fantasies arising from an almost willful misinterpretation of data and a perverse kind of political correctness. "I have seen no evidence that large numbers of people ever lived in the Beni," says Betty J. Meggers, of the Smithsonian Institution. "Claiming otherwise is just wishful thinking." Similar criticisms apply to many of the new scholarly claims about Indians, according to Dean R. Snow, an anthropologist at Pennsylvania State University. The problem is that "you can make the meager evidence from the ethnohistorical record tell you anything you want," he says. "It's really easy to kid yourself."

More important are the implications of the new theories for today's ecological battles. Much of the environmental movement is animated, consciously or not, by what William Denevan, a geographer at the University of Wisconsin, calls polemically, "the pristine myth"—the belief that the Americas in 1491 were an almost unmarked, even Edenic land, "untrammeled by man," in the words of the Wilderness Act of 1964, one of the nation's first and most important environmental laws. As the University of Wisconsin historian William Cronon has written, restoring this long-ago, putatively natural state is, in the view of environmentalists, a task that society is morally bound to undertake. Yet if the new view is correct and the work of humankind was pervasive, where does that leave efforts to restore nature?

The Beni is a case in point. In addition to building up the Beni mounds for houses and gardens, Erickson says, the Indians trapped fish in the seasonally flooded grassland. Indeed, he says, they fashioned dense zigzagging networks of earthen fish weirs between the causeways. To keep the habitat clear of unwanted trees and undergrowth, they regularly set huge areas on fire.

Over the centuries the burning created an intricate ecosystem of fire-adapted plant species dependent on native pyrophilia. The current inhabitants of the Beni still burn, although now it is to maintain the savannah for cattle. When we flew over the area, the dry season had just begun, but mile-long lines of flame were already on the march. In the charred areas behind the fires were the blackened spikes of trees—many of them, one assumes, of the varieties that activists fight to save in other parts of Amazonia.

After we landed, I asked Balée, Should we let people keep burning the Beni? Or should we let the trees invade and create a verdant tropical forest in the grasslands, even if one had not existed here for millennia?

Balée laughed. "You're trying to trap me, aren't you?" he said.

LIKE A CLUB BETWEEN THE EYES

According to family lore, my great-grandmother's great-grandmother's great-grandfather was the first white person hanged in America. His name was John Billington. He came on the *Mayflower,* which anchored off the coast of Massachusetts on November 9, 1620. Billington was not a Puritan; within six months of arrival he also became the first white person in America to be tried for complaining about the police. "He is a knave," William Bradford, the colony's governor, wrote of Billington, "and so will live and die." What one historian called Billington's "troublesome career" ended in 1630, when he was hanged for murder. My family has always said that he was framed—but we *would* say that, wouldn't we?

A few years ago it occurred to me that my ancestor and everyone else in the colony had voluntarily enlisted in a venture that brought them to New England without food or shelter six weeks before winter. Half the 102 people on the *Mayflower* made it through to spring, which to me was amazing. How, I wondered, did they survive?

In his history of Plymouth Colony, Bradford provided the answer: by robbing Indian houses and graves. The *Mayflower* first hove to at Cape Cod. An armed company staggered out. Eventually it found a recently deserted Indian settlement.

The newcomers—hungry, cold, sick—dug up graves and ransacked houses, looking for underground stashes of corn. "And sure it was God's good providence that we found this corn," Bradford wrote, "for else we know not how we should have done." (He felt uneasy about the thievery, though.) When the colonists came to Plymouth, a month later, they set up shop in another deserted Indian village. All through the coastal forest the Indians had "died on heapes, as they lay in their houses," the English trader Thomas Morton noted. "And the bones and skulls upon the several places of their habitations made such a spectacle" that to Morton the Massachusetts woods seemed to be "a new found Golgotha"—the hill of executions in Roman Jerusalem.

To the Pilgrims' astonishment, one of the corpses they exhumed on Cape Cod had blond hair. A French ship had been wrecked there several years earlier. The Patuxet Indians imprisoned a few survivors. One of them supposedly learned enough of the local language to inform his captors that God would destroy them for their misdeeds. The Patuxet scoffed at the threat. But the Europeans carried a disease, and they bequeathed it to their jailers. The epidemic (probably of viral hepatitis, according to a study by Arthur E. Spiess, an archaeologist at the Maine Historic Preservation Commission, and Bruce D. Spiess, the director of clinical research at the Medical College of Virginia) took years to exhaust itself and may have killed 90 percent of the people in coastal New England. It made a huge difference to American history. "The good hand of God favored our beginnings," Bradford mused, by "sweeping away great multitudes of the natives ... that he might make room for us."

By the time my ancestor set sail on the *Mayflower*, Europeans had been visiting New England for more than a hundred years. English, French, Italian, Spanish, and Portuguese mariners regularly plied the coastline, trading what they could, occasionally kidnapping the inhabitants for slaves. New England, the Europeans saw, was thickly settled and well defended. In 1605 and 1606 Samuel de Champlain visited Cape Cod, hoping to establish a French base. He abandoned the idea. Too many people already lived there. A year later Sir Ferdinando Gorges—British despite his name—tried to establish an English community in southern Maine. It had more founders than Plymouth and seems to have been better organized. Confronted by numerous well-armed local Indians, the settlers abandoned the project within months. The Indians at Plymouth would surely have been an equal obstacle to my ancestor and his ramshackle expedition had disease not intervened.

Faced with such stories, historians have long wondered how many people lived in the Americas at the time of contact. "Debated since Columbus attempted a partial census on Hispaniola in 1496," William Denevan has written, this "remains one of the great inquiries of history." (In 1976 Denevan assembled and edited an entire book on the subject. *The Native Population of the Americas in 1492*.) The first scholarly estimate of the indigenous population was made in 1910 by James Mooney, a distinguished ethnographer at the Smithsonian Institution. Combing through old documents, he concluded that in 1491 North America had 1.15 million inhabitants. Mooney's glittering reputation ensured that most subsequent researchers accepted his figure uncritically.

That changed in 1966, when Henry F. Dobyns published "Estimating Aboriginal American Population: An Appraisal of Techniques With a New Hemispheric Estimate," in the journal *Current Anthropology*. Despite the carefully neutral title, his argument was thunderous, its impact long-lasting. In the view of James Wilson, the author of *The Earth Shall Weep* (1998), a history of indigenous Americans, Dobyns's colleagues "are still struggling to get out of the crater that paper left in anthropology." Not only anthropologists were affected. Dobyns's estimate proved to be one of the opening rounds in today's culture wars.

Dobyns began his exploration of pre-Columbian Indian demography in the early 1950s, when he was a graduate student. At the invitation of a friend, he spent a few months in northern Mexico, which is full of Spanish-era missions. There he poked through the crumbling leather-bound ledgers in which Jesuits recorded local births and deaths. Right away he noticed how many more deaths there were. The Spaniards arrived, and then Indians died—in huge numbers, at incredible rates. It hit him,

Dobyns told me recently, "like a club right between the eyes."

It took Dobyns eleven years to obtain his Ph.D. Along the way he joined a rural-development project in Peru, which until colonial times was the seat of the Incan empire. Remembering what he had seen at the northern fringe of the Spanish conquest, Dobyns decided to compare it with figures for the south. He burrowed into the papers of the Lima cathedral and read apologetic Spanish histories. The Indians in Peru, Dobyns concluded, had faced plagues from the day the conquistadors showed up—in fact, before then: smallpox arrived around 1525, seven years ahead of the Spanish. Brought to Mexico apparently by a single sick Spaniard, it swept south and eliminated more than half the population of the Incan empire. Smallpox claimed the Incan dictator Huayna Capac and much of his family, setting off a calamitous war of succession. So complete was the chaos that Francisco Pizarro was able to seize an empire the size of Spain and Italy combined with a force of 168 men.

Smallpox was only the first epidemic. Typhus (probably) in 1546, influenza and smallpox together in 1558, smallpox again in 1589, diphtheria in 1614, measles in 1618—all ravaged the remains of Incan culture. Dobyns was the first social scientist to piece together this awful picture, and he naturally rushed his findings into print. Hardly anyone paid attention. But Dobyns was already working on a second related question: If all those people died, how many had been living there to begin with? Before Columbus, Dobyns calculated, the Western Hemisphere held ninety to 112 million people. Another way of saying this is that in 1491 more people lived in the Americas than in Europe.

His argument was simple but horrific. It is well known that Native Americans had no experience with many European diseases and were therefore immunologically unprepared—"virgin soil," in the metaphor of epidemiologists. What Dobyns realized was that such diseases could have swept from the coastlines initially visited by Europeans to inland areas controlled by Indians who had never seen a white person. The first whites to explore many parts of the Americas may therefore have encountered places that were already depopulated. Indeed, Dobyns argued, they must have done so.

Peru was one example, the Pacific Northwest another. In 1792 the British navigator George Vancouver led the first European expedition to survey Puget Sound. He found a vast charnel house: human remains "promiscuously scattered about the beach, in great numbers." Smallpox, Vancouver's crew discovered, had preceded them. Its few survivors, second lieutenant Peter Puget noted, were "most terribly pitted ... indeed many have lost their Eyes." In *Pox Americana* (2001), Elizabeth Fenn, a historian at George Washington University, contends that the disaster on the northwest coast was but a small part of a continental pandemic that erupted near Boston in 1774 and cut down Indians from Mexico to Alaska.

Because smallpox was not endemic in the Americas, colonials, too, had not acquired any immunity. The virus, an equal-opportunity killer, swept through the Continental Army and stopped the drive into Quebec. The American Revolution would be lost, Washington and other rebel leaders feared, if the contagion did to the colonists what it had done to the Indians. "The small Pox! The small Pox!" John Adams wrote to his wife, Abigail. "What shall We do with it?" In retrospect, Fenn says, "One of George Washington's most brilliant moves was to inoculate the army against smallpox during the Valley Forge winter of '78." Without inoculation smallpox could easily have given the United States back to the British.

So many epidemics occurred in the Americas, Dobyns argued, that the old data used by Mooney and his successors represented population nadirs. From the few cases in which before-and-after totals are known with relative certainty, Dobyns estimated that in the first 130 years of contact about 95 percent of the people in the Americas died—the worst demographic calamity in recorded history.

Dobyns's ideas were quickly attacked as politically motivated, a push from the hate-America crowd to inflate the toll of imperialism. The attacks continue to this day. "No question about it, some people want those higher numbers," says Shepard Krech III, a Brown University anthropologist who is the author of *The Ecological Indian* (1999). These people, he says, were thrilled when Dobyns revisited the subject in a book, *Their Numbers Become Thinned* (1983)—and revised his own estimates upward. Perhaps Dobyns's most vehement critic is David Henige, a bibliographer of Africana at the University of Wisconsin, whose *Numbers From Nowhere* (1998) is a landmark in the literature of demographic fulmination. "Suspect in 1966, it is no less suspect nowadays," Henige wrote of Dobyns's work. "If anything, it is worse."

When Henige wrote *Numbers From Nowhere*, the fight about pre-Columbian populations had already consumed forests' worth of trees; his bibliography is ninety pages long. And the dispute shows no sign of abating. More and more people have jumped in. This is partly because the subject is inherently fascinating. But more likely the increased interest in the debate is due to the growing realization of the high political and ecological stakes.

INVENTING BY THE MILLIONS

On May 30, 1539, Hernando de Soto landed his private army near Tampa Bay, in Florida. Soto, as he was called, was a novel figure: half warrior, half venture capitalist. He had grown very rich very young by becoming a market leader in the nascent trade for Indian slaves. The profits had helped to fund Pizarro's seizure of the Incan empire, which had made Soto wealthier still. Looking quite literally for new worlds to conquer, he persuaded the Spanish Crown to let him loose in North America. He spent one fortune to make another. He came to Florida with 200 horses, 600 soldiers, and 300 pigs.

From today's perspective, it is difficult to imagine the ethical system that would justify Soto's actions. For four years his force, looking for gold, wandered through what is now Florida, Georgia, North and South Carolina, Tennessee, Alabama, Mississippi, Arkansas, and Texas, wrecking almost everything it touched. The inhabitants often fought back vigorously, but they had never before encountered an army with horses and guns. Soto died of fever with his expedition in ruins; along the way his men had managed to rape, torture, enslave, and kill countless Indians. But the worst thing the Spaniards did, some researchers say, was entirely without malice—bring the pigs.

According to Charles Hudson, an anthropologist at the University of Georgia who spent fifteen years reconstructing the path of the expedition, Soto crossed the Mississippi a few miles downstream from the present site of Memphis. It was a nervous passage: the Spaniards were watched by several thousand Indian warriors. Utterly without fear, Soto brushed past the Indian force into what is now eastern Arkansas, through thickly settled land—"very well peopled with large towns," one of his men later recalled, "two or three of which were to be seen from one town." Eventually the Spaniards approached a cluster of small cities, each protected by earthen walls, sizeable moats, and deadeye archers. In his usual fashion, Soto brazenly marched in, stole food, and marched out.

After Soto left, no Europeans visited this part of the Mississippi Valley for more than a century. Early in 1682 whites appeared again, this time Frenchmen in canoes. One of them was Réné-Robert Cavelier, Sieur de la Salle. The French passed through the area where Soto had found cities cheek by jowl. It was deserted—La Salle didn't see an Indian village for 200 miles. About fifty settlements existed in this strip of the Mississippi when Soto showed up, according to Anne Ramenofsky, an anthropologist at the University of New Mexico. By La Salle's time the number had shrunk to perhaps ten, some probably inhabited by recent immigrants. Soto "had a privileged glimpse" of an Indian world, Hudson says. "The window opened and slammed shut. When the French came in and the record opened up again it was a transformed reality. A civilization crumbled. The question is, how did this happen?"

The question is even more complex than it may seem. Disaster of this magnitude suggests epidemic disease. In the view of Ramenofsky and Patricia Galloway, an anthropologist at the University of Texas, the source of the contagion was very likely not Soto's army but its ambulatory meat locker: his 300 pigs. Soto's force itself was too small to be an effective biological weapon. Sicknesses like measles and smallpox would have burned through his 600 soldiers long before they reached the Mississippi. But the same would not have held true for the pigs, which multiplied rapidly and were able to transmit their diseases to wildlife in the surrounding forest. When human beings and domesticated animals live close together, they trade microbes with abandon. Over time mutation spawns new diseases: avian influenza becomes human influenza, bovine rinder-pest becomes measles. Unlike Europeans, Indians did not live in close quarters with animals—they domesticated only the dog, the llama, the alpaca, the guinea pig, and, here and there, the turkey and the Muscovy duck. In some ways this is not surprising: the New World had fewer animal candidates for taming than the Old. Moreover, few Indians carry the gene that permits adults to digest lactose, a form of sugar abundant in milk. Non-milk-drinkers, one imagines, would be less likely to work at domesticating milk-giving animals. But this is guesswork. The fact is that what scientists call zoonotic disease was little known in the Americas. Swine alone can disseminate anthrax, brucellosis, leptospirosis, taeniasis, trichinosis, and tuberculosis. Pigs breed exuberantly and can transmit diseases to deer and turkeys. Only a few of Soto's pigs would have had to wander off to infect the forest.

Indeed, the calamity wrought by Soto apparently extended across the whole Southeast. The Coosa city-states, in western Georgia, and the Caddoan-speaking civilization centered on the Texas-Arkansas border, disintegrated soon after Soto appeared. The Caddo had had a taste for monumental architecture: public plazas, ceremonial platforms, mausoleums. After Soto's army left, notes Timothy K. Perttula, an archaeological consultant in Austin, Texas, the Caddo stopped building community centers and began digging community cemeteries. Between Soto's and La Salle's visits, Perttula believes, the Caddoan population fell from about 200,000 to about 8,500—a drop of nearly 96 percent. In the eighteenth century the tally shrank further, to 1,400. An equivalent loss today in the population of New York City would reduce it to 56,000—not enough to fill Yankee Stadium. "That's one reason whites think of Indians as nomadic hunters," says Russell Thornton, an anthropologist at the University of California at Los Angeles. "Everything else—all the heavily populated urbanized societies—was wiped out."

Could a few pigs truly wreak this much destruction? Such apocalyptic scenarios invite skepticism. As a rule, viruses, microbes, and parasites are rarely lethal on so wide a scale—a pest that wipes out its host species does not have a bright evolutionary future. In its worst outbreak, from 1347 to 1351, the European Black Death claimed only a third of its victims. (The rest survived, though they were often disfigured or crippled by its effects.) The Indians in Soto's path, if Dobyns, Ramenotsky and Perttula are correct, endured losses that were incomprehensibly greater.

One reason is that Indians were fresh territory for many plagues, not just one. Smallpox, typhoid, bubonic plague, influenza, mumps, measles, whooping cough—all rained down on the Americas in the century after Columbus. (Cholera, malaria, and scarlet fever came later.) Having little experience with epidemic diseases, Indians had no knowledge of how to combat them. In contrast, Europeans were well versed in the brutal logic of quarantine. They boarded up houses in which plague appeared and fled to the countryside. In Indian New England, Neal Salisbury, a historian at Smith College, wrote in *Manitou and Providence* (1982), family and friends gather with the shaman at the sufferer's bedside to wait out the illness—a practice that "could only have served to spread the disease more rapidly."

Indigenous biochemistry may also have played a role. The immune system constantly scans the body for molecules that it can recognize as foreign—molecules belonging to an invading virus, for instance. No one's immune system can identify all foreign presences. Roughly speaking, an individual's set of defensive tools is known as his MHC type. Because many bacteria and viruses mutate easily, they usually attack in the form of several slightly different strains. Pathogens win when MHC types miss some of the strains and the immune system is not stimulated to act. Most human groups contain many MHC types; a strain that slips by one person's defenses will be nailed by the defenses of the next. But, according to Francis L. Black, an epidemiologist at Yale University, Indians are characterized by unusually homogenous MHC types. One out of three South American Indians have similar MHC types; among Africans the corresponding figure is one in 200. The cause is a matter for Darwinian speculation, the effects less so.

In 1966 Dobyns's insistence on the role of disease was a shock to his colleagues. Today the impact of European pathogens on the New World is almost undisputed. Nonetheless, the fight over Indian numbers continues with undiminished fervor. Estimates of the population of North America in 1491 disagree by an order of magnitude—from 18 million, Dobyns's revised figure, to 1.8 million, calculated by Douglas H. Ubelaker, an anthropologist at the Smithsonian. To some "high counters," as David Henige calls them, the low counters' refusal to relinquish the vision of an empty continent is irrational or worse. "Non-Indian 'experts' always want to minimize the size of aboriginal populations," says Lenore Stiffarm, a Native American–education specialist at the University of Saskatchewan. The smaller the numbers of Indians, she believes, the easier it is to regard the continent as having been up for grabs. "It's perfectly acceptable to move into unoccupied land," Stiffarm says. "And land with only a few 'savages' is the next best thing."

"Most of the arguments for the very large numbers have been theoretical," Ubelaker says in defense of low counters. "When you try to marry the theoretical arguments to the data that are available on individual groups in different regions, it's hard to find support for those numbers." Archaeologists, he says, keep searching for the settlements in which those millions of people supposedly lived, with little success. "As more and more excavation is done, one would expect to see more evidence for dense populations than has thus far emerged." Dean Snow, the Pennsylvania State anthropologist, examined Colonial-era Mohawk Iroquois sites and found "no support for the notion that ubiquitous pandemics swept the region." In his view, asserting that the continent was filled with people who left no trace is like looking at an empty bank account and claiming that it must once have held millions of dollars.

The low counters are also troubled by the Dobynsian procedure for recovering original population numbers: applying an assumed death rate, usually 95 percent, to the observed population nadir. Ubelaker believes that the lowest point for Indians in North America was around 1900, when their numbers fell to about half a million. Assuming a 95 percent death rate, the pre-contact population would have been 10 million. Go up one percent, to a 96 percent death rate, and the figure jumps to 12.5 million—arithmetically creating more than two million people from a tiny increase in mortality rates. At 98 percent the number bounds to 25 million. Minute changes in baseline assumptions produce wildly different results.

"It's an absolutely unanswerable question on which tens of thousands of words have been spent to no purpose," Henige says. In 1976 he sat in on a seminar by William Denevan, the Wisconsin geographer. An "epiphanic moment" occurred when he read shortly afterward that scholars had "uncovered" the existence of eight million people in Hispaniola. *Can you just invent millions of people?* he wondered. "We can make of the historical record that there was depopulation and movement of people from internecine warfare and diseases," he says. "But as for how much, who knows? When we start putting numbers to something like that—applying large figures like ninety-five percent—we're saying things we shouldn't say. The number implies a level of knowledge that's impossible."

Nonetheless, one must try—or so Denevan believes. In his estimation the high counters (though not the highest counters) seem to be winning the argument, at least for now. No definitive data exists, he says, but the majority of the extant evidentiary scraps support their side. Even Henige is no low counter. When I asked him what he thought the population of the Americas was before Columbus, he insisted that any answer would be speculation and made me promise not to print what he was going to say next. Then he named a figure that forty years ago would have caused a commotion.

To Elizabeth Fenn, the smallpox historian, the squabble over numbers obscures a central fact. Whether one million or 10 million or 100 million died, she believes, the pall of sorrow that engulfed the hemisphere was immeasurable. Languages, prayers, hopes, habits, and dreams—entire ways of life hissed away like steam. The Spanish and the Portuguese lacked the germ theory of disease and could not explain what was happening (let alone stop it). Nor can we explain it: the ruin was too long ago and too all-encompassing. In the long run, Fenn says, the consequential finding is not that many people died but that many people once lived. The Americas were filled with a stunningly diverse assortment of peoples who had knocked about the continents for millennia. "You have to wonder," Fenn says, "What were all those people *up* to in all that time?"

BUFFALO FARM

In 1810 Henry Brackenridge came to Cahokia, in what is now southwest Illinois, just across the Mississippi from St. Louis. Born close to the frontier, Brackenridge was a budding adventure writer; his *Views of Louisiana,* published three years later, was a kind of nineteenth-century *Into Thin Air,* with terrific adventure but without tragedy. Brackenridge had an eye for archaeology, and he had heard that Cahokia was worth a visit. When he got there, trudging along the desolate Cahokia River, he was "struck with a degree of astonishment." Rising from the muddy bottomland was a "stupendous pile of earth," vaster than the Great Pyramid at Giza. Around it were more than a hundred small mounds, covering an area of five square miles. At the time, the area was almost uninhabited. One can only imagine what passed through Brackenridge's mind as he walked alone to the ruins of the biggest Indian city north of the Rio Grande.

To Brackenridge, it seemed clear that Cahokia and the many other ruins in the Midwest had been constructed by Indians. It was not so clear to everyone else. Nineteenth-century writers attributed them to, among others, the Vikings, the Chinese, the "Hindoos," the ancient Greeks, the ancient Egyptians, lost tribes of Israelites, and even straying bands of Welsh. (This last claim was surprisingly widespread; when Lewis and Clark surveyed the Missouri, Jefferson told them to keep an eye out for errant bands of Welsh-speaking white Indians.) The historian George Bancroft, dean of his profession, was a dissenter: the earthworks, he wrote in 1840, were purely natural formations.

Bancroft changed his mind about Cahokia, but not about Indians. To the end of his days he regarded them as "feeble barbarians, destitute of commerce and of political connection." His characterization lasted, largely unchanged, for more than a century. Samuel Eliot Morison, the winner of two Pulitzer Prizes, closed his monumental *European Discovery of America* (1974) with the observation that Native Americans expected only "short and brutish lives, void of hope for any future." As late as 1987 *American History: A Survey,* a standard high school textbook by three well-known historians, described the Americas before Columbus as "empty of mankind and its works." The story of Europeans in the New World, the book explained, "is the story of creation of a civilization where none existed."

Alfred Crosby, a historian at the University of Texas, came to other conclusions. Crosby's *The Columbian Exchange: Biological Consequences of 1492* caused almost as much of a stir when it was published, in 1972, as Henry Dobyns's calculation of Indian numbers six years earlier, though in different circles. Crosby was a standard names-and-battles historian who became frustrated by the random contingency of political events. "Some trivial thing happens and you have this guy winning the presidency instead of that guy," he says. He decided to go deeper. After he finished his manuscript, it sat on his shelf—he couldn't find a publisher willing to be associated with his new ideas. It took him three years to persuade a small editorial house to put it out. *The Columbian Exchange* has been in print ever since; a companion, *Ecological Imperialism: The Biological Expansion of Europe, 900–1900,* appeared in 1986.

Human history, in Crosby's interpretation, is marked by two world-altering centers of invention: the Middle East and central Mexico, where Indian groups independently created nearly all of the Neolithic innovations, writing included. The Neolithic Revolution began in the Middle East about 10,000 years ago. In the next few millennia humankind invented the wheel, the metal tool, and agriculture. The Sumerians eventually put these inventions together, added writing, and became the world's first civilization. Afterward Sumeria's heirs in Europe and Asia frantically copied one another's happiest discoveries: innovations ricocheted from one corner of Eurasia to another, stimulating technological progress. Native Americans, who had crossed to Alaska before Sumeria, missed out on the bounty. "They had to do everything on their own," Crosby says. Remarkably, they succeeded.

When Columbus appeared in the Caribbean, the descendants of the world's two Neolithic civilizations collided, with overwhelming consequences for both. American Neolithic development occurred later than that of the Middle East, possibly because the Indians needed more time to build up the requisite population density. Without beasts of burden they could not capitalize on the wheel (for individual workers on uneven terrain skids are nearly as effective as carts for hauling), and then never developed steel. But in agriculture they handily outstripped the children of Sumeria. Every tomato in Italy, every potato in Ireland, and every hot pepper in Thailand came from this hemisphere. Worldwide, more than half the crops grown today were initially developed in the Americas.

Maize, as corn is called in the rest of the world, was a triumph with global implications. Indians developed an extraordinary number of maize varieties for different growing conditions, which meant that the crop could and did spread throughout the planet. Central and Southern Europeans became particularly dependent on it; maize was the staple of Serbia, Romania, and Moldavia by the nineteenth century. Indian crops dramatically reduced hunger, Crosby says, which led to an Old World population boom.

Along with peanuts and manioc, maize came to Africa and transformed agriculture there, too. "The probability is that the population of Africa was greatly increased because of maize and other American Indian crops," Crosby says. "Those extra people helped make the slave trade possible." Maize conquered Africa at the time when introduced diseases were leveling Indian societies. The Spanish, the Portuguese, and the British were alarmed by the death rate among Indians, because they wanted to exploit them as workers. Faced with a labor shortage, the Europeans turned their eyes to Africa. The continent's quarrelsome societies helped slave traders

to siphon off millions of people. The maize-fed population boom, Crosby believes let the awful trade continue without pumping the well dry.

Back home in the Americas, Indian agriculture long sustained some of the world's largest cities. The Aztec capital of Tenochtitlan dazzled Hernán Cortes in 1519; it was bigger than Paris, Europe's greatest metropolis. The Spaniards gawped like hayseeds at the wide streets, ornately carved buildings, and markets bright with goods from hundreds of miles away. They had never before seen a city with botanical gardens, for the excellent reason that none existed in Europe. The same novelty attended the force of a thousand men that kept the crowded streets immaculate. (Streets that weren't ankle-deep in sewage! The conquistadors had never heard of such a thing.) Central America was not the only locus of prosperity. Thousands of miles north, John Smith, of Pocahontas fame, visited Massachusetts in 1614, before it was emptied by disease, and declared that the land was "so planted with Gardens and Corne fields, and so well inhabited with a goodly, strong and well proportioned people ... [that] I would rather live here than any where."

Smith was promoting colonization, and so had reason to exaggerate. But he also knew the hunger, sickness, and oppression of European life. France—"by any standards a privileged country," according to its great historian, Fernand Braudel—experienced seven nationwide famines in the fifteenth century and thirteen in the sixteenth. Disease was hunger's constant companion. During epidemics in London the dead were heaped onto carts "like common dung" (the simile is Daniel Defoe's) and trundled through the streets. The infant death rate in London orphanages, according to one contemporary source, was 88 percent. Governments were harsh, the rule of law arbitrary. The gibbets poking up in the background of so many old paintings were, Braudel observed, "merely a realistic detail."

The Earth Shall Weep, James Wilson's history of Indian America puts the comparison bluntly: "the western hemisphere was larger, richer, and more populous than Europe." Much of it was freer, too. Europeans, accustomed to the serfdom that thrived from Naples to the Baltic Sea, were puzzled and alarmed by the democratic spirit and respect for human rights in many Indian societies, especially those in North America. In theory, the sachems of New England Indian groups were absolute monarchs. In practice, the colonial leader Roger Williams wrote, "they will not conclude of ought ... unto which the people are averse."

Pre-1492 America wasn't a disease free paradise, Dobyns says, although in his "exuberance as a writer," he told me recently, he once made that claim. Indians had ailments of their own, notably parasites, tuberculosis, and anemia. The daily grind was wearing: life-spans in America were only as long as or a little longer than those in Europe, if the evidence of indigenous graveyards is to be believed. Nor was it a political utopia—the Inca, for instance, invented refinements to totalitarian rule that would have intrigued Stalin. Inveterate practitioners of what the historian Francis Jennings described as "state terrorism practiced horrifically on a huge scale," the Inca ruled so cruelly that one can speculate that their surviving subjects might actually have been better off under Spanish rule.

I asked seven anthropologists, archaeologists, and historians if they would rather have been a typical Indian or a typical European in 1491. None was delighted by the question, because it required judging the past by the standards of today—a fallacy disparaged as "presentism" by social scientists. But every one chose to be an Indian. Some early colonists gave the same answer. Horrifying the leaders of Jamestown and Plymouth, scores of English ran off to live with the Indians. My ancestor shared their desire, which is what led to the trumped-up murder charges against him—or that's what my grandfather told me, anyway.

As for the Indians, evidence suggests that they often viewed Europeans with disdain. The Hurons, a chagrined missionary reported, thought the French possessed "little intelligence in comparison to themselves." Europeans, Indians said, were physically weak, sexually untrustworthy, atrociously ugly, and just plain dirty. (Spaniards, who seldom if ever bathed, were amazed by the Aztec desire for personal cleanliness.) A Jesuit reported that the "Savages" were disgusted by handkerchiefs: "They say, we place

what is unclean in a fine white piece of linen, and put it away in our pockets as something very precious, while they throw it upon the ground." The Micmac scoffed at the notion of French superiority. If Christian civilization was so wonderful, why were its inhabitants leaving?

Like people everywhere, Indians survived by cleverly exploiting their environment. Europeans tended to manage land by breaking it into fragments for farmers and herders. Indians often worked on such a grand scale that the scope of their ambition can be hard to grasp. They created small plots, as Europeans did (about 1.5 million acres of terraces still exist in the Peruvian Andes), but they also reshaped entire landscapes to suit their purposes. A principal tool was fire, used to keep down underbrush and create the open, grassy conditions favorable for game. Rather than domesticating animals for meat, Indians retooled whole ecosystems to grow bumper crops of elk, deer, and bison. The first white settlers in Ohio found forests as open as English parks—they could drive carriages through the woods. Along the Hudson River the annual fall burning lit up the banks for miles on end; so flashy was the show that the Dutch in New Amsterdam boated upriver to goggle at the blaze like children at fireworks. In North America, Indian torches had their biggest impact on the Midwestern prairie, much or most of which was created and maintained by fire. Millenia of exuberant burning shaped the plains into vast buffalo farms. When Indian societies disintegrated, forest invaded savannah in Wisconsin, Illinois, Kansas, Nebraska, and the Texas Hill Country. Is it possible that the Indians changed the Americas more than the invading Europeans did? "The answer is probably yes for most regions for the next 250 years or so" after Columbus, William Denevan wrote, "and for some regions right up to the present time."

When scholars first began increasing their estimates of the ecological impact of Indian civilization, they met with considerable resistance from anthropologists and archaeologists. Over time the consensus in the human sciences changed. Under Denevan's direction, Oxford University Press has just issued the third volume of a huge catalogue of the "cultivated landscapes" of the Americas. This sort of phrase still provokes vehement objection—but the main dissenters are now ecologists and environmentalists. The disagreement is encapsulated by Amazonia, which has become *the* emblem of vanishing wilderness—an admonitory image of untouched Nature. Yet recently a growing number of researchers have come to believe that Indian societies had an enormous environmental impact on the jungle. Indeed, some antropologists have called the Amazon forest itself a cultural artifact—that is, an artificial object.

GREEN PRISONS

Northern visitors' first reaction to the storied Amazon rain forest is often disappointment. Ecotourist brochures evoke the immensity of Amazonia but rarely dwell on its extreme flatness. In the river's first 2,900 miles the vertical drop is only 500 feet. The river oozes like a huge runnel of dirty metal through a landscape utterly devoid of the romantic crags, arroyos, and heights that signify wildness and natural spectacle to most North Americans. Even the animals are invisible, although sometimes one can hear the bellow of monkey choruses. To the untutored eye—mine, for instance—the forest seems to stretch out in a monstrous green tangle as flat and incomprehensible as a printed circuit board.

The area east of the lower-Amazon town of Santarém is an exception. A series of sandstone ridges several hundred feet high reach down from the north, halting almost at the water's edge. Their tops stand drunkenly above the jungle like old tombstones. Many of the caves in the buttes are splattered with ancient petroglyphs—renditions of hands, stars, frogs, and human figures, all reminiscent of Miró, in overlapping red and yellow and brown. In recent years one of these caves, La Caverna da Pedra Pintada (Painted Rock Cave), has drawn attention in archaeological circles.

Wide and shallow and well lit, Painted Rock Cave is less thronged with bats than some of the other caves. The arched entrance is twenty feet high and lined with rock paintings. Out front is a sunny natural patio suitable for picnicking, edged by a few big rocks. People lived in this cave more than 11,000 years ago. They had no agriculture yet, and instead ate fish and fruit and built fires. During a recent visit I ate a sandwich atop a particularly inviting rock and looked over the forest below. The first Amazonians, I thought, must have done more or less the same thing.

In college I took an introductory anthropology class in which I read *Amazonia: Man and Culture in a Counterfeit Paradise* (1971), perhaps the most influential book ever written about the Amazon, and one that deeply impressed me at the time. Written by Betty J. Meggers, the Smithsonian archaeologist, *Amazonia* says that the apparent lushness of the rain forest is a sham. The soils are poor and can't hold nutrients—the jungle flora exists only because it snatches up everything worthwhile before it leaches away in the rain. Agriculture, which depends on extracting the wealth of the soil, therefore faces inherent ecological limitations in the wet desert of Amazonia.

As a result, Meggers argued, Indian villages were forced to remain small—any report of "more than a few hundred" people in permanent settlements, she told me recently, "makes my alarm bells go off." Bigger, more complex societies would inevitably overtax the forest soils, laying waste to their own foundations. Beginning in 1948 Meggers and her late husband, Clifford Evans, excavated a chiefdom on Marajó, an island twice the size of New Jersey that sits like a gigantic stopper in the mouth of the Amazon. The Marajoara, they concluded, were failed offshoots of a sophisticated culture in the Andes. Transplanted to the lush trap of the Amazon, the culture choked and died.

Green activists saw the implication: development in tropical forests destroys both the forests and their developers. Meggers's account had enormous public impact—*Amazonia* is one of the wellsprings of the campaign to save rain forests.

Then Anna C. Roosevelt, the curator of archaeology at Chicago's Field Museum of Natural History, re-excavated Marajó. Her complete report, *Moundbuilders of the Amazon* (1991), was like the anti-matter version of *Amazonia*. Marajó, she argued, was "one of the outstanding indigenous cultural achievements of the New World," a powerhouse that lasted for more than a thousand years, had "possibly well over 100,000" inhabitants, and covered thousands of square miles. Rather than damaging the forest, Marajó's "earth construction" and "large, dense populations" had *improved* it: the most luxuriant and diverse growth was on the mounds formerly occupied by the Marajóara. "If you listened to Meggers's theory, these places should have been ruined," Roosevelt says.

Meggers scoffed at Roosevelt's "extravagant claims," "polemical tone," and "defamatory remarks." Roosevelt, Meggers argued, had committed the beginner's error of mistaking a site that had been occupied many times by small, unstable groups for a single, long-lasting society. "[Archaeological remains] build up on areas of half a kilometer or so," she told me, "because [shifting Indian groups] don't land exactly on the same spot. The decorated types of pottery don't change much over time, so you can pick up a bunch of chips and say, 'Oh, look, it was all one big site!' Unless you know what you're doing, of course." Centuries after the conquistadors, "the myth of El Dorado is being revived by archaeologists." Meggers wrote last fall in the journal *Latin American Antiquity,* referring to the persistent Spanish delusion that cities of gold existed in the jungle.

The dispute grew bitter and personal; inevitable in a contemporary academic context, it has featured vituperative references to colonialism, elitism, and employment by the CIA. Meanwhile, Roosevelt's team investigated Painted Rock Cave. On the floor of the cave what looked to me like nothing in particular turned out to be an ancient midden: a refuse heap. The archaeologists slowly scraped away sediment, traveling backward in time with every inch. When the traces of human occupation vanished, they kept digging. ("You always go a meter past sterile," Roosevelt says.) A few inches below they struck the charcoal-rich dirt that signifies human habitation—a culture, Roosevelt said later, that wasn't supposed to be there.

For many millenia the cave's inhabitants hunted and gathered for food. But by about 4,000 years ago they were growing crops—perhaps as many as 140 of them, according to Charles R. Clement, an anthropological botanist at the Brazilian National Institute for Amazonian Research. Unlike Europeans, who planted mainly annual crops, the Indians, he says, centered their agriculture on the Amazon's unbelievably diverse assortment of trees: fruits, nuts, and palms. "It's tremendously difficult to clear fields with stone tools," Clement says. "If you can plant trees, you get twenty years of productivity out of your work instead of two or three."

Planting their orchards, the first Amazonians transformed large swaths of the river basin into something more pleasing to human beings. In a widely cited article from 1989, William Balée, the Tulane anthropologist, cautiously estimated that about 12 percent of the nonflooded Amazon forest was of anthropogenic origin—directly or indirectly created by human beings. In some circles this is now seen as a conservative position. "I basically think it's all human-created," Clement told me in Brazil. He argues that Indians changed the assortment and density of species throughout the region. So does Clark Erickson, the University of Pennsylvania archaeologist, who told me in Bolivia that the lowland tropical forests of South America are among the finest works of art on the planet. "Some of my colleagues would say that's pretty radical," he said, smiling mischievously. According to Peter Stahl, an anthropologist at the State University of New York at Binghamton, "lots" of botanists believe that "what the eco-imagery would like to picture as a pristine, untouched Urwelt [primeval world] in fact has been managed by people for millennia." The Phrase "built environment," Erickson says, "applies to most, if not all, Neotropical landscapes."

"Landscape" in this case is meant exactly—Amazonian Indians literally created the ground beneath their feet. According to William I. Woods, a soil geographer at Southern Illinois University, ecologists' claims about terrible Amazonian land were based on very little data. In the late 1990s, Woods and others began careful measurements in the lower Amazon. They indeed found lots of inhospitable terrain. But they also discovered swaths of *terra preta*—rich, fertile "black earth" that anthropologists increasingly believe was created by human beings.

Terra preta, Woods guesses, covers at least 10 percent of Amazonia, an area the size of France. It has amazing properties, he says.

Tropical rain doesn't leach nutrients from *terra preta* fields: instead the soil, so to speak, fights back. Not far from Painted Rock Cave is a 300-acre area with a two-foot layer of *terra preta* quarried by locals for potting soil. The bottom third of the layer is never removed, workers there explain, because over time it will re-create the original soil layer in its initial thickness. The reason, scientists suspect, is that *terra preta* is generated by a special suite of microorganisms that resists depletion. "Apparently," Woods and the Wisconsin geographer Joseph M. McCann argued in a presentation last summer, "at some threshold level … dark earth attains the capacity to perpetuate—even *regenerate* itself—thus behaving more like a living 'super'-organism than an inert material."

In as yet unpublished research the archaeologists Eduardo Neves, of the University of São Paulo; Michael Heckenberger of the University of Florida; and their colleagues examined *terra preta* in the upper Xingu, a huge southern tributary of the Amazon. Not all Xingu cultures left behind this living earth, they discovered. But the ones that did generated it rapidly—suggesting to Woods that *terra preta* was created deliberately. In a process reminiscent of dropping microorganism-rich starter into plain dough to create sourdough bread, Amazonian peoples, he believes, inoculated bad soil with a transforming bacterial charge. Not every group of Indians there did this, but quite a few did, and over an extended period of time.

When Woods told me this, I was so amazed that I almost dropped the phone. I ceased to be articulate for a moment and said things like "wow" and "gosh." Woods chuckled at my reaction, probably because he understood what was passing through my mind. Faced with an ecological problem, I was thinking, the Indians *fixed* it. They were in the process of terraforming the Amazon when Columbus showed up and ruined everything.

Scientists should study the microorganisms in *terra preta*, Woods told me, to find out how they work. If that could be learned, maybe some version of Amazonian dark earth could be used to improve the vast expanses of bad soil that cripple agriculture in Africa—a final gift from the people who brought us tomatoes, corn, and the immense grasslands of the Great Plains.

"Betty Meggers would just die if she heard me saying this," Woods told me. "Deep down her fear is that this data will be misused." Indeed, Meggers's recent *Latin American Antiquity* article charged that archaeologists who say the Amazon can support agriculture are effectively telling "developers [that they] are entitled to operate without restraint." Resuscitating the myth of El Dorado, in her view, "makes us accomplices in the accelerating pace of environmental degradation." Doubtless there is something to this—although, as some of her critics responded in the same issue of the journal, it is difficult to imagine greedy plutocrats "persuing the pages of *Latin American Antiquity* before deciding to rev up the chain saws." But the new picture doesn't automatically legitimize pacing the forest. Instead it suggests that for a long time big chunks of Amazonia were used nondestructively by clever people who knew tricks we have yet to learn.

I visited Painted Rock Cave during the river's annual flood, when it wells up over its banks and creeps inland for miles. Farmers in the floodplain build houses and barns on stilts and watch pink dolphins sport from their doorsteps. Ecotourists take shortcuts by driving motorboats through the drowned forest. Guys in dories chase after them, trying to sell sacks of incredibly good fruit.

All of this is described as "wilderness" in the tourist brochures. It's not, if researchers like Roosevelt are correct. Indeed, they believe that fewer people may be living there now than in 1491. Yet when my boat glided into the trees, the forest shut out the sky like the closing of an umbrella. Within a few hundred yards the human presence seemed to vanish. I felt alone and small, but in a way that was curiously like feeling exalted. If that place was not wilderness, how should I think of it? Since the fate of the forest is in our hands, what should be our goal for its future?

NOVEL SHORES

Hernando de Soto's expedition stomped through the Southeast for four years and apparently never saw bison. More than a century later, when French explorers came down the Mississippi, they saw "a solitude unrelieved by the faintest trace of man," the nineteenth-century historian Francis Parkman wrote. Instead the French encountered bison, "grazing in herds on the great prairies which then bordered the river."

To Charles Kay, the reason for the buffalo's sudden emergence is obvious. Kay is a wildlife ecologist in the political-science department at Utah State University. In ecological terms, he says, the Indians were the "keystone species" of American ecosystems. A keystone species, according to the Harvard biologist Edward O. Wilson, is a species "that affects the survival and abundance of many other species." Keystone species have a disproportionate impact on their ecosystems. Removing them, Wilson adds, "results in a relatively significant shift in the composition of the [ecological] community."

When disease swept Indians from the land, Kay says, what happened was exactly that. The ecological ancient régime collapsed, and strange new phenomena emerged. In a way this is unsurprising: for better or worse, humankind is a keystone species everywhere. Among these phenomena was a population explosion in the species that the Indians had kept down by hunting. After disease killed off the Indians, Kay believes, buffalo vastly extended their range. Their numbers more than sextupled. The same occurred with elk and mule deer. "If the elk were here in great numbers all this time, the archaeological sites should be chock-full of elk bones," Kay says. "But the archaeologists will tell you the elk weren't there." On the evidence of middens the number of elk jumped about 500 years ago.

Passenger pigeons may be another example. The epitome of natural American abundance, they flew in such great masses that the first colonists were stupefied by the sight. As a boy, the explorer Henry Brackenridge saw flocks "ten miles in width, by one hundred and twenty in length." For hours the birds darkened the sky from horizon to horizon. According to Thomas Neumann, a consulting archaeologist in Lilburn, Georgia, passenger pigeons "were incredibly dumb and always roosted in vast hordes, so they were very easy to harvest." Because they were readily caught and good to eat, Neumann says, archaeological digs should find many pigeon bones in the pre-Columbian strata of Indian middens. But they aren't there. The mobs of birds in the history books, he says, were "outbreak populations—always a symptom of an extraordinarily disrupted ecological system."

Throughout eastern North America the open landscape seen by the first Europeans quickly filled in with forest. According to William Cronon, of the University of Wisconsin, later colonists began complaining about how hard it was to get around. (Eventually, of course, they stripped New England almost bare of trees.) When Europeans moved west, they were preceded by two waves: one of disease, the other of ecological disturbance. The former crested with fearsome rapidity; the latter sometimes took more than a century to quiet down. Far from destroying pristine wilderness, European settlers bloodily *created* it. By 1800 the hemisphere was chockablock with new wilderness. If "forest primeval" means a woodland unsullied by the human presence, William Denevan has written, there was much more of it in the late eighteenth century than in the early sixteenth.

Cronon's *Changes in the Land: Indians, Colonists, and the Ecology of New England* (1983) belongs on the same shelf as works by Crosby and Dobyns. But it was not until one of his articles was excerpted in *The New York Times* in 1995 that people outside the social sciences began to understand the implications of this view of Indian history. Environmentalists and ecologists vigorously attacked the antiwilderness scenario, which they described as infected by postmodern philosophy. A small academic brouhaha ensued, complete with hundreds of footnotes. It precipitated *Reinventing Nature?* (1995), one of the few academic critiques of postmodernist philosophy written largely by biologists. *The Great New Wilderness Debate* (1998), another lengthy book on the subject was edited by two philosophers who earnestly identified themselves as "Euro-American men [whose] cultural legacy is patriarchal Western civilization in its current postcolonial, globally hegemonic form."

It is easy to tweak academics for opaque, self-protective language like this. Nonetheless, their concerns were quite justified. Crediting Indians with the role of keystone species has implications for the way the current Euro-American members of that keystone species manage the forests, watersheds, and endangered species of America. Because a third of the United States is owned by the federal government, the issue inevitably has political ramifications. In Amazonia, fabled storehouse of biodiversity, the stakes are global.

Guided by the pristine myth, mainstream environmentalists want to preserve as much of the world's land as possible in a putatively intact state. But "intact," if the new research is correct, means "run by human beings for human purposes." Environmentalists dislike this, because it seems to mean that anything goes. In a sense they are correct. Native Americans managed the continent as they saw fit. Modern nations must do the same. If they want to return as much of the landscape as possible to its 1491 state, they will have to find it within themselves to create the world's largest garden.

CRITICAL THINKING QUESTIONS

1. Why were Dobyn's population estimates of American Indian populations so controversial?
2. How did the transmission of European diseases to American Indian groups impact their cultures? Give specific examples.
3. What changed in the Mississippi River Valley between de Soto's 1539 visits and La Salle's visit in 1682? What do some researchers think may have been the catalyst for the changes and how?
4. What biological and cultural factors made American Indians particularly susceptible to European diseases?
5. Why do some people suggest that the idea of the Americas being "empty continents" in 1491 is appealing to some modern researchers and thinkers?
6. Why do some researchers believe that the idea of a densely populated North America is unsupportable?
7. According to James Wilson, what were the major cultural differences between the populations of Europe and North America?
8. How did American Indians manipulate their environments?

For Reasons Out of Our Hands: A Community Identifies the Causes of Language Shift

Joan Smith/Kocamahhul

What causes a community to shift from one language to another is generally a significant consideration for language maintenance programs. Yet research in specific language communities seldom investigates the community's ideas about the causes of its language shift. The researcher thus runs a risk of assuming that the attitudes of one or two key informants reflect the attitudes of the entire community. This assumption might in turn influence the direction of the research and may render it irrelevant to the community's needs. The ideas voiced by members of a community experiencing language shift and the implications these ideas have for the introduction and success of any future language maintenance efforts are discussed here. Assessing the community's understanding of the causes of its language shift is a crucial first step to take before attempting language maintenance. Community members need to be empowered to see language shift as something they can influence, rather than as something beyond their control.

SPEAKING ARABIC IN TURKEY

Speaking Arabic in a Muslim country might seem unremarkable to the uninitiated. In Turkey, however, the only official language is Turkish, and speaking any other mother tongue, even Arabic, is discouraged; for a time (1983–1991), some languages were prohibited outright.

Although there are no official statistics on language use or on ethnic groups in Turkey, it is clear that in the province of Hatay (in the south, bordering Syria), most people are descended from Arabic speakers. Arabic entered the area as a result of the Arab conquests in the seventh century. Prior to this, the cities were Greek-speaking; people in surrounding areas spoke Aramaic. (Trimingham, 1979) The area first came under Turkish rule for a brief time at the end of the eleventh century, when Seljuks and Turkmen began eroding Byzantine control. Crusader rule followed, and it has been alleged that from the eleventh to the thirteenth centuries even the "Christians were … (Arabs, both culturally and linguistically" (although Greek was the liturgical language for many more centuries). (Courbage & Fargues, 1997) The area subsequently came under Mameluke rule (from the thirteenth to the sixteenth centuries), then under Ottoman rule (from the sixteenth to the twentieth centuries). During both periods, the people spoke Turkish. As part of Greater Syria, Hatay was still largely Arabic-speaking when it was annexed by the Turkish Republic in 1938.[1]

Until annexation, Turkish and Arabic co-existed for centuries; under republican policies, however, the use of Arabic began to decline. Less than a generation ago, a child of an Arabic-speaking family would start school unable to speak Turkish; these days, most children of Arabic families start school unable to speak much, if any, Arabic. Some Arabic speakers will deny being "Arab," a term that can be derogatory in Turkey. I will therefore refer to the community as "Arabic," reflecting the fact that the ancestral connection to the language is the common characteristic.

Source: Reprinted from *Cultural Survival Quarterly*, Summer 2001.

Despite their linguistic connections, Arabic speakers in Hatay do not see themselves as one unified community, and religion, not language, is the primary marker of identity.[2] There are three main religious divisions: Christian (mostly Greek Orthodox), Sunni Muslim (like most Turks), and Alevi (a sect peripheral to Islam, but which shares some beliefs with Shiites). Most of the Arabic community in Hatay is Alevi.

Although the Treaty of Lausanne, signed in 1923 between the new Turkish Republic and the European allies, provided for non-Muslim communities in Turkey to teach their languages, no such provisions were made for Muslim communities. The Greek Christian community in Istanbul, for example, has its own schools which continue to teach Greek to this day. When Hatay was annexed fifteen years after the Treaty was signed, however, the Arabic-speaking Christian community did not avail itself of the right to teach Arabic. Had it tried to do so, the result would have been an untenable situation, with the Christian minority permitted to teach the language of the majority, but the majority itself being prohibited from doing likewise.

Turkey's policies on language have focused on imposing homogeneity. The degree of imposition peaked in 1983, when the military government introduced a law prohibiting (to varying degrees) languages other than Turkish. For speakers of some languages (those not using a first official language of a country recognized by Turkey), the law forbade the use of those languages, even during private conversation. (Rumpf, 1989) Although the law was repealed in 1991, the Constitution still prohibits any institution from teaching a language other than Turkish as a mother tongue (Article 42.9; provisions in international treaties are ostensibly upheld even today).

Although in theory Arabic-speaking Christians have more linguistic rights than Arabic-speaking Muslims, the government's treatment of Arabic as a community language (as opposed to a "liturgical" one) has been uniform irrespective of religion; the Muslim and Christian communities can thus be regarded as a single linguistic group. Modern Standard Arabic (the literary form for any contemporary dialect of Arabic) is, theoretically, permitted as foreign language—for Christians and Muslims alike. In reality, literary Arabic (albeit seldom used in Hatay) is not a foreign language, nor is it taught as such.[3] The notion of teaching Arabic as a foreign language as opposed to a mother tongue has many implications, including pedagogical ones.

COMMUNITY MEMBERS' IDEAS ABOUT LANGUAGE SHIFT

As part of a larger study (in progress) examining the role of code-switching in the language shift in Hatay (Myers-Scotton, 1998), a set of final interview questions was designed primarily to collect demographic information and subjective judgements on language use. The sample (an extended family and its social network, selected in order to obtain natural conversational data for the larger study) comprised 73 Arabic individuals, ranging from eleven to seventy-two years in age. Most (64) were from the city of Antakya (Antioch); the rest were from nearby villages. Most (53) were Christian; the rest were Alevi. Approximately half (39) were under 35. The participants were asked if Arabic was decreasing in Hatay. If they said "yes," they were asked why and whether they thought this was good or bad (or not important). The participants' responses suggest a sense of powerlessness on the part of speakers to affect language shift.

Eleven participants (15 percent of the sample)—let us call them the deny-ers—said that Arabic was not decreasing; yet some of their comments suggested an awareness of a shift:

A 63-year-old Christian man said:

"No. [It's] more … the Alevi more than us of course. The Alevi are all Arab. (Interviewer: Do they speak [it]?) [They're] all Arab; that is, they don't speak anything else."

A 29-year-old Christian woman said:

"No. … [There are] lots of Alevi. In general, Arabic is spoken."

A 46-year-old Alevi woman living in the city said:

"No. [There are] lots who speak, lots in the villages."

In choosing to focus their answers on a group other than their own, these speakers may have implied that Arabic had been decreasing in their own group (in the case of the Christians) or in their area (in the case of the city-dwelling Alevi). Yet, because they still heard the language being spoken by others, they believed that Arabic was not decreasing.[4]

Those who said Arabic was decreasing (62 respondents, 85 percent of the sample)—let us call them the realists—were then asked why. Three causes far outnumbered other responses: schools forbidding Arabic or not offering it as a subject (31 respondents, 50 percent); the older generation/parents not teaching the language (29 respondents, 47 percent) and the younger generation/children not wanting to learn it (18 respondents, 29 percent). All but two realists mentioned one or more of these three causes. Other answers varied, but were similar to causes cited in other studies:

- Arabic-speaking elders dying off, reducing the opportunity to learn the language (9 = 15 percent);
- the language as unnecessary for life in Turkey (9 = 15 percent);
- increased mobility around Turkey and higher education causing people to use Turkish more frequently (9 = 15 percent);
- Arabic a difficult language to learn (6 = 10 percent);
- the government's pursuit of assimilationist policies (6 = 10 percent); and
- Turkish used to camouflage "Arab" origins (4 = 7 percent).[5]

The three main causes—educational availability and the two generational behaviors—far outnumbered other responses. They were considered causally interconnected, since parents mentioned pressure from teachers not to speak Arabic with their children. One woman recalled that when she was a child, Arabic was forbidden at school (as it is today) and that she told her parents she didn't want to speak Arabic anymore. She added, however: "If [I had been] in my current state of mind, I definitely would have learned Arabic."

Bringing these responses together, there were 10 members of the older generation who saw the younger generation as the cause of the language shift, 22 of the younger generation who saw the older generation as causing the shift, four who blamed their peers but considered themselves exceptions, and 12 who blamed neither generation but indicted the educational system. Not including the two who blamed both generations, we end up with approximately 46 (74 percent of the "realists") who saw the causes of language shift as being, to quote one respondent, "for reasons out of our hands."

IMPLICATIONS FOR LANGUAGE MAINTENANCE

Community members' beliefs about the causes of language shift would be immaterial if the community were happy at the decline of Arabic, but it seems as if members of this group would prefer to maintain it. Of the realists, 40 (65 percent) said that the decline was a bad thing; another 12 (19 percent) had mixed feelings (the others did not think it was important). One (Christian) deny-er linked language maintenance to religion, saying that Arabic had to continue so that the Bible would be understood when it was read. In fact, a religious motivation to maintain Arabic was shared by all three religious groups; even Orthodox Christians stated that they used Arabic as their language of religion. One Alevi convert to Catholicism said that, although he could not understand Arabic (because his parents had not taught him the language), he found its use in the Orthodox service mystical. A cultural motivation to maintain Arabic was also mentioned by a number of respondents; 11 quoted an Arabic proverb affirming the value of multilingualism: "Every language is a person."

An apparent obstacle to language maintenance efforts exist, despite religious and cultural affirmations. If community members see the causes of language shifts as out of their hands, then language maintenance efforts may well seem doomed from the start, and are likely to suffer from a lack of impetus. The current lack of language maintenance efforts in Hatay is not necessarily due to indifference to the language; rather, it reflects the community's ambivalence as to whether it (can) have an effect on language shift.

WHERE TO START?

Since 50 percent of the realists cited the education system as a cause of language shift, perhaps language classes should be the starting point for a language maintenance program. Researchers in other parts of the world, however, have expressed concern that too much reliance is often placed on such programs. Furthermore, such programs require resources (teachers, classrooms, textbooks, etc.), and this need can lead to bureaucratic hurdles. Even with substantial state support, classroom efforts to maintain languages are not especially successful on their own. In Ireland, for example, where ample funding, resources, and incentives have increased knowledge of Irish at some levels, the number who speak it as a first language is still declining.

In Turkey, a classroom approach is impracticable for other reasons. As noted above, the Christian community could teach Arabic, but at the risk of creating resentment in the Muslim (Alevi and Sunni) communities. Arabic could be taught as a foreign language, but this would preclude a "language nest" approach to testing Arabic (language nests are implicitly about learning a language as a native, not a foreign, tongue).[6] Furthermore, moves to teach Arabic, even as a foreign language, might be interpreted by the authorities as evidence of affiliation with Syria and thus, with the promotion of separatist goals. Moreover, smaller minorities in Turkey are less likely to pursue structured language maintenance efforts until the Kurds have unambiguously secured cultural autonomy.[7] In this climate, even reporting the results of this research to the community needs to be done in such a way so as to avoid an antagonistic reaction from authorities.

Just because an education system was a major contributor to a language shift does not mean that it is the best means by which to "reverse" that shift. The causes of a language shift are only relevant when planning a language maintenance program (insofar as they sustain the shift). The key issue to be addressed is how to inhibit (and perhaps even eradicate) language shift itself. In the case of the Arabic speakers in Hatay, the perception that the causes of the language shift are out of their hands sustains the shift by implying that community members cannot have an effect on reversing it. To initiate a language maintenance program would require addressing this sense of powerlessness. Bearing this in mind, let us re-define the concept of language shift.

REDEFINING LANGUAGE SHIFT IN EMPOWERING TERMS

Language shift has been defined in various ways: "the loss of linguistic skills between generations" (De Bot, 1996); a community's giving up a language "completely in favor of another one" (Fasold, 1984); or, "speech communities whose native languages are threatened because their intergenerational continuity is proceeding negatively, with fewer and fewer users (speakers, readers, writers and even understanders) or uses every generation." (Fishman, 1991).

De Vries uses Weinreich's definition of language shift as his starting point: "the change from the habitual use of one language to that of another. ... " (Weinreich, 1952; de Vries, 1992) However, as De Vries points out, Weinreich's definition does not address the issue of choice. This is also true of many other definitions, not least because if reference is made to the speakers, the tendency is to define language shift in terms of societal entities (generations, communities), rather than in terms of individual speakers. However, as Fishman suggests, language shift rests in the non-use of the language by people. Fasold adds: "language maintenance and shift are the long-term, collective consequences of consistent patterns of language choice."

These patterns of language choice are not selected collectively, but on an individual basis, instance by instance. (The community is a group of individuals, and a living language exists only in the minds and mouths of the individuals who speak it.) Language shift, therefore, is the cumulative effect of a group of individuals increasingly using one language over another. For language maintenance, then, every individual has a contribution to make: the proficient speaker can use the language with less proficient speakers, the semi-speaker can become more proficient, the passive bilingual can become active. By using a definition of language shift which explicitly acknowledges the role of the individual in language shift and maintenance, individuals in any community may better understand the contribution they can make to language maintenance. Encouraging speakers to ask themselves, "What can I do differently?" could be a simple starting point.

In the case of the Arabic speakers in Hatay, the belief that the causes of language shift are out of their hands must be addressed. As noted above, a number of obstacles to pursuing a structured language maintenance program exist, yet the attitudes expressed by the Arabic community suggest receptiveness to language maintenance per se. It seems, then, that the safest approach is to encourage individuals to modify their speech behavior and use Arabic in preference to Turkish as much as is practical. Grandparents and other speakers of Arabic should be encouraged to use the language more with children. The frequent claim that speaking Arabic to children will be a long-term detriment to their acquisition of Turkish needs to be refuted. Some individuals may wish to explore the legal status of the language. Even the act of conducting research on the language—asking speakers to reflect on the language—may prompt individuals to think consciously about their attitudes toward Arabic and to consider ways of translating those attitudes into action. Individuals empowered with the knowledge that they have the ultimate "say" over what comes out of their mouths and how they can influence the future of the language need not be dependent on the government or the education system for support. The external causes of language shift may be out of their control, but the most crucial aspect of language maintenance, the speaking of it, is in their hands.

Notes

1. The name Hatay was given at the time of the annexation; prior to this, it was known as the Sanjak of Alexandretta. Syria still lays claim to Hatay, a point which continues to cause diplomatic tension.
2. This reality may have its roots in the fact that both the Ottoman Empire and the Turkish Republic place(d) an emphasis on classifying citizens according to religion. The term "minority" is only applied to nonMuslims. (*Turkish Daily News Online*, 9/11/00)
3. Arabic is taught as a foreign language at university level elsewhere in Turkey; it is not available at Mustafa Kemal University, Hatay's only (state) university, even though it is less than a hundred kilometers from the Syrian border.
4. This resonates with Schmidt's finding that speakers of Aboriginal languages may only belatedly recognize that their language is under threat. (Schmidt, 1990)
5. Fasold's list of causes includes most of those suggested by the "realists": migration (both emigration by community members and immigration by outsiders); industrialization and other economic changes; school language and other government pressures; urbanization; higher prestige for the language to which shift was occurring; and a smaller population of speakers of the language from which shift was taking place. (Fasold, 1984) Hyltenstam and Stroud's list is more extensive, factoring at societal, group, and individual levels. (Hyltenstam & Stroud, 1996).
6. The Kohanga Reo (or "language nest") movement began in New Zealand as a grassroots language revitalization strategy in the 1980s. Community elders provide a Māori-medium environment where preschool children acquire Māori naturally. The approach has been adapted for the Hawaiian and Saami languages (see Ole Henrik and Skutnabb-Kangas, this issue).
7. There does seem to be movement in this direction. Most recently, the head of Turkey's National Intelligence Agency stated that permitting Kurdish language broadcasts in the Southeast was a desirable way of counteracting pro-separatist broadcasts from outside Turkey. The Nationalist movement party, MHP, a member of the ruling coalition, is yet to be persuaded. (Parsons, 2000)

Joan Smith/Kocamahhul is a tutor in the School of Classics and Linguistics at the University of Canterbury, New Zealand.

Acknowledgments

I would like to thank Lyle Campbell, Susan Foster-Cohen, and Eileen Moore Quinn for helpful comments made on earlier drafts of this paper. Thanks are due also to Mişçel Kocamahhul for many unpaid hours of research assistance.

References and Further Reading

Courbage, Y. & Fargues, P. (1997). *Christians and Jews Under Islam*. London: I.B. Tauris.

De Bot, K. (1996). Language Loss. In *Contact Linguistics*. Goebl, H., Nelde, P.H., Stary, Z. & Wölck, W., Eds. Berlin: Walter de Gruyter. pp. 579–585.

De Vries, J. (1992). Language Maintenance and Shift: Problems of Measurement. In *Maintenance and Loss of Minority Languages*. Fase, W., Jaspaert, K. & Kroon, S., Eds. Amsterdam: John Benjamins. pp. 211–222.

Fasold, R. (1984). The Sociolinguistics of Society. Oxford: Basil Blackwell.

Fishman, J. A. (1991). *Reversing Language Shift*. Clevedon: Multilingual Matters.

Myers-Scotton, C. (1998). *A Way to a Dusty Death: the Matrix Language Turnover*.

The Republic of Turkey (2000, April 26). *The Constitution 1982* (English translation). www.mfa.gov.tr/grupc/ca/cag/I142.htm.

Rumpf, C. (1989). Das Sprachenverbot in der Türkei unter besonderer Berücksichtigung inhrer völkerrechtlichen Verpflichtungen.*Orient* 30, pp. 413–427.

Trimingham, J. S. (1979). *Christianity Among the Arabs in Pre-Islamic Times*. London: Longman.

Weinreich, U. (1952). *Languages in Contact*. Cambridge: Cambridge University Press.

CRITICAL THINKING QUESTIONS

1. Usually linguistic and ethnic communities are one and the same. What is different about the Arabic speakers of Hatay province?

2. Poll results suggest that the community was divided into two perception groups. What are these groups, and how do their perspectives on the loss of Arabic fluency differ?

3. Why would the Turkish government wish to suppress the use of Arabic in Hatay?

4. What are the causes identified by Smith as leading to a loss in fluency in Arabic, and how does she think that this trend could be reversed?

Queer Customs

Clyde Kluckhohn

In this selection, written more than half a century ago, Clyde Kluckhohn explains the anthropological concept of culture in a way that is eminently understandable for the beginning student of comparative cultures. Referring to culture as a "design for living," Kluckhohn, who for much of his career was the leading authority on the Navajo, used the anthropological perspective to explain what most nonanthropologists at the time considered to be "queer customs" He examined culture by showing how it is different from biological influences on our behavior, how culture influences biological process, how it is learned rather than being genetically transmitted, and how it functions to help people adapt to their environment. Even though some of his references are today politically incorrect (for example, the use of such terms as primitive and heathen), Kluckhohn's piece serves as a valuable reminder that the study of other cultures allows us to better understand our own culture.

Why do the Chinese dislike milk and milk products? Why would the Japanese die willingly in a Banzai charge that seemed senseless to Americans? Why do some nations trace descent through the father, others through the mother, still others through both parents? Not because different peoples have different instincts, not because they were designed by God or Fate to different habits, not because the weather is different in China and Japan and the United States. Sometimes shrewd common sense has an answer that is close to that of the anthropologist: "because they were brought up that way." By "culture" anthropology means the total life way of a people, the social legacy the individual acquires from his group. Or culture can be regarded as that part of the environment that is the creation of man.

This technical term has a wider meaning than the "culture" of history and literature. A humble cooking pot is as much a cultural product as is a Beethoven sonata. In ordinary speech a man of culture is a man who can speak languages other than his own. Who is familiar with history, literature, philosophy, or the fine arts. In some cliques that definition is still narrower. The cultured person is one who can talk about James Joyce, Scarlatti, and Picasso. To the anthropologist, however, to be human is to be cultured. There is culture in general, and then there are the specific cultures such as Russian, American, British, Hottentot, Inca. The general abstract notion services to remind us that we cannot explain acts solely in terms of the biological properties of the people concerned, their individual past experience, and the immediate situation. The past experience of other men in the form of culture enters into almost every event. Each specific culture constitutes a kind of blueprint for all of life's activities.

One of the interesting things about human beings is that they try to understand themselves and their own behavior. While this has been particularly true of Europeans in recent times, there is no group which has not developed a schema or schemes to explain man's actions. To the insistent human query "why?" the most exciting illumination anthropology has to offer is that of the concept of culture. Its explanatory importance is comparable to categories such as evolution in biology, gravity in physics, disease in medicine. A good deal of human behavior can be understood, and indeed predicted, if we know a people's design for living. Many acts are neither accidental nor due to personal peculiarities nor caused by supernatural forces nor simply mysterious. Even those of us who pride ourselves on our individualism follow most of the time a pattern not of our own making. We brush our teeth on arising. We put on pants—not a loincloth or a grass skirt. We eat three meals a day—not four or five or two. We sleep in a bed—not in a hammock or on a sheep pelt. I do not have to know the individual and his life history to be able to predict these and countless other regulations, including many in the thinking process, of all Americans who are not incarcerated in jail or hospitals for the insane.

To the American woman a system of plural wives seems "instinctively" abhorrent. She can not understand how any woman can fail to be jealous and uncomfortable if she must share her husband with other women. She feels it "unnatural" to accept such a situation. On the other hand, Koryak women of Siberia, for example, would find it hard to understand how a woman could be so selfish and so undesirous of femine companionship in the home as to wish to restrict her husband to one mate.

Some years ago I met in New York City a young man who did not speak a word of English and was obviously bewildered by American ways. By "blood" he was as American as you or I, for his parents had gone from Indiana to China as missionaries. Orphaned in infancy, he was reared by a Chinese family in a remote village. All who met him found him more Chinese than American. The facts of his blue eyes and light hair were less impressive than a Chinese style of gait, Chinese arm and hand movements, Chinese facial expression, and Chinese models of thought. The biological heritage was American, but the culture training had been Chinese. He returned to China.

Another example of another kind: I once knew a trader's wife in Arizona who took a somewhat devilish interest in producing a cultural reaction. Guests who came her way were often served delicious sandwiches filled with a meat that seemed to be neither chicken nor tuna fish yet was reminiscent of both. To queries she gave no reply until each had eaten his fill. She then explained that what they had eaten was not chicken, not tuna fish, but the rich, white flesh of freshly killed rattlesnakes. The response was instantaneous—vomiting, often violent vomiting. A biological process is caught in a cultural web.

A highly intelligent teacher with long and successful experience in the public schools of Chicago was finishing her first year in an Indian school. When asked her how her Navaho pupils compared in intelligence with Chicago youngsters, she replied, "Well, I just don't know. Sometimes the Indian's seem just a bright. At other times they just act like dumb animals. The other night we had a dance in the high school. I saw a boy who one of the best student in my English class standing off by himself. So I took him over to a pretty girl and told them to dance. But they just stood there with their heads down. They wouldn't even say anything." I inquired if she knew whether or not they were members of the same clan. "What difference would that make?"

"How would you feel about getting into bed with your brother?" The teacher walked off in a huff, but, actually, the two cases were quite comparable in principle. To the Indian the type of bodily contact involved in our social dancing has a directly sexual connotation. The incest taboos between members of the same clan are as severe as between true brothers and sisters. The shame of the Indians at the suggestion that a clan brother and sister should dance and the indignation of the white teacher at the idea that she should share a bed with an adult brother represent equally nonrational response, culturally standardized unreason.

All this does not mean that there is no such thing as raw human nature. The very fact that certain of the same institution are found in all known societies indicates that at bottom all human beings are very much alike. The files of the Cross-Cultural Survey at Yale University are organized according to categories such "marriage ceremonies," "life crisis rites," "incest taboos." At least seventy-five of these categories are represented in every single one of the hundreds of cultures analyzed. This is hardly surprising. The members of all human groups have about the same biological equipment. All men undergo the same poignant life experiences such as birth, helplessness, illness, old age, and death. The biological potentialities of the species are the blocks with which cultures are built. Some pattern every culture crystallize around focuses provided by the inevitables of biology; the difference between the sexes, the presence of persons of different ages, the varying physical strength and skill of individuals. The facts of nature also limit culture forms. No culture provides patterns for jumping over trees or eating iron ore.

There is thus no "either-or" between nature and that special form of nature called culture.

Culture determinism is as one-sided as biological determinism. The two factors are interdependent. Culture arises out of human nature, and its forms are restricted both by man's biology and by natural laws. It is equally true that culture channels biological processes—vomiting, weeping, fainting, sneezing, the daily habits of food intake and waste elimination. When a man eats, he is reacting to an internal "drive," namely, hunger contractions consequent upon the lowering of blood sugar, but his precise reaction to these internal stimuli cannot be predicted by physiological knowledge alone. Whether a healthy adult feel hungry twice, three times, or four times a day and the hours at which this feeling recurs is a question of culture. *What* he cats is of course limited by availability, but is also partly regulated by culture. It is a biological fact that some types of berries are poisonous; it is a cultural fact that, a few generations ago, most Americans considered tomatoes to be poisonous and refused to eat them. Such selective, discriminative use of the environment is characteristically cultural. In a still more general sense, too, the process of eating is channeled by culture. Whether a man eats to live, lives to eat, or merely eats and lives is only in part an individual matter, for there are also cultural trends. Emotions are physiological events. Certain situations will evoke fear in people from any culture. But sensations of pleasure, anger, and lust may be stimulated by cultural cues that would leave unmoved someone who has been reared in a different social condition.

Except in the case of newborn babies and of individuals born with clear-cut structural or functional abnormalities we can observe innate endowments only as modified by cultural training. In a hospital in New Mexico where Zuñi Indian, Navaho Indian, and white American babies are born, it is possible to classify the newly active infants as unusually active, average, and quiet. Some babies from each "racial" group will fall into each category, though a higher proportion of the white babies will fall into the unusually active class. But if a Navaho baby, a Zuñi baby, and a white baby—all classified as unusually active at birth—are again observed at the age of two years, the Zuñi baby will no longer seem given to quick and restless activity—*as compared will the white child* though he may seem so as compared with the other Zuñis of the same age. The Navaho child is likely to fall in between as contrasted with the Zuñi and the white, though he will probably still seem more than the average Navaho youngster.

It was remarked by many observers in the Japanese relocation centers that Japanese who were born and brought up in this country, especially those who were reared apart from any large colony of Japanese, resemble in behavior their white neighbors much more closely than they do their own parents who were educated in Japan.

I have said "culture channels biological processes." It is more accurate to say "the biological functioning of individuals is modified if they have been trained in certain ways and not in others." Culture is not a disembodied force. It is created and transmitted by people. However, culture, like well-known concepts of the physical sciences, is a convenient abstraction. One never sees gravity. One sees bodies falling in regular ways. One never sees an electromagnetic field. Yet certain happenings that can be seen may be given a neat abstract formulation by assuming that the electromagnetic field exists. Similarly, one never sees culture as such. What is seen are regularities in the behavior or artifacts of a group that has adhered to a common tradition. The regularities in style and technique of ancient Inca tapestries or stone axes from Melanesian islands are due to the existence of mental blueprints for the group.

Culture is a *way* of thinking, felling, believing. It is the group's knowledge stored up (in memories of men; in books and objects) for future use. We study the products of this "mental" activity: the overt behavior, the speech and gesture and activities of people, and the tangible results of these things such as tools, houses, cornfields, and what not. It has been customary in lists of "culture traits" to include such things as watches or lawbooks. This is a convenient way of thinking about them, but in the solution of any important problem we must remember that they, in themselves, are noting but metals, paper, and ink. What is important is that some men know how to make them, others set a value on them, are unhappy without them, direct their activities in relation to them, or disregard them.

It is only a helpful shorthand when we say "The cultural patterns of the Zulu were resistant to Christianization." In the directly observable world of course, it was individual Zulus who resisted. Nevertheless, if we do not forget that we are speaking at a high of abstraction, it is justifiable to speak of culture as a cause. One may compare the practice of saying "syphilis caused the extinction of the native population of the island." Was it "syphilis" or "syphilis germs" or "human beings who were carriers of syphilis?"

"Culture," then, is "a theory." But if a theory is not contradicted by any relevant fact and if it helps us to understand a mass of otherwise chaotic facts, it is useful. Darwin's contribution was much less the accumulation of new knowledge than the creation of a theory which put in order data already known. An accumulation of facts, however large, is no more a science than a pile of bricks is house. Anthropology's demonstration that the most weird set of customs has a consistency and an order is comparable to modern psychiatry's showing that there is meaning and purpose in the apparently incoherent talk of the insane. In fact, the inability of the older psychologies and philosophies to account for the strange behavior of madmen and heathens was the principal factor that forced psychiatry and anthropology to develop theories of the unconscious and of culture.

Since culture is an abstraction, it is important not to confuse culture with society. A "society" refers to a group of people who interact more with each other than they do with other individuals—who cooperate with each other for the attainment of certain ends. You can see and indeed count the individuals who make up a society. A "culture" refers to the distinctive ways of life of such a group of people. Not all social events are culturally patterned. New types of circumstances arise for which no cultural solutions have as yet been devised.

A culture constitutes a storehouse of the pooled learning of the group. A rabbit starts life with some innate responses. He can learn from his own experience and perhaps from observing other rabbits. A human infant is born with fewer instincts and greater plasticity. His main task is to learn the answers that persons he will never see, persons long dead, have worked out. Once he has learned the formulas supplied by the culture of his group, most of his behavior becomes almost as automatic and unthinking as if it were instinctive. There is a tremendous amount of intelligence behind the making of a radio, but not much is required to learn to turn it on.

The members of all human societies face some of the same unavoidable dilemmas, posed by biology and other facts of the human situation. This is why the basic categories of all cultures are so similar. Human culture without language is unthinkable. No culture fails to provide for aesthetic expression and aesthetic delight. Every culture supplies standardized orientations toward the deeper problems, such as death. Every culture is designed to perpetuate the group and its solidarity, to meet the demands of individuals for an orderly way of life and for satisfaction of biological needs.

However, the variations on these basic themes are numberless. Some languages are built up out of twenty basic sounds, others out of forty. Nose plugs were considered beautiful by the predynastic Egyptians but are not by the modern French. Puberty is a biological fact. But one culture ignotes it, another prescribes informal instructions about sex but no ceremony, a third has impressive rites for girls only, a fourth for boys and girls. In this culture, the first menstruation is welcomed as a happy, natural event; in that culture the atmosphere is full of dread and supernatural threat. Each culture dissects nature according to its own system of categories. The Navaho Indians apply the same word to the color of a robin's egg and to that of grass. A psychologist once assumed that this meant a difference in the sense organs, that Navahos didn't have the physiological equipment to distinguish "green" from "blue." However, when he showed them objects of the two colors and asked them if they were exactly the same colors, they looked at him with astonishment. His dream of discovering a new type of color blindness was shattered.

Every culture must deal with the sexual instinct. Some, however, seek to deny all sexual expression before marriage, whereas a Polynesian adolescent who was not promiscuous would he distinctly abnormal. Some cultures enforce lifelong monogamy, others, like our own, tolerate serial monogamy; in still other cultures, two or more women may be joined to one man or several men to a single woman. Homosexuality has been permitted pattern in the Greco-Roman world, in parts of Islam, and in various primitive tribes.

Large portions of the population of Tibet, and of Christendom at some places and periods, have practiced completely celibacy. To us marriage is first and foremost an arrangement between two individuals. In many more societies marriage is merely one facet of a complicated set of reciprocities, economic and otherwise, between two families or two clans.

The essence of the cultural process is selectivity. The selection is only exceptionally conscious and rational. Cultures are like Topsy. They just grew. Once, however, a way of handling a situation becomes institutionalized, there is ordinarily great resistance to change or deviation. When we speak of "our sacred beliefs," we mean of course that they are beyond criticism and that the person who suggests modification or abandonment must be punished. No person is emotionally indifferent to his culture. Certain cultural premises may become totally out of accord with a new factual situation. Leaders may recognize this and reject the old ways in theory. Yet their emotional loyalty continues in the face of reason because of the intimate conditionings of early childhood.

A culture is learned by individuals as the result of belonging to some particular group, and it constitutes that part of learned behavior which is shared with others. It is our social legacy, as contrasted with our organic heredity. It is one of the important factors which permits us to live together in an organized society, giving us ready-made solutions to our problems, helping us to predict the behavior of others, and permitting others in known what to expect of us.

Culture regulates our lives at every turn. From the moment we are born until we die there is, whether we are conscious of it or not, constant pressure upon us to follow certain types of behavior that other men have created for us. Some paths we follow willingly, others we follow because we know no other way, still others we deviate from or go back to most unwillingly. Mothers of small children known how unnaturally most of this comes to us—how little regard we have, until we are "culturalized," for the "proper" place, time, and manner for certain acts such as eating, excreting, sleeping, getting dirty, and making loud noises. But by more or less adhering to a system of related designs for carrying out all the acts of living, a group of men and women feel themselves linked together by a powerful chain of sentiments. Ruth Benedict gave an almost complete definition of the concept when she said, "Culture is that which binds men together."

It is true any culture is a set of techniques for adjusting both to the external environment and to other men. However, cultures create problems as well as solve them. If the lore of a people states that frogs are dangerous creatures, or that it is not safe to go about at night because of witches or ghosts, threats are posed which do not arise out of the inexorable facts of the external world. Cultures produce needs as well as provide a means of fulfilling them. There exists for every group culturally defined, acquired drives that may be more powerful in ordinary daily life than the biologically inborn drives. Many Americans, for example, will work harder for "success" than they will for sexual satisfaction.

Most groups elaborate certain aspects of their culture far beyond maximum utility or survival value. In other words, not all culture promotes physical survival. At times, indeed, it does exactly the opposite. Aspects of culture which once were adaptive may persist long after they have ceased to be useful. An analysis of any culture will disclose many features which cannot possibly be construed as adaptations to the total environment in which the group now finds itself. However, it is altogether likely that these apparently useless features represent survivals, with modifications through time, of cultural forms which were adaptive in one or another pervious situation.

Any cultural practice must be functional or it will disappear before long. That is, it must somehow contribute to the survival of the society or to the adjustment of the individual. However, many cultural functions are not manifest but latent. A cowboy will walk three miles to catch a horse which he then rides one mile to the store. From the point of view of manifest function this is positively irrational. But the act has the latent function of maintaining the cowboy's prestige in the terms of his own subculture. One can instance the buttons on the sleeve of a man's coat, our absurd English spelling, the use of capital letters, and a host of other apparently nonfunctional customs. They serve mainly the latent function of assisting individuals to maintain their security by preserving continuity with the past and by making certain sectors of life familiar and predictable.

Every culture is a precipitate of history. In more than one sense history is a sieve. Each culture embraces those aspects of the past which, usually in altered form and with altered meanings, live on in the present. Discoveries and inventions, both material and ideological, are constantly being made available to a group through its historical contacts with other peoples or being created by its own members. However, only those that fit the total immediate situation in meeting the group's needs for survival or in promoting the psychological adjustment of individuals will become part of the culture. The process of culture building may be regarded as an addition to man's innate biological capacities, an addition providing instruments which enlarge, or may even substitute for, biological functions, and to a degree compensating for biological limitations—as in ensuring that death does not always result in the loss to humanity of what the deceased has learned.

Culture is like a map. Just as a map isn't the territory but an abstract representation of a particular area, so also a culture is an abstract description of trends toward uniformity in the words, deeds, and artifacts of a human group. If a map is accurate and you can read it, you won't get lost; if you know a culture, you will know your way around in the life of a society. Many educated people have the notion that culture applies only to exotic ways of life or to societies where relative simplicity and relative homogeneity prevail. Some sophisticated missionaries, for example, will use the anthropological conception in discussing the special modes of living of South Sea Islanders, but seem amazed at the idea that it could be applied equally to inhabitants of New York City. And social workers in Boston will talk about the culture of a colorful and well-knit immigrant group but boggle at applying it to the behavior of staff members in the social-service agency itself.

In the primitive society the correspondence between the habits of individuals and the customers of the community is ordinarily greater. There is probably some truth in what an old Indian once said, "In the old days there was no law; everybody did what was right." The primitive tends to find happiness in the fulfillment of intricately involuted cultural patterns; the modern more often tends to feel the pattern as repressive to his individuality. It is also true that in a complex stratified society there are numerous exceptions to generalizations made about the culture as a whole. It is necessary to study regional, class, and occupational subcultures. Primitive cultures have greater stability than modern cultures; they change—but less rapidly.

However, modern men also are creators and carriers of culture. Only in some respects are they influenced differently from primitives by culture. Moreover, there are such wide variations in primitive cultures that any back-and-white contrast between the primitive and the civilized is altogether fictitious. The distinction which is most generally true lies in the field of conscious philosophy.

The publication of Paul Radin's *Primitive Man as a Philosopher* did much toward destroying the myth that an abstract analysis of experience was a peculiarity of literate societies.

CRITICAL THINKING QUESTIONS

1. What definition of culture does Kluckhohn use? In what ways is it similar and/or different from the version employed in your own anthropology class?
2. Kluckhohn argues that "culture channels biological processes." What does he mean by that? Provide supporting data from the article or your own experience to support your answer.
3. Why do people cling to their "sacred beliefs" provided to them by their culture? Can these beliefs change, and if so, how? Give an example from the article or American culture to support your answer.

Inventing Tibet

Lydia Aran

For quite some time now, the cause of Tibet and Tibetan Buddhism has enjoyed a phenomenal vogue in the advanced circles of the West. The "Tibetan cultural heritage," as it is known, is universally understood to be the repository of a precious spiritual wisdom—one, moreover, that is critically relevant to the future of the entire world. But Tibet's heritage is also seen to be highly endangered, in need of urgent support and rescue by the West.

One can date the emergence of the Tibetan cause fairly precisely. It occurred after the country was incorporated into the People's Republic of China in 1950, and especially after the 1959 flight to India of its spiritual and temporal leader, the 14th Dalai Lama. Before that time, Tibet barely registered in the West's consciousness. Indeed, for centuries it had effectively disappeared from the political map of the world.

In the 1960's and 70's new Tibet was born, not so much a country as a mental construct. Its progenitor was the Diaspora establishment headed by the Dalai Lama, centered in the Himalayan hill station of Dharamsala in North India. There, the leaders of a small community comprising no more than 5 percent of the Tibetan people as a whole undertook to construct a wholly new idea of Tibetan identity —and hugely succeeded.

One of the reasons Tibet went largely unnoticed until 1959 is that it had never been colonized by a European power. Colonialism, whatever its sins, has been a great producer of knowledge. It modernized the countries under its sway, bringing technology, infrastructure, school, and libraries. It also arranged for the education of native elites in the universities and professional schools of the colonial metropolis.

Tibet missed all this. Unlike in the case of India, no records, surveys, or reports about it accumulated in Western research institutes, no colonial scholar officers explored local history and culture, and no means existed through which Western-style knowledge might be disseminated to the inhabitants. The harshness of the country's landscape and climate, together with its self-imposed isolation, enhanced its reputation as a "forbidden land." Until the second half of the 20th century, it was known mostly by adventurers, missionaries, amateur explorers, and (following the 1904 British invasion) a few political officers disguised as trade agents.

Which is not to say that it was without its fans. Detached from history, transcending time and change, Tibet became for many a kind of utopia—a Shangri-La.

That, of course, is the name of the fictitious trans-Himalayan valley that provides the setting of James Hilton's 1933 novel *Lost Horizon,* and of the 1937 film by Frank Capra made from it. In that inaccessible valley, a spiritual community has taken refuge in a monastery housing the most valuable treasures of civilization—treasures to be restored to the world after the exiled Christian faith returns to prevail on earth. Members of the community, leading a serene, tranquil existence, their wants seen to by peaceful local Tibetans, enjoy the blessings of an illness-free longevity.

Hilton's novel is a Westernized and bowdlerized version of the ancient myth of Shambhala, a hidden kingdom somewhere north of Tibet where enlightened kings guard the secret core of Buddhist teachings until the moment when their armies will destroy the forces of evil and usher in a golden age. And here is but one aspect of the idealized notion of Tibet that would seize the imagination of the Western world: while Westerners look to Tibet as the locus of sublime ancient wisdom, Tibetans themselves have traditionally, as in the myth of Shambhala, looked for it somewhere else.

The Shangri-La view of Tibet would be given fresh impetus by the countercultural movements of the 1960's and 70's. Young (and not so young) Europeans and Americans proclaimed themselves to be in search of a new "paradigm," one based on moral and spiritual principles instead of the destructive forces of market capitalism and power politics. To many of them, Tibet seemed to offer such a paradigm, vague enough to serve as a kind of screen on which to project their own dreams and fantasies. Their Tibet, with its unique wisdom, not only was precious in itself but represented the last remaining hope for the ills of the materially rich but spiritually impoverished civilization of the West. It was a place inhabited by a simple, deeply religious, and inherently nonviolent people, ruled by an emanation of the Buddha in accordance with the tenets of benevolence, compassion, and the sanctity of all life.

HOW GENUINE IS THE VERSION OF TIBET'S RELIGIOUS AND CULTURAL HERITAGE?

The form of Buddhism practiced in Tibet is a blend of indigenous and imported elements that consolidated itself in the period following the disintegration of the Tibetan kingdom in the 9th century. By the 11th century, this branch of Buddhism had developed several monastic orders or lineages, which soon accumulated great wealth. Unlike in other form of Buddhism, the monastic establishment became strong enough to share power with the Tibetan aristocracy, and its hierarchs became not only prominent in political life but heads of Tibetan states.

As for the characteristic practices of Tibetan Buddhism, these comprise several strands. In the most familiar one, similar to forms of Buddhism found in other Asian societies, the primary pathway to ultimate enlightenment (buddhahood) lies through scholarship combined with monastic

discipline; the paradigmatic figure is the scholar-monk. But what truly distinguishes Tibetan Buddhism is something else, namely, the shamanic component: that is, the use of psychophysical techniques to create altered states of consciousness. This puts the practitioner in communication with a mode of reality more fundamental than that of everyday experience. Such shamanic techniques are found in many societies, but Tibet is the only known literal society in which they form a central rather than marginal element.

Shamanism operates in two distinct though overlapping areas of religious life. The first is folk religion. For the great majority of Tibetans, everyday existence is affected by a variety of spirits that populate forests, mountain peaks, lakes, rivers, rocks, caves, and house corners. Some these spirits hide in people's armpits, others take a ride on their shoulders. They are neither good nor bad; they help or harm, protect or attack, depending on how they are treated. Offense makes them dangerous; offerings pacify them. The domain they control is entirely mundane: health, wealth, crops, road safety, family and community life. Traffic with these spirits consists of pleasing, bribing, and paying ransom to them, and is mediated by shamanic specialists.

The second area, that of shamanic Buddhism proper, relates to the goal of achieving buddhahood. This state of being—conceived, as I have mentioned, in terms of an alternative mode of reality—is evoked through ritual, including the manipulation of consciousness by means of yoga, meditation, and the simulation of desired states of mind. The path toward enlightenment is represented by formulas like the mandala (most familiar to contemporary Westerners in the form of sacred sand paintings); the desired states of mind are symbolized by images of tantric divinities.

In shamanic Buddhism, the central figure is not a monk but the tantric lama, who need not be celibate or have formal monastic training but whose proficiency in ritual and yogic practice generates in him shamanic—i.e., "magical"— power. This he uses on behalf of the lay population. The Lama is well aware that his clients are concerned mainly with securing a better reincarnation or other mundane benefits, and his use of his magical power for the good of his followers and in the training of other shamanic practitioners is an expression of his compassion—a virtue helpful in his own progress toward enlightenment. The nexus between the pursuit of enlightenment by a small minority and the demand for shamanic services by the great majority is *the* hallmark of Tibetan Buddhism.

If these are the main components of Tibetan Buddhism and by extension the Tibetan "cultural heritage," whence the many other qualities imputed to it by Western admirers? Here we may return to the Dharamsala leaders, who were critically instrumented in re-positioning Tibet or, as we would say today, re-branding it, in a form palatable to Western audiences. They did so mainly by incorporating into Tibetan Buddhism a number of concepts and ideas that had never been part of Tibetan culture. These include the espousal of nonviolence, concern with the environment, human rights, world peace, feminism, and the like. At the same time, they brought forward the ethical element, hitherto minor in Tibetan Buddhism, and weeded out a number of specifically Tibetan features, especially the more esoteric and ritualistic ones.

They were abetted in this task by initiatives else where in the 19th and 20th centuries to "modernize" Buddhism by, for instance, dispensing with the parts of its cosmology that were in conflict with Western scientific through. This kind of Buddhist modernism, unknown in Tibet, was adopted by the Dalai Lama more or less simultaneously with his adoption of a philosophy of nonviolence derived from Tolstoy, Gandhi, and Martin Luther King, Jr. To this he eventually added the rhetoric of world peace, ecology, human rights, and the rest of the amorphous agenda that informs the liberal Western conscience.

Catering to the tastes of Western academics and New Age adepts alike, the diaspora establishment led by the Dalai Lama also began stressing the elements of the sacred and the mystical in Tibetan discourse. For both internal and foreign consumption, it selected for publication mostly religious texts, especially hagiographies, while barring critical historical analysis and allowing very few translations into Tibetan from other languages. For a long time, contact with foreign cultures was limited to a small, English-speaking elite.

The last fifteen years have witnessed watershed in academic research into the Tibetan past. Historians, anthropologists, political scientists, and sociologists, relying on extensive field work and critical readings of original documents, have shed new light on, among other things, Tibetan military expansionism in the imperial period (7th to late 9th century), the diversity of authority structures in different Tibetan states, and the practical workings of Tibet's relations with the Mongols and the Manchus. These studies have shown the inadequacy of treating Tibet solely as a victim of outside forces rather than as also an agent in much of its own history.

And yet, despite the achievements of recent scholarship, the Shangri-La image continues to enjoy wide currency in the West, and not only among activists and partisans but among reputable scholars at well. To illustrate, let me briefly focus on the quality perhaps responsible more than any other for Tibet's popularity in the West: namely, its allegedly deep-seated cultural affinity for nonviolence.

Even a cursory look at history reveals that nonviolence has never been a traditional Tibetan practice, or a societal norm, or, for that matter, a teaching of Tibetan Buddhism. Before the present Dalai Lama's encounter with the Gandhian concept of *ahimsa*, no Dalai Lama had ever invoked nonviolence as a virtue. Nor does *ahimsa*—meaning the abstinence from causing injury to any living creature—have any equivalent in Tibetan Buddhist tradition.

True, compassion (Tibetan *snying rje*, Sanskrit *karuva*) is an important religious and philosophical tenet, but it denotes above all the wish to save others from suffering by imparting to them Buddhist wisdom. In any case, it is not known ever to have been applied to political life in the way that, for instance, Gandhi took *ahimsa* as mandating a strategy of passive resistance to evil.

Pre-modern and modern Tibet engaged in many offensive campaigns against its neighbors, all of them sanctioned by Dalai Lamas. Domestically, too, Tibetan monasteries maintained private armies that were deployed in conflicts with the local government, and sometimes even among schools within the same monastery.

Fighting *"dobdos"* were known to constitute 15 percent of the monks of the great Gelugpa monasteries in and around Lhasa. Political rivalries were often settled by assassination. Some Dalai Lamas may have been kind and compassionate in person, but the historical record before 1960 unequivocally contradicts the image of a Dalai Lama preaching or practicing nonviolence.

Yet here is Robert Thurman, the well-known professor of Tibetan studies at Columbia University and a leading pro-Tibet activist— declaring that the great 5th Dalai Lama (1617–1682) was "a compassionate and peace-loving ruler who created in Tibet a unilaterally disarmed society." And here, by way of contrast, are the instructions of the 5th Dalai Lama himself to his commanders, who had been ordered to subdue a rebellion in Tsang in 1660:

> Make the male lines like trees that have had their roots cut; make the female lines like brooks that have dried up in winter; make the children and grandchildren like eggs smashed against rocks; make the servants and followers like heaps of grass consumed by fire; make their dominion like a lamp whose oil has been exhausted; in short, annihilate any traces of them, even their names.

Apart from creating a Tibetan past that never was, the diaspora leadership and its non-Tibetan advisers and collaborates have deployed selected aspects of Tibetan culture as tools in their effort to influence the global agenda. Examples include events co-produced by Western activists and Tibetan artists and monks in theaters, museums, and parks in the United States and other Western countries. Most of these shows are funded by American philanthropic institutions (like the Ford Foundation) and star the Dalai Lama and a Western intellectual (like Thurman) or celebrity (like Richard Gere). Their purpose is to reinforce the establishment's narrative of "Tibetanness" while recruiting new adherents to the agenda of support and rescue.

Here a genuinely Tibetan quality of mind is indeed manifest. The Dalai Lama has often stated that he sees his life's mission as "the preservation of the endangered Tibetan cultural heritage for the sake of all humanity." His formulation is rooted in a fundamental tenet of Mahayana Buddhism: individual practitioners should strive not solely for their own sake but for the sake of all sentient beings. This disposition, embodied in the figure of the *bodhisattva* (enlightened being) who out of compassion seeks to use his enlightenment for the good of others, is the principle on which the Dalai Lama—himself believed to be an emanation of the *bodhisattva* of compassion—rests his claim to relevance in the modern world.

And that relevance is indisputable. The Dalai Lama has been spectacularly successful in turning Buddhism into one of the world's great living religions and a force in global intellectual and political discourse. He has enriched Western cultural life not only by offering alternative paths of spiritual experience but by stimulating in some circles a reappraisal of accepted paradigms of both thought and practice. And he has placed his authority and popularity at the service of such global concerns as peace and respect for life.

But the task he considers his life's missions— "the preservation of the Tibetan cultural heritage"—is another matter. The effort to maintain an esoteric tradition, embodied in a numerically, politically, and economically negligible group of people, has confronted the Dalai Lama with a difficult dilemma. For a group dependent on others for its physical and cultural survival, the key consideration must be how it chooses to present itself to those who ultimately control its fate. The Dalai Lama seems to have chosen to buy a chance to continue the pursuit of scholarship and discipline within a very limited circle of insiders at the expense of offering an idealized and hybridized image of his culture for Western consumption.

That is idealized image, skillfully adapted to the needs and expectations of the Western public, has indeed succeeded in gathering much enthusiastic support, thereby keeping alive both the Tibetan issue and the diaspora community embodying it. Nor, in point of fact, is the Dalai Lama's use of Buddhism to recruit support or patronage without its own precedents in Tibetan history. Trading religious services and spiritual guidance for political, military, and material protection (Tibetan *chos-yon*, usually translated as patron-lama relationship) was the hallmark of Tibetan relations with the Mangol and later Manchu ruler of China since the 13th century.

Would it be far-fetched to see the whole complex of relations between the Tibetan exile community and the West, and in particular the Dalai Lama's relation with the world's rich, powerful, and glamorous, as a contemporary variant of the traditional patron-lama pattern? Is this how best to understand the public displays of embodied Buddhism: the ritual sand-mandala constructions by Tibetan monks in the foyers of museums staging exhibitions of Tibetan art, the mass initiations conducted by the Dalai Lama in New York's Central Park, the mass prayers he leads for world peace? Is all of this most plausibly viewed as a contemporary instance of the same strategy that successfully mediated relations between the Tibetan vassal states and their Mongol and Manchu overloads for hundred of years?

The historical ironies here are manifold, and quit delicious. Somehow, though, one doubts they would be appreciated by the Thurmans, the Geres, or any among the multitude of educated Westerners who have thrilled to the Shangri-La version of the Tibetan cultural heritage.

Lydia Aran, a specialist in Buddhism, taught in the department of Indian studies at the Hebrew University of Jerusalem until her retirement in 1998. Her books include Buddhism: An introduction to Buddhist Philosophy and Religion *(Hebrew, 1993) and* Destroying a Civilization: Tibet 1950–2000 *(Hebrew, 2007). Her memoir, "Krystyna's Gift," appeared in the February 2004 Commentary.*

CRITICAL THINKING QUESTIONS

1. What was the state of Western knowledge regarding Tibet prior to the Chinese invasion of 1950? What were the sources of this information?
2. Describe the form of Buddhism practiced in Tibet prior to the twentieth century.
3. Compare the current or modern image of Tibetan Buddhism with the pre-1959 version. What concepts have been added, or changed, that specifically appeal to modern Western sensibilities?
4. Using the concepts from the article, discuss whether there is an "idealized" version of American culture. In your answer, take what you believe to be an American cultural characteristic or concept, and explain how this concept does or does not reflect everyday reality.

Fieldwork among the Familiar and Strange

STATE OF THE ART: Fieldwork

In the early days of anthropology, professionals did not do fieldwork, the practice of living in the environment under study. The very first anthropologists, E. B. Tylor, Frazier, and their colleagues, were essentially "arm chair" anthropologists who relied on data gathered by nonanthropologists, missionaries, explorers, and colonial administrators, among others. These anthropologists then subjected the data to "scientific" examination. Thus, the field of anthropology relied on a purely experimental method which resembled that of the natural sciences—rigorous procedures of collecting and measuring data, subjecting the collected data to controlled experimentation and validity assessment, and using data to make generalizations about the human condition—the systematic rules of scientific investigation. Later, Franz Boas suggested a more humanistic approach to the study of human beings, which could be accomplished only through a close encounter with the people under study. Thus, fieldwork was born.

Since Boas introduced fieldwork in anthropology in 1883 (Rosman & Rubel 2004; Rosman, Rubel, & Weisgraw 2009), changes have occurred in the way it is conceived and carried out (Amit 2000; Wolcott 1995). Fieldwork combines scientific and humanistic approaches so the researcher is not bound by the systematic (scientific) rules of investigation. The current mode of fieldwork, the humanistic approach that involves participant observation—the direct involvement in the lives of the people under study—has been the preferred method of anthropological inquiry. Even so, fieldwork is fraught with difficulties as well as benefits.

Initially, fieldwork was about Western anthropologists studying faraway non-Western cultures. Their goal was to develop cultural pictures and to describe exotic ways of life that were thought to exist in closed systems, devoid of outside influences. Today, field sites are found not only in the non-Western cultures but also include societies and culture groups of the Western world. The city, which in the beginning was not a preferred site of anthropological study, has, for quite some time, been regarded as an appropriate field site. Employment facilities, organizations, assisted-living group homes, clubs, college environments, employment facilities, unions, and many other settings are now considered anthropological field "sites" and are studied within the framework of the wider society (Kingsolver 1998; Coleman 2009).

Also, it is no longer the norm to view and study cultures as isolated entities fit only for the outsider anthropologist. The combination of the insider and outsider traditions has been beneficial to the field of anthropology. Nonetheless, there are unique problems associated with the roles of insider (Ukaegbu 2004, 48–56) and outsider anthropologists. Fieldwork by insider and outsider anthropologists yields different types of data. The insider has access to cultural facts elusive to the outsider, while the outsider has perceptions elusive to the insider. Thus, the fieldwork enterprise now accommodates the relevance of both insider and outsider perspectives in increasing anthropological knowledge.

Fieldwork has taken on expanded meaning for the fieldworker. The role of the anthropologist/ fieldworker in the field from the start to the end of a project now involves ethical choices that affect the selection of research problems and data collection: experiences, encounters, how the work is done in the field, and how one immerses him- or herself into the culture under study as a participant observer. Such choices and concerns are difficulties in and of themselves (Wolcott 1995). Today, professionals also conceptualize fieldwork to include specific social issues of the culture under study and how the problems affect the social landscape as well as reflect emerging problems of the modern world. As a result, anthropological fieldworkers must seek new approaches while revising old ones. One such avenue of revision is *postmodernism,* which involves the critique and reexamination of old approaches to fieldwork, including participant observation. While participant observation has been the preeminent mode of anthropological research, anthropologists recognize its limitations in terms of our capacity to perceive the real features of the culture under study and the chances of participating and observing adequately in such a situation (Wolcott 1995). Anthropologists are taking stock of new issues in the way they conduct fieldwork. The capacity to establish rapport with people is one of the current challenges of fieldwork, including the nature and kinds of inquiries that anthropologists make in such interactions. There are the questions about who is best served by the study, the researcher or the observed; the feelings of betrayal or trust on the part of those under study; and the origin and source of the research questions one takes to the field. For example, there is the issue of whether the research question stems from bias and error or from correct assumptions about the group under study (Wolcott 1995).

Today, fieldwork continues to use the scientific (systematic) method, although it is not encumbered by it, amid problems that arise from its use. Though fieldwork follows the requirements of the scientific (systematic) method, in its actual implementation anthropologists have to grapple with the fact that the scientific method is not free from human judgment. Objectivity, the need to be uninfluenced by emotions or personal prejudices, is an important issue for fieldworkers. Nevertheless, fieldworkers understand the inevitability of some level of bias in the pursuit of fieldwork and that bias can stimulate inquiry if properly harnessed and directed. Fieldwork now entails coming to terms with the issues of *bias* and *neutrality,* especially as they are believed to affect research when applied in the research procedure (Wolcott 1995).

Some of the problems inherent in the scientific method are reliability, validity, and generalization. Fieldworkers must navigate through careful decision making in all aspects of the scientific process such as when identifying a problem (issue) and formulating testable hypotheses; when collecting, analyzing, and testing data in light of the scientific problem under investigation; and when arriving at a scientific conclusion and determining what generalizations (theory) can be made about the human condition (Wolcott 1995).

In reliability, the fieldworker must test for consistency by determining whether the measurement procedure in one setting will yield the same result in another setting. The criterion for the results must recognize the circumstances that obviate reliability as a central concern in fieldwork. The problem is thus handled through carefully documented ethnographic decision making, while not solving the issue of reliability as such (Wolcott 1995).

Validity is the degree to which researchers actually measure or record what they purport to measure through scientific observations. The problem of validity is that it is not an exact or precise procedure. As such the information provided by fieldworkers often may exemplify scientific procedures but not prove their accuracy. There is an increasing recognition on the part of fieldworkers of the need to grasp this process in order to understand what methods must be employed in ethnographic decision making and the measuring and recording of sociocultural data (Wolcott 1995).

Kenneth Feder (2010) notes that the technique itself is prone to errors, from the epistemological approach adopted (ways of knowing—i.e., observational first-hand experience or from external second-hand sources) to the actual application of the scientific procedure. Attempts at identifying the nature of a scientific problem can be beset with difficulties. The *inductive* and *deductive* processes used in determining the nature of a scientific problem and formulating hypotheses may present misleading data that lead to misinterpretations. Also there are problems associated with hypothesis testing. The last hypothesis on a list of *several hypotheses* should not be taken as the correct one until validated. Data collection may have little or no bearing on the validation of an hypothesis. The incidence of probable explanations by "chance" should not be ignored, as it could prove to be the valid explanation of the phenomenon.

In generalization, findings from a single case are applied to all human societies. Fieldworkers are faced with the problem that not all generalizations are adequate when drawn from a single case. As such single cases have their problems of adequacy for use in the generalizations of fieldwork.

ABOUT THE ARTICLES

The articles in this section are samples of the challenges of fieldwork. They deal with various theoretical and practical aspects of conducting fieldwork in both non-Western and Western cultures. All of the articles are linked together in several ways. The first article, by Durrenberger, discusses important theoretical and analytical issues in modern research. Anthropologists have been employing Western methods of data acquisition and analysis, defined as the *scientific method,* to conduct fieldwork. Durrenberger's work serves as an important counterpoint to that of traditional science. Durrenberger argues that science is actually a "cultural artifact" and thus intimately linked to Western culture and its views on the natural and cultural universe. Given this contention, he asks how we can ever be certain that what we report from the field is "true"? How accurate are our reports on our observations and interpretations from fieldwork? How do we get at data that are both valid and authentic?

The other three articles deal with practical and, at times, surprising facets of modern anthropological fieldwork. Womack and Barker discuss both the problems and potential advantages to being females when conducting fieldwork in cultural settings that are traditionally male-dominated, such as law enforcement and professional athletics. How they recognized, and adapted to, the issues specific to their fieldwork environment represents the art of fieldwork in a new and interesting light.

Arens's article is a classic example of how Westerners, in this case Americans, subconsciously view our own behaviors as "normal" and rarely think about the deeper cultural implications of our most cherished institutions. In this manner he mirrors many of the concepts suggested by Kluckhohn in his article in Section One. Arens examines the arena (pun intended) of American football, not from the emic (native) American viewpoint but from an etic (outsider) point of view. He interprets American football as a ritual activity that serves to legitimize certain American cultural values (competition, teamwork, specialization, etc.) and serves to integrate American culture across class and ethnic lines. Those who read this article may never view American culture in the same light.

Finally, Kusimba's article is a demonstration of how anthropological research and interpretation can be seen as being culturally influenced. He contrasts and compares the interpretations of eastern Africa's prehistory under the rule of Western colonial powers through his research in the region. Kusimba's findings are based on local knowledge corroborated by evidence from his own archeological research that legitimized Swahili civilization as an indigenous phenomenon. In so doing, Kusimba calls into question preconceived Western notions of Africa and Africans that in the past often led to misrepresentations of African realities. Such differing interpretations of the same data should lead the reader to reexamine the Durrenberger article from a fresh perspective.

References

Amit, V. *Constructing the Field: Ethnographic Fieldwork in the* Kingsolver, A. More than Class: Studying Power in U.S. Workplaces. Editor, and Introduction. Series in the Anthropology of Work. Albany: SUNY Press: 1998. 222p. *Contemporary World*. New York: Routledge, 2000.

Coleman, L. "Being Alone Together: From Solidarity to Solitude in Urban Anthropology," *Anthropology Quarterly*, (Summer 2009): 755–777.

Feder, K. "Epistomology: How You Know What You Know," in *Frauds, Myths, and Mysteries: Science and Pseudoscience in Archaeology*, 7th ed. New York: McGraw Hill, 2010.

Rosman, A., & Rubel, P. *The Tapestry of Culture: An Introduction to Cultural Anthropology*, 8th ed. New York: McGraw-Hill, 2004.

Rosman, A., Rubel, P., & Weisgraw, M. *The Tapestry of Culture: An Introduction to Cultural Anthropology*. Lanham: MD. Alta Mira Press, 2009.

Ukaegbu, D. Writing in Anthropology:the Sumary and the Critique Paper; *A Handbook for Beginners*. Upper Saddle River, NJ: Pearson/Prentice Hall, 2004. Forthcoming: 2nd. edition 2011.

Wolcott, H. F. *The Art of Fieldwork*. Walnut Creek, CA: AltaMira Press, 1995.

For Further Research

Nearly every ethnography contains a section on how the fieldwork used to obtain the data was conducted. There are several good introductory books on this topic that students should find enlightening. Anderson's *First Fieldwork: The Misadventures of an Anthropologist* (1989, Waveland Press) is a somewhat lighthearted look at the issues involved in fieldwork. DeWalt and Dewalt's *Participant Observation: A Guide for Fieldworkers* (2001, AltaMira Press) and Russell's *Research Methods in Anthropology: Qualitative and Quantitative Approaches* (4th ed., 2005, AltaMira Press) provide practical advice and approaches to professionals and amateurs alike. Finally, *Field Projects in Anthropology: A Student Handbook* (Crane and Angrosino, 1992, Waveland Press) is designed to give students some limited practical experience conducting fieldwork. For additional information on researching the topics discussed in the "State of the Art" section, please visit *www. mysearchlab.com*.

Are Ethnographies "Just So" Stories?

E. Paul Durrenberger

Some anthropologists think that ethnographies are "just so" stories, not necessarily to be believed as true. I don't agree. Here is why.

Skarp-Hedin leapt across the river, kept his footing as he hit the ice on the other side, went into a glide, and swooped down on Thrain, swinging an axe to split his head open to the jaw bone and spill Thrain's back teeth onto the ice. Skarp-Hedin didn't even slow down. One man threw a shield at him, but he jumped up and over it and just kept on going. Then Skarp-Hedin's four brothers came running up and killed three of Thrain's friends.

They let four of the young people who were in Thrain's group go because Skarp-Hedin couldn't bring himself to kill them. (Skarp-Hedin and his brothers were irritated at Thrain and his followers for insulting them.) Later on, the young men Skarp-Hedin didn't want to kill helped burn Skarp-Hedin and his brothers and father and mother in their house, but not before Skarp-Hedin had gouged out one man's eye with Thrain's back tooth, which he had saved from that day on the ice.

This story could be from a tabloid newspaper you see at the checkout counter at the grocery store or from a slasher movie. But it isn't. Here is another story.

There is a beautiful girl named Helga. When she is twelve, her father takes in a boy of the same age who doesn't get along with his own father. Helga and the boy, Gunnlaug, fall madly in love with each other. When Gunnlaug turns eighteen, he goes abroad to make his name and fortune, and Helga's father agrees that he won't make her marry anyone else for three years. Gunnlaug travels all over northern Europe composing poems for kings and raiding and pillaging. Because of a dispute over poetry, he makes a life-long enemy of another poet, named Hrafn. Gunnlaug gets delayed, and by the time he gets home more than the three years have passed and his enemy has married Helga.

Their families won't let them kill each other in a duel, so they agree to fight it out somewhere else. Gunnlaug manages to visit Helga a few times and gives her a cloak that a king had given him. He and Hrafn travel around until finally they meet, have a long and bloody fight, and both die. Helga now has no husband and no boyfriend. Her father finds another poet for her to marry, and she has some children with this man but never really loves him because she can never get her first love, Gunnlaug, out of her mind. Finally, she catches an epidemic disease. One day she lays her head in her husband's lap, has someone get the cloak Gunnlaug had given her, and dies holding it.

Are these true stories? Nobody knows. They are stories that Icelanders wrote in the thirteenth century as part of their sagas about things that were supposed to have happened two or three hundred years before. The first is from Njal's saga and the second is from Gunnlaug's saga.[1] Nobody even knows who wrote the sagas. All we know is that they were written in Icelandic. If these slasher-romances aren't true stories—and nobody can tell if they are true—why should we pay attention to them, especially in anthropology?

Source: Ember, Carol R.; Ember, Melvin; Peregrine, Peter N.; *New Directions in Anthropology*, 1st, © 2004. Electronically reproduced by permission of Pearson Education, Inc., Upper Saddle River, New Jersey.

Whatever else these stories are, they are cultural artifacts, just as much as a 1965 Chevy, a hand axe, or an episode of *Days of Our Lives* is a cultural artifact. If we want to learn about a culture, we study its artifacts, especially the ones that say something about social relations and the culture itself. But if someone made up the stories, what can they tell us about the culture or the society?

The imagination cannot go beyond culture. All of us are limited by our cultures. Our cultures define who we are and how we are, what we do, what we think and how we think. So, if you work this equation backward, you can learn a lot about a culture from looking at its artifacts, especially artifacts such as literature that talk about the culture itself.

We learn, for instance, that Icelandic people would kill each other over an insult, or even an imagined insult. We learn that they traveled abroad, raided, traded, made poetry, and fell in love. We learn that fathers could make daughters get married against their will, and many other details of the culture of medieval Iceland.

These are stories in books, and I like them as stories as well as for what they can tell us about medieval Iceland. I believe that we can use fiction for ethnography. If you want to learn about people, read their stories and you will see their culture reflected in the authors' imaginations. This is one of the things Ruth Benedict did in her perceptive study of Japanese culture "at a distance," *The Chrysanthemum and the Sword.*[2] This is what you do in your literature classes. Read Shakespeare's plays and you see a different culture. The manufactured parts of stories are names and events; the culturally given parts are motivations, emotions, judgments, social relations, and settings. To be good, fiction has to be true. The reason we can use fiction for ethnography is that everyone's imagination is a product of his or her culture, a reflection of the culture, so we can see the culture through the fictions.

The wrenching part of anthropology, what some people call culture shock, is being in places where people are doing things that we cannot imagine. You cannot imagine something you have never heard about or seen or done. But all of a sudden there you are, as anthropologist Bronislaw Malinowski was in the second decade of the twentieth century, in a canoe with a bunch of men blowing smoke and making magic to make things work out right.[3] The reason you are on this dangerous voyage in the middle of the ocean in a dugout canoe is that these men want to trade some shell bracelets for some necklaces on another island. To you it is all some kind of costume jewelry, but to them every individual piece has a history and a value. Their sense of prestige hangs on the trades they make, just as a medieval Icelander's prestige hung on never tolerating an insult, or yours hangs on the kind of car you drive, your credit rating, the clothes you wear, the music you listen to, who you date, and how you smell.

Blowing smoke and making magic to get a canoe across the ocean does not make sense to us. But it made sense to Trobriand Islanders when Malinowski was there early in the twentieth century. It was beyond his imagination, but it was an ordinary part of Trobriand culture.

Sometimes it is even more wrenching to come back to your own country and see that everything you thought was "just the way people do things" is really just another culture, another kind of imaginary construct that doesn't make that much sense.

When you think about it, many of the things we take for granted are pretty silly. Think about money, for example. Paper? Backed by the U.S. government? The only reason we can use money is that we all agree to believe that it has value. These days you can't even trade it for silver or gold, and when you think about it, what is the use of gold except for making wire and jewelry? Money is an incredible leap of the imagination, but an everyday part of our culture. And it gets even weirder than that. There are a lot of people who make a living just by pushing money from one place to another. And even stranger, they don't even push the actual money; they just enter figures in computers and things happen, and for this they make a nice living—making fictions of fictions. Stocks and bonds are stranger yet. You can take whole courses on how this stuff works in your school of business or economics department; you can learn all of the esoteric language and how to make a living doing this kind of magic. You can get a degree in it. It might seem strange to think of getting a B.A. in magic, but that's what business schools do. To anthropologists, it is just another kind of blowing smoke.

When people's assumptions are different from ours, we don't understand their motives, judgments, or sense of propriety. That is where anthropology comes in—trying to understand other people as well as ourselves.

So everything is a cultural artifact. That is one of the important lessons of anthropology. But if everything is a cultural artifact, isn't anthropology just another cultural artifact, like money, a 65 Chevy, a soap opera, or an Icelandic saga?

Whatever you can say about sagas, soap operas, and anthropology, a 65 Chevy will run. If it doesn't you can fix it so it will. There is a bottom line with some things: They work or they don't. You can try teleportation all you want, but if you want to get some place fast you will buy an airplane ticket. Airplanes work. So do computers. Cars, computers, and airplanes are all the result of scientific knowledge. So scientific knowledge must be "culture-free" right?

Wrong. Even science is a cultural artifact—something we make up, something we imagine. How do we know that? Because science changes from time to time and place to place. European science used to tell us that the earth was at the center of the universe and the sun went around it. European scientists didn't record any new stars. They couldn't. God made the heavens and the earth as they were and they did not change. Everyone knew that. If you saw what you thought was a new star, it was just one you had missed before. The Chinese, on the other hand, were looking at the heavens for signs and portents. They did not assume the heavens were changeless; they were looking for changes, and they saw and recorded new stars that astronomers today classify as novas.

Then an astrologer with strange religious ideas, a man named Copernicus, had the idea that the sun was at the center of the system. Everyone thought he was nuts until it turned out he could make a calendar that kept track of holidays better than the Ptolemaic system could. Easter stayed in the spring and Christmas stayed in the winter instead of straying all over the seasons. The Church wanted a consistent calendar, so they liked this calendar and the rest of the solar system came in on its coat tails. Evidence?

There wasn't any evidence one way or the other. In terms of observations you could make at the time, the Copernican system didn't work any better than the old Ptolemaic one that put the earth at the center of everything. Facts did not determine the choice. Imagination—culture—is stronger than facts.

But people who navigated with the Ptolemaic system could get where they wanted to go. It worked. It probably couldn't get them to the moon, but it could get them from Europe to America or Asia and that is what counted in those days. It will work as well today as it did then for navigation—as long as you don't leave our planet. The point is that just because something works does not necessarily mean that the ideas it is based on are correct. Even the pragmatic test of "working" is not always a good guide to truth. So what is left?

The answer is uncomfortable, but one that you might as well get accustomed to: Nothing is left. Everything we can think of, including science, is a cultural artifact. We cannot escape that. Culture is part of our being just as surely as is walking on two feet and talking and having an opposable thumb. It is built and bred into us and has been part of our evolutionary history since we walked out of Olduvai gorge or wherever we originated in our homeland in Africa.

What we try to do in anthropology is to move beyond our own cultures and understand other cultures. We try to do that in a scientific way. So what kind of artifact is science? It strives for reliable and valid knowledge. Valid means that we observe and measure what we think we are observing and measuring. Do Scholastic Aptitude Tests or entrance examinations really predict your college grades? If they do, they are valid. What do grades measure? Reliability means that anyone else would see and describe the same things if they did the same things. Science is cultural because the very terms for judging reliability and validity are cultural, thus anthropology is a cultural artifact.

This is not surprising when you think about it. But some anthropologists were very surprised when they figured it out. A long time ago, Aristotle wrote about rhetoric. These anthropologists discovered that all arguments are rhetorical, that they are all cultural artifacts. They discovered that Malinowski used rhetoric—that he was a writer. They acted like this was a big discovery and were very proud of themselves for making it, like the character in Moliere's play who learns that he has been speaking prose all his life.

In 1922, Malinowski said he was constructing interpretations of the kula, the trading of necklaces and shell arm bands; he made the analogy to a physicist constructing a theory from experimental data that everyone can understand but that falls into place when the physicist makes a consistent interpretation, a story. Malinowski was implying that he, like the physicist (a scientist), was constructing interpretations to help people understand things.[4]

In 1973, Clifford Geertz said he discovered that anthropological writings are interpretations, cultural artifacts, something anthropologists make, and he said they were fictions because they are cultural constructs.[5] (You should read some of Geertz's writings, just because anthropologists talk about him a lot. But be warned that Geertz gets confusing. If you find yourself scratching your head and wondering what he means, don't worry. He writes as if he wants to confuse you. And so he does.) He went on to say that these fictions are not untrue; they are just cultural artifacts, something someone makes, and in that sense they are just like any other kind of cultural artifact.

About ten years later, James Clifford and George Marcus got some anthropologists and other people together to talk about these things, and published a book of their essays in 1986.[6] In the introduction, Clifford discusses the idea of ethnographies as fiction, something made, and says they are not false, just incomplete—not unreal, just culturally determined. Some of the words he and the other anthropologists use are "irony," "hegemonic," "discourse," "trope," "interpretation," "hermeneutics," "subjectivity," "conflate," "elide," and "privilege" (as a verb).

Some of these anthropologists call themselves postmodernists. Don't worry if you haven't figured out exactly what that means; they don't want you to, so you are not likely to. Think of it as more of a riddle than a question, or a zen koan whose answer you aren't supposed to understand anyway. The difference is that a zen master will promise you enlightenment if you stick with it and think about the riddle. Enlightenment is

another cultural construct. But the postmodernists only promise more confusion. They are in the business of making confusion, not trying to understand it. When they pose you a riddle, if you know it, you know it, and if not, then you are in outer darkness. I am telling you that outer darkness is an "OK" place to be, and that we have to remember now and then to ask whether the emperor has any clothes.

In 1990, Katherine Hayles wrote a book about chaos theory.[7] She had studied chemistry and then English, so she knew something about scientific subjects as well as literature. Talking about postmodernists in literature, she asked about what she called the political economy of their discipline, the political and economic conditions of the people who write literary criticism. If there is only one correct view, she pointed out, these people would be out of business in no time flat. But if there are many equivalent views, none any better than the others, then they can keep on cranking out literary criticism and debating about how to do it until the cows come home. Maybe it is the same for postmodernism in anthropology.

Geertz recognizes the problem. You cannot be systematic about interpretations; if you can't be systematic, you can't evaluate them. It's like trying to figure out how to get an "A" in a course if nobody will tell you how you are being graded. Nobody wants to talk about how to grade interpretations. So they are all equally good. Listen to Geertz:

> For a field of study which, however timidly (though I, myself, am not timid about the matter at all), asserts itself to be a science, this just will not do. There is no reason why the conceptual structure of a cultural interpretation should be any less formulable, and thus less susceptible to explicit canons of appraisal, than that of, say, a biological observation or a physical experiment.

So far so good, and we think Geertz is right on track, but now comes the punch line to his joke:

> … no reason except that the terms of which such formulations can be cast are, if not wholly non-existent, very nearly so. We are reduced to insinuating theories because we lack the power to state them.[8]

Allow me to interpret. It would be nice to know how to grade interpretations, but we don't know how. So we don't. Instead of having theories, we guess.

If all stories are equivalent, how can we choose among them? Comparing personal interpretations is fundamentally undemocratic because, as Geertz suggested, the way to choose is to yield to the authority of the person who presents the interpretation. This person presents the interpretation and he or she is ... what? The most powerful? The loudest? The most fashionable? However, while Geertz's suggestion at first looks very liberal—it seems to say "entertain every point of view"—it really means "take my word for it and don't be critical or ask questions." On the other hand, if all interpretations are equally legitimate, then they might as well all be fiction.

If fiction can be ethnography and ethnography is fiction, can there be fictional ethnographies? There can be and there are, and it is something anthropologists talk about and even argue about. Maybe the most famous of these are the writings of Carlos Castaneda, who started with *The Teachings of Don Juan, A Yaqui Way of Knowledge*, which was published in 1968.[9] This was such a success that he went on to publish several others in the same vein. For a while there was a debate about whether Castaneda's books were "true."

Some people pointed out that he must have copied from well-known books about shamans and mysticism because of parallels in the texts. Others argued that the correspondences were universals of shamanic experience. Richard De Mille collected a number of assessments of Castaneda's work in 1980.[10] De Mille distinguishes between Validity and Authenticity. Validity means that a story corresponds to what we think we know, similar to the idea of validity for judging scientific work. New stars were not valid to early European astronomers, but they were to Chinese astronomers because of their different systems of reference—frameworks for validity, which are culturally variable. Authenticity means whether the events happened the way the stories say they did.

Did Skarp-Hedin really chop Thrain's teeth out of his head on the ice? The story is valid because it matches what we know about medieval Iceland and other such societies, but we don't know if it is authentic. Were Galileo's telescopic observations of the heavens accurate (authentic)? Check them for yourself. Anyone can do it. Science is democratic; it doesn't hide or confuse things.

Were Castaneda's stories authentic? It is more difficult to determine whether he really knew Don Juan. It isn't as simple as repeating an experiment or observation.

Because there are many authentic and valid ethnographic reports in libraries and books, De Mille suggested that people can use them to concoct valid but inauthentic reports. When you write a term paper, you cite your sources and do not pretend that you are the one who studied diet in China, or marriage customs in India, or religion in Peru. You and your professor are probably equally glad just to have the paper handed in by the due date without a five-year delay for you to go to the place, learn the language, and do the study yourself. You would have to take an incomplete for half a decade. That is what books are good for. But they require honest use. You get an "F" on your term paper if you plagiarize— another one of those cultural things.

When you read an ethnography, how do you know it is true? How do you know the author didn't make it up, as Castaneda did? The main reason is that the writer says, "I was there; this is based on my experience, on what I saw and heard." That experience is the writer's authority, the reason to believe what the writer says. But that is what Castaneda said to claim ethnographic authority, and he was not writing ethnography. In the 1986 book that Clifford and Marcus edited is a piece by Mary Louise Pratt of Stanford's Spanish and Portuguese Department. Pratt points out that you can write an accurate account of life in another culture without ever having been there.[11] Ruth Benedict did. And I have never been to medieval Iceland, but I wrote a book about it.[12] Pratt wonders why there was a big flap in anthropology journals over a book, by Florinda Donner, *Shabono*, published in 1982.[13] Was it fiction based on ethnographies and other sources like Castenada's works, or was it ethnography?

Pratt sees the threat to anthropologists in the missing link, the "being there" that gives ethnographers the "authority" to say they have given you an authentic account. I think the use of the word "authority" for this meaning is interesting, because an appeal to authority, in a somewhat different sense, is the only way to judge stories that are not scientific.

Pratt goes on to talk about how anthropologists establish that they were there, that their accounts are authentic. This is what all scientists do. Galileo said he looked through a telescope and this is what he saw. His authority, his claim to authenticity, came from his having looked through the telescope. If you don't believe him, you can read other books by other people who have looked through telescopes, look at their photos or drawings, or look through a telescope yourself. If other people cannot see the same things, the observations are not reliable. And so it is for ethnography.

Pratt says that ethnographic writing is boring. How, she wonders, could such interesting people doing such interesting things produce such dull books? Boredom, of course, is self-generated. It isn't in what we see but in how we respond to it. Have you ever tried to explain why you were fascinated by an experiment you did in chemistry lab to someone who was so bored with science that he didn't even want to discuss it? If people are bored with something, we can't change their minds about it. It's like what they say about trying to teach pigs to sing. It is a waste of your time and it irritates the pig. People of the English persuasion have tried to explain cricket to me, but I would just as soon watch paint dry.

I must confess that I find some art and some ethnography boring and some exciting. I never could get into *Gravity's Rainbow,* though my wife swears by it. I know Joyce's *Ulysses* is a great work, but I can't get into it. Or Jane Austen. But I once spent an afternoon absorbed in an ethnography of Timbuktu.

Fiction writers are obliged to try not to bore their readers; ethnographers can be irritatingly indifferent to their audience and use the most atrocious obfuscatory language. Among the most obfuscatory and boring writers of modern anthropology, by the way, are those who discovered that they were writing rhetoric. Richard de Mille suggests that Castaneda perpetrated his hoaxes because the competition was too great in the fiction market. Castaneda's stories are short on plot, lack detail, have unconvincing characters who never develop and who show stereotyped emotions, and have nothing in the way of human relations. That is not good fiction—it would never sell—but it makes pretty good reading as fact because readers love supposedly true adventures, even if they aren't well written.

In fiction, the ideas of truth are a little different, and that is why Pratt didn't understand the big flap about authenticity in anthropology. John Gardner, in his book about writing, *The Art of Fiction,*[14] suggests that telling truth in fiction can mean one of several things: being factually correct, being coherent so that it does not feel like lying, or affirming a moral truth about human existence. Like Pratt, he considers authenticity to be trivial, except in creating an appearance of truth that makes a story interesting and compelling (what literary people call "verisimilitude"). He regards validity—making the story fit a cultural framework—as more important. Universal morality he appreciates as the highest form of truth, the goal of art.

This highest truth, as any anthropologist will tell you, is cultural. But reality is just there. Science is the job of trying to match the two. Skarp-Hedin was affirming a truth when he chopped out Thrain's teeth, but his actions would not be considered quite so praiseworthy today. Skarp-Hedin would wind up pleading insanity and hoping to get committed to an asylum rather than death row. But to know that, we have to know something about our culture and other cultures; and to know those things, we have to describe and understand them; and to do that, we have to tell truth as best we can, as Galileo did. Other people and their actions, thoughts, words, and deeds are realities that anthropologists try to understand.

Ethnographers, if they are honest and authentic, must be willing to say, "If you don't believe our stories, you can go there yourself and see for yourself." They have to believe that if you do what they did you will see the same things. So the stories to establish authenticity are more than just figures of speech or rhetorical tactics or ploys—tropes, as they say—or they are no less so than any other such rhetoric of any scientific report. And to say that everything is a trope is about as enlightening as to say that we speak in prose. Sometimes people do go and check others' work, and sometimes, though not all the time, it leads to disputes about who was using the better telescope because different people may present equally valid and equally authentic but different pictures of what they saw.

Try it out sometime. You and two of your friends each get cameras and all go to an event like a wedding or a carnival or a graduation—anything at all. Then compare the pictures you took. You all will have been at the same place with the same people, but I will bet that you each took different pictures to emphasize different things. This is one reason different anthropologists can tell different stories—they concentrate on different things. (This may be what was at stake in the differences between Oscar Lewis and Robert Redfield in their understandings of Mexican peasant life.[15]) On the other hand, maybe you went to different weddings and one was in Texas and the other in New Jersey. Or maybe you are comparing pictures from this year's wedding with your grandfather's wedding. There can also be differences of time and location.

The more precisely you can tell people what you did, the better they can try to see things the way you saw them. That is the reason anthropologists have to spend some time on methodology—talking about how they know what they are talking about (to establish reliability), as well as theory. Methodology is the framework for validity.

If everything is a cultural construct and all ethnographic accounts are stories like any other kind of science, does it make any difference whether we make them up in libraries or in some foreign place? Isn't one story as good as another?

Remember that inauthentic ethnographies depend on authentic ones. The only reason people can make up ethnography in a library is that someone did the real job of description before. Without that kind of aid they could not move beyond the imaginative limits of their own culture and would have to write poor fiction rather than fake ethnography.

How you judge a story depends on what you want it for. If its only job is to amuse you, then popular television writing will win over any academic or scientific writing any day of the week. That is what makes popular writing and television popular. Maybe that is why academic writers are so poorly paid. If you are trying to get from Europe to America or Asia, or from the earth to the moon, you need a different kind of story. If you want the kind of story that makes a computer work, you don't ask how amusing it is, you ask how well it works.

And so it is for understanding other cultures and your own culture. That which leaves you with the most authentic and valid account is the best ethnography. That is the ethnography upon which you can base a sound search for those higher truths. Ask anyone who has tried to understand your culture and its moral truths. Talk to some foreign students as they are getting used to American ways and see what they tell you. You will be surprised at what surprises them.

One young woman confided to me her amusement on hearing at an orientation session that Americans were very conscious of smells in their love lives. She laughed as she regaled me with stories she had heard and this whole new dimension of social relations she had never thought about before. In the United States, that is the foundation for a whole neurosis and the industry based on it. While Icelanders think Americans silly to bathe every day, Thai think Americans uncouth for bathing only once a day.

When you see yourself through others' eyes, you never see what you thought you would see, what you see through your own eyes. Watching yourself in a video is an alienating experience. You don't look like you thought you would. The person holding the camera didn't see things the way you saw them.

Horace Miner wrote an essay called "Body Ritual among the Nacirema," which was published in 1956 in the *American Anthropologist*.[16] "Nacirema" is "American" spelled backwards. In the article, he describes how Americans brush their teeth as he imagines an anthropologist might describe this ritual. It seems strange because he puts it in a different context than we do when we brush our teeth. So ethnographic accounts often have an air of strangeness about them to the people they describe. Different people see things differently—that is one of the great lessons of anthropology. Texans, for instance, didn't much like Michener's treatment of their state in his novel. But Texans didn't like

Ferber's *Giant* either. Only a Texan, they argue, can really understand the uniqueness of that people and that land. Anything that doesn't agree with our own self images, anything that doesn't confirm the rightness of our own prejudices and opinions, we are likely to dismiss as wrongheaded at worst or innocent fiction at best. Texans say they are heirs to a proud historical tradition, while others see this kind of attitude as boorish, ethnocentric bigotry.

If you are an athlete and your coach tells you how to improve your stroke, your serve, the swing of your golf club, your gait when you are running, or how to hold the bat to hit the ball, you can view the tapes, concede that you don't look to others as you imagined you did, and listen to your coach's advice. Your game will improve. Or you can insist that your view is the only right one and suffer the consequences. It is your choice. It is the same in music, writing, art, computer science, engineering … you name it. And it is our choice. We may not like what de Toqueville said about America, but it might help us to listen, whether we like the story or not, whether it is amusing or not.

Three of my favorite writers died on motorcycles. One of them, C. Wright Mills, was a sociologist. He wrote that ordinary people felt they were living in traps because of large social forces beyond their control. To understand a person's life or the history of his or her society, you have to understand both together.[17] Another, John Gardner, wrote fiction and also wrote about writing fiction. He wrote that fiction seeks out truth. We cannot sort universals into moral codes, but fiction interests us because it helps us learn how the world works, how we and all other human beings can resolve conflicts we share, what values we agree with, and what the moral risks are. He said that a writer who cannot distinguish truth from a peanut butter sandwich can't write good fiction.[18] The third, T. E. Lawrence, wrote something that was sociology, fiction, history, and autobiography as well.[19] All three of these men met the same end. Maybe we should learn to wear helmets when we get on motorcycles.

Some of my favorite writers are still alive. Halldor Laxness is an Icelandic novelist who wrote with such precision that I once despaired that he left nothing for anthropologists to do—regarding

Iceland, at least.[20] Like Texans, Icelanders didn't much like his writing, until he won a Nobel prize. Then it was OK because foreigners thought it was good. Richard Condon wrote the definitive work on economics in his novel *Money Is Love*.[21] Miles Richardson is an anthropologist who captured what it is to be an anthropologist.[22]

Richardson talks about how he became an anthropologist and how anthropologists accuse each other of every imaginable sin. He wonders how to explain such accusations when they contrast so with the image of anthropologists as people who are sympathetic to differences. He talks about doing fieldwork and the conditions of fieldwork—that we have to drop the idea that the world is the same as it was for Malinowski seventy years ago. We have to accept the contemporary world on its own terms. When we do this, we can begin to see clearly, we can listen carefully, and we can hear what we must. There are different ways to listen, as there are different ways to take photographs. We can be detached; we can be revolutionaries, bureaucrats, apologists. There are a lot of ambiguities because of the differences in power among people and among peoples and countries.

How can we get anything out of this enterprise besides a bunch of equally good if not equally entertaining "just so" stories? Richardson says that there is another way to think of anthropology—something like what Gardner had in mind for writers: They are myth-tellers, people who stand on the edge of the society in the outer darkness, away from the hot glow of the campfires that comfort us, and tell the myth of humanity with skill and passion. We cannot falsify what we are. We work with all the pieces of the puzzles we have: what we can develop, what our predecessors developed, what our students are developing. We try to understand it all. We stand between the most and the least powerful social orders and feel the tensions. To tell the story well, Richardson says, we need the passion of the radical, the detachment of the scientist, and the practicality of the liberal. That is our job, he concludes—to tell the human story, to tell it well, to tell it truly.

But why does Richardson call it a myth, this story of our selves and our fellow humans? Isn't it a "just so" story, along with all the other myths science banishes with its valid and reliable analyses? He calls the story of humanity a myth not because it is untrue but because it reaches for that higher truth that Gardner spoke of. Such myths are true. Anthropology tells those stories, and it is up to us to tell them well and truly.

Notes

1. Anonymous, *Njal's Saga*, trans. Magnus Magnusson and Hermann Pálsson (New York: Penguin, 1960); Anonymous, *The Saga of Gunnlaugur Snake's Tongue with an Essay on the Structure and Translation of the Saga*, trans. E. Paul Durrenberger and Dorothy Durrenberger (Rutherford, NJ: Fairleigh Dickinson University Press, 1992).
2. Ruth Benedict, *The Chrysanthemum and the Sword* (Boston: Houghton Mifflin, 1946).
3. Bronislaw Malinowski, *Argonauts of the Western Pacific: An Account of Native Enterprise and Adventure in the Archipelagoes of Melanesian New Guinea* (Prospect Heights, IL: Waveland Press, 1984; originally published in 1922).
4. Ibid.
5. Clifford Geertz, *The Interpretation of Cultures* (New York: Basic Books, 1973).
6. James Clifford and George E. Marcus, eds., *Writing Culture: The Poetics and Politics of Ethnography* (Berkeley: University of California Press, 1986).
7. Katherine N. Hayles, *Chaos Bound: Orderly Disorder in Contemporary Literature and Science* (Ithaca: Cornell University Press, 1990).
8. Geertz, *The Interpretation of Cultures*, p. 24.
9. Carlos Castaneda, *The Teachings of Don Juan: A Yaqui Way of Knowledge* (Berkeley: University of California Press, 1968).
10. Richard De Mille, *The Don Juan Papers: Further Castaneda Controversies* (1980; reprint Belmont, CA: Wadsworth Publishing, 1992).
11. Mary Louise Pratt, "Fieldwork in Common Places," in James Clifford and George E. Marcus, eds., *Writing Culture: The Poetics and Politics of Ethnography* (Berkeley: University of California Press, 1986), pp. 27–50.
12. E. Paul Durrenberger, *The Dynamics of Medieval Iceland: Political Economy and Literature* (Iowa City: University of Iowa Press, 1992).
13. Florinda Donner, *Shabono: A True Adventure in the Remote and Magical Heart of the South American Jungle* (New York: Laurel Books, 1982).
14. John Gardner, *The Art of Fiction* (New York: Alfred A. Knopf, 1984).
15. Robert Redfield, *Tepoztlán, a Mexican Village: A Study of Folk Life* (Chicago: University of Chicago Press, 1930); Oscar Lewis, *Life in a Mexican Village: Tepoztlán Restudied* (Urbana: University of Illinois Press, 1951).
16. Horace Miner, "Body Ritual among the Nacirema," *American Anthropologist* 58 (1956): 503–507.
17. C. Wright Mills, *The Sociological Imagination* (New York: Oxford University Press, 1959).
18. Gardner, *The Art of Fiction*.
19. T. E. Lawrence, *The Seven Pillars of Wisdom: A Triumph* (Garden City, NY: Doubleday, 1938).
20. Halldor Laxness, *Salka Valka*, trans. F. H. Lyon (London: George Allen & Unwin Ltd., 1936); Halldor Laxness, *Independent People* (New York: Alfred A. Knopf, 1946).
21. Richard Condon, *Money Is Love* (New York: Dial Press, 1975).
22. Miles Richardson, *Cry Lonesome and Other Accounts of the Anthropologist's Project* (Albany: State University of New York Press, 1990).

Suggested Readings

Condon, Richard. *Money Is Love.* New York: Dial Press, 1975. A novel that treats the mysteries of money and economic systems. Many of Condon's other novels are equally interesting.

Durrenberger, E. Paul. *The Dynamics of Medieval Iceland: Political Economy and Literature.* Iowa City: University of Iowa Press, 1992. Discusses the relationships between politics, economics, and literature in medieval Iceland.

Geertz, Clifford. *The Interpretation of Cultures.* New York: Basic Books, 1973. Not a very good book, definitely not well written, but anthropologists talk about it a lot. Read it some time if you want to see what they are talking about.

Hayles, Katherine N. *Chaos Bound: Orderly Disorder in Contemporary Literature and Science.* Ithaca: Cornell University Press, 1990. Discusses chaos theory.

Kuhn, Thomas S. *The Copernican Revolution: Planetary Astronomy in the Development of Western Thought.* New York: Vintage Books, 1957. Accessible discussion of astronomy in European cultures. Shows how Ptolemaic astronomy made sense with the observations they had at that time and how sun-centered theories made no more sense than earth-centered ones. This is a good portrayal of the relationship between facts and theories and how ideas about astronomy influenced other areas of thought. Kuhn later wrote the influential book *Structure of Scientific Revolutions.* Chicago: University of Chicago Press, 1962.

Malinowski, Bronislaw. *Argonauts of the Western Pacific An Account of Native Enterprise and Adventure in the Archipelagoes of Melanesian New Guinea.* 1922; reprint Prospect Heights, IL: Waveland Press, 1984. Better than you might guess as a book just to read and a classic of anthropology. Good summer vacation book.

Mills, C. Wright. *The Sociological Imagination.* New York: Oxford University Press, 1959. Mills is a good writer. His work is generally accessible, no nonsense, to the point, sensible, and necessary reading for anyone going on in anthropology or any social science.

Richardson, Miles. *Cry Lonesome and Other Accounts of the Anthropologist's Project.* Albany: State University of New York Press, 1990. The best account of what it is like to be an anthropologist.

CRITICAL THINKING QUESTIONS

1. Define the term *cultural artifact*. Why does Durrenberger define anthropology as a "cultural artifact"?
2. Is science a culture-free enterprise? Why or why not?
3. What do Durrenberger and Western science mean by the terms *validity, reliability,* and *authenticity*?
4. How do anthropologists establish the validity and authenticity of their research?
5. What is a *myth,* and what purposes do myths serve in all cultures?
6. Why does Durrenberger call anthropologists "myth tellers"? What does he mean by this expression?
7. Describe and discuss an American or a Western myth. How would you interpret that myth in the light of Durrenberger's article?

Adventures in the Field and in the Locker Room

Mari Womack and Joan C. Barker

When Mari Womack decided to study rituals of professional team sport athletes, virtually all of whom are male, she was advised by several anthropologists to work with a male co-researcher. It was feared she would not have access to such key sites as the locker room and that male athletes would be reluctant to discuss their magic with a woman. There were also suggestions that, as a female and an outsider, she might be labeled a "jinx" if the teams went into a slump while she was studying them.

Joan Barker found herself in a similarly equivocal position when she studied officers in the Los Angeles Police Department. Her research began at a time when the organization had recently implemented affirmative action policies which, in some cases, created tensions between men and women on the force. As women studying male-dominant groups, the two researchers discovered that being an obvious outsider conferred some unanticipated advantages and that the experience shed new light on the traditional relationship of anthropologists to the people they study.

GENDER, PARTICIPANT OBSERVATION AND THE INSIDER PERSPECTIVE

The gender of the anthropologist has been identified as an important issue in conducting field work. Most of the discussion has centered on the implications of men studying women or, even more problematic, men studying men and allowing that to stand for society as a whole. E. E. Evans-Pritchard pondered whether it were possible to gain access to the women's viewpoint, or whether one could get the "native view about life" from men alone (1973:7). In her now-classic article "Woman The Gatherer: Male Bias in Anthropology," Sally Slocum answers this question with a resounding "NO!": "The perspective of women is, in many ways, ... foreign to an anthropology that has been developed and pursued primarily by males. There is a strong male bias in the questions asked, and the interpretations given" (1975:37).

On the other hand, James R. Gregory (1984) notes that the emphasis on gender as a factor in limiting access to certain kinds of information obscures the fact that, by the nature of field work, anthropologists are subject to being misled by the people they study:

> ... the myth of the male ethnographer and the woman's world is a false statement in the sense that it implies that such problems with distortions, omissions, and half-truths are unique and that there are no comparable problems for male ethnographers in working with male informants. In my experience, nothing could be farther from the truth.... (1984:321)

Gregory suggests that gender is one of a number of factors that may affect the anthropologist's ability to gain information. The process of collecting data can be influenced by such conditions as the nature of the information being sought (whether it is sensitive or dangerous), the group's previous experience with outsiders, and whether the information is provided privately or in the presence of others. This view is consistent with the experiences of Womack and Barker.

Participant-observation is a preferred methodology for the field but, as Gregory points out, the ability of anthropologists to "participate" in any society has probably been exaggerated. The researcher is prevented—due to barriers of sex, age or differential status—from having access to many customs and practices of a culture. Suspension of norms is typically allowed only when the anthropologist is considered a nonperson or outsider. In one case, a Japanese woman anthropologist was barred from observing certain Shinto ceremonies, whereas an American woman anthropologist was permitted to observe them (Lisa Cerroni-Long, personal communication, 1989). As an insider, the Japanese anthropologist was bound by rules that define women as ritually polluting. The American woman—an outsider and non-person—was not. The same logic favored a male anthropologist who, during his study in New Guinea, observed some female rituals normally forbidden to males (Philip Newman, personal communication). Hortense Powdermaker (1966) notes that she was invited to attend men's feasts on the island of Lesu and even to observe closely guarded male circumcision rituals.

Suspension of rules for outsiders often favors the female researcher in an all-male group. In studying police, Barker discovered that being female relieved her of the necessity of being an "O.K." male, a category with standards almost impossible for a non-police officer to meet. She did not have to be athletic, a skilled fisherman or have mastery over large and powerful motorcycles. She did not have to have "command presence," or have an acceptable profession, such as police officer, firefighter or professional athlete. She could eschew risk taking, but could participate in these activities as an onlooker. This is acceptable behavior for a woman, but not for a man.

Barker also learned that being female was a partial solution to overcoming "clannishness" among police officers because it allowed her to interact with them in a relaxed, off-duty setting. Her research began when she was challenged by a police officer, one of her students, to apply the concept of cultural relativism to a study of "cops." She was invited to socialize with off-duty officers at a "cop bar." She later discovered that her entry into the group was greatly facilitated by the fact that her initial contact was a highly respected officer who, in effect, vouched for her good behavior and signalled to other officers that she was trustworthy.

Barker and Womack were obvious outsiders, since there was no likelihood that either would become a member of the group. Womack was barred from becoming a professional athlete by her gender and lack of adequate playing skills. Barker had not undergone the rigorous training and graduation ceremony of the police academy.

Womack began her study as the inadvertent result of becoming friends with a professional hockey player, who introduced her to teammates and their wives. It was in this casual context that she became aware of the importance of sporting rituals. Thus, both researchers experienced a transition from informal participant-observation to formal interviews, and both found the quality and kinds of information gathered differed when the context of information gathering shifted from "conversation" to "interview."

Both Womack and Barker were assisted in their research by the fact that their field site, Los Angeles, is a media center. Athletes and police officers are accustomed to being the focus of the media spotlight. Though both groups express a great deal of hostility toward journalists, they do not question cultural norms that accord strangers with note pads and tape recorders the right to ask intrusive questions.

However, the transition from "conversation" to "interview" was more acute for Barker, who discovered that police reacted warily to being "interviewed." Many officers avoided scheduled interviews altogether, and many of those who were interviewed initially tended to give idealized and very brief responses, with little of the elaboration open-ended interviews are designed to encourage. Police are adept at giving minimal information, especially in situations that resemble questioning by news media.

Athletes, on the other hand, are usually relaxed during interviews. However, they are more likely to try to "shape" an interview by listening for the question behind the question and by framing their answers so they sound good on the air or in print. In informal conversations, athletes are more reflective and less concerned with controlling the outcome of the exchange.

Because of their different research settings and research questions, the two anthropologists took opposite approaches in asking questions. In fact, this is probably a key difference between

Womack's research context and that of Barker. Barker conducted her study in informal settings and downplayed any associations with media; Womack emphasized her journalistic connections. Barker was most effective by "being the person who wasn't there." Because her interactions with police officers took place in recreational contexts where women are accepted, Barker could, in effect, disappear into the woodwork. Womack couldn't disappear. She was treading the hollowed ground of baseball dugouts and team locker rooms, where few women had gone before. Therefore, Womack underscored her visibility. She gained access to high-level athletes through her credentials as a professional journalist, access that would be difficult to achieve in any other way. Her press pass allowed her to interact with athletes before and after games and during practice.

Womack relied on visual cues to enhance or downplay her association with sportswriters as the research required. For example, she displayed a note pad or tape recorder to signal her purpose for being there. Athletes are accustomed to being followed around by reporters bearing tape recorders, note books, and television cameras and lights. They are suspicious and disdainful of strangers without these paraphernalia who hang around locker rooms and playing fields. Females are usually assumed to be "groupies"; males are part of the despised social category known as "jocksniffers." Reporters are also viewed as "jocksniffers," but athletes acknowledge that journalists are required to hang around because of their jobs, which is a more acceptable motivation than simple curiosity.

To avoid undesirable aspects of being associated with journalists, Womack distanced herself from them by always dressing in skirts and dresses, since almost all sportswriters at the time she began her research were male. At the same time, she dressed discreetly in a businesslike "uniform" to distinguish herself from "groupies," women who gain access to the group through sexual favors. Womack also distanced herself behaviorally from sportswriters by avoiding the kind of "good old boy" display that sportswriters often affect. She refrained from giving the athletes pointers on their games, as sportswriters sometimes do, and generally

avoided conveying a sense of superior knowledge about sports. Although males commonly use this means to get to know each other and establish patterns of dominance and deference, it infuriates professional athletes when they are subjected to it by outsiders. In fact, being a woman was an advantage in this respect, because athletes presumed her innocent of any knowledge of sports and, therefore, found her non-threatening. This became apparent one day in the Dodger dugout when Womack was chatting casually with a high-ranking member of the team. A male visitor began to instruct her on the finer points of baseball, while affecting an easy familiarity with the team. The athlete looked at him disdainfully and scornfully made his exit. This incident, and others like it, definitively resolved for Womack the issue of whether she was correct in choosing not to work with a male co-researcher.

MALE SOLIDARITY

Both police officers and professional athletes adhere to an ethic of "esprit de corps," in which they strongly ally themselves with their fellows. A number of athletic customs and rituals emphasize the solidarity of the group and link the identity of the individual player to his position on the team. For example, a hockey player new to a team is subjected to a ritual shaving by his teammates. This forcible removal of head and body hair is usually administered when the new team member demonstrates a disregard for his teammates by inconveniencing them in some way. Professional football teams serve communal meals on the day of a game, and some hold vesper services as well.

The custom in baseball of shaking hands after hitting a home run reminds the triumphant athlete that he is still a member of the team. During the course of Womack's field work, Reggie Jackson created a scandal by refusing to shake hands with his teammates on the New York Yankees. When a member of another baseball team was asked about the incident, he replied: "That would never happen on our team. We're all one team, you know. (Getting a home run) is part of a team effort. I don't know what Reggie had in mind—maybe there's something there I don't know about—but it's like taking it all for yourself."

This sports figure is expressing the pull of two loyalties created by the emphasis on solidarity among athletes. He is reluctant to criticize a fellow insider in baseball to an outsider, but it was evident in the context of the interview that he strongly disapproved of Jackson's behavior because it emphasized the individual over the team.

Team (and police) solidarity is generated and maintained by excluding outsiders, especially those who might threaten the integrity of the group. As Mary Douglas (1966) has noted, it is ambiguity and mixing of cultural categories that is particularly threatening. Thus, *male* outsiders are more "dangerous" than *female* outsiders, who are members of a "safer" conceptual category because they can never become insiders.

During Womack's field work, a court decision was handed down that forced teams to admit women to their locker rooms. The announcement came on a day she made a scheduled visit to the Los Angeles Dodgers, resulting in the only overt display of hostility Womack experienced while studying the team. A member of the coaching staff approached her in the dugout and said, "Why don't you go on into the locker room?" Womack correctly interpreted this as a challenge and replied, "I think I'll pass on it today." Rebuffed in his attempt to attack her directly, the team member launched into a tirade against women reporters in general, concluding his speech with the assertion: "Women who want to go into the locker room aren't women at all. The players have nothing but contempt for them."

Although this team member was the only one who verbalized his anger, his attitude was no doubt generally shared, as evidenced by Womack's later experiences on entering the locker room. On one occasion, she was taking a picture of a fully clothed athlete when his unclad teammate deliberately stepped into the frame, affording the anthropologist a photograph of a full frontal male nude. Admitting women to the locker room was perceived as a challenge to the solidarity of the group because it permitted "outsiders" to invade the male team realm. Women, who were "safe" in a clearly delineated external role, became "dangerous" when they were

allowed to get too close. In another context, male "wanna-bes" or "jocksniffers" are dangerous because their attempts to get close to the athletes are experienced as threatening the solidarity of the in-group.

Police display a similar reaction to outsiders who fail to observe the proper distance. Many people seeking to ingratiate themselves with police officers drop names of other officers and try to impress them with "inside" knowledge. This has the opposite effect, since police view such attempts as inappropriate familiarity.

No outsider will ever be perceived as an insider by police or by professional athletes. However, an outsider who occupies a clearly defined, delimited, and non-threatening role—and who conveys an understanding of that role—will be accepted and even welcomed. As noted later in this paper, Womack and Barker discovered that both athletes and police were eager to tell their stories after they learned to trust the researcher. For both, earning trust included passing a few well-chosen tests.

PASSING THE TEST

Womack and Barker were forced to establish early in their research that they were not "groupies," part of the experience of professional athletes and police officers alike, and both researchers were subjected to various types of tests in the field. Early in her research, Barker discovered that police officers would deliberately try to shock her by describing a grisly event on the job or by making a provocative political statement. At these times, their emphasis was different from when they discussed such subjects among themselves. Barker learned to distinguish whether they were exchanging information among themselves and allowing her to overhear, or whether they were directly addressing her and, in many cases, trying to assess her reaction.

In one sense, police officers were trying to determine whether she was "for" or "against" them. This went beyond a simple insider-outsider distinction, and was an attempt to find out more general kinds of information about her. They wanted to know whether she was a "pushover for the image" or, conversely, whether she would be hypercritical of them.

In the first instance, they would disdain her for being gullible; in the second, they would be offended by her close-mindedness. They were asking the tacit question: Are you interested in me because of what you think I am or because of who I really am?

In another sense, Barker was being subjected to a test of character. Officers value the ability to be noncommittal until, as they put it, they "know all the knowns"—that is, until all the facts are in. Yet street officers must often respond instantly to situations in which they do not "know all the knowns," and they must draw conclusions based on fragmentary information. These conflicting abilities are essential in the performance of their jobs, and the ability to sort out complex social situations is required of fellow officers and valued in people generally.

Also as a result of their jobs, police officers automatically try to find out "where you're coming from." They are trained interviewers and know many tricks of the trade designed to gain information from others while revealing little about themselves. Barker found herself subject to many of the techniques officers rely on to elicit information from suspects and victims. She would be conversationally "set up" by officers introducing a subject about which they knew she had information and then waiting to see her response. This was a test of her discretion and trustworthiness. On some occasions, Barker found herself the object of an adapted version of "good cop, bad cop."

Like police officers, professional athletes are accustomed to being courted or vilified because of their image, and they are scornful of those who are blinded by the uniform. Womack was often offered a chew of tobacco by baseball players intent on putting her on the spot. Just as with police officers, the real test was how she felt about them. If she had reacted with disgust, she would have been scorned as one who wanted the glory of being associated with them but was unwilling to accept them as they are. Had she accepted, she would have earned the contempt athletes reserve for women who try to be men or for outsiders who try to be insiders. Passing the test required an understanding of how to maintain the proper distance while demonstrating the ability to take the heat. In other words, the athletes wanted to know whether Womack possessed the appropriate qualities of innate character and social sensitivity. Once she demonstrated her ability to reject the tobacco but not the man, the discussion proceeded comfortably and cordially.

There was one particularly severe test that Womack failed honorably, however. While interviewing a hockey player on the sidelines during practice, other players carefully aimed hockey pucks so they would sail within ten feet of her and the athlete. This is no gentle threat, since hard-hit hockey pucks have been timed at ninety miles an hour, and can cause serious injury. After enduring this aggressive display for several minutes, the researcher confessed, "This is making me a little nervous."

The hockey player replied, "It's making me pretty nervous, too."

Come to think of it, Womack may have passed that test.

MACHISMO AND THE "EMPATHY" FACTOR

Both researchers discovered unexpected advantages to being a woman studying a male-dominant group, and some of these are due to the values of machismo culture. Women are non-threatening, whereas men are competitors. Women are viewed as sympathetic listeners, especially when the discussion involves a revelation of self. Womack found that athletes were often eager to talk to her about rituals, a subject so personal one team member said it was "like asking them what brand of shorts they wore." In general, talking about magic is viewed as dangerous, both because athletes fear being considered "superstitious" and because, as baseball player Ron Cey put it, "If I told you my rituals, they wouldn't work."

Whereas talking with another male can be an encounter fraught with danger, talking with a woman can be an opportunity for display. Barker discovered that police officers were flattered by the attention and pleased that an outsider was interested in them as individuals, as well as the work they did. She also feels she may have been aided by the fact that they viewed her project as being of little consequence and, therefore, non-threatening.

The empathy factor—and face-to-face inter-action—played an important part in getting athletes to talk about their rituals, yielding information that is virtually impossible to get any other way. After presenting some of her data at a conference, Womack was approached by a researcher conducting a study on athletes, who asked, "How did you get all this information? I tried to get a group of athletes to answer a questionnaire and got all negative results." Athletes are experts at refusing to answer a question they don't like, or seeming to answer a question without actually doing so, and at misleading an interviewer they don't particularly like.

In some ways, Womack's and Barker's equivocal role as women in male-dominant groups provided a service to the subjects, in that they were able to talk about their lives in a way that was customarily denied them. Barker notes that police could reveal vulnerability with her, and describe their emotional reactions to some of their experiences. They were especially disturbed by brutality to children and frustrated by their sense of being unable to intervene effectively. However, in spite of their strong reaction to scenes of children who were killed, beaten or sexually abused, police were limited in their ability to distance themselves from it. Unlike the public, police must focus on the experience in filling out their reports, but report writing emphasizes detachment rather than emotion. Police are subject to extended contact with events that provoke strong emotion, but are generally deprived of an outlet for expressing it. Barker's research drew this description of his work from one officer:

I can take anything the job throws at me except the kids. First fatal [case involving a death] I drew was my third day on and there were two children and their mom. She lost control and T-boned a telephone pole. The infant in the child seat, the three-year-old and the mom. We were the first on the scene and the three-year-old kept asking for her mother, and you could see the mother was dead. The baby was gone, and this little girl was so broken up, and all you could do was talk to her—you couldn't pick her up, or hold her, because of the injuries. I kept talking to her, but she never even

made it out of the wreck. Welcome to the wonderful world of public service. That almost ended my career. I thought I could never go through that again. On every call I just pray there are no kids, no children.

As another officer put it, "Police must be pretty well balanced to take the 'stuff' over and over again." Most male police attempt to protect their wives from such experiences, so they don't talk about them at home. Police may talk about such events with their partners, who have gone through the experience with them, but in this case a fellow officer is too intimately involved to provide a useful sounding board, and there may be some reluctance to let down all professional barriers. Even if the partner is a woman, she is not viewed as quite so understanding as a woman who has not been through the rigorous police training and toughening experiences of the street. A policewoman is one of them and, therefore, "tough." She is also subject to the same professional constraints that prevent officers from venting their feelings as openly as they did with Barker. It may well be that to do so would add to their sense of frustration and powerlessness since, in their view, they are admitting to being unable to "take it."

Barker occupied the appropriate position to bridge the empathy gap: she knew the job and was also a woman. The researcher provided an opportunity to reprocess the experiences, this time including the outrage, pain and frustration. Barker was more knowledgeable about the job of policing than officers' wives, who are removed and "protected," but at the same time she was enough removed from the experience to provide scope for reflection. Barker provided the perfect sounding board because she was softer than a policewoman and more knowledgeable than a wife.

Womack found much the same to be true of professional athletes. She was softer than reporters or athletes and more knowledgeable than fans. On a number of occasions she was told, "I'm glad you're doing this. People need to know what it's really like to be an athlete." Although they are the focus of much attention and are grilled for information about everything from their attitudes to their weight, athletes as human beings attract little interest. They are in the unique position that everyone wants to know them, but no one cares who they are. Womack asked them to reflect upon their experiences.

Like police, athletes are subject to intense stress and lack of understanding from outsiders. Both need a well-considered approach to life to survive in a highly stressful social environment and perform consistently beyond the capacity of most humans. The careers of many physically gifted athletes are cut short by the inability to handle stress. Most athletes have thought carefully about who they are and what their performance means, but no one wants to hear about it. Athletes are presumed to be unintellectual, so no one is interested in their opinions. When a sympathetic listener sits down and asks, "What do you think about ... ?" and is willing to listen to the answer, they are only too happy to talk. This is especially true if the listener is a woman and, therefore, assumed to be sympathetic. Womack observed men settling in for a chat with athletes and noted that, often, the exchange held an edge of tension related to competition. The male outsider appeared eager to demonstrate his knowledge of the game, and the athlete appeared eager to avoid being put on the spot.

The willingness to listen is a key factor in Womack's and Barker's research experiences and is probably a crucial aspect of anthropological research in general, transcending gender. The importance of empathy in anthropological methodology is often overlooked. Books on field work may devote a great deal of space to discussing how to ask questions, but virtually none considers the perhaps more important aspect of conducting interviews—how to listen. This is an issue that transcends differences of gender and distinctions of insider and outsider and goes to the heart of anthropological research. It is not enough to ask the good question. Whether female or male, the anthropologist who wants to understand the insider perspective must turn off the internal dialogue, settle back, and really *listen* to the answer.

THE FEMININE FACTOR

Males who are part of a machismo culture often seem to view it as incumbent upon them to please a woman by giving her what she wants or what they *think* she wants. Therefore, they feel an obligation to answer questions posed by a woman in a one-on-one context, even if they view the question as intrusive. This circumstance favors the female researcher, but the advantage is lost if the interview takes place in the presence of other males. For example, in her job as a sports reporter, Womack was conducting an interview in the locker room of a professional boxer immediately after he had lost a fight. "What are your plans now?" she asked. The boxer's manager flew at her in a rage, saying, "How can you be so insensitive? This man has just lost a fight. How can you ask a question like that?" Just then a male reporter entered the locker room and, not hearing the previous exchange, asked the same question, "What next?" Without a moment's hesitation, the manager answered the question.

This episode illustrates one disadvantage of being a female researcher in an all-male group—becoming a scapegoat. As an onlooker with distinctive characteristics, a woman is likely to be singled out for blame in times of trouble. Just as women have the power to sink ships, they are also capable of sinking a baseball team. In this respect, the outsider status of female is more risky than the traditional outsider role of the anthropologist, since women are viewed as polluting by many groups, including professional sports teams. Elsewhere, Womack (1982) has noted that women are barred from group interactions organized around male solidarity because female-male pair bonding threatens the male-male group bond. Similarly, Rena Lederman (1989) notes that male rhetoric that purports to devalue women is actually aimed at shaming men into fulfilling their assigned responsibilities in the all-male group.

It is impossible to assess whether a male researcher could have acquired the kinds of information about athletes and police officers available to two female researchers. Certainly, none has so far done so. However, this may be because male researchers have not posed the same questions, rather than that they would not have received the same kinds of answers. On the basis of their experiences, however, both Womack and Barker concluded that being a woman researcher working with a male-dominated group offered certain key advantages:

1. As women, they were able to transcend traditional male rivalries.
2. They were able to negotiate their equivocal status to gain access to information not otherwise available.
3. They were perceived as empathic listeners.

Gender as a factor in field research shares some advantages associated with the traditional outsider role of the anthropologist. However the female researcher/male-dominant group dynamic is further influenced by concepts of femaleness and maleness. Thus, negotiating the relationship of insider and outsider is necessarily more complex.

CRITICAL THINKING QUESTIONS

1. Why has gender traditionally been seen as an obstacle or limiting factor to conducting adequate anthropological fieldwork?
2. What are the "suspensions of norms" that the article discusses? How do they occur, and how can they actually work to the advantage of an anthropologist in the authors' views?
3. How was male solidarity expressed among athletes and policemen?
4. How did Womack and Barker differentiate themselves from the individuals whom athletes and policemen normally deal with—journalists and groupies?
5. What pressures and stresses do athletes and policemen face in the course of their professions?
6. In the authors' opinion, how did being women present both advantages and disadvantages in conducting their research?

Professional Football: An American Symbol and Ritual

William Arens

O, you sir, you! Come you hither, sir. Who am
I, sir?
OSWALD: My lady's father.
LEAR: 'My lady's father'! my lord's knave! you
whoreson dog! you slave! you cur!
OSWALD: I am none of these, my lord; I be-
seech your pardon.
LEAR: Do you bandy looks with me, you ras-
cal? [striking him.]
OSWALD: I'll not be strucken, my lord.
KENT: Nor trip'd neither, you base football
player.
—*King Lear, Act I, Scene 4*

"A school without football is in danger of dete-
riorating into a medieval study hall."
—*Vince Lombardi*

Attitudes toward football players obviously
have changed since Shakespeare's time. Today,
the once "base football player" occupies the
throne and rules the land. In fact, to have played
too many games without a helmet seems to be a
prerequisite for high office in our country. The
prominent role football assumes in our society
deserves comment. I would contend that
although only a game, it has much to say about
who and what we are as a people.

Although I am a professional anthropologist
by training and have carried out field work in
another culture, this essay owes its impetus to
the years I have sat in front of a television watching hundreds of football contests. Out of a feeling of guilt, I began to muse in a more academic
fashion about this game and turned to the
numerous books written by players and to the
rare anthropological accounts of sport in other
societies. This has led me to believe that if an
anthropologist from another planet visited here,
he would be struck by the American fixation on
this game and would report on it with the glee
and romantic intoxication anthropologists normally reserve for the exotic rituals of a newly
discovered tribe. This assertion is based on the
theory that certain significant symbols are the
key to understanding a culture. It might be a
dreadful thought, but nonetheless true, that if
we understood the meaning of football, we
might better understand ourselves.

I emphasize a symbolic analysis because this
game that intrigues us so much is engaged in by
relatively few, but highly skilled individuals.
Most of us at one time or another have played
golf, tennis, basketball, softball, or even baseball,
but only the "pros" play football. Touch football
must be discounted because it lacks the essential
ingredients of violent physical contact and complexity of game plan. The pleasure derived from
football therefore is almost totally vicarious. This
sport's images and messages satisfy our collective
mind, not our individual bodies.

An appreciation of this argument requires an
initial short detour in time to examine the evolution of this American sport from its European
origins. The enshrined mythology states that the
game was first played by a group of English soldiers who celebrated their victory over a Viking
settlement by entering the losers' burial ground
and using the skulls of the enemies' dead in a
kicking match. Sometime later, an animal's in-
flated bladder was substituted for the skull, and
the sport of "Dane's Head" became known as
football. During the early Middle Ages, the
game was a disorganized all-day competition
between neighboring towns. The ball was placed

Source: Reprinted from *Natural History*, October 1975, pp. 72-81; copyright © Natural History Magazine, Inc., 1975.

midway between two villages and the object was to kick it along the countryside into the village and finally onto the green of the opposing community for a score. The game became so popular with the English peasantry that Henry II banned the pastime in the twelfth century because it interfered with the practice of archery. The sport was not reinstated until the seventeenth century, by which time the longbow had become an obsolete weapon.

According to Reisman and Denny (1969), who have charted the game's evolution, the kicking aspect remained dominant until 1823 when, as popular legend has it, a scoundrel named William Ellis, of Rugby School, "with a fine disregard for the rules of football, as played in his time, first took the ball in his arms and ran with it." This innovation on soccer was institutionalized at the school, and shortly thereafter was adopted by others; hence the name "rugby"— and the association of this sport in England with the educated elite.

Although both games were exported to America, only rugby was modified in the new setting. The claim has been made by the participants, and officially adopted by the National Collegiate Athletic Association, that the first intercollegiate game took place between Rutgers and Princeton in 1869. However, because that contest followed soccer rules, the honor of having played the first game of what was to emerge as American football rightly should go to Harvard and McGill in 1874, when rugby regulations were the order of the day. In the remaining decades of the nineteenth century, the sport began to take on a more American form as a definite line of scrimmage and the center snap, replaced the swaying "scrum" and "heal out" of English rugby. This meant that possession of the ball was now given to one team at a time. However, the introduction of the forward pass in the early years of this century signaled the most radical break with the past. These revisions on rugby resulted in greater structure and order, but at the same time more variety and flexibility, because running, kicking, and forward passing were incorporated as offensive maneuvers. Football had become an American game.

As a result of this process, football has emerged as an item of our cultural inventory that we share with no other country but Canada, where it is not nearly so popular. Does football's uniqueness and popularity say something essential about our culture? Rather than dismiss this question as trivial, we should be aware that we share our language, kinship system, religions, political and economic institutions, and a variety of other traits with many nations, but not our premier spectator sport. This is important when we consider that other societies have taken up baseball, a variation of cricket, and basketball, a homegrown product. Like English beer, the American brand of football is unexportable, even to the colonies. No one else can imagine what the natives see in it. On the other hand, soccer, the world's number one sport, has not been a popular success in America. In a peculiar social inversion, though, the educated and well-traveled American middle class has taken some interest in this sport of the European working classes. Nonetheless, football is uniquely American and little else can be included in this category.

Also, football as compared to our language and many values, is not forced upon us. It is an optional aspect of our culture's inventions, which individuals choose to accept. Our society, like any other complex one, is divided by race, ethnicity, income, political affiliation, and regionalism. However, seventy-nine percent of all the households in the country tuned in to the first Super Bowl on TV, implying that the event cut through many of the divisive factors just mentioned. Personally, I can think of precious little else that I have in common with our former or current president, with a rural Texan, or an urban black man other than a mutual passion for this game. Football represents not only "Middle America," as is so often claimed, but the whole of America. When we consider football, we focus on one of the few things we share with no one outside our borders, but do share with almost everyone within it.

The salient features of the game and the society that created and nourishes it reflect some striking similarities. The sport combines the qualities to an extent, but in football the process has surely reached the zenith. Every professional and major college team finds it necessary today to include a player whose only function is place kicking, and another for punting. Some have individuals whose sole responsibility is to center or hold the ball for the point after touchdown. Football is also a game in which success now demands an extensive reliance on sophisticated electronic technology from telephones to computers while the match is in progress. In short, football, as opposed to its ancestor, rugby, epitomizes the spirit and the form of contemporary American society.

Violence is another of our society's most apparent features. This quality of American life and its expression in football clearly accounts for some of the game's appeal. That football involves legitimate bodily contact and territorial incursion defines it as an aggressive sport par excellence. It is hardly surprising therefore that books by participants are replete with symbolic references to war. For example, Jerry Kramer, a Green Bay Packer during their glory years of the 1960s, divides his book, *Instant Replay,* into the following sections: Preliminary Skirmishes; Basic Training; Mock Warfare; Armed Combat; War's End. Frank Leahy, a former coach of Notre Dame and in his time a living symbol of America, wrote in his memoirs:

> ... the Stars and Stripes have never taken second place on any battlefield. With this in mind, we ask you to think back and ask yourself where our young men developed the qualities that go to make up a good fighting man.... These rafts are something that cannot be found in textbooks nor can they be learned in the lecture room. It is on the athletic fields that our boys acquire these winning ways as much a part of the American life as are freedom of speech and of the press (1949: 230).

Mike Holovak (1967), a former coach of the New England Patriots, waxed even more lyrical in reminiscing about his World War II military service. He refers to those years as the time he was on "the first team" in the "South Pacific playground" where the tracers arched out "like a long touchdown pass" and the artillery fired "orange blobs—just like a football."

To single out violence as the sole or even primary reason for the game's popularity is a tempting oversimplification. There are more violent sports available to us, such as boxing, which

allows for an even greater display of legitimate blood spilling. Yet, boxing's popularity has waned over the last few decades. Its decline corresponds with the increased interest in professional football, in which aggression is acted out in a more tactical and sophisticated context. Football's violence is expressed within the framework of teamwork, specialization, mechanization, and variation, and this combination accounts for its appeal. A football contest more adequately symbolizes the way in which our society carries out violence than does a sport that relies on naked individual force. An explanation of football's popularity on the basis of violence alone also overlooks the fact that we are not unique in this respect. There have been many other violent nations, but they did not enshrine football as a national symbol.

Although the "national pastime" may not have suffered the same fate as boxing, interest in baseball also has ebbed. If my analysis of football is correct, then baseball is not in step with the times either. The action in baseball does not entail the degree of complexity, coordination, and specialization that now captures our fancy. I think this is what people mean when they say that baseball is boring. The recent introduction of the designated hitter and the occasional baserunning specialist who never bats or fields are moves to inject specialization and to heighten the game's appeal to modern America. In essence, baseball belongs to another era, when life was a bit less complicated.

To return to our original interest, one final point must be made on the symbolism of football. Earlier, I wrote that football represented the whole of America and overcame traditional differences in our society. However, the importance of the division between the sexes, which has more recently become part of our consciousness, was not mentioned. Football plays a part in representing this dichotomy in our society because it is a male preserve that manifests and symbolizes both the physical and cultural values of masculinity. Entrance into the arena of football competition depends on muscle power and speed possessed by very few males and beyond that of most females. Women can and have excelled in a variety of other sports, but football generally excludes them from participation. It was reported in a local newspaper that during a game between female teams the players' husbands appeared on the sidelines in women's clothes and wigs. The message was clear: If the women were going to act as men then the men were going to transform themselves into women. These "rituals of rebellion" involving an inversion of sex roles have been recorded often by anthropologists. It is not surprising that this symbolic rebellion in our culture was aimed at a bastion of male supremacy.

If this argument seems farfetched, consider the extent to which the equipment accents the male physique. The donning of the required items results in an enlarged head and shoulders and a narrowed waist, with the lower torso poured into skin-tight trousers accented only by a metal cod-piece. The result is not an expression, but an exaggeration of maleness. Dressed in this manner, the players engage in handholding, hugging, and bottom patting, which would be ludicrous and disapproved of in any other context. Yet, this is accepted on the gridiron without a second thought. Admittedly, there are good reasons for wearing the gear, but does that mean we must dismiss the symbolic significance of the visual impression? The game could just as easily be played without the major items, such as the helmet, shoulder pads, and cleats. They are as much offensive as defensive in function. Indeed, in comparison, rugby players seem to manage quite well in the flimsiest of uniforms.

The preceding discussion puts us in a better position to ask the question hinted at earlier—are we in effect dealing with an American ritual of some meaning? The answer depends upon how ritual is defined. A broad anthropological view suggests that it is a standardized, repetitive activity carried out for the purpose of expressing and communicating basic cultural ideals and symbols. A ritual therefore does not necessarily imply communication with the supernatural. The inauguration of a president or the playing of the national anthem are common examples of nonreligious rituals in America. An objective evaluation of the problem also demands recognizing that an act can have a sacred and a secular character at the same time. Consequently, at one level, football can be viewed simply as a sport

and at another level as a public ritual. Considering some of the players' activities from this perspective furnishes some interesting and supportive observations.

If we view the game as a ritual and, therefore, in some respects as a sacred activity, we would expect the participants to disengage themselves from the profane world of everyday affairs. This is a common aspect of ritual behavior in any part of the world. Especially relevant for the participants is the avoidance of what anthropologists refer to as "pollution"—an impure ritual state—as the result of contact with contaminating acts or situations. Association with this profane realm renders a participant symbolically unfit to engage in a sacred performance.

In many rituals performed entirely for and by males, sexual contact with females must be avoided. Abstinence under these conditions is almost a cultural universal because the sexual act is an expression of man's animal or profane nature. In many a rite of passage for boys about to enter adulthood, the participants are taken out of the community, isolated from the opposite sex, and may not be seen by them. In other societies, prior to a significant activity such as the hunt or warfare, the community members are admonished to refrain from sexual behavior for fear of disastrous consequences. Is it really surprising then that in the world of sport, and with football in particular, sex before the event is viewed with suspicion? In this context, I am reminded of Hoebel's (1960) statement that "The Cheyenne feeling about male sexuality is that it is something to be husbanded and kept in reserve as a source of strength for the great crises of war." This compares well with the attitude at the virtually monastic world of football training camps. At these facilities, all the players, including those married, are sequestered together during practice days. They are allowed to visit their wives, who must be living off the grounds, on Saturday night only, because there is no practice on Sunday. As is to be expected, they must return to the all-male atmosphere on Sunday evening in consideration of Monday's activities. The result is that sex and football, the profane and the sacred, are segregated in time and space. During the season, a variation of the procedure prevails. The players and staff spend Saturday night together because the contest takes place on Sunday. In each instance there is a clear-cut attempt to avoid the symbolic danger of contact with females prior to the event.

This was impressed on me when I traveled with my university's team by chartered bus to a game to be played at the opponent's field. Because there were a few unoccupied seats, two of the players asked the coach if their girlfriends could ride along. He said in all seriousness that they could not ride to the game with us, but that they could join us on the bus on the way home. A writer who spent the season with the Rice University football squad mentioned a similar instance (Tippette 1973). When the team bus pulled up in front of the dormitory where they would spend the night on the opponent's campus, a number of the girls from the college entered the vehicle and began to flirt with the players. The Rice coach, who was in an accompanying car, stormed onto the bus and ordered the girls off immediately. He then told the players that they should have known better—the incident was a dirty trick instigated by their foe. Dirty trick or not, somebody planned the exercise, well aware of the unsettling effect that it would have on the team.

One further example is from the professional arena. Describing the night before the first Super Bowl, when the Green Bay Packers were allowed to bring along their wives as a reward for championship play, Jerry Kramer wrote: "My wife's been here for the past few days, and so has Chandler's. Tonight we're putting the girls in one room, and Danny and I are sharing one. It's better for the girls to be away from us tonight. We're always grumpy and grouchy before a game" (1968).

There are, of course, some perfectly reasonable arguments for segregating the players prior to a game. For one, the coaches argue that they are assured that the team members get an undistracted night's sleep. Thus it is assumed that the players will be better able to concentrate on the upcoming event. At the same time, when these vignettes are considered, the theme of possible pollution through contact with females is not altogether absent. In any event, the inhibition of sexual activity prior to an athletic event has no apparent scientific rationale. The latest position based on research argues that sex is actually beneficial, because it induces a more restful night's sleep.

The *New York Times* recently reported that a British physician who has advised and interviewed his country's Olympic competitors mentioned that one informant admitted setting the world record in a middle distance track event an hour after sexual intercourse. Another confessed that he ran the mile in less than four minutes an hour and a half after the same activity. One must look beyond rationality for an explanation of the negative attitude toward sex on the part of the elders who control professional football. However, if we grant that the sport involves a significant ritual element, then the idea does make some sense. From this standpoint, scientific reasoning is not relevant.

Accounts of rituals in other cultures also indicate the prevalent belief in symbolic contamination through contact with illness or physical imperfection. Examples of this sort of avoidance also crop up in football. Players report that those who become sick to their stomachs in the summer heat of training camp are avoided and become the objects of ridicule. In a similar vein, participants are rightfully admonished to stay away from an injured player so that the trainer can attend to him. However, they do not appear to need the advice because after a momentary glance they studiously avoid a downed colleague. Injured, inactive players on the team I was associated with as a faculty sponsor were not allowed to mingle with the active participants during the game. The loquacious professional Jerry Kramer also writes that when he was hurt and disabled, he felt like an "outsider," "isolated" and "separated" from the rest of the group. Others have written that they were ignored during these times by their teammates and coaches. I do not want to push this argument too far because there are many sound reasons to explain this patterned reaction. At the same time, I can think of similar arguments for the behavior of people in other cultures after having come into contact with illness or death.

Eating is another profane act, because it is a further indication of our animal nature. As in every society, contact with certain foods renders an individual unfit to participate in rituals. However, in contrast to sexuality and physical imperfection, nourishment cannot be avoided for any length of time. Instead, under controlled conditions, the act of eating is incorporated into the ritual, and the food becomes charged with a sacred character. Consequently, not just any type of food is acceptable, but only specified types with symbolic significance may be ingested by ritual participants. What would be more appropriate in our society than males eating beef prior to the great event? Imagine the scorn that would be heaped upon a team if it were known that they prepared themselves for the competition by eating chicken.

The problem with a purely functional interpretation is that this meat, which, it is believed, must be eaten on the day of the competition, is not converted into potential energy until hours after the game has ended. Although the players must appear for this meal because it is part of the ritual, actually very few eat what is presented to them. Instead, in contradiction to the ritual experts, the participants prefer a high-energy snack, such as a pill, which they realize has more immediate value. Nevertheless, those who control the players' behavior, as in the other instances, adhere to a less functional course by forcing their charges to confront a meaningful symbolic substance. If this situation were presented to an anthropologist in the heart of the Amazon, I wonder how long it would take to suggest ritual cannibalism on the part of the natives.

I have tried to make it clear that I am well aware that there are a number of secular, functional explanations for the behavior that has been described. However, it bears repeating that a ritual has a variety of levels, components, and consequences. The slaughter of a white bull during a rite of passage for males among cattle-keeping people in Africa has an obvious nutritional benefit for those who consume it. At the same time, though, this does not obviate the ritual significance of the act. If I am making too much of the symbolic element of American football, then perhaps we ought to reconsider the ease with which we accept this type of analysis for other supposedly simpler cultures. Accounts of team log racing among the Shavante Indians of Brazil as an attempt to restore harmony to a social order beset by political divisions (Maybury-Lewis, 1967) and the analysis of cock fighting in Bali (Geertz, 1972) as an expression of national character have caused little stir. Unless we consider ourselves something special, our own society is equally suited to such anthropological studies. It is reasonable that if other people express their basic cultural themes in symbolic rituals, then we are likely to do the same.

References

Geertz, Clifford. 1972. "Deep Play: Notes on a Balinese Cockfight." *Daedalus* Winter.

Hoebel, E. Adamson. 1960. *The Cheyenne*. New York: Holt, Rinehart and Winston.

Holovak, Mike. 1967. *Violence Every Sunday*. New York: Coward-McCann.

Kramer, Jerry. 1968. *Instant Replay*. New York and Cleveland: World Publishing Company.

Leahy, Frank. 1949. *Notre Dame Football*. New York: Prentice-Hall.

Maybury-Lewis, David. 1967. *Akwe-shavante Society*. Oxford: Clarendon Press.

Reisman, David, and Reuel Denny. 1969. "Football in America: A Study in Cultural Diffusion." In J. W. Lory, Jr. and G. S. Kenyon, eds., *Sport, Culture and Society*. New York: Macmillan.

Tippette, Giles. 1973. *Saturday's Children*. New York: Macmillan.

CRITICAL THINKING QUESTIONS

1. Why does Arens state that football is the quintessential American sport?
2. What essential American values does football reflect and reinforce?
3. According to Arens, how does football enhance "maleness" in American culture?
4. Can any aspect of football be defined as ritual in the cultural or religious sense?
5. Using Arens's article and class discussion material, define why the Super Bowl can be seen as the ultimate American secular, and perhaps religious, ritual?

Kenya, Land of My Fathers: A Time Traveler in Kenya

Chapurukha M. Kusimba

Thirty-five years ago, I was born and given the name Cullen, in honor of an Irishman who was then my father's boss at the Kilembe mines in Uganda. My parents were from western Kenya, but I spent the first five years of my life in Uganda, where Father had found work as a civil engineer. After the two neighboring nations failed to resolve the labor migration crisis, Kenyans were forced to leave Uganda, and we settled in Father's village of Kaptola, where my parents had a modest two-bedroom house. This is where my two brothers, my sister, and I first became acquainted with our extended family. Having been born and raised in Uganda, we spoke Luganda, Lutoro, and some English, but none of our family's mother tongue, Lubukusu. Mother and Father decided that we should spend some time in the village to learn the ways of our people.

Our home was about one hundred yards from my grandparents' huge, six-bedroom house, which always seemed to be a beehive of activity. Here, in the evenings after school and dinner, all the grandchildren gathered to complete their homework, listen to Bible stories or fairy tales, sing traditional and Christian hymns, and, quite often, take refuge from irritated parents. For the next twelve years, in the great house that Grandfather built and Grandmother managed, I and my expanding family of cousins and siblings were raised. We were growing up in a recently independent and fast-changing society, little realizing that our generation enjoyed a unique link to the past.

Occasionally, one of us would bring home an arrowhead or stone tool, and our grandparents would patiently explain how people lived in former times. The Bukusu, to which I belong, are a Bantu-speaking people and inhabit the area around Mount Elgon on the Kenya-Uganda border. Traditionally, the Bukusu lived in large fortress villages, farming and grazing cattle in scattered meadows. They were surrounded by the Nilotic-speaking Iteso, Sabaot, and Nandi; by other Bantu groups; and by the Ndorobo, who were hunter-gatherers. In times of peace and prosperity, these peoples engaged in trade and intermarried. In times of famine, they competed for land and stole from one another's herds. Skirmishes, raids, and counterraids were somehow accepted as a way of life.

Born in 1904, Grandfather was a skilled hunter, wonderful teacher, and excellent farmer. He became a Quaker in 1916 and was one of the first local missionaries to set up a meetinghouse among the pastoral Sabaot people of western Kenya. Our grandparents made it clear that we were in one way or another connected with our neighbors, including the hunter-gatherers, who brought us baskets, mats, dried meats, honey, and dried bamboo shoots in exchange for grains (mostly millet, sorghum, and maize).

Grandfather spoke all the languages of his neighbors, among whom he preached the Quaker message of peace and brotherhood. Few Kenyans can now speak more than four indigenous languages, in addition to English and Kiswahili. That people were traditionally multilingual is testimony to the interactions that existed among them. At the time I was growing up, however, the history of African groups was little known, and what we were taught in school was that African cultures were static until European missionaries and colonists arrived in the late nineteenth century.

Source: Published as "A Time Traveler in Kenya" by Chapururkha Kusimba. Reprinted from *Natural History,* June 1997, pp. 38-47; copyright © Natural History Magazine, Inc., 1997.

Kenyan peoples that I learned about in childhood included the Swahili of the coast, whose Arab ties and history as slave traders gave them a less than favorable reputation. Grandfather remembered that Swahili caravans used to stop and trade in western Kenya on their way to Uganda. On one such visit, Grandfather, then five years old, approached one of the Swahili men, borrowed his rifle, and carried the heavy object for a few minutes to the amazement of all those present. One Swahili man declared, *Huyu mtoto ana nguvu kama ya simba,* "This child is as powerful as a lion." Grandfather then got the nickname Kusimba, or Big Lion, a name that he later formalized.

The history of the Swahili also came up when I accompanied Grandfather on a hunting expedition on the slopes of Mount Elgon. There I saw many rock shelters and caves, some with paintings. Because we were learning in school that ancient people used to live in caves, I asked Grandfather whether our people lived in some of them. His response was that people took refuge in the mountains and caves from the slave trade and slavery, which continued at least into the 1880s. He explained that Islamic Swahili people from the coast would attack whole villages and take people away. He also said that one of our ancestors, who had been engaged as a porter by Swahili traders when Grandfather was a young man, had never returned. It was widely believed that he had been taken into slavery. Even in my own childhood there were stories of lost children who were believed to have suffered a similar fate, and the books we used in school were replete with images of caravans led by ferocious, bearded Arab and Swahili men, wielding whips over emaciated slaves tied together and carrying ivory to the coast.

Grandfather's stories helped me understand that the cultural diversity of African people preceded European colonization; that trade, friendships, and alliances among different communities led to the exchange of ideas, information, and often genes. At the same time, Grandfather laid much of the blame for the destruction of East African societies on the slave trade and slavery. As a Quaker and a product of a missionary school, he laid that blame on the Muslim peoples of the coast.

When I got older, I began to learn about the Swahili firsthand. In 1984, I was in a group of one hundred students from Kenyatta University in Nairobi who traveled to the coast to see historical and archeological sites. I was greatly impressed by the great palace and main mosque at Gede (Gedi), built more than 700 years ago. Our guides attributed this and other significant sites to seafaring Arabs and Arabized Persians who came to East Africa to trade and to colonize the coast. Archeologists and historians thought that although these seafaring people intermixed with Africans, their coastal settlements developed in isolation from the up-country African settlements that surrounded them and with which they traded. In the words of archeologist Neville Chittick, then director of the British Institute of Eastern Africa, the coastal settlements were economically dependent on Africa but "it was seawards that they faced, looking out over the great maritime region constituted by the Indian Ocean."

This view did not seem convincing to me, and I determined to delve into the question of Swahili origins. I returned to Mombasa to begin archeological research in the autumn of 1986. There I met Mohammed Mchulla, a curatorial assistant in the department of archeology at the Fort Jesus Museum. Mohammed invited me to live with his family—his wife, Maimuna, and their two young boys, Abubakr and Abdillatif. Over the next ten months, before I left for graduate school in the United States, Mohammed's house was my home away from home, and I have returned every year since. Through this personal contact, I have been helped to understand Swahili society today and have enjoyed enlightening conversations with sages, poets, midwives, blacksmiths, potters, boat makers, tourist guides, and friends.

The resources of the Swahili coast, which extends from Somalia through Kenya, Tanzania, Mozam-bique, Madagascar, and the Comoros, have attracted many different peoples. Although most coastal inhabitants speak Kiswahili, a Bantu language, other ethnic groups also inhabit the area, including the hunter-gatherer Dahalo, Waata, and Boni (Sanye); the pastoral Orma and Somali; and the agricultural Malakote, Pokomo, and Mijikenda. To understand the roots of Swahili culture requires more than sorting through all these groups. Five hundred years of colonization also have to be unscrambled. This includes conquest by the Portuguese, who first rounded the Cape of Good Hope in search of a trade route to India; rule by the Omani Arabs, who followed in the eighteenth century after the coast enjoyed a brief period of independence; and finally, occupation by the Western European industrial powers, which met in Berlin in 1884 and partitioned Africa.

Influenced in part by local explanations of Swahili origins and by the abundance of Arabic loan words, the colonizing European intellectual community was convinced that Swahili peoples, especially the elite, were not African, even when they grudgingly accepted that Kiswahili was a Bantu language. All the monuments found in East Africa were assigned to various foreign societies—Phoenicians, Sabaens, Persians, Egyptians, Indians, Omanis—but never to the indigenous Africans. In recent years, however, historians and linguists have begun to question the common assumptions. And since 1980 several major archeological excavations and more than ten doctoral research projects have been carried out, mostly by African archeologists, that have shed new light on the complex origins and development of the Swahili states.

For an archeologist, understanding a place that has seen so many political changes can be a nightmare. But a chronology of the Swahili coast has been constructed based upon radiocarbon dates, coins, imported ceramics, and local pottery. The earliest sites that have been excavated date to the second century A.D. These finds suggest that coastal people lived in village communities, where they fished, farmed, kept domestic animals (chickens, donkeys, camels), and smelted and forged iron. Shards of Partho-Sassanian ware at some of these sites suggest that Egyptians and Ethiopians would round the Horn to trade with communities along the Somali coast. Such contact is mentioned in *Periplus of the Erythraean Sea*, written about A.D. 50, and Claudius Ptolemy's second-century *Geography*.

In the absence of earlier sites, archeologists speculate that the coast was settled sometime between 500 B.C. and A.D. 1. Based on linguistic evidence, Derek Nurse and Thomas Spear believe that Bantu-speaking people spread to the coast from what is now Zaire. The rivers and sea yielded fish and shellfish; the forested floodplains could be cleared, providing both fertile farmland and wood fuel for smelting and forging the region's abundant iron ore; and the clay deposits in the swamps were suitable for pottery making.

Chris Ehret and other linguists suggest that when the Bantu speakers arrived on the coast, the ancestors of present-day Eastern Cushites, Somali, Boni, and Aweera inhabited the hinterland and may also have been rapidly settling along the northern coast of Kenya and Somalia. The Cushites were mostly hunter-gatherers and nomadic pastoralists. Interactions among the various groups, each exploiting specific resources, would have promoted friendships, alliances, gift exchanges, barter, and occasional skirmishes.

Sites dating from the eighth century on are better known, and among their artifacts are local cowries and shell beads, evidence of trade with neighboring and interior groups by such craft specialists as potters, ironworkers, shell bead makers, and boat and canoe builders. By the ninth century, the annual monsoon winds were bringing foreign merchants bearing cloth, clothing, ceramics, and beads in exchange for ivory, rhino horns, hides and skins, ebony, ostrich feathers, ambergris, *bêche-de-mer*, copal, iron, gold—and slaves. As shown by archeologist Mark Horton, Islamic influence began to leave a mark in the ninth century, when a timber mosque was built at Shanga. But Horton found no evidence of foreign settlement at the site in terms of burials or monumental architecture.

Between 1000 and 1200, trade between the coast and the interior, Madagascar, and the Middle East increased. Along the length of the coast, pots were traded for sorghum, millet, rice, and other cereals. Pots, cowrie shells, shell beads, textiles, and cereals were exchanged with hinterland peoples up the rivers for honey, cattle, hides, ghee, and such luxuries as gold, copper, and ivory. Cereals, especially rice, were among the export items from East Africa, bringing in such maritime trade goods as beads and ceramics (primarily from India and China). According to a twelfth-century account by the Arab geographer Idrisi, Indians preferred iron from East Africa over their own because of its malleability.

(Galu, a village site I excavated, produced the world's oldest crucible steel, a high-carbon steel dated to the seventh century. Before the Galu discoveries, crucible steel was known only from tenth-century India, Sri Lanka, and Arabia.)

As the population grew and settlements became more permanent, an emerging elite began to exercise control over resources, crafts, and trade. By 1300, Islam had become a widespread part of coastal culture. Islam provided a connection between the local elite and other Muslim elites and traders that helped catapult the East African coast into international commerce. The next two centuries witnessed the importation of Chinese porcelain, Islamic pottery, glass beads, and other trade goods. At the same time, local manufacturing surged, not only of pottery and iron but also of new products, notably cotton and kapok clothing.

While early inhabitants built their dwellings of wattle and daub or unfired mud brick on a wooden frame, buildings of unfired mud brick with coral mortar foundations and of coral blocks in lime mortar began to appear after 1200. The buildings, including distinct mosques, were clustered by type of construction, suggesting that place of residence was determined by wealth, social status, and perhaps religious affiliation. Many of the elite, including merchants and political leaders, interred their dead in monumental tombs that show ranking among the townspeople. Nineteenth-century accounts by missionaries and explorers suggest that individuals of lower rank were prohibited from wearing daggers and silk dresses, building coral houses, learning to read the Koran, and buying and displaying expensive jewelry and porcelain.

The civilization of East Africa reached its zenith between 1300 and 1500. Many towns, including Mogadishu, Pate, Lamu, Mombasa, Kilwa, and Mahilaka, burgeoned into major cosmopolitan centers. Traders and merchants began to wrest more political and economic power from the farmers, fishers, potters, and ironworkers. They forged alliances and connections outside the community through contracts (including intermarriage) with potential trading partners and, in general, were the ones to welcome innovations. As the coast became more involved in trade, more and more people from the interior and abroad settled among the coastal people, creating a society that was dynamic, tolerant, and enterprising.

The question that intrigues scholars who study these developments is the extent to which Swahili civilization was an indigenous phenomenon. The vital role of local production and trade with interior African peoples argues for a strong indigenous basis. In contrast, foreign influence is represented in the spread of Islam. The identity of the Swahili elite is harder to ascertain. Nevertheless, important clues suggest that the intermediary between the hinterland and the foreign merchants was an indigenous business community.

In *Islamic Architecture on the East African Coast* (1966), British archeologist Peter Garlake examined the structures generally regarded as evidence of a Middle Eastern or Arabic colonial presence. He concluded that in basic features, such as construction techniques, ornamental and decorative detail, and composition and planning of mosques and domestic buildings, Swahili architecture evolved from local patterns. Also suggestive of the indigenous identity of coastal elites are fourteenth- and fifteenth-century tombs with circular, rectangular, or polygonal pillars and paneled façades. Called phallic pillars by the locals, they are decorated with porcelain bowls and Arabic scripts, often citations from the Koran. Unknown in the Middle East, these structures are widespread among the Oromo of Somalia and Kenya, where they symbolize manhood and show that those interred are men.

Dutch anthropologist A. H. J. Prins has argued that the traditional Swahili system of land tenure would have established a land-owning elite among the original settlers and their descendants, enabling them to control vast tracts of land, labor, and goods through a council of elders. According to their system, virgin land that an ancestor had cleared and walled in for cultivation was inherited and owned communally by patrilineal descendants. The landowners could thus levy taxes on commoners and immigrants; forge patronage relationships that provided labor for fishing, craft production, and other enterprises; and deny immigrants from the interior and abroad the right to own land.

Whatever the nature of the elite, Swahili civilization as a whole was never politically unified.

When the Portuguese arrived in 1500, the region put up little organized resistance. The conflict was unlike any that East Africans had experienced. Instead of occasional raids, this conquest saw the burning and destruction of whole villages, with the vanquished often taken wholesale into slavery. Many of these people were shipped to Portuguese colonies in the New World or sold to other European and Arab slavers. Local as well as foreign mercantile traders lost control of the Indian and Red Seas and stopped coming to East Africa. Long-established trade relationships between the coast and hinterland were destabilized.

Colonization brought increased immigration of Europeans, Arabs, and Asians into East Africa. Swahili towns were composed of numerous and diverse clans claiming different ethnic origins, ranging from the African mainland, the Arabian Peninsula, Persia, India, Portugal, and the Far East. Members of the former elite, no longer in a position of control, conspired against one another, allying with colonizers through marriage and becoming political puppets. Those who revolted were defeated and hanged or took refuge in the hinterland in hill fortresses.

The loss of independence and freedom drove many coastal people to seek the safety of the interior. This period of separation must have fostered cultural, linguistic, and ethnic differentiation between coastal and hinterland peoples. The exile continued until slavery was abolished at the end of the nineteenth century. Then, many coastal peoples and others began to move more freely and to reestablish alliances. After some sixteen generations, they had a lot to relearn, including an understanding of cultural ties. In present-day Kenya, centered on the national capital of Nairobi, there is a tendency to regard the Swahili as an alien people. Unfavorable stereotypes of them as lazy urbanites who neglect their rich lands are being used to justify land grabbing and destruction of coastal archeological sites.

This summer marks the final season of my excavations at Mtwapa, a coastal settlement nine miles north of Mombasa. Inhabited from 1100 to 1750, it was, at its height in the fifteenth century, a port town with several wards, each with its own wells, mosques, and cemeteries. Imported beads, textiles, and iron tools passed through Mtwapa in exchange for such hinterland products as cereals, ivory, rhino horns, iron, hides, and skins. Salinization of the wells, together with the Portuguese conquest of the region and a southward expansion of the Oromo, eventually led to abandonment of the town, whose ruins cover about nine acres. My next project, beginning this fall, is to survey and excavate sites in the hinterland of Mtwapa in order to understand their relationship to the coastal settlement.

I hope my work will help unravel the myths that exclude the Swahili from participation in Kenya's post-colonial national identity. Grandmother may think I'm a well-paid gravedigger, but I have managed to convince some of the folks back home that the Swahili are our brothers. Grandfather passed on in 1982 but, as an ancestor, continues to inspire my work.

CRITICAL THINKING QUESTIONS

1. Who are the Swahili, and what is their importance in eastern African history?
2. What were African students taught about the early history and prehistory of eastern Africa?
3. What political, cultural, and ideological reasons were behind the European interpretation of the remains and archaeological sites of eastern Africa?
4. What were the earliest dates of settlement in eastern Africa? What sort of lifestyle did the earliest inhabitants of the region practice?
5. What were intergroup relationships like throughout eastern African prehistory and history? What impact did these relationships have on the settlement of the region?
6. What cultural changes occurred in the late nineteenth and twentieth centuries as a result of the European colonization of eastern Africa?
7. How has recent archaeological research changed ideas regarding the prehistory of eastern Africa?

SECTION THREE

Subsistence and Economics

STATE OF THE ART: SUBSISTENCE AND ECONOMICS

From its inception, anthropology has been concerned with how various cultures go about producing food, since food production is dependent on the natural provisions of the environment, the technology available to a society, its cultural values, and the methods it employs in subsistence.

This *substantive view* of economic anthropology differed from earlier conceptions which tried to apply a general theory of economics to non-Western economies based on the *formalist view* of the Western capitalist system that is based on production for market exchange and the maximization of profit. Although it is centered on tribal and peasant societies whose primary goal was production for consumption purposes, the concern of the substantive theory was how people made a living from their own environment, regardless of whether or not it resembled the Western market system. Kin-based or lineage-based redistribution and reciprocal exchanges were the cultural values of these societies. For anthropologists the challenge was how, and if, economic theories of Western industrial society could be applied to non-Western societies that were different in so many ways. They concluded that "a universal theory of economics" borne out of the West was unsuitable for "non-Western, tribal" societies (Dalton 1969; Polyani 1944, 1968). Thus the field of anthropology has studied the various strategies of subsistence found around the world. These include hunting and gathering, pastoralism, and types of farming systems such as horticulture, grain agriculture, and intensive agriculture. In this context, anthropology also focuses on the various changes that arise from globalism and technological changes in the modern world (Bonvillain 2010; Ember & Ember 2007; Haviland 2002; Rosman & Rubel 2004; Scupin 2008).

Anthropologists noted that every society has an economic system. Various economic systems produce food and material goods differently. Hence Gudeman (1986) introduced the concept of *culturalism,* an alternative economic model that opposed substantivism on the grounds that it gave a weak critique of the universal application of Western economic theories to non-Western societies. *Culturalism* promotes a cultural relativist view involving the unique ways in which a culture goes about provisioning its members—processes which he says are culturally constructed. Anthropology continues to collect new data on the modes of production by looking at what natural resources are available to a particular society, and how resources are accessed, converted, and distributed.

Anthropologists are also interested in various types of production, division and organization of labor, the commercialization of goods, and how the world is becoming a single market system (Bonvillain 2010; Ember & Ember 2007; Haviland 2002; Rosman & Rubel 2004). The present-day economic reality of non-Western societies is different from that of sixty or seventy years ago. The coexistence of multiple modes of production in a given environment has forced economic anthropologists to characterize these production modes as *mixed economies* (the capitalist mode operating alongside traditional modes). Despite their shortcomings and criticisms (Carrier 2005; Ensminger 2002; Narotsky 1997), formalism, substantivism, and culturalism can be applied to the mixed economies of today.

Anthropology has focused on societies' access to natural resources. Though some cultures practice private ownership while others stress the collective, every society makes use of its local resources and develops its own particular technology for production depending on its environment. Anthropology is witnessing accelerating trends in the borrowing of technology from other societies and the changes brought about on the borrower society.

Anthropology has sought to understand the particulars of labor and found that labor involves its division by gender and age and that there are formal and informal rules and incentives for labor and its organization. Commercialization and distribution of goods and services are classified under various methods that anthropology has identified for the world societies. Redistribution is tied into political power locally and globally. Anthropology continues to study the changing market as the world becomes a single unit in which the circulation of goods involves global interchange (Ember & Ember 2007; Rosman & Rubel 2004; Scupin 2008). This mileu has included the "ethnography of subsistence and economics" as a methodological framework that traces the linkages of local patterns to the world capitalist market and the historical, political, gendered, and ethnic complexities surrounding trading. One example is Gracia Clark's *Onions Are My Husband* (1994), in which she analyzes the market system in West Africa, highlighting the social organization of the marketplace and the technical aspects of trading women routinely employ, including methods of bargaining and the use of credit.

In the twenty-first century, anthropology is faced with new research problems—the exploitation of labor is now an international phenomenon as corporations seek to employ cheap labor and profit-generating mechanisms from local sources. In addition, new consumption styles are emerging in the various regions of the world.

ABOUT THE ARTICLES

The articles in Section Three reflect the different types of subsistence and economic organization as defined by anthropology. The Roscoe article deals with the most basic form of human subsistence organization—hunting and gathering. He discusses the data on this subsistence form in New Guinea and attempts to place it within the larger field of hunter-gatherer studies. He emphasizes the differences between the "classic" anthropological formulation of this lifestyle and the nature of the lifestyle in New Guinea.

The next two articles deal with agriculture from different perspectives. Fuller discusses the evidence for early agriculture in southern India and the impact it had on human social and technological organization. The data parallel and enhance information from other areas of early agriculture, mainly southern China and the Fertile Crescent area of Mesopotamia, regarding the origins and impact of agriculture on Neolithic peoples. The student may also wish to read the article *The Magic Flutes* by Juzhong and Kuen in Section Eight for additional information on the Chinese Neolithic period.

Hames's article deals with one of the classic groups in the anthropological literature, the Yanamamö. Although classified as horticulturalists ("simple farmers"), his article demonstrates how even minor environmental differences can affect the organization of subsistence activities and villages from the same cultural tradition located in a generally homogenous environmental zone. It also shows how foraging can remain a vital component of people's subsistence at this level of organization.

Rasmussen's article examines a rare form of subsistence. She discusses the concept of pastoralism as a definitional category and how it functions in Tuareg life and culture. She then examines this subsistence form in terms of the sexual division of labor and the different factors, both internal and external, that affect the sexual division of labor among pastoral groups. She ends the article with an examination of the impact which the incorporation of the Tuareg into modern nation-states has had on their culture.

Leyton's article discusses a vital economic issue, the inheritance of goods and property. The patterns of inheritance in the northern Irish town of Aughnaboy are scrutinized not only from the perspective of *who* gets the goods but also *how* and *why*. He examines the local ideologies that define not only what kinds of property are inheritable but also why specific relatives receive certain categories of goods and under what conditions. What results is an illumination of family and cultural traditions that impact patterns of inheritance in a rural area that is embedded in a larger industrialized society.

References

Bonvillain, N. *Cultural Anthropology,* 2nd ed. Upper Saddle River, NJ: Pearson/Prentice Hall, 2010.

Carrier, J. G. *A Handbook of Economic Anthropology.* Cheltenham, England: Edward Elgar Publishing Company, 2005.

Clark, G. *Onions Are My Husband: Survival and Accumulation by West African Women.* Chicago, IL: The University of Chicago Press, 1994.

Dalton, G. Theoretical Issues in Economic Anthropology. *Current Anthropology* 10, no. 1 (1969): 63–102.

Ember, C., & Ember, M. *Cultural Anthropology,* 11th ed. Upper Saddle River, NJ: Pearson/Prentice Hall, 2007.

Ensminger, J. *Theory in Economic Anthropology.* Lanham, MD. Alta Mira Press, 2002.

Gudeman, S. *Economics as Culture: Models and Metaphors of Livelihood.* London: Routledge, 1986.

Haviland, W. *Cultural Anthropology,* 10th ed. Belmont, CA: Wadsworth, 2002.

Narotsky, S. *New Directions in Economic Anthropology.* London, England: Pluto Press, 1997.

Polyani, K. *The Great Transformation.* New York: Rhinehart, 1944.

Polyani, K. The Economy as Instituted Process. In *Economic Anthropology,* E. LeClair and H. Schneider (eds.). New York: Holt, Rinehart, and Winton, 1968.

Rosman, A., & Rubel, P. *The Tapestry of Culture: An Introduction to Cultural Anthropology,* 8th ed. New York: McGraw-Hill, 2004.

Scupin, R. *Cultural Anthropology,* 7th ed. Upper Saddle River, NJ: McGraw-Hill, 2008.

For Further Research

Two anthropological journals that deal with issues of economics and subsistence are *Anthropology of Work Review* and *Culture and Agriculture*. A good recent general overview of different subsistence strategies is Bates's *Human Adaptive Strategies: Ecology, Culture, and Politics* (3rd ed., 2005, Pearson/Allyn & Bacon). For hunter-gatherers a good general source is Burch and Ellanna's *Key Issues in Hunter-Gatherer Research* (1994, Berg Publishers). For horticulture there is Sahlin's *Tribesmen* (1968, Prentice Hall). *The Origins of Agriculture: An Evolutionary Perspective* (1984, Academic Press) by Rindos provides an archaeological perspective on the origins of intensive agriculture. A classic examination of pastoralists is E. E. Evans-Pritchard's *The Nuer: A Description of the Modes and Political Institutions of a Nilotic people* (1969, Oxford University Press). For additional information on researching the topics discussed in the "State of the Art" section, please visit *www.mysearchlab.com*.

The Hunters and Gatherers of New Guinea[1]

Paul Roscoe

If humans may be characterized by the balance of their history on earth, then they are a hunter-gatherer species. As a result, scholars who have surveyed or theorized humanity, from Hobbes and Rousseau through Marx and Freud, have felt duty-bound to make at least a passing nod, if not a more lingering genuflection, towards some more or less fanciful notion of the foraging life. In anthropology, with the sweep of human history as its subject matter, hunters and gatherers have featured prominently as an assumed baseline in numerous theories of economic, social, political, and cultural evolution.

Unfortunately, ethnographic information on hunter-gatherer life is limited in proportion to its importance. Hunter-gatherer species we may be, but the record of non-hunter-gatherer societies is infinitely richer than that of foragers. From the 1966 Man the Hunter conference to the present, surveys routinely identify fewer than 100 or so hunter-gatherer groups upon which some ethnographic and/or historical data are available (e.g., Bailey et al. 1989: 62–67; Hayden 1981:345, 354–55; Keeley 1988:382–83; Kelly 1995:4–5; Lee 1968:44–48; Murdock 1968:14).

None of these surveys has ever identified New Guinea as home to a hunter-gatherer group—even the recent, authoritative *Cambridge Encyclopedia of Hunters and Gatherers* (Lee and Daly 1999) includes no entry on a New Guinean society—so one might conclude that there are no hunters and gatherers among its 1,000 or so cultures. Certainly, this is the conventional wisdom: introductory textbooks routinely turn to New Guinea for ethnographic examples of horticulturalists and agriculturalists but never of hunters and gatherers. Rosman and Rubel (1989:27; see also Ayres 1980:736) are hardly alone in presuming that "the subsistence base for all New Guinea societies is root crop horticulture. There are no societies in New Guinea which only hunt, forage, and collect; every society is dependent to some extent on horticulture."

In fact, close scrutiny of the New Guinea literature turns up many scattered references to "hunters and gatherers," and in this article I seek to document that contact-era New Guinea was home to numerous foraging societies. My primary aim, as a Melanesian scholar, is to alert hunter-gatherer specialists to this substantial, largely unexploited body of comparative ethnographic data and to attract their attention to the significant opportunities that still exist for fieldwork in New Guinea among groups that continue to rely predominantly on foraged resources. Along the way, I seek to demonstrate the value of this overlooked ethnographic resource by sketching how it illuminates recent arguments connecting aquatic resources to the development of hunter-gatherer sociocultural complexity. In conclusion, I note that it also buttresses concern about the analytical utility of the concept of a hunter-gatherer "type."

HUNTERS AND GATHERERS

Any attempt to identify New Guinea's hunters and gatherers should begin by defining what constitutes a hunter-gatherer group, but this

Source: Roscoe, P. The Hunters and Gatherers of New Guinea, *Current Anthropology* 2002 43(1): 153–162. © 2002 The University of Chicago Press.

simple task quickly runs aground on a shoal of well-known difficulties (e.g., Barnard 1983: 208–10; Ellen 1982:170–76; Harris 1989:16–23; Lee and DeVore 1968:4). According to common definition, hunters and gatherers are those who subsist by gathering wild plants and hunting wild animals, these activities usually being extended to include fishing. Yet these criteria beg a number of questions, not least the issue of what constitutes "wild." The very presence of consuming humans on a landscape affects food resources, blurring the lines between wild and domesticated and, hence, between hunting and pastoralism and between gathering and cultivation (e.g., Harris 1977, Ingold 1974). It is unclear, moreover, whether "domestication" should mean breeding, nurturing, or both. Is it hunting or pastoralism if people capture and raise (but do not breed) the piglets of a wild sow they have killed, and is it gathering, pastoralism, or cultivation when wild palms are felled and chopped up to encourage "larvae plantations" (e.g., Clastres 1972:160–61, 166–67; Oosterwal 1961:70; Townsend 1969:51; Schwab 1940a:242)?

It is likewise unclear how groups should be classified that are hunters and gatherers in their procurement strategies but cultivators or pastoralists in their consumption patterns—subsisting, for example, by trading wild foods to neighbors in return for domesticated crops. And there are significant differences over whether the definition should be nonparametric or parametric. Must a group depend exclusively on foraging—however defined—to be considered a hunter-gatherer society, or is it sufficient that it depends for 50%, 75%, or some other percentage of its subsistence on wild resources (e.g., Barry 1968:208; Keeley 1988:377–78; Lee 1968:41; Murdock 1968:15; Service 1979:3, 13; Whiting 1968:336–37; Yesner 1990:728)? If the latter, should percentage dependence be measured in calories, protein, weight, labor invested, or what—bearing in mind that each of these measures could yield a different classificatory result?

If I have belabored these definitional difficulties, it is only to underscore the impossibility of definitively surveying "the hunters and gatherers of New Guinea." For pragmatic reasons alone, I have chosen to identify as a hunter-gatherer group any that appears to derive at least 75% of its subsistence calories by procuring wild resources—"wild" meaning resources that living members have not themselves deliberately bred or planted. This decision is unavoidably arbitrary but not entirely so: for space reasons, I have ignored many New Guinea groups that derive 50–74% of their calories from wild resources, groups that the most liberal definitions include as hunter-gatherers.

THE HUNTERS AND GATHERERS OF NEW GUINEA

The most comprehensive sources on the subsistence regimes of New Guinea are the reports by the Human Geography Department of the Australian National University on the agricultural systems of Papua New Guinea. Unfortunately, these cover only the eastern half of the island; no equivalent exists for the western half, the Indonesian province of Irian Jaya. Other subsistence data are contained in an enormous corpus of published and unpublished ethnographic, missionary, and administrative writings, in particular the sections of early Australian and Dutch patrol reports on native subsistence.

In addition to the usual difficulties of interpreting these historical materials, several particular problems complicate the identification of New Guinea's hunters and gatherers. Although numerous lowland groups depend on sago for their staple, the literature often fails to specify whether the palms exploited are wild, planted, or both. Where the planting of sago is mentioned, it is a rare report that estimates in even rough terms the ratio of planted to wild palms and a rarer one yet that surveys variations in this ratio. (In several societies, some villages seem to have depended wholly on wild palms while others practiced some sago planting.) Caution must also be exercised with regard to claims that a society depended wholly on wild sago: sago planting is usually so casual and undemanding that, on brief visits, observers can easily overlook its presence.

The effects of Western contact pose special difficulties for evaluating the state of contact-era subsistence patterns. At an early point in New Guinea history, administrative and missionary agents began to pressure local people into greater use of domesticated resources. Other contact-related developments inclined native people to accept them. Following pacification, and often under administrative pressure, for example, numerous groups abandoned their hilltop and swampland settlements and migrated to lower or firmer ground, often consolidating in large villages along coastlines, river banks, or newly constructed roads. By extending distances between settlements and traditional foraging reserves and by increasing population pressure, however, these moves enhanced the attractions of domestication (e.g., Report 1947:83, 129; cf. Ulijaszek and Poraituk 1983:581–82; Dye and Dye Bakker 1991:2 n.2; Haberland and Seyfarth 1974:236, 241–42). The scale of such changes is often difficult to judge, but at contact most of New Guinea's hunter-gatherers probably depended to a significantly greater extent on foraging than they did subsequently.

These difficulties notwithstanding, it is possible to identify a large number of contact-era New Guinea hunter-gatherer groups. Table 1 catalogues those I have been able to identify with some confidence. Some 10–20 societies seem to have been almost entirely dependent on wild foods; another score or so derived at least 90% of their food by foraging, and a further score probably obtained 75–90% of their food in this way. These are conservative figures: if the ethnography of contact-era New Guinea—in particular, the prevalence of sago planting—were better known, Table 1 probably would include as many as 100 societies.[2]

Table 1 is organized by the approximate percentage of their subsistence calories these foragers procured from wild resources and by three distinct subsistence strategies that, it transpires, they pursued. Every group depended for its main carbohydrate source on the starch of the wild sago palm (Metroxylon sp.). In its natural state, the sago palm grows in shallow freshwater swamps, taking 10–15 years to mature and reaching heights of 30–50 feet (Barrau 1958:151; Flach 1983:5; Ruddle et al. 1978:5–10). The palm is felled shortly before maturity, the pith is hacked out and leached to extract its starch, and the dried flour is then stored—often for months—for future consumption (Ruddle et al. 1978:11–40). Yields from wild palms are typically less than from their cultivated congeners, but wild Metroxylon is nevertheless a productive means of provisioning a community. Hard data are scarce, but five to ten harvestable palms per hectare of stand per year appears to be a typical yield, requiring around 150 work hours to produce a million calories (pp. 61–67). Calories aside, however, sago starch is nutrient-poor, containing negligible fat and less than 0.3% of protein by dry weight (p. 57). Typically, therefore, New Guinea's hunters and gatherers supplemented sago with varying combinations of aquatic and terrestrial game, and it is on this score that the three subsistence strategies in Table 1 are distinguished.

The first rank of Table 1 lists groups that secured very little meat protein in any form and/or obtained most of it from terrestrial and arboreal rather than aquatic game. Few, if any, procured a significant portion of their diet through trade. The second rank lists groups that obtained meat protein largely (and through their own efforts) from rich aquatic resources rather than from terrestrial or arboreal game. Groups in the third rank are similar to those in the second except that they procured a large proportion of their sago or aquatic resources through trade.

Given the number of New Guinea foraging societies in Table 1, it is a challenge to explain why they should have remained so long invisible to general anthropological attention. Suffice it to say that they provide hunter-gatherer scholars with a substantial new body of comparative ethnographic data and furnish continuing opportunities for fieldwork among groups that subsist more by foraging than perhaps any other contemporary groups in the world.

TABLE 1 The Hunters and Gatherers of New Guinea (a)

	Approximate Percentage of Calories from Foraging		
Subsistence Staples	*97–100*	*90–96.9*	*75–89.9*

Sago, game, limited aquatic resources	Northern Irian Jaya
	  Bonerif
	  Iau
	  Kwerba
	  Sikaritai??
		Northern Irian Jaya
		  Bauzi?
		  Berik
		  Edopi?
		  Isirawa
		  Mander
		  Soromadja??
		  Tause?	

	Sepik
	  Arafundi (Lowland)
	  Mianmin (Kime,
	  Sebai groups)
		Sepik
		  Alamblak
		  Bahinemo
		  Bisis??
		  Bitara/Berinmo??
		  One??
		  Sanio-Hiowe
		  Inland Warapu??
		  Watakatauwi
		  Yabio??
			Sepik (b)
			  Ama/Sawiyano
			  Changriwa??
			  Kwoma (Nukuma)?
			  Marl??
			  Mekmek??
			  Sumariup??

	South Coast
	  Sawuy?
	  Siagha-Yenimu?
		South Coast
		  Kombai?
			South Coast
			  Mappi River

Sago, aquatic resources, limited game		Northern Irian Jaya
		  Biak, Coastal?
		  Waropen, Kai?
			Northern Irian Jaya
			  Waropen, Napan??

	Sepik
	  Kaningara??
	
	  Kapriman
	  Karawari
	  Yimas?
		Sepik
		  Kambot
		   (Swampland)?
		  Mongol?
			Sepik (b)
			  Kambot
			   (High-ground)?
			  Langam??
			  Miyak??
			  Yaul??

	South Coast
	  Asmat (Central)
	  Asmat (Casuarina
	   Coast)
		South Coast
		  Asmat (North)
		  Boazi
		
		  Jaquai
		  Morigi
		  Mimika, Western
		  Zimakani??
			South Coast
			  Fly Estuary Kiwai??

Sago and aquatic resources obtained largely by trade, limited game		Sepik
		  Murik
		  Kwoma (Hill)
			Sepik
			  Kaunga?
			  Sawos
			
			South Coast
			  Koriki/Purari

Sources: Alamblak, Angoram Patrol Report, National Archives, Port Moresby (hereafter ANG) 6–54/55:n.p. and 12–59/60:n.p., Bruce (1974:169, 182–83), Edmiston and Edmiston (1989:2, 30–32), Haberland (1968:iv), Haberland and Seyfarth (1974:224–51); Arafundi (Lowland), ANG 6–54/55:n.p., Haberland (1966:37, 56–57, 59), Karawari Patrol Report, National Archives, Port Moresby 3–61/62:n.p.; Ama/Sawiyano, Guddemi (1992:43–44, 46–53); Asmat, Casuarina Coast, Trenkenschuh (1982a:56–57); Asmat, Central, Eyde (1967: preface, 6, 8–12, 18–40, 58–68, 71–72), Trenkenschuh (1982b:11–12; 1982c),

(*continued*)

TABLE 1   (*continued*)

van Arsdale (1975:85–86, 89, 94–96, 98–102, 105–10, 398–99; 1978:453, 459 n.2), Zegwaard (1959:1021); Asmat, North, Eyde (1967:117, 122); Bahinemo, Ambunti Patrol Report, National Archives, Port Moresby (hereafter AMB) 6–62/63:9, 11 and 9–62/63:9, Bakker (1994:49), Dye (1983:6), Dye and Dye Bakker (1991:2), Kawasaki (1998:81–82); Bauzi, Briley (1983:3; 1991:117), Sterner (1990:105); Biak, Coastal, Oomen (1959:39, 45); Bisis, ANG 6–54/55; n.p.; Bitara/Berinmo, AMB 6–62/63:9–10, Davidoff, Davies, and Roberson (1999: 203); Boazi, Busse (1987:54–55), Maunsell and Partners (1982:24); Bonerif, Oosterwal (1959:830; 1961:57–58, 62, 67, 70, 72–77); Berik, Kalmbacher (1983:25); Oosterwal (1959:830; 1961:57–58, 62, 67, 70, 72–77); Changriwa, ANG 18–49/50, Ag. Note:1; Edopi, Green (1986:69), Kim (1997:201); Iau, Bateman (1982:40), Miehle (1985:82 n.1); Isirawa, Erickson (1976:42 n.2; 1981:36); Oosterwal (1959:830; 1961:57–58, 62, 67, 70, 72–77); Jaquai, Boelaars (n.d. [1958]:16, 20, 24, 26–27, 39–40; 1975 [1955]:13), Gajdusek and Salazar (1982:109, 111); Kambot (Swampland and High-ground), ANG 19–49/50, Ag. Note: 1, 5–56/57:5, 7–8, table, 7–56/57:5, 8, and 3–59/60:2, Bjerre (1958:141), Territory of New Guinea (1931:97), Snack (1988:17–18, 48, 77–80). Schwab (1938:134; 1940a:242, 243; 1940b:259), Simpson (1955:61); Kaningra, ANG 6–54/55:n.p., Department of Human Geography (1993:22); Kapriman, AMB 9–29/30:7, ANG 6–54/55:n.p. and 12–56/57:3, Kumagai (1998:47); van den Broek D'Obrenan (1939:208); Karawari, ANG 11–49/50, Ag. Note: 1; Geo Note: 1–2; 18–49/50, Ag. Note:1; 6–54/55:n.p., Telban (1998: 19–24 and personal communication, 1999); Kaunga, AMB 2–49/50:3; Kiwai, Fly Estuary, Beaver (1920:153, 160, 214–15, 250), Maunsell and Partners (1982:24); Kombai, Venema (1989:40); Koriki, Report (1947:16, 83–86, 129–32), Chalmers (1895:105), Holmes (1924:28, 241–47, 255–57), Williams (1924:2–3); Kwerba, de Vries (1988:2, n. 2, 3), Ooster-wal (1959:830; 1961:57–58, 62, 67, 70, 72–77); Kwoma (Hill), AMB 2–51/52:3 and 3–52/53:4, Bowden (1983:9, 11–12), Whiting (1941:5, 110–12, 115–19); Kwoma (Nukuma), AMB 2–49/50:3 and 2–51/52:3; Langam, ANG 5–56/57:8; Mander, Oosterwal (1959:830; 1961:57–58, 62, 67, 70, 72–77); Mappi River, Eng (1983: 1–2, 6, 9–10); Mari, Toyoda (1998:65); Mekmek, ANG 18–49/50, Ag. Note:1; Mianmin (Kime, Sebai), Gardner (1981:49); Mimika, Western, Pouwer (n.d.[1955]:5, 12, 14, 34–35, 37, 39–45, 47, 49, 53–54), Wollaston (1912:101); Miyak, ANG 14–56/57:n.p.; ANG 18–49/50, Geo. Note:1; ANG 18–49/50, Ag. Note:1, Mongol, ANG 5–56/57:5, 7, 8, table; Morigi, Department of Human Geography (1993b:19–20), Austen (1946); Murik, ANG 2–55/56:5; Lipset (1997:17–20, 39, 46–47), Marienberg Patrol Report 2–30/31:3, Microfilm no. 616, Pacific Manuscripts Bureau, Canberra; Schmidt (1922–23:702, 715–16); Kenneth H. Thomas, Notes on the natives of villages between Marienberg and the coast, visited during above patrol, Attachment to ANG 4–32/33, File 47, Thomas Archives, South Australia Museum, p. 10; One, Aitape Patrol Report, Somare Library, University of Papua New Guinea, Port Moresby (hereafter AIT) 2–24/25; 13, 17, 20, 28–29; Sanio-Hiowe, AMB 1–61/62b:2, 6–1962/63:9–10, and 2–68/69b:3–4; Townsend (1969:23, 47, 51, 55–56, 59–65; 1974: 230; 1990:746); Sawos, Schindlbeck (1980:103–14, 131–44, 154–95; 1981:12; 1983:5); Sawuy, Mills (1986:49), Yost (1988:60–61, 64); Siagha-Yenimu, Gajdusek and Salazar 1982:109, 111); Sikaritai, Martin (1997:126); Soromadja, Oosterwal (1967:165); Sumariup, ANG 12–59/60:n.p.; Tause, Munnings and Munnings (1990:2, 15–21); Warapu, AIT 2–24/25:3, 6, 10, 28; Waropen, Kai, Held (1957:10–11, 342, 345, 347–48, 350–54, pl. 3); Oomen (1959:39, 43, 45); Waropen, Napan, Held (1957:350); Watakatauwi, ANG 1–47/48:2–3 and 6–54/55:n.p., Yamada (1997:1–3, 7–9, 21); Yabio, AMB 1–61/62:2 and 2–68/69:4, 5, Department of Human Geography (1993a:61), Saito (1998:95, 107, 111); Yaul, ANG 5–56/57:5, 7, 8, table: Yimas, ANG 11–49/50, Ag. Note:1; Foley (1991:11–13); Zimakani, Maunsell and Partners (1982:24).

(a) A single question mark denotes significant uncertainty about whether a group is placed in the correct column. Double question marks denote a group for which data are fragmentary; it follows that there is also significant uncertainty about whether it is placed in the correct column.

(b) In some Sepik cases, the sago staple is known to be entirely wild. In others, a minority of palms are planted, but it is difficult to estimate with confidence the ratio involved. Were this figure known, however, it would likely reveal that a number of these groups actually acquired 90% or more of their subsistence from wild resources.

NEW GUINEA FORAGERS IN COMPARATIVE PERSPECTIVE

The comparative value of these groups lies in New Guinea's remarkable ethnolinguistic diversity and its status as the "Last Unknown." Most of the island's societies were pacified within just the past 30 to 80 years, and their ethnographic, historic, environmental, and demographic record is consequently as rich as any in the nonindustrial world. One of the more instructive points to emerge from these comparative data is their documentation and illumination of the contention that foraging supports considerable social and cultural variability and even highly complex lifeways (Arnold 1996; Kelly 1995; Price and Brown 1985). Although New Guinea's foragers exploited a similar suite of resources (sago, aquatic resources, game, and bush foods), they exhibited a striking range of cultural forms that appear to correlate strongly with the three subsistence types detailed in Table 1.

Groups that secured very little meat protein in any form and/or obtained most of it from terrestrial and arboreal game markedly resemble the classic stereotype of the "simple" hunter-gatherer, typified by the !Kung, Inuit, Mbuti, and many Australian Aboriginal groups. At contact, their typical densities averaged 0.7/km², ranging from about 0.2 to 1.7/km². Their settlements were small, and they tended to be semi- to fully nomadic, spending most of their time in small, dispersed bush camps of 5 to 25 people but every few weeks or months congregating in a single large central settlement of between 30 and 150 people for defensive, social, or ritual purposes. Political life was relatively egalitarian: inequities in power and influence were uncommon, though status often rewarded fighting prowess, hunting ability, ritual expertise (including sorcery), and/or (occasionally) economic generosity. Ritual life was comparatively unelaborated, and there was little visual art, though nonvisual arts such as song were sometimes highly developed. Contradicting the common stereotype that war is attenuated or absent among hunters and gatherers, fighting was endemic.

Groups heavily dependent for meat protein, either directly or indirectly, on rich aquatic resources rather than terrestrial and arboreal game typically exhibited a cultural complexity that rivaled or surpassed that of many intensive agriculturalists. Among these groups, contact densities were higher, typically averaging 4.0/km² and ranging from about 1.1 to 9.4/km². Settlements were larger, typically one hundred to several hundred people. Located for defensive purposes on ridges, hilltops, or small tributaries just off major waterways, they were relatively permanent, with lifetimes of at least three years and, more usually, a generation or more. Hierarchy was often pronounced, some villages even exhibiting descent-group ranking. Leadership took various forms, including gerontocracy, big-manship, and small-scale chieftainship. Differences in both power and status were pronounced and depended on factors such as prowess in war, access to economic resources, and command of esoteric knowledge. Finally, in stark contrast to their simpler counterparts, these groups were remarkable for their highly developed ritual and visual art: some, such as the Asmat, Karawari, Kwoma, and Purari, are among the most famous of New Guinea's ritual artists. Nowhere was this productivity and proficiency more in evidence than in the monumental architecture of their elaborately carved and decorated spirit houses, which sometimes approached in size and artistry the spirit houses of the Ilahita Arapesh (whose construction required at least 10,000 man-days of work [Tuzin 1980:166 n. 45]). These structures were usually the ritual focus of highly developed initiation and headhunting cults that sometimes also involved cannibalism.

What is especially revealing about these differences in cultural complexity is the apparent absence of any significant correlation with dependence on cultivation. The Asmat, Kapriman, and Karawari, who derived little or none of their contact-era subsistence from domestication, were vastly more complex than the Ama, Bahinemo, Sanio, and Yabio, who procured 4–25% of their subsistence from domesticated resources. Indeed, the complexity of many New Guinea foragers outstripped that of horticulturalists such as the Daribi, Mianmin, and Mountain Arapesh (Gardner 1981; Mead 1947; Wagner 1967), and even the intensive agriculturalists of the Central Highlands—the Chimbu, Kuma, and Melpa—seem to have boasted hardly more sociocultural complexity than the Asmat, Kapriman, and Karawari.

New Guinea's hunters and gatherers are unusual among modern foragers for their access to a particularly rich carbohydrate source, sago. For this reason, they provide especially useful ethnographic analogies for understanding the lifestyle of prehistoric foragers who inhabited more abundant environments than the marginal habitats of most contemporary groups. With New Guinea's simple and complex foragers depending equally on sago for their carbohydrate source, however, the nature of meat-protein resources emerges as the critical subsistence variable for understanding variations in their sociocultural complexity. Whereas simple foragers obtained only limited meat protein (e.g., Arafundi, Tor groups) or procured it primarily from terrestrial and arboreal game (e.g., Ama, Bahinemo), complex foragers could depend on concentrated aquatic resources either directly (e.g., Asmat, Kapriman, Mimika, Murik) or indirectly through trade (e.g., Sawos).

The importance of aquatic resources to sociocultural complexity among foraging groups has been incidentally noted for a long time (e.g., Murdock 1968:15; Service 1979:3) and more recently has generated increasing theoretical consideration, mostly with reference to maritime adaptations (e.g., Moseley and Feldman 1988: 126; Palsson 1988; Quilter and Stocker 1983; Renouf 1984; Yesner 1980). In the New Guinea case, the conjoint properties of subsistence and warfare—a badly neglected institution in hunter-gatherer studies—emerge as the important determinants of complexity. Everywhere in contact-era New Guinea, endemic warfare exerted defensive pressures to increase the size and compactness of settlements, principally against the threat of attack at night (Roscoe 1996). Counteracting these centripetal military pressures, however, were the demands of resource exploitation during the day, which favored dispersal and mobility in the interests of efficient exploitation. On the larger rivers and lakes inhabited by groups such as the Asmat, Kapriman, Karawari, and Murik, rich, localized aquatic resources allowed defensive nucleating tendencies to triumph over fissive subsistence pressures, producing large, permanent settlements. These in turn facilitated and possibly stimulated (through such scale-related factors as increased potential conflict in large settlements) the production of social and symbolic culture. The stunning visual art of these societies, for example, was a means by which individuals and kin groups within a settlement could assert and emotionally experience their identity, prestige, and dominance over others without resorting to the physical violence that would destroy them (Roscoe 1995).

By contrast, among peoples such as the Arafundi and Tor groups, who depended for meat protein on terrestrial game or small-scale fishing rather than on concentrated aquatic resources, fissive tendencies were more powerful. Game was scattered in comparatively low densities across the landscape, forcing hunters to disperse and pursue their quarry and producing smaller, more mobile settlements and a concomitant reduction in the possibilities and demands for complex social and symbolic culture.

NEW GUINEA HUNTER-GATHERERS TODAY

In something of an iconoclastic assessment of hunter-gatherer research, Burch (1998:201) has noted as a pressing practical issue that there are "few if any societies of foragers left in the world that have not been profoundly affected by, and to some extent integrated into, much larger-scale systems." As a result, "hunter-gatherer research may soon become historically oriented rather than field oriented." It would be naive to disagree: as many scholars have observed (e.g., Headland and Reid 1989:43; Kent 1992:52), virtually all modern hunter-gatherers now engage in nonforaging subsistence activities, with dramatic changes having taken place even among the standard exemplars of hunter-gatherer life. For some time now, the !Kung have been sedentized, procuring only 30% of their calories by hunting and gathering. For many years, the Efe of the Ituri Forest have obtained more than 60% of their calories from crop foods, primarily by working in the gardens of neighboring agriculturalists. Together with other BaMbuti groups, they have increasingly become commercial hunters and, most recently, have had to wrestle with the chaos and dislocation of guerrilla war and Hutu refugee camps. Fieldwork to test optimal-foraging theories of hunter-gatherer life is frequently conducted among groups like the Cree and Inuit, who now have snowmobiles and satellite TVs and depend partly on wage labor and welfare payments, or the Ache, who have become sedentized around a mission station, spend only 25% of their days foraging, and procure a significant part of their subsistence from agriculture (Bailey and Aunger 1989:279; Hawkes, Hill, and O'Connell 1982:381–82; Hill et al. 1987:5; Lee 1993:153–67; Smith 1981:54; Winterhalder 1981:70).

Nevertheless, some hunter-gatherer groups have been considerably less affected and encapsulated by the industrial world than others, and this is a second reason that New Guinea's foragers deserve the attention of hunter-gatherer scholarship. Because of their comparatively recent contact history and general inaccessibility, many of the island's hunters and gatherers are among the least acculturated of contemporary foraging groups. To be sure, Western contact has had significant influences, but in comparison with better-known hunter-gatherer groups their acculturation is strikingly limited. Groups such as the Sanio-Hiowe, Lower Arafundi, Karawari, and Watakatauwi maintain a largely hunter-gatherer lifestyle (e.g., Telban 1998; personal communication, 1999; Yamada 1997). They still procure a greater proportion of their subsistence by foraging than the 85% that characterized the !Kung when Lee (1993:156) first studied them in 1963. Indeed, in the early 1990s some of the Lower Arafundi group were still living wholly by hunting and gathering in rock caves at the base of the central cordillera (Telban, personal communication, 999). In sum, it would be unfortunate if hunter-gatherer scholars prematurely resigned themselves to the archives when New Guinea continues to provide an array of viable field opportunities.

CONCLUSION: WHY HUNTERS AND GATHERERS?

I began this paper by noting a number of difficulties in distinguishing hunting and gathering from cultivation and pastoralism, and I should like, in conclusion, to return to this issue. For at least half a century, anthropology's principal classification of human societies has been by their mode of subsistence: hunting and gathering, pastoralism, horticulture, and (intensive) agriculture. Hardly an introductory text exists that fails to reproduce this scheme, the rationale apparently being that these four modes primarily determine four main types of culture and social organization among the societies of the world. Thus, for hunters and gatherers, as Arcand (1981:39–40; see also Hamilton 1982) observes, the assumption is that "the fact of producing food solely from hunting and gathering must correlate in a significant way with other aspects of the society."

Over the years, a number of scholars have cautioned that these notions are overly typological. In hunter-gatherer studies, the principal concern has been that lifestyles within the foraging mode of subsistence are far from the monolithic unity suggested by a "hunter-gatherer type" (e.g., Ember 1978:447; Kelly 1995; Kent 1996). Some, though, have also questioned whether lifestyles are necessarily so different across subsistence types. In forager studies, Feit (1994:422; see also Hallpike 1988:165–66) goes so far as to suggest that "a universal concept of socially distinctive hunter-gatherer societies may not be a credible anthropological category."

The New Guinea data cast this concern into particularly sharp relief. To begin with, as noted earlier, there appears to be no clear correlation between dependence on wild or domesticated resources on the one hand and sociocultural form and complexity on the other. Many of the region's cultivators have a sociocultural complexity no greater than that of foragers dependent on hunting for their meat protein, while foragers with access to rich aquatic resources rival the sociocultural complexity of the most intensive agriculturalists in the Highlands.

Moreover, whether sago is wild or cultivated seems to be of minimal importance to understanding the social-cultural forms practiced by those dependent upon it. Although sago cultivation can sometimes require significant labor inputs in areas with limited swampland (e.g., Rhoads 1980:26), it usually involves minimal work in absolute terms and almost none in comparison with the labor of harvesting a palm. Planting out a sago sucker is seldom more than a few moments' work, and subsequent management involves little more than an occasional clearing of surrounding undergrowth over the next decade or two (Flach 1983:5; Kawasaki 1998:82; Schindlbeck 1980:143–44). The reward from planting can be a higher starch yield—some studies suggest that a cultivated palm can yield two to six times as much as a wild palm (Flach 1983:5, 8). But the overall differences in labor investment and yield—rough figures from the Sepik suggest that exploiting wild as opposed to planted sago may require as little as four minutes' extra work/ person/day[3]—and the minimal impact on mobility patterns seem far too small to have the kinds of social-cultural effects that would warrant classifying wild sago gatherers and sago cultivators as two qualitatively different types, foragers and cultivators. Indeed, the Angoram and Iatmul, who depend heavily on cultivated sago, are culturally very similar to the Asmat, Kapriman, and Karawari, who exploit the same resource suites but depend entirely on wild palms.

In asserting that the wild or domesticated nature of subsistence resources is of limited value to understanding sociocultural forms, I do not mean to endorse the proposition that subsistence and the material world are but subsidiary influences on hunter-gatherer life (cf. Lourandos 1997). Rather, the New Guinea data indicate that categorizing societies and analyzing their social forms on the basis of whether they exploit wild or domesticated food resources may be of less value than attending to the conjoint consequences of the physical properties of these resources and the manner of their exploitation. We have known for a long time, of course, that the contours of the resource/exploitation interface significantly influence other realms of culture. This was Steward's point, and it is the basis of optimal-foraging theory and behavioral ecology (e.g., Kelly 1995: 62–63; Winterhalder and Smith 1981, 2000). Yet, this idea is usually only applied within subsistence types—to explain, for example, diversity within the hunter-gatherer type—when it deserves to be more rigorously pursued across subsistence types (e.g., Dyson-Hudson and Smith 1978).

In New Guinea, for example, access to rich aquatic resources seems to be a significant determinant of sedentism and social and cultural complexity. What appears to matter, however, is not that fish are wild rather than domesticated but that they provide a large, localized, stable, and rapidly regenerating food mass. In this respect, they resemble large herds of pigs (and, to a somewhat lesser degree, sweet-potato crops on rich agricultural land), and their exploitation may have similar consequences for sociocultural form. Conversely, dependence on small game seems to be a significant determinant of mobility, small settlements, and limited social and cultural complexity. What matters, however, is not that the game is wild but that it is scattered thinly; in this respect, it appears to have social-cultural sequelae similar to those of cultivating scattered pockets of thin soil. In other parts of the world, dependence on large, mobile game animals and dependence on rich fishing grounds appear to be associated with significantly different social-cultural forms, even though both resources are wild. Conversely, even though they involve domesticated and wild resources respectively, herding of large domesticated animals such as reindeer and camels has social-cultural consequences rather more akin to those of hunting large game animals than to those of exploiting rich fishing grounds. What appears to matter in relating sociocultural realms to environment and ecology, in sum, is not the wild as opposed to domesticated nature of exploited resources but rather their patchiness, spatial and temporal stability, perishability, and abundance and the technologies, capital and labor investment, and social strategies (e.g., individual or cooperative) required to raise and/or harvest them.

To describe the peoples of the world as "foragers," "pastoralists," "horticulturalists," and "agriculturalists" is innocuous enough if these categories are used merely as crude, "hand-waving" guides to general areas on what is a multidimensional continuum of human social and cultural forms. Indeed, it is hard to imagine how this spectrum could be discussed without some such broad categorization, and since they represent anthropology's received categories it is equally difficult to avoid them and remain intelligible— witness their liberal use in this article. If we must refer to peoples and social lives by capacious and radically underdetermined subsistence categories, however, it might be less misleading and more useful to describe them as practicing, for example, "hunting and gathering"—among other things—rather than referring to them as "hunters and gatherers," thereby surrendering to the Western tendency to reduce people to, or essentialize them as, their socioeconomic occupations (doctor, lawyer, forager, farmer).

Notes

1. I deeply appreciate the assistance and/or comments of George Appell, Ulrike Class, Terry Hays, Benjamin Orlove, Brian Robinson, Dave Sanger, Eric Alden Smith, Borut Telban, John Terrell, and Pat Townsend. I owe a special debt to Hays for sharing his New Guinea bibliography and language files and for locating for me more than half of the hunter-gatherer groups in Northern Irian Jaya. Much of the documentary material for this paper was gathered and/or processed with the financial assistance of the American Philosophical Society, Friends of the Geisel Library (San Diego), Fulbright-Hays, and the National Science Founda-

tion, to all of which I am also grateful. No one but myself, however, bears any culpability for my mistakes.

2. Major areas containing other possible foraging groups include the Upper Sepik (e.g., the Abau, Left May groups, May River Iwam, and Sepik Iwam), the West Sepik, north of the Sepik River (e.g., the Ak, Kwieftim, Nagatman), the floodplain of the Ramu River (e.g., the Anor, Giri, Rao), and the South Coast of New Guinea (e.g., the Suki, Lower Morehead). Conversely, there are no obvious hunter-gatherer groups in the provinces of Bougainville, Central, Chimbu, East New Britain, Eastern Highlands, Enga, Milne Bay, Morobe, New Ireland, West New Britain, and Western Highlands. For lack of survey data, no similar list can be compiled for Irian Jaya.

3. Townsend (1969:43) calculates that the Sanio Hiowe expend 157 hours of work (travel time excluded) to produce one million calories from wild sago. Among the Abelam, who plant their sago, the equivalent figure is 154 hours (Lea 1964:121–29). Thus, to feed an average Sanio-Hiowe hunter-gatherer, who consumes 1,900 calories of sago per day (Townsend 1969:77), it would take 22 minutes of work/day for wild sago and 17 minutes for planted sago.

References Cited

Arcand, B. 1981. The Negritos and the Penan will never be Cuiva. *Folk* 23:37–43.

Arnold, Jeanne E. 1996. Archaeology of complex hunter-gatherers. *Journal of Archaeological Method and Theory* 3: 77–126.

Austen, Leo. 1946. Notes on the food supply of the Turamarubi of Western Papua. *Mankind* 3:227–30.

Ayres, William S. 1980. Comment on: *Maritime hunter-gatherers: Ecology and prehistory,* by David R. Yesner. *Current Anthropology* 21:736.

Bailey, Robert C., and Robert Aunger. 1989. Net hunters vs. archers: Variation in women's subsistence strategies in the Ituri Forest. *Human Ecology* 17:273–97.

Bailey, Robert C., Genevieve Head, Mark Jenike, Bruce Owen, Robert Rechtman, and Elzbieta Zechenter. 1989. Hunting and gathering in tropical rain forest: Is it possible? *American Anthropologist* 91:59–82.

Bakker, Edie. 1994. Return to Hunstein Forest. *National Geographic* 185(2):40–63.

Barnard, Alan. 1983. Contemporary hunter-gatherers: Current theoretical issues in ecology and social organization. *Annual Review of Anthropology* 12:193–214.

Barrau, Jacques. 1958. Subsistence agriculture in Melanesia. Honolulu: Bernice P. Bishop Museum.

Barry, Herbert, III. 1968. Regional and worldwide variations in culture. *Ethnology* 7:207–17.

Bateman, Janet. 1982. Iau kinship and marriage. *Irian* 10(3): 34–74.

Beaver, Wilfred N. 1920. *Unexplored New Guinea: A record of the travels, adventures, and experiences of a resident magistrate amongst the head-hunting savages and cannibals of the unexplored interior of New Guinea.* London: Seeley, Service.

Bjerre, Jens. 1958. *The last cannibals.* London: Pan Books.

Boelaars, J. n.d. (1958). *Papoea's aan de Mappi.* Utrecht-Antwerpen: De Fontein.

———. 1975 (1955). The Jaqai: Thoughts about the past, present, and future of a people. Translated by H. Hockmuller and F. Trenkenschuh. *Asmat Sketch Book* 3:9–40.

Bowden, Ross. 1983. *Yena: Art and ceremony in a Sepik society.* Oxford: Pitt Rivers Museum.

Briley, Joyce E. 1983. "The Bauzi view of ritual and magic," in *Gods, heroes, kinsmen: Ethnographic studies from Irian Jaya, Indonesia.* Edited by William R. Merrifield, Marilyn Gregerson, and Daniel C. Ajamiseba, pp. 3–23. Jayapura and Dallas: Cenderawasih University and the International Museum of Cultures.

———. 1991. Controls of red and white in the Bauzi cycle of reproduction. *Irian* 19:116–35.

Bruce, Leslie. 1974. "Alamblak kinsmen: To give is better than to receive (and you'll get it back)," in *Kinship studies in Papua New Guinea.* Edited by R. Daniel Shaw, pp. 169–86. Ukarumpa, PNG: Summer Institute of Linguistics.

Burch, Ernest S. 1998. "The future of hunter-gatherer research," in *Limited wants, unlimited means: A reader on hunter-gatherer economics and the environment.* Edited by John Gowdy, pp. 201–17. Washington, D.C.: Island Press.

Busse, Mark William. 1987. Sister exchange among the Wamek of the Middle Fly. Ph.D. diss., University of California, San Diego, Calif.

Chalmers, James. 1895. *Pioneer life and work in New Guinea 1877–1894.* London: Religious Tract Society.

Clastres, Pierre. 1972. "The Guayaki," in *Hunters and gatherers today: A socioeconomic study of eleven such cultures in the twentieth century.* Edited by M. G. Bicchieri, pp. 138–74. New York: Holt, Rinehart and Winston.

Davidoff, Jules, Ian Davies, and Debi Roberson. 1999. Colour categories in a Stone-Age tribe. *Nature* 398:203–4.

Department of Human Geography, Australian National University. 1993a. Agricultural systems of Papua New Guinea, working paper no. 2: East Sepik Province. Canberra.

———. 1993b. Agricultural systems of Papua New Guinea, working paper no. 5: Gulf Province. Canberra.

De Vries, Jim. 1988. Kwerba supernatural beliefs. *Irian* 16: 1–16.

Dye, Sally. 1983. What disrupts Bahinemo marriage. Melanesian Institute for Pastoral and Socio-Economic Service, Working Papers in Melanesian Marriage and Family Life 6.

Dye, T. Wayne, and Edith Dye Bakker. 1991. The response of Bahinemo foragers to imposed land tenure changes: An-word gemic perspective. Paper presented at the annual meetings of the American Anthropological Association, Chicago, Ill.

Dyson-Hudson, Rada, and Eric Alden Smith. 1978. Human territoriality: An ecological reassessment. *American Anthropologist* 80:21–41.

Edmiston, Patrick, and Melenda Edmiston. 1989. *Alamblak background study.* Ukarumpa, PNG: Summer Institute of Linguistics.

Ellen, R. 1982. *Environment, subsistence, and system.* Cambridge: Cambridge University Press.

Ember, Carol. 1978. Myths about hunter-gatherers. *Ethnology* 17:439–48.

Eng, Joan. 1983. *Sago and nutrition in Bomakia.* Jayapura: Irian Jaya Development Information Service Center.

Erickson, Carol J. 1976. Isirawa kinship and exchange marriage. *Irian* 5(1):22–44.

———. 1981. Spirit alliances and possession among the Isirawa. *Irian* 9 (1):33–54.

Eyde, David Bruener. 1967. Cultural correlates of warfare among the Asmat of South-west New Guinea. Ph.D. diss., Yale University, New Haven, Conn.

Feit, Harvey A. 1994. "The enduring pursuit: Land, time, and social relationships in anthropological models of hunter-gatherers and in subarctic hunters' images," in *Key issue in hunter-gatherer research.* Edited by E. S. Burch and L. J. Ellana, pp. 421–39. Oxford: Berg.

Flach, M. 1983. The sago palm. FAO Plant Production and Protection Paper 47.

Foley, William A. 1991. *The Yimas language of New Guinea.* Stanford: Stanford University Press.

Gajdusek, D. Carleton, and Andres M. Salazar. 1982. Amyotrophic lateral sclerosis and Parkinsonian syndromes in high incidence among the Auyu and Jakai people of West New Guinea. *Neurology* 32:107–26.

Gardner, Donald Stanley. 1981. Cult ritual and social organisation among the Mianmin. Ph.D. diss., The Australian National University, Canberra, Australia.

Green, Ivor. 1986. Dou kinship terms. *Irian* 14:68–77.

Guddemi, Phillip V. 1992. We came from this: Knowledge, memory, painting, and "play" in the initiation rituals of the Sawiyano of Papua New Guinea. Ph.D. diss., University of Michigan, Ann Arbor, Mich.

Haberland, Eike. 1966. Zur Ethnographie der Alfendio-Region (Sudlicher Sepik-Distrikt, Neuguinea). Jahrbuch des Museums fur Volkerkunde zu Leipzig 23:33–67.

———. 1968. *The caves of Karawari.* New York: D'Arcy Galleries.

Haberland, Pike, and Siegfried Seyfarth. 1974. Die Yimar am Oberen Korowori (Neuguinea). Wiesbaden: Franz Steiner.

Hallpike, C. R. 1988. *The principles of social evolution.* Oxford: Clarendon.

Hamilton, Annette. 1982. "The unity of hunting-gathering societies: Reflections on economic forms and resource management," in *Resource managers: North American and Australian hunter-gatherers.* Edited by Nancy M. Williams and Eugene S. Hunn, pp. 229–47. Boulder: Westview Press.

Harris, David R. 1977. "Subsistence strategies across Torres Strait," in *Sunda and Sahul: Prehistoric studies in Southeast Asia, Melanesia, and Australia.* Edited by Jim Allen, Jack Golson, and Rhys Jones, pp. 421–63. London and New York: Academic Press.

———. 1989. "An evolutionary continuum of people-plant interaction," in *Foraging and farming: The evolution of plant exploitation.* Edited by David R. Harris and Gordon C. Hillman, pp. 11–26. London: Unwin Hyman.

Hawkes, Kristen, Kim Hill, and James F. O'Connell. 1982. Why hunters gather: Optimal foraging and the Ache of Eastern Paraguay. *American Ethnologist* 9: 379–98.

Hayden, Brian. 1981. "Subsistence and ecological adaptations of modern hunter/gatherers," in *Omnivorous primates: Gathering and hunting in human evolution.* Edited by Robert S. O. Harding and Geza Teleki, pp. 344–421. New York: Columbia University Press.

Headland, Thomas N., and Lawrence A. Reid. 1989. Hunter-gatherers and their neighbors from prehistory to the present. *Current Anthropology* 30:43–66.

Held, G. J. 1957. The Papuas of Waropen. The Hague: Martinus Nijhoff.

Hill, Kim, Hillard Kaplan, Kristen Hawkes, and A. Magdalena Hurtado. 1987. Foraging decisions among Ache hunter-gatherers. *Ethology and Sociobiology* 8:1–36.

Holmes, J. H. 1924. *In primitive New Guinea: An account of a quarter of a century spent amongst the primitive Ipi & Namau groups of tribes of the Gulf of Papua, with an interesting description of their manner of living, their customs & habits, feasts & festivals, totems & cults.* New York: Putnam.

Ingold, T. 1974. On reindeer and men. *Man,* n.s., 9:523–38.

Kalmbacher, Carol. 1983. "Came, female cannibal culture hero," in *Gods, heroes, kinsmen: Ethnographic studies from Irian Jaya, Indonesia.* Edited by William R. Merrifield, Marilyn Gregerson, and Daniel C. Ajamiseba, pp. 23–41. Jayapura and Dallas: Cenderawasih University and the International Museum of Cultures.

Kawasaki, Ippei. 1998. "Pigs, two women, and an island: A reality of subsistence in Bahinemo mythology," in *Fringe area of highlands in Papua New Guinea.* Edited by Shuji Yoshida and Yujio Toyoda, pp. 79–91. Senri Ethnological Series 47.

Keeley, Lawrence H. 1988. Hunter-gatherer economic complexity and "population pressure": A cross-cultural analysis. *Journal of Anthropological Archaeology* 7:373–411.

Kelly, Robert L. 1995. *The foraging spectrum: Diversity in hunter-gatherer lifeways.* Washington, D.C., and London: Smithsonian Institution.

Kent, Susan. 1992. The current forager controversy: Real versus ideal views of hunter-gatherers. *Man,* n.s., 27:45–70.

———. Editor. 1996. *Cultural diversity among twentieth-century foragers: An African perspective.* Cambridge: Cambridge University Press.

Kim, Yun Hwa. 1997. "Edopi kinship, marriage, and social structure," in *Kinship and social organization in Irian Jaya: A glimpse of seven systems.* Edited by Marilyn Gregerson and Joyce Sterner, pp. 199–220. Jayapura and Dallas: Cenderawasih University and Summer Institute of Linguistics.

Kumagai, Kei Chi. 1998. "Migration and shifting settlement patterns among the Kabriman people of East Sepik Province, Papua New Guinea," in *Fringe area of highlands in Papua New Guinea.* Edited by Shuji Yoshida and Yujio Toyoda, pp. 43–60. Senri Ethnological Series 47.

Lea, D. A. M. 1964. Abelam land and sustenance. Ph.D. diss., The Australian National University, Canberra, Australia.

Lee, Richard S. 1968. "What hunters do for a living, or, How to make out on scarce resources," in *Man the hunter.* Edited by Richard B. Lee and Irven DeVore, pp. 30–48. Chicago: Aldine.

———. 1993. *The Dobe Ju/'hoansi.* Fort Worth: Harcourt Brace.

Lee, Richard B., and Richard Heywood Daly. 1999. *The Cambridge encyclopedia of hunters and gatherers.* Cambridge and New York: Cambridge University Press.

Lee, Richard B., and Irven DeVore. 1968. "Problems in the study of hunters and gatherers," in *Man the hunter.* Edited by Richard B. Lee and Irven DeVore, pp. 3–12. Chicago: Aldine.

Lipset, David. 1997. *Mangrove man: Dialogics of culture in the Sepik Estuary.* Cambridge: Cambridge University Press.

Lourandos, Harry. 1997. *Continent of hunter-gatherers: New perspectives in Australian prehistory.* Cambridge: Cambridge University Press.

Martin, David L. 1997. "The social functions of polygyny in relation to Sikaritai kinship and marriage," in *Kinship and social organization in Irian Jaya: A glimpse of seven systems.* Edited by Marilyn Gregerson and Joyce Sterner, pp. 121–67. Jayapura and Dallas: Cenderawasih University and Summer Institute of Linguistics.

Maunsell and Partners. 1982. *Ok Tedi environmental study.* Vol. 5. *Population and resource use: Ethnobiology.* Melbourne.

Mead, Margaret. 1947. The Mountain Arapesh: 3. Socioeconomic life; 4. Diary of events in Alitoa. *Anthropological Papers of the American Museum of Natural History* 40:159–419.

Miehle, Helen. 1985. What's in a name? A descriptive study of Iau personal names. *Irian* 13:66–84.

Mills, A. John. 1986. My row of birds: A short history of the Sawi village of Kamur, an analysis of their kinship system, and a description of related marriage customs. *Irian* 14:46–67.

Moseley, Michael E., and Robert A. Feldman. 1988. "Fishing, farming, and the foundations of Andean civilisation," in *The archaeology of prehistoric coastlines*. Edited by Geoff Bailey and John Parkington, pp. 125–34. Cambridge: Cambridge University Press.

Munnings, Peter, and Mary Jane Munnings. 1990. *Between two worlds: A photo documentary of the Tause culture of Irian Jaya, Indonesia*. Jayapura: Uncen-SIL Cooperative Program.

Murdock, George Peter. 1968. "The current status of the world's hunting and gathering peoples," in *Man the hunter*. Edited by Richard B. Lee and Irven DeVore, pp. 13–20. Chicago: Aldine.

Oomen, H. A. P. C. 1959. Poor-food patterns in New Guinea. *Nieuw-Guinea Studien* 3:35–46.

Oosterwal, G. 1959. The position of the bachelor in the Upper Tot territory. *American Anthropologist* 61:829–39.

———. 1961. *People of the Tor: A cultural-anthropological study on the tribes of the Tot territory (Northern Netherlands New-Guinea)*. Assert: Royal van Gorcum.

———. 1967. "Muremarew: A dual organized village on the Mamberamo, West Irian," in *Villages in Indonesia*. Edited by Koentjaraningrat, pp. 157–88. Ithaca: Cornell University Press.

Palsson, Gisli. 1988. "Hunters and gatherers of the sea," in *Hunters and gatherers x: History, evolution, and social change*. Edited by Tim Ingold, David Riches, and James Woodburn, pp. 189–204. Oxford: Berg.

Pouwer, Jan. n.d. (1955). Enkele aspecten van de Mimikacultuur (Nederlands Zuidwest Nieuw Guinea).'s-Gravenhage: Staatsdrukkerij- en Uitgeversbedrijk.

Price, T. Douglas, and James Allison Brown. 1985. *Prehistoric hunter-gatherers: The emergence of cultural complexity*. Orlando: Academic Press.

Quilter, J., and T. Stocker. 1983. Subsistence economies and the origins of Andean complex societies. *American Anthropologist* 85:545–62.

Renouf, M. A. P. 1984. Northern coastal hunter-fishers: An archaeological model. *World Archaeology* 16:18–27.

Report of the New Guinea Nutrition Survey Expedition. 1947. Sydney: Pettifer, Government Printer.

Rhoads, James W. 1980. Through a glass darkly: Present and past land-use systems of Papuan sagopalm users. Ph.D. diss., The Australian National University, Canberra, Australia.

Roscoe, Paul B. 1995. Of power and menace: Sepik art as an affecting presence. *Journal of the Royal Anthropological Institute*, n.s., 1:1–22.

———. 1996. War and society in Sepik New Guinea. *Journal of the Royal Anthropological Institute* 2:645–66.

Rosman, Abraham, and Paula G. Rubel. 1989. "Stalking the wild pig: Hunting and horticulture in Papua New Guinea," in *Farmers as hunters: The implications of sedentism*. Edited by Susan Kent, pp. 27–36. Cambridge: Cambridge University Press.

Ruddle, Kenneth, Dennis Johnson, Patricia K. Townsend, and John D. Rees. 1978. *Palm sago: A tropical starch from marginal lands*. Honolulu: University Press of Hawaii for the East-West Center.

Saito, Hisafumi. 1998. "We are one flesh: Unity and migration of the Yabio," in *Fringe area of highlands in Papua New Guinea*. Edited by Shuji Yoshida and Yukio Toyoda, pp. 93–112. Senri Ethnological Series 47.

Schindlbeck, Markus. 1980. *Sago bei den Sawos (Mittelsepik, Papua New Guinea): Untersuchungen uber die Bedeutung von Sago in Wirtschaft, Sozialordnung und Religion*. Basel: Ethnologisches Seminar der Universitat und Museum fur Volkerkunde.

———. 1981. "Sawos (New Guinea, Middle Sepik): Burning patterns into the skin," in *Publikationen zu Wissenschaftlichen Filmen, Ethnologie*, Series II, no. 3, pp. 12–17. Gottingen: Institut fur den Wissenschaftlichen Film.

———. 1983. Kokospalme und Brotfruchtbaum: Siedlings-Vorstellungen der Sawos und Kwanga, Sepik-Gebiet, Papua-Neuguinea. *Geographica Helvetica* 38:3–10.

Schmidt, J. 1922–23. Die Ethnographie der Nor-Papua (Murik-Kaup-Karau) bei Dallmannhafen, Neu-Guinea. *Anthropos* 18–19:700–732.

Schwab, Ignaz. 1938. Winterfreuden in Moskitania. *Steyler Missionsbote* 65:134–35.

———. 1940a. Jagderlebnisse auf einer Missionsfahrt. *Steyler Missionsbote* 67:242–43.

———. 1940b. Ein alter Haudegen. *Steyler Missionsbote* 67: 259–60.

Service, Elman R. 1979. *The hunters*. Englewood Cliffs: Prentice-Hall.

Shack, Kathryn Wetherell. 1988. Effects of agricultural development and resettlement on nutritional status and dietary intakes of mothers and children: A study of three ethnic groups in lowland Papua New Guinea. Ph.D. diss., University of California, Davis, Calif.

Simpson, Colin. 1955. *Islands of men*. Sydney: Angus and Robertson.

Smith, Eric Alden. 1981. "The application of optimal foraging theory to the analysis of hunter-gatherer group size," in *Hunter-gatherer foraging strategies: Ethnographic and archaeological analyses*. Edited by Bruce Winterhalder and Eric Alden Smith, pp. 36–65. Chicago and London: University of Chicago Press.

Sterner, Joyce K. 1990. The role of women in traditional Irian Jaya societies as exemplified among the Bauzi and Ketengban. *Irian* 18:102–8.

Telban, Borut. 1998. *Dancing through time: A Sepik cosmology*. Oxford: Clarendon.

Territory of New Guinea. 1931. *Report to the League of Nations for 1929–30*. Canberra: Government Printer.

Townsend, Patricia Kathryn Woods. 1969. Subsistence and social organization in a New Guinea society. Ph.D. diss., University of Michigan, Ann Arbor, Mich.

———. 1974. Sago production in a New Guinea economy. *Human Ecology* 2:217–36.

———. 1990. On the possibility/impossibility of tropical forest hunting and gathering. *American Anthropologist* 92:745–48.

Toyoda, Yukio. 1998. "To which bird do you belong? Totemic belief among the Mari, Papua New Guinea," in *Fringe area of highlands in Papua New Guinea*. Edited by Shuji Yoshida and Yukio Toyoda, pp. 61–77. Senri Ethnological Series 47.

Trenkenschuh, F. 1982a. "The Asmat people of the Casuarina coast," in *An Asmat sketch book no. 1*. Edited by Frank A. Trenkenschuh, pp. 55–59. Hastings. Nebr.: Crosier Missions.

———. 1982b. "The physical environment of Asmat," in *An Asmat sketch book no. 1*. Edited by Frank A. Trenkenschuh, pp. 11–12. Hastings, Nebr.: Crosier Missions.

———. 1982c. "Asmat sago gathering practices," in *An Asmat sketch book no. 1*. Edited by Frank A. Trenkenschuh, pp. 45–53. Hastings, Nebr.: Crosier Missions.

Tuzin, Donald F. 1980. The voice of the Tambaran: Truth and illusion in Ilahita Arapesh religion. Berkeley: University of California Press.

Ulijaszek, S. J., and S. P. Poraituk. 1983. "Subsistence patterns and sago cultivation in the Purari River," in *The Purari: Tropical environment of a high rainfall basin*. Edited by T. Petr, pp. 577–88. The Hague: Dr. W. Junk.

Van Arsdale, Peter Wayne. 1975. Perspectives on development among Irian Jaya's Asmat: Cultural and demographic correlates of induced change. Ph.D. diss., University of Colorado, Denver, Colo.

———. 1978. Activity patterns of Asmat hunter-gatherers: A time budget analysis. *Mankind* 11:453–60.

Van Den Broek D'Obrenan, Charles. 1939. *Le voyage de "La Korrigane."* Paris: Payot.

Venema, Hank. 1989. Sago grub festival. *Irian* 17:38–63.

Wagner, Roy. 1967. *The curse of Souw: Principles of Daribi clan definition and alliance in New Guinea*. Chicago: University of Chicago Press.

Whiting, John W. M. 1941. *Becoming a Kwoma: Teaching and learning in a New Guinea tribe*. New Haven: Yale University Press.

———. 1968. "Discussions, Part 7," in *Man the hunter*. Edited by Richard B. Lee and Irven DeVore, pp. 336–39. Chicago: Aldine.

Williams, F. E. 1924. *The natives of the Purari Delta*. Port Moresby: Government Printer.

Winterhalder, Bruce. 1981. "Foraging strategies in the boreal forest: An analysis of Cree hunting and gathering," in *Hunter-gatherer foraging strategies: Ethnographic and archaeological analyses*. Edited by Bruce Winterhalder and Eric Alden Smith, pp. 66–98. Chicago and London: University of Chicago Press.

Winterhalder, Bruce, and Eric Alden Smith. 1981. *Hunter-gatherer foraging strategies: Ethnographic and archaeological analyses*. Edited by Bruce Winterhalder and Eric Alden Smith. Chicago and London: University of Chicago Press.

———. 2000. Analyzing adaptive strategies: Human behavioral ecology at twenty-five. *Evolutionary Anthropology* 9:51–72.

Wollaston, A. F. R. 1912. *Pygmies and Papuans: The Stone Age to-day in Dutch New Guinea*. London: John Murray.

Yamada, Yoichi. 1997. *Songs of spirits: An ethnography of sounds in a Papua New Guinea society*. Translated by Jun'ichi Ohno. Boroko, PNG: Institute of Papua New Guinea Studies.

Yesner, David R. 1980. Maritime hunter-gatherers: Ecology and prehistory. *Current Anthropology* 21:727–35.

Yost, Jim. 1988. Traditional Sawi religion. *Irian* 16:50–113.

Zegwaard, Gerard A. 1959. Headhunting practices of the Asmat of Netherlands New Guinea. *American Anthropologist* 61:1020–41.

CRITICAL THINKING QUESTIONS

1. Hunting and gathering groups have been normatively defined as an organizational "type" in the anthropological literature. How do the New Guinea groups differ from this classic definition, and what defining characteristics does the author use to classify the New Guinea groups?

2. What impact does the author say Western contact has had when evaluating contact-era subsistence patterns in New Guinea?

3. Roscoe categorizes different New Guinea hunting and gathering groups based on specific subsistence strategies. What are these strategies, and how does Roscoe say these strategies affect these groups' social and organizational complexity?

4. What are the dangers in using general categories to define cultures as "types"?

Ashmounds and Hilltop Villages: The Search for Early Agriculture in Southern India

Dorian Q. Fuller

Archaeological research on the origins and early development of agriculture in Asia has largely focused on the continent's western and eastern margins, with much less attention paid to the vast intervening regions of Central and South Asia. Now a bioarchaeological research project led by a new member of the Institute's staff is discovering how and when cultivation and pastoralism began in southern India.

Large heaps of ash are dotted across the landscape of southern India, spanning an area roughly the size of the whole of Ireland. These mysterious ashmounds, which are associated with fragments of pottery, stone tools and animal bones, puzzled many nineteenth-century British administrators. The new archaeological research reported here shows how these sites provide important clues to the lifeways of the earliest farmers and herders in southern India. Other ancient sites of human habitation, usually located on the tops of dramatic granite hills, share the landscape with the ashmounds. My investigation of ancient plant remains from these hilltop sites, as well as observations on the ashmounds, is helping us to understand the beginnings of agriculture in southern India.

THE ASHMOUNDS AND THE VILLAGES

This research project, which is raising new questions about, and bringing new methods to bear on, the prehistoric archaeology of southern India, is not the first occasion on which a member of staff of the Institute of Archaeology has worked in the region. Although many important observations on the ashmounds were made by the nineteenth-century Scottish geologist, Robert Bruce Foote, scientific methods were first used to establish their origin in the 1950s by Frederick Zeuner, who was then Professor of Environmental Archaeology at the Institute.[1] Zeuner collected samples of ash from the mounds, including the sites of Kupgal and Kudatini, and also fragments of slag-like material present in them. He subjected the samples to chemical analysis and microscopic examination and found that they resembled experimentally burnt cattle dung. The microscopic evidence showed that the ash included large quantities of silica (natural glass) derived from grass cells (known to specialists as phytoliths) which one would expect to find in the dung of grazing animals. The slag-like chunks of material came from dung that was burned at such high temperatures (1000°C or more) that the silica in these plant cells actually melted and fused. Also in the 1950s, excavations by the British archaeologist Raymond Allchin at one of the ashmounds (Utnur) revealed that the layers of dung had accumulated in an area that had been enclosed by a large stockade, and in some layers cattle hoof prints were preserved in the cement-like ashy mud. Thus, the mounds appear to have been places where cattle were penned, where the dung was allowed to accumulate, and where it was episodically burned, perhaps ritually, as part of seasonal festivals.[2]

Source: Reprinted from *Archaeology International 2000/2001* with permission of the Institute of Archaeology, University College, London.

The pottery and stone tools from the mounds link them to the hilltop habitation sites. Radiocarbon dates place early sites of this culture at 2800 BC, with most sites beginning by about 2200 BC, during the southern Indian Neolithic period. By 1200–1000 BC most of them had been abandoned and societies had changed to become more hierarchical. The hilltop sites and some of the ashmounds are clustered in what may have been interlinked communities. But whereas the hilltop sites may have been villages inhabited throughout the year, the ashmounds appear to have been seasonal sites where cattle were penned. Although some of the mounds are located near the hilltop villages, and probably represent sites at which the population came together at certain times of the year, others are isolated and distant from the villages and they probably represent encampments of pastoral groups who followed cyclical patterns of movement during the year. The ashmounds, and the bones of domesticated animals found there (mostly cattle, but also sheep and goat), indicate that herding was important in the economy, but it has been unclear what plant foods the people used and whether cultivation formed the economic basis of the hilltop villages.

EVIDENCE OF NATIVE AND INTRODUCED CROPS

To answer these questions, I have been collaborating with Indian archaeologists from Karnatak University.[3] We have undertaken sampling at five of the hilltop sites with the specific aim of recovering the small remains of plants that were missed by previous generations of archaeologists, and we have also sampled seven other contemporary sites in adjacent regions. We have recovered substantial quantities of charred plant remains from the bulk samples of archaeological sediment by flotation (a method of using water to separate the light charred plant remains from the heavier sediment), In order to obtain a large sample of ancient plant material from a range of sites, flotation was carried out on soil samples taken from new test excavations and from re-cleared profiles of old excavations.

The remains of crops that were recovered include species introduced from outside southern India and some others that were probably domesticated within the region. Of particular interest are two pulses (plants of the pea and bean family), mung bean (*Vigna radiata*, which is used in Britain for beansprouts) and horsegram (*Macrotyloma uniflorum*), and two small millet-grasses that are native to southern India, known as browntop millet (*Brachiaria ramosa*) and bristly foxtail grass (*Setaria verticillata*).[4] These pulses and millets appear to have been the staple crops at all the sites—a finding that represents the first direct archaeological evidence for the early use of these species in the region where that may have been domesticated. All these species are summer crops naturally adapted to growing and producing seed during the annual monsoons. We also recovered from our samples some charred fragments of parenchyma (starchy storage tissue that occurs in roots and tubers), which suggests that some (as yet unidentified) tuberous foods were also cultivated or gathered as wild plants. Tubers may have been available through much of the year but are likely to have been most important as a food source in the winter (December–February) and in the dry season (March–June).

In addition to the two millets and two pulses that appear to have been the staple foods of this part of southern India, we have found evidence of several other crops that originated elsewhere in the world. At some but not all the sites we have studied, there is evidence of wheat and barley, both of which originated in Southwest Asia and spread gradually eastwards into India. Although both were cultivated in Pakistan as early as 6000 BC, they did not penetrate India until after 3000 BC. Our evidence suggests that they reached southern India by about 2200 BC, but they do not appear to have bean cultivated widely, perhaps only by select communities. Wheat and barley are conventionally grown in the dry winter months in India, in contrast to the summer-monsoon crops. Therefore, their cultivation is likely to have required some form of irrigation, which implies that some communities in southern India undertook new forms of labor to increase agricultural production during the Neolithic period. Several crops from other regions were also adopted by some communities. They include pigeon pea (*Cajanus cajan,* which almost certainly originated to the northeast in the Indian state of Orissa), pearl millet (*Pennisetum glaucum*) and hyacinth bean (*Lablab purpureus*). Both of the latter originated in Africa and must have reached India as a result of some form of early long-distance contact. Taken as a whole, the evidence indicates that the Neolithic people of southern India grew native plants as well as crops that they acquired through trade with other regions.

THE NEOLITHIC LANDSCAPE AND ECONOMY

With this basic knowledge of southern Indian Neolithic agriculture, and its seasonal context, we can begin to understand how the ashmound sites and the hilltop villages were linked in the Neolithic landscape and through annual cycles. They can be interpreted as groups of related sites, such as those around the village of Sanganakallu. In this group of sites there are two hilltop settlements, both of which have produced evidence for monsoon and winter crops. These sites also have evidence for the processing of seed foods, in the form of many often large grinding or pounding hollows formed in the granite boulders around the sites, as well as separate grinding stones found on the sites. These locations are likely to have been sites where crops that were grown on the surrounding plains were routinely processed, and they may have been inhabited all year round.

In this group of sites near Sanganakallu village there are also two ashmound sites, one of which is a small hilltop mound on a peak between the two hilltop settlements and the other consists of a group of three substantial mounds at Kupgal. The archaeology associated with these ashmounds suggests shorter periods of habitation and much less, or no, processing of seed foods. They are likely to represent seasonal camps where cattle were penned (and dung accumulated) and some people camped near them. It is likely that such seasonal gatherings occurred during the period of harvest after the monsoon (October–November), when additional labor may have been needed to help with the harvests, and cattle could be grazed on the stubble of recently harvested fields. Conversely, the herds

would have been kept away from the fields during the growing season when they might have damaged crops. As is often the case, the harvest season was probably a time of festivals and the apparently ritual burning of dung at some of the ashmounds (those near to the hilltop sites) is likely to have taken place during this period. Indeed, the modern southern Indian harvest festival of Pongal, although now associated with the rice harvest in January, may have inherited elements from the Neolithic, as it includes bull chasing, ritual fires (which often include dung), and in some areas the driving of cattle across smouldering fires.[5]

In the winter months as the dry season (which begins in February) approached, most of each cattle herd probably dispersed with its masters into the wider territories around the villages. It is during this period that small-scale cultivation of wheat and barley would have been carried out and, as the dry season progressed, an increasing number of wild fruits and tubers would have become available for collection by both the village cultivators and the pastoralists. At some stage during the dry season, the pastoralists seem to have camped at isolated points on the landscape where their cattle were again penned, the dung accumulated and ritual burning took place. The remnants of these dispersed camps can be found in many isolated ashmounds, distant from any permanent Neolithic villages. These camps were located at natural boundaries between clusters of villages and ashmounds, such as the one near Sanganakallu. Thus, the isolated ashmound sites may have played an important role in interactions between adjacent group territories.

CONCLUSION

Southern India is a region where the beginnings of agriculture have remained mysterious. Our continuing research promises to elucidate the nature of early agriculture there and to suggest how these early food-producing societies were organized. In our future work we aim to investigate how food production began, including both plant cultivation and animal herding, and what changes took place in the natural environment. The abundance of the remains of native plants in the earliest levels so far sampled indicates that indigenous crops played an important role in the local development of agriculture, a conclusion that counters the widely held view that the beginnings of agriculture in most parts of the world resulted from dispersal from one of a few primary centers. Agriculture appears to have begun in southern India during a period when monsoon rainfall was declining, and the effects of this on vegetation and human communities may be important for understanding the transition from hunting and gathering to agriculture—a process that transformed the cultural and natural landscape from one used by hunter–gatherers in the late Palaeolithic period to one transformed in the Neolithic through the practices of village agriculturalists.

Notes

1. F. E. Zeuner, "On the origin of the cinder mounds of the Bellary district, India," *Bulletin of the Institute of Archaeology* 2, 37–44, 1959.
2. See F. R. Allchin, *Neolithic cattle keepers of south India: a study of Deccan ashmounds* (Cambridge: Cambridge University Press, 1963); and R. Korisettar, P. C. Venkatasubbaiah, D. Q. Fuller, "Brahmagiri and beyond: the archaeology of the southern Neolithic," in *Indian archaeology in retrospect*, volume I: *Prehistory*, S. Settar & R. Korisettar (eds), 151–356. (New Delhi: Manohar, 2000).
3. My principal collaborators in this project are Professor Ravi Korisettar and Dr P. C. Venkatasubbaiah of the Department of Ancient History and Archaeology, Karnatak University, Karnataka.
4. For background on the botany and. agriculture of the pulses see J. Smartt, *Grain legumes* (Cambridge: Cambridge University Press, 1990). For background on the millets see J. M. J. de Wet, "Minor cereals." In *Evolution of crop plants*, 2nd edn, J. Smartt & N. Simmonds (eds), 202–8 (London: Longman, 1995) and M. Kimata, E. G. Ashok, A. Seetharam, "Domestication, cultivation and utilization of two small millets, *Brachiaria ramosa* and *Setaria glauca* (Poaceae), in South India," *Economic Botany* 54, 217–27, 2000. For a review of native and introduced crops and archaeological evidence for their use in South Asia see D. Q. Fuller, "Fifty years of archaeobotanical studies in India: laying a solid foundation." In *Indian archaeology in retrospect*, volume III: *archaeology and interactive disciplines*, S. Settar & R. Korisettar (eds), 247–363 (New Delhi: Manohar, 2000).
5. Modern festivals in various parts of India are discussed by Allchin (*n*. 2, above) in relation to the Neolithic ashmounds. A general overview of Pongal and other Indian fire festivals in comparative context can be found in James Frazer's *The golden bough*, 3rd edn, part V, *Spirits of the corn and the wild*, volume II, 56, and part VII, *Balder the beautiful. The fire festivals of Europe and the doctrine of the external soul*, volume II, 1–3 (London, Macmillan, 1912–1913).

CRITICAL THINKING QUESTIONS

1. Ashmounds dot the south Indian landscape. What role does the author say these localities played in prehistoric Indian settlement and subsistence systems?
2. What crops were employed by the prehistoric farmers of southern India? What techniques were used to acquire this evidence, and what did this evidence consist of?
3. Agriculture inevitably brings on changes in a culture. What technological and social changes occurred among the populations of southern India as a result of the advent of agriculture?

Yanomamö: Varying Adaptations of Foraging Horticulturalists

Raymond B. Hames

The documentation of behavioral variation in cultural anthropology is key to scientific description and explanation. Early ethnographers were content to describe typical patterns of behavior to give readers an idea of what was expected or customary in a given culture. To understand variation in cultural practices, anthropologists who are engaged in cross-cultural comparison use individual societies as data points or exemplars of particular traits. Although comparative or cross-cultural approaches have been enormously productive, they are not the only useful approach to a scientific understanding of cultural variation. Within each society, individuals or even whole regions may vary enormously in how they conduct their social, economic, and political lives. Accurately documenting this intracultural variation and attempting to associate it with explanatory factors is an important alternative approach. This is not to say that intracultural comparisons are superior to or in competition with cross-cultural approaches. In fact, I would expect them to complement each other. For example, one might demonstrate cross-culturally that warfare is strongly associated with a particular environmental variable. This then might lead us to test that proposition within a particular cultural group if that environmental variable had enough variation.

The goal of this chapter is to describe variation in Yanomamö economic activities at cross-cultural, regional, and individual comparative levels. I will first compare Yanomamö horticultural adaptation to other horticultural groups. The striking finding here is that compared to other horticulturalists the Yanomamö spend an enormous amount of time in the foraging activities of hunting, gathering, and fishing. In many ways, they behave like hunters and gatherers, peoples without agriculture. I will then turn to a regional comparison of Yanomamö economic adaptations by comparing how highland and lowland Yanomamö adapt to the rain forest. Here we will find that highland Yanomamö are much more dedicated to a sedentary horticultural life than lowland Yanomamö. Finally, I will turn to an analysis of individual Yanomamö to describe how sex and age determine the division of labor and the amount of time that individuals work.

DEMOGRAPHY, GEOGRAPHY, AND ENVIRONMENT

The Yanomamö are a tribal population occupying the Amazonian border between Venezuela and Brazil. In Venezuela, the northern extension of the Yanomamö is delimited to the north by headwaters of the Erebato and Caura rivers, east along the Parima mountains, and west along the Padamo and Mavaca in a direct line to the Brazilian border. In Brazil, they concentrate themselves in the headwaters of the Demini, Catrimani, Araca, Padauari, Urari Coera, Parima, and Mucajai rivers. In both countries, the total area inhabited by the Yanomamö is approximately 192,000 square kilometers. Dense tropical forest covers most of the area. Savannas are interspersed in forests at high elevations. In general, the topography is flat to gently rolling, with elevations ranging from 250 to 1,200 meters.

Area Exploited

The area village members exploit in the course of their economic activities is probably best characterized as a *home range*. Home ranges differ from territories because they are not defended, but like territories they tend to be used exclusively by a single group. This exclusiveness is not determined by force but by the following simple economic considerations. Important food resources tend to be evenly distributed in the tropical forest. When Yanomamö establish a new village they intensively exploit and deplete resources near the village. Through time, they must travel greater distances where higher return rates compensate for greater travel costs needed to reach areas of higher resource density. At a certain point, they will begin to reach areas that are exploited by neighboring villages and if they were to travel still further they would begin to enter areas close to neighboring villages that have been depleted. At this point, it is not economic to travel further since the costs of gaining resources increases (more travel time) while resource density decreases. Thus, the borders of home ranges are established with some overlap with the home ranges of adjacent villages. The point to understand here is that a village has near-exclusive use of its home range but that exclusivity is determined by economic factors and not by aggression or threat of aggression.[1]

Where warfare is intensive, home ranges may become more like territories if enemy villages are neighbors. In such cases, exclusive use of an area is maintained through aggression or threat of aggression. However, it is difficult to determine what is being defended. It may be that the Yanomamö want to keep enemies out of their foraging areas so that they may hunt and gather without the worry of meeting a raiding party; or it may be that a powerful village decides to press its advantage over a weaker neighbor by expanding its range into a neighbor's area to monopolize all the resources in the area. The way in which Yanomamö verbally rationalize their reasons for warring complicates this matter further. Yanomamö may claim that they go to war in order to avenge an insult, a previous killing, an abduction of a woman, or the illness-causing spells cast by a neighboring shaman. Therefore,

Yanomamö explain war in terms of vengeance for harm caused by an enemy. The problem here is that neighboring villages invariably have members who have done one or more of the above to a neighbor or a neighbor's ancestor. Why some past wrongs are ignored or acted upon may be determined by economic (territorial) and political (opponent's strength or perceived threat) factors. Further complexities of Yanomamö warfare are described in the section on conflict below.

We have little comparative data on sizes of the home ranges of Yanomamö villages. Differences in home range may be the result of ecological differences in resource density or the distribution of neighboring villages. The limited data we have indicate that home ranges vary from three hundred to seven hundred square kilometers, roughly a circular area with a radius of ten to fifteen kilometers. This radius is approximately the distance one can easily walk through the forest in less than a day.

Demography and Settlement Pattern of Yanomamö Villages

Although ethnographers have done extensive and excellent demographic research on some Venezuelan and Brazilian Yanomamö, a complete census for Venezuelan and Brazilian Yanomamö is lacking. Current estimates are 12,500 and 8,500 Yanomamö in Venezuela and Brazil, respectively, for a total of 21,000. However, the figures for Brazil may be significantly less because of epidemics and white-Yanomamö fighting caused by incursions of Brazilian gold miners starting about 1987. I discuss this problem later. In Venezuela and Brazil, there are approximately 363 villages ranging in size from 30 to 90 residents each. But some Venezuelan villages in the Mavaca drainage may reach two hundred or more. Napoleon A. Chagnon[2] provides evidence that warfare intensity is associated with village size: Where warfare is intense, villages are large. People are forced to associate in large villages both to deter attackers and enable themselves to mount effective counterattacks. Population density ranges from about 6.7 square kilometers per person to 33.5 square kilometers per person.

Anthropologists consider stable settled life one of the important consequences of the agricultural revolution. Although the Yanomamö are agriculturalists, villages are unstable in duration, location, and membership. A typical Yanomamö village *(shabono)* has the shape of a giant circular "lean-to" with a diameter of fifty meters or more depending on the number of people living in the village. Each house or apartment section of a village has a roof and a back wall but no front or side walls. Individual family lean-tos are joined in a circle. When a Yanomamö sits in his hammock and looks left or right he sees his next-door neighbor; if he looks straight ahead he sees a broad plaza and the dwellings of neighbors on the other side of the village. A village structure rarely lasts more than a few years before the roof thatch begins to rot and the entire village becomes filled with vermin. On such occasions, a new village may be constructed adjacent to the old one.

Aside from the reasons stated above, Yanomamö villages are relocated about every five years because of economic and political considerations.[3] The practice of shifting cultivation forces the Yanomamö to use extensive tracts of land. This is because garden land is used for only two to three years, and then, abandoned to the encroaching forest. Through time gardens become increasingly distant from the village. When gardens or easily accessible garden land become too distant, the village may move several kilometers to be in the midst of good garden land. Raiding provides a political cause for village relocation. When a village is repeatedly raided by a more powerful enemy, the entire village may be forced to relocate. Such moves are designed to put as much distance as possible between themselves and an enemy and may cause great privation due to loss of easy access to productive gardens.

Highland and Lowland

There is good reason to suspect that there are fundamental differences in environmental quality for Yanomamö who occupy highland and lowland elevations. Defining a precise boundary between the highlands and lowlands is impossible at this point. However, I tentatively define highland populations as villages found in areas higher than 500 to 750 meters of elevation and occupying areas of highly dissected and hilly terrain with small fast flowing streams and occasional savannas. The lowland environment is flatter with slowly moving, larger streams and rivers. This highland-lowland distinction appears to have important implications for the fundamental economic activities of gathering, hunting, fishing, and agriculture.

General ecological research provides considerable evidence that plant biomass and diversity decrease with increases in altitude. Detailed ethnographic research on the Yanomamö points to a similar conclusion. For example, ethnobotanical research by Lizot[4] shows a greater variety of edible plants are available to lowland groups, more plants are restricted to lowland environments, and, on average, more edible plants are available on a monthly basis for lowland groups. In addition, the cultural geographer William Smole[5] notes a decrease in edible plants with increasing elevation. Although it cannot be positively concluded that gathering is more productive in lowland areas because plants differ enormously in food value, processing costs, density, and seasonal availability, available data show that the rate of return in gathering wild forest resources is much greater in lowland than in highland areas.[6]

It is well established that fish are more abundant and larger in the wider, slower moving rivers in lower elevations.[7] A comparison of sites reveals that groups living along large streams or rivers consume twice as much fish and other aquatic prey (frogs, caimans, and crabs).[8] In addition, these lowland groups gain fish at efficiencies two to three times higher than highland groups.[9]

The evidence on game density is less direct. However, it is my impression (based on Yanomamö statements and direct observation) and that of other Yanomamö researchers[10] that game animals are much less abundant in higher elevations. In terms of kilograms of game killed per hour of hunting, Colchester shows that the highland Sanema Yanomamö hunt much less efficiently than lowland Yanomamö.[11] Because both highland and lowland groups use the same bow and arrow technology and are equally adept hunters, it can be concluded that the greater hunting success of lowlanders is the result of greater game densities in the lowlands. A review of the ecological and biogeographical literature on altitude and animal biomass gradients suggests that huntable biomass declines with increasing elevation.[12]

We have no convincing comparative data to indicate significant differences between highland and lowland areas for agricultural pursuits. Agricultural productivity is a complex interplay of many factors, such as soil quality, quantity and distribution of rain, and temperature extremes. It is clear, as I show below, that significant differences in garden size correspond to a highland and lowland divide. What is not clear, however, is whether these differences are the result of environmental, economic, or socio-political factors to be discussed below.

YANOMAMÖ ECONOMICS

Economically, the Yanomamö, along with most other tribal peoples living in the tropics, are classified as shifting cultivators because most of their dietary calories come from horticulture. However, a significant amount of time is allocated to the foraging activities of hunting, gathering, and fishing. In fact, as we shall see later, the Yanomamö allocate more time to foraging activities than they do to agriculture. Their dedication to foraging is greater than any other Amazonia group and any other horticultural group that we know of.[13] Given this huge investment in foraging activities it might be more accurate to refer to the Yanomamö as "foraging horticulturalists." In this section, I describe the basic productive components of the Yanomamö economy.

Technology

Until the mid-1950s, the Yanomamö relied on a locally produced "stone age" technology, which was dependent on local, non-metal resources. For example, axes were made of stone, knives of bamboo, fish hooks of bone, and pots of clay. Since that time, much of their traditional technology has been replaced by steel cutting tools (machetes and axes), aluminum pots, and other industrial items given or traded

to the Yanomamö primarily by missionaries. The main impact of such introductions has been to reduce labor time and increase Yanomamö dependence on non-Yanomamö to satisfy these new needs.[14] In many instances the Yanomamö no longer possess the skills to make or use traditional technology, such as clay pots or fire drills.

Gardening

In shifting cultivation, forest is cleared with machetes, axes, and fires. The newly opened forest is then planted with plantains, root crops (manioc, sweet potatoes, and taro) and a large variety of plants that serve as relishes, medicines, and technology sources. After about two to three years of cultivation, the garden is abandoned to the encroaching forest. In most years, Yanomamö add to the size of a current garden by clearing adjacent forest. As yields begin to diminish and weeding becomes time consuming, they cease to work old areas of the garden and let them naturally revert to scrub and, later, to forest. Men do nearly all the heavy work involved in clearing, such as slashing the undergrowth and felling large forest trees. Men and women work together to plant the garden and women are responsible for the nearly daily trips to the garden to harvest and weed.

There is considerable variation, as Figure 1 clearly indicates, in the amount of land under cultivation per capita in Yanomamö villages. Per capita land cultivated in highland villages averages five times as much as in lowland villages, a difference that is statistically significant. At least

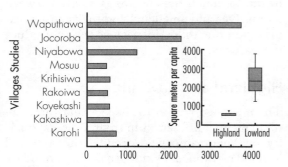

FIGURE 1 Garden Land Per-Capita (m²) in Nine Villages, and Low-land/Highland Contrasts

two possible ecological and economic explanations exist for these differences. Garden land may not be as fertile in higher elevations, or basic crops may not be as productive because of the cooler temperatures in highland areas.[15] As a result, highlanders are forced to increase garden size to produce the same quantity of plantains as lowlanders. A second reason to cultivate less land in lowland areas is that foraging success (efficiency) is greater in lowland areas, therefore lowlanders may gain a larger fraction of their diet from foraging, which lessens their dependence on garden food.

There is a basic contrast in subsistence crops relied upon by highland and lowland groups that may have far-reaching consequences in helping us understand their economic differences. Lowland groups rely on plantains and bananas as the basic subsistence crop while some highland groups rely more heavily on manioc, a very productive root crop. Where either crop is a staple, it contributes up to forty percent or more of all dietary calories. This difference leads us to ask why some highland groups depend on manioc and what impact dependence on one or the other has on the overall Yanomamö economy. Colchester suggests that manioc is a recent introduction from neighboring groups such as the Ye'kwana.[16] Where manioc has been introduced, the Yanomamö have taken it up because it appears to be a forty percent more efficient source of calories than plantains. However, this alleged advantage may disappear because the comparative data on efficiency do not consider processing costs. Some varieties of manioc become poisonous ("bitter") soon after harvesting and must be detoxified. In addition, many varieties require a laborious process of peeling, grating, and baking before consumption. Plantains, in contrast, are easily peeled and quickly cooked by roasting or boiling. Chagnon makes an opposite argument by suggesting that manioc was aboriginal with the Yanomamö and it was replaced by plantains (an Old World crop introduced by the Spanish more than four hundred years ago) because plantains were a more efficient producer of calories.[17] Unfortunately, neither Colchester or Chagnon have quantitative data to back up their claims. Clearly, relatively simple research could help settle this issue.

Whether or not manioc or plantains are ancient or recent introductions, dependence on one or the other may have a strong impact on the Yanomamö economy. The key issue here is not one of efficiency but of reliable and predictable yield. Tropical forest peoples tend to rely on crops that can be harvested over a long time. In contrast to temperate horticulturalists, many tropical peoples who grow root crops or plantains do not harvest their entire field during a single harvest period and do not store the crop to tide them through seasons when crop growth is impossible or risky. Instead, tropical cultivators stagger-plant throughout the year so that what is needed can be harvested from the field every few days or weeks. For example, one can harvest manioc six, twelve, or eighteen or more months after it is planted. This allows the manioc cultivator considerable flexibility in insuring a steady and reliable yield. Plantains, in contrast, have much less flexibility. Although Yanomamö attempt to stagger-plant plantains to gain a reliable weekly or half-weekly yield, a variety of environmental factors thwart this strategy. Dry spells can hasten maturation while prolonged wet spells slow maturation. Also, heavy winds that accompany violent thunderstorms may blow down plantains with heavy maturing racemes (bunches). Yanomamö can salvage blown down bunches of plantains (if they're close to maturation) by hanging them in the village. When the plantains ripen there will be a momentary glut of food, but there will be a lack of plantains in the near future when they would have otherwise matured.

Heavy dependence on plantains by lowland groups may help us to understand their greater reliance on gathering compared to manioc-producing highland groups. Since plantains are far less reliable than manioc, lowland Yanomamö may be forced to gather because of periodic underproduction of plantains. Evidence consistent with this idea is presented in Table 1. The only highland group on which we have time allocation (Sanema, in the table) shows that the average adult spends only twenty-six minutes each day gathering, which is the lowest figure in the table and fully one-half of the average time allocated to this task in lowland villages.

If manioc is more reliable than plantains we must ask why plantain-growing lowlanders do

TABLE 1 Time Allocation in Eight Yanomamö Villages (Minutes per Day)

Village	Hunt	Fish	Garden	Gather	Cook	Manufacture	Misc	Total	Source
Bisaasi	83	86	29	51	42	43	33	367	2
Hasubë	65	19	40	100	ND	ND	ND	a	4
Koyekashi	42	85	85	66	26	36	17	357	3
Krihi	32	108	32	54	26	58	65	375	2
Mishi	13	109	81	53	37	149	17	459	1
Rakoi	12	109	44	24	27	68	76	360	2
Sanema	70	15	52	26	59	118[b]	ND	350	5
Toropo	61	56	43	55	41	69	35	359	1
Yanomami	38	40	38	45	54	52	84	357	2
Mean	50	64	45	52	37	62	49	359	

Sources: 1 = Hames, 1989; 2 = Hames, b; 3 = Lhermillier, 1974; 4 = Good, 1989; 5 = Colchester, 1984. ND = no data.
[a]total not given because of incomplete data
[b]technology and maintenance activities are combined and column mean ignores these figures

not grow more manioc than they currently do. Because lowland gathering is about twice as efficient as highland gathering, it may mean that unreliable plantain production is buffered by highly productive gathering. Because the overall work effort for the highland Sanema is essentially identical to the average level of work for lowland villages (see the Total column in Table 1), I suggest that this is clear evidence that plantain gardening coupled with a high reliance on gathering causes no discernible hardship in overall work effort.

Foraging

Foraging is the simple extraction of resources from the environment without any attempt to modify the environment (as agriculture does) to increase the yield of that which is harvested. Hunting, gathering, and fishing are the basic foraging activities. Foraging is the most ancient technique humans use to exploit the environment and is an adaptation that humans share with all other animals. What is interesting about Yanomamö foraging is the large amount of time they allocate to it. As time allocation statistics in Table 1 indicate, Yanomamö allocate more than twice as much time to foraging as they do to gardening.

Given the amount of time the Yanomamö spend foraging on a daily basis, the term *foraging horticulturalists* might be an apt designation for their economic adaptation to the tropical forest.

The logic of this designation is reinforced further by the Yanomamö practice of *waiyumö*, or trekking. Trekking is camping in the forest and subsisting mostly by foraging. It usually occurs in the dry season when there is an abundance of forest fruit and the dryness makes walking and camping out pleasant. The probable motivation behind most trekking is to save travel time by taking advantage of abundant vegetable resources distant from the village. However, trekking may also be stimulated by a shortage of garden food or the presence of powerful enemies. If the latter is the cause, then trekking is an adaptation designed for concealment against enemies. Treks may last a week to more than a month and normally include all village members. Dependence on wild resources is not total; young men are sent from forest camps to gardens to harvest plantains if the wild resources are scarce.

Hunting

Hunting is the main source of dietary protein for the Yanomamö. As we shall see in the time allocation statistics, hunting is essentially a male activity with important social and ritual functions. Bows and arrows, which measure approximately two meters in length, are the main weapons of the hunt. The long arrow is not accurate beyond about thirty meters. This is of little significance in dense tropical forest where it is rare to have a clear shot at a greater distance.[18] Skills in locating game and stalking it to a short distance are abilities that differentiate good from poor hunters. Game sought ranges from 1-kilogram birds, to 25-kilogram peccaries, and to the occasional 175-kilogram tapir (the largest terrestrial animal in South America). Yanomamö quivers contain large lancelotate (spear shaped) tips for big game, poisoned pencil-shaped tips for monkeys, and harpoon points for birds and small terrestrial game. Because arrows are two meters long, a hunter can carry no more than three arrows on a hunt; however, hunters carry a case that contains a repair kit of thread, resin, and a hand tool to repair damaged arrows.

Although most hunting is done by individuals or pairs, organized group hunts occur under two important circumstances. If a hunter discovers a herd of white-lipped peccaries (a distant relative of the pig weighing twenty to thirty kilograms), he carefully notes the location and immediately returns to the village to alert other hunters who return to cooperatively hunt the herd. To prepare for a feast *(reahu)*, organized hunting parties travel great distances and may continuously hunt for a week in order to amass a large quantity of game to provide high-quality meals for visiting allies on a variety of social occasions *(reahu* and *braiai* rituals). During these excursions hunters especially seek highly esteemed game, such as peccaries, turkey-like birds, and monkeys.

Gathering

The harvesting of wild plant resources is an activity that includes all ages and sexes and is commonly organized by families and groups of families. Important resources include honey, palm fruits, brazil nuts, palm heart, and cashew fruit. Men specialize in the risky task of climbing trees to shake loose fruit or to sever fruit-laden branches. The peach palm is especially important. It is planted in gardens but it only begins to yield several years after a garden has been abandoned and it continues to bear for a decade or more. The Yanomamö assert that peach palms are owned by those who planted them and it is not uncommon for disputes to arise over ownership. With the exception of the peach palm, the Yanomamö make little or no effort to harvest fruit trees or palms so they may be harvested on

a sustained basis. The Yanomamö fell small, fruit-laden trees to make harvesting easier but never such forest giants as Brazil nut or cashew trees because of the enormous labor required.

Fishing

Most Yanomamö villages occupy areas between major rivers that are crossed by small streams. Fish found here are seldom larger than a few kilograms. Nevertheless, fishing is widely and avidly pursued by all ages and sexes, especially in the dry season through hand catching, stream poisoning, and archery. In the dry season, small streams begin to shrink, leaving fish in large ponds or cutoffs. The Yanomamö will use a vegetable poison to stun fish and cause them to rise to the surface where they can be grabbed or shot with a miniature bow and arrow. Women sometimes will jointly push a long, broad palm frond through the water to herd fish towards a bank where they can be trapped.

MARRIAGE AND FAMILY

Yanomamö marriage rules prescribe that marriage partners ought to be cross-cousins. Ideally, mates are double cross-cousins, a result of the practice of sister exchange. Soon after their first menses, women typically marry men in their early twenties. Although women are required to reside in their husband's village after marriage (patrilocal marriage), a husband must initially live with his in-laws for several years and work diligently for them, performing what is known as bride service. This requirement may be relaxed for high-status males. Polygyny (a man having more than one wife) is permitted; ten to twenty percent of all males at any time are polygynists. Ideally, polygynists marry sisters (sororal polygyny) because the Yanomamö believe that sisters get along better. If a woman's husband dies, she may be required to marry his brother (levirate marriage) and if a man's wife dies he may claim her sister as a bride (sororate marriage). Men and women average 2.8 marital partners during their lifetime, with about seventy-five percent of those marriages ending as a result of divorce with the balance as a result of death of one of the partners.[19]

Monogamous or polygynous nuclear families are the rule among the Yanomamö. Deviations from this pattern occur when aged parents live closely associated with married children or when newly-weds dwell with one or the other's parents. Each family has a garden or gardens and is responsible for basic subsistence activities.

POLITICAL ORGANIZATION

Each Yanomamö village is an autonomous political entity, free to make war or peace with other villages. Coalitions between villages are important; nevertheless, such coalitions tend to be fragile and ephemeral. Although the Yanomamö are an egalitarian people, age, sex, and personal accomplishments are important in status differentiation. Yanomamö men acquire high status through valor in combat, accomplished oratory, and expertise in shamanism. However, high status cannot be inherited—it must be earned. Mature men dominate positions of political authority and religious practice. Local descent groups play important roles in regulating marriages and settling disputes within the village.

The village headman is the dominant political leader and comes from the largest local patrilineage (a kin group whose members trace descent through male relatives). When a village is large or when two local descent groups are approximately equal in size, a village may have several headmen. The headman must rely on demonstrated skills in settling disputes, representing the interests of his lineage, and successfully dealing with allies and enemies. Styles of leadership vary: some headmen lead through practiced verbal skills while others resort to bullying. Concerted action requires the consensus of adult males. However, an individual is free to desert collective action if it suits him.

Villages range in size from about forty residents to more than two hundred. As a village increases in size it has a tendency to break into two groups of approximately equal size, which form new villages. As villages become large, kinship relationships become weaker and village headmen are less able to amicably settle disputes.[20] In addition, local resources tend to be more quickly depleted, which causes an increase in work effort.[21] However, if warfare is intense village members are more likely to realize the value of large size as a deterrent against enemies and are more likely to tolerate irksome co-villagers and increased work loads.

Social Control

Conflicts typically arise from accusations of adultery, failure to deliver a betrothed woman, personal affronts, stinginess, or thefts of coveted garden crops such as tobacco and peach palm. For men, if such conflicts move past a boisterous shouting match, a variety of graded, formal duels may occur. If a fight becomes serious, respected men may intervene to cool tempers and prevent others from participating. Frequently, duels end in a draw, which allows each contestant to preserve his dignity. For women, dueling is rare. Instead, a direct attack is made by the aggrieved woman using hands and feet or makeshift weapons.

Conflict

Warfare between villages is endemic among the Yanomamö. While the initial cause of a conflict may be frequently traced to a sexual or marital issue, conflicts are self-perpetuating since the Yanomamö lack any formal mechanisms to prevent aggrieved parties from exacting the amount of vengeance or counter-vengeance they deem sufficient once a conflict has started. The primary vengeance unit is the lineage, but co-resident non-kin have some obligation to assist, because co-residence with a feuding faction is seen as implicit support of the faction by the faction's enemies. Most combat is in the form of stealthy raids. The goal is to quickly kill as many of the enemy as possible (who frequently are found on the outskirts of the other village engaging in mundane activities), abduct nubile women if possible, and return quickly home. Although the primary goal is to kill mature men and their kin believed to be responsible for a previous wrong, unrelated co-villagers may be killed if there is no safe opportunity to kill primary targets. Endemic warfare has a profound effect on politics and settlement size and location. Each village needs at least one allied village it can call upon for assistance if it is over-matched by a more powerful enemy; and village size and distance between villages tend to increase with the intensity of conflict. Peace between villages may develop if conflict has remained dormant for a long period and there is a mutual need for an alliance in the face of a common enemy. It begins with a series of ceremonially festive visits. If old antagonisms do not flare, visits may lead to joint raids and intermarriage between villages that strongly solidify an alliance. Proximity of missions and government agencies has had little impact on warfare.

MAJOR CHANGES

Over the last twenty years, most Yanomamö have become totally dependent on outside sources of axes, machetes, aluminum cooking pots, and fish hooks and line. These metal goods have replaced much of their stone-age technology. Most of these items have come from missionaries as gifts and wages. Through mission-organized cooperatives, the Yanomamö recently have begun to market baskets and arrows and some agricultural products.

Missionary presence also has distorted the traditional Yanomamö settlement pattern. Yanomamö attempt to gain easy access to mission outposts by moving their villages near a mission. As a result, the normal spacing of about a day's walk between villages has diminished dramatically. For example, around the Salesian mission at Mavaca there are five villages and numerous small settlements with a total population of about nine hundred people within one day's walk. This population density is unprecedented for the Yanomamö and has led to severe depletion of wild resources. In addition, a significant fraction of that population no longer lives in traditional round communal villages but rather in small settlements of two to three houses occupied by a few families. Despite these changes, missionaries have failed to gain significant numbers of Yanomamö converts to Christianity. The Yanomamö have enormous pride in their culture and have strong doubts about the authenticity or superiority of Christian beliefs.

However, the greatest change and threat to the Yanomamö are the thousands of Brazilian gold miners who have infiltrated Yanomamö territory in Brazil and who have again (July 1993) illegally entered into Venezuela and this time killed seventeen men, women, and children. The situation in Brazil is similar to the situation in the United States in the 1800s when whites expanded into the lands of Native Americans. Miners bring epidemics of measles and influenza that lead to high mortality rates among the Yanomamö. Gold processing pollutes streams with mercury, killing fish and ruining a village's water supply. And open warfare between miners and Yanomamö has killed numerous Yanomamö and disrupted village life.[22]

TIME ALLOCATION

In the West, we tend to think of work as something done away from the home for forty hours a week. In subsistence-based tribal populations, this sort of definition is as inadequate for them as it is for us. Although it is true that the Yanomamö, for example, leave the village to travel to garden, forest, and stream to acquire resources, much work takes place in the village. But the same thing is true in the West. Driving to work, mowing the lawn, shopping for food, washing clothes, and all those other household chores that must be done are not what we would call leisure time activities. We do these tasks to maintain our material well-being. I believe that most of us would define leisure time activities as including dining out, going to the movies, visiting friends, and playing sports. Therefore, one can define work as all those other activities we must do to maintain or enhance our material existence. Clearly, adults in the West work more than 40 hours per week if we use this expansive definition of work. Researchers who have investigated time allocated to work in the West show that urban European and North Americans work on average 55 to 65 hours per week, or 7.8 to 9.3 hours per day, seven days a week.[23]

Table 1 presents time allocation data for adults in eight Yanomamö villages on a basic set of work activities. The table reveals that the Yanomamö work about 6 hours per day (360 minutes) or 42 hours per week. This is significantly less than the 55 to 66 hours of work in modern societies. Furthermore, if we compare Yanomamö and related simple tropical horticulturalists to other types of economies (hunters and gatherers, pastoralists, agriculturists, etc.), we find that they are among the most leisured people in the world.[24]

Although Table 1 shows little variation in overall labor time (mean 359, SD 7.88), considerable variation exists among villages in time allocated to various subsistence tasks. Much of the variation can be attributed to local conditions, such as the season in which the researcher collected the data, the degree to which a village is associated with missionaries, or special environmental conditions. Nevertheless, the only highland site, Sanema, shows some interesting patterns. This village allocates the third-most time to gardening, the least time to fishing, the second-least amount of time to gathering, and the second-most amount of time to hunting. Gathering and gardening times are probably related, as I suggested earlier. Because the density of wild sources of plant food is lower in the highlands, foraging is not as productive, which leads highlanders to spend more time gardening. Related to this is the higher reliability of manioc gardening, which makes gathering less of an important alternative source of vegetable foods. Another way of expressing the contrasting dependence on foraging (hunting, gathering, and fishing) and gardening in highland and lowland locales is to note that the highland population spends the least amount of time foraging and has the lowest ratio of foraging time to gardening time (2.13:1.0 compared to a mean of 4.43:1.0 for the lowlanders).[25]

The extremely low amount of time highlanders allocate to fishing and the relatively high amount of time they allocate to hunting are also related. Highlanders do little fishing because of difficulties exploiting steep and narrow highland streams. Because fishing and hunting are the only ways of gaining sufficient high-quality protein to the diet and fishing is unprofitable, highlanders are forced to hunt more intensively.

DIVISION OF LABOR

As Figure 2 indicates, women spend significantly more time in cooking, fishing, gathering, and caring for children than men do, whereas

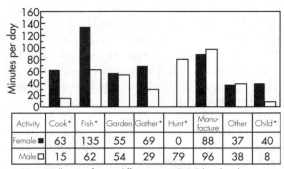

Activity	Cook*	Fish*	Garden	Gather*	Hunt*	Manu-facture	Other	Child*
Female ■	63	135	55	69	0	88	37	40
Male □	15	62	54	29	79	96	38	8

* Statistically significant difference at 0.05 level or better

FIGURE 2 Male and Female Time Allocation to Basic Economic Tasks

men spend more time hunting than women. From what we know about the division of labor cross-culturally, these differences in time allocation are not surprising. In all cultures, hunting is either predominately or wholly a male activity. Although the data indicate that Yanomamö women do almost no hunting, some qualifications are necessary. Yanomamö women occasionally accompany men on hunting forays to act as spotters and to assist in the retrieval of game. Rarely do they ever make kills while with men. However, they occasionally make fortuitous kills of their own while gathering or fishing. Such kills are made without the use of bows and arrows.

Although the data show no significant difference between men and women in gardening, there are important differences in garden tasks performed. Men almost exclusively do the heavy work of felling large trees, slashing the undergrowth, and burning the resulting debris prior to planting. Both sexes share in planting, whereas the daily tasks of weeding and harvesting fall almost exclusively to women. The pattern of men doing tasks which are dangerous and/or take them far from home is consistent with Judith Brown's model of the division of labor.[26] Brown suggests that women tend to dominate tasks that are compatible with simultaneous child care. Such tasks are not dangerous, can be accomplished near to home, and can be interrupted and resumed with no loss of efficiency.

While Brown's model usefully captures much of the variation in the division of labor among the Yanomamö and other groups, it does not explain why women who are post-menopausal or otherwise unencumbered with intensive child care do not, for example, engage in hunting or tree felling. For dangerous and arduous activities, such as tree felling, it is probable that models that focus on physical strength differences may be useful. Or perhaps task linkages are required to complement Brown's model.[27] However, lack of female participation in hunting may require yet another explanation. Hunting is a highly skilled activity that is not easily learned and requires frequent practice to maintain proficiency. On average, little Yanomamö boys spend sixty to eighty minutes per day playing with bows and arrows and spotting, tracking, and stalking small birds and other tiny game near the village. It may be the case that women don't hunt because they never acquired the skills necessary to become proficient hunters.

The question of whether men or women work more can be answered only if we have a reasonable definition of work. Generally, economic anthropologists define work as all of those activities required to directly maintain and enhance survival and reproduction. Thus, it includes rather obvious activities such as the provisioning and preparing of food, construction and repair of tools and shelter, and the acquisition and management of fuel (or firewood, in the case of the Yanomamö). If we use this definition of work, Yanomamö women work about twelve minutes per day more than men, but the difference is not statistically significant. This finding is rather interesting because, in the vast majority of horticultural tribal populations on which we have time allocation data, women work significantly more than men.[28] The only societies in which men work significantly more than women are hunters and gatherers. That Yanomamö men and women work approximately equally is therefore consistent with the point made earlier: That they can be best characterized as foraging horticulturalists because their time allocation patterns fall between horticulturalists and hunter-gatherers.

Some may consider this definition unnecessarily restrictive because it ignores a task that is critical for the long-term survival of the Yanomamö: child care. The tropical forest harbors many sources of environmental trauma that are very dangerous to infants and small children. Inside and outside the village there are stinging and biting insects, dangerous plant spines, and poisonous plants, snakes, and insects. Infants and small children are protected from these threats by being carried in slings much of the time and actively watched when they are set down.[29] Although caring for infants and small children in this way may be pleasurable, it is also exhausting and difficult. And recall that I defined work as those things we do to enhance or maintain our physical well-being. Just as the Yanomamö labor to provide food for their children, they also physically care for them. To assess the impact of child care on overall labor time differences, I must restrict my analysis to data I collected on four Yanomamö villages (Mishimishimaböwei, Rakoiwä, Krihisiwä, and Bisaasi) because none of the other studies collected child care data. When I include direct child care activities (carrying, feeding, nursing, holding, etc.),[30] female work time increases by forty-three minutes per day while male work time increases by only eight minutes per day. If child care activities are added to conventionally defined labor, then Yanomamö women work more than men.

Status and the Allocation of Labor

The Yanomamö, like all people, exhibit strong individual differences in the amount of labor they perform that are independent of sex. Factors such as age, number of dependents, and marital status should logically help us to understand much of the variation. For example, one would expect that a married couple with numerous dependent children to labor more than newlyweds with no dependents. Such a prediction is based on a number of assumptions, such as each family is wholly responsible for supplying its economic needs and economic resources are freely available. Although this latter assumption is correct for the Yanomamö, the former is suspect, as I will later explain. In this section, I will examine the degree to which age determines individual labor time allocation.

Child Labor Trends

On the basis of our own experiences we expect that the amount of work one does will increase with age and that it eventually begins to diminish when one retires or becomes physically incapacitated. We also tend to believe that childhood should be a carefree time with little in the way of work responsibilities—a time for play, exploration, and learning. An examination of Yanomamö time allocation data will allow us to evaluate all of these ideas; and, because the Yanomamö are relatively typical representatives of the tribal world, we can get a sense of whether our Western experience is in any way typical over the history of humankind.

Figure 3 shows the amount of time children from ages five through eighteen allocate to labor time activities.[31] As can be easily seen, labor time does generally increase with age of the child. The rate of increase is uneven only because of small sample sizes in some of the age groups. Over the chart, I have superimposed adult male and female labor time. You will note in this graph that the females work significantly more (421 min./day) than males (372 min./day). These figures differ from the ones given earlier in the ten-village comparison because they derive from the four villages I studied. I use this smaller data set here because it is the only one broken down by age. As the figure indicates, boys and girls begin to achieve adult labor time levels by the time they become teenagers.

The data presented seem to indicate that childhood is brief and children are quickly

recruited into the family work force. To some extent these figures are an artifact of the method I used to collect time allocation data. If I could not observe someone when I was sampling behavior, I had to rely on reports of what they were doing. For example, someone would tell me that all the members of a particular family were in the forest gathering wild palm nuts or weeding the garden. When I was able to accompany families on their economic activities, I found that children did work but not as hard or as constantly as adults: They worked about forty to eighty percent as much as adults when, for example, a garden was being weeded. Nevertheless, the data tell us something important about work and family life that provides a strong contrast to what occurs in the urban West. Yanomamö children work alongside their parents and are important to the household economy. The family unit does not separate in the morning; children and adults do not go their separate ways to school and work only to rejoin each other in the evening. "School" for a Yanomamö child is in the context of the family economy where they learn how to hunt, gather, garden, fish, and perform all the other activities necessary for them to become competent adults.

Adult Labor Trends

If we extend the analysis of time allocated to work across the entire life span, we expect to see labor time increase to a point and then decrease. This pattern, an inverted U-shaped curve, is evident for both men and women in Figure 4. However, the shapes of the curves are quite different. Male allocation of labor time begins at a lower level but increases rapidly until it peaks around age thirty-five, and then rapidly decreases thereafter. Females, in contrast, begin at initially higher levels, ascend more slowly to a peak at age fifty and then decrease their efforts much more slowly. The last point is rather interesting: the curve shows that women at ages thirty and sixty work about the same amount of time. The factors that account for these patterns are quite complex. Women

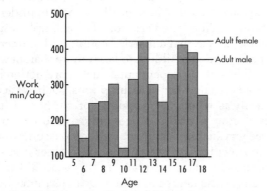

FIGURE 3 Labor Time of Children

Males

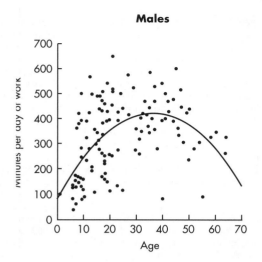

Females

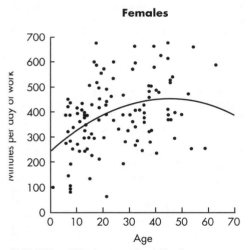

FIGURE 4 Work over the Life Span

more rapidly. Related to this trend is that as men become older they work more at relatively sedentary tasks, such as manufacturing and the gardening tasks of weeding and harvesting, and work significantly less in hunting and clearing new gardens.

CONCLUSION

Since 1975, when Allen Johnson reintroduced anthropologists to methods for measuring time allocation,[33] studies of how people use their time have become increasing popular among anthropologists. In this chapter, I have attempted to show some of the uses to which time allocation can be put by showing how it can elucidate fundamental ethnographic problems in intracultural variation. I showed that differences in environment between lowland and highland Yanomamö lead to differences in the allocation of time to basic economic activities. We found that highland groups are much more tied to agricultural pursuits because of a lack of high-quality foraging resources. In the area of the sexual division of labor, we found that men and women work nearly the same amount of time but allocate their efforts much differently. In addition, we found that if child care activities are included in labor time, then women work significantly more than men. Finally, I showed that time allocation patterns show significant patterns associated with age. Both boys and girls are quickly absorbed into the family's labor pool and adult male labor effort peaks earlier and declines more quickly than it does for women.

In closing I should note that time allocation studies are not simply restricted to the documentation of variation in work effort. Researchers now use the method to quantify patterns of social interaction such as how much time husbands and wives spend together, the size and composition of play groups among children, and patterns of cooperation among co-villagers. So long as ethnographers are interested in quantitative measures of variation in social life we can expect that time allocation studies will play a central role.

engaged in active child care (for example, nursing) work less than women who are not.[32] This fact probably accounts for female labor time peaking after menopause. Male labor time decreases quite rapidly after age thirty-five, but I am not sure why the rate of decrease is so much greater than for women. There are two inter-related possibilities. Because males have higher rates of mortality than women at all ages, they may also have higher rates of decrepitude than women, that is, their ability to do physically demanding labor may decrease

Notes

1. R. Hames, "The Settlement Pattern of a Yanomamö Population Bloc," in R. Hames and W. Vickers, eds., *Adaptive Responses of Native Amazonians* (New York: Academic Press, 1983), pp. 192–229.

2. N. Chagnon, *Studying the Yanomamö* (New York: Holt, Rinehart & Winston, 1974).

3. N. Chagnon, *Studying the Yanomamö*; R. Hames, "The Settlement Pattern of a Yanomamö Population Bloc."

4. J. Lizot, *Les Yanomami Centrau* (Paris: Editions de L'Ecole des Hautes Etudes en Sciences Sociales, 1984), p. 54, Table 2.

5. W. Smole, *The Yanoama Indians: A Cultural Geography* (Austin: University of Texas Press, 1976).

6. M. Colchester, "Rethinking Stone Age Economics: Some Speculations Concerning the Pre-Columbian Yanoama Economy," *Human Ecology* 12 (1984): 291–314.

7. M. Goulding, *The Fishes and the Forest* (Berkeley: University of California Press, 1980).

8. G. Saffirio and R. Hames, "The Forest and the Highway," in K. Kensinger and J. Clay, eds., *Working Papers on South American Indians #6 and Cultural Survival Occasional Paper #11*, joint publication (Cambridge, MA: Cultural Survival, 1983), pp. 1–52.

9. R. Hames, "Time, Efficiency, and Fitness in the Amazonian Protein Quest," *Research in Economic Anthropology* 11 (1989): 43–85. Anthropologists measure the efficiency of subsistence activities in kilograms of food gained per hour of work or kilocalories of food gained per kilocalorie of work.

10. W. Smole, pp. 81 and 227.

11. M. Colchester, p. 300, Table 2; Hames, "Time, Efficiency, and Fitness in the Amazonian Protein Quest," p. 64, Table 6.

12. J. Eisenberg, "The Density and Biomass of Tropical Mammals," in M. Soule and B. Wilcox, eds., *Conservation Biology: An Evolutionary-Ecological Perspective* (Sunderland, MA: Sinauer Associates, 1980), pp. 35–55; J. Eisenberg, M. O'Connell, and V. August, "Density, Productivity, and Distribution of Mammals in the Northern Neotropics," in J. Eisenberg, ed., *Vertebrate Ecology in the Northern Neotropics* (Washington, DC: Smithsonian Institution Press, 1979), pp. 187–207.

13. R. Hames, "Time, Efficiency, and Fitness in the Amazonian Protein Quest."

14. R. Hames, "A Comparison of the Efficiencies of the Shotgun and Bow in Neotropical Forest Hunting," *Human Ecology* 7 (1979): 219–252.

15. Data on Yanomamö garden size is from the following sources: E. Fuentes, "Los Yanomami y las plantas silvestres," *Antropologica* 54 (1980): 3–138; Smole, *The Yanoama Indians*, pp. 36–37; J. Lizot, "Economie Primitive et Subsistence: Essai sur Le Travail et L'alimentation Chez les Yanomami," *Libre* 4 (1980): 69–113; and J. Lizot, "La Agricultural Yanomami," *Anthropologica* 53 (1980): 3–93. Information on cultivated bananas and plantains can be found in N. W. Simmonds, *The Evolution of Bananas* (London: Longmans & Green, 1979).

16. M. Colchester, p. 301.

17. N. Chagnon, *Yanomamö: The Fierce People* (New York: Harcourt Brace Jovanovich, 1992).

18. R. Hames, "A Comparison of the Efficiencies of the Shotgun and Bow in Neotropical Forest Hunting."

19. T. Melancon, "Marriage and Reproduction among the Yanomamö of Venezuela" (Ph.D. diss., Pennsylvania State University, 1982). Cross-cousins are offspring of siblings of the opposite sex. For example, your father's sister's children are your cross-cousins and so are your mother's brother's children. Double cross-cousin marriage is set up when two men marry one another's sisters. The Yanomamö prescribe that the offspring of such unions should marry. These people are double cross-cousins because (using the male as an example) a male is marrying a woman who is simultaneously his father's sister's daughter and his mother's brother's daughter.

20. N. Chagnon, Yanomamö: The Fierce People.

21. R. Hames, "The Settlement Pattern of a Yanomamö Population Bloc."

22. N. Chagnon, *Yanomamö: The Last Days of Eden* (New York: Harcourt Brace Jovanovich, 1993); N. Chagnon, "Covering Up the Yanomamö Massacre," *New York Times*, October 23, 1993; see also Saffirio and Hames, on the impact of road construction on Yanomamö economy, and N. Chagnon and T. Melancon, "Reproduction, Epidemics, and the Number of Kin in Tribal Populations: A Case Study," in N. Keyfitz, ed., *Population and Biology: A Bridge between Two Disciplines* (Liege: Ordina Editions, 1984), pp. 147–167, on the effects of epidemics spread by whites.

23. R. Hames, "Time, Efficiency, and Fitness in the Amazonian Protein Quest." Adult labor time is the average of male and female labor time.

24. Sources for time allocation data in Table 1 are as follows: Colchester, p. 299; K. Good, "Yanomami Hunting Patterns: Trekking and Garden Relocation as an Adaptation to Game Availability in Amazonia, Venezuela" (Ph.D. diss., University of Florida, 1989); Hames, "Time, Efficiency, and Fitness in the Amazonian Protein Quest"; A. Lhermillier and N. Lhermillier, "Vie Economique et Sociale d'une Unite Familliale Yanomami" (thesis, L'Ecole Pratique des Hautes Etudes, 1974); Lizot, "Economie Primitive et Subsistence."

25. Ibid.

26. J. Brown, "A Note on the Division of Labor," *American Anthropologist* 72 (1970): 1073–1078.

27. G. P. Murdock and C. Provost, "Factors in the Division of Labor by Sex: A Cross-Cultural Analysis," *Ethnology* 12 (1973): 206–212; M. Burton and D. White, "Sexual Division of Labor in Agriculture," *American Anthropologist* 86 (1984): 568–583. In their task linkage model Burton and White show that the sex that begins a task that has a series of steps is more likely to complete the subsequent steps. For example, if women harvest food they are more likely to perform the processing and storage tasks that immediately follow harvesting.

28. R. Hames, "Time, Efficiency, and Fitness in the Amazonian Protein Quest."

29. R. Hames, "Variation in Paternal Care among the Yanomamö," in B. Hewlett, ed., *The Father's Role: Cultural and Evolutionary Perspectives* (Chicago: Aldine de Gruyter, 1992), pp. 85–110.

30. Ibid.

31. The data reported here on the division of labor, male and female labor time, and child labor time are taken from data I collected in the villages of Mishimishimaböwei-teri, Rakoiwä-teri, Bisaasi-teri, and Krihisiwä-teri in 1986 and 1987. The data set consists of seventy-three adult females and seventy-six adult males. Adults are defined as anyone over the age of fifteen years who is married or has been married.

32. Ibid.
33. A. Johnson, "Time Allocation in a Machiguenga Community," *Ethnology* 14 (1975): 301–310. See also the continuing series of studies of time allocation, in various societies, that are published by the Human Relations Area Files.

Suggested Readings

Biocca, E. *Yanoama: The Narrative of a White Girl Kidnapped by Amazonian Indians*. New York: E. P. Dutton, 1970. Helena Valero was captured by Brazilian Yanomamö when she was twelve years old. This book is the exciting account of her capture, problems in adjusting to Yanomamö social life, marriage to several Yanomamö men, and eventual release to missionaries.

Chagnon, N. *Yanomamö: The Fierce People*. 4th ed. New York: Holt, Rinehart & Winston, 1992. This is perhaps the most popular ethnography written in the last several decades. It is an introductory yet detailed ethnography of the Yanomamö with a special focus on kinship, social organization, and politics.

———. *Yanomamö: The Last Days of Eden*. New York: Harcourt Brace Jovanovich, 1993. A more personal and accessible account of the Yanomamö than Chagnon's standard ethnography listed above. It presents a lucid picture of what it is like to do fieldwork with the Yanomamö and some contemporary problems faced by the Yanomamö.

Early, J., and J. Peters. *The Population Dynamics of the Mujacai Yanomamö*. New York: Academic Press, 1991. This monograph describes Brazilian Yanomamö with a special emphasis on demography in relation to social organization. In addition, it presents a novel explanation of mother-in-law avoidance by the son-in-law, a moderately common cross-cultural phenomenon.

Lizot, J. *Tales of the Yanomami: Daily Life in the Venezuelan Forest*. Cambridge: Cambridge University Press, 1985. Jacques Lizot is a French social anthropologist who has worked with the Yanomamö for nearly two dozen years. He presents vignettes of Yanomamö life in novelistic fashion with stories of romance, vengeance, politics, shamanism, and women's lives.

CRITICAL THINKING QUESTIONS

1. Who are the Yanomamö, and where do they live?
2. Define the differences, in terms of topography, available resources, soil productivity, forest cover, and other factors, between the highland and lowland environments of the Yanomamö.
3. What is trekking, and how does it supplement the Yanomamö horticultural economy?
4. What changes have occurred in Yanomamö culture since their introduction to Western goods and ideas?
5. Discuss the division of labor among the Yanomamö. What tasks are allocated to what group, and who seems to put more effort into the food production economy?

Pastoral Nomadism and Gender: Status and Prestige, Economic Contribution, and Division of Labor among the Tuareg of Niger

Susan Rasmussen

INTRODUCTION

Gender in Anthropology

This is a discussion of women's perceived economic contributions in relation to status, prestige, and division of labor in a traditionally pastoral nomadic, stockbreeding society, the Tuareg of the African Sahara and Sahel. I also offer a critique of some interpretations of gender and pastoralism in predominantly seminomadic communities moving toward sedentarization and migrant labor. First, I situate my own analysis in current approaches to gender in anthropology, and present an overview of studies of women's and men's roles in pastoral society. Following this section, I focus upon the Tuareg, a seminomadic, Islamic, socially stratified people who live in Niger, Mali, Burkina Faso, and Algeria, with an emphasis on data from my research among the Air Tuareg of northern Niger Republic.[1] I conclude with a brief discussion of socioeconomic and political transformations that impinge upon Tuareg gender, relations between the sexes, and issues raised for the future.

Gender is socially and culturally constructed, and can usefully be understood as a comparative, relational concept (Di Leonardo 1990; Butler 1990:6; Davison 1997). Critical to gender structuring are intertwined modalities: social variables such as ethnicity, class, religion, and age,

among many (Ortner and Whitehead 1981; Di Leonardo 1990). Regional variations may also impinge on inter- and intragender identities and relationships (Meena 1992; Gaidzanwa 1985; Mannathoko 1992; Davison 1997). Each of these modalities, singly or in combination, interacts dialectically with gender in a given society at a specific point in time, altering the way women and men are perceived and how they perceive themselves and each other. Constructions of gender therefore depend heavily upon positionality.[2]

In recent years, a number of scholars have called for studies that treat gender dynamically, as occurring in processes generated by discrete locales and through particular histories; they assert that gender is not fixed either across time or in location (di Lauretis 1984; Scott 1988, 1992; Kondo 1990; Probyn 1990; Butler 1992; Flax 1993; Barlow 1996). Thus although I use the term "women," I also try to make clear that the Tuareg women about whom I write do not constitute an undifferentiated category of "essentialized woman." They interact with men and are defined by their age, social origins, occupations, kinship roles, and other locations in Tuareg society. I insist that specifics of time and place are critical; I aim to tease out the relationship of historical and social contexts to certain configurations of gender.[3] My point is not to argue for

Source: From Brettell, Caroline B. and Sargent, Carolyn F., *Gender in Cross-Cultural Perspective*, 4/e. Copyright © 2005, pp. 155–169. Reprinted by permission of Pearson Education, Inc., Upper Saddle River, NJ.

some timeless, quintessentially Tuareg sense of woman, but to show how gender and knowledge are constructed in a particular place and time, namely, of seminomadism: in a pastoralist nomadic community undergoing transitions whose directions are difficult to predict over the long term, but who now include some sedentary oasis gardening and migrant labor, within a larger, multiethnic nation-state experiencing ecological disaster, economic crisis, and political tensions.

Women and Men in Pastoral Nomadism

Some researchers (Barth 1961; Martin and Voorhies 1975:332–366) view pastoralism as one extreme on a continuum of dependence upon herd animals and cultivation for subsistence, in which segments of sedentary tilling communities may, during periods of scarce resources (i.e., droughts, overpopulation) come to depend increasingly on the products of their herd animals for subsistence. Much Tuareg data, however, contradicts this: in the difficulties of drought, many Tuareg have been pressured to become more sedentary, and to depend increasingly on products of their oasis gardens rather than herd animals for subsistence. Despite this, however, a pastoralist ideology persists. Many Tuareg yearn to return to pastoral nomadism but realize the necessity today for mixing subsistence modes of herding, oasis gardening, caravan and other itinerant trading, and migrant labor, and among the more specialized artisan social strata, arts/crafts production (Rasmussen 1992, 1994, 1996). Martin and Voorhies also observe that during periods of plenty, when the size of herds becomes cumbersome or provides the wherewithal for purchase of arable land, pastoral segments may be repatriated to villages. But among the Tuareg, exactly the opposite occurs: during periods of stress and deprivation when herds become greatly diminished or even depleted, population segments tend to be repatriated to villages.

Tuareg patterns therefore suggest the need to modify or refine some prevalent representations of the cyclical pattern of pastoralism (Martin and Voorhies 1975:334). They offer contradictions, or at least variations, of some previous interpretations of gender in pastoral nomadic societies,

and show the need to deconstruct concepts in both pastoralist and gender studies. In a classic study, Martin and Voorhies (1975:351) acknowledge that it is difficult to point to any single pattern of economic adaptation or social juxtaposition of the sexes among pastoralists as a whole, and correlations cannot always be converted to causal connections. Based upon their ethnological, cross-cultural and historical secondary data, these authors make several tentative generalizations. They note that the sexual division of labor seems related to the degree and nature of mobility required for the successful execution of subsistence activities (Martin and Voorhies 1975:352). They argue that gender variations among pastoralists are influenced by at least three factors: (1) their specific adaptation to a given environment (settlement pattern, interaction of herding and cultivation); (2) cultural history of society (common culture areas such as sedentary community origins in Africa south of the Sahara correlate with economic independence, the hoe, polygyny, and sexual freedom; those in the Middle East and of agricultural origins display the opposite pattern); and (3) recent diffusion of ideas rather than cultural origins (Islam, for example—although the Tuareg are an exception to other Muslim pastoralists, in demonstrating less emphasis on the patriarchal family and on gender inequalities) (Martin and Voorhies 1975:365–366).

From their study of forty-four pastoral societies, Martin and Voorhies conclude that the female contribution to the diet of herders is small. Men do almost all herding and women dairy in only about one-third of societies. Men also do most of the cultivation in half of their sample, however, where cultivation is based on horticultural techniques, women are either the exclusive cultivators, or men and women share equally in cultivation (Martin and Voorhies 1975:339–343; O'Kelly and Carney 1986:66). Martin and Voorhies and O'Kelly and Carney suggest that among herders with a high dependence on crops, variations found in the gender division of labor may be a result of the influence of the parent cultural community out of which pastoral society developed. Hence it is instructive to acknowledge the cultures of neighbors. However, the reverse also holds true. Cultural flows are multidirectional, and Tuareg influences are also present in their neighboring sedentary farming cultures. Thus it is difficult to determine the direction of cultural and social influences, and it is not easy to generalize that all nomadic cultures with a horticultural background are more likely to share tasks, or that all those with an agricultural background are more likely to assign primary productive tasks to men.

O'Kelly and Carney (1986:66) argue that gender division of labor within many pastoral societies is "tipped toward male dominance" of economically productive tasks. These authors explain this in terms of the strength required to handle large animals. Males tend to be exclusive herders of large animals. Females may, however, herd smaller animals and serve as dairy maids for large and small species. Women and children contribute by gathering food, carrying water, and processing byproducts such as milk, wool, hides, and dung. But the lack of firm differentiation between domestic and public spheres encourages gender egalitarianism. Where women have some economic control, women's status may be raised. Boulding (1976:288–299) argues that women participate more fully in the total life of these societies than they do in settled agricultural communities. But Martin and Voorhies (1975) argue that male dominance of economic production gives rise to male dominance in the wider culture and social structure of pastoral societies. Lois Beck, on the other hand, found a flexible division of labor, economic interdependence between genders, and a low degree of gender segregation among the Qashqai of Iran (Beck in Beck and Keddie 1978:365–367). Furthermore, because of the small size of independent households of these pastoralists, males and females were partners in economically independent units, and neither males nor females formed strong separate solidarity groups.

Many authors agree that, however diverse the forms it takes, the division of labor among herders does not create a sharp dichotomy between domestic and public spheres. Women's tasks are more likely to take place in camp than men's tasks, but they do not isolate women in the household. Much women's work is done in cooperation with other women. Both men and women participate in collective work patterns with other members of the same gender. Camps are typically divided into women's spaces and men's spaces, but almost all activities are carried out in the open, avoiding development of private domestic spheres for women versus public spheres for men (O'Kelly and Carney 1986:67). Women's work may be household work, but it is public household work; public/domestic domains thus emerge as overly rigid and bound to western cultures.[4,5]

In many pastoral nomadic societies, ownership and control over the disposition of livestock appear to be predominantly in male hands. However, females are sometimes at least nominal owners of some livestock through inheritance, dowries, or purchase (O'Kelly and Carney 1986:68). But even owners of livestock cannot usually dispose freely of their animals: they are bound by an intricate web of kinship-based exchanges, which requires giving periodically large numbers of animals to close kin, as bridewealth to the bride's family, dowries to the groom, and as compensation for violation of certain rules, for example, homicide (Evans-Pritchard 1956; Hutchinson 1996) and adultery (Rasmussen 1998a). Furthermore, certain animals in a herd may be held jointly with others or in their interest, and are subject to many limitations on use and disposal. Males who control large herds thus do not necessarily derive significant economic power from these herds; rather, use rights are important considerations. But large herds bring prestige and influence to owners.

Other factors influencing gender are the defense needs and warfare practices of herders and patricentric kinship systems. In terms of Peggy Sanday's (1981:181) typology, many pastoralists appear to fall under the rubric of "real male dominance," because in most cases the environment is sufficiently dangerous for the society to depend on the strength and aggressiveness of their men for survival. Sanday argues that under such conditions of stress, for the sake of social and cultural survival, women "accept real male dominance." Once again, the Tuareg data suggest modifications of this hypothesis. Tuareg men's frequent absence from home in past raiding and more recent separatist warfare against the central state governments of Mali and Niger, and also men's peaceful trading, have encouraged, indeed necessitated women's independence in some domains of activity (education of children and work). However, some high-status men remain at home and control official political decisions. Thus a warrior aristocracy does not produce gender inequality in all respects; rather, there is a mixed bag here. In fact, some authors report legends of "warrior queens" in Tuareg and other pastoralist nomadic cultures (Boulding 1976:303–312; Rodd 1926:170). While difficult to verify, they suggest that women's elevated position in the class structure may modify their gender roles; thus class cross-cuts gender (Ortner and Whitehead 1981; Di Leonardo 1990).

The pastoral-nomadic/gender relationship is therefore complex, and defies facile generalizations or typologies. There are numerous cross-cultural contradictions and forces that tend toward both gender egalitarianism and male dominance. These suggest the importance of examining local cultures and histories.

THE TUAREG CASE

Tuareg Gender Roles and Relations between the Sexes: Women's Status and Prestige

Tuareg pastoral nomads today are predominantly seminomadic and practice, to varying degrees, mixed subsistence patterns. Most Tuareg live in the central Sahara and along its borders, in the Sahel. More nomadic Tuareg herd camels, sheep, goats, cattle, and donkeys. They are Muslims of Berber origin. Most Tuareg of the Air Mountain region in Niger originated in the Fezzan and other areas of Libya. Eight politically distinct descent groups (drum groups) all speak mutually intelligible dialects of a Berber-derived language, Tamajaq, and are designated by geographic region. Two of these, Kel Ajjer and Kel Ahaggar, are the northern Tuareg in Algeria. The other six—Kel Adar, Kel Air, and Kel Geres, Iwllemmeden Kel Dennek, and Iwllemmeden Kel Ataram, and Kel Tademaket—live on the southern fringes of desert in Mali, Niger, and Burkina Faso, and are the southern Tuareg. Within the Kel Air are the political confederations of Kel Ewey, Kel Ferwan, and Kel Fadey, those groups emphasized in the present essay.

Precolonial social organization was divided into free nobles, religious scholars, tributaries, smiths/artisans, and servile peoples. In most regions, slavery was abolished by the mid-twentieth century.

In general, many Tuareg women enjoy considerable rights and privileges. They are not sequestered, do not veil their faces (although Tuareg men do), and have much social and economic independence and freedom of movement. Separation of the sexes is relatively minimal. Men and women regularly meet and socialize in public. Women are singers and musicians, and organizers of many social events, such as drum playing and dance gatherings, which feature much flirting and courtship. Throughout their lives, many Tuareg women enjoy freedom of choice in sexual involvement and actively pursue romantic preferences (King 1903:280; Rodd 1926:174–175). They may regularly have male visitors, though not always lovers, when their husbands are absent (Rodd 1926:174–175); Nicolas 1946:225; Lhote 1955:335; Murphy 1964; Claudot-Hawad 1993).

Although many of these gender roles and relationships apply to most Tuareg, there is the need to refine and specify, rather than generalize, interpretation of some aspects of Tuareg women's status. Many Tuareg groups display variation in gender arrangements according to relative degrees of nomadism and sedentarization, devotion to official Islam, and regional and confederational differences, as well as age, kinship roles, and social stratum origins. The Kel Ewey *ineslemen* clans of maraboutique Islamic scholars, for example, attempt to control their women slightly more by placing greater emphasis upon virginity and application of Koranic inheritance laws. Even among these clans, however, women own property, are not secluded, and go about unveiled and relatively freely visit and receive male visitors, and although extramarital affairs are less tolerated, men, not women, are fined or punished in reprisals (Rasmussen 1994, 1998a, 1998b).

There are gender transformations over the life course: for example, age and marital status make a difference in women's status, prestige, and property ownership, as well as work and economic independence. Older women enjoy security as mothers-in-law and grandmothers. They specialize in herbal medicine, divination, and bone-setting healing specialties. Urbanization and nation-state policies also influence Tuareg women's status, roles, prestige, and economic bases of power. For example, much property in the Saharan town of Agadez is not independently owned by the married woman, but merged together with that of her husband in civic records.

There are, moreover, seasonal variations in residential spatial arrangements that symbolically convey gender-related socioeconomic processes. In seminomadic carvanning Air villages, the basic residential unit, *eghiwan*, is highly flexible, undergoing fission and fusion according to season and subsistence strategy. Men are often gone from five to seven months a year on caravan trade and migrant labor. Young, unmarried girls and older post-childbearing-age women often go out and establish temporary camps with their herds, intermittently for four months during the dry season; elderly women in the rainy season leave for several weeks to gather leaves and roots and grasses for sauces, and herbal healers are often absent on trips to collect medicines from trees on Mount Bagzan.

During the cold, dry caravanning season, women construct their tent doors to face outward, toward the compounds of their female relatives, the more matrifocal or matricentric space reflecting these women's greater cooperation and sharing at this time. In contrast, in the hot and rainy seasons while many men are at home, the women close these doors and construct doors opening onto the interior courtyard of the nuclear-household compound; the emphasis here is more patrifocal, and patricentric, reflecting greater focus within the nuclear household. Ties with maternal female kin become less emphasized during this time (women visit each other less, and do more housework such as cooking within their own kitchen while husbands are at home).

Most women prefer monogamous unions, and polygyny is a rare occurrence, except among some prominent chiefs, Islamic scholars, and prosperous, more sedentarized gardeners and merchants. I frequently heard women in monogamous marriages tease those who were co-wives

about polygyny, and many women initiate divorce upon husbands' attempts to contract polygynous marriages. Polygynous men try to avoid co-wives' jealousy by installing wives in separate compounds and even distant villages. Co-wives never share cooking facilities or sleep in the same compound. A widow or divorcee may become a household head in advanced age; if younger, she usually returns to her parental household.

There is a tendency toward late marriages and preference for political marriages within the descent group or *tawsit* and chiefly among families in many noble groups. The idea in Tuareg marriage is an enduring relationship based upon romantic love. Tuareg often say they prefer to marry cross-cousins because the joking relationship that ordinarily obtains between them is conducive to a strong marital bond (Bernus 1981:149). On the other hand, some such marriages do not last because some Tuareg say close cousins continue to "feel like brother and sister" (Nicolaisen 1963; Murphy 1964). As the marriage stabilizes, the joking relationship is supposed to become a more serious relationship of mutual respect, with some aspects of a respect/reserve relationship in public between the spouses. Name avoidance does not entail wife-to-husband deference among the Tuareg as Schlegel (1975:167–168) inferred from the data available on Tuareg through the HRAF (Human Relations Area Files). The use of teknonymy and sobriquets is symmetric, applying to both sexes. The term for a new spouse is "friend," and later on, "wife" and "husband." Wife-to-husband deference is not a feature of Tuareg society, as it is among the Hausa, for example, where a wife ritually kneels when serving her husband. Tuareg women do not ritually kneel, bow their heads, or engage in any other extreme gestures of subservience to their husbands. Husbands, at least ideally, should regularly "defer" to their wives' wishes about as much as wives to husbands, in a mutual-respect relationship. One man, for example, commented that he had been considering polygyny, but had decided to refrain from taking a co-wife in deference to his wife's wishes, because he "respected" her. A woman may show her contempt for her husband's behavior by returning to her mother's camp, removing the tent and its contents, and leaving the man without a shelter. Direct expression of anger on the part of a man toward his wife is considered shameful.

The creation of a home and its furnishing in nomadic societies is usually part of the dowry institution: this occurs in the context of marriage. Tuareg women receive their nuptial tent as part of their dowry. It is constructed communally on the evening of the wedding by elderly female relatives of the bride, and torn down and reconstructed to be larger on each successive evening of the seven-day wedding ritual (Ramussen 1997). A tent thus comes into being with the wedding ritual, and is a metaphor for the institution of the family. Because descent is bilateral and the tent is matrilineally defined and transmitted, the tent also becomes a metaphor for matriliny and an allegory for maternity (Prussin 1995:92). A woman has the same status in her own tent as she has in her mother's; she is at home in both. Conversely, a man is a guest in his wife's tent.

The wedding tent, which after the marriage will be the tent of the newly married couple's residence, is erected near the camp of the bride's family. For seven days, this tent remains empty during the day, occupied by the couple only at night. The two spouses subsequently may choose to move with their tent to the husband's family camp. Since the tent is inherited matrilineally, it moves from one camp to another, as when the bride's relatives bring her tent to her husband's camp or village. An unmarried man usually lives in a straw and mat conical building called *tettrem*, or in more sedentarized communities, in an adobe mud house. These single men's buildings are located either within or just adjacent to their parents' compound. Traditionally, the only men who owned their own tent were noble drum-group chiefs. So Tuareg men and women do not inhabit tents in the same way. In general, only a married woman can have a tent. Thus the number of tents in a camp or village generally indicates the number of married women.

In Tuareg culture, the nuptial tent is therefore women's property, brought to the marriage as dowry, a central symbol in the wedding, and used as the married couple's sleeping room, but

also much more: it symbolizes the traditional ideal of monogamy. Recently, however, many men have been constructing adobe mud houses that the married man owns. These houses now often stand next to the tent owned by a married woman within the married couple's household compound (Rasmussen 1994, 1996, 1997). The more nomadic Tuareg groups still count women as owners of compounds, as well as tents, in identifying the household compounds. But the semisedentarized Kel Ewey have begun to identify compounds by the names of husbands, as belonging to men, as they do the men's adobe mud houses in many of these compounds, standing next to the women's tents. These processes indicate some important changes in gender roles, status, and power upon sedentarization, which disrupts the property balance between the sexes. To what extent, then, does the tent confer women's control? The key issue, as Moore (1988:52–53) points out, is the relationship between women's productive and reproductive roles, in the descent and inheritance system.

Legal/Jural Rights, Property, Descent, and Inheritance

The Tuareg official political structure is male-dominated. Among the more nomadic groups, the camping group (*eghiwan*) is an extended family headed by a male elder (*amghar*). In more sedentarized, seminomadic groups this term *eghiwan* refers to the village or hamlet, which may include a number of families, many of whom are related, and today often also includes households whose members vary in occupation and degree of nomadism, sometimes combining or alternating between several different subsistence forms (for example, a man of diverse social stratum origins might practice caravan trade, herding, oasis gardening, and migrant labor within a single lifetime, in different seasons). Allied descent groups comprise a drum group or confederation under the power of a drum chief called *ettebel*, a legitimate male successor from the dominant noble group within it. The confederation is socially stratified into noble and vassal named groups.

Most Tuareg descent groups are bilateral, combining patrilineal influences from Islam with local matrilineal institutions. Many descent groups trace their origins matrilineally to female ancestresses or culture heroines, although some more devoutly Muslim groups and men in general tend to downplay these ancestresses and emphasize patrilineal descent and male ancestors or culture heroes. For example, many Kel Ewey Tuareg men and marabouts in rural Air communities where I conducted research mentioned Boulkhou, a patrilineal ancestor of the current *ettebel,* as their important founder. He had sunk the first well, built a mosque, and resisted enemies in battles in that region. By contrast, many women tended to emphasize Tagurmat, the female ancestor of the Kel Igurmaden descent group within the Kel Ewey confederation, who in a myth gave birth to twin daughters who founded the professions of herbalism and Islamic/Koranic healing. The Kel Fadey say their people descend from two sisters who came from the east, bringing with them livestock, herds, and a large wooden drum (the drum, kept by the chief's wife, is used to call the tribal sections together for political or military action) (Worley 1992:56). The Kel Fadey reckon their most important kinship connections through women (matrilineally), so a child's closest relationships are usually with his or her mother's people, especially the mother's brother. In the past, both property inheritance and succession to the chieftainship followed maternal lines, from a man to his sister's sons and daughters.

A recurring question in Tuareg ethnography has been the extent to which Tuareg practice matrilineal inheritance and descent and succession. In matriliny, theoretically, mothers and sisters of heirs enjoy status. A problem here is the use of the term to mean certain institutions, or "society" and "culture" in general (Oxby 1977). Also often ignored are variations among the different Tuareg groups and according to social context. Thus the issue becomes, which kin links are most important and what factors other than kinship are important in determining relationships between the generations and the sexes? Descent group (*tawsit*) allegiance is, in practice, through the mother. Ideally, however, political office passes from father to son in all groups but the

Kel Geres, where it goes from maternal uncle to sister's son. Hence both matrilateral and patrilateral kin ties are important. There are also important criteria apart from kinship in political leadership: for example, wealth and personal qualities of leadership.

Women's property is passed down mainly from mother to daughter; men's, from father to son. Objects acquired by women before marriage include jewelry, blankets, a bed, other household items, and sometimes cloth and sandals. In the past, noble women brought a slave to their married household; today, rural noble women still inherit an attached smith/artisan client family. Inheritance of livestock is predominantly Koranic: daughters receive one-third to one-half of sons' shares. Children are considered, among most Air Tuareg, more important heirs than spouses and siblings. If there are only daughters, a brother receives the son's share. The mother's brother is a less significant figure in some groups than in others, but everywhere the mother's brother/sister's son tie features, at minimum, affection, and frequent gifts, and security in assistance. The sibling tie in fact sometimes competes with the husband-wife tie. Each spouse, regardless of postmarital residence, if possible spends much time during the day (for example, eating meals) at the residence of his/her own kin. Individuals often try to return to maternal kin in latter years of life. Women often refuse to follow husbands to remote places, for example, to start new gardens, and divorce often ensues (although this may be changing recently). Men are present with their sisters during the funeral sacrifice of meat in the event of their sisters' children's death. An older sister is described as "like a mother" to her younger brother; older brothers are supposed to take care of younger sisters, accompanying them on travel and assisting them in legal cases. Brothers and sisters are supposed to be allies, and brothers ideally should look out for sisters' legal and other interests. Often, brothers do support sisters upon the divorce, and also contribute to the support of widowed sisters' children. The father's sibling group is equated with the father, as a source of authority and possible conflict; the mother's sibling group, by contrast, is a source of love and aid, generosity, and support. A man has the right to take domestic animals from his true and classificatory mother's brothers. He must inform them of this act through a third party.

Some Tuareg say, "It is the stomach that colors the child." Another source of shared maternal identity is breast milk: those who are nursed by the same woman cannot marry. Possession by spirits not curable by Koranic verses is believed to be inherited matrilineally from mother to daughter in breast milk. Formerly, matrilineal clans were associated with specific totems. Sultan Goma allotted land to noble women in these clans in order to prevent it from passing out of the clan's ownership (Nicolaisen 1963; Norris 1972, 1975). Many Tuareg believe that the maternal nephew inherits intelligence from his maternal uncle. But Kel Ewey do not use separate kinship terms for a maternal versus paternal nephew; they refer to both as *tegazay*.

Nowadays, however, the concept of maternal kinship identity tends to be submerged in most legal practice. Koranic and patrilineal influence extend to naming, ideas about children's affiliation and identity, and marriage. Men refer to the offspring of a polygynous man and one of his co-wives as the "children of men." They tend to disparage an older form of naming a girl "daughter of" (*oult*) as "only done with an illegitimate child." Rural women are now called Madame plus the name of husband's father as surname, in postal addresses, clinic rosters, and school registration. Illegitimacy is considered shameful, antisocial, and greatly stigmatizing to the mother. A child belongs to the descent group or clan of his or her father. Men insist that the secret, Tamajaq name which older female relatives bestow on the child in the unofficial naming ritual the evening before the official Islamic naming by the father and marabout at the mosque, is "not important, it means nothing," but women dispute this, saying the latter name is as important to the child's identity as the Arabic, Koranic name. Women's property is sometimes subject to dispute and challenge in Koranic-based rulings by marabouts. For example, although a woman has the right to eject her husband from her tent, a woman's bridewealth is only reimbursed to the person the marabout rules is not at fault in divorce; many marabouts rule the woman at fault if she requests divorce to protest polygyny.

Nonetheless women's opinions are highly valued, and they are normally consulted by men on decisions that affect the life of the camp or village (Bernus 1981:146–147). Yet there are some contexts in which women defer to some men: namely, before Islamic scholars and important chiefs, and toward elders in general, particularly those on the patrilineal side. Female herbal medicine women, for example, referred patients to marabouts for diagnosis of illness, more often than vice versa. But women participate in public discussions over matters of concern to the group, represent themselves in legal cases, and exert great influence in the public sphere. For example, a smith/artisan woman in Agadez held a position as head of a smith/artisan women's cooperative, and also gave radio addresses on women's health issues.

Tuareg women generally enjoy a high degree of economic independence, since they own significant property in livestock. Under optimum conditions, therefore, livestock does constitute great security for women. But this can fluctuate according to climate and nation-state conditions. During droughts and armed conflicts, many herds were diminished, lost, or dispersed. Elderly women often survive off herds of donkeys, which are easy to care for (only requiring salt licks and free roaming for water) and which they sell off gradually at markets. A number of authors (Bernus 1981; Casajus 1987; Claudot-Hawad 1993; Keenan 1977; Lhote 1955; Murphy 1964), correctly I believe, have noted the importance of a custom among the Tuareg that allows women to acquire more property in livestock, and sometimes date palms, than they would normally have right to under Koranic law. This practice, known as *akh hudderan*, allows an individual to make a pre-inheritance gift of livestock to female relatives, usually daughters, sisters, and nieces, which they then own and control corporately. This property cannot be sold or otherwise disposed of.

Additionally, Tuareg women accumulate livestock through important gifts (*alkhalal*) from both parents and other relatives after birth, which form the basis of their own herds. Women may receive outright gifts of livestock from consanguine kin throughout their lives, and in all marriages after the first, it is usually the wife herself who accepts the bridewealth (*taggalt*). As a result of these gifts and pre-inheritance practices, therefore, some women under optimum conditions (of plentiful pasture, regular rainfall, cooperative male kin and spouses, and peace) may indeed become quite wealthy in livestock. Even in the recent droughts and warfare, some women manage to support themselves. In more prosperous and peaceful eras, it was not uncommon for a woman to be wealthier than her husband. But it is difficult to assess the extent to which women still enjoy these ideal property arrangements, in the light of recent upheavals. More nomadic nobles, in particular, have lost much property over the past twenty years. But these losses affect both sexes, not solely women. There are strong pressures to settle down and practice oasis gardening more extensively, and there is evidence that women's bases of property are increasingly altered by all these processes. In semisedentarized communities, for example, men's houses complicate property disputes on divorce. For example, after the divorce of Aghaly and Mariama (pseudonyms), Aghaly retained his mud house and Mariama her tent in the same compound on the same land. At first, the ex-husband did not want to leave his house. The couple took their case to the secular courts in Agadez, which ruled a compromise: each party changed the door on his or her respective structure, so that the buildings faced the exterior, rather than the interior courtyard. Aghaly ate his meals at his mother's home. This solution divided the property and also saved the divorced couple from daily interaction. Aghaly eventually moved back into his old house adjacent to his parents' compound in a neighboring village (Rasmussen 1996:18).

Some married women residing virilocally (with the husband's family) have very different spatial and social arrangements in their new home, which affect work and authority patterns. In initial postmarital uxorilocality (residence with the wife's family), most visiting and sharing of resources and work occurs between maternally related women (mothers and sisters and daughters); whereas in virilocal residence, the wife is more isolated from her own kin, and more dependent upon her husband and his family. She is also subject to a strict reserve relationship with her parents-in-law. She also obtains a bit less assistance with household tasks from her sisters-in-law than she would from her own sisters.

Sexual Division of Labor

Domestic work in more nomadic groups takes a minimum of women's time. Mothers can support pregnancy and breastfeed children while performing the physically demanding work of pastoralism, milking the livestock, and packing and moving the tents they own. One noble woman in a seminomadic village, the daughter of a local chief, has managed her own small store since 1997. Another woman has a small restaurant on a road from Agadez into the rural area. Older children usually watch small children and toddlers. Infants may be carried on the mother's back while she is working. There is little house cleaning to contend with. The tent needs to have the wall mats adjusted several times a day as the direction of the wind changes (Worley 1988:278), and it is swept out occasionally. Fresh clean sand is gathered at intervals for the tent floor. Grinding and sifting and crushing millet and other cereals is arduous work that all women, nowadays, do (in the past, slaves did this labor). In nomadic Kel Fadey camps, Worley reported that this task takes approximately two hours a day (Worley 1988:278); in the seminomadic villages of the Kel Ewey Tuareg, I noticed, pounding millet took up far more of women's time, up to approximately 90 percent of their day's work. In more sedentarized communities, therefore, women's time is taken up more extensively with food-processing work within the compound than is more nomadic women's time; these latter, by contrast, often circulate more widely away from the compound herding their own livestock at outlying pastures. Other cereal grains were traditionally crushed on a flat stone. Recently, several mills have been built in this area and women no longer crush corn and wheat on flat stone as I had observed them do earlier in my research (in the 1970s and 1980s). In all Tuareg rural communities, women's communal work parties do mat and tent construction and repair, together in reciprocal gatherings called *gaya* (derived from Hausa).

Subsistence work regularly takes many women outside the village or camp for the collection of firewood, gathering of wild grains, berries, and other plants, and the daily drawing of water at a well, which may be several miles from the camp. Women view these tasks differently, however: some welcome tasks such as herding and gathering for the freedom they confer; others, however, view going to the well and herding as hot, arduous tasks. In semisedentarized communities around Mount Bagzan, some women are described as "housewives" (called by the French term *menageres*). These women have given up herding (though not always herd ownership), and have relegated this task to kinspersons. A few gardeners' wives have even given up their tents. Reasons given for this included scarcity of materials, and also no further need for a tent in the presence of a husband's house. But most women still own and use tents, even alongside men's houses, and still own herds. Some women married to gardeners are giving up herding and (if smiths) leatherwork, as well. Very few women individually own gardens, which are traditionally inherited and owned mostly by men (though a few women have date-palms through matrilineal *akh huderan* inheritance). Upon herds' depletion in drought, theft, or war, women are at a disadvantage because livestock herds are more difficult to reconstitute than oasis gardens. Traditionally, planting was done by men and harvesting done only by elderly women; recently, however, over the summer of 1998 I noticed some hints of change in these patterns. A development agency had established a women's garden cooperative, and some women had begun enclosing and gardening in this designated space, known as the "women's garden (enclosure)" (*afarag n tchidoden*). In order to prevent erosion, a fence was being constructed: each woman is paid an amount to participate in the work party, provide wood, and construct the fence. A female "president" supervises this project, in which the women take up a collection (250 CFA or approximately 50 cents each) from each household to build a well (cost: 25,000 CFA, approximately $50). When the well is completed, the project organization will give the group an animal. Women have also recently been involved in projects selling millet on the market

in Agadez. It remains to be seen how extensively Tuareg women will pursue gardening tasks on these semisedentarized oases. This may constitute a significant departure from women's traditional work patterns, and become a new property base and source of economic power.

Many women who own animals, however, continue to herd small livestock—goats, sheep, and donkeys, and on occasion, camels when men are absent. Women milk the small livestock and process the milk into cheese and butter, consuming them within the household and also selling some of the surplus to travelers and other local residents. Women's subsistence work is considered critical in Tuareg pastoral production, and they must be capable of taking over some of the men's work on occasion when men are absent. In the 1960s, 1970s, and 1980s, for example, many young men left in exile from the droughts of 1973 and 1984, in search of jobs. In 1990, the Tuareg rebellion broke out. Therefore many young marriageable men became marginalized economically and politically, resisted some elders' efforts to arrange matches, or found it difficult to raise bridewealth to marry at all. A few men are beginning to sell Tuareg silver and leatherwork items abroad in international art fairs. Other men work on farms in Italy and Libya. Male migrant workers are forbidden by Libya to send or bring money home to Niger, however. So they must hide it, and/or wives must support their families on their own at home. Many women, not solely smith/artisans, do this by making basketry and embroidery for sale in craft shops in Niger and France, though very few Tuareg women travel to France.

Smith/artisan men and women derive much income from arts and crafts. Metal and woodworking are smith men's work; most leatherworking is smith women's work. Women of diverse social origins tan hides, but mostly smith/artisan women cut and embroider them. Smith/artisan women in rural areas obtain cash and food gifts through leatherworking and rites-of-passage services for nobles. In Saharan towns, women smiths continue to do leatherwork, but with fewer raw materials, which cost more in the sedentarized setting, and also fewer customers, for demand there is lower than in rural communities where herders and gardeners need hide containers and implements, and tourists and functionaries buy more metal jewelry than leatherwork. Recently, some religious and human rights and aid organizations in France purchased millet while it was at a low price and gave it to Air Tuareg groups to store during the period of higher millet prices. These organizations also bring art objects made in workshops (by both men and women specialists) to sell in France at fairs. They sponsor women's basketry and weaving workshops, where artists modify traditional designs for sale in France.

CONCLUSIONS

Socioeconomic and Political Changes; Implications; Issues and Questions Raised for Future Trends

One of the key changes affecting the organization of nomadic pastoralism is the nomads' loss of autonomy after incorporation into sedentary nation-states, in the wake of the military advantage of sedentary states and revolutions in transportation technology during the past century (Barfield 1993:207). Upon sedentarization, there is disruption of traditional ties and undermining of important sources of defense and security. As men are increasingly obliged to travel as migrant laborers and children are sent to school, the workload of women extends from their traditional routines to a heavier involvement in supplementary tasks. In Niger, colonial and postcolonial eras saw pastoralist border zones farmed, depleting the soil and disrupting ecological and socioeconomic balance and relations between groups and lands. Mobility has been curtailed, censuses, schools and taxes imposed by colonial governments, and by postcolonial central state governments. Sometimes these have imposed a patrilineal bias. Tuareg are unique among pastoralists in the enduring significance their matrilineal institutions have for gender roles and relations between the sexes. Although these remain significant in the bilateral system, there is evidence that matriliny is under duress. This is shown by the transformations in property balance described in this article and elsewhere (Rasmussen 1994, 1996, 1997, 1998). It is also shown in Gast's (1992:151–172) description of Tuareg cultural

encounters with more powerful neighbors: nation-state policies toward Tuareg nomads brought many workers, functionaries, soldiers, and tourists into rural Tuareg communities. Often, they were ignorant of and disrespectful toward traditional beliefs and practices; for example, they misunderstood evening festival and courtship customs as opportunities to seduce women, whereas traditionally, Tuareg cultural values emphasize music, poetry, flirting, visits, and conversation without necessarily including sexual intercourse. Some camps along routes became labeled by outsiders as places of license and prostitution (Gast 1996:169). In some respects, then, Tuareg women appear to have become the wards of men in encounters with outside males, and in national systems of registration/ naming, food relief and medical distribution programs, taxation and census counts. However, as shown, there are also new opportunities—in new cooperative agencies and projects offering some benefits for women, as well as men.

The question raised is how nomadic pastoral Tuareg women actively respond to forces of sedentization, urbanization, and nationalism. Do they gain or lose? How? For example, women can use the urban setting to escape from an extended household ruled over by a mother-in-law. It is therefore hazardous to generalize too sweepingly about pastoralism, women, and gender, or to base observations solely upon structural as opposed to situational meanings and practices. Pastoral nomadic societies display a wide range of variation in economics, culture, and gender relations, and divergent transformations. Rather than building models and typologies, anthropologists need to deconstruct and refine pastoral and gender-related categories and processes.

Notes

1. In these projects—on spirit possession, aging and the life course, herbal healers, and rural and urban smith/artisans, I gratefully acknowledge assistance from Fulbright Hays (1983,1998); Wenner Gren Foundation for Anthropological Research (1991,1995,1998); Social Science Research Council (1995); National Geographic Society for Research and Exploration (1995,1998); Indiana University (1983), and University of Houston (1991).

2. For example, Mohanty (1992) criticizes western feminists for essentializing women's experience regardless of race, class, or nationality. Mohanty faults western feminists for

universalizing women's oppression, as well. She argues that western feminists psychologize complex and often contradictory historical and cultural realities that mark differences among women. Differences among women need to be engaged rather than transcended. She also warns against globalizing women as victims; there is the need to acknowledge women's active agency. Yet feminists in these areas are diverse; they come from various schools of thought depending on their national and cultural orientations.

3. Despite very valuable work on women and gender in the Muslim world, there have been some tendencies to deploy "Islam" and "Muslim" as a gloss for very diverse cultural interpretations of official religion, their sharing of common themes notwithstanding. Mernissi's (1987) famous analysis of gender relations in Moroccan society is complemented and enriched by perspectives from scholars on other Muslim societies in Africa, for example Afonja (1986).

4. Pastoralist societies therefore break down the assumed dichotomy of private/public or domestic/public domains, a tenacious concept in some early feminist anthropology (Rosaldo and Lamphere 1974) later critiqued in more recent anthropology of gender studies (Ong 1987).

5. These observations raise interesting issues. For example, traditionally, men's honor depended upon women's praise music upon their victorious return from battles; thus women control men's reputations. Women's praise songs of men often welcomed them after successful raids or migrant labor or caravan trade, but women could also mock and scorn men who returned less victorious or without money. Women still hold power over men's reputations, but many men have not returned victorious or wealthy in recent years. Some men have attempted to find social recognition through participation in the 1990–95 nationalist/separatist military conflict. Much new music of the Tuareg rebellion composed by both sexes, as well as women's traditional songs, perhaps is responding to these new predicaments and in effect, conveys men's and women's efforts to reconstruct social prestige and independent socioeconomic status in Tuareg gender-role relationships.

References Cited

Afonja, S. 1986. Changing Modes of Production and the Sexual Division of Labor among the Yoruba. In *Women's Work*, E. Leacock and H. Safa, eds. South Hadley, MA: Bergin and Garvey.

Barfield, Thomas J. 1993. *The Nomadic Alternative*. Upper Saddle River, NJ: Prentice Hall.

Barlow, Tani. 1996. Theorizing Women: Funu, Guojia, Jiating. (Chinese Women, Chinese State, Chinese Family). In *Feminism and History*, Joan W. Scott, ed. Oxford: Oxford University Press.

Barth, Fredrik. 1961. *Nomads of South Persia: The Basseri Tribe of the Khamseh Confederacy*. Oslo: Oslo University Press.

Beck, Lois. 1978. Women among Qashqai Nomadic Pastoralist in Iran. In *Women in the Muslim World*, Lois Beck and Nikki Keddie eds. Cambridge, MA.: Harvard University Press.

Bernus, Edmond. 1981. *Touaregs Nigeriens: Unité Culturelle et Diversité Regionale d'un Peuple Pasteur*. Paris: Office de la Recherche Scientifique et Technique Outre-Mer.

Boulding, Elise. 1976. *The Underside of History*. Boulder, CO: Westview Press.

Butler, Judith. 1990. *Gender Trouble*. New York: Routledge Press.

Casajus, Dominique. 1987. *La Tente dans l'Essuf*. London and Paris: Cambridge.

Claudot-Hawad, Hélène 1993. *Les Touaregs: Portrait en Fragments*. Aix-en-Provence: Edisud.

Davison, Jean. 1997. *Gender, Lineage, and Ethnicity in Southern Africa*. Boulder, CO: Westview Press.

di Lauretis, Teresa. 1984. *Alice Doesn't: Feminism, Semiotics, Cinema*. Bloomington: Indiana University Press.

Di Leonardo, Michaela. 1990. *Gender at the Crossroads of Knowledge*. Berkeley: University of California Press.

Evans-Pritchard, E. E. 1956 *Nuer Religion*, Oxford: Oxford University Press.

Flax, Jane. 1993. *Disputed Subjects: Essays on Psychoanalysis, Politics, and Philosophy*. New York: Routledge.

Gaidzanwa, R. B. 1985. *Images of Women in Zimbabwean Literature*. Harere: College Press.

Gast, Marcel. 1992. Relations Amoureuses chez les Kel Ahaggar. In *Amour, Phantasmes, et Sociétés en Afrique du Nord et au Sahara*, Tassadit Yacine, ed. Paris: L'Harmattan-Awal.

Hutchinson, Sharon. 1996. *Nuer Dilemmas*. Berkeley: University of California Press.

Keenan, Jeremy. 1977, *Tuareg: People of Ahaggar*. New York: St. Martin's Press.

King, William J. Harding. 1903. *A Search for the Masked Tawaraks*. London: Smith, Elder and Co.

Kondo, Dorinne. 1990. *Crafting Selves*. Chicago: University of Chicago Press.

Lhote, Henri. 1955. *Les Touaregs du Hoggar*. Paris: Payot.

Mannathoko, C. 1992. Feminist Theories and the Study of Gender in Southern Africa. In *Gender in Southern Africa*, R. Meena, ed. Harare: SAPES Books.

Martin, M. Kay, and Barbara Voorhies 1975. *Female of the Species*. New York: Columbia University Press.

Meena, R. 1992. Gender Research/Studies in Southern Africa: An Overview. In *Gender in Southern Africa: Conceptual and Theoretical Issues*, R. Meena, ed. Harare: SAPES Books.

Mernissi, Fatima. 1987. Beyond the Veil: Male-Female Dynamics in *Modern Muslim Society*. Bloomington: Indiana University Press.

Mohanty, C.T. 1992. Feminist Encounter: Locating the Politics of Experience. In *Destabilizing Theory: Contemporary Feminist Debates*, M. Barrett and A. Phillips, eds. Palo Alto: Stanford University Press.

Moore, Henrietta. 1988. *Feminism and Anthropology*. Minneapolis: University of Minnesota Press.

Murphy, Robert. 1964. Social Distance and the Veil. *American Anthropologist* 66:1257–1274.

Nicolaisen, Johannes. 1963. *Ecology and Culture of the Pastoral Tuareg*. Copenhagen: Royal National Museum.

Nicolas, Francis. 1946. *Tamesna: Les Ioullemmeden de l'Est, ou Tuareg Kel Dinnik, Cercle de T'awa—Colonie du Niger*. Paris: Imprimerie Nationale.

Norris, H. T. 1972. *Saharan Myth and Saga*. Oxford: Clarendon Press.

———. 1975. *The Tuaregs: Their Islamic Legacy and Its Diffusion in the Sahel*. Warminster, England: Aris and Phillips.

O'Kelly, Charlotte G. and Larry S. Carney 1986. *Women and Men in Society: Cross-Cultural Perspectives on Gender Stratification*. Belmont, CA: Wadsworth Publishing Company.

Ong, Aihwa. 1987. *Spirits of Resistance and Capitalist Discipline: Factory Women in Malaysia*. Albany: State University of New York Press.

Ortner, Sherry. and Harriet Whitehead, eds. 1981. *Sexual Meanings*. Cambridge: Cambridge University Press.

Oxby, Clare. 1978. Sexual Division and Slavery in a Tuareg Community. Ph.D. dissertation, London School of Economics.

Probyn, Elspeth. 1990. Travels in the Postmodern: Making Sense of the Local. In *Feminism/Postmodernism*, Linda J. Nicholson, ed. New York: Routledge.

Prussin, LaBelle. 1995. *African Nomadic Architecture: Space, Place, and Gender*. Washington, DC: Smithsonian Institution Press.

Rasmussen, Susan. 1992. Disputed Boundaries: Tuareg Discourse on Class and Ethnicity. *Ethnology* 31: 351–366.

———. 1994. Female Sexuality, Social Reproduction, and Medical Intervention: Kel Ewey Tuareg Perspectives. *Culture, Medicine, and Psychiatry* 18:433–462.

———. 1995. *Spirit Possession and Personhood among the Kel Ewey Tuareg*. Cambridge: Cambridge University Press.

———. 1996. Tuareg Tent as Field Space and Cultural Symbol. *Anthropological Quarterly*, 69:14–27.

———.1997. *The Poetics and Politics of Tuareg Aging: Life Course and Personal Destiny in Niger*. DeKalb, IL: Northern Illinois University Press.

———. 1998a. Within the Tent and at the Crossroads: Travel and Gender Identity among the Tuareg of Niger. *Ethos* 26:153–182.

———. 1998b. Only Women Know Trees: Medicine Women and the Role of Herbal Healing in Tuareg Culture. *Journal of Anthropological Research* 54:147–171.

Rodd, Francis, Lord of Rennell. 1926. *People of the Veil*. London: MacMillan and Co.

Rosaldo, Michele. and Louise Lamphere, eds. 1974. *Women, Culture, and Society*. Stanford: Stanford University Press.

Sanday, Peggy. 1981. *Female Power and Male Dominance: On the Origins of Sexual Inequality*. Cambridge: Cambridge University Press.

Schlegel, Alice. 1975. Three Styles of Domestic Authority: A Cross-Cultural Study. In *Being Female: Reproduction, Power, and Change*, Dana Raphael, ed. The Hague, Paris: Mouton Publishers.

Scott, Joan W. 1988. *Gender and the Politics of History*. New York: Columbia University Press.

Scott, Joan W. 1992. Experience. In *Feminists Theorize the Political*, Judith Butler and Joan W. Scott, eds. New York: Routledge.

Worley, Barbara. 1988. Bed Posts and Broad Swords: Tuareg Women's Work Parties and the Dialectics of Sexual Conflict. In *Dialectics and Gender: Anthropological Approaches*, Richard R. Randolph, David M. Schneider, and May N. Diaz, eds. Boulder: Westview Press.

———. 1992. Where All the Women Are Strong. *Natural History* 101 (11):54–64.

CRITICAL THINKING QUESTIONS

1. How do the Tuareg fit into the traditional anthropological definition of pastoralists?

2. How does Rasmussen define and use the concept of "gender" in her article?

3. What factors does the author cite as affecting the sexual division of labor among pastoralists? Give examples from the article.

4. Describe in outline form the basics of Tuareg culture.

5. In which domestic and economic activities do Tuareg women participate?

6. Describe, in terms of rights and privileges, the status of women in Tuareg culture. How does this differ from the status of women in other Muslim societies you have discussed or read about?

7. What impact has incorporation into modern nation-states had on Tuareg culture?

Spheres of Inheritance in Aughnaboy[1]

Elliott H. Leyton

This paper uses the concept of spheres to analyze the transmission of goods between the generations in Aughnaboy. It argues that a concept such as a sphere is necessary to unravel the complex patterns of inheritance in this rural sector of a complex Western industrial society, and it concludes that there are three spheres of inheritance; each sphere distinguished by the movement of different items through different modes of exchange, and each sphere characterized by a distinct ideology and a distinct pattern of flow.

The analysis of the patterns of inheritance is basic to social anthropology and few monographs published in the last thirty years have failed to make some reference to the mechanisms regulating this transmission. Within European studies, the material is surprisingly full; there does however appear to be great variation among different European societies regarding the conventions concerning the transmission of property. Among Campbell's Sarakatsani, for example, the family is a corporation controlling property in common—the elder brother succeeding not to the estate but to the office of leader—and from this property "are drawn the dowries of the daughters, which sometimes exceed in value the patrimony of a brother" (Campbell 1964:188). When the last of the daughters is married and division of the estate begins, each son is entitled to one share of the family herd, one additional share being reserved for the parents; this passes on their deaths to the youngest son, with whom they traditionally spend the remainder of their lives. The parents' share that passes to the youngest son is regarded as his compensation for caring for them in their old age, which, "although a sacred duty, is also in their declining years of mental and phys-

ical feebleness a considerable burden" (Campbell 1964:188). This contrasts with Arensberg and Kimball's (1940) County Clare, where inheritance was a structural hinge intimately linked with marriage, with the transfer of economic control during the life of the parents, and with the reformation of family ties as the new couple moved into the house and slowly established control of the household and farm. Here, only one son could be provided for on the farm—and one daughter married into another farm—and the remaining children "must travel." Contrasting with this pattern of patrilaterality and primogeniture is the complex clan system described by Fox (1966) for Tory Island, off the coast of County Donegal, where inheritance of land "is bilateral in the sense that both men and women can own and transmit land, and that all a person's children, regardless of sex, have a *claim* on his/her land." The situation in Aughnaboy differs once again partially because most of the villagers are wage laborers who possess relatively little property of major importance to pass on to the next generation, but, more importantly, because the complex local ideology distinguishes between different types of property and assigns separate norms and expectations to their transmission.

THE CONCEPT OF SPHERES

This paper uses the concept of spheres as explored by Bohannan (1955), Bohannan and Dalton (1965), and Barth (1967) to analyze the patterns of inheritance of all forms of property in one village in Northern Ireland—Aughnaboy. The notion of sphere of exchange has been most useful in the analysis of economic systems, spheres being distinguished by the movement of different items through different modes of exchange. Bohannan and Dalton (1965) have used the Trobriand material to exemplify this process and have shown that there are two transactional spheres, the *kula* exchange of treasure items on the basis of the principle of reciprocity, and the *gimwali* exchange of subsistence items on the market principle. Referring to the Darfur economy, Barth (1967) has discussed the unity within and the barriers between spheres and shown that the flow of goods and services is patterned in two discrete spheres, "one that embraces a large variety of material items . . . and is associated with the market . . . and another that exists for the exchange of labor and beer." These patterns exhibit the characteristics of spheres in that each constitutes a "set of freely exchangeable material items and services." In general, this work uses the concept of sphere in the context of exchange in an economic system. This paper attempts to pick up Barth's (1967) suggestion that it might be fruitful to apply the concept to the analysis of inheritance. In the empirical material presented below, I try to show that there are three spheres of inheritance in Aughnaboy: each sphere is characterized by the transmission of different material items, by a different ideology, and by a different statistical pattern regarding the actual direction of the transmission.

THE IDEOLOGY OF INHERITANCE IN AUGHNABOY

The material on which this analysis is based is taken from Aughnaboy, a Protestant laboring/fishing/farming village in Northern Ireland with a total population of 900, distributed among 259 households. The kinship system of Aughnaboy is bilateral with an agnatic bias, and cognates form what Goodenough (1955) and Fox (1965) call an "Ego-focused group," which is normally traced to second cousins. Each household, typically parents and their unmarried children, is related through its natal families to members of the wider kindred. Moral obligations of general kind—essentially an injunction to help all family and kindred when they are in need—are extended to the full range of kinsmen incorporated in the kindred, though the strength of these obligations tends to diminish at the peripheries of the kindred. A man's supreme obligations are to his parents and his children. Once his children have completed their education, these obligations include ensuring that his daughter "marry well" into a "decent" family capable of caring for them and that sons are placed in careers that will enable them to support their own children with pride and dignity. During his working life a man will, if he can afford it, loan or give money to his children. When his working life is over, and his income correspondingly reduced, it is expected that his children will reciprocate his gifts and attentions in ensuring that he is well housed and well clothed and able to face the prospect of old age and death in comfort and serenity.

A man's last act in life, an act whose repercussions do not make themselves felt until after his death, is to pass what property he has to his children or, lacking children, to members of his kindred. As it is his last act, it is also the discharge of his final obligation; accordingly, he must ensure that his property is passed with justice to the person or persons who, in Aughnaboy's ideology, are most entitled to it and deserve it the most. As such, a man has several fundamental duties to discharge when he is deciding who shall inherit his worldly goods. One is to provide as many of his children as possible with as many material goods as he can, and particularly to provide as many of his sons as is possible with the resources for their occupations—funds for the continuation of their education, or items of fixed capital such as trawlers, farms, or businesses. Additionally, he must ensure that his goods are so divided that they reflect the measure and quality of his love and esteem for the various members of his family and kindred; for inheritance is the appropriate mechanism to finally reward those who have done the most to earn his affection and trust. Thus, from the children's point of view, inheritance is not only a source of financial or material gain; it is also a source of psychic gain, for it is a measure of love and esteem. Finally, a man is obliged to ensure the well-being of his wife for the remainder of her widowhood and to provide for any of his daughters who may have remained unmarried or stayed at home to care for him during his old age. These basic obligations are reinforced by the state,[2] and government legislation holds a man responsible for maintaining four types of kin, regardless of the direction in which he wishes to will the remainder of his estate. No individual can refuse to provide for his wife until she remarries, his unmarried daughter until she marries, his infant son until he reaches the age of twenty-one and his mentally or physically disabled child until he or she is cured—unless it can be proven in court that the conduct of the dependent toward the deceased justifies this refusal.

Within the general context of the broad obligations I have described there are a number of additional ideals and preferences that influence the patterns of inheritance. One ideal is simply that no property of any kind should ever be passed beyond the range of recognized kin, that is, the kindred. Though no deviations from this ideal were recorded in Aughnaboy, the village is full of appalling tales of such occurrences, which are reputed to have happened in neighboring villages: here, sons stayed loyally unmarried at home working on their widowed father's farm, only to find the farm passing on his death not to the sons who so richly deserved it, but to some village trollop who had "entertained him" during his dotage. These stories, however, are clearly sanctions in the form of examples of moral depravity or expressions of nightmarish anxiety, for no specific named examples could ever be given by the villages. A second preference is what can be called the Lear principle, that is, that no property should be transferred until the death of the owner. The belief here is that money and property tie the children to their parents and to transfer these before one's death is to risk losing not only the control but also the affection and attentions of one's children. It is not just the actual transfer of goods that is delayed; the decision itself is often not made until the owner finds himself on his deathbed. Consequently, it is often necessary for relatives, usually sons, to compete with one another for the esteem of the owner until his death. This principle is closely followed in Aughnaboy, and the only exceptions occur when it is necessary for the individual to dispose of his property in order to obtain the old-age pension or the welfare benefits of national assistance. Thus, even when operational control of a farm or business affairs may have passed to the son, the retired father normally retains legal control of the enterprise—and social control of the son—unless his income is sufficiently low to necessitate formal transmission in order to obtain the pensions.

The final set of general ideals and preferences relevant to all spheres of inheritance concerns the priorities assigned to different types of kin. Essentially, the villagers use two sets of oppositions, oppositions of kinship category (cognate/affine, patrikin/matrikin) and oppositions of genealogical distance (family/kindred, first cousin/second cousin) to determine the relative strength of their obligations to a given kinsman. This method or reckoning obligation is of considerable importance to a man deciding which way his estate shall be willed, and it is worth examining these in greater detail. At the broadest level is the priority of cognates over all affines. This is an inflexible value that nevertheless gives rise to much anxiety in Aughnaboy, for the countryside is filled with stories—once again generally unsubstantiated—of men who gave their property without condition to their wives, who in turn remarried and "gave it to a stranger." Accordingly then, when there is a surviving spouse to be provided for, the property is normally passed directly to the children, with the proviso that the spouse be cared for "for her time," or it may be passed to the spouse with the provision that, on her death or remarriage, the property reverts to the owner's cognates. This is illustrated in the case of McKeague, a chronically unemployed laborer from Belfast, who, when he married Annie, came to live with her in her house in Aughnaboy. When Annie died she left her house to her son Henry, with the proviso that her husband be allowed to remain in the house until he died or remarried. Two years later, when McKeague remarried, he left the house.

A second principle here is the priority of "the name." If a man dies leaving no children, then those kindred who bear the same name—his brother's sons and his patrilateral parallel cousins—have "greater entitlement" to his property. This emphasis is, as we shall see below, of particular strength in the case of major items of fixed capital, such as farms or trawlers, for land is scarce, and the land that belongs to a man is what Buchanan (1958) has called "the object of his passionate attachment." A man's land is inextricably bound up with his being and substance, and as such it is inextricably stamped with his family's name. To "keep the name on the land" is a matter of great concern, and it is because of this that land is much more likely to pass to brother's son than to a sister's son, to a patrilateral parallel cousin than to any other cousin, for the former bear the same name and the latter do not.

The primary principle regulating inheritance however is the paramount significance of a man's family of marriage—of his sons and daughters—over all others; for it is here that his supreme obligations lie. It is not to be thought, however, that sons and daughters are undifferentiated, for there is a tendency to give rather more to sons than to daughters—for daughters have husbands of their own who can provide for them—and there is a tendency for the eldest son to receive more than the younger sons. It is concerning this latter expectation that consensus in the village fails, and it is this principle that contains the greatest inherent conflict. Some, including of course eldest sons, feel that eldest sons should be given preference in inheritance, that they have the "greatest entitlement" to major items of fixed capital, and that they are entitled to a somewhat larger share of whatever goods there may be to inherit. The majority of the villagers however (fifty-five percent of a sample of forty-three informants) feel that the property rightfully belongs to the son who "deserves it the most," to the son "that sticks to the old people the longest," and who takes the most devoted care of his parents. Such disunity of expectation is likely to produce conflict. In fact, however, of a recorded seventy-four disputes in Aughnaboy (see Leyton 1966), only three cases of major disputes over inheritance were recorded. The relevant illustration here concerns the two Pendennis brothers who did not speak to each other for twenty years after their father's shop went to the eldest son who had "been away working in England." The younger son felt that the shop was rightfully his because he had stayed behind and helped his father in the shop; the elder brother felt it rightfully belonged to him because he was the eldest son, and the "eldest son is the most entitled." However, serious disputes over inheritance are relatively rare in Aughnaboy.

This is partially because in relatively few cases is the sum involved considered to be of overriding concern, for there are few men of wealth in Aughnaboy, and a laborer is likely to leave goods with a total value ranging from £100 to £1,000. Thus, when Willy Tague died, a pensioner for more than twenty-five years, he left only his savings of £120, old pieces of furniture with almost no market value, and his clothing. When Hugh Wilson, a forty-seven-year-old lorry driver, died, he left his four-year-old Ford valued at some £300, savings of some £250, and his personal possessions and furniture. These are not estates of sufficient value to overstimulate the cupidity of the younger and more prosperous generation of Aughnaboy. Disputes over inheritance are also rare because the bulk of the major items of fixed capital, such as shops, trawlers, and farms, provide life styles that are not always attractive to young men. Many young sons of farmers, for example, despise farming and "want no part of it." Often, too, the inheritance of these major items tends to be solved gradually over the years, one son by inclination and agreement with his father and brothers gradually stepping into the role of prospective heir. But the absence of many serious disputes over inheritance is primarily a consequence of the fact that to quarrel over an inheritance is to risk alienating all future support of one's family and kindred; for to quarrel openly or vehemently about an inheritance is to expose oneself and one's family to the social disgrace that, in Aughnaboy, must accompany familial discord. For these reasons, though there may be, and often is, open competition and rivalry before a will is made, the bitterness and discord a will may provoke are normally repressed or denied in order to maintain stable relations with a man's primary source of support—his family and his kindred.

This lack of open discord does not denigrate the importance of inheritance in Aughnaboy, for it is in fact important in the lives of the villagers. But the loss of an inheritance is not irreparable, as it might be, for example, among Campbell's (1964) Sarakatsani shepherds who have few alternative sources of income; in Aughnaboy, men can and do become, without debilitating loss of face or income, wage laborers or employees rather than farmers or shopkeepers. Rather, to lose an inheritance is to be publicly insulted—for it implies lack of love and esteem—and to be deprived perhaps of added luxuries in one's life. But it is rarely a major economic catastrophe, for no father will see his child so afflicted.

INDIVIDUAL SPHERES OF INHERITANCE

I have described the inheritance ideology as essentially a familial one: property is only passed to the kindred when a man's family is old or dead; here, the matter of the name and genealogical "closeness" are the primary influences. The actual situation regarding the patterns of inheritance is more complex than this, and we must examine the individual spheres of inheritance. The three spheres can perhaps best be seen as falling at different points along a broad continuum. (1) Major items of fixed capital are at one end of the continuum and flow monosexually through males and within the family (eighty-two percent of recorded transmissions were within the family). (2) The sphere of money is at the other end of the continuum; it flows bisexually to and from both sexes and is even more likely to flow to members of the wider kindred than within the family (only forty-two percent of transmissions were within the family). (3) The sphere of houses falls at an intermediate point between the other spheres, falling halfway between the monosexual/bisexual and family/kindred extremes of the continuum (seventy-three percent of houses were transmitted within the family). Though the bulk of all inheritances in all spheres take place between parents and children and, less frequently, between siblings

(see Table 2, which shows that 149 of the 215 recorded inheritances occurred within the family), members of the kindred are still important, forty-four of the 215 inheritances involving extrafamilial kin. Table 1 summarizes the characteristics of the three spheres.

Sphere 1: Fixed Capital

This sphere includes such pieces of property as farms, businesses, and trawlers from which the owners derive their primary source of income. In general, the ideology regarding transmission within this sphere emphasizes the significance of the family, the name, and monosexuality through males. It is strongly believed that these capital items should remain within the family and within the name. Thus, if a man has no sons, "the mother's side drops out; a McPherson wants to leave it to a McPherson, holding it in the one name." Men wish to leave their farms and trawlers to their sons; if they have no sons, the emphasis on the family will force them to give it to their daughters; if they have no children, they prefer to give it to male members of their kindred who bear the same name. This monosexual and male/male emphasis is related to the ideas that occupational affairs are matters between men and that sons must be provided for before daughters, because daughters will marry men with other names who will provide for them. McLintock, a "big farmer" with more than 100 acres, had one son and one daughter. His son had married and gone into the civil service and ignored McLintock, whereas his daughter had married a relatively poor fisherman and "could have used the farm." But the farm

TABLE 1   Characteristics of the three spheres of inheritance in Aughnaboy

	Fixed Capital	Houses	Money	Totals
Within family	57	72	20	149
Between kindred	12	19	24	55
Between affines	0	7	4	11
Between nonkin	0	0	0	0
Totals	69	98	48	215
Male recipient	62	60	16	138
Female recipient	7	38	32	77
Totals	69	98	48	215

went to McLintock's son: "I want it kept in the name."

Within these general preferences, however, there are additional factors. As I have already mentioned, there is a widely held belief that the eldest son is "most entitled," but there is also a widely held and contrary belief that major items of property should go to the son who deserves it the most, to "whichever son was the best to the homestead, was the best to the father, and worked the hardest." This ambiguity is extended to nephews when there are no children, and to first cousins when there are neither nephews nor children. Consequently, villagers of the appropriate category of prospective heirs must go to considerable lengths to prove that they are the most deserving: "Both would be making strenuous efforts to get the farm. There'd be no scruples. There'd be a battle to get in with him. One of the family would be sitting up nights to get it from the other." Eldest sons then, though often given preference, do not invariably inherit. Their parents may believe that another son deserves it more; often the eldest son is unwilling to wait the many years until his father's death before he will fall heir to the enterprise, and he frequently takes up another occupation, passing the rights to the farm or business to a younger son. But it must be emphasized that these broad patterns of monosexuality and "keeping things in the name" are preferences and expectations, not rigid prescriptions—in fact, five of the twelve inheritances that went to members of the kindred went to those who did not bear the same name—and the pattern of transmission in any given case can be changed if circumstances or need dictate. Jack McCulla was a bachelor who lived in the back of his hardware shop. He had two nephews, Ned McCulla, his brother's son, and Hugh Leach, his sister's son. Normally, the need to keep the property in the name might automatically pass the shop and house to Jack's brother's son Ned; but Ned was a prosperous builder whereas Hugh was unemployed through no fault of his own. Recognizing the greater need of his sister's son, Jack willed the shop and attached house to Hugh. Hugh kept the shop and maintained it as an adequate source of income; his wife died shortly after the birth of the last of his three children—two sons and one daughter. When Hugh died after a

short illness in 1969, his children were all in their twenties and unmarried. The house was willed to his spinster daughter, who was most in need of a place to live, for she had no one else to care for her if the boys married; the shop was willed jointly to all three of his children.

On the whole however, the principles of family-centeredness and male/male monosexuality prevail in the flow of major items of fixed capital; this is illustrated in Table 1, which summarizes the actual behavior regarding the transfer of sixty-nine items of fixed capital. The fundamental obligations are that these must be kept in the family or, failing that, within the name. But this must be balanced against the "closeness" of the genealogical relationship, for a man is regarded as being colder to his sister's son than he is to his father's brother's son and closer to his daughter than to his brother's son. Thus, the order of preference tends to be eldest son/son/daughter/brother or brother's son/any sibling's child/ patrilateral parallel cousin/all other cousins. This is borne out in the actual transmissions, in which the vast majority flow from father to son, and the only substantial minorities to inherit major items of fixed capital are from father to daughter and from father's brother to brother's son. The cases given below illustrate the normal application of the principles dominant in the sphere of major items of fixed capital.

1. Abraham MacAlinden set up a business in the stone trade in the mid-nineteenth century—quarrying, cutting, and polishing local granite. Abraham had three sons: his eldest son Isaac inherited the stone business and the house, the largest piece of property owned by Abraham; the second son was given a small farm; and the third son inherited a small grocery that Abraham also owned. In the next generation, the house and stone business passed from Abraham's eldest son Isaac to Isaac's only son Russell. In addition, Isaac's two brothers, who had remained childless, passed the grocery and the farm to Russell on their deaths. Though actual control of the stone yard—which gives its owner an annual income in excess of £5,000—was in Russell's hands well before his father's death, no legal

provisions for this passage were made until shortly before his father's death—"I was the only son, it just drifted on from year to year."

2. A second case involves the inheritance of a fifty-five acre farm, with a present-day market value of approximately £15,000: Willy McAnn, whose father was a stonecutter, was interested in farming. Willy's father's brother, James, who was childless and a farmer, took Willy into his home as an adolescent and raised him, and Willy accordingly inherited James's farm. At Willy's death, the farm passed to his second son Geordie, who had stayed at home and not married, whereas Willy's two other sons were provided with smaller farms elsewhere in the district.

3. Charlie Fairleigh had two farms, with a combined market value of approximately £24,000. Charlie was survived by two sons and four daughters—three of the daughters had married, and the fourth had remained unmarried and stayed at home to "take care" of Charlie. Charlie left his largest farm, with a market value of some £16,000 to his eldest son (his youngest son was a builder with no interest in farming), and the smaller £8,000 farm to the daughter who had remained single and looked after him. The remaining son and three daughters were each given a token sum of £30, which infuriated them and, indeed, left the family in a state of extreme tension. Nevertheless, the community regarded the inheritance as a just one, if unnecessarily unkind to the remaining children.

Sphere 2: Houses

The sphere of houses falls at an intermediate point between the family-centered and monosexual male/male sphere of fixed capital and the bilateral and bisexual sphere of money (which flows to kindred as well as to the family). The primary criteria on the basis of which houses are transmitted are "deserts" and "need": a house should go to whomever deserves it the most or needs it the most, and matters of "the name" are relatively unimportant. Houses are not regarded as having the same value as major items of fixed capital or large sums of money, and the rivalry

for houses is muted in comparison. Houses in Aughnaboy are of relatively little financial value—the market value of the average workman's cottage is in the range between £400 and £1,000—and, more important, cheap rented housing is readily available through the housing trust, the county council, and private landlords, with rents ranging from ten to forty shillings per week. This does not suggest that the villagers place no value on houses, for they do, and there is a sentimental value attached to "the home place" where the family was raised. But because alternatives are readily available, villagers rarely feel that houses are worth fighting over and disturbing the delicate balance of family and kindred—"the main thing is to preserve the family friendship." The notions relevant here are illustrated in the case of Frankie Jordan, who died leaving three children and two houses. Rather than offend one of his children by leaving him out of the will, he simply left the two houses jointly to the three children, asking that they settle the division themselves. One of the daughters had recently built her own house, so she "didn't need it"; the only son was already living in one of the father's housed, and the other daughter "had stayed with them (the parents) and was most entitled to it, so she got it." Table 1 summarizes the actual behavior regarding the inheritance of houses, which are in fact passed to females as well as to males and to kindred as well as family. There would be a greater proportion of houses passed to females were it not for the fact that many houses are associated with major items of fixed capital—such as farms or businesses with attached houses—and in these cases the house is automatically transmitted along with the farm or shop. There is also a preference that the "home place" should stay in the name, as long as this does not conflict with the needs of daughters. The large number of females who have inherited houses normally do so by remaining unmarried and staying at home to care for their aging parents, an act that gives them greater "entitlement" to the house. But the house is normally passed to them "for their time" only, after which the house is most often passed back into the name.

1. Anna Prentice, a spinster embroiderer, lived with her widowed father and "nursed" him

until he died, by which time she was in her sixties herself. Anna's brother and sister had both married and emigrated to England, and the house naturally passed to Anna who needed it the most and who deserved it because she had "sacrificed her own life" to help her father.

2. Andrew Smith and his two unmarried brothers jointly inherited their house and the attached farm from their father during the 1940s, the farm and house passed to Andrew's eldest son Adam, with the proviso that Andrew's spinster daughter have "a place" in the house until she married or died.

3. A third case involves the widowed shopkeeper Hugh Arnett, who lived with his two sons and unmarried sister in a house adjacent to the shop. Arnett willed his house and shop jointly to his two sons, but stipulated that his sister would have a room in the house for her lifetime.

In sum then, houses form a sphere intermediate between fixed capital and money; houses are transmitted to both men and women, and the primary criteria governing their transmission are need and deserts, while the notion of keeping things in the name plays a secondary, if important, role.

Sphere 3: Money

Money constitutes the third sphere of inheritance, and it is this sphere that demonstrates a pattern very different from the others. Though fixed capital tends to flow primarily within the family and monosexually to males and houses modify these characteristics by using need and deserts as the primary criteria, money flows freely to kindred as well as family, to females as well as males, and without reference to "the name." Money—the amounts recorded in the inheritances ranged from £100 to £100,000, with the bulk under £2,000—is normally a reward for services performed and a means of acknowledging the favorite(s) among one's family and kindred—"money usually goes to whoever treated them the best." At the same time however, no child wishes to think that his parents love him less than a sibling or other kinsman,

and there is likely to be considerable offense taken if the money is not shared with at least a semblance of rough equality between all children. Thus, the individual drawing up his will must exercise the greatest delicacy in the distribution of his money, for to give a substantially greater sum to one child than to another creates possible jealousy and resentment, a condition that few men like to leave in their wake. Money is not rigidly attached to males or to the name, and if a man or woman is childless, he does not feel the same need to transmit it to a brother's son and is free to give it to any favored member of his kindred. In addition, money is readily divisible, unlike fixed capital or houses, and a man or woman can divide his money to reflect with greater accuracy the measure of his love and esteem for the various members of his family and kindred. This is the normal situation, and as can be seen in Table 2, money is even more likely to come from kinsmen other than parents and from kindred rather than family, a characteristic that is displayed by no other sphere. The only exception to these general patterns occurs in the extremely rare instances when the sum involved is so large that it can provide a living for its owner, that is, it virtually becomes an item of fixed capital; in these cases it tends to be treated as fixed capital. Table 1 summarizes the patterns of actual transmissions, in which it is clear that women are even more likely than men to receive money (if a son gets a farm, a daughter will get some of the money), and individuals can and do receive money from any category or degree of kinsman. In contrast to fixed capital in which inheritances are almost entirely between father and son, father and daughter, father's brother and brother's son, in the sphere of money the inheritances are spread throughout the family and the kindred and include mother's brother-sister's daughter, father's father's brother-brother's son's daughter, mother's mother-daughter's daughter, as well as the full range of intrafamily roles. The cases that follow illustrate the general patterns of transmission in the sphere of money.

1. Robbie Hale, a widowed farmer with three sons and one daughter, willed £2,000 as compensation to his eldest son who had been most entitled to the farm but had turned it down

TABLE 2   Inheritance in all three spheres, by kin type

	Fixed capital	House	Money	Totals
From parents	55	68	17	140
From siblings	2	4	3	9
From paternal grandparents	1	4	0	5
From maternal grandparents	1	2	4	7
From paternal uncles or aunts	6	9	5	20
From maternal uncles or aunts	0	3	8	11
From paternal great-uncles or great-aunts	2	1	3	6
From maternal great-uncles or great-aunts	1	0	4	5
From husband	1	7	4	12
From nonkin	0	0	0	0
Totals	69	98	48	215

and emigrated to Australia, £500 to the youngest son who worked in a Belfast factory, no money to the middle son who had inherited the farm and house in the eldest son's place, £300 to his daughter who was married to a policeman, and £100 to his sister's daughter who, though resident for twenty-five years in the United States, spent every summer with Robbie in Aughnaboy.

2. Bertie Foster, an elderly widowed farmer, left a total of £2,000, which was willed in equal portions to his three daughters and two sons.

3. The third case is more complex and involves the inheritance of the largest sum of money recorded in the village. Gordie McOnachie, a bachelor whose father and mother had each married twice, emigrated to south Africa during the early 1920s. Though he accumulated a "fortune" of approximately £100,000 in his South African business operations, he never returned to Aughnaboy—though he continued to write members of his family. When he died, he was survived by one brother's daughter, four half-siblings by his father's second marriage, and six half-siblings by his mother's first marriage. McOnachie willed his money as follows: the £100,000 was divided into six shares, one full share going to each of his father's second wife's four children, one full share going to his dead brother's daughter, one-half share to one of the son of his mother's first marriage, who had corresponded faithfully with McOnachie over the years, keeping him intimate touch with the affairs of the family and community,

and one-half share to this same half-brother's spinster daughter.

4. Cissy Cromwell, widowed hospital matron, with an estate of £8,000, was survived by her only daughter, middle-aged and married, and her daughter's two children, Cissy's grandson and granddaughter. Cissy had "never got on that well" with her own daughter, who had "married badly," but "worshipped" her grandchildren. She divided her money equally between her two grandchildren, leaving nothing to her daughter.

CONCLUSIONS

The inhabitants of Aughnaboy distinguish three separate spheres[3] of inheritance: fixed capital, houses, and money. There are seven basic principles that inform the individual's decision-making regarding inheritance: (1) genealogical distance, (2) kinship category, (3) birth order, (4) sex, (5) "deserts," (6) "need," and (7) esteem. These seven principles are assigned different significance in the three spheres of inheritance, and this weighting enables the individual to make the necessary decisions regarding the transmission of his worldly goods to the next generation. The common denominator to all spheres is the overriding importance of the family, though this is least important in the sphere of money, where the estate can be divided easily and smaller gifts given to extrafamilial kin. Beyond the basic first priority of the family, each sphere weights the variables differently. In the sphere of fixed capital, genealogical distance, kinship category, sex, and birth order are given the greatest priority and matters of deserts or need are regarded as of lesser significance. Thus, here those with the greatest entitlement to the fixed capital are, in order of preference, eldest son/son/daughter/ brother or brother's son/any sex sibling's any sex child/father's brother's son/any cognatic cousin. This grading of entitlement on the exclusive basis of formal kinship criteria is only altered by cases of need or waywardness such as a dissolute and improvident eldest son who may be passed by in favor of a hard-working and reliable younger brother, or in the case of favoritism between two individuals of the same kin type, such as two brother's sons. However, in the sphere of money, deserts and esteem are assigned a far greater weight, and the significance of the formal criteria of distance, category, sex, and birth order tends to be minimized. Thus, the individual will transfer his money to his favorite son or daughter, share the money equally between all his children, or share it with his children and favored members of his kindred, according to his own feelings toward them and the degree of his concern for giving offense. Though the four formal criteria still carry considerable weight in this sphere—a favorite cousin will not normally, for example, inherit before a disliked son—deserts and esteem are assigned the greatest weight. The sphere of houses falls between the two spheres of fixed capital and money in the weighting of the five criteria: here all seven principles are assigned roughly equal weights, and depending on the individuals and their circumstances, any criterion or criteria may be used in the process of decision-making. Thus, an individual may transmit his house to his eldest son, to the daughter who nursed him in his old age, or to his favorite nephew. In Aughnaboy there are norms or prescriptions regulating inheritance other than the stipulations of the legal system that wife, unmarried daughter, and minor or disabled son be cared for. There are only sets of preferences and moral obligations: preferences for certain categories of kin and certain individuals, and moral obligations to provide for the welfare of the family, for whom all men's loyalty is paramount. The willing of his property is a man's last act, in which he discharges for all time his duties to

family and kindred, provides for the welfare of his descendants, and is given his last opportunity to express his love and esteem. Thus his individual preferences must be delicately balanced against his moral obligations to members of his family and close kin. In such a situation, the different patterns of transmission for different types of goods—what I call "spheres"—are convenient mechanisms for maintaining this balance between individual preferences and moral obligations.

NOTES

1. A summary version of this paper was read at the annual meeting of the American Anthropological Association in November 1968 in Seattle, Washington. The field research on which this article is based was carried out in Aughnaboy between October 1964 and November 1966, when I was in the Department of Social Anthropology at The Queen's University of Belfast, and between June and November of 1969, when I held a joint appointment between the Memorial University of Newfoundland's Department of sociology and Anthropology and the institute of social and Economic Research. I am indebted to both these institutions for generous assistance with research time and expenses and to Mr. Rex Clark, Dr. Robin Fox, Dr. Jean La Fontaine, and Dr. Robert Paine for criticism of this paper.

2. Though this legislation reinforces Aughnaboy custom, the government legislation regarding the distribution of the estates of those who died without making a will run counter to Aughnaboy ideology. This conflict lies in five areas: (1) the government legislation makes no distinctions on the basis of birth order, whereas Aughnaboy custom holds an inherent bias for the eldest son; (2) government legislation makes no distinction on the basis of sex whereas Aughnaboy custom strongly favors the passage of fixed capital through males only; (3) legislation expresses a purely bilateral kinship ideology, whereas Aughnaboy custom expresses a strong patrilateral bias; (4) legislation makes no distinction between full and half-blood relatives, whereas Aughnaboy custom assigns much greater weight to full-blood relatives; and (5) legislation gives one affine priority over cognates—Ego's second wife—and this contrasts sharply with Aughnaboy custom, in which the second wife is not entitled to inherit money or property. The effect of this legislation on the aged villagers is not however to produce great actual conflict, but rather to force the men of Aughnaboy to ensure that their wills are made before they die; for otherwise, their property will be distributed according to bizarre and foreign notions of "entitlement."

3. A note should be made here about the level of conceptualization of these sphere ideologies. These ideologies do exist as separate entities, but at what might be called a subliminal level. If the observer simply inquires, "How does inheritance work?" he will get a single answer, most likely stressing the importance of "keeping it in the name." If however he inquires further and asks if any distinctions are made in fact between different types of property, he will then elicit

the response of the different ideologies and statistical patterns that are here described as spheres.

References Cited

ARensberg, Conrad, and S. T. Kimball. 1940 Family and community in Ireland. Cambridge, Mass.: Harvard University Press.

Barth, Fredrik. 1967 Economic spheres in Darfur. *In* Themes in economic anthropology. R. Firth, ed. London: Tavistock.

Bohannan, Paul. 1955 Some principles of exchange and investment among the Tiv. American Anthropologist 57:60–70.

Bohannan, Paul, and George Dalton. 1965 Markets in Africa. New York: Double-day (Anchor).

Buchannan, R. H. 1958 Rural change in an Irish townland. Advancement of science 2:291–300.

Campbell, J. K. 1964 Honour, family and patronage. Oxford: Oxford University Press.

Fox, Robin. 1965 Prolegomena to the study of British kinship. *In* Penguin survey of the social sciences. J. Gould, ed. Harmondswort: penguin.

1966 Kinship and land tenure on Tory Island. Ulster Folklife 12:1–17.

Goodenough, W. H. 1955 A problem in Malayo-Polynesian social organization. American Anthropologist 57:71–83.

Leyton, Elliott. 1966 Conscious models and dispute regulation in an Ulster village. Man (n.s.) 1:534–542.

CRITICAL THINKING QUESTIONS

1. Describe the family and kinship organization that operates in Aughnaboy.
2. What "fundamental duties" does Leyton say a man has to discharge when he arranges for the inheritance of his worldly goods? Give examples from the article to support your answer.
3. What ideals and preferences influence patterns of inheritance in Aughnaboy?
4. Define and describe the three "spheres of inheritance" that impact the inheritance of goods and properties within families in Aughnaboy.
5. How does government legislation about inheritance when there is no will conflict with the ideology of inheritance in Aughnaboy? (Hint: Read Note 2 at the end of the article.)

Family, Marriage, and Kinship

STATE OF THE ART: FAMILY, MARRIAGE, AND KINSHIP

The earliest anthropological studies of kinship date back to the late 1800s when L. H. Morgan discovered that human societies differ in the types, conditions, and uses of kinship terms (mother, brother, uncle, cousin, nephew, etc.) to refer to categories of relatives. This is commonly known as "kinship terminology system." Although the goal of collecting "kinship terminologies" had evolutionary foundations in terms of primitive societies serving as the pristine image of advanced societies, the approach did not yield a universal (formalist) schema for all societies (Peletz 1995). A recent attempt to interpret a culture's kinship system and family based upon another culture's own system resulted in problems of translation and unsuitable explanations, highlighting the differences (Murphy 2006). For instance, although the Eskimo kinship terminology system that emphasizes the nuclear family and distinguishes other types of relatives by generation and gender is shared by modern north Americans and the Eskimo tribe, different cultural rules operate. Kinship relations in primitive societies based on "blood ties" differed in form and practice from those of advanced societies that are based on "soil" and the "state"(Holy 1996). Anthropologists realized that variation in "kinship system" ("system of determining who one's relatives are and what one's relationship is to them"—Bonvillain 2010), including the values, beliefs and sentiments, obligations and expectations toward one another abound and needed to be understood.

Hence the study of kinship as a specialized and separate analytical domain in anthropology became very popular. A knowledge of the kinship terminology system was perceived as the key to understanding kinship relations and their social dynamics. Anthropologists sought in vain to develop a semantic meaning to account for the similarities and differences of kinship terminologies worldwide. Later, the study of kinship as a "terminological system" succumbed to the general paradigm shift (methodological and theoretical changes) that confronted the discipline of anthropology. By the 1950s, the *structure* of kin groups (descent groupings like clan, lineage) and how they *functioned* (statuses and roles) were emphasized. It appeared that political and kinship institutions in tribal societies were often one and the same. By the late 1950s to the 1960s, emphasis on *structure* yielded to the *process* approach. The study of process examines, for instance, the *reproduction* of "structural forms" such as the developmental cycle of the domestic unit (the household)—how kinship perpetuates itself through marriage and other types of social relations (Goody 1958, Holy 1996). In essence, "process analysts seek to examine how these same units (groups and roles) come into being, change form or function" (Faulkingham 1970), and interact through time. Anthropologists analyze *how* societies in which kinship is important tie together individuals with different sets of kin, whether tied through males or females.

Anthropology has been concerned with the varying patterns of marriage in different societies, working within the traditional definition of marriage as a union between a man and a woman and viewing marriage as a system of exchange, as are relations between groups through marriage. Some anthropologists offer a genderless definition of marriage as "between two people." Others have argued that definitions of marriage vary cross-culturally (Stone 2004). Nonetheless, they all agree that kinship, marriage, and the family are interlocking institutions that perpetuate society.

Schneider's (1984) critique of kinship studies resulted in the shift from the concern with facts (objective science) to the conditions of acquiring knowledge (epistemic concerns). He conceptualized kinship as a "symbolic system," full of meanings, linked to and capable of rendering meaning to other domains of sociocultural life (Schneider 1968, 1980). He recognized the interrelationship between kinship, social class, ethnicity, religion, and gender. Therefore, kinship was to be studied as a domain of "social relations" (Peletz 1995). Michelle Rosaldo, Louise Lamphere, and other feminist anthropologists thus viewed kinship and gender as "mutually constructed" (Holy 1996) rather than as separate analytical domains. They linked kinship to major gender issues and systems of inequality (Ortner &Whitehead 1981, Stone 2009). By the 1970s, a major change occurred in the study of kinship. Kinship was subsumed under the various subfields of anthropology including legal and political anthropology. Its role was thematic and sometimes tangential. Hence, kinship studies lost its centrality in anthropology. Furthermore, the late twentieth century, properly referred as the era of *rethinking difference,* attempted to overhaul the analytical foci—similarities and differences—that have been the basis of comparative studies in anthropology. It was argued that extending static kinship models of primitive societies to civilizing societies of Asia and the Orient made the latter primitive. They recommended that the focus should be on common variables such as religious practices, modes of production, and so on (Peletz 1995).

Today anthropology looks at how the modern world has been destabilized through political and economic changes brought on by the spread of capitalism and its relationships to kinship, marriage, and the family. The twentieth century witnessed increased divorce and related incidences of dysfunction in the stepfamily, single parenting roles, juvenile delinquency, and general breakdown in the nuclear family structure (Peletz 1995). These legacies continue in the twenty-first century. Anthropology today views the family as a changing unit of new focus and research, with implications for kinship studies.

In response to these developments, anthropologists have repatriated kinship by returning to the study of contemporary American kinship—compiling an impressive corpus of data on various ethnic groups, adoptions, foster parenting, and gay and lesbian families of diverse social, racial, and ethnic backgrounds (Sherman 1992; Peletz 1995).

As modern society adopts new reproductive strategies through sperm banks, test-tube fertilization, and surrogate motherhood, anthropology consequently has the task of reevaluating definitions of kinship and seeking new meanings of motherhood and fatherhood and making sense of the new patterns of social relationships that result from these trends. Anthropologists are examining the issues of surrogate motherhood and its relationship to the concept of marriage (Stone 1994). Rosman, Weisgrau, and Rubel (2009) have examined the impact of new reproductive technologies.

Contemporary anthropology is concerned with the "practice of social reproduction" (Peletz 1995) in the wider political and economic context, that is, the *process* of social relations through which members of society are cared for, sustained, and enabled to contribute to the well-being of society. Social reproduction is extended to sexuality and gender reconstructions, self-concepts, and personhood. Anthropology explores how the institutions of marriage, family, and kinship serve as agents of such reproduction. Kinship is at the center of these processes.

ABOUT THE ARTICLES

Marriage, family, and the concepts of kinship are human universals. The articles in this section deal with these issues and are related to one another at a number of levels.

Cohen's article deals with the basic question of human interrelationships, namely, how does one define the universe of individuals who are potential mates? Cohen discusses, and dismisses, the earliest theories suggested to explain the *incest taboo.* He concludes that alliance building for group survival is the primary force behind the taboo, a reason that was of vital importance to the survival of smaller human social groups. In examining the reduced size and scope of the modern Western incest taboo, he suggests that as alliance building through marriage is no longer necessary for group survival, the taboo may have run its course of usefulness.

McCurdy's article examines arranged marriages and how they interrelate with other social institutions, particularly marriage and kinship ties. Parents attempt to pair off children in marriage in ways that benefits the family and kin group first, and then as a secondary issue, the children themselves. Upon finishing the article, students may want to exercise their anthropological imaginations in thinking about how different their own lives would be if they lived in a culture that, unlike modern Western tradition, did not allow for the completely free individual choice of a mate.

Lindholm and Lindholm's article examines social customs that Westerners are unfamiliar with except through short news reports: *purdah* and the ideology of male dominance pervasive in the Pakhtun culture of northwestern Pakistan. Their writing reveals the intricate interconnections between segmentary lineage organization, marriage, purdah, and male–female relationships among this group—in a way that three-minute news segments on Western television never could. This research can illuminate for the student how and why the custom of purdah is so widespread in the Islamic world.

The article by Yuan and Mitchell demonstrates that not all systems of reproduction and child rearing are based on marriage as defined traditionally. The Mosuo institution of *sisi* (walking marriage) is based on the permanence of matrilineal kin groups, not a specific marital union, and provides a different path toward solving the basic issues of reproduction and enculturation.

The final article by Sheper-Hughes and Hoffman looks at the breakdown of family structure under conditions of extreme poverty and societal disintegration. The *moleques* (homeless children) of Brazil are the product of these trends. In the last three decades, Brazilian society's attitude toward these children has changed significantly, from seeing them as tolerable and sometimes loveable nuisances, to menaces to public order who need to be controlled and repressed through violence if necessary. Given current trends in American society, this situation could be viewed as a cautionary tale of our own possible cultural future.

References

Bonvillain, N. *Cultural Anthropology.* New Jersey: Upper Saddle River. Prentice Hall, 2010.

Faulkingham, R. H. Political Support in a Hausa Village. Dissertation. Michigan State University, 1970.

Goody, J. (ed.) *The Development Cycle of the Domestic Group.* Cambridge, UK, 1958.

Holy, L. *Anthropological Perspectives on Kinship.* London: Pluto Press. 1996.

Murphy, F. Lost in Translation? Remote Indigenous Households and Definitions of the Family. Family Matters 73 (2006). Australian Institute of Family Studies.

Ortner, S. B., & Whitehead, H. *Sexual Meanings: The Cultural Construction of Gender and Sexuality.* Cambridge: Cambridge University Press, 1981.

Peletz, M. Kinship Studies in Late Twentieth-Century Anthropology. *Annual Review of Anthropology* 24 (1995): 343–372.

Schneider, D. *American Kinship: A Cultural Account,* 1st ed. Englewoods Cliffs, NJ: Prentice Hall, 1968.

Schneider, D. *American Kinship: A Cultural Account,* 2nd ed. Chicago: University of Chicago Press, 1980.

Schneider, D. M. *A Critique of the Study of Kinship.* Ann Arbor: University of Michigan Press, 1984.

Sherman, S. *Lesbian and Gay Marriage: Private Commitments, Public Ceremonies.* Philadelphia: Temple University Press, 1992.

Stone, L. Gay Marriage and Anthropology. *Anthropology News* 45, no. 5 (2004). American Anthropological Association.

Stone, L. *Kinship and Gender: An Introduction,* 4th ed. Westview Press, 2009.

Rosman, A., Weisgrau, M., & Rubel, P. *The Tapestry of Culture: An Introduction to Cultural Anthropology,* 10th ed. New York: Alta Mira Press, 2009.

For Further Research

Kinship is one of the first, and great, abiding loves of anthropology. As with fieldwork, nearly every ethnography published has a section on kinship and marriage. One of the most influential discussions of the subject is *The Elementary Structures of Kinship* (1971, Beacon Press) by Claude Levi-Strauss. It has influenced nearly every major study of kinship since the 1970s. Also enlightening are Fox's *Kinship and Marriage: An Anthropological Perspective* (1984, Cambridge University Press) and Ladslav Holy's *Anthropological Perspectives on Kinship* (1996, Pluto Press). These three references gives the student a broad overview of kinship studies in anthropology, while the last two in particular also provide something of a historical perspective on the field. For additional information on researching the topics discussed in the "State of the Art" section, please visit *www.mysearchlab.com*.

The Disappearance of the Incest Taboo

Yéhudi Cohen

Several years ago a minor Swedish bureaucrat, apparently with nothing better to do, was leafing through birth and marriage records, matching people with their natural parents. To his amazement he found a full brother and sister who were married and had several children. The couple were arrested and brought to trial. It emerged that they had been brought up by separate sets of foster parents and never knew of each other's existence. By a coincidence reminiscent of a Greek tragedy, they met as adults, fell in love, and married, learning of their biological tie only after their arrest. The local court declared their marriage illegal and void.

The couple appealed the decision to Sweden's Supreme Court. After lengthy testimony on both sides of the issue, the court overturned the decision on the grounds that the pair had not been reared together. The marriage was declared legal and valid. In the wake of the decision, a committee appointed by Sweden's Minister of Justice to examine the question has proposed that criminal sanctions against incest be repealed. The committee's members were apparently swayed by Carl-Henry Alstrom, a professor of psychiatry. Alstrom argued that psychological deterrents to incest are stronger than legal prohibitions. The question will soon go to Sweden's Parliament, which seems prepared to follow the committee's recommendation.

Aside from illustrating the idea that the most momentous changes in human societies often occur as a result of unforeseen events, this landmark case raises questions that go far beyond Sweden's (or any other society's) borders. Some people may be tempted to dismiss the Swedish decision as an anomaly, as nothing more than a part of Sweden's unusual experiments in public welfare and sexual freedom.

But the probable Swedish decision to repeal criminal laws against incest cannot be regarded so lightly; this simple step reflects a trend in human society that has been developing for several thousand years. When we arrange human societies along a continuum from the least to the most complex, from those with the smallest number of interacting social groups to those with the highest number of groups, from those with the simplest technology to those with the most advanced technology, we observe that the incest taboo applies to fewer and fewer relatives beyond the immediate family.

Though there are exceptions, the widest extension of incest taboos beyond the nuclear family is found in the least complex societies. In a few societies, such as the Cheyenne of North America and the Kwoma of New Guinea, incest taboos extend to many remote relatives, including in-laws and the in-laws of in-laws. In modern industrial societies, incest taboos are usually confined to members of the immediate household. This contraction in the range of incest taboos is reaching the point at which they may disappear entirely.

The source of these changes in incest taboos lies in changing patterns of external trade. Trade is a society's jugular. Because every group lives in a milieu lacking some necessities that are available in other habitats, the flow of goods and resources is a society's lifeblood. But it is never sufficient merely to encourage people to form trade alliances with others in different areas. Incest taboos force people to marry outside their own group, to form alliances and to maintain trade networks. As other institutions—governments, business organizations—begin to organize trade, incest taboos become less necessary for assuring the flow of the society's lifeblood; they start to contract.

Other explanations of the incest taboo do not, under close examination, hold up. The most common assumption is that close inbreeding is biologically deleterious and will lead to the extinction of those who practice it. But there is strong evidence that inbreeding does not materially increase the rate of maladies such as albinism, total color blindness, or various forms of idiocy, which generally result when each parent carries the same recessive gene. In most cases these diseases result from chance combinations of recessive genes or from mutation.

According to Theodosius Dobzhansky, a geneticist, "The increase of the incidence of hereditary diseases in the offspring of marriages between relatives (cousins, uncle and niece or aunt and nephew, second cousins, etc.) over that in marriages between persons not known to be related is slight—so slight that geneticists hesitate to declare such marriages disgenic." Inbreeding does carry a slight risk. The progeny of relatives include more stillbirths and infant and early childhood deaths than the progeny of unrelated people. But most of these deaths are due to environmental rather than genetic factors. Genetic disadvantages are not frequent enough to justify a prohibition. Moreover, it is difficult to justify the biological explanation for incest taboos when many societies prescribe marriage to one cousin and prohibit marriage to another. Among the Lesu of Melanesia, a man must avoid sexual contact with his parallel cousins, his mother's sisters' daughters and his father's brothers' daughters, but is supposed to marry his cross cousins, his mother's brothers' daughters and his father's sisters' daughters. Even though both types of cousins have the same genetic relationship to the man, only one kind is included in the incest taboo. The taboo is apparently a cultural phenomenon based on the cultural classification of people and cannot be explained biologically.

Genetic inbreeding may even have some advantages in terms of natural selection. Each time a person dies of a hereditary disadvantage, his detrimental genes are lost to the population. By such a process of genetic cleansing, inbreeding may lead to the elimination, or at least to reduced frequencies, of recessive genes. The infant mortality rate may increase slightly at first, but after the sheltered recessive genes are eliminated, the population may stabilize. Inbreeding may also increase the frequency of beneficial recessive genes, contributing to the population's genetic fitness. In the end, inbreeding seems to have only a slight effect on the offspring and a mixed effect, some good and some bad, on the gene pool itself. This mild consequence hardly justifies the universal taboo on incest.

Another explanation of the incest taboo is the theory of natural aversion, first produced by Edward Westermarck in his 1891 book, *The History of Human Marriage*. According to Westermarck, children reared in the same household are naturally averse to having sexual relations with one another in adulthood. But this theory has major difficulties. First, it has a basic logical flaw: If there were a natural aversion to incest, the taboo would be unnecessary. As James Frazer pointed out in 1910, "It is not easy to see why any deep human instinct should need to be reinforced by law. There is no law commanding men to eat and drink or forbidding them to put their hands in the fire ... The law only forbids men to do what their instincts incline them to do; what nature itself prohibits and punishes, it would be superfluous for the law to prohibit and punish ... Instead of assuming, therefore, from the legal prohibition of incest that there is a natural aversion to incest, we ought rather to assume that there is a natural instinct in favor of it."

Second, the facts play havoc with the notion of natural aversion. In many societies, such as the Arapesh of New Guinea studied by Margaret Mead, and the Eskimo, young children are betrothed and raised together, usually by the boy's parents, before the marriage is consummated. Arthur Wolf, an anthropologist who studied a village in northern Taiwan, describes just such a custom: "Dressed in the traditional red wedding costume, the bride enters her future husband's home as a child. She is seldom more than three years of age and often less than a year ... [The] last phase in the marriage process does not take place until she is old enough to fulfill the role of wife. In the meantime, she and her parents are affinally related to the groom's parents, but she is not in fact married to the groom."

One of the examples commonly drawn up to support Westermarck's theory of aversion is the Israeli *kibbutz,* where children who have been raised together tend to avoid marrying. But this avoidance has been greatly exaggerated. There is some tendency among those who have been brought up in the same age group in a communal "children's house" to avoid marrying one another, but this arises from two regulations that separate young adults from their *kibbutz* at about the age when they might marry. The first is a regulation of the Israel Defense Forces that no married woman may serve in the armed forces. Conscription for men and women is at 18, usually coinciding with their completion of secondary school, and military service is a deeply felt responsibility for most *kibbutz*-reared Israelis. Were women to marry prior to 18, they would be denied one of their principal goals. By the time they complete their military service, many choose urban spouses whom they have met in the army. Thus the probability of marrying a person one has grown up with is greatly reduced.

The second regulation that limits intermarriage on a *kibbutz* is a policy of the federations to which almost all *kibbutzim* belong. Each of the four major federations reserves the right to transfer any member to any other settlement, especially when a new one is being established. These "seeds," as the transferred members are called, are recruited individually from different settlements and most transfers are made during a soldier's third or fourth year of military service. When these soldiers leave the army to live on a *kibbutz,* they may be separated from those they were reared with. The frequency of marriage among people from working-class backgrounds who began and completed school together in an American city or town is probably higher than for an Israeli *kibbutz;* the proclivity among American college graduates to marry outside their neighborhoods or towns is no more an example of exogamy or incest avoidance than is the tendency in Israel *kibbutzim* to marry out.

Just as marriage within a neighborhood is accepted in the United States, so is marriage within a *kibbutz* accepted in Israel. During research I conducted in Israel between 1967 and 1969, I attended the wedding of two people in a *kibbutz* who supposedly were covered by this taboo or rule of avoidance. As my tape recordings and photographs show, it would be difficult to imagine a more joyous occasion. When I questioned members of the *kibbutz* about this, they told me with condescending smiles that they had "heard of these things the professors say."

A third, "demographic," explanation of the incest taboo was originally set forth in 1960 by Wilson Wallis and elaborated in 1959 by Mariam Slater. According to this theory, mating within the household, especially between parents and children, was unlikely in early human societies because the life span in these early groups was so short that by the time offspring were old enough to mate, their parents would probably have died. Mating between siblings would also have been unlikely because of the average of eight years between children that resulted from breast feeding and high rates of infant mortality. But even assuming this to have been true for the first human societies, there is nothing to prevent mating among the members of a nuclear family when the life span is lengthened.

A fourth theory that is widely subscribed to focuses on the length of the human child's parental dependency, which is the longest in the animal kingdom. Given the long period required for socializing children, there must be regulation of sexual activity so that children may learn their proper role. If the nuclear family's members are permitted to have unrestricted sexual access to one another, the members of the unit would be confused about their roles. Parental authority would be undermined, and it would be impossible to socialize children. This interpretation has much to recommend it as far as relationships between parents and children are concerned, but it does not help explain brother-sister incest taboos or the extension of incest taboos to include remote relatives.

The explanation closest to my interpretation of the changes in the taboo is the theory of alliance advocated by the French anthropologist Claude Lévi-Strauss, which suggests that people are compelled to marry outside their groups in order to form unions with other groups and promote harmony among them. A key element in the theory is that men exchange their sisters and daughters in marriage with men of other groups.

As originally propounded, the theory of alliance was based on the assumption that men stay put while the women change groups by marrying out, moved about by men like pieces on a chessboard. But there are many instances in which the women stay put while the men change groups by marrying out. In either case, the result is the same. Marriage forges alliances.

These alliances freed early human societies from exclusive reliance on their own limited materials and products. No society is self-sustaining or self-perpetuating; no culture is a world unto itself. Each society is compelled to trade with others and this was as true for tribal societies as it is for modern industrial nations. North America, for instance, was crisscrossed with elaborate trade networks before the Europeans arrived. Similar trade networks covered aboriginal New Guinea and Australia. In these trade networks, coastal or riverline groups gave shells and fish to hinterland people in exchange for cultivated foods, wood, and manufactured items.

American Indian standards of living were quite high before the Europeans destroyed the native trade networks, and the same seems to have been true in almost all other parts of the world. It will come as no surprise to economists that the material quality of people's lives improves to the extent that they engage in external trade.

But barter and exchange do not automatically take place when people meet. Exchange involves trust, and devices are needed to establish trust, to distinguish friend from foe, and to assure a smooth, predictable flow of trade goods. Marriage in the tribal world established permanent obligations and reciprocal rights and privileges among families living in different habitats.

For instance, when a young Cheyenne Indian man decided on a girl to marry, he told his family of his choice. If they agreed that his selection was good, they gathered a store of prized possessions—clothing, blankets, guns, bows and arrows—and carefully loaded them on a fine horse. A friend of the family, usually a respected old woman, led the horse to the tepee of the girl's elder brother. There the go-between spread the gifts for everyone to see while she pressed the suitor's case. The next step was for the girl's brother to assemble all his cousins for a conference to weigh the proposal. If they agreed to it, the cousins distributed the gifts among themselves, the brother taking the horse. Then the men returned to their tepees to find suitable gifts to give in return. Within a day or two, each returned with something roughly equal in value to what he had received. While this was happening, the bride was made beautiful. When all arrangements were completed, she mounted one horse while the return gifts were loaded on another. The old woman led both horses to the groom's camp. After the bride was received, her accompanying gifts were distributed among the groom's relatives in accordance with what each had given. The exchanges between the two families did not end with the marriage ceremony, however; they continued as a permanent part of the marriage ties. This continual exchange, which took place periodically, is why the young man's bridal choice was so important for his entire family.

Marriage was not the only integral part of external trade relationships. Another was ritualized friendship, "blood brotherhood," for example. Such bonds were generally established between members of different groups and were invariably trade partnerships. Significantly, these ritualized friendships often included taboos against marriage with the friend's sisters; sometimes the taboo applied to all their close relatives. This extension of a taboo provides an important key for understanding all incest taboos. Sexual prohibitions do not necessarily grow out of biological ties. Both marriage and ritualized friendships in primitive societies promote economic alliances and both are associated with incest taboos.

Incest taboos force people into alliances with others in as many groups as possible. They promote the greatest flow of manufactured goods and raw materials from the widest variety of groups and ecological niches and force people to spread their social nets. Looked at another way, incest taboos prevent localism and economic provincialism; they block social and economic inbreeding.

Incest taboos have their widest extensions outside the nuclear family in those societies in which technology is least well developed and in which people have to carry their own trade goods for barter or exchange with members of other groups. Often in these small societies, everyone in a community is sexually taboo to the rest of the group. When the technology surrounding trade improves and shipments of goods and materials can be concentrated (as when people learn to build and navigate ocean-going canoes or harness pack animals), fewer and fewer people have to be involved in trade. As this happens, incest taboos begin to contract, affecting fewer and fewer people outside the nuclear family.

This process has been going on for centuries. Today, in most industrial societies, the only incest taboos are those that pertain to members of the nuclear family. This contraction of the range of the taboo is inseparable from the fact that we no longer engage in personal alliances and trade agreements to get the food we eat, the clothes we wear, the tools and materials we use, the fuels on which we depend. Goods are brought to distribution points near our homes by a relatively tiny handful of truckers, shippers, merchants, entrepreneurs, and others. Most of us are only vaguely aware of the alliances, negotiations, and relationships that make this massive movement of goods possible. When we compare tribal and contemporary industrialized societies, the correspondence between the range of incest taboos and the material conditions of life cannot be dismissed as mere coincidence.

Industrialization does not operate alone in affecting the degree to which incest taboos extend beyond the nuclear family. In the history of societies, political institutions developed as technology advanced. Improvements in packaging and transportation have led not only to reductions in the number of people involved in external trade, but also to greater and greater concentrations of decision making in the hands of fewer and fewer people. Trade is no longer the responsibility of all members of a society, and the maintenance of relationships between societies has become the responsibility of a few people—a king and his bureaucracy, impersonal governmental agencies, national and multinational corporations.

To the extent that trade is conducted and negotiated by a handful of people, it becomes unnecessary to use incest taboos to force the majority of people into alliances with other groups. Treaties, political alliances, and negotiations by the managers of a few impersonal agencies have replaced marital and other personal alliances. The history of human societies suggests that incest taboos may have outlived their original purpose.

But incest taboos still serve other purposes. For social and emotional reasons rather than economic ones, people in modern industrial societies still need to prevent localism. Psychological well-being in a diversified society depends largely on the ability to tap different ideas, points of view, life styles, and social relationships. The jugulars that must now be kept open by the majority of people may no longer be for goods and resources, but for variety and stimulation. This need for variety is what, in part, seems to underlie the preference of Israelis to marry outside the communities in which they were born and brought up. The taboo against sex within the nuclear family leads young people to explore, to seek new experiences. In a survey of a thousand cases of incest, Christopher Bagley found that incestuous families are cut off from their society's social and cultural mainstream. Whether rural or urban, he writes, "the family seems to withdraw from the general community, and initiates its own 'deviant' norms of sexual behavior, which are contained within the family circle." "Such a family," he continues, "is an isolated cultural unit, relatively untouched by external social norms." This social and cultural inbreeding is the cause of the profound malaise represented by incest.

To illustrate the correspondence between incest and social isolation, let me describe an incestuous family reported by Peter Wilson, an anthropologist. Wilson sketched a sequence of events in which a South American family became almost totally isolated from the community in which it lived, and began to practice almost every variety of incest. The decline into incest began many years before Wilson appeared on the scene to do anthropological research, when the father of five daughters and four sons made the girls (who ranged in age from 18 to 33) sexually available to some sailors for a small sum of money. As a result, the entire household was ostracized by the rest of the village. "But most important," Wilson writes, "the Brown family was immediately cut off from sexual partners. No woman would have anything to do with a Brown man; no man would touch a Brown woman."

The Brown's isolation and incest continued for several years, until the women in the family rebelled—apparently because a new road connecting their hamlet to others provided the opportunity for social contact with people outside the hamlet. At the same time the Brown men began working in new light industry in the area and spending their money in local stores. The family slowly regained some social acceptance in Green Fields, the larger village to which their hamlet belonged. Little by little they were reintegrated into the hamlet and there seems to have been no recurrence of incest among them.

A second example is an upper middle class, Jewish urban American family that was described to me by a colleague. The Erva family (a pseudonym) consists of six people—the parents, two daughters aged 19 and 22, and two sons, aged 14 and 20. Mr. Erva is a computer analyst and his wife a dentist. Twenty-five years ago, the Ervas seemed relatively normal, but shortly after their first child was born, Mr. and Mrs. Erva took to wandering naked about their apartment, even when others were present. They also began dropping in on friends for as long as a week; their notion of reciprocity was to refuse to accept food, to eat very little of what was offered them, or to order one member of their family not to accept any food at all during a meal. Their rationale seemed to be that accepting food was receiving a favor, but occupying a bed was not. This pattern was accompanied by intense family bickering and inadvertent insults to their hosts. Not surprisingly, most of their friends wearied of their visits and the family was left almost friendless.

Reflecting Bagley's general description of incestuous families, the Ervas had withdrawn from the norms of the general community after the birth of their first child and had instituted their own "deviant" patterns of behavior. They thereby set the stage for incest.

Mr. Erva began to have intercourse with his daughters when they were 14 and 16 years old. Neither of them was self-conscious about the relationship and it was common for the father to take both girls into bed with him at the same time when they were visiting overnight. Mrs. Erva apparently did not have intercourse with her sons. The incest became a matter of gossip and added to the family's isolation.

The Erva family then moved to the Southwest to start over again. They built a home on a parcel of land that had no access to water. Claiming they could not afford a well of their own, the family began to use the bathrooms and washing facilities of their neighbors. In the end these neighbors, too, wanted nothing to do with them.

Mr. and Mrs. Erva eventually separated, he taking the daughters and she the sons. Later the younger daughter left her father to live alone, but the older daughter still shares a one bedroom apartment with her father.

Social isolation and incest appear to be related, and social maturity and a taboo on incest are also related. Within the modern nuclear family, social and emotional relationships are intense, and sexuality is the source of some of the strongest emotions in human life. When combined with the intensity of family life, sexually stimulated emotions can be overwhelming for children. Incest taboos are a way of limiting family relationships. They are assurances of a degree of emotional insularity, of detachment on which emotional maturity depends.

On balance, then, we can say that legal penalties for incest were first instituted because of the adverse economic effects of incestuous unions on society, but that today the negative consequences of incest affect only individuals. Some will say that criminal penalties should be retained if only to protect children. But legal restraints alone are unlikely to serve as deterrents. Father-daughter incest is regarded by many social workers, judges, and psychiatrists as a form of child abuse, but criminal penalties have not deterred other forms of child abuse. Moreover, incest between brothers and sisters cannot be considered child abuse. Some have even suggested that the concept of abuse may be inappropriate when applied to incest. "Many psychotherapists," claims psychologist James McCary in *Human Sexuality,* "believe that a child is less affected by actual incest than by seductive behavior on the part of a parent that never culminates in any manifest sexual activity."

Human history suggests that the incest taboo may indeed be obsolete. As in connection with changing attitudes toward homosexuality, it may be maintained that incestuous relations between consenting mature adults are their concern alone and no one else's. At the same time, however, children must be protected. But questions still remain about how they should be protected and until what age.

If a debate over the repeal of criminal laws against incest is to begin in earnest, as it surely will if the Swedish Parliament acts on the proposed reversal, one other important fact about the social history of sexual behavior must be remembered. Until about a century ago, many societies punished adultery and violations of celibacy with death. When it came time to repeal those laws, not a few people favored their retention on the grounds that extramarital sexual relationships would adversely affect the entire society. Someday people may regard incest in the same way they now regard adultery and violations of celibacy. Where the threat of punishment once seemed necessary, social and emotional dissuasion may now suffice.

References

Bagley, Christopher, "Incest Behavior and Incest Taboos," *Social Problems,* Vol. 16, 1969, pp. 505–519.

Birdsell, J. B., *Human Evolution: An Introduction to the New Physical Anthropology,* Rand McNally, 1972.

Bischof, Norbert, "The Biological Foundations of the Incest Taboo," *Social Science Information,* Vol. 11, No. 6, 1972.

Fox, Robin, *Kinship and Marriage,* Penguin Books, 1968.

Slater, Mariam, "Ecological Factors in the Origin of Incest," *American Anthropologist,* Vol. 61, No. 6, 1959.

Wilson, Peter J, "Incest: A Case Study," *Social and Economic Studies,* Vol. 12, 1961, pp. 200–209.

CRITICAL THINKING QUESTIONS

1. What is the incest taboo, and what relatives does it generally cover?
2. Discuss some of the various theories suggested to explain the origins of the incest taboo. What are their strengths and weaknesses?
3. Cohen suggests that incest taboos force people to forge alliances between groups. What purposes do such alliances serve?
4. In Cohen's view, what are the major problems caused by incestuous behavior?
5. Why does Cohen suggest that the need for the incest taboo is disappearing? Do you agree or disagree with his conclusions, and why?

Family and Kinship in Village India

David W. McCurdy

On a hot afternoon in May, 1962, I sat talking with three Bhil men in the village of Ratakote, located in southern Rajasthan, India.[1] We spoke about the results of recent national elections, their worry over a cattle disease that was afflicting the village herds, and predictions about when the monsoon rains would start. But our longest discussion concerned kin—the terms used to refer to them, the responsibilities they had toward one another, and the importance of marrying them off properly. It was toward the end of this conversation that one of the men, Kanji, said, "Now sāb (Bhili for sāhīb), you are finally asking about a good thing. This is what we want you tell people about us when you go back to America."

As I thought about it later, I was struck by how different this social outlook was from mine. I doubt that I or any of my friends in the United States would say something like this. Americans do have kin. We have parents, although our parents may not always live together, and we often know other relatives, some of whom are likely to play important parts in our lives. We grow up in families and we often create new ones if we have children. But we also live in a social network of other people whom we meet at work or encounter in various "outside" social settings, and these people can be of equal or even greater importance to us than kin. Our social worlds include such non-kin structures as companies and other work organizations, schools, neighborhoods, churches and other religious groups, and voluntary associations, including recreational groups and social clubs. We are not likely to worry much about our obligations to relatives with the notable exceptions of our children and grandchildren (middle-class American parents are notoriously child-centered), and more grudgingly, our aging parents. We are not supposed to "live off" relatives or lean too heavily on them.

Not so in Ratakote. Ratakote's society, like many agrarian villages around the world, is kinship-centered. Villagers anchor themselves in their families. They spend great energy on creating and maintaining their kinship system. This actually is not so surprising. Elaborate kinship systems work well in agrarian societies where families tend to be corporate units and where peoples' social horizons are often limited to the distance they can walk in a day. For the same reasons, families in the United States were also stronger in the past when more of them owned farms and neighborhood businesses.

What may come as a surprise, however, is how resilient and strong Indian kinship systems such as Ratakote's have been in the face of recent economic changes, especially the growth of wage labor. Let us look more closely at the Bhil kinship system, especially at arranged marriage, to illustrate these ideas.

ARRANGING A MARRIAGE

If there is anything that my American students have trouble understanding about India, it is arranged marriage. They cannot imagine sitting passively by while their parents advertise their charms and evaluate emerging nuptial candidates. The thought of living—to say nothing of have sex with—a total stranger seems out of the question to them. In our country, personal independence takes precedence over loyalty to family.

Not so in India. There, arranged marriage is the norm, and most young people, as well as their elders, accept and support the custom. (They often find it sexually exciting, too.) There are many reasons why this is so, but one stands out for

Source: Reprinted from Spradley, James, & McCurdy, David: *Conformity and Conflict, Readings in Cultural Anthropology,* 9/e. Published by Allyn & Bacon, Boston, MA. Copyright © 1997 by Pearson Education, reprinted by permission of the publisher.

discussion here. Marriage constructs alliances between families, lineages, and clans. The resulting kinship network is a pivotal structure in Indian society. It confers social strength and security. People's personal reputations depend on the quality and number of their allied kin. There is little question in their minds about who should arrange marriages. The decision is too important to leave up to inexperienced and impressionable young people.

As an aside I should note that young Indians play a greater part in the process than they used to. Middle-class boys often visit the families of prospective brides, where they manage to briefly "interview" them. They also tap into their kinship network to find out personal information about prospects. Young women also seek out information about prospective grooms. Bhils are no exception. They often conspire to meet those to whom they have been betrothed, usually at a fair or other public event where their contact is likely to go unnoticed. If they don't like each other, they will begin to pressure their parents to back out of the arrangement.

The importance of arranging a marriage was brought home to me several times during fieldwork in Ratakote, but one instance stands out most clearly. When I arrived in the village for a short stay in 1985, Kanji had just concluded marriage arrangements for his daughter, Rupani.[2] What he told me about the process underscored the important role kinship plays in the life of the village.

Kanji started by saying that he and his wife first discussed Rupani's marriage the previous year when the girl first menstruated. She seemed too young for such a union then so they had waited nine months before committing to the marriage process. Even then, Rupani was still only 15 years old. Kanji explained that everyone preferred early marriage for their children because young people were likely to become sexually active as they grew older and might fall in love and elope, preempting the arrangement process altogether. Now they figured that the time had come, and they began a series of steps to find a suitable spouse that would eventually involve most of their kin.

The first step was to consult the members of Kanji's *lineage*. Lineage is an anthropological term, not one used by Bhils. But Bhils share membership in local groups of relatives that meet the anthropological definition. Lineages (in this case, patrilineages) include closely related men who are all descended from a known ancestor. Kanji's lineage consists of his two married brothers, three married sons of his deceased father's brother (his father is also dead), and his own married son when the latter is home. All are the descendants of his grandfather who had migrated to Ratakote many years earlier. He had talked with all of them informally about the possibility of his daughter's marriage before this. Now he called them together for formal approval.

The approval of lineage mates is necessary because they are essential to the marriage process. Each one of them will help spread the word to other villages that Rupani is available for marriage. They will loan money to Kanji for wedding expenses, and when it comes time for the wedding ceremony, they will provide much of the labor needed to prepare food and arrange required activities. Each family belonging to the lineage will host a special meal for the bride (the groom is similarly entertained in his village) during the wedding period, and one or two will help her make offerings to their lineal ancestors. The groom will also experience this ritual.

The lineage also has functions not directly related to marriage. It has the right to redistribute the land of deceased childless, male members, and it provides its members with political support. It sees to memorial feasts for deceased members. Its members may cooperatively plow and sow fields together and combine their animals for herding.

With lineage approval in hand, Kanji announced Rupani's eligibility in other villages. (Bhils are village exogamous, meaning they prefer to marry spouses from other communities.) Kanji and his lineage mates went about this by paying visits to feminal relatives in other villages. These are kin of the women, now living in Ratakote, who have married into his family. They also include the daughters of his family line who have married and gone to live in other villages, along with their husbands and husbands' kin.

Once the word has been spread, news of prospective candidates begins to filter in. It may arrive with feminal kin from other villages when they visit Ratakote. Or it may come from neighbors who are acting as go-betweens in Ratakote for kin who live in other villages and who seek partners for their children. Either way, a process of evaluation starts. Does the family of the suggested boy or girl have a good reputation? Are they hospitable to their in-laws? Do they meet their obligations to others? What is the reputation of the boy or girl they are offering in marriage? Is he or she tall or short, light or dark, robust or frail, cheerful or complaining, hard working or lazy? What about their level of education? Does the family have sufficient land and animals? Have they treated other sons- and daughters-in-law well?

The most fundamental question to ask, however, is whether the prospective spouse is from the right clan. In anthropology, the term *clan* refers to an aggregate of people who all believe they are descended from a common ancestor. In Ratakote this group is called an *arak*. Araks are named and the names are used as surnames when Bhils identify themselves. Kanji comes from the pargi arak and is thus known as Kanji Pargi. There is Lalu Bodar, Naraji Katara, Dita Hiravat, Nathu Airi—all men named for one of the 36 araks found in Ratakote. Women also belong to their father's clan, but unlike many American women who adopt their husband's surname at marriage, they keep their arak name all their lives.

Araks are based on a rule of patrilineal descent. This means that their members trace ancestry through males, only. (Matrilineal descent traces the line through females only, and bilateral descent, which is found in U.S. society, includes both sexes.) Patrilineal descent not only defines arak membership, it governs inheritance. (Sons inherit equally from their fathers in Ratakote; daughters do not inherit despite a national law giving them that right.) It says that the children of divorced parents stay with the father's family. It bolsters the authority of men over their wives and children. It supports the rule of patrilocality. It even defines the village view of conception. Men plant the "seeds" that grow into children; women provide the fields in which the seeds germinate and grow.

The arak symbolizes patrilineal descent. It is not an organized group, although the members of an arak worship the same mother goddess no matter where they live. Instead it is an identity, an indicator that tells people who their lineal blood relatives are. There are pargis in hundreds of other Bhil villages. Most are strangers to Kanji but if he meets pargis elsewhere, he knows they share a common blood heritage with him.

It is this sense of common heritage that affects marriage. Bhils, like most Indians, believe that clan (arak) mates are close relatives even though they may be strangers. Marriage with them is forbidden. To make sure incest is impossible, it is also forbidden to marry anyone from your mother's arak or your father's mother's arak, to say nothing of anyone else you know you are related to.

This point was driven home to me on another occasion when a neighbor of Kanji's, Kamalaji Kharadi, who was sitting smoking with several other men, asked me which arak I belonged to. Instead of letting it go at "McCurdy," I said that I didn't have an arak. I explained that Americans didn't have a kinship group similar to this, and that was why I had to ask questions about kinship.

My listeners didn't believe me. After all, I must have a father and you get your arak automatically from him. It is a matter of birth and all people are born. They looked at each other as if to say, "We wonder why he won't tell us what his arak is?" then tried again to get me to answer. My second denial led them to ask, "OK, then what is your wife's arak?" (If you can't get at it one way, then try another.) I answered that she didn't have an arak either. This caused a mild sensation. "Then how do you know if you have not married your own relative?" they asked, secretly (I think) delighted by the scandalous prospect.

The third step that occurred during the arrangement of Rupani's marriage came after the family had settled on a prospective groom. This step is the betrothal, and it took place when the groom's father and some of his lineage mates and neighbors paid a formal visit to Kanji's house. When they arrive, Kanji must offer his guests a formal meal, usually slaughtering a goat and distilling some liquor for the occasion. The bride, her face covered by her sari, will be brought out for a brief viewing, as well. But most of the time will be spent making arrangements—when will the actual wedding take place?; who will check the couple's horoscopes for fit?; how much will the bride price (also called bride wealth by many anthropologists) be?

Bride price *(dapa)* deserves special comment. It is usually a standard sum of money (about 700 rupees in 1985), although it may also include silver ornaments or other valuables. The dapa is given by the groom's father and his line to the parents of the bride. Bhils view this exchange as a compensation for the loss of the bride's services to her family. It also pays for a shift in her loyalty.

The exchange points up an important strain on families in patrilineal societies, the transfer of a woman from her natal family and line to those of her husband. This transfer includes not only her person, but her loyalty, labor, and children. Although she always will belong to her father's *arak*, she is now part of her husband's family, not his.

This problem is especially troublesome in India because of the close ties formed there by a girl and her parents. Parents know their daughter will leave when she marries, and they know that in her husband's house and village, she will be at a disadvantage. She will be alone, and out of respect for his parents her husband may not favor her wishes, at least in public. Because of this, they tend to give her extra freedom and support. In addition, they recognize the strain she will be under when she first goes to live with her new husband and his family. To ease her transition, they permit her to visit her parents frequently for a year or two. They also may try to marry her into a village where other women from Ratakote have married, so that she has some kin or at least supporters.

After her marriage, a woman's parents and especially her brothers find it hard not to care about her welfare. Their potential interest presents a built-in structural conflict that could strain relations between the two families if nothing were done about it.

A solution to this problem is to make the marriage into an exchange, and bride price is one result. Bride price also helps to dramatize the change in loyalty and obligation accompanying the bride's entrance into her new family.

Bhils have also devised a number of wedding rituals to dramatize the bride's shift in family membership. The bride must cry to symbolize that she is leaving her home. The groom ritually storms the bride's house at the beginning of the final ceremony. He does so like a conquering hero, drawing his sword to strike a ceremonial arch placed over the entrance while simultaneously stepping on a small fire (he wears a slipper to protect his foot), ritually violating the household's sacred hearth. At the end of the wedding, the groom, with some friends, engages in a mock battle with the bride's brothers and other young men, and symbolically abducts her. The meaning of this ritual is a dramatic equivalent of a father "giving away the bride" at American weddings.

One additional way of managing possible tension between in-laws is the application of respect behavior. The parents of the bride must always treat those of the groom and their relatives with respect. They must not joke in their presence, and they must use respectful language and defer to the groom's parents in normal conversation. In keeping with the strong patrilineal system, a groom may not accept important gifts from his wife's family except on ritual occasions, such as weddings, when exchange is expected. A groom may help support his own father, but he should not do so with his in-laws. That is up to their sons.

Bride price exchange also sets in motion a life-long process of mutual hospitality between the two families. Once the marriage has taken place, the families will become part of each other's feminal kin. They will exchange gifts on some ritual occasions, open their houses to each other, and, of course, help one another make future marriages.

THE FUTURE OF INDIAN KINSHIP

On our last trip to India in 1994, my wife and I learned that Rupani had delivered three children since her wedding. Kanji had visited them a few months before we arrived, and he said that Rupani was happy and that he had wonderful grandchildren. But he also mentioned that her husband now spent most of his time in the nearby city of Udaipur working in construction there. He sent money home, but his absence left Rupani to run the house and raise the children by herself, although she did so with the assistance of his parents and lineage mates.

Rupani's case is not unusual. Every morning 70 or 80 men board one of the 20 or so busses that travel the road, now paved, that runs through Ratakote to the city. There they wait to be recruited by contractors for day labor at a low wage. If they are successful, gain special skills, or make good connections, they may get more permanent, better-paying jobs and live for weeks at a time in the city.

The reason they have to take this kind of work is simple. Ratakote has more than doubled in population since 1962. (The village had a population of 1,184 in 1963. By 1994 an estimate put the number at about 2,600.) There is not enough land for everyone to farm nor can the land produce enough to feed the growing population, even in abundant years. Work in the city is the answer, especially for householders whose land is not irrigated like Kanji's.

Cash labor has a potential to break down the kinship system that Bhils value so highly. It frees men and women from economic dependence on the family (since they make their own money working for someone else). It takes up time, too, making it difficult for them to attend the leisurely eleven-day weddings of relatives or meet other obligations to kin that require their presence. With cash labor, one's reputation is likely to hinge less on family than on work. For some, work means moving the family altogether. Devaji Katara, one of Kanji's neighbors, has a son who has moved with his wife and children to the Central Indian city of Indore. He has a good factory job there, and the move has kept them together. By doing so, however, he and they are largely removed from the kinship loop.

Despite these structural changes, kinship in Ratakote and for India as a whole remains exceptionally strong. Even though they may live farther away, Bhil sons and daughters still visit their families regularly. They send money home, and they try to attend weddings. They talk about their kin, too, and surprisingly, they continue the long process of arranging marriage for their children.

Perhaps one reason for kinship's vitality is the use to which kinship is put by many Indians. The people of Ratakote and other Indians have never given up teaching their children to respect their elders and subordinate their interests to those of the family. Family loyalty is still a paramount value. They use this loyalty to help each other economically. Family members hire each other in business. They take one another in during hard times. They offer hospitality to each other. Unlike Americans who feel guilty about accepting one-sided help from relatives, Indians look to the future. Giving aid now may pay off with a job or a favor later. Even if it doesn't, it is the proper thing to do.

Instead of breaking up the kinship network, work that takes men and families away from the village has simply stretched it out. An Indian student I know has found relatives in every American city he has visited. He knows of kin in Europe and southeast Asia too. Anywhere he goes he is likely to have relatives to stay with and to help him. When he settles down he will be expected to return the favor. Another Indian acquaintance, who went to graduate school in the United States and who continues to work here, has sent his father thousands of dollars to help with the building of a house. This act, which would surprise many Americans, seems perfectly normal to him.

Kanji is not disturbed by the economic changes that are overtaking the quiet agricultural pace of Ratakote. I last left him standing in front of his house with a grandson in his arms. His son, who had left the village in 1982 to be a "wiper" on a truck, returned to run the farm. He will be able to meet the family's obligation to lineage and feminal kin. For Kanji, traditional rules of inheritance have pulled a son and, for the moment at least, a grandson, back into the bosom of the family where they belong.

Notes

1. Ratakote is a Bhil tribal village located 21 miles southwest of Udaipur, Rajasthan, in the Aravalli hills. I did ethnographic research in the village from 1961 to 1963, and again in 1985, 1991, and 1993 for shorter periods of time.
2. Kanji and Rupani are not real people. Their experiences are a composite of several life histories.

CRITICAL THINKING QUESTIONS

1. What is an arranged marriage?
2. Why are arranged marriages the norm in India, and what purposes do such marriages serve?
3. What characteristics do Indian families look for in a potential spouse when arranging marriages for their children?

4. What pressures do the institutions of marriage and kinship face in India? What problems can these pressures cause?

Life Behind the Veil

Cherry Lindholm and Charles Lindholm

Harvard professors Cherry Lindholm and Charles Lindholm metaphorically remove the veil from Moslem women in Pakistan, who are of a strict purdah society, to reveal how this "institution of female seclusion" influences all Pakhtun societal practices and institutions.

The bazaar teems with activity. Pedestrians throng the narrow streets, wending past donkey carts, cyclists, and overloaded vehicles. Vendors haggle in the dark doorways of their shops. Pitiful beggars shuffle among the crowds, while bearded religious mendicants wander about, their eyes fixed on a distant world.

Drifting among the mobs of men are, here and there, anonymous figures hidden beneath voluminous folds of material, who float along like ships in full sail, graceful, mysterious, faceless, instilling in the observer a sense both of awe and of curiosity. These are the Moslem women of the Middle East. Their dress is the customary *chador,* which they wear when obliged to leave the privacy of their homes. The *chador* is but one means by which women maintain their *purdah,* the institution of female seclusion, which requires that women should remain unseen by men who are not close relatives and strikes Westerners as so totally foreign and incomprehensible.

Sometimes the alien aspect is tempered with a touch of Western familiarity. A pair of plastic sunglasses may gleam from behind the lace that covers the eyes, or a platform shoe might peep forth from beneath the hem of the flowing *chador.* Nevertheless, the overall presence remains one of inscrutability and is perhaps the most striking image of Middle Eastern societies.

We spent nine months in one of the most strict of all the *purdah* societies, the Yusufzai Pakhtun of the Swat Valley in the North-West Frontier Province of Pakistan. ("Pakhtun" is the designation preferred by the tribesmen, who were generally called Pathans in the days of the British *raj.*)

We had come to the Swat Valley after a hair-raising ride on a rickety bus from Peshawar over the 10,280-foot Malakand Pass. Winston Churchill came this way as a young war correspondent attached to the Malakand Field Force in 1897. As we came into the valley, about half the size of Connecticut, we passed a sign that said WELCOME TO SWAT. We were fortunate to have entrée into the community through a Swati friend we had made eight years before. In Swat, women are secluded inside the domestic compound except for family rituals, such as marriage, circumcision, and funerals, or visits to saint's tombs. A woman must always be in the protective company of other women and is never allowed out alone. It tells a great deal about the community that the word for husband in Pakhto, the language of the Pakhtun, is *kwawund,* which also means God.

However, as everywhere, rules are sometimes broken or, more frequently, cleverly manipulated. Our Pakhtun host's stepmother, Bibi, an intelligent and forceful woman, was renowned for her tactics. Once, when all the females of the household had been forbidden to leave the compound to receive cholera inoculations at the temporary clinic next door, Bibi respectfully bowed her head and assured the men they could visit the mosque with easy minds. Once the men had gone, she promptly climbed the ladder to the flat roof and summoned the doctor to the door of her compound. One by one, the women extended their bare arms through the doorway and received their shots. Later, Bibi could honestly swear that no woman had set foot outside the compound walls.

Source: Reprinted by permission of the authors from THE GENDER READER 2/e, edited by Evelyn Aston-Jones et al. (Longman, 2000).

Despite such circumventions, *purdah* is of paramount importance in Swat. As one Pakhtun proverb succinctly states: "The woman's place is in the home or the grave." Years ago in Swat, if a woman broke her *purdah*, her husband might kill her or cut off her nose as punishment and as a means of cleansing his honor. If a woman is caught alone with an unrelated man, it will always be assumed that the liaison is sexual, and public opinion will oblige her husband to shoot her, even if he does not desire her death; to go unavenged is to be known henceforth as *begherata*, or man without honor. As such, he would no longer have the right to call himself Pakhtun.

A shameless woman is a threat to the whole society. Our host remembered witnessing, thirty years ago when he was a child, the entire village stoning an adulteress. This punishment is prescribed by Islamic law, though the law requires there be four witnesses to the sexual act itself to establish guilt. Nowadays, punishments for wifely misdemeanors have become less harsh, though adulterous wives are still killed.

In the rural areas, poorer families generally cannot maintain *purdah* as rigorously as their wealthier neighbors, for often a wife must help her husband in the fields or become a servant. Nevertheless, she is required to keep her hair covered at all times and to interact with men to a minimum. Here again, the rules are sometimes flouted, and a poor woman might entice a man with her eyes, or even, according to village men who claimed personal experiences, become more aggressive in her seductive attempts and actually seize a man in a deserted alleyway and lure him into her house. Often, the man is persuaded. Such a woman will accept money from her lover, who is usually a man from a wealthy family. Her husband is then a *begherata*, but some men acquiesce to the situation because of the money the wife is earning or because of fear of the wife's socially superior and more powerful lover. But most poor men, and certainly all the elite, keep their women under strict control.

In the Islamic Middle East, women are viewed as powerful and dangerous beings, highly sexual and lacking in personal discipline and discrimination. In Middle Eastern thought, sexual intercourse itself, though polluting, lacks the same negative connotations it has in the West. It has always been believed that women have sexual climaxes, and there is no notion of female frigidity. Male impotence, however, is well-documented, and some middle-aged and even young men admitted to us that they had lost their interest in women. Sometimes, though rarely, a young bridegroom will find himself incapable of consummating his marriage, either because he finds his bride unattractive or because he has been previously enchanted by a male lover and has become impotent in a heterosexual relationship. Homosexuality has never been seen as aberrant in the Middle East. As a famous Afghan saying humorously declares: "A woman is for bearing children, a boy is for pleasure, but ecstasy is a ripe watermelon!" However, with Western influence, homosexuality in the Middle East is now less overt. But even when it was common and open, the man was still expected to marry and produce children.

Men must marry, though women are regarded as a chaotic and anarchic force. They are believed to possess many times the sexual desire of men and constitute a potential threat to the family and the family's honor, which is based in large measure on the possession and control of women and their excessive and dangerous sexuality.

Among the Pakhtun of Swat, where the male-female relation is one of the most hostile in the Middle East, the man avoids showing affection to his wife, for fear she will become too self-confident and will begin to assert herself in ways that insult his position and honor. She may start by leaving the compound without his permission and, if unchecked, may end by bringing outside men into the house for sexual encounters, secure in the knowledge that her husband, weakened by his affection for her, will not take action. This course of events is considered inevitable by men and women alike and was illustrated by a few actual cases in the village where we lived.

Women are therefore much feared, despite the pronouncements of male supremacy. They must be controlled, in order to prevent their alarming basic natures from coming to the fore and causing dishonor to their own lineages. *Purdah* is generally described as a system that serves to protect the woman, but implicitly it protects the men and society in general from the potentially disruptive actions of the powerful female sex.

Changes are occurring, however, particularly in the modern urban centers. The educated urban woman often dispenses with the *chador*, replacing it with a simple length of veiling draped over the head or across the shoulders; she may even decide to adopt modest Western dress. The extent of this transformation will depend partly upon the attitude of the community in which she lives.

In the urban centers of the stricter *purdah* regions the public display of *purdah* is scrupulous, sometimes even more striking than that of the tribal village. Behind the scenes, though, the city-dwelling woman does have more freedom than she would have in the village. She will be able to visit not only relatives but friends without specific permission from her husband, who is out at work all day. She may, suitably veiled, go shopping in the bazaar, a chore her husband would have undertaken in the village. On the whole, the city woman will have a great deal more independence, and city men sometimes lament this weakening of traditional male domination.

The urbanized male may speak of the custom-bound tribesmen (such as the Swat Pakhtun, the Bedouin nomads of Saudi Arabia or Qashqai herdsmen of Iran) as country bumpkins, yet he still considers their central values, their sense of personal pride, honor, and autonomy, as cultural ideals and views the tribesmen, in a very real way, as exemplars of the proper mode of life. Elite families in the cities proudly emphasize their tribal heritage and sometimes send their sons to live for a year or so with distant tribal cousins, in order to expose them to the tribesman's integrity and moral code. The tribesman, on the other hand, views his urbanized relatives as weak and womanly, especially with reference to the slackening of *purdah* in the cities. Though the *purdah* female, both in the cities and in the tribal areas, rarely personifies the ideal virtues of silence, submission, and obedience, the concept of *purdah* and male supremacy remains central to the male identity and to the ideology of the culture as a whole.

The dynamic beneath the notion of male supremacy, the institution of *purdah*, and the ideology of women's sexual power becomes apparent when one takes an overall view of the social structure. The family in the Middle East, particularly in the tribal regions, is not an isolate element; kinship and marriage are the underlying principles that structure action and thought. Individuals interact not so much according to personal preference as according to kinship.

The Middle Eastern kinship system is known to anthropologists as a segmentary-lineage organization; the basic idea is that kinship is traced through one line only. In the Middle East, the system is patrilineal, which means that the male line is followed, and all the links through women are ignored. An individual can therefore trace his relationship to any other individual in the society and know the exact genealogical distance between them; i.e., the distance that must be traced to reach a common male ancestor. The system obliges men to defend their patrilineal relatives if they are attacked, but if there is no external force threatening the lineage, then men struggle against one another according to the principle of genealogical distance. This principle is nicely stated in a famous Middle Eastern proverb: "I against my brothers, my brothers and I against my cousins; my cousins, my brothers, and I against the world." The cousins in question are of course patrilineal.

Within this system, women appear to have no role, though they are the units of reproduction, the mothers of the sons who will carry on the patriline. Strange as it may seem, this is the core contradiction of the society: The "pure" patriline itself is actually descended from a woman. This helps explain the exaggerated fear of women's promiscuity and supposedly voracious sexuality. In order to protect the patriline, women must be isolated and guarded. Their sexuality, which threatens the integrity of the patriline, must be made the exclusive property of their husbands. Women, while being absolutely necessary for the perpetuation of the social order, are simultaneously the greatest threat to it.

The persistent denigration of women is explained by this core contradiction. Moslem society considers women naturally inferior in intelligence and ability—childlike, incapable of discernment, incompetent to testify in court, prey to whims and fancies. In tribal areas, women are prohibited from inheritance, despite a Koranic injunction, and in marriage they are purchased from their fathers like a commodity.

Were woman not feared, these denials of her personhood would be unnecessary.

Another unique element of Middle Eastern culture is the prevalence of marriage with the father's brother's daughter. In many areas, in fact, this marriage is so favored that a boy must give explicit permission to allow his patrilineal female cousin to marry elsewhere. This peculiar marriage form, which is found nowhere else in the world, also serves to negate the woman by merging her lineage with that of her husband, since both are members of the same patriline (indeed, are the offspring of brothers). No new blood enters, and the sanctity of the patriline is steadily maintained.

However, this ploy gives rise to other problems. Cousin marriage often divides the brothers rather than uniting them. Although the brideprice is usually reduced in such marriages, it is always demanded, thus turning the brothers into opponents in a business negotiation. Furthermore, giving a woman in Swat carries an implication of inferiority; historically, victors in war took women from the vanquished. Cousin marriage thus renders the brothers' equality questionable. Finally, the young couple's fights will further alienate the brothers, especially since such marriages are notoriously contentious. This is because patrilineal male cousins are rivals for the common grandfather's inheritance (in fact, the Swati term for father's brother's son is *tarbur*, which also means enemy), and a man who marries his patrilineal cousin is marrying the sister of his life-long opponent. Her loyalty is with her brother, and this is bound to cause frequent disputes.

Though the girl is treated like goods, she does not see herself as such. The fundamental premise of tribal life is the equality of the various landed families. There are very few hierarchies in these societies, and even the leaders are often no more than first among equals. Within this system, which has been described as a nearly perfect democracy, each *khan* (which means landowner and literally translates as king) family sees itself as superior to all others. The girls of the household feel the same pride in their lineage as their brothers and cannot help but regard their husband's families through jaundiced eyes. The new bride is prepared to defend the honor of her family, even though they have partially repudiated her by negotiating the marriage. Her identity, like that of a man, rests on her lineage pride, which she will fight to uphold. The husband, meanwhile, is determined to demonstrate his domination and mastery, since control of women is the nexus of a man's sense of self-respect.

Hostility is thus built into marriage by the very structure of the society, which pits every lineage against every other in a never-ending contest to maintain an equilibrium of power within this markedly egalitarian culture. The hostility of the marriage bond is evident from its beginnings. The reluctant bride is torn from her cot in her family's house and ensconced on a palanquin that strongly resembles a bier. The war drums that announce the marriage procession indicate the nature of the tie, as does the stoning of the palanquin by the small boys of the village as it is carried through the dusty streets. When the bride arrives at her new husband's house, his family triumphantly fires their rifles into the air. They have taken a woman! The young wife cowers in her veils as she is prodded and poked curiously by the females of the husband's house who try to persuade her to show her face. The groom himself is nowhere to be seen, having retreated to the men's house in shame. In three days, he will creep to her room and consummate the marriage. Taking the virginity of the bride is a highly charged symbolic act, and in some areas of the Middle East the display of the bloody nuptial sheet to the public is a vital part of the wedding rite. Breaking the hymen demonstrates the husband's possession of his wife's sexuality. She then becomes the junior adult in the household, subordinate to everyone, but, most especially, under the heavy thumb of her mother-in-law.

The household the bride enters will be that of her husband's father, since the system, as well as being patrilineal, is also patrilocal. She will be surrounded by his relatives and will be alone with her husband only at night. During the day he will pay no attention to her, for it is considered shameful for a man to take note of his wife in front of others, particularly his father and mother. Within the compound walls, which shield the household from the rest of the world, she is at the mercy of her new family.

Life within the compound is hardly peaceful. Wives squabble among themselves, and wives who have built a power base by having sons even quarrel with the old matriarch, their mother-in-law. This is usually a prelude to a couple moving out of the house into their own compound, and husbands always blame their wives for the breakup of the extended family, even though they, too, will be glad to become the masters of their own homes and households.

But the worst fights among women are the fights between women married to the same man. Islam permits polygamous marriage, and legally a man may have four wives. Not all men are financially able to take more than one wife, but most men dream of marrying again, despite the Swati proverb that says "I may be a fool, but not so much of a fool as the man with two wives." Men who can afford it often do take a second wife. The reason is not sexual desire, for wives do not mind if their husbands have liaisons with prostitutes or promiscuous poor women. Rather, the second wife is brought in to humiliate an overly assertive first wife. Bringing in a second wife is a terrible insult; it is an expression of contempt for the first wife and her entire lineage. The insult is especially cutting in Swat, where divorce is prohibited (though it is permitted in the Koran) and where a disliked wife must either endure her lot or retreat to her family's household and a life of celibacy. Small wonder then that households with two wives are pits of intrigue, vituperation, and magical incantation, as each wife seeks to expel the other. The Koran says a man should only practice polygamy if he is sure he can treat each wife equally; the only man we met who was able to approximate this ideal was a man who never went home. He spent his time in the men's house, talking with his cronies and having his meals sent to him.

The men's house is the best-built structure in any village, along with the mosque, which is also prohibited to women. It is a meeting place for the clan, the center for hospitality and refuge, and the arena for political manipulation. This is where the visitors will be received, surrounded by men who gossip, doze, or clean their rifles. Here, the guest might well imagine that women do not even exist. Only the tea and food that is sent over from the compound nearby tell him of the women working behind the walls.

Formerly, in Swat, most men slept in the men's house, visiting their wives secretly late at night and returning before daybreak. But now only a few elders and some ne'er-do-well youths live permanently in the elegant, aging buildings. Sometimes, however, a man may be obliged to move to the men's house for a few days if his wife makes his home too uncomfortable, for women have their own weapons in the household battles. Arguments may flare up over almost anything: the husband buying a rotten piece of meat or forgetting to bring home a length of material, the wife ruining some curd or gossiping too much with a neighbor. The wife may then angrily refuse to cook, obliging the husband to retreat to the men's house for food. The man's weapon in fights is violence, while the woman can withdraw domestic services at will.

In the early days of a marriage, when the bride is new to the household and surrounded by her husband's people, she may be fairly meek. But when her status has improved as a result of producing sons, she will become more aggressive. Her lacerating tongue is renowned, and she will also begin to fight back physically as well as verbally. Finally, her exasperated husband may silence her with a blow from a heavy stick he keeps for that purpose. No shame is attached to beating one's wife, and men laugh about beatings they have administered. The women themselves, though they decry their men's brutality, proudly display their scars and bruises, characterizing a neighbor who is relatively gentle to his wife as "a man with no penis."

The older a woman gets, the more powerful and fearless she becomes. She is aided by her sons who, though respecting their father, regard him as an obstacle to their gaining rights in land. The old man, who gains his stature from his landholding, is always reluctant to allot shares to his grown sons. Furthermore, the sons' ties of affection are much stronger with the mother. The elderly father, who is generally ten or fifteen years older than his wife, is thus surrounded by animosity in his own house. The situation of the earlier years has reversed itself, and the wife, who began alone and friendless, gains allies in her old age, while the husband becomes isolated. Ghani Khan, a modern Pakhtun writer, had described the situation well: "The Pakhtun thinks he is as good as anyone else and his father rolled into one and is fool enough to try this even with his wife. She pays for it in her youth, and he in his old age.''

But many women do not live to see their triumph. In northern Swat, for every 100 women over the age of sixty there are 149 men, compared to the more equal 100 to 108 ratio below sixty. The women are worn out by continual childbearing, breast feeding, and a lack of protein. Though fertile in places, the Swat valley is heavily overpopulated with an estimated 1 million people, and survival is always difficult. The diet consists chiefly of bread, rice, seasonal vegetables, and some dairy products. Meat is a rarity and goes to the men and boys as a matter of course. They perpetuate the patrilineal clan and must survive, while women can always be replaced. The lives of men are hard, but the lives of women are harder, as witnessed by their early deaths.

In this environment, people must learn to be tough, just as they must learn to fit the structure of the patrilineal system. Child rearing serves both functions.

The birth of a boy in Swat is greeted by rejoicing, while the birth of a girl is an occasion for gloom. But the first few years for both sexes are virtually identical. Like most Middle Easterners, the Swatis practice swaddling, binding the baby tightly so that it is immobilized. Ostensibly, this is to help the baby sleep and prevent it from blinding itself with its flailing hands, but anthropologists have hypothesized that swaddling actually serves to develop a certain character type: a type which can withstand great restraint but which also tends to uncontrolled bursts of temper. This hypothesis fits Swat, where privation and the exigencies of the social structure demand stoicism, but where violent temper is also useful. We often saw Swati children of all ages lose themselves in tantrums to coerce their parents, and such coercion was usually successful. Grown men and women as well are prone to fits of temper, and this dangerous aspect makes their enemies leery of pressing them too hard.

Both sexes are indoctrinated in the virtues of their family and its lineage. In marital fights this training is obvious, as both partners heatedly assert, "Your ancestor was nothing, and mine was great!" At a man's death his sister, not his wife, is his chief mourner. And if a woman is killed it is her brother, not her husband, who avenges her.

Child training in Swat produces strong characters. When they give affection, they give it wholeheartedly, and when they hate, they hate bitterly. The conditions under which they live are cruel and cramped, and they respond with cruelty and rigidity in order to survive. But at the same time, the people are able to bear their hard lives with pride and dignity.

CRITICAL THINKING QUESTIONS

1. In Pakhtun society the *chador* and the concept of *purdah* are interrelated. What is *purdah*, and how is it reflected in the *chador*?
2. The Lindholms discuss Pakhtun men's fear of female sexuality and the ideology of male dominance. How is women's sexuality viewed among the Pakhtun? How is the ideology of male dominance and the treatment of women a reflection of these fears?
3. Despite *purdah*, women in urban areas have a lot of freedoms that their counterparts in the rural areas do not have. What are these freedoms, and how do women employ them?
4. How are *purdah*, protection of the patriline, and the Pakhtun view of women interrelated?
5. Why and how is hostility built into the institution of marriage by the structure of Pakhtun society?

Land of the Walking Marriage

Lu Yuan and Sam Mitchell

For the Mosuo of China, a woman's world.
There are so many skillful people, but none can
  compare with my mother.
There are so many knowledgeable people, but
  none can equal my mother.
There are so many people skilled at song and
  dance, but none can compete with my mother.

We first heard this folk song around a blazing fire
in southwestern China in the spring of 1995. It
was sung enthusiastically by women of Luoshui
village—members of the Nari, an ethnic group
more commonly known to outsiders as the
Mosuo. During the past few years, we have
returned several times to visit these people, who
celebrate women in more than song. Although
the majority of China's ethnic groups follow a
strong patrilineal tradition, the Mosuo emphasize matrilineal ties, with matrilineally related
kin assisting one another to farm, fish, and raise
children. Women also head most households and
control most family property.

Marriage as other cultures know it is uncommon among the Mosuo; they prefer a visiting relationship between lovers—an arrangement they
sometimes refer to in their language as sisi (walking back and forth). At about the age of twelve, a
Mosuo girl is given a coming-of-age ceremony,
and after puberty, she is free to receive male visitors. A lover may remain overnight in her room
but will return in the morning to his own
mother's home and his primary responsibilities.
Children born from such a relationship live with
their mother, and the male relatives responsible
for helping to look after them are her brothers.
Many children know who their fathers are, of
course, but even if the relationship between
father and child is quite close, it involves no social

or economic obligation. And lovers can end their
relationship at any time; a woman may signal her
change of heart by simply no longer opening the
door. When speaking Chinese, the Mosuo will
call the sisi arrangement zou hun (walking marriage) or azhu hunyin (friend marriage, azhu
being the Mosuo word for friend); nevertheless,
the relationship is not a formal union.

Chuan-kang Shih, an anthropologist at the
University of Illinois at Urbana-Champaign and
an authority on the Mosuo, points out that many
aspects of their family system have parallels elsewhere in the world. For example, although in
most societies a husband and wife live together
(usually near his relatives or hers), in others they
continue to live in separate households, and one
spouse must make overnight nuptial visits. Matrilineal kinship systems, in which a man looks after
the interests of his sisters' children, are also well
known. And although men commonly wield the
power, even in matrilineal societies, women may
play important political and economic roles. But
the absence of a formal marital union may quite
possibly be unique to the Mosuo. In this respect,
only the precolonial practices of the matrilineal
Nayar of southern India come close. As Shih explains, among some Nayar groups, a woman
would take lovers (with due regard for social
class), who would establish and maintain their relationships to her through a pattern of gift giving.
Despite being expected to acknowledge paternity,
the lovers incurred no obligations to their offspring. Still, the Nayar had a vestigial form of
marriage: shortly before puberty, a girl would be
wed to a young man; although this marriage lasted
only three days and was often purely ceremonial
in nature, the union marked the girl's transition to
adult life and legitimized the birth of her children.

Source: "Land of the Walking Marriage" by Lu Yuan and Sam Mitchell. Reprinted from Natural History, November 2000. Copyright ©
Natural History Magazine, inc., 2000.

In Luoshui we stayed with thirty-year-old A Long, who runs a small guesthouse. His family consisted of his mother, grandmother, younger brother and sister, and sister's two-year-old son. Each evening A Long departed with his small overnight bag; each morning he returned to help his mother and sister. After several days of eating with the family and becoming friendly with them, we asked A Long what he thought about the sisi system. " 'Friend marriage' is very good," he replied. "First, we are all our mother's children, making money for her; therefore there is no conflict between the brothers and sisters. Second, the relationship is based on love, and no money or dowry is involved in it. If a couple feels contented, they stay together. If they feel unhappy, they can go their separate ways. As a result, there is little fighting." A Long told us that he used to have several lovers but started to have a stable relationship with one when she had her first child.

"Are you taking care of your children?" we asked.

"I sometimes buy candy for them. My responsibility is to help raise my sister's children. In the future, they will take care of me when I get old."

A Long's twenty-six-year-old sister, Qima, told us that the Mosuo system "is good because my friend and I help our own families during the daytime and only come together at night, and therefore there are few quarrels between us. When we are about fifty years old, we will not have 'friend marriage' anymore."

Ge Ze A Che is the leader of Luoshui, which has a population of more than 200 people, the majority of them Mosuo, with a few Han (China's majority ethnic group) and Pumi as well. He spoke proudly of this small settlement: "I have been the leader of the village for five years. There has been little theft, rape, or even argument here. 'Friend marriage' is better than the husband-wife system, because in large extended families everyone helps each other, so we are not afraid of anything. It is too hard to do so much work in the field and at home just as a couple, the way the Han do."

The Mosuo live in villages around Lugu Lake, which straddles the border between Yunnan and Sichuan provinces, and in the nearby town of Yongning. They are believed to be descendants of the ancient Qiang, an early people of the Tibetan plateau from whom many neighboring minority groups, including the Tibetans themselves, claim descent. As a result of Han expansion during the Qin dynasty (221–206 B.C.), some Qiang from an area near the Huang (Yellow) River migrated south and west into Yunnan. The two earliest mentions of the Mosuo appear during the Han dynasty (A.D. 206–222) and the Tang dynasty (A.D. 618–907), in records concerning what is now southwestern China.

The Mosuo do not surface again in historical accounts until after Mongol soldiers under Kublai Khan subjugated the area in 1253. During the Yuan dynasty (1279–1368), a period of minority rule by the Mongols, the province of Yunnan was incorporated into the Chinese empire, and many Mongol soldiers settled in the Mosuo region. In fact, during the 1950s, when the government set out to classify the country's minority nationalities, several Mosuo villages surrounding Lugu Lake identified themselves as Mongol, and some continue to do so today. When we walked around the lake, as the Mosuo do each year in the seventh lunar month—a ritual believed to ensure good fortune during the coming year—we passed through villages that identified themselves variously as Mosuo, Mongol, Naxi, Pumi, and Han. The "Mongol" people we encountered dressed the same as the Mosuo and spoke the same language. Their dances and songs, too, were the same, and they sometimes even referred to themselves as Mosuo.

Tibetan Buddhism first entered the region in the late thirteenth century and has greatly influenced the lives and customs of the Mosuo. Before the area came under the control of the Communist government, at least one male from almost every family joined the monastic community. The local practice of Buddhism even incorporated aspects of the sisi system, although the women did the "commuting." On the eighth day of the fifth lunar month, monks traveling to Tibet for religious study would camp in front of Kaiji village. That night, each monk would be joined by his accustomed lover—a ceremonial practice believed to enable the monks to reach Lhasa safely and to succeed in completing their studies. And the local Mosuo monks, each of whom lived with his own mother's family, could also receive lovers. Such arrangements seem to defy the injunctions of many schools of Tibetan Buddhism, but by allowing the monks to live and work at home, outside the strict confines of monastic life, they helped the Mosuo maintain a stable population and ensure an adequate labor force to sustain local agriculture.

The area around Lugu Lake did not come under the full control of China's central government until 1956, seven years after the founding of the People's Republic. In 1958 and 1959, during the Great Leap Forward, the nearby monasteries, notably the one at Yongning, were badly damaged. Now, however, with a combination of government funds and donations from local people, they are slowly being rebuilt. One element of recent religious revival is the Bon tradition, which is accepted by the Dalai Lama as a school of Tibetan Buddhism but believed by many scholars to be derived from an earlier, animist tradition. During our walk around Lugu Lake, we witnessed a Bon cremation ceremony and visited the Bon temple on the eastern shore of the lake. The Mosuo also retain a shamanic and animist tradition of their own, known as Daba.

In the twentieth century, the West became acquainted with the Mosuo through the work of French ethnographers Edouard Chavannes and Jacques Bacot and through the contributions of Joseph Rock, a Vienna-born American who first journeyed to Yunnan in 1922 while on a botanical expedition. A flamboyant character, Rock traveled through remote Tibetan borderlands accompanied by trains of servants and bodyguards and equipped with such dubious necessities as a collapsible bath-tub and a silver English tea set. He made the Naxi town of Lijiang his home for more than twenty years, until the victory of the Chinese Communist Party in 1949 spelled an end to foreign-funded research and missionary activity in the area.

Besides conducting botanical surveys and collecting plant and animal specimens, Rock took many photographs and became the West's foremost expert on the region's peoples and their shamanic practices. He identified the Mosuo as a subgroup of the Naxi, who, although their kinship system is patrilineal, speak a language closely related to that of the Mosuo. The Mosuo strongly contest this classification, but it has been retained by the present government, which has been reluctant to assign the Mosuo the status of a distinct minority. The Communists claim that the Mosuo do not fit the criteria for nationality status as defined for the Soviet Union by Joseph Stalin. According to Stalin, as he phrased it in a 1929 letter, "A nation is a historically constituted, stable community of people, formed on the basis of the common possession of four principal characteristics, namely: a common language, a common territory, a common economic life, and a common psychological make-up manifested in common specific features of national culture."

In keeping with Marxist interpretations of historical development, Chinese ethnologists have also regarded Mosuo society as a "living fossil," characterized by ancient marriage and family structures. This view draws on theories of social evolution formerly embraced by Western anthropologists, notably the American ethnologist Lewis Henry Morgan (1818–81). Morgan proposed that societies pass through successive natural stages of "savagery" and "barbarism" before attaining "civilization." He also proposed a sequence of marriage forms, from a hypothetical "group marriage" of brothers and sisters to monogamy. Chinese scholars have argued that a minority such as the Mosuo, with its unusual kinship system, fits into this scheme and thus validates Marxist views. Of course, the application of Morgan's theories to minority cultures in China has also enabled the Han majority to see itself as more advanced in the chain of human societal evolution. This kind of thinking, long discredited in the West, is only now beginning to be reexamined in China.

With the coming of the Cultural Revolution (1966–76), the Mosuo were pressured to change their way of life. According to Lama Luo Sang Yi Shi (a Mosuo who holds a county-government title but is primarily a spiritual leader), "during the Cultural Revolution, the governor of Yunnan came to Yongning. He went into Mosuo homes and cursed us, saying that we were like animals, born in a mess without fathers. At that time, all of the Mosuo were forced to marry and to adopt the Han practice of monogamy; otherwise, they would be punished by being deprived of food." During this period Mosuo couples lived with the woman's family, and divorce was not permitted. But even though they held marriage certificates and lived with their wives, the men kept returning to their maternal homes each morning to work.

Luo Sang Yi Shi criticized this attempt to change the Mosuo and explained that "at the end of the Cultural Revolution, the Mosuo soon returned to their former system of 'friend marriage.' A small family is not good for work. Also, mothers and their daughters-in-law cannot get along well."

Today the Mosuo maintain their matrilineal system and pursue sisi relationships. Yet how long will this remain the case? The government of Yunnan recently opened Lugu Lake to tourism, and vans full of visitors, both Chinese and foreign, are beginning to arrive. To some

degree, this added exposure threatens to envelop the Mosuo in a society that is becoming increasingly homogeneous. Yet the tourists are drawn not only by the beauty of the lake but by the exotic qualities of the Mosuo people. Ironically, their unique qualities may well enable the Mosuo to endure and prosper.

We asked Ge Ze A Che, the Luoshui village leader, if tourism would change the lives of the Mosuo. "It has already changed their lives to some extent," he observed. "Our young people now like to wear Han clothes, speak Chinese, and sing Chinese songs. In the future they will lose our people's traditions and customs."

And what would happen to "friend marriage"? we wondered.

"It will also change—but very, very slowly!"

CRITICAL THINKING QUESTIONS

1. How are the Mosuo different from other Chinese social groups with regard to their descent system?
2. Describe the system of "walking marriage" (*sisi*) in terms of partner commitment, child rearing, and other responsibilities.
3. How did Buddhism affect, and was affected by, the customs of the Musuo?
4. How are the Mosuo officially classified and regarded by the Chinese government, and why?

5. The attitude of many Americans toward marriage has undergone significant change in the last generation, with cohabitation, gay marriage, and other "alternative" approaches to marriage being experimented with. Given this, do you think a system like that of the Mosuo could work in the United States, at least among some social groups? Why or why not?

Brazil: Moving Targets

Nancy Scheper-Hughes and Daniel Hoffman

In the 1960s ubiquitous street urchins in Brazil were referred to with a blend of annoyance and affection as moleques, meaning ragamuffins, scamps, or rascals. Moleques were streetwise, cute, and cunning, sometimes sexually precocious, and invariably economically enterprising. The moleque was an amusing enough popular stereotype that an ice cream bar, chocolate-covered and flaked with "dirty" bits of coconut and almonds, was later named the pé de moleque, "ragamuffin's foot." Moleques tried to make themselves useful in myriad ways, some bordering on the criminal and deviant. Think of Fagin's boys in Dickens's Oliver Twist, especially the Artful Dodger, and you have it. Shoppers would slap their heads in exasperation when a nameless scamp they had hired to carry home a market basket on his head made off with their watch in the quick final transaction. While the victims of a moleque's street tactics might alert local police and the boy might be found—perhaps beaten by a police officer or sent to a state-sponsored reform school—there was no sense that street children as a class were a pressing social problem against which certain interest groups (homeowners, shopkeepers, business people) should aggressively organize. Instead, they were seen as a potential source of cheap domestic or agricultural labor.

In the Brazil of the 1990s, however, poor children on the loose are more often viewed as a scandal, a public nuisance, and a danger. This shift is reflected in the stigmatizing terms by which the children are now known. Yesterday's cunning moleque is today's pivete (young thief), trombadinha (pickpocket, purse snatcher) and maloqueiro (street child, thief). (Ours is a perspective informed by more than thirty years of intermittent anthropological fieldwork in the interior sugar plantation market town of Bom Jesus da Mata in the state of Pernambuco, and more recently in the cities of Rio de Janeiro, São Paulo, and Recife, as well as contact and communications with children's rights activists.)

Street urchins have long been a feature of urban life in Brazil, as elsewhere in Latin America, where children are simultaneously drawn to, and in flight from, different kinds of labor. But in 1981 Hector Babenco's film Pixote: a lei do mais fraco (Pixote: The Law of the Weakest) stunned audiences with its savage images of the lives of marginalized children both on the streets and in detention. Filmed during the final stages of the military dictatorship in Brazil, Pixote focused on a child in the generation left behind by the failed "economic miracle" of the 1970s. Rapid industrial expansion made Brazil into the world's eighth strongest economy, but one whose wealth was more unequally distributed than in any other modern, industrialized nation.

The country's much-vaunted move to democratization was especially hard on street children. The authoritarian police state that had ruled Brazil for twenty years had kept the social classes safely apart, with "dangerous" poor children confined to the favelas (slums) or in prison-like reform schools. But with the transition to democracy in 1985, the shantytowns ruptured. Poor black street children descended from hillside slums and seemed to be everywhere, flooding downtown boulevards and praças (plazas), flaunting their misery and their needs. Children who in the 1960s might have been viewed with mild annoyance were now feared and often became targets of violence and even murder.

Perhaps the very process of democratization (accompanied by economic austerities imposed by the World Bank's model of development

Source: Reprinted with permission of the author.

through "structural adjustment"), occurring in the absence of economic and social justice, provoked a crisis for street children. Not only had they become part of a more visible, desperately poor population, but new democratic laws and liberal institutions now promised them civil rights protections that used to be the province of the affluent and the educated. Many middle-class Brazilians felt insecure, unprotected, and threatened by these newly empowered children. Paradoxically, vigilante and police-linked violence increased during and following the transition from military to democratic politics, with children included as targets.

The crisis has been complicated by a lack of precision regarding the numbers of street children, the nature of their existence (alternating between home and street), and the number of crimes committed by and/or against them. Estimates of their population vary from tens of thousands to millions. In São Paulo alone, survey estimates vary from as low as 5,000 to as high as 500,000, depending in part on whether they include those children who have homes but spend most of the day and occasional nights on the streets.

In a 1989 interview, a group of boys who survived by begging on the streets of Bom Jesus da Mata discussed public perceptions of them. "They say we will turn into thieves," said nine-year-old Josenildo. Marcelo, two years older, broke in with, "Thanks be to God that up until now I have never stolen anything, and I never want to either!" The quietest and most reflective of the group, ten-year-old Adevaldo (nicknamed Deo), said, "We do become thieves. But I myself am going to be different. I am going to return to school until I am graduated and then I will find a good job. I am going to have a wife and children and I will never put any of them out in the streets to beg."

"And where do you hope to find a job, Deo?"

"I want to work in the Bank of Brazil," he replied proudly, to laughter all around.

"Do you think they will trust you in a bank, Deo? Won't they say, 'Oh, I remember him; wasn't he the one who used to beg outside the Santa Terezinha bakery?"

"But I am going to quit soon, and no one will remember me. I am already looking for a job, but the woman who said she would hire me has changed her mind. And now I only beg because I am hungry."

"When you go home, isn't there food for you?"

"My mother only cooks for my father, not for me."

"Doesn't your mother care for you?"

[After a slight hesitation] "She likes a part of me."

"Which part?"

"That I sometimes bring home things for her that I get in the street."

"You mean that you steal?"

"Yes, sometimes. But I don't like doing these things and I want to 'reform.'"

Casa and *rua*, "house" and "street," are keywords in Brazil that refer to more than physical spaces. The terms are moral entities, spheres of social action, and ethical provinces. *Casa* is the realm of relational ties and privilege that confers social personhood, human rights, and full citizenship. *Rua*, in contrast, is an unbounded, impersonal, and dangerous realm, the space of the masses *(o povo)*. Shantytown homes are overcrowded and families often unstable. Consequently "home," especially for boys, is not so much a place to eat and sleep as an emotional space, the place where one comes from and where one returns, at least periodically. As denizens of the street, poor and semiautonomous children are separated from all that can confer relationship and propriety, without which rights and citizenship are impossible. Yet, while street children may be almost autonomous, they often remain emotionally dependent on home and deeply attached to the idea of family. When we asked nine-year-old Chico, a street boy of Bom Jesus da Mata, if his mother still loved him, he replied without hesitation, "She's my mother, she has to love me!" But Chico knew as well as we did that his mother had tried several times to give him away to distant relatives when he was a baby and had later forced him out of the house.

From the point of view of shantytown dwellers, nothing is extraordinary or problematic about its children flowing onto the streets, for the streets, especially in the city center, are primary sites of employment and economic survival for both poor children and adults. The term "street child" is not even used in the shantytowns; parents sometimes do speak critically of local boys and young men, *malandros*, who "spend their lives doing bad things on the street." Perhaps the closest that people in the shantytowns come to thinking of a street child is the oft-expressed fear of "losing" a child to the streets, to the uncontrolled realm beyond the home.

Like Chico, most street children work. They sell candy or Popsicles, guard and wash cars, carry groceries, and shine shoes. The outward signs that a child is working—the shoeshine box, the tray of candy, the pail of roasted nuts—signify that the child is "good" and should not be perceived as a threat. The empty-handed street child, traveling in a group and obviously not working, is far more likely to suffer discrimination. Most children return home at night to sleep, while a minority alternate sleeping outdoors with sleeping at home. An even smaller group lives full-time in the streets. This smallest group, truly homeless and very visible, fuels the negative stereotypes of dangerous and uncontrollable street children. Commonly associated with theft, gang life, and drugs, they are the most likely to be targets of exploitation and of violence that includes police brutality.

The most notorious assault on Brazilian street children, one that renewed international concern for their plight, was the Candelária massacre of July 23, 1993. On that night a group of off-duty policemen opened fire on more than fifty children who were sleeping in the elegant square in front of Rio de Janeiro's Candelária Cathedral. Eight died, six on the spot, and two at a nearby beach, where they were taken and killed execution-style. Many others were wounded. Opinion polls showed considerable public support for the police action. Many "ordinary" citizens reported being "fed up" with the criminal and disorderly behavior of street children. Rascally *moleques* truly had been transformed into dangerous *meninos de rua* (street children).

In the past decade a new fear has been added, that of untimely death at the hands of paid death squads. Beginning in the 1980s—well into Brazil's democratic transition—reports surfaced of a deadly campaign against street children involving kidnapping, torture, and assassination by paid vigilantes and off-duty police recruited in

projects of "urban hygiene." They seemed to operate with relative impunity, especially in large cities. But even in small interior towns such as Bom Jesus da Mata, street children live in daily fear of police, state institutions, kidnappers, and, more fantastically, people who are rumored to steal human organs. Between 1988 and 1990, close to 5,000 street children and adolescents were murdered in Brazil, but few of these homicides were deemed worthy of official investigation. This lack of bureaucratic attention is not surprising when police officers are among the suspected perpetrators. Most of the victims were males fifteen to nineteen years old, although younger children were also victims.

In his 1991 denunciation of violence, *Brazil: War on Children*, journalist Gilberto Dimenstein identified the role of off-duty policemen and hired killers—working in concert with small businessmen and shopowners—in sustaining the death squads. Street children were said to be bad for business and for tourism, threats to public health and safety. A report by the São Paulo chapter of the Brazilian Bar Association implicated military police in death squads funded by shopkeepers that killed most of nearly 1,000 street children who were slain in that city in 1990.

The vast majority of full-time street children do not so much run away or "choose" the streets as they are thrown out of, or driven from, homes where exposure to chronic hunger, neglect, and physical or sexual abuse makes life under bridges, in bus stations, and in public rest rooms seem preferable, or even—as one child living in an abandoned building in Bom Jesus da Mata put it—more "peaceful" and "happy" than life at home. Those who live on the streets full-time mostly boys, although girls are also forced there, often following escape from exploitative work as domestic servants or as child prostitutes in cabarets. For some girls, however, the reverse is true: they may seek out prostitution, believing it provides a "safe house" away from the anarchy of the streets.

Rumor plays a significant part in justifying discrimination against these children. In the May 29, 1991, issue of *Veja*, a weekly magazine, it was reported that the street children who congregate in the Praça de Sé, the central plaza of São Paulo, commit more than 32,000 thefts and robberies a year, that is, about three thefts a day by each child. The sources of these statistics were vague. In 1992 newspapers and radio carried reports about roving gangs of shantytown children, some of whom were said to stream across the southern beaches of Rio de Janeiro, robbing anyone within reach. These reports were based on a single incident later attributed to youths from a particular slum, none of whom were homeless. Nonetheless, the stories caused considerable panic in middle- and working-class people, fearful of new "invasions" of the desperately poor into their social spaces.

It's true that some street children, especially older ones, survive, at least in part, through petty crimes. However, Padre Bruno Secchi, a Salesian missionary who has been working with the poor and street children for thirty years in the Amazonian city of Belem contends that what is striking is not how many poor children are criminals but, considering the misery of their lives, how few resort to crime. Many survive by begging, but as soon as they show signs of physical maturity, they cease to evoke compassion. Seventeen-year-old Marcos Julio spent nine years living on the streets of Bom Jesus da Mata. He said that as long as he was "little and cute" he could make his way by begging, but after he turned about fourteen, people suddenly became afraid of him and chased him away.

Exchanging sex for food and affection is also a survival strategy, especially for boys who were initiated into sex at an early age. And for young girls escaping from the "slavery" of domestic service, prostitution can seem like liberation. "The first time I sold my body was the first time I felt like it really belonged to me," a teen-age girl confided at a meeting for younger sex workers in São Paulo, organized by an AIDS awareness group. The girl, who had run away from Pernambuco, had a family history that included incest.

Glue sniffing is another badge of street identity, along with sniffing perfume, gasoline, or shoe polish. In Bom Jesus da Mata, children as young as eight years old explained that glue was pleasant (*bom*) and smelled nice (*cherioso*). Some said that it helped them to sleep especially when hungry. Pedro, age twelve, described himself as nervous and emotional. He said glue sniffing made him more calm. For some small children, it

was used interchangeably with thumb sucking or pacifier sucking, practices that street children (as well as other children in the shantytowns) sometimes engage in as late as adolescence.

During the military years (1964–85) the primary mechanism to control loose and wayward children was FEBEM; the State Federation for the Well-being of Minors, a network of reform schools that were often jail-like and inspired fear in shantytown children. ("You won't ever turn me in to FEBEM, will you?" street children often nervously asked Nancy during the military regime years.) But even after the passage of new laws designed to reform these institutions, real change has been slow, and in many small municipalities like Bom Jesus da Mata, local jails have replaced the reform schools as "holding tanks" for dangerous and endangered youth. During fieldwork in 1992, we met several underage youths locked up alongside adult offenders in Bom Jesus da Mata's small, dingy municipal jail. Some of them had been there for periods ranging from several weeks to six months with no clear indication of just when they might be tried or released. A local judge explained that these boys were at risk of retaliatory attacks by other children and by paid vigilantes. Without relatives to claim or protect them, with the FEBEM mandate curtailed under new laws, and in the absence of a formal network of foster homes, jail seemed the only reasonable option.

Decisions about the fate of individual street children are made in the context of a deep national preoccupation with the country's future. So many factors feed public fears—chaotic urbanization, the AIDS epidemic, and the political liberalization that provided new legal protections for the poor, homosexuals, and the sick or disabled—that it is increasingly difficult to remove or incarcerate "unwanted" populations legally. At the same time Colombian cartels and the Italian Mafia, trafficking in cocaine, brought upscale firearms into the shantytowns and distributed them to youths and even to street children, whom they also recruited as messengers. The expansion and reorganization of crime in the shantytowns interrupted and confounded the growth of participatory democracy that so many grassroots organizations—residents' associations, trade unions, and local church communities—had long struggled to introduce.

A classified document produced at Brazil's Superior War College in 1989 played on people's fears:

Let us suppose, for the sake of argument, that there are some 200,000 unattached minors (which is a conservative estimate). By the beginning of the next century we will have a contingent of criminals, malefactors, and murderers the size of our current army. … At that time, if police lack the means to confront such a situation, the constituted executive, legislative, and judicial powers could request the co-operation of the armed forces to take on the difficult task of neutralizing them [that is, "destroying them"] in order to maintain law and order.

Something like this is already happening. In November 1994, soldiers, backed by tanks and helicopters, were used in a crackdown on crime in Rio de Janeiro shantytowns. According to Human Rights Watch, the first victims included young people caught in the crossfire. Paradoxically, shantytown dwellers strongly support various police actions against their own populations, according to opinion polls. What makes people there assume that violent attacks on them and their children are an acceptable form of social control, the legitimate "business" of the police? For one thing, the very ubiquity of violence against the poor makes them view their own violent deaths as predictable, natural. There are also racial undertones to the "normalization" of police and vigilante attacks on people in the shantytowns. The crimes of the poor, the petty thievery of older street children, are viewed as "race" crimes and as "naturally" produced. Poor, young, unemployed blacks are said to steal because it is "in their blood" to do so. They are described in crudely racist terms as *bichos da Africa*, "animals from Africa." Increasingly today, race hatred and unconscious racism have emerged as explanations for popular support of violent and illegal police actions in shantytowns and on the street. Indeed, the subtext of the discourse on street children is color-coded in "race-blind" Brazil, where most street children are black. Of the more than 5,000 children and youths murdered between 1988 and 1990, most

of the victims were black males between the ages of fifteen and nineteen years.

Fundamentally, Brazil's street children are poor children in the wrong place; as long as they remain in the shantytowns, they are not viewed as an urgent problem about which something must be done. But by "invading" the city centers, frequenting upper-class beaches, and engaging in petty crimes against the middle class, they defy the segregated order. The wealthy retreat into private enclaves with private schools, private security, and private transportation, and the public sphere is abandoned to its own turmoil: lack of security, paucity of resources, and vigilante justice. The risks and hazards for street children are great: illiteracy, toxicity from inhalant drugs, chronic hunger and undernutrition, sexual exploitation, and AIDS.

Although the overall picture is not encouraging, there are hopeful signs. In the past decade, a large social movement on behalf of children's rights has arisen, involving thousands of individuals and many small grassroots groups. They have organized street youth in the cities, exposed routine violence and assassinations, advanced constitutional reforms and legislation, and defended the right of children to be *in* the street, while recognizing that a life *of* the streets can only be self-destructive in the long term. Despite the backlash against its liberal reforms, the new Brazilian constitution (1988), and particularly the *Estatuto da Cruinça e de Adolescente* (the Child and Adolescent Statute), which became law in 1990, are remarkable documents. The child statute—the result of intensive lobbying by a broad coalition of nongovernmental organizations and activists—radically transformed the legal status of children and redefined the responsibilities of the state and civil society. But as enviable as the new laws are, they have not yet been claimed by the majority, nor have they become internalized popular standards and everyday practice in Brazil. They remain elusive ideals that are daily subverted by those who regard the lives of poor children as undesirable and expendable.

Brazil's street children have challenged and redefined the boundaries between public and private, adult and child, normal and deviant behavior. Because they violate conventional ideas about childhood innocence, vulnerability, and dependency, they are seen not as children at all but as dangerous young people in revolt. The choices offered such children at present are extremely limited: to return home to their "proper" childhoods—which is not an option for most—or to accept the risks of a semiautonomous life on the streets. The true test of Brazil's democracy will be the nation's ability to think of childhood and citizenship in radically new ways. Will it be possible for street children—who cannot depend on nuclear families for support—to find protection, rather than bullets, on the elegant streets of modern Brazil?

CRITICAL THINKING QUESTIONS

1. The image of street children in Brazil has undergone a dramatic change since the 1960s. Compare the attitudes of Brazilians toward street children in the 1960s and today.
2. What social conditions and events appeared to lead to the crisis that led thousands of children to be set loose in the streets of Brazil's major cities?
3. How are the terms *casa* (house) and *rua* (street) used in the worldview of Brazilian language and social life?
4. How do most street children survive?
5. What efforts, both peaceful and violent, have been directed toward dealing with the problem of the street children?

Realities of Gender

STATE OF THE ART: Gender

In anthropology's infancy, anthropologists focused on men's roles in society to the exclusion of women's roles. The societies from which these anthropologists came viewed most matters of recognizable importance as deriving from the male sex alone. Hence attention was given to men's roles, which resulted in a male bias in anthropology. Female ethnographers argued that women were indispensable actors in all areas of sociocultural life and sought "an anthropology of women," or one that is inclusive of both sexes (Rosaldo & Lamphere 1974, Reiter 1975, Milton 1979). The 1970s laid the foundation for "the anthropology of gender" even though analyses of gender as we know it today had not developed. The early feminists used conceptual frameworks that aimed at the "universality of women's experiences." Their approaches were rooted in "essentialism"—the belief that men and women have inherent, basic qualities (masculinity and femininity) that are "biologically driven," and explain their behavior. The 1970s work on the anthropology of gender focused on gender stratification. Since then anthropologists have found that natural or biological differences alone do not account for male and female roles, including economic roles, but rather arise from different socializing practices in the society. Male and female roles differ from society to society as a reflection of cultural differences that exist around the world.

Often male economic roles are assigned higher cultural value in a given society (Strathern 1972, Friedl 1975, 1978) although anthropologists have revealed cases where women contributed more to subsistence (Bonvillain 2010). The 1970s work on the anthropology of gender is noted for its emphasis on gender stratification: the nature of male dominance, the status of women, the conditions of female subordination—these were compared cross-culturally for the purpose of making generalizations. Thus, anthropologists have sought causes for differences in the social, legal, political, and economic status of men and women, and the actual manifestations of these differences (Schlegel 1977; Rosman, Rubel, & Weisgrau 2009). In the 1980s anthropologists began to challenge the generalized, "essentialist" views of men and women that tended to subsume specific cases, and masked the conditions of male dominance and female subordination. Feminist anthropologists argued that women worldwide do not share similar experiences of oppression, therefore, should not be perceived as a unitary group. Experiences vary across race, ethnicity, culture, caste, and class. Hence anthropologists returned to "defacto particularism"—the study of particular groups. The 1990s continued with unresolved issues regarding the existence of a universal "sexual asymmetry" (status inequality). Ortner proposed an alternative theoretical argument that consists of a combination of factors: (1) no culture has a single "gender model" or standard, (2) women are not a unitary group, (3) the idea of a "gender hegemony" recognizes both "order and contradiction" in a society's gender practices (Delcore 2007) that may unveil situations in which women exercise power over men. Ortner called for the "historicization of gender studies" (Delcore 2007) to reveal the actual gender situation of a particular time and place. By the end of the twentieth century and into the present anthropologists such as Gurvin & Hill (2009) and several others continue to study gender roles and are raising more issues that call into question the "essentialist" views in earlier studies.

As the world changes, the conditions of males and females, including their roles, change accordingly. Globalization has impacted women negatively in some areas of the world in terms of the central role they once played in subsistence (Bonvillain 2010). Others have gained tremendously from it. Views about men and women vary cross-culturally—some cultural participants still believe in the "cult of domesticity," "machismo," and any other such labels as each culture designates. Anthropologists study the impacts of these gender ideologies to the extent to which they perpetuate inequality in society.

Earlier studies revealed how males and females are assigned different spaces, with the women often getting the domestic realm because of mothering and the home, while the public realm is often reserved for men (Rosman & Rubel 2004). Furthermore, in a sociocultural context "space" is configured, and "spatial relations" are enacted, re-configured, and "consciously mediated," (Persson 2007), contested (Zhang 2006), transformed (Toren 2007), and actively contrived to produce added meaning. Today the realms are blurring, with men and women moving into each other's spheres; some societies are redefining tasks and roles, and gender is becoming less significant in making such decisions.

Later, anthropologists began to focus on male–female relationships and the way roles are culturally constructed. The cross-dressing of persons in many societies reflects the shifting of gender. Anthropologists have identified societies in which four types of gender categories exist as the norm (Epple 1998; Rosman & Rubel 2004; Rosman, Rubel & Weisgrau 2009).

Apart from the "heuristic"—general traditional theories that anthropology uses to study the human condition—there are minor (middle range) theories and concepts that apply in gender studies. For example, the heuristic "functionalist theory" (Section One—State of the Art) can be applied to the study of gender roles in a given society. Recent theoretical advances in gender studies are "post-structuralist, post-colonial, and performance approaches" (Delcore 2007). Post-structuralism is a critical extension of the theory of "structuralism," derived from the techniques of "decontruction" (see Section One—State of the Art). Post colonial theory is a critical response to the oppressive conditions of a historical period (colonialism), and the ensuing resistance. Non-Western scholars living in the West are at the forefront of this intellectual discourse. Performance theory sees gender as a practice, a ritualized behavior, and the enactment of sex/gender identities. Linguistically, it refers to actual language usage by men and women that differs from the performer's knowledge of proper grammar. It complements "linguistic competence." Another is the *queer theory,* a term some anthropologists use to designate the investigation of nontraditional sexual practice (Rubel 2004). Sexual minorities use queer theory to contest and renegotiate their social identities ascribed on the basis of difference from the acceptable norm—"heteronormativity." They reject taxonomic or sexual labels that categorize people as homosexual, heterosexual, the psychologically impaired or sexual deviant, etc. (Voss 2000, 2008).

Anthropologists have always looked at how gender intersects with other areas of culture and domains of social life such as art, symbols, religion, ritual, government and politics, political organizations, and other areas. Some have explored the applicability of the concept of feminism to non-Western societies and, in those societies, found different brands of feminism that differ in many ways from the Western brand. Also, the meanings of gender symbols are derived from the symbolic system of the society that created them. New contexts of study are emerging in gender studies. Within the past four decades, focus has shifted from the conditions of males in society to the conditions of women, almost to the point that the study of women was synonymous with that of gender. Feminist anthropologists were much in favor of *deconstructionist* views (see Section One, State of the Art: *The Subfields*). Anthropological ethnographies were subjected to a rigorous deconstructionist analysis that revealed inaccuracies in the rendition of women's actual circumstances. The deconstructionist exercise also encouraged new perspectives in examining women's lives. The result was a female bias in anthropology. *Postmodernist* approaches (see Section One, State of the Art: *The Subfields*) further encouraged a serious introspection in feminist anthropology. In recognition of the female bias in the study of gender, anthropologists began to give equal attention to both sexes. As a result, masculinity studies are gaining momentum. According to Gutmann (1997) masculinity studies should focus on "studying men as men" rather than utilizing previous frameworks used to study manhood. Presently, anthropologists are reexamining old concepts used in gender studies such as "patriarchy" and "matriarchy," and addressing epistemological flaws in ethnographies such as "unrecognized female status" in patriarchal systems and the theoretical view of a "stable, universal homosexual subject" that do not account for individual or group differences. Anthropologists are attempting to redefine these concepts and revamp ideas based upon new ethnographic findings that show evidence of active female status and power in the domain of apparent male hegemony; propose an alternative meaning of matriarchy that is based upon "maternal symbols" in which both men and women take part in nurturing, contrary to a view of matriarchy as "a woman-ruled" system; a representation of homosexual subjects as individuals with differing self presentations, ideologies, and types (Sanday 2002; Sinnot 2004; Symonds 2004; Stockett 2005; Delcore 2007; Zuo & La Rossa 2009). These approaches worked simultaneously with a reconsideration of analytical frameworks like cross-cultural comparison upon which these studies were based, in the process uncovering new patterns and processes that were obscured by generalizations (Delcore 2007). In a new ongoing study, a team of anthropologists (Smith et al 2010; Mulder et al 2010; & Shenk et al 2010) are revisiting an old question—the state of "inequality" in the so-called egalitarian society (the hunting and gathering, pastoral, and premodern agricultural types) that is characterized by "pervasive equality" and maintained through the institution of redistribution. Through rigorous, standardized scientific procedures, they explored the role of the transmission of "intergenerational wealth" (hunting ability and successes, healthy and productive kin members, mental acumen, inherited assets and material resources) in promoting or mitigating inequality. Findings suggest a reassessment of egalitarianism given the degree of inequality found in the midst of supposed equality. The bigger question is, what are the implications for gender studies, and anthropology in general?

ABOUT THE ARTICLES

The articles in Section Five examine the role of gender and gender formation from the perspective of several cultures and several different approaches.

Stockard and Johnson present a general overview of research into the relationship between human biology and gender behavior. While acknowledging the role that biology plays in gender formation and behavior, they sound a cautionary note regarding the interpretation and application of such data from either a masculine or a feminine perspective. They call for a more evenhanded, non-gender-biased approach to the investigation of gender roles.

Estioko-Griffin and Griffin present data on what, from the anthropological perspective, is an unusual cultural circumstance. The Agta are a culture where women, contrary to generally accepted anthropological ideas and observations, heavily participate in hunting and other "traditionally male" activities. These activities, and the reasons behind them, are discussed in light of both the traditional cultural patterns of the Agta and the impact of outside cultural influences. The reader could ask if female hunting and participation in other "male" activities make Agta women the social and economic equals of Agta men.

Dubisch's article examines not only gender behavior in a Greek village but also the ideologies that inform and construct gender relationships in that village. She argues that gender has to be seen in multiple contexts, ranging from the personal and domestic all the way to the national. This article may help the student examine how his or her own concept of gender has been derived from multiple sources and may vary according to the social context in which gender is expressed.

The last article in the section is perhaps the most revealing. Herdt raises a series of important issues about the cultural construction of gender, particularly how male gender identity is constructed. Unlike American society, the Sambia believe that masculinity is not a biological given but that boys' masculinity must be constructed at the hands of older initiated males of the society. They believe that only an initiated adult male can turn a boy into an adult male. Their procedure may be disconcerting to Western sensibilities, but it serves to create a masculine persona that has served the Sambia well, given their social and political conditions.

References

Bonvillain, N. *Cultural Anthropology,* 2nd ed. Upper Saddle River, NJ. Prentice Hall, 2010.

Delcore, H. D. "New Reflections on Old Question in the Anthropology of Gender." *Reviews in Anthropology* 36, (2007): 109–130.

Epple, C. "Coming to Terms with Navaho Nadleehi: A Critique of bederche, Gay, Alternative Gender, and Two-Spirits." *American Ethnologist* 25, no. 2 (1998): 267–290.

Friedl, E. *Women and Men: An Anthropologist's View.* Holt, Rhinehart and Winston, 1975.

Friedl, E. "Society and Sex Roles." *Human Nature.* April, 1978.

Gurvin, M., & Hill, K. "Why Do Men Hunt?: A Reevaluation of 'Man the Hunter' and the Sexual Division of Labor," *Current Anthropology* 50, no.1 (2009).

Gutmann, M. C. "Trafficking In Men." *Annual Review of Anthropology* 26 (1997): 385–409.

Milton, K. "Male Bias in Anthropology." *Man 14,* New Series, no.1 (1979): 40–54.

Mulder, M. B. et al. "Pastoralism and Wealth Inequality: Revisiting an Old Question." *Current Anthropology* 51, no.1 (Feb. 2010), 35–48.

Persson, A. "Intimate Immensity: Phenomenology of Place and Space in an Australian Yoga Community." *American Ethnologist* 34, no.1 (Feb. 2007): 44–56.

Reiter, R. "Toward an Anthropology of Women." *Monthly Review Press,* 1975.

Rosaldo, M. Z. & Lamphere, L. *Women, Culture and Society.* Stanford University Press, 1974.

Rosman, A., & Rubel, P. *The Tapestry of Culture: An Introduction to Cultural Anthropology,* 8th ed. New York: McGraw–Hill, 2004.

Rosman, A., Rubel, P., & Weisgrau, M. *The Tapestry of Culture: An Introduction to Cultural Anthropology,* 10th ed. New York: Alta Mira Press, 2009.

Sanday, P. R. *Women at the Center: Life in a Modern Matriarchy.* Ithaca, NY: Cornell University Press, 2002.

Schlegel, A. *Sexual Stratification: A Cross-Cultural View.* Columbia University Press, 1977.

Shenk, M. K. et al. "Intergenerational Wealth Transmission among Agriculturalists: Foundations of Agrarian Inequality." *Current Anthropology* 51, no.1 (Feb. 2010): 65–83.

Sinnott, M. J. *Toms and Dees: Transgender Identity and Female Same-Sex Relationships in Thailand.* Honolulu: University of Hawaii Press, 2004.

Smith, E. A. et al. "Wealth Transmission and Inequality among Hunter—Gatherers." *Current Anthropology* 51, no.1 (Feb.2010): 19–34.

Stockett, M. K. "On the Importance of Difference: Re-Envisioning Sex and Gender in Ancient Mesoamerica." *World Archaeology* 37, no.4 (Dec. 2005): 566–578.

Strathern, M. *Women in Between: Female Roles in a Male World.* Academic Press, 1972.

Symonds, P. V. *Calling in the Soul: Gender and the Cycle of Life in a Hmong Village. Seattle:* University of Washington Press, 2004.

Toren, C. "Sunday Lunch in Fiji: Continuity and Transformation in Ideas of the household." *American Anthropologist* 109, no.2 (June 2007): 285–295.

Voss, B. L. "Feminisms, Queer Theories, and the Archaeological Study of Past Sexualties." *World Archaeologies* 32, no. 2 (Oct. 2000): 180–192.

Voss, B. L. "Sexuality Studies in Archaeology." *Annual Review of Anthropology* 37, (2008): 317–336.

Zhang, L. "Contesting Spatial Modernity in Late Socialist China." *Current Anthropology* 47, no.3 (June 2006): 461–484.

Zuo, J. & La Rosa, R. "Rethinking Family Patriarchy and Women's Positions in Presocialist China." *Journal of Marriage and the Family* 71, no. 3 (Aug., 2009): 542–557.

For Further Research

Gender has emerged as a topic of intense research since the mid-1980s. Numerous articles on gender have been published in the various anthropological journals cited elsewhere. There are several books that will provide the student with a solid overview of anthropological perspectives on gender, and provide further, more in-depth references. The first is *Gender and Anthropology* (1999, Waveland Press) by Frances Mascia-Lees and Nancy Black. Another is *Gender Diversity: Crosscultural Variations* (1999, Waveland Press) by Serena Nanda. A view of the homoerotic in a cross-cultural perspective is provided by Gilbert Herdt's *Same Sex, Different Cultures: Exploring Gay and Lesbian Lives* (1998, Westview Press). From the archaeological perspective, a good introduction is Joan Gero and Margaret Conkey's *Engendering Archaeology: Women and Prehistory* (1991, Wiley-Blackwell). For additional information on researching the topics discussed in the "State of the Art" section, please visit *www.mysearchlab.com.*

Biological Influences on Gender

Jean Stockard and Miriam M. Johnson

Popularized theories claim that one biological factor or another determines other psychological and social phenomena. Usually, these analyses try to justify male dominance and the traditional gender division of labor on the basis of some male capacity or female incapacity. This misuse of biology has understandably led many feminists to be extremely leery of any biological perspectives on gender differences. Actually, biological data need not, and in fact do not, imply that women are inferior to men nor that societal systems of male dominance or female mothering are inevitable.

There are obviously biological differences between females and males. There also probably are some psychological gender differences that have a biological base. However, because many studies of these differences have been based on a masculine paradigm, it is important to try to analyze these differences without a masculine bias. At the same time, we must avoid a possible feminist bias, a tendency to distort findings or overlook contradictory evidence because we want to believe certain "congenial truths" (Mackie 1977).

Few people now would argue for the exclusive importance of either nature or nurture in explaining sex gender differences. Biology by no means fully determines what happens to individuals or to social groups. Although physiological variables may prompt individuals to move in certain directions, the social situation, including economic and cultural factors, or individual desires, may overrule or drastically alter these biological predilections.

THE DEVELOPMENT OF SEX DIFFERENCES IN UTERO

Biological gender is first determined when the male's sperm unites with the female's egg to form the zygote. Both the sperm and the egg cell have 23 chromosomes. These chromosomes are then paired in the fertilized egg, yielding 23 pairs of 46 individual chromosomes. One of the pairs of chromosomes determines genetic sex. The egg contributes an X sex chromosome; the sperm contributes either an X or a Y chromosome. If the embryo has two X sex chromosomes, it is a genetic female; if it has an X and a Y chromosome, it is a genetic male. Because the female always contributes an X chromosome, it is the male's sperm that determines a child's sex. Scientists estimate that almost 140 XY conceptions occur for every 100 XX conceptions. However, more XY conceptions fail to develop and so, at birth, the ratio of males to females is about 105 to 100 (Money and Tucker 1975:41–42).

For the first six weeks after conception, embryos with either an XX or an XY sex chromosome structure appear the same, although they can be differentiated microscopically. All embryos have "growth buds" that can develop into male or female organs. Differentiation takes place in stages, starting first with the gonads or sex glands (the ovaries and testes), moving then to the internal reproductive structures, and finally to the external genitalia.

If the embryo has XY sex chromosomes, at about the sixth week after conception the bud of the gonads begins to develop into testicles, the male gonads. If the embryo has XX chromosomes, nothing will happen for about six more weeks, when the buds begin to differentiate into ovaries. These will contain many egg cells for reproduction in later life.

The testicles then begin to produce sex hormones: progesterone, androgen, and estrogen. Although we normally think of estrogen as the female hormone and androgen as the male hormone because of the relative proportion of the

Source: Reprinted from Stockard, Jean; Johnson, Miriam M., *Sex and Gender in Society,* 2nd Edition, © 1992. Reprinted by permission of Pearson Education, Inc., Upper Saddle River, NJ.

hormone each sex group produces, it is important to remember that both males and females have all three hormones in their bodies. The proportion of hormones varies both between men and women and between individuals within each sex group and over the life cycle. Testicles produce more androgen than estrogen, and ovaries produce more estrogen than androgen.

At around the third to fourth month after conception, hormones produced by the testicles cause the *wolffian* structures, which are present in all fetuses, to develop as *seminal vesicles*, the *prostate*, and the *vasa*. These are the internal male genitalia. During this time of prenatal life, the testicles also produce a substance that inhibits or stops the *mullerian* structures, also present in all fetuses, from developing into female organs. If testicles have not developed and none of these hormones has been produced, female internal genitalia develop. No hormones appear to be needed to prompt the *mullerian* structures to develop into the *uterus*, *fallopian tubes*, and upper *vagina*, the internal female genitalia (Money and Tucker 1975:46–47). It is possible, however, that hormones from the placenta and the mother, as well as even the ovaries, may influence the development of female genitalia (Fausto-Sterling 1985:81; Otten 1985:160).

Although the male and female internal genitalia develop from different structures, both present in all fetuses, the external genitalia develop from the same preliminary structure. Again, the hormonal mix determines how the preliminary genital tubercle becomes a penis and a scrotum to hold the testicles when they descend. If hormones generally secreted by the testicles are not present, the tubercle stays small to become the clitoris, and the two folds of skin, instead of joining to form the scrotum, stay separate to become the labia minora and head of the clitoris, separating the vagina from the urethra, which connects to the bladder.

One of the most important differences between males and females is the cyclic nature of female hormonal activity. In all female mammals, hormone production follows a regular cycle. Estrogen production is higher from the menstrual period to the time of highest fertility, and progesterone levels are higher after that. These cycles are controlled by the pituitary gland. Males do not have such specific or regular patterns of hormonal activity. Scientists have concluded from experiments on animals that prenatal secretion of androgen by the testicles influences how the pituitary gland will behave later. If androgen is lacking in prenatal life, the female pattern of cyclical secretion develops in later years. Other aspects of the brain are also affected by the prenatal hormone mix including, perhaps, some aspects of personality and behavior.

THE NATURE OF PHYSICAL DIFFERENCES

Physiological differences between the sex groups continue to appear and develop after birth. Some of these differences, primarily involving traits such as skin sensitivity and strength, first appear at birth. Others become important only at puberty, when sex differences in hormonal levels again occur. Below, we discuss differences in size and strength, susceptibility to illness and disease, and perception.

Size and Strength

At birth, boy babies tend to be slightly longer and weigh slightly more than girl babies. Females' lungs and hearts are proportionally smaller than those of males, and females have a lower percentage of their body weight in muscle, but a higher percentage in fat. Despite these size differences, females mature more rapidly than males. This difference first appears seven weeks after conception. By the time of birth, the female is four weeks ahead of the male baby. Females learn to walk and talk and are toilet trained more quickly than males. They also reach puberty and full physiological maturity earlier.

At birth, male metabolism is faster than female, although the difference may not be statistically significant. From the age of two months, males consume more calories than females. Adult males also have a lower resting heart rate, higher blood pressure, greater oxygen-carrying capacity, and more efficient recovery from muscular activity. These physiological characteristics are one basis of male superiority in strength. Females may certainly develop their strength and endurance through exercise programs. In recent years, as more funds have been devoted to training women athletes, they have rapidly improved their athletic performance (Dyer 1985, 1986). However, it is not yet known whether they will match men athletically in all endeavors.

Illness and Disease

A well-known sex difference that appears even prenatally is the male's greater susceptibility to illness and death. As we noted in the previous section, many more male than female fetuses are conceived, but the sex ratio is almost equal at birth. After birth, males also tend to be more susceptible to both disease and death. In this country, one-third more males than females die before their first birthday. Even as life expectancy in a society lengthens, the benefits accrue faster for women than for men, although this may result from the decline of female deaths associated with pregnancy and birth (Barfield 1976:67; Stillion 1985).

Males are susceptible to physical difficulties that pass females by. Such well-known problems as color blindness, hemophilia, and even baldness result from the males' XY chromosome structure. These inherited conditions arise from genetic information on the X chromosome that the child receives from the mother. Girls may also receive this condition-carrying X chromosome. But because the gene related to hemophilia or color blindness is recessive, the corresponding gene on the girls' other X chromosome can prevent the appearance of the condition in the female. The boy has no other X chromosome to block this effect and thus exhibits the defect. The girl remains a carrier and can pass the characteristic on to her offspring.

The incidence of other disorders may be influenced by our culture. Both males and females have physiological reactions to stress. But in our culture men more often develop peptic ulcers and skin disorders, and women exhibit headaches, migraines, backaches, and insomnia. Sex differences also appear in the incidence of many other diseases and conditions, although the reasons underlying all of these differences are not yet clear. For instance, women develop diabetes, phlebitis, and diseases of the thyroid gland more often than

men, whereas men more often develop most forms of cancer and cardiovascular and immunodeficiency diseases (Otten 1985:204–206). In middle age, women more often develop nonfatal chronic diseases, and men more often develop fatal diseases (Verbrugge 1989:345). Differences also occur in the incidence of mental illness. Women more often suffer from depression; men more often suffer from substance abuse and personality disorders that include problems with aggression and impulse control.

Finally, some sex differences in physical vulnerability may come from environmental and activity differences. A higher proportion of male deaths than female deaths results from accidents and injuries. Males also smoke cigarettes more and die from lung cancer more than females. However, as women become more involved in dangerous activities and as they increase their smoking, their death rate in these areas also rises (Travis 1988). Although it is popularly assumed that the stresses men face in the occupational world contribute to the higher number of heart attacks, there is now some evidence that women's hormonal secretions somehow protect them from heart disease. When these secretions diminish at menopause, women's susceptibility to heart disease rises. Females' lower death rate may also be promoted by their tendency to seek medical help more quickly than men (Verbrugge 1976; Hibbard and Pope 1983, 1986).

PHYSIOLOGY AND PSYCHOLOGICAL GENDER DIFFERENCES

Some differences we think of as "psychological" may have a physiological basis, including gender differences in nurturance, aggression and mood change.

Nurturance

We use the term *nurturance* to describe the "giving of aid and comfort to others" (Maccoby and Jacklin 1974:214–215). Nurturant behavior often involves responding to bids for help and comfort from others who are younger, weaker, or for some other reason, such as illness or old age, in a dependent position. Nurturant care of the young is essential for the survival of the human species, for human young depend totally on others for their care for a number of years.

Sex differences in the propensity to nurture appear in studies of adolescent animals and in studies of humans. Field studies show that young male langurs and baboons mainly play with other males and that young females spend a great deal of time with adult females and help take care of infants (Jay 1963; DeVore 1963; Fedigan 1982). Similar results have also been observed with human children in a wide cross-section of cultures (Whiting and Whiting 1975; Whiting and Edwards 1988). Similarly, experimenters who gave young monkeys to preadolescent pairs of male and female monkeys found that the preadolescent females were four times as likely as the males to act maternally toward young monkeys. The males were ten times as likely as the females to exhibit hostile behaviors (Chamove et al. 1967). Both males and females exhibit nurturant behaviors; females simply seem to show a greater interest in learning to do so.

Although biological factors influence nurturance, other factors also play an important part. Some authors emphasize the importance of physical contact in the postpartum period in cementing maternal-child ties (e.g., Fabes and Filsinger 1988). Similarly, however, greater contact between fathers and children appears to increase fathers' nurturance (e.g., LaRossa and LaRossa 1989). Attachment and nurturant behaviors appear to develop as parent and child interact and communicate with each other. Although the prenatal hormone doses males receive may hinder their interest in nurturing young children, they by no means eliminate their capacity for nurturing, as shown by experiences of fathers of newborns. Even among young boys, those with younger siblings at home show more nurturance in doll play than other boys. Girls show nurturance whether or not they have younger siblings (Ehrhardt and Baker 1974:38).

Aggression

Males exhibit more aggressive behavior than females in all known societies. Male nonhuman primates also exhibit more aggression than their female counterparts. Certainly, aspects of these differences are socially learned. Most important, the patterns of aggressive behavior that individuals exhibit depend on the social and cultural context. For instance, young boys may wrestle and fight during school recess, but they know that such behavior is not permitted in the classroom. Brawls and fights may occur regularly in some areas of town, but almost never in others.

Prenatal influences

As with nurturance, prenatal hormone doses are believed to have an organizing function on aggressive behavior. Evidence from research with animals indicates that males receiving lower than normal prenatal doses of androgens tend to exhibit less aggressive behavior in later life, whereas females who receive higher than normal prenatal doses of androgens exhibit more fighting in adulthood (Edwards 1969; Tieger 1980).

Although one may generalize from such animal studies to humans only with caution, studies with humans do suggest some connection between prenatal hormone doses and later aggression. Some studies indicate that boys and girls who received unusually high doses of androgen were more likely to have a higher level of energy and prefer boys' toys and activities, involving a high degree of rough, outdoor play (Ehrhardt 1973, 1985; Ehrhardt and Baker 1974).

The increased activity of the children with excessive hormonal doses may not be the same as aggression, which is usually defined as actions with intent to hurt another. It may be that in acting out a female gender identity, these girls learn to pattern their activity in nonaggressive ways. This finding suggests that because the feminine role does not include aggressiveness, hormones cannot produce it. The hormones do influence the young women, but the influence is expressed in ways compatible with a feminine identity.

Postnatal influences

For both animals and humans, hormonal levels can fluctuate markedly as a result of changes in the social environment. Studies on humans that try to link the level of testosterone within individuals' bloodstream with their level of aggressive or criminal behavior have yielded conflicting results. The relationship may be stronger with certain types of aggressive behaviors and with younger men, but more evidence is needed. Testosterone levels do appear to be associated with positions of dominance. Evidence from studies of nonhuman primates indicates that the more dominant animals have higher androgen levels than the less dominant animals (Moyer 1987), and some have suggested that this model might apply to human groups as well (e.g., Mazur 1985).

Under certain conditions, females are aggressive. Maternal aggression is found in many different species. This behavior, whether involving attacks toward strangers or just general irritability, is usually directly related to pregnancy, parturition, and lactation. Among the primates, this aggression appears to be elicited largely by the distress of the young and is shown by others as well as the mother. Males in a primate troop and other females besides the mother may display strong defensive reactions for the young.

In some cases animal mothers kill their young. However, this probably arises from a different endocrine basis than maternal aggression, including an abnormally high level of androgen (Moyer 1976:182).

Moods

Almost 60 percent of all women report that they experience discomfort or changes with their monthly menstrual period (Ramey 1976:139; Ericksen 1984:178). Some of the shifts in mood that women experience may result from negative attitudes toward the bodily functions, but some may result from the influence of different hormonal levels within the body. All living creatures experience cyclic changes. Sleep, pain tolerance, and cell division all appear to vary in regular cycles. Yet, among humans, women's mood changes during the monthly menstrual cycle have received the most research and popular attention. Women secrete hormones in a fixed pattern, corresponding with the menstrual cycle. During the first half of the menstrual cycle, after menstruation, the secretion of estrogen rises. Midway through the cycle, ovulation occurs, as an egg is released from a follicle in one ovary. Estrogen secretion then drops, but begins to rise again about the twentieth day of the cycle and finally drops quickly just before menstruation. Progesterone, also called the pregnancy hormone, increases after ovulation and peaks around the twentieth day

of the cycle. Its function is to prepare the body for pregnancy in case sperm fertilizes the egg. Just before menstruation the level of progesterone production falls markedly. There is some evidence that testosterone, a type of androgen, is secreted more heavily just before menstruation and also at ovulation (Bardwick 1974:29; Money and Ehrhardt 1972:222; Barfield 1976:70–71).

Hormones travel through the bloodstream and thus can potentially affect all parts of the body. Although some women have much wider mood changes than others, a good deal of evidence indicates that hostility, anxiety, and depression appear more during the premenstrual stage than in other parts of the cycle. Self-esteem and self-confidence seem to be highest in midcycle at ovulation (Hoyenga and Hoyenga 1979:145–153). Yet, as research in this area accumulates, it has become clear that no simple generalizations can be made about the incidence, symptoms, or source of "premenstrual syndrome" or "PMS." Only a relatively small percentage of women experience the extremely debilitating symptoms associated with a clinical definition of this syndrome. Moreover, cultural beliefs about menstruation and women's cycles are extremely widespread, and hormonal secretions are influenced by environmental variables such as stress. Thus, complete understanding of premenstrual syndrome must consider its multiple dimensions and the interaction of hormonal, cultural, and social influences.

Some evidence suggests that men as well as women experience cycles of hormonal secretions and mood. Several studies have documented relatively regular fluctuations of emotions or moods of both sex groups over a variety of time periods (e.g., Englander-Golden, et al. 1986). Other studies have noted fluctuations in the testosterone levels of males, with over half experiencing repeating cycles (e.g., Doering, et al. 1975). Even though men may have cyclical changes in mood and other bodily functions, it is not known if individual fluctuations in hormones are related to these changes. Relatively little research has examined this issue, and almost no work has compared women's mood fluctuations with men's.

Whatever may eventually be found with regard to hormonal and mood fluctuations in men, we can say now that the attention given to these matters in women has often been used to disparage them. Both women and men have fluctuations in mood from one time to another. Yet, to say that women should not hold responsible positions because their monthly changes in hormonal secretions affect their moods is akin to saying that men should not hold responsible positions because of their biologically based aggressiveness!

AVOIDING A MASCULINE BIAS

In general, sex differences in physical characteristics appear at birth or develop at puberty. Males are larger and stronger, and they have well-developed visual-spatial ability more often than females. Females mature more quickly, are less susceptible to disease, live longer, and may be more sensitive to taste, smell and touch than males are. Although women have a regular pattern of hormone secretion after puberty, no regular pattern has yet been found for men.

Although these physical differences generally appear cross-culturally, the meaning given to them varies from one society to another. For example, in this society, we have tended to stress women's relative lack of strength and men are expected to be the burden carriers. In other societies, relative strength is apparently unimportant and women carry the heavy loads. Biological differences are also used to justify differential evaluation of the sex groups, but here again the connection is by no means obvious. If one focuses on endurance and freedom from physical defect, one could argue for the natural superiority of women. If one focuses on size and strength, men might be called naturally superior.

Biological influences appear to affect psychological traits by increasing the likelihood that certain behaviors such as aggression or nurturance will appear. It is probably easier to prompt women to nurture and men to be aggressive because of prenatal hormonal influences and hormonal changes later in life. Yet, under certain circumstances, both women and men can nurture and both women and men can be aggressive. Hormones are neither necessary nor sufficient for these behaviors. Thus, that nurturance and aggression are influenced by biology does not mean that the social assignment of mothering to women and warfare to men is inevitable.

Although both men and women are subject to changes in mood, women's moods are somewhat more predictable than men's because they are more clearly influenced by cyclic hormonal changes. It is a masculine bias to assume that these cyclic changes are in themselves bad.

Some writers contend that male dominance itself can be explained by biology. Yet the activities and roles toward which females are biologically prompted are more important to the long-term survival of the group than those of males. For example, the affectional bonds between mother and young and between female members of primate groups promote group cohesion and survival much more than dominance and aggression. Although biology can help explain the social role divisions between women and men, it cannot explain why men's activities are valued more highly than women's. In order to explain this, one must look for theories that take into account the unique capacity of humans to imagine, to interpret, and to create meaning from their physical and social world.

CRITICAL THINKING QUESTIONS

1. What biological changes occur in utero that determine a fetus's sex?
2. Although generally stronger and faster than women, men are more susceptible to certain illnesses and physical disabilities. Name and discuss some of these illnesses.
3. Although males *tend* to be more aggressive than females, what influences this tendency more: biology? culture? or a combination of factors?
4. How do the authors explain the general differences in mood states between men and women?
5. Relate this article to another article in this section. Do you believe that the behaviors discussed in the other article are biologically influenced, culturally influenced, or a combination of both factors? Cite data from your chosen article to support your answer.

Woman the Hunter: The Agta

Agnes Estioko-Griffin and P. Bion Griffin

Among Agta Negritos of northeastern Luzon, the Philippines, women are of special interest to anthropology because of their position in the organization of subsistence. They are substantial contributors to the daily subsistence of their families and have considerable authority in decision making in the family and in residential groups. In addition, and in contradiction to one of the sacred canons of anthropology, women in one area frequently hunt game animals. They also fish in the rivers with men and barter with lowland Filipinos for goods and services.[1]

In this chapter, we describe women's roles in Agta subsistence economy and discuss the relationship of subsistence activities, authority allocation, and egalitarianism. With this may come an indication of the importance of the Agta research to the anthropology of women and of hunter-gatherers in general....

Women, especially women in hunting-gathering societies, have been a neglected domain of anthropological research. The recent volume edited by Richard Lee and Irven DeVore (1976) and the *!Kung of Nyae Nyae* (Marshall 1976) begin to remedy the lack but focus solely on the !Kung San of southern Africa. Other works are either general or synthetic (Friedl 1975; Martin and Voorhies 1975), or report narrowly bounded topics (Rosaldo and Lamphere 1974). Sally Slocum, writing in *Toward an Anthropology of Women* (Reiter 1975), has provided impetus for the Agta study. Slocum points out a male bias in studying hunter-gatherers, showing how approaching subsistence from a female view gives a new picture. From the insights of Slocum we have sought to focus on Agta women, to compare the several dialect groups, and to begin investigating the nature and implications of women as not "merely" gatherers but also hunters.

THE AGTA

The Agta are Negrito peoples found throughout eastern Luzon, generally along the Pacific coast and up rivers into the Sierra Madre interior.... Although perhaps fewer in numbers, they are also located on the western side of the mountains, especially on the tributary rivers feeding the Cagayan. In general terms, the Agta of Isabela and Cagayan provinces are not dissimilar to other present and past Philippine Negritos. (See Vanoverbergh 1925, 1929–30, 1937–38; Fox 1952; Garvan 1964; and Maceda 1964 for information on Negritos outside the present study area.) In the more remote locales, hunting forest game, especially wild pig, deer, and monkey, is still important. Everywhere, collection of forest plant foods has been eclipsed by exchange of meat for corn, rice, and cultivated root crops. Fishing is usually important throughout the dry season, while collection of the starch of the caryota palm (*Caryota cumingii*) is common in the rainy season. An earlier paper (Estioko and Griffin 1975) gives some detail concerning the less settled Agta; both Bennagen (1976) and Peterson (1974, 1978*a,b*, n.d.) closely examine aspects of subsistence among Agta in the municipality of Palanan.

A brief review of Agta economic organization will be sufficient for later discussion of women's activities. Centuries ago all Agta may have been strictly hunter-gatherers. Since at least A.D. 1900 the groups near the towns of Casiguran (Headland and Headland 1974) and Palanan have been sporadic, part-time horticulturalists, supplementing wild plant foods with sweet potatoes, corn, cassava, and rice. The more remote, interior Agta, sometimes referred to as *ebuked* (Estioko and Griffin 1975), plant small plots of roots, a few square meters of corn, and a banana stalk or two. They usually plant only in the wet season, harvesting an almost immature crop when staples are difficult to obtain by trade. *Ebuked* neglect crop production, preferring to trade meat for grains and roots.

Lee and DeVore (1968:7) argue that women produce much of the typical hunter-gatherers' diet and that in the tropics vegetable foods far outweigh meat in reliability and frequency of consumption. The Dipagsanghang and Dianggu-Malibu Agta strikingly contradict this idea. They are superb hunters, eat animal protein almost daily, and, as noted above, may have both men and women hunting. (The Tasaday, to the south in Mindanao, may represent an extreme nonhunting adaptation, one in which plant food collection is very dominant [Yen 1976].) Hunting varies seasonally and by techniques used among various groups, but is basically a bow and arrow technology for killing wild pig and deer, the only large game in the Luzon dipterocarp forests. Monkey, although not large, is a reliable rainy season prey. Among Agta close to Palanan and Casiguran, hunting is a male domain. Many hunters pride themselves on skill with bow and arrow; less able hunters may use traps. Dogs to drive game are very desirable in the dry season when the forest is too noisy for daylight stalking of animals.

The collecting of wild plant food is not a daily task. Most Agta prefer to eat corn, cassava, and sweet potatoes, and neglect the several varieties of roots, palm hearts, and greens procurable in the forest.... Forest foods are difficult to collect, necessitate residence moves over long distances, and do not taste as good as cultivated foods. Emphasis of trade networks with lowland farmers favors deemphasis of forest exploitation of plants. Only in the rainy season do Agta actively process a traditional resource, the sago-like caryota palm. Fruits are often picked on the spur of the moment; seldom do parties leave camp solely for their collection.

Trade with farmers is practiced by all Agta known to us. Rumors of Agta "farther into the mountains" who never trade (or cultivate) seem to be without substance. In the report of the Philippine Commission (1908:334), evidence of lowland-Agta trade around 1900 indicates the

ibay trade partner relationship to have some antiquity. As the lowlander population has increased since World War II, trade has also increased. Agta are more and more dependent on goods and foodstuffs gained from farmers; adjustments of Agta economic behavior continue to be made, with labor on farms being one aspect of change. Agta formerly simply traded meat for carbohydrates. Around Palanan they may now work for cash or kind when residing close to farmers' settlements. Hunting decreases as the demands of cultivation are met. A cycle is created, and further withdrawal from forest subsistence occurs. Farmers live in areas once solely owned by Agta. Debts to farmers increase with economic dependence; freedom of mobility and choice of activity decrease; and Agta in farming areas become landless laborers.

At the same time, Agta seek to get out of the cycle by emulating the farmers. Many Agta within ten kilometers of Palanan Centro are attempting to become farmers themselves. While the success rate is slow, the attempt is real. Again, when questioned by an early American anthropologist, Agta close to Palanan Centro claimed to be planting small rainy season plots with corn, roots, and upland rice (Worcester 1912:841). Living informants confirm the long practice of cultivation, but suggest a recent expansion of Agta fields and commitment to abandoning forest nomadism (especially over the last fifteen years). Around the areas of Disuked-Dilaknadinum and Kahanayan-Diabut in Palanan, Agta are well known for their interest in swidden cultivation. Even the most unsettled Agta farther upriver claim small fields and sporadically plant along the rivers well upstream of lowland farmsteads.

The horticultural efforts of the Agta appear less than is the case, since the social organization and settlement patterns are very different from those of the farmers. Agta throughout Isabela and Cagayan are loosely organized into extended family residential groups. A group, called a *pisan*, is seldom less than two nuclear families and very rarely more than five (in the dry season—perhaps slightly higher average during the wet season). The nuclear family is the basic unit of Agta society, being potentially self-sufficient under usual circumstances. The residential group is organized as a cluster of nuclear families united either through a common parent or by sibling ties. Non-kin friends may be visitors for several weeks, and any nuclear family is able to leave and join another group of relatives at will.

As is typical of hunting-gathering societies, no formal, institutionalized authority base exists. The nuclear family is the decision maker concerning residence, work, and relations with other people. Older, respected individuals, often parents and grandparents of group members, may be consulted, but their opinions are not binding. Often group consensus is desired; people who disagree are free to grumble or to leave.

The settlement pattern is determined, in part, by the seasonal cycle of rains and sunny weather, and by these influences on the flora and fauna exploited for food. Rainy season flooding restricts forest travel, brings hardships in exchange, but is compensated by good condition of the game animals. The dry season permits travel over greater distances and into the remote mountains. Predictable fish resources enhance the advantages of human dispersal; only the need to carry trade meats to farmers inhibits distant residence placement.

WOMEN'S ACTIVITIES

Women participate in all the subsistence activities that men do. Women trade with farmers, fish in the rivers, collect forest plant foods, and may even hunt game animals. Tasks are not identical, however; a modest sexual division of labor does exist. Furthermore, considerable variation is found among the groups of Agta of Isabella and Cagayan provinces. These differences may possibly be ascribed to degree of adjustment of Agta to lowland Filipino culture. Some differences may be due to unique culture histories and to little contact.

Although in Isabela most Agta women do not hunt with bow and arrows, with machetes, or by use of traps, most are willing to assist men in the hunt. Not uncommonly, women help carry game out of the forest. Since mature pig and deer are heavy and the terrain is difficult, this is no small accomplishment. Even in areas around Palanan and Casiguran, women are known to accompany men and dogs into the forest and to guide the dogs in the game drive. Some women are famous for their abilities to handle dogs; one informant, a girl about fifteen years of age, was especially skilled. In Palanan and Casiguran, women and men laugh at the idea of women hunting. Such a practice would be a custom of wild, uncivilized Agta (*ebuked*) far in the mountains, they say. Many of the attributes of *ebuked* seem to be old-fashioned customs still practiced by interior groups.

Two groups studied as part of the present research do have women who hunt. Among the Dipagsanghang Agta, several mature women claim to have hunting skills; they learned these in their unmarried teen years. They only hunt under extreme circumstances, such as low food supplies or great distances from farmers and a supply of corn. All these Agta are found in southern Isabela between Dipagsanghang and Dinapiqui.

In the northernmost section of Isabela and well into Cagayan province, women are active and proficient hunters. While we have termed the Agta here as the Dianggu-Malibu group, we are actually referring to speakers of the southeast Cagayan dialect who live on the river drainage areas of the Dianggu and Malibu rivers.[2] Both the dialect and women who hunt are found over a considerably greater territory, according to informants, reaching north to Baggao, Cagayan, and at least to the Taboan River.

Among the Dianggu-Malibu women some variation, perhaps localized, perhaps personal, is found. On the Dianggu, some of the women questioned, and observed hunting, carried machetes and were accompanied by dogs. They claim to prefer the machete to the bow and arrow, allowing dogs to corner and hold pigs for sticking with the knife. Our sample of actual observations is too small to argue that only immature pigs are killed, but we do know that in the dry season adult male pigs are dangerous in the extreme. Dogs may be killed during hunts. Since Agta dogs are seldom strong animals, we wonder if mature pigs are acquired only occasionally. On the other hand, so many dogs are owned by these Agta that sheer numbers may favor large kills. We have observed two Agta women with as many as fifteen dogs. Other Dianggu women prefer the bow.

On the Malibu River, Agta women are expert bow and arrow hunters. On both of our brief visits to this group, women were observed hunting. They claim to use bows always, and they seek the full range of prey animals. Wild pig is most desired, while deer are often killed. Future work must quantify the hunting details, but women seem to vary slightly from men in their hunting strategies. Informants say they hunt only with dogs. On closer questioning they admit to knowing techniques that do not involve dogs—for example, they may climb trees and lie in wait for an animal to approach to feed on fallen fruit. Among all Agta, hunting practices vary considerably between the rainy and dry seasons. Our fieldwork in Malibu has been confined to the dry season, when dogs are important. In the rainy season solitary stalking is practiced. Field observations should eventually provide quantitative data on women hunting in this season; we must stress that our data are primarily from interview and brief observation. We have not resided among Cagayan Agta long enough to advance quantitatively based generalizations.

Women not only hunt but appear to hunt frequently. Like men, some enjoy hunting more than others. The more remotely located Agta seem most to favor hunting. Even among Agta certain males and females are considered lacking in initiative, a fault that may not be confined to hunting.

Informant data indicate that while women may make their own arrows, the actual blacksmithing of the metal projectile points is a male activity. More field research is necessary to confirm the universality of this detail. Other items of interest pertain to the composition of hunting parties. Most people in any one residence group are consanguineally or affinely related. We have observed several combinations of hunting parties. Men and women hunt together or among themselves. Often sisters, or mother and daughter, or aunt and niece hunt together. At Malibu, two sisters, co-wives of one male, hunt together, and either or both sisters join the husband to hunt. When young children exist, one of the two wives may stay at the residence while the husband and the other wife hunt and fish. Also, sisters and brothers cooperate on the hunt. A woman would not hunt with, for example, a cousin's husband unless the cousin were along.

The only real argument, in our opinion, that has been advanced to support the contention that women must gather and men hunt relates to childbearing and nurture. Among the Agta, during late pregnancy and for the first few months of nursing, a woman will not hunt. In spite of the small size of each residential group, however, some females seem always to be around to hunt, although one or more may be temporarily withdrawn from the activity. Women with young children hunt less than teenagers and older women. On the occasion of brief hunts—part of one day—children are cared for by older siblings, by grandparents, and by other relatives. Occasionally a father will tend a child. Only infants are closely tied to mothers.

Girls start hunting shortly after puberty. Before then they are gaining forest knowledge but are not strong. Boys are no different. We have no menopause data, but at least one woman known to us as a hunter must have passed childbearing age. She is considered an older woman, but since she is strong, she hunts. The pattern is typical of men also. As long as strength to travel and to carry game is retained, people hunt. Our best informant, a young grandmother, hunts several times a week.

Both Agta men and women fish. In fact, from early childhood until the infirmity of old age all Agta fish. If most adults are gone on a hunting trip for several days, the remaining adults and children must obtain animal protein by themselves. Only women in late pregnancy, with young infants, or into old age, withdraw from fishing, which makes considerable demands of endurance as well as skill. Some men excel at working in rough, deep, and cold waters. The everyday techniques for fishing are limited to underwater spear fishing. Glass-lensed wooden goggles, a heavy wire spear or rod varying according to size of fish sought, and an inner-tube rubber band complete the equipment. To fish, people simply swim underwater, seeking fish in the various aquatic environments known for each species. Girls in their teens are very capable at fishing. When fishing individually, women may be major contributors to the daily catch.

When group fishing is undertaken, a drive is conducted. In this operation, a long vine is prepared by attaching stones and banners of wild banana stalks. Two people drag the vine, one on each end and on opposite sides of the river, while the people in the water spear fish startled by the stones and stalks. Women join men in the drives, with older men and women dragging the vine while all able-bodied youths and adults work in the water.

Difficulty of fishing may be characterized as a gradient upon which men and women become less and less able as age and debilities increase. The elderly, when mobile, may still be productive, but instead of true fishing, their activities may be termed collecting. Both the coastal reef areas and freshwater rivers and streams have abundant shellfish, shrimp, and amphibians that may be caught by hand. Elderly women and grandchildren are especially eager to harvest these resources. Older men are not ashamed to follow suit, although the enthusiasm of others for the task seldom gives old men incentive. Men are much less eager to give up riverine fishing after middle age than are women. Clearly some emphasis on males securing protein is found among Agta. Women, however, seem to have traditionally been active in fishing. Interestingly, as a few Agta adopt lowland fishing technology, especially nets, women seldom participate. Like their female counterparts in lowland society, women are deemed not appropriate in net fishing.

One might expect that, on the basis of worldwide comparison, tropic hunters would really be gatherers, and that women would be the steady and substantial providers. Agta do not fit the generalizations now accepted. Few Agta women regularly dig roots, gather palm hearts, seek fruit, or pick greens. Most Agta daily consume domesticated staples grown by the farmers. Women are, however, very knowledgeable concerning flora and its use, and among the less settled Agta, young girls are still taught all traditional forest lore. Brides-to-be among these Agta are partially evaluated on the basis of their knowledge, skill, and endurance in collecting jungle plant foods.

Roots are collected by women whenever more desirable food is unobtainable, when several wild pigs have been killed and the men want to eat "forest food" with pig fat, or when a visit to relatives or friends calls for a special treat. The interior groups may actually combine meat and wild roots for weeks when camped so far from farmers that exchange for corn is impossible. Downriver Agta consider such a practice a real hardship, not to be willingly endured. Men are known to dig roots, even though they say it is women's work. On long-distance hunts men do not as a rule carry food, and they may occasionally dig roots to alleviate the all meat-fish diet.

As hunting is thought of as a "sort of" male activity among many Agta (in Isabela), processing the starch of the caryota palm is a female activity. Women cruise the forest searching for trees containing masses of the starch; they also chop down the trees, split the trunks, adze out the pith, and extract the flour. Often parties of women and girls work together, speeding up the laborious task. On occasion, men will assist. Extracting the flour starch is moderately heavy work, and tiring. Husbands may help when wives have a pressing need to complete a task quickly. Since much of the final product is given in gift form, the need for haste occurs frequently. Perhaps most important to note is the male participation. Sexual division of labor is tenuously bounded among all Agta. Emphases may exist, but a man can even build a house (i.e., tie the fronds to the frame—a female task).

As noted at the beginning, trade, exchange, and horticulture are not new to Agta. Informants, early photographs, and writings indicate that all but the most remote Agta were not "pure" hunter-gatherers after about A.D. 1900. Since the mountains have been a final retreat—from the earliest Spanish attempts to conquer the Cagayan Valley until the present—Agta must have been in contact with former farmers/revolutionaries in hiding. Keesing (1962), summarizing the peoples of northern Luzon, documents several societies of pagan swiddeners adjacent to or in Negrito territory. The Palanan River drainage area was inhabited by farmers before Spanish contact in the sixteenth century. Doubtless, Agta have participated in economic exchange and social intercourse for centuries. Agta now have institutionalized trade partnerships, at least in Palanan and Casiguran municipalities. Trade partners are called *ibay* (Peterson [1978a,b] discussed the *ibay* relationship in detail), and partnerships may last between two families over two or more generations. *Ibay* exchange meat for grains and roots, or meat for cloth, metal, to-bacco, beads, and other goods. Services may be exchanged, especially in downriver areas. Fields may be worked by Agta, who then borrow a carabao, receive corn or rice, and satisfy any of a number of needs. What is important in relation to this chapter is that Agta women may engage in *ibay* partnerships. Among the lowland farmers almost all *ibay* are males. An Agta woman may be an *ibay* with a lowland man. According to our data, an Agta husband often is not also *ibay* with his wife's *ibay*, but he must treat the farmer as he would his own *ibay*. Of course Agta men and women trade with any farmer they choose, but such exchange is without the consideration given to an *ibay*. (Considerations include credit, acts of friendship, and first choice/best deal on goods.) Not only do women have *ibay*, but they very frequently are the most active agents of exchange. In areas where the trade rests mostly on meat and where men do most of the hunting, women are likely to carry out the dried meat and bring back the staple. They therefore gain experience in dealing with the farmers. We should note that many farmers attempt to cheat the Agta by shortchanging them on counts or weights, but they do so on the basis of gullibility or naiveté of the Agta, not on the basis of sex. Agta women are actually more aggressive traders than are men, who do not like confrontation.

Among the Dipagsanghang Agta, women seldom hunt today, and infrequently dig roots. They do carry out meat to trade. They seem to have an easier life, with emphasis on corn, rice, and roots instead of gathering wild foods. However, downriver, close to farmers, Agta women have reversed this trend, and are working harder and longer hours.[3] Intensification of the *ibay* relationship and need to own and cultivate land has forced women to become horticulturalists and wage laborers for farmers. On their own family plots (family-owned, not male- or female-owned) they, together with adult males and youths, clear land, break soil, plant, weed, and harvest. When clearing virgin forest of large trees, women do not participate. They do clear secondary growth in fallowed fields.

In the families that reside close to Palanan ... men and women work almost daily in the fields of farmers. Women go to the forest to collect the lighter raw materials for house construction, mats, betel chews, medicines, and so on. Men follow a similar pattern, giving up hunting for field labor and a corn and sweet potato diet supplemented by small fish. Again we see a remarkable parallel in the activities of males and females.

Looking more closely at specialized women's activities, one may suggest increasing importance in downriver areas. Women have several domains that they use to gain cash or kind income. As just stated, income from labor in fields adds to the economic power of women. A small-scale traditional pursuit, shared by men and women, is the gathering of copal, a tree resin common to trees (*Agathis philippinensis*) found scattered in the Sierra Madre. Women often collect and carry the resin out to lowland "middlemen," who sell it to the depot in town. While corn and cash may be sought in exchange, cloth is desired in order to make skirts. Medicine and medical treatments for ailing children may be paid for by copal collection. Another example of entrepreneurship by females is a small-scale mobile variety store effort. After working in fields for cash and building a surplus, families may cross the Sierra Madre to the towns of San Mariano, Cauayan, and Ilagan. There Agta, often women, purchase in markets and stores goods for use and resale in Palanan. Palanan Centro itself has no real market, only several small general stores selling goods at highly marked up prices. Since no road reaches Palanan, all manufactured supplies must enter town by airplane from Cauayan or boat from Baler. Freight costs are high. Some Agta women are very eager to hike outside to get tobacco, which always commands a high price and a ready market.

DISCUSSION

The role of women in Agta economic activities has been reviewed. Assessment of an hypothesized egalitarian position of women may be more difficult, and rests on assertions and interpretations drawn from the economic roles. First, drawing in part from Friedl (1975), an argument can be made that women in Agta society have equality with men because they have similar authority in decision making. The authority could be based on the equal contribution to the subsistence resources. Working back, we see that among many Agta, women do contribute heavily to the daily food supply, do perform maintenance tasks with men, and may initiate food acquisition efforts through their own skills. They do control the distribution of their acquired food, sharing first with their own nuclear family and extended family, then trading as they see fit. They may procure nonfood goods as they desire. Men may do the same; generally spouses discuss what work to do, what needs should be satisfied, and who will do what. Whole residential groups frequently together decide courses of action. Women are as vocal and as critical in reaching decisions as are men. Further examples could strongly validate the hypothesis that women do supply a substantial portion of foods, and the assertion that women have authority in major decision making. Two questions arise. May we accept a causal relationship between percentage of food production and equality? Certainly there are cases to the contrary. According to Richard A. Gould (personal communication), Australian Aboriginal women in various areas collected the bulk of the food, yet remained less than equal (as we will define equality). Second, we may ask if Agta males and females are actually "equal."

Two avenues may suffice in answering this question. First, one might explore a definition of equality, surely a culturally loaded concept. Since Agta women have authority or control of the economic gain of their own labor, they may be equal in this critical domain. Equality must surely be equated with decision-making power and control of one's own production. The second avenue of equality validation by the scientist may be to examine the female's control over herself in noneconomic matters. These could include selection of marriage partner, lack of premarital sexual intercourse proscription, spacing of children, ease of divorce, and polygyny rules.

In marriage, two forms are typical of Agta. One, the less common, is elopement by young lovers. While such marriages admittedly are fragile, elopement is not uncommon. In this case both partners must be willing. Rape and abduction are rare. Rape by Agta men is not known to the authors. Abduction must involve a slightly willing female, and is not done by young people. A mature man might abduct a married woman, crossing the mountains to a safe locale. To abduct a young girl would be difficult. Parents of eloping couples may be enraged, but usually reconcile themselves to the marriage. If the newlyweds stay together, no more is made of it.

The proper form of marriage is one arranged by customary meetings and discussions, as well as exchange of goods between two families. Often neither the bride nor the groom has had much say in the matter, although serious dislike by either would probably kill the negotiations before the marriage. Mothers are the most important in choosing who will marry whom. Even when their children are young, they are looking about for good partners. Word filters around when a young girl is marriageable, and efforts are made to get the appropriate young man and his family into negotiations before an undesirable family appears. Once any family with a prospective groom formally asks, a rejection is given only for strong and good reasons, since the denied family loses considerable face and may be angry enough to seek revenge.[4]

Criteria for choice of a marriage partner are varied. Often a young man in his early twenties marries a girl about fifteen. Girls entering marriage before puberty are not uncommon. In such cases the husband may help raise the girl until the time the marriage is consummated and full wifehood is recognized. Other combinations are seen. One much discussed case was the marriage of a woman in her forties to a man in his mid-twenties. The couple seemed very happy, with the wife paying rather special attention to her husband. The man's mother, a friend of the wife's, decided that the marriage was peculiar but acceptable.

Premarital female chastity is not an idea of much currency. Agta close to farmers will pay lip service to the idea, but should a girl become pregnant she will take a husband. There are no illegitimate Agta children, although an occasional rape of an Agta by a lowland male may produce a child. Since by the time a girl is fertile she likely will be married, illegitimacy is not the issue. Although some data are difficult to collect concerning sex, almost certainly girls are able to engage in sexual activity with relative ease; promiscuity is not favored in any circumstance. Males may have as little or great difficulty in engaging in sex as females. The Agta are widely dispersed in extended family groups; hence appropriate sexual partners are seldom seen. No homosexuality is known to exist.

Agta gossip suggests that many Agta, male and female, married and unmarried, constantly carry on extramarital sexual relations. This may be a function of gossip and a gross exaggeration. Whatever reality, neither males nor females seem to be especially singled out for criticism.

Women say they space their children. The practice certainly varies hugely from person to person, as does fecundity and luck in keeping children alive. The Agta use various herbal concoctions that supposedly prevent conception, cause abortions shortly after conception, and have several functions related to menstruation. These medicines are known to all Agta and are frequently used. Our census data indicate that some women seem to be successful in spacing births. Other cases note high infant mortality yet no infanticide, female or male. All Agta abhor the idea.

Divorce is infrequent among Agta, with elopement being more prone to failure than are arranged marriages. Divorce does happen often enough, however, for us to look at the causes and relate them to an inquiry into female equality. First, either sex may divorce the other with equal ease. Agta have no possessions. Some gift giving between the two families establishes the marriage, but most of the gifts are food. Cloth, kettles, and minor items make up the rest. Return of marriage gifts is unlikely. Spouses simply take their personal possessions and return to the residential group of close relatives.

Causes for divorce are mainly laziness or improvidence, excessive adultery, or personality clashes and incompatibility, usually caused by a combination of the first two conditions. Skill and success in subsistence activities is of primary importance to marriage. While some Agta are less industrious and less skilled than others, all

Agta expect a mate to work hard at all appropriate tasks. Should a male fail, divorce is likely. Occasionally, very young couples experience extra difficulties. These may be accentuated by displeased parents of either party.

Polygamy is not found in most of Isabela. Census data collected to date reveal only monogamy or serial monogamy. That is, spouses may be divorced or widow(er)ed several times in a lifetime. In Cagayan the data are incomplete but startling. Probably some of the strongest support for the equality of women hypothesis, when added to the facts of women as hunters, comes from a study of Agta polygamy. We noted earlier that two co-wives, sisters, hunted together in Malibu. South of Malibu at Blos, another husband and two sisters/co-wives arrangement was found. In the same residential unit we recorded a woman residing with her two co-husbands. They were not brothers; one was older than the wife, one younger. The other women considered this arrangement as humorous, but acceptable. An insight into the male sexual jealousy found in many societies worldwide is the comment of a Palanan Agta man. This old man, when told of the polyandrous marriage to the north, thought for a moment and commented, "Well, perhaps one man with two wives is OK, but a woman with two husbands? I find that totally bad." The women laughed at him.

Notes

1. Although the authors have worked among the Agta about fourteen months, visits to the northerly group in the Dianggu-Malibu area have been brief. The practice of women hunting was first observed during a survey trip in 1972. We again visited the Dianggu group in 1975. In August 1978 we returned for one week to Dianggu and Malibu, where we verified in greater detail the subsistence activities of women. Data were collected using the Palanan Agta dialect and Ilokano.
2. Dianggu and Malibu are river names used by Agta and nearby Malay Filipinos. On the Board of Technical Surveys and Maps (Lobod Point, Philippines), the Dianggu is named the Lobod and the Malibu is named the Ilang.
3. Peterson (n.d.) argues that "downriver" Agta women are highly variable in their devotion to labor, older women being hardworking and young mothers not at all industrious.
4. Thomas Headland tells us that rejection of a prospective spouse may be a less serious matter among Casiguran Agta than among those we know.

References

Bennagen, Ponciano. 1976. Kultura at Kapaligiran: Pangkulturang Pagbabago at Kapanatagan ng mga Agta sa Palanan, Isabela. M.A. thesis, Department of Anthropology, University of the Philippines, Diliman, Quezon City.

Briggs, Jean L. 1974. Eskimo women: makers of men. In *Many sisters: women in cross-cultural perspective*, ed. Carolyn J. Matthiasson, pp. 261–304. New York: Free Press.

Estioko, Agnes A., and P. Bion Griffin. 1975. The *Ebuked* Agta of northeastern Luzon. *Philippines Quarterly of Culture and Society* 3(4):237–44.

Flannery, Regina. 1932. The position of women among the Mescalero-Apache. *Primitive Man*. 10:26–32.

———. 1935. The position of women among the eastern Cree. *Primitive Man* 12:81–86.

Fox, Robert B. 1952. The Pinatubo Negritos, their useful plants and material culture. *Philippine Journal of Science* 81:113–414.

Friedl, Ernestine. 1975. *Women and men: an anthropologist's view*. New York: Holt, Rinehart and Winston.

Garvan, John M. 1964. *The Negritos of the Philippines*, ed. Hermann Hochegger, Weiner beitrage zur kulturgeschichte und linguistik, vol. 14. Horn: F. Berger.

Goodale, Jane C. 1971. *Tiwi wives: a study of the women of Melville Island, north Australia*. Seattle, Wash.: University of Washington Press.

Gough, Kathleen. 1975. The origin of the family. In *Toward an anthropology of women*, ed. Rayna R. Reiter, pp. 51–76. New York: Monthly Review Press.

Hammond, Dorothy, and Alta Jablow. 1976. *Women in cultures of the world*. Menlo Park, Calif.: Benjamin/Cummings.

Harako, Reizo. 1976. The Mbuti as hunters—a study of ecological anthropology of the Mbuti pygmies. *Kyoto University African Studies* 10:37–99.

Headland, Thomas, and Janet D. Headland. 1974. *A Dumagat (Casiguran)—English dictionary*. Pacific Linguistics Series C. No. 28. Australian National University, Canberra: Linguistics Circle of Canberra.

Howell, F. Clark. 1973. *Early man*, rev. ed. New York: Time-Life Books.

Isaac, Glynn L. 1969. Studies of early culture in East Africa. *World Archaeology* 1:1–27.

———. 1971. The diet of early man: aspects of archaeological evidence from lower and middle Pleistocene sites in Africa. *World Archaeology* 2:278–98.

———. 1978. The food-sharing behavior of proto-human hominids. *Scientific American* 238(4):90–109.

Jenness, Diamond. 1922. *The life of the Copper Eskimos. Report of the Canadian Arctic Expedition 1913–1918*, vol. XII, pt. 9. Ottawa: Acland.

Keesing, Felix. 1962. *The ethnohistory of northern Luzon*. Stanford, Calif.: Stanford University Press.

Lancaster, Jane B. 1978. Carrying and sharing in human evolution. *Human Nature* 1(2):82–89.

Landes, Ruth. 1938. *The Ojibwa Woman*. New York: Columbia University Press.

Lee, Richard B., and Irven DeVore. 1968. Problems in the study of hunters and gatherers. In *Man the Hunter*, ed. Lee and DeVore. Chicago: Aldine.

———. 1976. *Kalahari hunter-gatherers: studies of the !Kung San and their neighbors*. Cambridge, Mass.: Harvard University Press.

Maceda, Marcelino M. 1964. *The culture of the mamanuas (northeast Mindanao) as compared with that of the other Negritos of Southeast Asia*. Manila: Catholic Trade School.

Marshall, Lorna. 1976. *The !Kung of Nyae Nyae*. Cambridge, Mass.: Harvard University Press.

Martin, M. Kay, and Barbara Voorhies. 1975. *Female of the species*. New York: Columbia University Press.

Peterson, Jean Treloggen. 1974. An ecological perspective on the economic and social behavior of Agta hunter-gatherers, northeastern Luzon, Philippines. Ph.D. dissertation, University of Hawaii at Manoa.

———. 1978a. Hunter-gatherer farmer exchange. *American Anthropologist* 80:335–51.

———. 1978b. The ecology of social boundaries: Agta foragers of the Philippines. *Illinois Studies in Anthropology No. 11*. University of Illinois, Urbana-Champaign, Ill.

———. n.d. Hunter mobility, family organization and change. In *Circulation in the Third World*, ed. Murray Chapman and Ralph Mansell Prothero. London: Routledge & Kegan Paul.

Philippine Commission. 1908. *8th Annual Report of the Philippine Commission: 1907*. Bureau of Insular Affairs, War Department. Washington, D.C.: Government Printing Office.

Quinn, Naomi. 1977. Anthropological studies on women's status. In *Annual review of anthropology*, ed. Bernard J. Siegel, pp. 181–225. Palo Alto, Calif.: Annual Reviews.

Reiter, Rayna R., ed. 1975. *Toward an anthropology of women*. New York: Monthly Review Press.

Rosaldo, Michelle Zimbalist, and Louise Lamphere, eds. 1974. *Woman, culture, and society*. Stanford, Calif.: Stanford University Press.

Slocum, Sally. 1975. Woman the gatherer: male bias in anthropology. In *Toward an anthropology of women*, ed. Rayna R. Reiter, pp. 36–50. New York: Monthly Review Press.

Tanner, Nancy, and Adrienne Zihlman. 1976. Women in evolution. Part I: Innovations and selection in human origins. *Signs: Journal of Women in Culture and Society* 1:585–608.

Tanno, Tadashi. 1976. The Mbuti net-hunters in the Ituri Forest, Eastern Zaire—their hunting activities and band composition. *Kyoto University African Studies* 10:101–35.

Turnball, Colin M. 1965. *Wayward servants: the two worlds of the African pygmies*. Garden City, N.Y.: Natural History Press.

Vanoverberg, Maurice. 1925. Negritos of northern Luzon *Anthropos* 20:148–99.

———. 1929–30. Negritos of northern Luzon again. *Anthropos* 24:1–75, 897–911; 25:25–71, 527–656.

———. 1937–38. Negritos of eastern Luzon. *Anthropos* 32:905–28; 33:119–64.

Washburn, Sherwood L., and C. S. Lancaster. 1968. The evolution of hunting. In *Man the hunter*, ed. Richard B. Lee and Irven DeVore, pp. 293–303. Chicago: Aldine.

Worcester, Dean C. 1912. Head-hunters of northern Luzon. *National Geographic* 23(9):833–930.

Yen, D. E. 1976. The ethnobotany of the Tasaday: III. Note on the subsistence system. In *Further studies on the Tasaday*, ed. D. E. Yen and John Nance. Makati, Rizal: PANAMIN Foundation Research Series No. 2.

CRITICAL THINKING QUESTIONS

1. Discuss, in general terms, Agta economic organization and activities.
2. How do Agta women's activities contradict the traditional anthropological view of women's roles in hunting-and-gathering societies?
3. Describe women's hunting activities in general terms.
4. Based on the data and discussion portions of the article can it be said that Agta women are the social and economic equals of Agta men? Support your opinion with specific evidence from the article.

Rituals of Manhood: Male Initiation in Papua New Guinea

Gilbert H. Herdt

Sambia are a mountain-dwelling hunting and horticultural people who number some 2,000 persons and inhabit one of New Guinea's most rugged terrains. The population is dispersed through narrow river valleys over a widespread, thinly populated rain forest; rainfall is heavy; and even today the surrounding mountain ranges keep the area isolated. Sambia live on the fringes of the Highlands, but they trace their origins to the Papua hinterlands; their culture and economy thus reflect a mixture of influences from both of those areas. Hunting still predominates as a masculine activity through which most meat protein is acquired. As in the Highlands, though, sweet potatoes and taro are the staple crops, and their cultivation is for the most part women's work. Pigs are few, and they have no ceremonial or exchange significance; indigenous marsupials, such as possum and tree kangaroo, provide necessary meat prestations for all initiations and ceremonial feasts (cf. Meigs 1976).

Sambia settlements are small, well-defended, mountain clan hamlets. These communities comprise locally based descent groups organized through a strong agnatic idiom. Residence is patrivirilocal, and most men actually reside in their father's hamlets. Clans are exogamous, and one or more of them together constitute a hamlet's landowning corporate agnatic body. These men also form a localized warriorhood that is sometimes allied with other hamlets in matters of fighting, marriage, and ritual. Each hamlet contains one or two men's clubhouses, in addition to women's houses, and the men's ritual life centers on their clubhouse. Marriage is usually by sister exchange or infant betrothal, although the latter form of prearranged marriage is culturally preferred. Intrahamlet marriage is occasionally more

frequent (up to fifty percent of all marriages in my own hamlet field site) than one would expect in such small segmentary groupings, an involutional pattern weakened since pacification.

Sambia male and female residential patterns differ somewhat from those of other Highlands peoples. The nuclear family is an important subunit of the hamlet-based extended family of interrelated clans. A man, his wife, and their children usually cohabit within a single, small, round hut. Children are thus reared together by their parents during the early years of life, so the nuclear family is a residential unit, an institution virtually unknown to the Highlands (Meggit 1964; Read 1954). Sometimes this unit is expanded through polygyny, in which case a man, his co-wives, and their children may occupy the single dwelling. Girls continue to reside with their parents until marriage (usually near the menarche, around fifteen to seventeen years of age). Boys, however, are removed to the men's clubhouse at seven to ten years of age, following their first-stage initiation. There they reside exclusively until marriage and cohabitation years later. Despite familial cohabitation in early childhood, strict taboos based on beliefs about menstrual pollution still separate men and women in their sleeping and eating arrangements.

Warfare used to be constant and nagging among Sambia, and it conditioned the values and masculine stereotypes surrounding the male initiatory cult. Ritualized bow fights occurred among neighboring hamlets, whose members still intermarried and usually initiated their sons together. At the same time, though, hamlets also united against enemy tribes and in staging war parties against them. Hence, warfare, marriage, and initiation were interlocking institutions; the

Source: Adapted and condensed from "Fetish and Fantasy in Sambia Initiation" by Gilbert Herdt from *Rituals of Manhood: Male Initiation in Papua New Guinea*, ed. by Gilbert Herdt. Reprinted by permission of the author.

effect of this political instability was to reinforce tough, strident masculine performance in most arenas of social life. "Strength" (*jerundu*) was—and is—a pivotal idea in this male ethos. Indeed, strength, which has both ethnobiological and behavioral aspects, could be aptly translated as "maleness" and "manliness." Strength has come to be virtually synonymous with idealized conformity to male ritual routine. Before conquest and pacification by the Australians, though, strength had its chief performative significance in one's conduct on the battlefield. Even today bitter reminders of war linger on among the Sambia; and we should not forget that it is against the harsh background of the warrior's existence that Sambia initiate their boys, whose only perceived protection against the inconstant world is their own unbending masculinity.

Initiation rests solely in the hands of the men's secret society. It is this organization that brings the collective initiatory cycle into being as jointly performed by neighboring hamlets (and as constrained by their own chronic bow fighting). The necessary feastcrop gardens, ritual leadership, and knowledge, dictate that a handful of elders, war leaders, and ritual experts be in full command of the actual staging of the event. Everyone and all else are secondary.

There are six intermittent initiations from the ages of seven to ten and onward. They are, however, constituted and conceptualized as two distinct cultural systems within the male life cycle. First-stage (*moku*, at seven to ten years of age), second-stage (*imbutu*, at ten to thirteen years), and third-stage (*ipmangwi*, at thirteen to sixteen years) initiations—bachelorhood rites—are collectively performed for regional groups of boys as agemates. The initiations are held in sequence, as age-graded advancements; the entire sequel takes months to perform. The focus of all these initiations is the construction and habitation of a great cult house (*moo-angu*) on a traditional dance ground; its ceremonialized building inaugurates the whole cycle. Fourth-stage (*nuposha:* sixteen years and onward), fifth-stage (*taiketnyi*), and sixth-stage (*moondangu*) initiations are, conversely, individually centered events not associated with the confederacy of interrelated hamlets, cult house, or dance ground. Each of these initiations, like the preceding ones, does have its own

ritual status, social role, and title, as noted. The triggering event for the latter three initiations, unlike that for the bachelorhood rites, is not the building of a cult house or a political agreement of hamlets to act collectively, but is rather the maturing femininity and life-crisis events of the women assigned in marriage to youths (who become the initiated novices). Therefore, fourth-stage initiation is only a semipublic activity organized by the youths' clansmen (and some male affines). Its secret purificatory and other rites are followed by the formal marriage ceremony in the hamlet. Fifth-stage initiation comes at a woman's menarche, when her husband is secretly introduced to additional purification and sexual techniques. Sixth-stage initiation issues from the birth of a man's wife's first child. This event is, de jure, the attainment of manhood. (The first birth is elaborately ritualized and celebrated; the next three births are also celebrated, but in more truncated fashion.) Two children bring full adulthood (*aatmwunu*) for husband and wife alike. Birth ceremonies are suspended after the fourth birth, since there is no reason to belabor what is by now obvious: a man has proved himself competent in reproduction. This sequence of male initiations forms the basis for male development, and it underlies the antagonistic tenor of relationships between the sexes.

It needs stating only once that men's secular rhetoric and ritual practices depict women as dangerous and polluting inferiors whom men are to distrust throughout their lives. In this regard, Sambia values and relationships pit men against women even more markedly, I think, than occurs in other Highlands communities (cf. Brown and Buchbinder 1976; Meggitt 1964; Read 1954). Men hold themselves as the superiors of women in physique, personality, and social position. And this dogma of male supremacy permeates all social relationships and institutions, likewise coloring domestic behavior among the sexes (cf. Tuzin 1980 for an important contrast). Men fear not only pollution from contact with women's vaginal fluids and menstrual blood but also the depletion of their semen, the vital spark of maleness, which women (and boys, too) inevitably extract, sapping a man's substance. These are among the main themes of male belief underlying initiation.

The ritualized simulation of maleness is the result of initiation, and men believe the process to be vital for the nature and nurture of manly growth and well-being. First-stage initiation begins the process in small boys. Over the ensuing ten to fifteen years, until marriage, cumulative initiations and residence in the men's house are said to promote biological changes that firmly cement the growth from childhood to manhood. Nature provides male genitals, it is true; but nature alone does not bestow the vital spark biologically necessary for stimulating masculine growth or demonstrating cold-blooded self-preservation.

New Guinea specialists will recognize in the Sambia belief system a theme that links it to the comparative ethnography of male initiation and masculine development: the use of ritual procedures for sparking, fostering, and maintaining manliness in males (see Berndt 1962; Meigs 1976; Newman 1964, 1965; Poole 1981; Read 1965; Salisbury 1965; Strathern 1969, 1970). Sambia themselves refer to the results of first-stage collective initiation—our main interests—as a means of "growing a boy"; and this trend of ritual belief is particularly emphatic.

Unlike ourselves, Sambia perceive no imminent, naturally driven fit between one's birthright sex and one's gender identity or role.[1] Indeed, the problem (and it is approached as a situation wanting a solution) is implicitly and explicitly understood in quite different terms. The solution is also different for the two sexes: men believe that a girl is born with all of the vital organs and fluids necessary for her to attain reproductive competence through "natural" maturation. This conviction is embodied in cultural perceptions of the girl's development beginning with the sex assignment at birth. What distinguishes a girl (*tai*) from a boy (*kwulai'u*) is obvious: "A boy has a penis, and a girl does not," men say. Underlying men's communications is a conviction that maleness, unlike femaleness, is not a biological given. It must be artificially induced through secret ritual; and that is a personal achievement.

The visible manifestations of girls' fast-growing reproductive competence, noticed first in early motor coordination and speech and then later in the rapid attainment of height and secondary sex traits (e.g., breast development), are attributed to inner biological properties.

Girls possess a menstrual-blood organ, or *tingu*, said to precipitate all those events and the menarche. Boys, on the other hand, are thought to possess an inactive tingu. They do possess, however, another organ—the *kere-ku-kereku*, or semen organ—that is thought to be the repository of semen, the very essence of maleness and masculinity; but this organ is not functional at birth, since it contains no semen naturally and can only store, never produce, any. Only oral insemination, men believe, can activate the boy's semen organ, thereby precipitating his push into adult reproductive competence. In short, femininity unfolds naturally, whereas masculinity must be achieved; and here is where the male ritual cult steps in.

Men also perceive the early socialization risks of boys and girls in quite different terms. All infants are closely bonded to their mothers. Out of a woman's contaminating, life-giving womb pours the baby, who thereafter remains tied to the woman's body, breast milk, and many ministrations. This latter contact only reinforces the femininity and female contamination in which birth involves the infant. Then, too, the father, both because of postpartum taboos and by personal choice, tends to avoid being present at the breast-feedings. Mother thus becomes the unalterable primary influence; father is a weak second. Sambia say this does not place girls at a "risk"—they simply succumb to the drives of their "natural" biology. This maternal attachment and paternal distance clearly jeopardize the boys' growth, however, since nothing innate within male maturation seems to resist the inhibiting effects of mothers' femininity. Hence boys must be traumatically separated—wiped clean of their female contaminants—so that their masculinity may develop.

Homosexual fellatio inseminations can follow this separation but cannot precede it, for otherwise they would go for naught. The accumulating semen, injected time and again for years, is believed crucial for the formation of biological maleness and masculine comportment. This native perspective is sufficiently novel to justify our using a special concept for aiding description and analysis of the data: masculinization (Herdt 1981:205 ff). Hence I shall refer to the overall process that involves separating a boy from his mother, initiating him, ritually treating his body, administering homosexual inseminations, his biological attainment of puberty, and his eventual reproductive competence as masculinization. (Precisely what role personal and cultural fantasy plays in the negotiation of this ritual process I have considered elsewhere: see Herdt 1981: chaps. 6, 7, and 8.)

A boy has female contaminants inside of him which not only retard physical development but, if not removed, debilitate him and eventually bring death. His body is male: his tingu contains no blood and will not activate. The achievement of puberty for boys requires semen. Breast milk "nurtures the boy," and sweet potatoes or other "female" foods provide "stomach nourishment," but these substances become only feces, not semen. Women's own bodies internally produce the menarche, the hallmark of reproductive maturity. There is no comparable mechanism active in a boy, nothing that can stimulate his secondary sex traits. Only semen can do that; only men have semen; boys have none. What is left to do, then, except initiate and masculinize boys into adulthood?

Note

1. I follow Stroller (1968) in adhering to the following distinctions: the term *sex traits* refers to purely biological phenomena (anatomy, hormones, genetic structure, etc.), whereas *gender* refers to those psychological and cultural attributes that compel a person (consciously or unconsciously) to sense him- or herself, and other persons, as belonging to either the male or female sex. It follows that the term *gender role* (Sears 1965), rather than the imprecise term *sex role*, refers to the normative set of expectations associated with masculine and feminine social positions.

References

Berndt, R. M. 1962. *Excess and Restraint: Social Control among a New Guinea Mountain People.* Chicago: University of Chicago Press.

Brown, P., and G. Buchbinder (eds.). 1976. *Man and Woman in the New Guinea Highlands.* Washington, DC: American Anthropological Association.

Herdt, G. H. 1981. *Guardians of the Flutes: Idioms of Masculinity.* New York: McGraw-Hill.

Meggitt, M. J. 1964. Male-Female Relationships in the Highlands of Australian New Guinea. In *New Guinea: The Central Highlands*, ed. J. B. Watson, *American Anthropologist*, 66, pt. 2 (4):204–224.

Meigs, A. S. 1976. Male Pregnancy and the Reduction of Sexual Opposition in a New Guinea Highlands Society. *Ethnology* 15 (4):393–407.

Newman, P. L. 1964. Religious Belief and Ritual in a New Guinea Society. In *New Guinea: The Central Highlands*, ed. J. B. Watson, *American Anthropologist* 66, pt. 2 (4):257–272.

———. 1965. *Knowing the Gururumba.* New York: Holt, Rinehart and Winston.

Poole, F. J. P. 1981. Transforming "Natural" Woman: Female Ritual Leaders and Gender Ideology Among Bimin-Kuskumin. In *Sexual Meanings*, ed. S. B. Ortner and H. Whitehead. New York: Cambridge University Press.

Read, K. E. 1954. Cultures of the Central Highlands, New Guinea. *Southwestern Journal of Anthropology* 10(l):1–43.

———. 1965. *The High Valley.* London: George Allen and Unwin.

Salisbury, R. F. 1965. The Siane of the Eastern Highlands. In *Gods, Ghosts, and Men in Melanesia*, P. Lawrence and M. J. Meggitt, pp. 50–77, Melbourne: Melbourne University Press.

Sears, R. R. 1965. Development of Gender Role. In *Sex and Behavior*, ed. F. A. Beach, pp. 133–163. New York: John Wiley and Sons.

Stoller, R. J. 1968. *Sex and Gender.* New York: Science House.

Strathern, A. J. 1969. Descent and Alliance in the New Guinea Highlands: Some Problems of Comparison. Royal Anthropological Institute, *Proceedings*, pp. 37–52.

———. 1970. Male Initiation in the New Guinea Highlands societies. *Ethnology* 9 (4):373–379.

Tuzin, D. F. 1980. *The Voice of the Tambaran: Truth and Illusion in Ilahita Arapesh Religion.* Berkeley, Los Angeles, and London: University of California Press.

CRITICAL THINKING QUESTIONS

1. Outline Sambia culture based on information from the article: economics, social and political organization, and other facets of life.
2. How do warfare, marriage, and male initiation rites operate as interlocking institutions in Sambia culture?
3. What is the purpose of male initiation rites? How many stages are there in the rites before the goal of adult male status is reached?
4. How do Sambia men's attitudes toward women and sex contribute to the functioning and cultural understanding of the purpose of the rites?
5. How do the Sambia explain their understanding of the biological basis of maleness and femaleness, and how does that understanding affect their behavior?
6. Relate the Sambian ideas regarding masculinity and femininity to those found in the United States.

"Foreign Chickens" and Other Outsiders: Gender and Community in Greece

Jill Dubisch

The anthropological study of the Mediterranean has provided an important arena for discussions of gender and gender roles, in part because concepts of gender have themselves been key elements in debates over the definition of a "Mediterranean area." Some analysts have presented the ideology of "honor and shame," a complex of values and practices that stresses the cultural control of female sexuality and its relationship to notions of "honor" and masculinity, as a distinctive feature of "the Mediterranean."[1] Reacting against the emphasis on honor and shame, other analysts have focused on the contrast between "appearance" and "reality"—that is, on the ways in which cultural ideologies regarding gender roles may misrepresent or obscure the actual power Mediterranean women wield in daily life.[2] The concern in such analyses is not so much with defining a region as with considering the implications for the anthropological study of gender, and context and experience are emphasized while the consequences of specific gender ideologies for women's roles are explored.

Both "honor and shame" and the concern with women's concrete roles and exercise of power, however, are shaped by particular agendas of a Western anthropology that has tended to analyze gender in terms of sexuality, gender "identity," or issue of power and dominance in the relations between men and women. Such approaches generally fail to consider gender and sexuality, both in the Mediterranean context and elsewhere, in a wider, more complex social and cultural web.[3] And only recently have anthropologists begun to address the variations in conceptions of gender within specific national contexts (see, for example, Loizos and Papataxiarchis 1991a).

In this article I focus on a particular social context, a modern Greek Village, in order to explore some of the ways gender can enter into a larger social discourse. In the village, concepts of gender are not simply "about" men and women and their behavior; they serve to construct and interpret other areas of social experience as well, including social segmentation and communal boundaries. In my analysis I seek to heed Ortner and Whitehead's suggestion that the study of sex and gender be, in part at least, "a matter of symbolic analysis and interpretation, a matter of relating such symbols and meaning to other cultural symbols and meaning on the one hand, and to the forms of social life and experience on the other" (1981:1–2). In particular, I focus on the ways in which boundaries between social groups are established and maintained and on the opposition and conflict that may exist both within and between such groups. I begin with an incident from my fieldwork, using it as a metaphor to help explicate some of the relationships between gender, boundaries, and groups.

Anthropological discussions of gender in the Mediterranean have tended to focus on two related issues: the control of female sexuality, particularly in terms of concepts of "honor and shame," and women's power and its relationship to the public and private spheres of community life. This article seeks to move beyond these issues to a broader examination of gender ideology. It suggests that gender needs to be seen in a shifting context of boundaries, representations, and conflicts at the domestic, communal, and even national level. Using data from a Greek village, the article explores women's positions as representations of both "inside" and "outside" and relates such representations to ongoing discourses about personal, village, and national identities [gender, women's roles, Greece, the Mediterranean, social boundaries].

INSIDE/OUTSIDE AND THE ANTHROPOLOGIST AS HEN

The incident took place in a small agricultural village on the island of Tinos, one of a group of Aegean island known as the Cyclades. Like many of the Cycladic islands, Tinos has a settlement pattern of nucleated, mostly agricultural villages, scattered across a somewhat rugged and rocky landscape, with a large main town that serves as the island's port (see Dubisch 1976). At the time of my original fieldwork in 1969–70, the village in question had a population of approximately 370. In the last 20 years, the population has gradually dwindled, as have those of many other Greek island villages, through out-migration to Athens and to the island's main town.

At the beginning of my original fieldwork, my husband and I rented the upper part of a house in the village. One day as my landlady was showing me around the grounds of the house, she indignantly chased away some chickens that were pecking in the yard. They were not her chickens, she explained to me, but rather *ksénes kótes.* Still in the early phases of learning Greek, I mentally translated the phrase as "foreign chickens": *kséni* (feminine singular), meaning "foreign" or "foreigner"; *kóta* (singular), meaning "chicken," more specifically, "hen." It was not until I later heard the words *kséni* and *ksénos* (masculine singular) in a number of contexts that I came to appreciate their range or meanings and to see the ways in which my own original translation was both inaccurate and yet, in its own way, appropriate.

A more suitable translation of my landlady's phrase, I later realized, would have been "someone else's chickens." Nonetheless, the term "foreign chickens"—my original thought—was not entirely inaccurate, given what I came to learn of Greek village social life and gender roles. It was also appropriate that the term *kóta* is feminine, denoting "hen" (rather than "chicken"), for, as will be seen, it provides an apt metaphor for women. In Greek, *kóta* is applied to a certain kind

of woman, one who is proper and bustling about her own business. In addition, foreign women pursued by Greek men may be referred to as "chickens" (Zinovieff 1991:212). The term *kséni* has a reflexive significance for the anthropologist as well. I myself was a "foreign chicken," at least in certain periods and situations of my fieldwork.[4]

The terms *ksénos* (plural *kséni*), which can signify "foreign," "foreigner," "stranger," "nonvillager," "nonrelative," or simply "not us," and *dhikós mas* (plural *dhikí mas*), meaning "own" or "our own," together denote a division between two important realms of Greek social life. These realms are not demarcated by fixed boundaries but rather expand and contract depending upon context. Thus, in some situations *kséni* may be used to refer to those who are not members of one's immediate family; in others it may mean nonvillagers; in still others, non-Greeks. Likewise, *dhikí mas* may include only relatives, all fellow villagers, all Greeks, or any other group one is contrasting with "others," that is, "those who are not us." For example, a villager referring to migrants who had returned from Athens to the village for a religious festival labeled them *kséni,* emphasizing by his choice of word their "outsiderness" and the fact that they were not regular actors in the daily social world of the village. On other occasions, however, villagers referred to migrants as *dhikí mas,* emphasizing the villagers' and the migrants' continuing mutual interest in, and connection to, each other. Thus, the concepts of "inside" and "outside" provide a kind of rhetoric of segmentation, merging or separating social units according to specific situations.[5]

The contextual nature of the terms also holds when they are applied to the ethnographer, and this has implications for the kind of information obtained during fieldwork, as a number of researchers in Greece have noted (see, for example, Herzfeld 1986:220–221; also see Caraveli 1986; Clark 1983; Cowan 1990). In any given situation, what is observed often depends upon the observer's status, since what is presented to an insider will differ from what an outsider is permitted to observe. In order to see how this inside/outside distinction is linked to gender, we must first briefly consider certain aspects of village social life, the nature of gender roles, and the ways these are related both to the representation of boundaries and to the shifting of such boundaries.

WOMEN AND MEN: ROLES AND IDEOLOGY

A number of ethnographers have portrayed Greek women as subordinated to men in both ideology and practice (see, for example, Campbell 1964; du Boulay 1974, 1986), generally describing the ideological dimension of this subordination in terms of "honor and shame." Women, they have claimed, are viewed as inherently weak, associated with the devil and with Eve, and saddled with a sinful nature that must be controlled by themselves and others and redeemed through motherhood. In order to guard their own reputations and their families' honor, women must restrict their public activities, maintain their chastity, and in general cultivate their sense of shame (*dropí*).

Although I was familiar with such ethnographic descriptions when I arrived in the village, what first drew my attention was not so much women's subordination as the separation of their daily lives from the village men's. Men's and women's activities tended to take place in different areas of the village. Women performed their tasks in or near the house (making occasional trips to the store, to nearby fields or stables, or to church), while men ranged farther, to distant fields, to other villages, or to the island's main town for business or wage labor. In the evening, man congregated in the coffeehouse (*kafenío*) while women socialized on the porches or steps of their houses. Men and women generally sought to retain a certain amount of authority over their respective spheres. A man called home by his wife from drinking with his friends at the *kafenío*, for example, would typically delay for a while, thus demonstrating to his male peers that he was not simply at his wife's beck and call.[6] Women, on the other hand, managed their own households and would scold men who interfered with their tasks.

The greater presence of men in public spaces hasfrequently been interpreted as an indication of their greater power and/or prestige, particularly in the literature on the Mediterranean. Such an interpretation, however, has been challenged on several grounds. Ernestine Friedl, for example, has argued that it is necessary to consider both the "appearance" of men's public prestige and he "reality" of women's power in the domestic realm (1967; see also Collier 1974). She has suggested that given the importance of the family in Greek society, the significance of "domestic power" should not be overlooked. Similarly, Susan Carol Rogers has suggested that male dominance in peasant societies is a "myth" to which both men and women acquiesce, men because they wish to preserve a public appearance of authority, and women because the myth leads men to claim the public sphere, leaving women in charge of the domestic realm, the real source of power in peasant societies (Rogers 1975; for a revision of this argument see Rogers 1985). Others have focused on social class and gender, arguing that it is peasant men's lack of power in a class-stratified society, coupled with their exclusion from the domestic sphere, that accounts for their spending so much time in all-male activities in the public space (see, for example, Brandes 1980; Driessen 1983; Papataxiarchis 1985). Additionally, the very use of such concepts as public and private as a framework for the analysis of power and gender roles has itself been subject to increasing scrutiny and criticism (see, for example, Collier and Yanagisako 1987).

In some respects the spatial/social separation between village women and men can be seen as a reflection of their differing tasks. In the island village, women's work was more or less continuous throughout the day. Even when socializing together on their porches, women were usually performing some domestic task such as mending, knitting, or cleaning vegetables. On the other hand, women's work was more readily interrupted and women were more likely than men to make social excursions during the course of the day—for coffee at a friend's house, to a local church for a saint's day service. For those village men engaged in agriculture, daily work was generally not a social activity, since they labored alone in the fields (see also du Boulay 1974), and hence they experienced a more definite break between work and leisure.[7] When men returned from the fields or their jobs in the late afternoon or early evening, they were free to stroll down to the *kafenío* for a drink with friends.[8] Men's lesser participation in religious activities was sometimes even justified to me (by women) on the grounds of their work. Men, women would say, could not attend church because they were too busy, and the difficulty of their physical labor made it hard for them to observe religious fasts.[9] In such a manner, women laid claim to religious "work" as their own (cf. Dubisch 1991).

However, differing uses of space did not reflect simply the utilitarian requirements of the gendered division of labor in the village, and social rules were often more restrictive for women than for men. Women were more confined in their spatial movements, and their breaches of the rules for such confinement would elicit comment and criticism. Whereas men, both young and old, were basically free to roam where they wished, women were usually restricted to the village and home (and even in the village they were expected not to spend too much time outside the house). They made excursions only in the company of related men or (particularly for religious events) in the company of other adult women. While these restrictions were connected in part with the control of women's sexual behavior, they were also one aspect of a larger social and symbolic dimension of village life: woman's association with the house and with the "inside."

The "inside" begins with dimensions of physical space. Village houses are clustered closely together but are raised above the street, shuttered, and angled in such a way that few houses face each other directly, thus guarding family privacy as much as is possible within the close confines of village life.[10] This does not mean, however, that there is a simple isomorphism between the house and the concept of "inside." Village dwellings are divided both physically and symbolically into several different kinds of space. Most houses have a porch or veranda linking them to the public world of the street. Here activities are on public view and people socialize informally with neighbors on their own verandas or with passersby (see also Hirschon 1989; Hirschon and Gold 1982). The porch usually opens into the kitchen, where family members not only prepare and eat meals but also visit casually with relatives and close friends. Connected to the kitchen is the *saloni*, which functions as a kind of a parlor. An area where the family displays its photographs and prized possessions— handicrafts produced by women, purchased items, heirlooms—the *saloni* is the site of more

formal entertaining, including celebrations connected with name days, weddings, baptisms, and other family rites. In the *saloni* the family is on public display (see Danforth 1979). One could say that in the kitchen visitor are received as *dhikí mas*, whereas in the *salóni* they are received as *kséni*.[11] It would mark a turning point in our relationship with a village family when my husband and I were received in their kitchen during our visits rather than in the *salóni*. Villagers themselves explicitly recognized the change. "They're not *kséni*," one woman remarked when a friend of hers suggested that we go into the *salóni* rather than the kitchen. And not surprisingly, it was in the kitchen, observing the comings and goings of family members and the round of daily activities, that I learned more about the private aspects of family life than I ever did in a *salóni* visit where I was subjected to the rituals of hospitality and to a formal exchange of greetings and questions.[12]

The house is par excellence the realm of the woman: women maintain the boundaries of the household and guard its integrity (see Dubisch 1986b). This boundary maintenance includes the control of sex, the responsibility for which rests chiefly (through not entirely) on women. Sex, however, is not necessarily considered bad in and of itself. (I was somewhat startled by the amount of sexual banter and innuendo I encountered in daily village conversation.) It is important, however, that sexuality be controlled and not become a threat to social order.[13] Sex must either be brought "inside" through the institution of marriage or confined to the margins of the social group. Young people in the village, for example, had sex in fields or in the shadowy places of village life—in dark corners behind buildings or other clandestine locations (cf. Harris 1980)—and young men went to town, to Athens, or to other "outside" places to find women for sex. Greek men frequently pursue foreign women, who are particularly "outside," a practice so common that it is institutionalized under the term *kamáki* (literally, "fishing spear"; see Zinovieff 1991).

But it was not only village men who had affairs. Though it was more difficult for them, some young women arranged to meet young men clandestinely outside the village. However, a woman had to be more discreet than a man. Given the importance of a woman's control of her sexuality to the preservation of family integrity, a woman who seemed to lack such control was not likely to be perceived as a desirable mate. One village man, commenting about a young unmarried woman with a "reputation," said that she might very well make a good wife but that one simply couldn't know. There was always the danger that she might deceive her husband "in the street" (see also Hirschon 1978).[14] Thus, while male sexuality may be tolerated or even positively valued, at least by men (for an example of Greek women's view see Cowan 1991:192), women's sexuality requires concealment and, ideally, domestication so that the "sexual identity of women is subordinated to their kinship role as mothers and guardians of the domestic order" (Loizos and Papataxiarchis 1991b:223).

Similarly, sexual joking and innuendo are to be kept "inside"; that is, they are to be indulged in only among familiars and avoided in the presence of those from "outside." As Herzfeld puts it, "Sexual humor is a mark of intimacy" (Herzfeld 1987b:117; see also Clark 1983).

Sexuality thus becomes a marker of the boundaries between outside and inside, between *kséni* and *dhikí*. Women's sexuality in particular comes to represent both familial and communal integrity, to be kept inside and guarded against penetration. By controlling their own behavior, women maintain the coherence and purity of the family. A woman should be "of the house" (*tou spitiú*), concerned with and confined to appropriate domestic matters. A woman who lets things "out," into the "street," whether these things are gossip (uncontrolled words), family secrets, or her own sexuality, is behaving inappropriately and will be subject to communal censure. Likewise, she must guard house and family against any intrusions from the outside, including dirt, illicit sexuality, and other "foreign" matter (Dubisch 1986a). Sexuality, women's in particular, becomes a marker of the boundaries of social groups.

Thus, while both men and women bear burdens in the agonistic arena of Greek village life, they bear them differently. Men carry the brunt of public competition in the "outside" world, the world of the *kafenío* and the *agorá*, while women maintain the solidarity of the "inside," the world

of domestic life centered in the house, and experience the restrictions this task imposes.[15] By extension, women may represent other oppositions as well, including the opposition between the "us" of the community and the "outside" of the state (see Dimen 1986; Herzfeld 1986).[16] In this way they become what Goddard has termed "carriers of the problematic of 'us versus them' " (Goddard 1987:185).

The inside/outside, female/male association, however, must not be seen only in terms of opposition or as a simple equation of life. The two arenas of social experience are in a dialectical relationship, simultaneously defining and sustaining each other. The boundaries between them are not fixed but shift according to context. Both men and women have public as well as domestic roles (see Dubisch 1983; Herzfeld 1986; Hirschon 1983), and one can argue that even women's domestic roles are in a sense "public" since upon their performance rests, in part at least, the reputation of the family (see, for example, Stanton and Salamone 1986).

Women also serve as mediators between the inside and the outside (see Dubisch 1986a). Moreover, it is through women that men are tied to domestic life. The literature on Greece has tended to emphasize the importance of marriage for a woman—as a rite of passage to adulthood, as the context in which she can direct her sexuality into the "destiny" of motherhood, as a continuation of the process by which she is socially defined through her attachment to men (see, for example, du Boulay 1986; Hirschon 1978; Loizos and Papataxiarchis 1991b). But it is clear that a man's full adult status also depends upon his marriage.[17] A man may delay marriage longer than a woman, and a single man certainly enjoys more freedom than does a single woman (through some village women I knew looked back nostalgically on the days of their unmarried youth). But it is expected that a man will eventually marry and so become a full-fledged adult member of the community. In the village, young men who had delayed marriage might be teased or admonished to find a wife, and a young retarded man was frequently saluted with the joking toast "to your wedding." The "joke" was that, being retarded, he was incapable of marrying and becoming an adult.[18]

Men, too, mediate between the inside and the outside, though to a lesser extent than women. Men are expected to provide women passage into the public world. With a brother or other male relative to escort her, a young unmarried woman in the village could move more freely through public space. Married village women usually relied on their husbands as escorts, and a man who did not take his wife out to the *kafenío* for saint's day or other festivals might be criticized by other villagers for leaving her confined to the house.

Connected to issues of women's virtue and the *kséni/dhikí* contrast is the concern with appearances that is an important feature of Greek village life. A family maintains or loses its reputation together. While a woman or man may be judged as an individual, regardless of how other members of the family are judged (a good person may have a bad spouse, for example, or a virtuous mother may produce a delinquent child), such judgments do not entirely ignore the behavior and character of other family members. The defects of one member can raise doubts about the character of all. At the same time, because reputation is a matter of public judgment and therefore depends upon the opinions and knowledge of others, wrongdoing is not necessarily damaging in and of itself; what counts is whether or not others find out about it. Thus, one's duty to the family mandates that one conceal that which might undermine the family's reputation.[19] This concern with what the community thinks was demonstrated to me by a villager who explained why she did not attend church services during a period of mourning for a close family member. "Better," she said, quoting proverb, "to fear the people than God."[20]

In an ideological system that emphasizes appearance, what one does "inside" may be viewed quite differently from what one does "outside." For example, sexual activity carried on "outside"—that is, outside the village—is less likely to become village knowledge and therefore less likely to be disruptive or to damage one's reputation. Fellow villagers who learn of such activity may even tolerate it because it takes place outside the village, as in the cases Papataxiarchis reports of adultery by women whose husbands were absent for long periods of time (1988:116–117). Indicative of the link between moral relativity and social boundaries is a comment I heard a village man make to his wife. She had scolded him for eating cheese pies in a neighboring village during Lent. The man jokingly defended himself by saying that it wasn't a sin *(amartía)* to have broken the Lenten fast, since he had done so in a village not his own.

THE CASE OF THE "FOREIGN CHICKENS"

Up to this point I have discussed "the village" as if it were a self-evident and clearly bounded unit. In fact, "the village" is a concept whose definition and boundaries fluctuate. Although presented in Greek ideology as enduring social and physical entities, many villages have in fact moved, merged, and split over time (see Sutton 1988). Moreover, in the particular village I studied, as in villages in many other areas of Greece, out-migration, both temporary and permanent, has been a fact of life for generations. Migrants from the village are often referred to collectively as "our villager" or (if they have gone to Athens) as "our Athenians," and may continue to take an active interest in village life after they have left.[21] Thus, the social unit of "the village" transcends a particular physical locale. The boundaries of the village are further blurred by marriage, as outsiders, bearing their own attachments to natal village and kin, enter the community.

It is precisely for these reasons that the processes of boundary definition and maintenance take on particular importance. That is, because boundaries are not only shifting (for example, *dhikí mas* may mean fellow villagers, immediate family, relatives who have migrated, and so on) but are also constituted in social processes, they must constantly be recreated and affirmed. The anthropologist, alternately (or, sometimes, simultaneously) insider and outsider, participates in such social processes, becoming a reference point for boundary definition by villagers. The more I was "inside" (at least to some of the villagers) and the more I was seen as knowledgeable about and in some vague sense at least as "belonging" to the village, the more I was likely to be allowed to see that the village was not seamless but divided by a variety of conflicts and feuds. At the same time, as an outsider to whom these conflicts were being represented, I could observe the ways in which boundaries were defined. Here again, gender enters the picture.

During my fieldwork several quarrels arose between women in the village. In one case, two friends had a falling out, reportedly over the use of some land as an animal pen. ("She is a 'pig', a 'mule'," one woman said of the other, drawing upon a variety of animal imagery.) Details of the quarrel were recounted to me with a certain amount of disgust (and some relish) by the other villagers, who dismissed the incident by pointing out that both of the women involved were *ksénes kopéles,* women from elsewhere who had married into the village. (One woman was from another village on the island, the other from mainland Greece.) The husband of one of them had been deliberately deceived about her character when her brothers were seeking a husband for her,[22] I was told, and she had proved extremely quarrelsome, alienating all of her in-laws and driving her mother-in-law to her death. In addition, my informants added, she was a poor housekeeper, cook, and mother. Thus, weak or defective character, revealed in one's failure to be a proper woman, explained the higher incidence of quarreling among these *ksénes.*

The villagers were not wrong in pointing out that such quarrels usually erupted among "outside" women (or between such outsiders and "native" villagers). They were clearly implying that what came from outside could not be trusted. I came to realize, however, that such quarrels were less an indication of flawed character than of the weak structural position of the *ksénes* in the village social system.

Postmarital residence in the Aegean islands of Greece tends to be uxorilocal (see Casselberry and Valavanes 1976), with young couples setting up house in neighborhood of the bride's parents. Village endogamy is (or was) common, and the bride's family frequently gives the couple a house by way of dowry (see, for example, Kenna 1976). Neolocal households were the norm in the village in which I lived, and they seem to be the norm throughout the islands, in contrast to areas of mainland Greece, where extended patrilocal families are, or have been, more common (see Campbell 1964; Danforth 1979; Friedl 1967). In the village, the only couples I encountered who

lived with parents were those in which the wife was from outside the village or those who had taken in a widowed parent of either the husband or the wife. Although one might argue that even a village wife living in her own house and near parents' house can be considered an "outsider" vis-à-vis her husband's family (see Hoffman 1976), nonetheless her position differs significantly from that of a woman living patrilocally or a woman married into the village from outside (see Dubisch 1974). Village wives who were *ksénes* thus found themselves in a more difficult situation than those who came from the village.

Removed from sources of direct familial aid (particularly fathers, brothers, and mothers) and usually without a dowry to bolster their position within the family (see Friedl 1967), such women often formed friendships and alliances with one another. However, because of these women's difficult, isolated position within village social networks and because of their conflicting allegiances, their alliances were subject to strain and breakage. In addition, lacking other resources, the *ksénes* often resorted to quarreling and nagging to achieve their ends. They were pursuing the limited political strategies available to them as outsiders, but villagers interpreted their socially disapproved behavior as an indication of defective character.[23] This pattern accords with Jane Collier's observation that while conflicts between men may be explained "in terms of culturally recognized rules, women's quarrels are often attributed to personal idiosyncrasies or to particularistic circumstances" (1974:89–90).

A woman's status as a *kséni* was not automatic, however. While any woman from outside could be labeled a *kséni,* some women never were. It was only when I obtained the life histories of these women that I found they were not originally from the village. Disapproved or disruptive behavior, then, makes one an outsider, simultaneously establishing the inside/outside boundary and reaffirming the "norm" of internal village solidarity. Disruptive individuals are, after all, not "one of us."

We see a similar, albeit more inclusive, process in the virilocal joint and extended families found in areas of mainland Greece. These families eventually split up, usually after the father/father-in-law dies, and the split is frequently blamed on the in-marrying wives, who, it is claimed, cannot get along (Friedl 1962). In fact, the split is due more to the diverging interests of the brothers' nuclear families. The in-marrying wives, whose primary ties are unambiguously to their own husbands and children, can promote these interests more straightforwardly than can the brothers, for whom an acknowledgment of the interest conflicts with the idea of fraternal solidarity and loyalty to the larger family. The brothers, to phrase it in the terms used in this article, are torn between two different concepts of the "inside": the *dhikí mas* of the extended family and the *dhikí mas* of the conjugal unit. While ideally these should be in harmony, in fact often they are not. An in-marrying daughter-in-law is a breach in the security of the domestic sphere, for she is both insider and outsider. Many of the restrictions placed on the daughter-in-law are attempts to preserve the integrity of the inside in the face of this intrusion, as Campbell has noted (1964). In a virilocal, exogamous, extended family situation, then, *all* women are *ksénes* and potentially disruptive. By contrast, the in-marrying husband (*sógambros*) who takes up residence in his wife's family, although he may not enjoy the strongest position of domestic authority (Dubisch 1974), does not experience the problems of the in-marrying wife and does not pose the same conceptual inside/outside ambiguity, for he, as a man, does not bear the same sort of responsibility for the integrity of the family and the maintenance of its boundaries that a woman does.

In both the village I studied and elsewhere, then, the anthropologist may see conflicts between women as part of a struggle to exercise power in order to meet personal needs, to provide for children, and to gain domestic control, but the actors themselves often explain such conflict in terms of defects in women's individual or collective character. To misinterpret or deny women's exercise of power is to deny tensions inherent in (ideally) solid social units by interpreting such tensions in terms of interpersonal conflict. Women both represent and maintain the "inside" and the loyalty, solidarity, and intimacy that should characterize it. Restrictions are placed upon them in areas where they threaten the cohesion and well-being of the family. Whereas competitiveness among men has an

ironic double edge—it is part of the "agonistic" nature of village life but also binds villagers together (see Herzfeld 1985)—women's conflicts only disrupt and divide.

Michael Herzfeld has remarked on "the tension between individual and totality that constitutes the segmentary quality of society" and on Greek villagers' recognition of this tension as they explain the difficulty of living in perfect harmony with a shrug and the phrase "We are human (*ánthropi*)" (1987b:171). The cooperation and harmony that should characterize the "inside"—whether the inside is family or the community or the nation—are ideals not always realized. Insofar as women come to represent the "inside" and to be seen as maintainers of its harmony through their control of forces of disorder and pollution (see Dubisch 1986a), they can also, conversely, be blamed for failure of that ideal, that is, for conflict that occurs within social units. And since the exercise of power implies competition and self-seeking, it is inappropriate within the family. In such situations women are turned into outsiders, *ksénes*. But even when women become *ksénes*, to acknowledge that their behavior is political (that is, goal-oriented and to some extent "rational") would be to admit that the reasons for such behavior inhere in the structure of familial and communal life. So quarrels within the village are blamed on *ksénes*. The break-up of a joint household is blamed on the brothers' wives and not on the diverging interests of the families. It is "foreign chickens," scratching around where they do not belong, who cause all the trouble—not one's own hens. Thus, particular breaches of the integrity of social units are ascribed to the disruptive nature of feminine character, whether individual or collective, and not to the segmentary nature of social life itself. The shifting nature of the concepts of *kséni* and *dhikí mas* is what makes such ascription possible.[24]

I do not wish to suggest that villagers never recognize or acknowledge the strains and tensions of village unity. The terms *dhikí* and *kséni* are not mutually exclusive but contextual, and they apply to the anthropologist as well. When I was viewed as a *kséni*, the villagers stressed village unity. When, however, I was considered *dhikí mas*, at least in certain contexts, they tended to inform me of conflicts, feuds, and scandals. The shifts in my status were related not only to the amount of time spent in the field and to the nature of particular situations but also to the variations in my relationships with individual villagers and families. Like more anthropologists, I tended to gravitate to those who treated me as an "insider," because from them I could obtain the most personal and comprehensive information. And yet information one obtains as an "outsider" can be equally useful (Herzfeld 1986) because of what it reveals about boundaries and the ways in which members represent their social units to outsiders.

Thus, gender must not be seen just in the context of the domestic/public distinction. In Greece at least, notions of domestic and public not only mark shifting sets of boundaries but are themselves an aspect of a larger system of opposition between inside and outside.[25] Women may symbolize the character of any social unit to which the inside/outside dichotomy pertains. It was women marrying into the *village* who were the *ksénes kopéles*. And women, along with wine and water, figure most prominently in villagers' discussions of communal character in other regions of Greece, suggesting the general importance of purity in such evaluation. "We don't put chemicals [*fármaka*] in our wine," villagers would say when praising the local vintage. Or, "Our water is pure here." Similarly, to say of a community of region that its men respond violently to any advances to their women is an expression of praise. The untainted and the unpenetrated serve as emblems of integrity. Women's virtue and men's willingness to defend it signify communal character. Likewise, loose women and complaisant men render a community an object of contempt. Thus gender becomes part of a discourse about reputation and boundaries, and about the power and willingness to defend them.

BEYOND HONOR AND SHAME

I have sought to expand discussions of gender in the Mediterranean beyond the concepts of honor and shame and beyond a focus on women as social actors, attempting to place gender in a wider social and conceptual context. Exploration of the relationships between gender, power, and community suggests that concepts such as public and private, rather than being represented as ideological and analytical dichotomies, need to be grounded firmly in specific ethnographic contexts. In the case of Greece, the opposition between inside and outside (of which a domestic/public contrast is only one manifestation) must be seen as a segmentary and dynamic process of social life, one more inclusive and more extensive in its relationship to gender than the opposition between public and private suggests. Gender itself becomes one way of representing the *kséni/dhikí* contrast, and analysis of notions of gender elucidates the flexible, situational nature of the boundaries that this contrast serves to demarcate. Moreover, where there is a strong concern with boundary definition and maintenance, as there is in Greece, the exercise of power by certain individuals (in this case women, who represent the "inside") may be ignored, denied, or interpreted as a malevolent or disruptive force.[26]

The relationship between inside and outside, "our own" and "strangers," and male and female also has implications for our understanding of Greek society beyond the household and the village. Sofka Zinovieff has analyzed the institution of *kamáki,* the systematic "hunting" by Greek men of foreign women, as both a competitive male activity and a playing out of "the sense of antagonism that many Greeks have toward 'Europe or the West' " (1991:203). In conquering the foreign women these men gain a sort of revenge and overcome their sense of inferiority as members of a poorer, more backward society. The foreign woman (*kséni*), being an outsider, is fair game. Deception is common in the "chase," and the Greek man may preserve his privileged "insider" position by speaking Greek with his friends in front of his conquest, sometimes referring to her disparagingly without her knowledge. Such behavior would of course not be possible with a Greek woman; it can be carried out only with those who are outside the moral norms of the community. (A paradox arises when a Greek man marries one of these foreign women, for then the outsider must be brought inside the domestic sphere—a situation that does not always turn out happily. The marriage often remains "in the liminal zone of culture contact" [Loizos and Papataxiarchis 1991a:19], that is, neither inside nor out.)

At another level, gender provides a framework for discourse about national identity. Herzfeld, for example, sees a tension between two conceptions of Greekness: what he terms the "Hellenic," a model drawn from images of classical Greece and oriented toward the outsider's (particularly the western European's) view of Greece; and the "Romeic," the insider's view, a model of a more "intimate" Greece, revealed more often by Greeks among themselves (1982, 1987b). This "insider's" Greece, Herzfeld argues, may be symbolized by women, who are associated with the intimate, interior sphere of life and are kept "covered" (literally or symbolically) from the view of outsider (Herzfeld 1986:227, 1987b). Women thus "stand for" Greece, and the relationships between women and men (particularly "outsider" men) stand for Greece's relationships with other nations (just as in *kamáki*, foreign women come to represent foreign nations). Discourse on gender thus becomes discourse on nationalism as well.

Gender can also come into play in the religious definitions of boundaries and community. Villages, ethnic groups, islands, and regions as well as the nation of Greece itself are represented by individual saints, devotion to whom is centered on particular icons and churches, each of which celebrates its own saint's day. Such representations have gender implications at several levels. Not only do women represent their individual households in ritual activities, tending household shrines and family graves (Danforth 1982; Dubisch 1983; Hirschon 1983) and making vows and pilgrimages on their families' behalf (Dubisch 1990), but the most venerated holy figure in Greece is a female, the Madonna (Panayía). Although a wide variety of saints are venerated in Greece (see, for example, Danforth 1989), the Madonna is a focus for the sort of segmentation discussed by Herzfeld (1987b), for she represents both the Greek nation as a whole (see Dubisch 1988) and specific localities or communities (see, for example, Kenna 1977). But she reflects a particular aspect of Greece. In discussing why the Assumption of the Madonna has never been proclaimed a dogma of the Orthodox church, Timothy Ware states that "the doctrines of the Trinity and Incarnation have been proclaimed as dogmas, for they belong to the public preaching of the Church; but the glorification of Our Lady belongs to the Church's inner Tradition" (1963:265). Ware goes on to quote Vladimir Lossky: "while Christ was preached on the housetops, and proclaimed for all to know, ... the mystery of His Mother was revealed only to those who were within the Church" (Lossky, cited in Ware 1963:265). A clearer statement of Mary's role as representative of the "inside" would be difficult to find. This view may be one key, Herzfeld suggests, to understanding how widespread devotion to the Madonna can exist simultaneously with the blasphemous expression "screw your Panayía." By such an expression, "a blasphemous Greek can divide up the holy image of the Virgin between rival factions or regions" (Herzfeld 1987b:159; also see 1984). The rival unit is then violated by the verbal penetration of the (feminine) "inside." The speaker impugns the purity of the Madonna herself, the highest symbol of womanhood (see du Boulay 1986), as a means of insulting those of another social group who have failed to maintain the integrity of their own boundaries. It is only in the context of the relationships between gender, social groups, and social boundaries that such expressions become intelligible.

POSTSCRIPT: SOME FURTHER QUESTIONS

I have phrased much of my ethnographic description of the village in the past tense, for the village changed considerably since the time of my fieldwork.[27] Already experiencing high out-migration at that period (Dubisch 1977), it has continued to lose population, both to Athens and to the island's main town. Although some farms continue to be worked, and some business remain (particularly those catering to summer visitors), the village is gradually becoming a place of summer house and summer visitors, serving both former residents and Greek and foreign tourists. It has not lost its identity completely, nor have those who have migrated necessarily ceased to think of themselves as in some manner "belonging" to the village; the terms *kséni* and *dhikí mas* are still heard. But these terms of attachment and separation have become more flexible and ambiguous, as the connection to the village by a new generation born and raised in the city, or abroad, becomes less certain. For the migrant generations, the village has become more and more a place of retreat as well as symbol of "traditional" values and practices, rather than the context of daily social life.[28]

Given such changes, it is reasonable to ask what the implications are for social boundaries, both familial and communal, and for what I have argued here about women's representation of the "inside." In particular, one might ask whether women are becoming less significant as representations of communities, as well as whether they themselves are less concerned with reputation in a bounded social group and more concerned with demonstrating "modernity" in an urban setting (see, for example, Collier 1986) and with establishing their own senses of personhood (Cowan 1990). With increasing affluence, does Greek women's maintenance of family reputation now rest more on their role as consumers, demonstrating a family's material status in both urban and village settings, and less on the control of sexuality and the maintenance of the integrity of the "inside"?[29] And if so, does this affect the representation of both nation and community?

Although the answer to all these questions is at least an equivocal yes, the relationship between gender and boundaries is not necessarily sundered completely in a changing Greece. Women may mark off new boundaries, as for example when villagers disapprovingly contrast the freer behavior of urban girls with that of their village cousins, the former typifying, for those who remain in the village, the looser morals of city life. (By contrast, the restriction of women in the village may represent for urbanites the "backwardness" of village life, just as in *kamáki* the foreign woman may represent both the immorality of the outside—in contrast to the virtue of the Greek woman—and the progress, sophistication, and wealth of Western Europe.) Radical changes in village life may also shift gender-represented boundaries away from strictly local manifestations and toward regional or national systems. In a recent sermon on the Day of the Dormition

(15 August) at Tinos' famous Church of the Annunciation, for example, the local bishop railed against young women who came improperly attired to pay their respects to the church's famous icon of the Madonna. Their behavior, according to the bishop, indicated that they had "left the proper road [*dhrómo*]." His criticism of the inappropriate crossing of boundaries by women, and his use of such a metaphor for moral and religious decline in Greece, illustrate the ways in which gender, articulated as a representation of community integrity at the village level, can be incorporated into a national level of discourse as well. Concepts of gender thus serve both as a means of representing—and in the process creating—social units and social boundaries and as a means of talking about social experience itself.

Within such a framework of understanding, we can also see some of the significance of women's own crossing of boundaries as they seek to change social definitions of gender and self. From the village woman who indignantly recounted the bishop's speech to me and refused an invitation to a saint's day banquet because priests would be there, to the young women in the town studied by Jane Cowan (1991) who seek altered definitions of their personhood in the newly created public space of the *kafetería*, to a generation of young Greek women whose relatively greater sexual freedom blurs (to some extent at least) their demarcation from the *ksénes* and reduces the sexual justification for *kamáki* (Zinovieff 1991), Greek women themselves strive to alter their own association with the inside and their symbolic position as the emblems of its integrity.

Notes

1. On honor and shame, see particularly Campbell (1964), Gilmore (1982, 1987) Peristiany (1966), and Pitt-Rivers (1977). For critiques, see Herzfeld (1980, 1987a) and Lever (1986).

2. The classic article on this topic is by Friedl (1967); see also Dubisch (1986b), Rogers (1975, 1985), and, more recently, Gilmore (1990).

3. For a recent analysis of these issues (though not in the Mediterranean), see Strathern (1988).

4. On the use of metaphor, and particularly animal metaphors, see Fernandez (1986). I should emphasize that the use of the "chicken" metaphor, while not unrelated to the villagers' usage, is my own device for understanding, organizing, and analyzing certain observations.

5. On the application of the concept of segmentation to Greece, see Herzfeld (1985, 1987b).

6. Such a scene is beautifully described in Stratis Myrivilis' novel *The Mermaid Madonna* (1959).

7. In other areas of Greece, however, women are more extensively involved in agricultural work.

8. There is some stigma attached to a man's spending too much of his time in the house (see Kennedy 1986; Loizos 1981; Pavlides and Hesser 1986).

9. A number of authors have noted that women participate in religious activities more than men do, in Greece and in other areas of the Mediterranean. On Greece, see Dubisch (1983, 1989) and Hirschon (1983). On Greek men's ambivalence toward religion and priests, see Campbell (1964) and Herzfeld (1985).

10. Village houses were arranged for purposes of defense during the centuries when the islands were beset by pirates and other raiders. The original fortifications can still be seen in some villages (see Kharitonidou 1984). Newer houses, however, are still built to preserve a sense of privacy, by means of their spatial arrangement and/or shutters that can be closed or lowered. In the summers, open doors always have curtains hung over them, both to guard against insects and to shield the interior from view.

11. It is interesting to note that the word *salóni* is itself a foreign one (Herzfeld 1987b:118).

12. Even in the kitchen, however, rules of hospitality were not abandoned; they were simply relaxed.

13. Sex is one of a number of bodily functions that can be considered polluting (see Dubisch 1986a).

14. Male sexuality also has a dangerous quality, however. As Gilmore suggests, "sexuality is a form of social power" (1987:4). As such, it can be highly disruptive. (Also see Cowan 1990.)

15. There is a psychological state that can result from confinement. It is called *stenohória*, which is often translated as "depression" or "anxiety" and which literally means "being in a narrow place." (See Danforth 1989:122–124.)

16. My argument differs somewhat from that of Schneider, who, in analyzing the problem of female purity in the Mediterranean, describes women as a "contested resource" and sees the common interest in preserving female virginity as a unifying force for social groups (1971). See Ortner (1978) for a critique of Schneider's analysis.

17. The importance of marriage in the life cycle is illustrated by the custom of the "death wedding," in which a young person who dies without having been married goes through a wedding ceremony as part of the funeral, thus completing the life cycle that would have been expected if death had not intervened. (On the death wedding in Romania, see Kligman 1988.)

18. Marriage connects men to the spiritual world as well as to the domestic world, since women perform religious rituals on behalf of their families (tending graves, making vows and pilgrimages, lighting the lamp in front of family icons). (I am indebted to Charles Stewart [personal communication, 1986] for this observation.)

19. As Juliet du Boulay was told by a villager in Euboea, "God wants people to cover up (*O Theós théli sképasma*)" (1976:406).

20. Compare the situation noted by Lever in a Spanish community: "A girl who lost a parent should wear mourning and go to mass, not because it is 'right,' but to avoid criticism. If she is outside the pueblo, she can do as she pleases" (1986:95). Also see Collier (1986) on changing observances of mourning in a Spanish village.

21. Migrants abroad may be referred to in similar fashions as "our Canadians" or "our Congolese," for example.

22. Compare Campbell's discussion of deception in marriage negotiations among Sarakatsani shepherds (1964).

23. Women's friendships are generally difficult and somewhat suspect in Greek village life. Indeed, anthropologists working in Greece have recently debated whether or not such friendships even exist (see Kennedy 1986; Loizos and Papataxiarchis 1991b). Women's friendships, especially those of married women, may be seen as a threat to familial integrity. In addition, women themselves may downplay or deny time spent with friends lest others view it as time stolen from household affairs. Such situations exist elsewhere in the Mediterranean as well. In discussing women's friendships in a Spanish community, Brandes, for example, notes that "adult female friendships are anomalous" and occur mainly among women who have moved into the community from outside (1985:116).

24. It is important to emphasize again that villagers do not simply equate public and domestic with male and female roles. Women have acknowledged public roles, and when they pursue familial interests, their public activity is acknowledged and acceptable.

25. Herzfeld (1986) has convincingly argued this point.

26. One might ask whether such explanations were offered only to me, as an outsider, by attempting to present the essential nature of the village as one of unity, or whether they were also the accepted "insider's" explanations. Even if only the former were true, it would serve to support my point.

27. My use of changing tenses in this article raises the issue of the so-called ethnographic present as a form of anthropological writing. Some elements of my description still hold true for the present, while some apply to the village only as it was in the recent past. I have tried to combine past and present verb tenses in order to avoid both the sense of a "timeless" village and the sense of a radical break between past and present or between "tradition" and "change." (On writing and the ethnographic present, see Clifford and Marcus 1986 and Marcus and Cushman 1982.)

28. By "traditional" I mean what urban Greeks construct as traditional, which may conflict with how life is (or ever was) actually lived in villages. (For a discussion of the concept of the "traditional" Greek village, see Sutton 1988.)

29. This possibility has been suggested in, for example, Pavlides and Hesser 1986 and Dubisch 1989.

Acknowledgments

I did fieldwork in 1969–70 under a grant from the National Institute of Mental Health and made return trips to the village in 1972, 1973, 1975, and 1979. My more recent research on the island (including several return trips to the village) took place in 1986, 1988, and 1990, funded in part by the Fulbright Foundation and by the University of North Carolina, Charlotte, and the UNCC Foundation.

References cited

Brandes, Stanley. 1980 Metaphors of Masculinity: Sex and Status in Andalusian Folklore. Philadelphia: University of Pennsylvania Press. 1985 Women of Southern Spain: Aspirations, Fantasies, Realities. Anthropology 9(1/2):111–128.

Campbell, John K. 1964 Honour, Family, and Patronage: A Study of Institutions and Moral Values in a Greek Mountain Community. Oxford: Clarendon Press.

Caraveli, Anna. 1986 The Bitter Wounding: The Lament as Social Protest in Rural Greece. *In* Gender and Power in Rural Greece. J. Dubisch, ed. pp. 169–194. Princeton, NJ: Princeton University Press.

Casselberry, Samuel E., and Nancy Valavanes. 1976 "Matrilocal" Greek Peasants and a Reconsideration of Residence Terminology. American Ethnologist 3:215–226.

Clark, Mari. 1983 Variations on Themes of Male and Female: Reflections on Gender Bias in Fieldwork in Rural Greece. Women's Studies 10:117–133.

Clifford, James, and George E. Marcus, eds. 1986 Writing Culture: The Poetics and Politics of Ethnography. Berkeley: University of California Press.

Collier, Jane. 1974 Women in Politics. *In* Woman, Culture, and Society. M. Z. Rosaldo and L. Lamphere, eds. pp. 89–96. Stanford, CA: Stanford University Press. 1986 From Mary to Modern Woman: The Material Basis of Marianismo and Its Transformation in a Spanish Village. American Ethnologist 13:100–107.

Collier, Jane, and Sylvia Yanagisako. 1987 Gender and Kinship: Essays toward a Unified Analysis, Stanford, CA: Stanford University Press.

Cowan, Jane. 1990 Dance and the Body Politic in Northern Greece. Princeton, NJ: Princeton University Press. 1991 Going out for Coffee? Contesting the Grounds of Gendered Pleasures in Everyday Sociability. *In* Contested Identities: Gender and Kinship in Modern Greece. P. Loizos and E. Papataxiarchis, eds. pp. 180–202. Princeton, NJ: Princeton University Press.

Danforth, Loring. 1979 Women's Strategies and Powers: A Rural Greek Example. Paper presented at the American Anthropological Association Annual Meeting, November, Cincinnati, OH. 1982 The Death Rituals of Rural Greece. Photography by A. Tsiaras. Princeton, NJ: Princeton University Press. 1989 Firewalking and Religious Healing: The Anastenaria of Greece and the American Firewalking Movement. Princeton, NJ: Princeton University Press.

Dimen, Muriel. 1986 Servants and Sentries: Women, Power, and Social Reproduction in Kriovrisi. *In* Gender and Power in Rural Greece. J. Dubisch, ed. pp. 53–62. Princeton, NJ: Princeton University Press.

Driessen, Henk. 1983 Male Sociability and Rituals of Masculinity in Rural Andalusia. Anthropological Quarterly 56(3):125–133.

Dubisch, Jill. 1974 The Domestic Power of Women in a Greek Island Village. Studies in European Society 1:23–33. 1976 The Ethnography of the Islands: Tinos. *In* Regional Variation in Modern Greece and Cyprus: Toward a Perspective on the Ethnography of Greece. M. Dimen and E. Friedl, eds. pp. 314–327. Annals of the New York Academy of Sciences, Vol. 268. New York: New York Academy of Sciences. 1977 The City as Resource: Migration from a Greek Island Village. Urban Anthropology 6(1):65–83. 1983 Greek Women: Sacred or Profane. Journal of Modern Greek Studies 1(1):185–202. 1986a Culture Enters through the Kitchen: Women, Food and Social Boundaries in Rural Greece. *In* Gender and Power in Rural Greece. J. Dubisch, ed. pp. 195–214. Princeton, NJ: Princeton University Press. 1986b Introduction. *In* Gender and Power in Rural Greece. J. Dubisch, ed. pp. 3–41. Princeton, NJ: Princeton University Press. 1988 Golden Oranges and Silver Ships: An Interpretive Approach to a Greek Holy Shrine. Journal of Modern Greek Studies 6(1):117–134. 1989 Death and Social Change in Greece. Anthropological Quarterly 62(4):189–200. 1990 Pilgrimage and Popular Religion at a Greek Holy Shrine. *In* Religious Orthodoxy and Popular Faith in European Society. E. Badone, ed. pp. 113–129. Princeton, NJ: Princeton University Press. 1991 Gender, Kinship and Religion: "Reconstructing" the Anthropology of Greece. *In* Contested Identities: Gender and Kinship in Modern Greece. P. Loizos and E. Papataxiarchis, eds. pp. 29–46. Princeton, NJ: Princeton University Press.

du Boulay, Juliet. 1974 Portrait of a Greek Mountain Village. Oxford: Clarendon Press. 1976 Lies, Mockery and Family Integrity. *In* Mediterranean Family Structures. J. G. Peristiany, ed. pp. 389–406. Cambridge: Cambridge University Press. 1986 Women—Images of Their Nature and Destiny in Rural Greece. *In* Gender and Power in Rural Greece. J. Dubisch, ed. pp. 139–168. Princeton, NJ: Princeton University Press.

Fernandez, James. 1986 Persuasions and Performances: The Play of Tropes in Culture. Bloomington: Indiana University Press.

Friedl, Ernestine. 1962 Vasilika: A Village in Modern Greece. New York: Holt, Rinehart, and Winston. 1967 The Position of Women: Appearance and Reality. Anthropological Quarterly 40(3):97–108.

Gilmore, David D. 1982 Anthropology of the Mediterranean Area. Annual Review of Anthropology 11:175–205. 1987 Introduction: The Shame of Dishonor. *In* Honor and Shame and the Unity of the Mediterranean. D. Gilmore, ed. pp. 2–21. American Anthropological Association Special Publication No. 22. Washington, DC: American Anthropological Association. 1990 Men and Women in Southern Spain: "Domestic Power" Revisited. American Anthropologist 92:953–970.

Goddard, Victoria. 1987 Honour and Shame: The Control of Women's Sexuality and Group Identity in Naples. *In* The Cultural Construction of Sexuality. P. Caplan, ed. pp. 166–192. London: Tavistock.

Harris Olivia. 1980 The Power of Signs: Gender, Culture and the Wild in the Bolivian Andes. *In* Nature, Culture and Gender. C. P. MacCormack and M. Strathern, eds. pp. 70–94. Cambridge University Press.

Herzfeld, Michael. 1980 Honour and Shame: Some Problems in the Comparative Analysis of Moral Systems. Man (n.s.) 15:339–351. 1982 Ours Once More: Folklore, Ideology, and the Making of Modern Greece. Austin: University of Texas Press. 1984 The Significance of the Insignificant: Blasphemy as Ideology. Man (n.s.) 19:653–664. 1985 The Poetics of Manhood: Contest and Identity in a Cretan Mountain Village. Princeton, NJ: Princeton University Press. 1986 Within and Without: The Category of "Female" in the Ethnography of Modern Greece. *In* Gender and Power in Rural Greece. J. Dubisch, ed. pp. 215–233. Princeton, NJ: Princeton University Press. 1987a "As in Your Own House": Hospitality, Ethnography, and the Stereotype of Mediterranean Society. *In* Honor and Shame and the Unity of the Mediterranean. D. Gilmore, ed. pp. 75–89. American

Anthropological Association Special Publication No. 22. Washington, DC: American Anthropological Association. 1987b Anthropology through the Looking-Glass: Critical Ethnography in the Margins of Europe. Cambridge: Cambridge University Press.

Hirschon, Renée. 1978 Open Body, Closed Space: The Transformation of Female Sexuality. *In* Defining Females. S. Ardener, ed. pp. 66–88. New York: John Wiley and Sons. 1983 Women, the Aged and Religious Activity: Oppositions and Complementarity in an Urban Locality. Journal of Modern Greek Studies 1(1):113–130. 1989 Heirs of the Greek Catastrophe: The Social Life of Asia Minor Refugees in Piraeus. Oxford: Clarendon Press.

Hirschon, Renée, and John R. Gold. 1982 Territoriality and the Home Environment in Greek Urban Community. Anthropological Quarterly 55(2):63–73.

Hoffman, Susannah. 1976 The Ethnography of the Islands: Thera. *In* Regional Variation in Modern Greece and Cyprus: Toward a Perspective on the Ethnography of Greece. M. Dimen and E. Friedl, eds. pp. 328–340. Annals of the New York Academy of Sciences, Vol. 268. New York: New York Academy of Sciences.

Kenna, Margaret. 1976 Houses, Fields and Graves: Property and Ritual Obligation on a Greek Island. Ethnology 15:21–34. 1977 Greek Urban Migrants and Their Patron Saint. Ethnic Studies 1:14–23.

Kennedy, Robinette. 1986 Women's Friendships on Crete: A Psychological Perspective, *In* Gender and Power in Rural Greece. J. Dubisch, ed. pp. 121–138. Princeton, NJ: Princeton University Press.

Kharitonidou, Angeliki. 1984 Greek Traditional Architecture: Tinos D. Hardy, trans. Athens Melissa Publishing House.

Kligman, Gail. 1988 The Wedding of the Dead: Ritual, Poetics, and Popular Culture in Transylvania. Berkeley: University of California Press.

Lever, Alison. 1986 Honor as a Red Herring. Critique of Anthropology 6(3):83–106.

Loizos, Peter. 1981 The Heart Grown Bitter: A Chronicle of Cypriot War Refugees. Cambridge: Cambridge University Press.

Loizos, Peter, and Evthymios Papataxiarchis. 1991a [eds.] Contested Identities: Gender and Kinship in Modern Greece. Princeton, NJ: Princeton University Press. 1991b Gender, Sexuality, and the Person in Greek Culture. *In* Contested Identities: Gender and Kinship in Modem Greece. P. Loizos and E. Papataxiarchis, eds. pp. 221–234. Princeton, NJ: Princeton University Press.

Marcus, George E., and Dick Cushman. 1982 Ethnographies as Texts. Annual Review of Anthropology 11:25–69.

Myrivilis, Stratis. 1959 The Mermaid Madonna. A. Rick, trans. New York: Crowell.

Ortner, Sherry B. 1978 The Virgin and the State. Feminist Studies 4(3):19–35.

Ortner, Sherry, and Harriet Whitehead, eds. 1981 Sexual Meanings: The Cultural Constitution of Gender and Sexuality. New York: Cambridge University Press.

Papataxiarchis, Evthymios 1988 Kinship, Friendship and Gender Relations in Two East Aegean Villages. Ph.D. dissertation, University of London. 1985 The Dancing Efes: Notions of the Male Person in Aegean Greek Fiction. Paper presented at the Modem Greek Studies Association Symposium on Greeks and Asia Minor, Anatolia College, Thessaloniki.

Pavlides, Eleftherios, and Jana Hesser. 1986 Women's Roles and House Form and Decoration in Eressos, Greece. *In* Gender and power in Rural Greece. J. Dubisch, ed. pp. 68–96. Princeton, NJ: Princeton University Press.

Peristiany, Jean G., ed. 1966 Honour and Shame: The Values of Mediterranean Society. Chicago: University of Chicago Press.

Pitt-Rivers, Julian. 1977 The Fate of Sechem, or the Politics of Sex: Essays on the Anthropology of the Mediterranean. Cambridge: Cambridge University Press.

Rogers, Susan Carol. 1975 Female Forms of Power and the Myth of Male Dominance: A Model of Female/Male Interaction in Peasant Society. American Ethnologist 2:727–756. 1985 Gender in Southwestern France: The Myth of Male Dominance Revisited. Anthropology 9(1/2):65–86.

Schneider, Jane. 1971 Of Vigilance and Virgins: Honor, Shame and Access to Resources in Mediterranean Society. Ethnology 10:1–24.

Stanton, Jill, and Stephen Salamone. 1986 Introducing the Nikokyra: Ideality and Reality in Social Process. *In* Gender and Power in Rural Greece. J. Dubisch, ed. pp. 97–120. Princeton, NJ: Princeton University Press.

Strathern, Marilyn. 1988 The Gender of the Gift: Problems with Women and Problems with Society in Melanesia. Berkeley: University of California Press.

Sutton, Susan Buck. 1988 What Is a "Village" in a Nation of Migrants? Journal of Modem Greek Studies 6(2):1 87–216.

Ware, Timothy. 1963 The Orthodox Church. New York: Penguin Books.

Zinovieff, Sofka. 1991 Hunters and Hunted: Kamaki and the Ambiguities of Sexual Predation in a Greek Town. *In* Contested Identities: Gender and Kinship in Modern Greece. P. Loizos and E. Papataxiarchis, eds. pp. 203–220. Princeton, NJ: Princeton University Press.

CRITICAL THINKING QUESTIONS

1. How do the meanings of the Greek words *ksénos* and *dhikós mas* change depending on the context the words are used in?

2. What was the "traditional" ethnographic description of Greek women, and how does that differ from what Dubisch observed?

3. How are men and women spatially/socially separated in the village Dubisch studied?

4. How and why are women associated with the world of the "inside"? Give specific examples.

5. Why is boundary maintenance important in the village? How are these boundaries developed and maintained? Give specific examples.

6. How is gender used to define and delineate social boundaries in the local, national, and religious spheres?

Politics: Who Gets What, When, and How

STATE OF THE ART: Politics

Anthropology has always been concerned with politics—the process by which power is accrued and exercised in a society. Before 1940, anthropological studies of politics were part of the general study of culture. The theory of *cultural evolution* that was used for such studies emphasized stages of cultural development, from the "primitive" to the "civilized." Ethnographic descriptions of culture included the evolution of political activity in terms of *who* gets *what* (positions of power or rulership, valued resources, etc.), *when* they get them, and *how* they get them. The art of exercising power, of deciding who rules or who governs, was an aspect of every culture, including cultures of preindustrial societies, which had to maintain political or social order through personal relations, the *gens* (corporate lineage), and other social units such as the clan.

Franz Boas's reaction against this early evolutionism—the classification of cultures into primitive and civilized, and generalizations of cultural realities—led to an emphasis on the detailed study of particular cultures. The study of politics was neither emphasized nor isolated from other cultural institutions such as religion, kinship, and age–grade associations in which politics was manifest. *Structural functionalism* appeared later to challenge evolutionism. Structural functionalism was concerned with how cultural institutions *functioned politically* in the maintenance of social order. It looked for the basis of integration and group harmony and how they relate to decision making, power, and authority in society. The study conducted by Meier Fortes and E. E. Evans-Pritchard in 1940 on African political systems was an example of this theoretical trend and provided the foundation for the emergence of the subfield of political anthropology. Fortes and Evans-Pritchard identified two types of political systems in Africa: primitive states with centralized authority and judicial systems (the chiefdom and the state), and stateless societies that lack centralized authority and institutions (the band and the tribe). As structural functionalists, Fortes and Evans-Pritchard focused on how lineages in the tribes they studied functioned politically (Lewellen 2003).

Because functionalism assumed that social equilibrium was a normal feature of society, subsequent studies attempted to show how conflict and interest groups operated in the stability of the society. Subsequently, A. L. Southall challenged the functionalist idea of the lineage as the center of political activities, and proposed the idea that, in a stateless society, institutions such as age-grades, women's associations, and secret societies cut across lineage boundaries for political action (Lewellen 2003).

In the early 1950s, Edmund Leach found three political systems, rather than the usual two, among the Kachins of Burma. There was the small-scale centralized state, and a traditional system with dual facets, one anarchic (lacking in significant government) and the other unstable and neither anarchic nor centralized. Both the traditional and state systems were distinct communities of several linguistic, cultural, and political subgroups, which formed an interrelated whole. Leach understood that this whole could not be in equilibrium, but he treated the society as though it was in equilibrium in order to untangle the web of realities. He found constant tension and change among the various subsystems of Kachin society. His work laid the foundation for the *process approach* in the anthropological study of politics. In his study of African societies in the late 1950s and in 1960, Max Gluckman pointed out that equilibrium is neither characterized by stability nor is it static. Gluckman believed that equilibrium is a process in which conflicts and sets of relations interact with other sets of relations, for instance, when cross-cutting loyalties unite the wider society in settling intragroup feuds.

Claude Lévi-Strauss's *structuralism* offered new challenges to earlier theoretical approaches. The structuralist approach sought the underlying structures of a culture, which were believed to operate like language in their relationship to one another. The main contribution of structuralism to the study of politics was the identification of *political structure* as one of the underlying structures of culture (Lewellen 2003).

In the 1940s, when the alternative theoretical orientations were dominant, a new form of evolutionism—*neoevolutionism*—appeared to revive and revise the earlier nineteenth-century evolutionism. Leslie White and Julian Steward were concerned with the factors that triggered evolution. For White, cultural evolution occurred with efficient use of the energy from the environment. Steward insisted that the interaction between the environment, subsistence methods, and the political institutions of a society determined evolution (Rosman & Rubel 2004). In the 1960s, Elman Service and other neoevolutionists emphasized the characteristics of each level of sociocultural integration rather than how each level evolved into the next (Lewellen 2003). Political hierarchy or *political evolution* was demonstrated through the band, tribe, chiefdom, and state-level political organizations (Kurtz 2001). The characteristics of such themes as power, authority, and decision making and how they *differ* from one level to the next were sought. Since then, more elaborate political classifications have been formulated and political evolution continues to be favored among neoevolutionists, although it is not a major focus of political anthropology. Rather, functionalist theory was also embraced and continued to be relevant in political anthropology. It held sway until political anthropologists began to lose interest, although some continue to use it to this day. As functionalism began to wane in popularity, emphasis on political processes and decision making gained attention among political anthropologists. They focused on how power is used and manipulated to achieve public goals. The process approach highlights how political agents use a variety of strategies to obtain power (action theory). Studies of political process focus on political support, legitimacy, conflict, authority code, characteristics of the political field, and the nature of the political arena. Ralph Faulkingham's 1970 study of political support in a Hausa village is one example. His work is an analysis of political processes, highlighting the kinds of support generated and used by those vying for the position of village chiefship. The process approach continues to be used in the anthropological studies of politics (Kurtz 2001; Lewellen 2003). Anthropologists who have worked in the tradition of Clifford Geertz applied his symbolic analysis to the study of politics. Ukaegbu's study of political conflict in her native Ogwa sought to uncover the cultural meanings of political behavior as interpretive acts of her people (Ukaegbu 1995).

The phenomenon of globalization has created a flow of people, money, ideas, culture, and trade within the context of rapidly changing communications and travel technology and the spread of corporate capitalism. Reaction to these changes is forcing new conceptions in political anthropology, as the field faces "new definitions of culture" (Borofsky et al. 2001; Lewellen 2003), community, locality, and identity. Since the onset of globalization, power is both more diffuse and locally concentrated as it gravitates downward from states to multinational corporations to community-level nongovernmental groups and ethnic organizations (Lewellen 2003). Consequently, political anthropologists analyze the nature of power relations between such entities. Political anthropologists have watched with keen interest the political developments of the last few decades of the twentieth century to the present, including the recent worldwide movement toward *internal democratic changes*. The political elite who were once unwilling to concede to demands made by ordinary citizens for the inclusion of their voices in the polity are now "broadening citizens' access to political participation" (Bonvillain 2010:323). The new reforms are the consequences of globalization.

Today, political anthropology looks at politics from a broad perspective that includes the place of religion and ritual and the role of the individual in politics, the structure of power and its application in the current world in which we live, the results of people's resistance and rebellion against the social order, and the particular relations of gender and power in the society. Also of interest to anthropologists are the ways of socializing individuals to develop a political identity in the context of ethnicity and national identity (Lewellen 2003).

ABOUT THE ARTICLES

Anthropology has a long history of interest in and fascination with politics and the different forms political systems take. All political systems, from the simplest to the most complex, perform two basic functions. First they have to regulate and control issues of internal harmony and intragroup cooperation. Part of this includes how the population is linked to natural resources and the means of distributing these resources throughout the group. The second function involves how groups regulate their relationships with external groups. These relationships can involve trade, communication, war and peace, and myriad other issues. The articles in Section Six discuss how various groups deal with both sets of functions. With two exceptions, they deal with these functions from the perspective of modern states and issues.

Watanabe's article deals with a system of sociopolitical organization that has fascinated anthropology and archaeology for years, the hunting-and-gathering band. He reviews the "classic" view of the band from an anthropological perspective and then discusses the band from the perspective of New Guinean ethnography. He then presents a cultural evolutionary continuum classifying bands from both the prehistoric and modern perspectives, explaining how modern band societies cannot be used as surrogate models for prehistoric band groups.

The selection from Trigger's book, *The Huron: Farmers of the North,* examines what can be defined as a "tribal" level society. Trigger discusses the basic political structure of this culture from a historic perspective, as this group no longer exists as an autonomous entity as it did in the seventeenth century. Trigger talks about the role of chiefs and how they are selected, their powers and perhaps more importantly, how such powers are limited by cultural tradition and attitudes. In some ways their political organization mirrored that of the early American state, so the student may want to ask how the Huron avoided the concentration of power that sometimes occurs in cultures larger than a band-level society.

The next two articles examine the issues of the formation (ethnogenesis) of ethnic and national identity. Shahrani attempts to delineate the relationship between individual, ethnic, and national identity in Afghanistan by examining how ideas about kinship, ethnicity, and Islam interweave. He demonstrates how Western concepts regarding the nation-state, imposed on Afghanistan from the outside, do not fit well within this framework. Shahrani then argues that it was the impropriety of this model of nationhood and interference by outside forces that led to the collapse of the Afghan state in the 1990s and the rise of the Taliban. This article may provide insights into how Western powers embroiled in the region could improve the situation within the country.

Lefkowitz also examines ethnic and national identity, though he does so from an Israeli perspective. By highlighting the way the Israeli media tend to categorize and codify various ethnic groups in Israel, he examines the process of group and national identity building.

The final article by Altran considers one of the more intractable and misunderstood phenomena in modern politics: the suicide bomber. He begins by exploring formal definitions of what terrorism is and then focuses on what he calls "suicide terrorism," defined as the targeting of noncombatant populations by self-destructing human beings for political purposes. Altran delves into the history of such behavior, as well as its most recent incarnation among Muslim groups. The Western definition of the individuals who commit such acts—cowardly lunatics and loners motivated by poverty, oppression, and ignorance—is shown to be wanting as the data indicate that most such actors are at least as educated and economically well-off as their surrounding populations. Muslim communities contribute to the motivation of suicide terrorists by actively supporting the institutions (political groups) that create "fictive communities" which articulate the political, economic, and religious grievances that motivate the attackers. Altran ends the article with a tentative exploration of ways communities can be induced to abandon their support for such groups as a way to begin to end the cycle of violence.

References

Bonvillain, N. *Cultural Anthropology,* 2nd ed. Upper Saddle River, NJ. Prentice Hall, 2010.

Borofsky, R., Barth, F., Shweder, R. A., Rodseth, L., & Stolzenberg, M. N., "When: A Conversation about Culture." *American Anthropologist* 103, no. 2 (June 2001): 432–446.

Faulkingham, R. H. Political Support in a Hausa Village. Ph.D. dissertation. Michigan State University, 1970.

Kurtz, D. V. *Political Anthropology: Power and Paradigms.* Boulder, CO: Westview Press, 2001.

Lewellen, T. C. *Political Anthropology: An Introduction,* 3rd revised ed. Westport, CT: Praeger, 2003.

Rosman, A., & Rubel, P. *The Tapestry of Culture: An Introduction to Cultural Anthropology,* 8th ed. New York: McGraw-Hill, 2004.

Ukaegbu, D. C. *The Expression of Ndorondoro, Ituaka, and Igbakoaka among Contemporary Ogwa Igbo: An Interpretive Act.* Ph.D. dissertation. University of Massachusetts at Amherst, 1995.

For Further Research

Politics and political structure have formed an abiding source of study for the field. As with every other section, articles on political anthropology are published in most journals. Two discussions of political structure that have seriously influenced anthropology and archaeology are Morton Fried's *The Evolution of Political Society: An Essay in Political Anthropology* (1967, McGraw-Hill) and Elman Service's *Primitive Social Organization: An Evolutionary Perspective* (2nd ed., 1971, Random House). These will give the student a historical perspective on more recent discussions regarding political organization. A good general overview is Joan Vincent's *The Anthropology of* *Politics: A Reader in Ethnography, Theory, and Critique* (2002, Oxford: Blackwell). A subsequent volume is *A Companion to the Anthropology of Politics* edited by David Nugent and Joan Vincent (2004, Oxford: Blackwell). Another overview is John Gledhill's *Power and its Disguises: Anthropological Perspectives on Politics* (2nd. ed., 2000, London: Pluto Press). A fourth insightful book is *The Anthropology of the State* edited by Aradhana Sharma and Akhil Gupta (2006, Oxford: Blackwell). For additional information on researching the topics discussed in the "State of the Art" section, please visit *www. mysearchlab.com.*

Social Classification of Hunter-Gatherers: An Evolutionary Perspective

Hitoshi Watanabe

Abstract *Based on my own work among the Ainu in northern Hokkaido and ethnographic literatures for many modern hunting-gathering societies in the northern Pacific rim in particular, this paper presents that such societies are classified into "Every-Male-the-Hunter" type and "Not-Every-Male-the-Hunter" type, which are distinctive from each other in their ecological and socioeconomic adaptive mechanisms; here, hunter refers to a big-game hunter. This occupational differentiation of males, reflecting different levels of sociocultural complexity, is judged to play a significant role in social evolution. This classification is considered in relation to hominization process.*

Keywords: *hunter-gatherer, big-game hunter, occupational differentiation, social evolution, ethnoarchaeology, Ainu*

INTRODUCTION

While I was making ethnographic field researches among the Ainu of northern Japan in the 1950s, I came to notice a new fact that their traditional hunting-gathering communities included two different types of families, i.e. hunting-oriented families and fishing-oriented ones.

This differentiation of subsistence pattern between families within the community was based on the occupational differentiation of males between hunters who were specialized in large-game hunting and non-hunters who were not regular hunters of large game. The large-game hunters were also engaged in fishing as their primary subsistence activity, while the non-hunters were primarily fishermen and were never engaged in large-game hunting as a regular occupation.

Some simple description of the new field data was published for the first time in my monograph on the Ainu ecosystem in 1964 (Watanabe, 1964).

Then, in the course of my comparative ecological studies of northern food-gatherers with special reference to the Ainu, I came to realize the following two facts:

1. The first fact is that the same phenomenon, as seen within the Ainu community, i.e., differentiation of adult male members between hunters and non-hunters, is found widely distributed among sedentary hunter-gatherers of the northern Pacific rim who have often been designated as "fishermen" and who are apt to be excluded from the category of hunter-gatherers;
2. The second fact is that the occupational differentiation mentioned above is deeply concerned with the social stratification of freemen into two classes of the upper and the lower ones. My first paper on this point was published as an article of the *Current Anthropology* in 1983, under the title of "Occupational differentiation and social stratification: the case of northern Pacific maritime food-gatherers" (Watanabe, 1983).

After having published this report, I began to realize firstly (a) that the differentiation of fishermen from hunters is nothing but the differentiation of non-hunters from hunters, and secondly (b) that the presence or absence of such non-hunters within one and the same community can

Source: Reprinted from *Anthropological Science* (1998), The Anthropological Society of Nippon.

be a significant criterion for the socioecological or socioeconomic classification of hunter-gatherers.

This point of view was mentioned briefly in my comment to an article of the *Current Anthropology* in 1988 (Watanabe, 1988a).

THE SYSTEM OF CLASSIFICATION

From the above point of view, I would like to present here a new system of socioecological or socioeconomic classification of hunter-gatherers based on variation in the male's occupation, i.e. the presence or absence of non-hunters within the community.

The result is that modern hunter-gatherers' societies can be classified into two categories, (I) societies in which every adult male is expected to be a large-game hunter (Every-Male-the-Hunter type), and (II) societies in which non-large-game-hunters are accepted (Not-Every-Male-the-Hunter type).

The possibility of such a classification has already been implied in such an early ethnographic publication as "Indians of the United States" by Clark Wissler (Wissler, 1940). He states in it: "Since the pre-Columbian society of the United States was maintained by hunting and this was the man's job, the three R's of a boy's education were the techniques of hunting; he must major in deer or bison according to where he lived. In the northeast, one of his minors would be moose; in the bison area, he would have two minors, elk and deer. No youth could qualify to respectability unless well trained in these hunting techniques. There is no evidence that all the graduates from the hunting school were rated at A+, and as in all societies the able provider fed more than his share, but made up for it in prestige and power. We may summarize with the remark that the desirable standard of living in aboriginal United States was based upon hunting large game, meat being the staple and the preferred food. It is recorded more than once in literature that Indians said, "When there is no meat, starvation stalks through the camp." In general, then, the basic occupation among the United States Indians was hunting large game. The only possible exception might be in the Puget Sound area, where fishing was important, and in Arizona and New Mexico, where maize was cultivated intensively. Yet, even in those areas, the hunting of deer was important. The killing of large game not only results in food, but many inedible products" (Wissler, 1940: 243–244).

As shown above, Wissler suggests that pre-Columbian societies of the United States Indians can be divided into two major types: one is the society in which man's job was large-game hunting and the other is that in which man's job was not large-game hunting. My idea of classifying societies of modern hunter-gatherers into two types, Categories I and II previously mentioned, has been greatly encouraged by the classic statement of Wissler.

The subject of my classification to be presented here is aboriginal societies of non-mounted and non-mechanized hunters. Accordingly, such peoples as Indians of Arizona and New Mexico with intensive cultivation of maize by males or the Pueblo Indians, and the Plains Indians as mounted hunters of the bison are excluded from my classification.

[I] Society of Category I: Every-Male-the-Hunter Type

This is the society in which every adult male is expected to become a large-game hunter or man's job is large-game hunting.

Hunter-gatherers' society of this type is represented by nomadic and semi-nomadic groups of the world including Greenland, North America, Asia, Australia, and Africa.

In the society of this type the developmental cycle of the boy's hunting skill is the focus of public interest, and various communal customs are found formed around the cycle. The commonest and most important of them may be the first kill rite and marriage regulation based on hunting skill.

(A) Typical Ethnographic Examples of the Every-Male-the-Hunter Society Ethnographic reports including full or careful descriptions of the boy's life cycle from the above point of view show the following elements:

1. Boy's first killing of large game celebrated or publicly marked.
2. Large-game hunting as condition for marriage or responsibility of husband.

TABLE 1 Hunting-gathering Groups Classified as the Every-Male-the-Hunter Type with (A)-1 and (A)-2 Elements

Area	First Game	Ethnographic Source
Greenland		
West Greenland Eskimo	Seal	Birket-Smith, 1924: 422; Kleivan, 1984: 608, 613, 617
Polar Eskimo	Polar Bear	Murdock, 1934: 212
Nunivak Eskimo	Bearded Seal	Oswalt, 1967: 204; Fitzhugh and Kaplan, 1982: 152
North America		
Arctic		
Quebec Eskimo	Seal	D'Anglure, 1984: 492, 496
Caribou Eskimo	Seal/Caribou	Birket-Smith, 1929: 292
Copper Eskimo	Seal/Caribou	Jenness, 1922: 158
Kobuk River Eskimo	Bear	Giddings, 1956: 26
Nunivak Eskimo	Seal	Lantis, 1984a: 219–220, 1947: 6
	Bearded Seal (Adult)	Fitzhugh and Kaplan, 1982: 152
Nelson Is. Eskimo	Bearded Seal	Fienup-Riordan, 1983: 267
Subarctic		
Ojibwa	Deer/Bear	Jenness, 1935: 94, 98; Landes, 1971: 11–12, 131
Slavey	Large Game	Asch, 1981: 339–340, 344
Great Basin		
Washoe	Deer	D'Azevedo, 1963: 26, 36, 108; Downs, 1966: 36
Northern Paiute	Large Game/Deer	Fowler and Liljeblad, 1986: 449–450*-
Africa		
!Kung (Nyae Nyae)	Large Game	Marshall, 1976: 130
!Kung (Dobe)	Antelope	Lee, 1979: 230, 235–236
Pygmies (Mbuti)	Large Antelope	Turnbull, 1965b: 139–140

*Element (A)-2 is absent and (B)-2 present instead.

Hunter-gatherers showing the combination of those elements, (A)-1 and (A)-2, are listed in Table 1.

Hunting of large game as a man's job is usually regarded by hunter-gatherers themselves as the most difficult of their occupations because it requires hard and long training and the highest level of skill and knowledge. But small-game hunting is much easier because it does neither need such hard and long training nor such high-level of skill and knowledge. Furthermore, range of activity for a small-game hunter is much narrower than that for a large-game hunter (Watanabe, 1985a: 178). In consequence, hunting of small game (the size limit roughly being hare [Watanabe, 1985a: 145]) is universally woman's job in the division of labor among hunter-gatherers (Watanabe, 1985a: 146). From the above comparison it may be evident that there are some fundamental differences between large-game hunting and small-game one. It is therefore essential and indispensable to make a terminological distinction between the two types of hunting in ethnographic description. But in practice it is not the case with the majority of ethnographic reports I have surveyed. The examples are shown below.

(B) Other Ethnographic Examples of the Every-Male-the-Hunter Society Many ethnographic reports show the following elements concerned with the boy's life cycle:

1. Boy's first killing of game celebrated or formally marked.
2. Hunting as condition for marriage or responsibility of husband.

Hunter-gatherers showing the combination of those elements, (B)-1 and (B)-2, are listed in Table 2.

TABLE 2 Hunting-gathering Groups Classified as the Every-Male-the-Hunter Type with (B)-1 and (B)-2 Elements

Area	People	Ethnographic Source
North America		
Arctic	Baffinland Eskimo	Kemp, 1984: 473
Subarctic	Mistassini Cree	Rogers, 1972: 91, 126; Rogers and Rogers, 1960: 26–27
	Kaska	Honigmann, 1954: 131, 134, 1981: 445, 447
Great Basin	Southern Paiute	Kelly and Fowler, 1986: 375, 377
Northeast	Illinois	Callendar, 1978: 674–675

TABLE 3 Hunting-gathering Groups Classified as the Every-Male-the-Hunter Type with One of the Elements of (A)-1, (A)-2, (B)-1, and (B)-2

Area	People	Element	Ethnographic Source
Greenland	Polar Eskimo	(A)-2	Murdock, 1934: 212
		(B)-2	Gilberg, 1984: 586–587
N. America			
Arctic	Central Eskimo	(B)-2	Boas, 1888: 63, 170–171
	Iglulik Eskimo	(B)-2	Mary-Rousseliere, 1984: 440
	Netsilik Eskimo	(B)-2	Balikci, 1970: 102, 176
	N. Alaskan Eskimo	(B)-2	Spencer, 1959: 237, 241, 244
Subarctic	Northern Naskapi	(B)-2	Graburn and Strong, 1973: 116
	Ojibwa	(A)-2	Jenness, 1935: 98–99
	W. Woods Cree	(A)-1	Smith, 1981: 260
	Hare	(A)-1	Savishinsky and Hara, 1981: 320; Savishinsky, 1974: 18, 20, 23
	Kutchin	(B)-1	Slobodin, 1981: 516, 527
	Cordillera (general)	(A)-1	McLellan and Denniston, 1981: 376, 385
	Chipewyan	(B)-2	Smith, 1981
Northwest	Delaware	(A)-1	Axtell, 1981: 41–2; Goddard, 1978: 216
	Huron	(B)-2	Trigger, 1969: 44; Tooker, 1964: 126
Plains	Gros Ventres	(A)-1	Flannery, 1953: 53, 55, 162
Plateau	Modoc	(A)-1	Ray, 1963: 106, 182
Asia	Yukaghir	(B)-2	Graburn and Strong, 1973: 47
Australia	Murngin	(A)-1	Warner, 1937: 117–119
	Murdudjara	(B)-2	Tonkinson, 1978: 34, 35, 67, 80
Africa	Mbuti	(B)-2	Turnbull, 1965a: 126, 141, 151; 1965b: 224, 225
	Bushman (N.W.)	(A)-2	Shapera, 1930: 122, 125, 128

It is evident from the original ethnographic contexts concerned that the term "game" or "hunting" used in the descriptions of the above elements in the ethnographic reports listed in Table 2 actually means large game or large-game hunting respectively.

(C) Additional Ethnographic Examples of the Every-Male-the-Hunter Society Hunter-gatherers listed in Table 3 show any one of the aforementioned elements, (A)-1 and -2, and

(B)-1 and -2. Those examples suggest lack of systematic description of the developmental cycle of boy's hunting skill.

[II] Society of Category II: Not-Every-Male-the-Hunter Type

This is the society in which not all adult males are large-game hunters or any adult male is allowed to be a non-large-game hunter.

Hunting-gathering societies of this type are distributed among sedentary and semi-sedentary groups (Watanabe, 1990c: 18, Table 1) of northern Pacific rim. Many of them show one or both of the following elements:

1. Large-game hunting as a specialized occupation.
2. Only selected or promising boys are professionally trained to become large-game hunters.

Concrete examples of such peoples are given in Table 4.

Speaking of hunter-gatherers of this social category on the Asian side, considerable amount of data on the occupational differentiation and specialization of large-game hunters were obtained from the Ainu of northern Japan by the present writer, having been published elsewhere (Watanabe, 1964, 1973, 1983, 1990a, 1990c).

Stages of Social Evolution

According to the current system of classification popular among modern anthropologists, hunter-gatherers mean nomadic ones or those of the band type, and such sedentary groups as the Northwest Coast Indians or hunter-gatherers of the northern Pacific rim are omitted from the list of hunter-gatherers or excluded from the category of hunter-gatherers, on account of their sociocultural complexity.

Such exclusive dichotomy, however, is not appropriate even from a viewpoint of the spectrum-like variation in their residential stability and food economy as already shown in my published papers (Watanabe, 1968, 1978, 1990a).

Hunter-gatherers' societies of Category II, i.e. those of the northern Pacific rim characterized by the sociocultural complexity of farmer's level,

---

TABLE 4 Hunting-gathering Groups Classified as the Not-Every-Male-the-Hunter Type

People	Element	Ethnographic Source
California		
Tipai-Ipai	(1) (2)	Luomala, 1978: 601
Nomlaki	(1) (2)	Goldschmidt, 1951: 317, 326, 405
Pomo	(1) (2)	Loeb, 0926: 170, 180, 182; Bean and Theodoratus, 1978: 289–290, 294
Yurok	(2)	Pilling, 1978: 141–142
Northwest Coast		
Alsea	-	Drucker, 1939: 82–84, 96
Quinault	(1)	Olson, 1936: 41, 44, 94
Quileute	(1)	Pettitt, 1950: 10–11
Klallam	(1)	Gunther, 1927: 198, 205, 216, 261
Upper Stalo	(1) (2)	Duff, 1952: 72
Nootka	(1) (2)	Drucker, 1951: 253, 273, 1955: 142; Gunther, 1927: 214–215
Bella Coola	(1)	Government of British Columbia, 1972: 53
Tsimshian	(1)	Garfield and Wingert, 1966: 15–l6
Tlingit	(1) (2)	Oberg, 1973: 30–32
Alaska		
Pacific Eskimo	(1)	Oswalt, 1967: 130–131, 206, 246
Aleut	(1)	Lantis, 1984b: 176
Far East		
Kamchadal	-	Chard, 1953: 24*
Nivkhi	(1)	Black, 1973: 19
Ainu (Hokkaido)	(1) (2)	Watanabe, 1973: 24, 47, 145, 1983: 217, 1988a: 490, 1990a: 22–24, 1990b: 258–260, 262–264

See text for elements (1) and (2).

*As regards the Kamchadal who were classified as a fishing people by Jochelson (1926: Map 9), ethnographic data on the occupational differentiation are scanty, but there is some evidence to show that they belong to this social category. Chard (1953: 24) states that the average Kamchadal does not seem to have been interested in hunting until pressed by necessity, which is understandable in view of the relative ease with which the bulk of his livelihood was obtained.

are nothing but the products of sociocultural evolution resulted from their adaptation to the rich and diverse environment of the region. The specific resource environment and residential stability made the occupational differentiation of males possible. This factor of the occupational differentiation appears to have been of fundamental importance to the development of the complexity represented by such traits as the presence of a group of elite families within the community, social stratification associated with wealth differentiation, and complex systems of communal rites (Watanabe, 1983, 1988a, 1990a, 1990c).

On the other hand, hunter-gatherers' societies of Category I which are not associated with the occupational differentiation, i.e. socially undifferentiated hunter-gatherers of nomadic type, are not only simpler and more generalized than the socially differentiated hunter-gatherers of Category II mentioned above but also are much more widely distributed than the latter, the distribution extending from the tropical zones to the arctic zones.

Judging from the differences in the sociocultural complexity and the size of the geographical range of distribution, the societies of Category I, i.e. the occupationally undifferentiated societies, can be regarded as representing an evolutionary stage earlier in sequence than those of Category II or the occupationally differentiated societies.

From the above point of view, aforementioned two types of hunter-gatherers' societies, [I] Every-Male-the-Hunter type and [II] Not-Every-Male-the-Hunter type, can be regarded as representing

two successive stages of social evolution, Type I (Category I) representing the earlier stage and Type II (Category II) the later one (Fig. 1-A).

The above result of the classification of modern hunter-gatherers into the two groups representing two successive evolutionary stages raises an interesting question whether or not modern hunter-gatherers represent all the stages of their social evolution.

The reason is that even the earlier one of the two stages represented by modern hunter-gatherers appears to be too much developed or specialized to be regarded as the earliest stage of their social evolution. This fact suggests the possibility of the presence of some stage or stages which precede the two stages represented by modern hunter-gatherers and it means that modern hunter-gatherers cannot represent all the stages of their social evolution. This implies some limitation of applicability of ethnographic data to Palaeolithic archaeology or the study of hunter-gatherers' social evolution.

The first or earliest stage of their social evolution as seen from the change of male's occupational role as mentioned above must have been the one in which every male was a gatherer as every female was. That is the Every-Male-the-Gatherer stage in which all males were collectors of plant foods and hunters of small animals just as females (and children) were (Fig. 1-B).

Then another question yet to be answered is that on the change from the Every-Male-the-Gatherer stage to the Every-Male-the-Hunter stage. There is a gap between the two. Therefore there must be a transitional stage between them. It may be assumed to be the Not-Every-Male-the-Gatherer stage, in which not all adult males were gatherers (Fig. 1-B).

It seems that Australopithecines were representatives of the earliest stage. This interpretation is based on the result of my ethnoarchaeological researches on hominization that Australopithecines were plant collectors and small-animal hunters (Watanabe, 1985a: 126–151, 217–221). The transitional stage was probably reached in the age of *Homo erectus*. This interpretation is also based on the results of my ethnoarchaeological studies (Watanabe, 1985a: 212–221, 1985b). The beginning of the fourth stage or Not-Every-Male-the-Hunter stage may not have been earlier

Possible Age of the Beginning of Each Stage

Age of Australo-pithecus	Age of *Homo erectus*	Age of *Homo sapiens:* Upper paleo-lithic or later	Age of *Homo sapiens:* Mesolithic or later
[I] Every-Male-the-Gatherer Stage	[II] Not-Every-Male-the-Gatherer Stage	[III] Every-Male-the-Hunter Societies	[IV] Not-Every-Male-the-Hunter Societies

Stages in the Social Evolution of Hunter-Gatherers

FIGURE 1 Stages in the Social Evolution of Hunter-Gatherers.

B. Stages in the Social Evolution of Hunter-Gatherers

[I]	[II]	[III]	[IV]
Every-Male-the-Gatherer Stage	Not-Every-Male-the-Gatherer Stage	Every-Male-the-Hunter Stage	Not Every-Male-the-Hunter Stage
		Every-Male-the-Hunter Societies	Not-Every-Male-the-Hunter Societies

A. Modern Hunter-Gatherers

FIGURE 2 Stages in the Social Evolution of Hunter-Gatherers and their possible corresponding ages.

than the Mesolithic age because modern representatives of the stage, i.e. sedentary hunter-gatherers of the northern Pacific rim, are largely concerned with fishing (Watanabe, 1988b, 1990a) (Fig. 2).

References

Asch M.I. (1981) Slavey. In *Handbook of North American Indians*, Vol. 6, Smithsonian Institution, Washington, D.C., pp. 338–349.

Axtell J. ed. (1981) *The Indian Peoples of Eastern America*. Oxford University Press, New York.

Balikci A. (1970) *The Netsilik Eskimo*. Natural History Press, New York.

Bean L.J., and Theodoratus D. (1978) Western Pomo and Northeastern Pomo. In *Handbook of North American Indians*, Vol. 8, Smithsonian Institution, Washington, D.C., pp. 289–305.

Birket-Smith K. (1924) *Ethnography of the Egedesminde District with Aspects of the General Culture of West Greenland*. Nationalmuseets Skrifter, Ethnografisk Raekke, Copenhagen.

Birket-Smith K. (1929) *The Caribou Eskimos: Materials and Social Life and Their Cultural Position*, 1. Descriptive Part. *Report of the Fifth Thule Expedition 1921–24*. Gyldendalske Boghandel, Copenhagen.

Black L. (1973) The Nivkh (Gilyak) of Sakhalin and the Lower Amur. *Arctic Anthropology*, 10(1), 1–117.

Boas F. (1888) *The Central Eskimo*. Bureau of American Ethnology, 6th Annual Report, Smithsonian Institution, Washington, D.C.

Callendar C. (1978) Illinois. In *Handbook of North American Indians*, Vol. 15, Smithsonian Institution, Washington, D.C., pp. 673–680.

Chard C.S. (1953) *The Kamchadal: a synthetic sketch*. Kroeber Anthropological Society Papers, 8/9, 20–44.

D'Anglure B.S. (1984) Inuit of Quebec. In *Handbook of North American Indians*, Vol. 5, Smithsonian Institution, Washington, D.C., pp. 476–507.

D'Azevedo W.L. (1963) *The Washo Indians of California and Nevada*. Anthropological Papers, 67, Department of Anthropology, University of Utah.

Downs J.F. (1966) *The Two Worlds of the Washo*. Holt, Rinehart and Winston, New York.

Drucker P. (1939) *Contributions to Alsea ethnography*. University of California Publications in American Archaeology and Ethnology, 35(7), 81–102.

Drucker P. (1951) *The Northern and Central Nootka Tribes*. Bureau of American Ethnology Bulletin, 144.

Drucker P. (1955) *Indians of the Northeast Coast*. American Museum of Natural History, Anthropological Handbook, 10.

Duff W. (1952) *The Upper Stalo Indians of the Fraser River of B.C.* Anthropology in British Columbia, Memoir No. 1, British Columbia Provincial Museum, Victoria.

Fienup-Riordan A. (1983) *The Nelson Island Eskimo: Social Structure and Ritual Distribution*. Alaska Pacific University Press, Anchorage.

Fitzhugh W.W., and Kaplan S.A. (1982) *Inua, Spirit World of the Beiring Sea Eskimo*. Smithsonian Institution Press, Washington, D.C.

Flannery R. (1953) *The Gros Ventres of Montana*, Part I: *Social Life*. Catholic University of America, Anthropological Series, Vol. 15.

Fowler C.S., and Liljeblad S. (1986) Northern Paiute. In *Handbook of North American Indians*, Vol. 11, Smithsonian Institution, Washington, D.C., pp. 435–465.

Garfield V.E., and Wingert P.S. (1966) *The Wolf and the Raven: Totempoles of Southeastern Alaska*. University of Washington Press, Seattle.

Giddings J.L., Jr. (1956) *Ancient Men of the Arctic*. Knopf, New York.

Gilberg R. (1984) Polar Eskimo. In *Handbook of North American Indians*, Vol. 5, Smithsonian Institution, Washington, D.C., pp. 577–594.

Goddard I. (1978) Delaware. In *Handbook of North American Indians*, Vol. 15, Smithsonian Institution, Washington, D.C., pp. 213–239.

Goldschmidt W. (1951) *Nomlaki ethnography*. University of California Publications in American Archaeology and Ethnology, 42(4), 303–443.

Government of British Columbia (1972) *Bella Coola*. British Columbia Heritage Series, Ser. 1, Vol. 10, Provincial Museum, Victoria.

Graburn N.H.H., and Strong B.S. (1973) *Circumpolar Peoples: An Anthropological Perspective*. Good-year Publishing Co., Pacific Palisades, California.

Gunther E. (1927) *Klallam ethnography*. University of Washington Publications in Anthropology, 1, 171–314.

Honigmann J.J. (1954) *The Kaska Indians: An Ethnographic Reconstruction*. Yale University Publications in Anthropology, Vol. 51.

Honigmann J.J. (1981) Expressive aspects of subarctic Indian culture. In *Handbook of North American Indians*, Vol. 6, Smithsonian Institution, Washington, D.C.

Jenness D. (1922) *The Life of the Copper Eskimo: Report of the Canadian Expedition, 1913–18*. F.A. Acland, Ottawa.

Jenness D. (1935) *The Ojibwa Indians of Parry Island: Their Social and Religious Life*. National Museum of Canada Bulletin 78, Ottawa.

Jochelson W. (1926) *The Yukaghir and Yukaghirized Tungas*. American Museum of Natural History, Memoir 13, New York.

Kelly I.T., and Fowler C.S. (1986) Southern Paiute. In *Handbook of North American Indians*, Vol. 11, Smithsonian Institution, Washington, D.C., pp. 368–397.

Kemp W.B. (1984) Buffinland Eskimo. In *Handbook of North American Indians,* Vol. 5, Smithsonian Institution, Washington, D.C., pp. 463–475.

Kleivan I. (1984) West Greenland before 1950. In *Handbook of North American Indians,* Vol. 5, Smithsonian Institution, Washington, D.C., pp. 595–621.

Landes R. (1971) *Ojibwa Religion and the Medewiwin.* University of Wisconsin Press, Madison.

Lantis M. (1947) *Alaskan Eskimo Ceremonialism.* University of Washington Press, Seattle.

Lantis M. (1984a) Nunivak Eskimo. In *Handbook of North American Indians,* Vol. 5, Smithsonian Institution, Washigton, D.C., pp. 209–223.

Lantis M. (1984b) Aleut. In *Handbook of North American Indians,* Vol. 15, Smithsonian Institution, Washington, D.C., pp. 161–184.

Lee R.B. (1979) *The !Kung San: Men, Women, and Work in a Foraging Society.* Cambridge University Press, London.

Loeb E.M. (1926) *Pomo folkways.* University of California Publications in American Archaeology and Ethnology, 19(2), 149–405.

Luomala K. (1978) Tipai and Ipai. In *Handbook of North American Indians,* Vol. 8, Smithsonian Institution, Washington, D.C., pp. 592–609.

Marshall L. (1976) *The !Kung of Nyae Nyae.* Harvard University Press, Cambridge, Massachusetts.

Mary-Rousseliere G. (1984) Iglulik. In *Handbook of North American Indians,* Vol. 5, Smithsonian Institution, Washington, D.C., pp. 431–446.

McLellan C., and Denniston G. (1981) Environment and culture in the Cordillera. In *Handbook of North American Indians,* Vol. 6, Smithsonian Institution, Washington, D.C., pp. 372–386.

Murdock G.P. (1934) *Our Primitive Contemporaries.* Macmillan, New York.

Oberg K. (1973) *The Social Economy of the Tlingit Indians.* University of Washington Press, Seattle.

Olson R.L. (1936) *The Quinault Indians.* University of Washington Publications in Anthropology, 6(1), 1–190.

Oswalt W.H. (1967) *Alaskan Eskimo.* Chandalar Publishing Co., Scranton, Pennsylvania.

Pettitt G. (1950) *The Quileute of La Push, 1775–1945.* University of California, Anthropological Records, 14, 1–120.

Pilling A.R. (1978) Yurok. In *Handbook of North American Indians,* Vol. 8, Smithsonian Institution, Washington, D.C., pp. 137–154.

Ray F. (1963) *Primitive Pragmatists: The Modoc Indians of Northern California.* University of Washington Press, Seattle.

Rogers E.S., and Rogers J.H. (1960) *The individual in Mistassini society from birth to death.* National Museum of Canada, Bulletin, 190, 10–36.

Rogers E.S. (1972) The Mistassini Cree. In *Hunters and Gatherers Today* (Bicchieri, M.G., ed.), Holt, Rinehart and Winston, New York, pp. 90–137.

Savishinsky J.S. (1974) *The Trail of the Hare: Life and Stress in an Arctic Community.* Gordon & Breach, New York.

Savishinsky J.S., and Hara H. (1981) Hare. In *Handbook of North American Indians,* Vol. 6, Smithsonian Institution, Washington, D.C., pp. 314–325.

Shapera I. (1930) *The Khoisan Peoples of South Africa: Bushmen and Hottentots.* Routledge & Kegan Paul, London.

Slobodin R. (1981) Kutchin. In *Handbook of North American Indians,* Vol. 6, Smithsonian Institution, Washington, D.C., pp. 514–532.

Smith J.G.E. (1981) Chipewayan. In *Handbook of North American Indians,* Vol. 6, Smithsonian Institution, Washington, D.C., pp. 271–284.

Spencer R.F. (1959) *The North Alaskan Eskimo: A Study in Ecology and Society.* Smithsonian Institution, Bureau of American Ethnology, Bulletin 171, Washington, D.C.

Tooker E. (1964) *An Ethnography of the Huron Indians, 1615–1649.* Smithsonian Institution, Bureau of American Ethnology, Bulletin 190, Washington, D.C.

Tonkinson R. (1978) *The Mardudjara Aborigines: Living the Dream in Australian Desert.* Holt, Rinehart & Winston, New York.

Trigger B.G. (1969) *The Huron: Farmers of the North.* Holt, Rinehart & Winston, New York.

Turnbull C.M. (1965a) *Wayward Servants: The Two Worlds of the African Pygmies.* Eyre & Spottiswoode, London.

Turnbull C.M. (1965b) *The Mbuti Pygmies: an ethnographic survey.* Anthropological Papers of the American Museum of Natural History, 50(3), 139–282.

Warner W.L. (1937) *A Black Civilization: A Social Study of an Australian Tribe.* Harper and Bros, New York.

Watanabe H. (1964) The Ainu: a study of ecology and the system of social solidarity between man and nature in relation to group structure. *Journal of the Faculty of Science, University of Tokyo,* Sect. 5, Vol. 2, Pt. 6.

Watanabe H. (1968) Subsistence and ecology of northern food gatherers with special reference to the Ainu. In *Man the Hunter* (Lee, R.B., and DeVore, I., eds.), Aldine Publishing Co., Chicago, pp. 69–77.

Watanabe H. (1973) *The Ainu Ecosystem: Environment and Group Structure.* American Ethnological Society Monograph 54. University of Washington Press, Seattle.

Watanabe H. (1978) Shuryo saishuumin no shokusei no bunri: shinkateki seitaigakuteki kenchi kara (Systematic classification of hunter-gatherers' food habits: an ecological-evolutionary perspective). *Journal of the Ethnological Society of Japan,* 43(2), 111–137.

Watanabe H. (1983) Occupational differentiation and social stratification: the case of northern Pacific maritime food gatherers. *Current Anthropology,* 24(2), 217–219.

Watanabe H. (1985a) *Hitowa Naze Tachiagatta ka; Seitaigakuteki Kasetsu to Tenbo (Why Did Man Stand Up? An Ethnoarchaeological Model for Hominization).* University of Tokyo Press, Tokyo.

Watanabe H. (1985b) The chopper-chopping tool complex of eastern Asia: an ethnoarchaeological-ecological reexamination. *Journal of Anthropological Archaeology,* 4(1), 1–18.

Watanabe H. (1988a) On the social anthropology of hunter-gatherers. *Current Anthropology,* 29(3), 489–490.

Watanabe H. (1988b) Kitataiheiyo engan bunkaken: shuryo saishumin kara no shiten (The northern Pacific maritime culture zone: a viewpoint from hunter-gatherers I). *Bulletin of the National Museum of Ethnology,* 13(2), 297–356.

Watanabe H. (1990a) *Jomonshiki Kaisoka Shakai (Prehistoric Jomon Stratified Society).* Rokko Shuppan, Tokyo.

Watanabe H. (1990b) Hoppo shuryo saishumin no seizan shinko (Northern hunter-gatherers' belief in the sacred mountains as the dwelling of the game-giver or gamelord: a functional perspective centering around the Ainu). In *Comparative Studies on Northern Cultures* (Kotani Y. ed.), University of Nagoya, Faculty of General Education, pp. 237–279.

Watanabe H. (1990c) *Hokuyo engan bunkaken: shuryo saishumin bunka no kyotsusei to sono kaishaku mondai (The northern*

Pacific maritime culture zone: similarity of hunter-gatherers cultures and problems on interpretation). Proceedings of the Symposium on "Language of Northern People and Their

Histories," University of Hokkaido, Department of Linguistics, Sapporo.

Wissler C. (1940) *Indians of the United States.* Doran, New York.

CRITICAL THINKING QUESTIONS

1. Based on his research on the Ainu, Watanabe concludes that many modern hunter-gatherer communities contained two different types of families. What are these family types, and what is their economic orientation?
2. Watanabe suggests a new evolutionary classification for hunter-gatherer groups. Outline and define this classification system, discussing the proposed characteristics of each stage. How does this differ from the "traditional" classifications presented in your introductory anthropology class?
3. Why does Watanabe suggest that the last stages of his classificatory scheme are applicable only to modern hunter-gatherer groups?

The Huron Farmers of the North: Government and Law

Bruce G. Trigger

The thousands of Huron who lived south of Matchedash Bay had evolved a social and political organization, as well as a subsistence economy, that permitted a far larger number of people to live together and cooperate than was the case among the Algonkian hunting bands that inhabited the Canadian Shield. By 1610, the Huron confederacy had expanded to embrace four peoples and over twenty communities. The largest settlements each contained as many as six clan segments and a total population of 1500–2000 people.

The confederacy effectively suppressed all blood feuds among its members. This permitted the Huron peoples to live side by side, to cooperate in their mutual defense, and to share a lucrative trade with the north. The unity of the Huron was not a temporary development brought about by the personality of an outstanding chief and likely to perish with him; instead it was founded on a carefully organized system of government that linked clan segments together to form communities, communities to form peoples, and peoples to form the confederacy. Through an elaborate series of councils, which began informally within each extended family and reached to the confederacy level, the activities of these groups were coordinated with one another in the general interest.

In spite of the size and complexity of the Huron confederacy, nothing about its organization shows any sign of being a radical departure from the egalitarian ideas about government that prevailed among the smaller-scale societies of the Lower Great Lakes region. The Huron confederacy had developed out of Iroquoian institutions that predated the adoption of a horticultural economy. Each household remained economically self-sufficient, and clan segments were willing to brook no interference in their internal

affairs. Moreover, disagreements and disputes between clan segments, settlements, and even peoples were not uncommon. The Huron confederacy was not invested with any special powers to curb these tendencies; instead it attempted to resolve each crisis as it arose. Government, whether at the community, national, or confederacy level, strove to achieve a balance between the integrative and divisive forces that were inherent in Huron society. The confederacy respected the rights of its constituent clan segments, settlements, and peoples and elicited only enough support from these groupings to act for their common good. While the confederacy was a fragile structure built on an endless series of pragmatic compromises concerning specific issues, it was able to cope with the political challengers that confronted the Huron people prior to the arrival of the Europeans.

CHIEFS

All public offices were held by men. In part this was true because office holders had to visit other Huron communities and sometimes confront their counterparts among far-off and even hostile peoples—all of this being behavior that Huron considered appropriate for men rather than women. It also reflected the Huron belief that the focus of a woman's interest and power remained within her family and household.

The Huron term for chief (*yarihwa*) meant literally "he is great of voice." This does not mean that a chief was person who gave orders. His primary duty was to announce decisions that were arrived at through a process of consensus that involved all the adult men and women of his group. Chiefs were not supposed to decide

---

Source: From Bruce Trigger, THE HURON, first edition. Copyright © 2002 Wadsworth, a part of Cengage Learning, Inc. Reproduced by permission. www.cengage.com/permissions.

matters on their own and would not be obeyed if they did. Instead, they were expected to act as speakers or chairmen, first helping their own people come to an agreement about a course of action and then representing them in negotiations with other groups. No decision could be considered final until it had received the individual consent of every person who was expected to be bound by it. The ideal chief was not a man who argued with others or attempted to dominate them, but one who spoke softly and respected the opinions of others. It was also a fundamental rule of Huron society that any public respect accorded to a chief had to be reciprocated by a lavish distribution of food and other goods to his followers and anyone else he hoped to influence.

The Huron had two principal kinds of chiefs: *yarihwa endionhra* and *yarihwa ondoutayuehte*. The first were civil or peace chiefs who were concerned with problems of everyday life. They negotiated all foreign treaties, settled disputes, and arranged feasts, dances, and games. The second were war chiefs, who were concerned with waging war and killing witches. This division of responsibility represented the application to the political order of the distinction between peace and war, and more generally between reason and emotion, that played a major role in Huron thinking (Steckley 1978). The Huron believed that duties requiring quiet persuasiveness and the exercise of violence could not be successfully combined at the same time in the same person. Significantly, civil chiefs were the more important of the two. Each clan segment had two chiefs, one for peace and another for war. Thus, in large communities there were several chiefs of either sort, representing the various clan segments that composed the settlement.

Being a chief, especially a civil chief, required the expenditure of considerable time and wealth. They were expected to entertain their supporters as well as to provide hospitality for visitors. They also had to travel considerable distances to attend meetings, sometimes in very bad weather. The chief at whose house a meeting was held was obliged to provide food and entertainment for his visitors. This required him and his family to work harder than anyone else to produce the food that had to be given away to validate his

public office. Likewise, most of the goods that chiefs received as presents or form their control of trade routes had to be given away to maintain the reputation for generosity without which a chief would have no support. The more influential a chief, which meant the larger were the number of people in whose name he spoke, the greater was the scale on which he had to provide feasts and give away exotic goods.

Civil chiefships were hereditary in particular lineages, the office passing from a chief to one of his brothers, and in the next generation to one of his sister's sons. While the hereditary nature of chiefship may have conflicted to some degree with the egalitarian ideals of Huron society, it served to minimize what might have been a potentially disruptive competition for public office among households and lineages. Chiefs were supported by the members of their clan segments but, unlike the situation among the Indians of the Northwest Coast, there appears to have been little overt status rivalry among them. The additional prestige that accrued to members of chiefly lineages was balanced by the need for members of those lineages to work extra hard to produce the food and other goods that a chief needed to give away to validate his status.

There was also no rule to determine which individual within a particular lineage should inherit an office. Instead, the lineage members, and in particular the older women of the lineage, selected the new chief. In doing so they considered the qualifications of each candidate to represent their clan segment. These included their intelligence, oratorical abilities, willingness to work, popularity, and above all their courage, as demonstrated by their past performance as warriors. Individuals who did not wish to play an active role in community life would refuse the offer of a chiefship. Chiefs who failed to perform the duties expected of them, and hence became objects of public complaint or ridicule, could be dismissed at any time by the women of their lineage.

The investiture of new chiefs usually took place at the annual meeting of the confederacy council. The main event of this ceremony was conferring on the new officeholder the ceremonial name of his predecessor, which henceforth replaced his previous personal name. The name of a man holding a particular office therefore remained unchanged from generation to generation. The Huron placed a strong emphasis on structural continuity in their political organization, which they considered to be more imporant than historical or genealogical considerations. A chief was expected not only to assume the name of his predecessor but also to exhibit similar personal qualities and to behave as much as possible like him.

Prior to an investiture, a magnificent feast was hosted by the newly selected chief's clan segment. The other chiefs who attended were well fed and provided with rich presents in order to win their support for the candidate. While each clan segment had the right to choose its own chief, the respect and goodwill of other chiefs were vital if he was to discharge the duties of his office successfully. Hence, the women of his lineage took care to select a candidate who would be acceptable to other chiefs and to win their support. After the new chief's appointment by his lineage was approved by the various chiefs of the confederacy, his new name was conferred on him. He was further identified with his predecessor by being symbolically drawn from the grave by the assembled chiefs. They then presented him with gifts on behalf of all the clan segments, communities, and peoples they represented. Each present was accompanied by an explanation of its symbolical meaning. Presents were given to draw the deceased from the grave, give him weapons to repel his enemies, and make the earth solid under his feet so that he would remain immovable during his tenure of office. Two women, probably the senior ones of his clan segment and lineage, were expected to attend the investiture; if they did not, this was believed to betoken misfortune for the officeholder.

New chiefs were presented with special insignia of office, which were passed from each officeholder to his successor and regarded as the most treasured objects in the country. These took the form of distinctive personal ornaments. Each chief also had a package of council sticks (*atsatonewai*), which functioned as his books and papers. They were mnemonic devices that served a purpose similar to strings and belts of wampum among the Iroquois, outlining the structure and seating plans of councils and the order in which speeches were to be made. Some of these sticks were buried with dead chiefs.

After the investiture, a second magnificent feast was held to celebrate what had happened. At this event old men recited Huron myths and traditions so that the young people could hear and remember them. These included the Huron account of the creation of the world. Following this celebration, a new chief often recruited young men to accompany him on a war expedition. His aim was to perform some daring exploit that would make it apparent that he had inherited the powers as well as the name of his predecessor. Hereafter, while civil chiefs might continue to join military expeditions, they left the expeditions' organization in the hands of the war chiefs.

The relatives of civil chiefs served them as assistants and counselors. At least one of these assistants was a deputy who frequently accompanied the chief and made public announcements in his name. An Iroquoian tendency to equate silence or soft-spokenness with power made it desirable for each civil chief to have a deputy who spoke publicly in his name. Hence, it was often difficult for strangers to determine who the actual chiefs were, and who were merely speaking for them. The various meetings and consultations by means of which a civil chief managed the affairs of his clan segment were attended by the representatives of the constituent households and lineages, as well as by all of the older men, whose opinions were considered seriously.

The office of war chief, while less prestigious than civil ones, was also hereditary within a particular lineage of each clan segment. War chiefs were often closely related to civil chiefs, and both offices normally seem to have been inherited within the same lineage. Some war chiefs held the office into old age and possibly for life. Others, who displayed desirable qualities, relinquished the war chief's position to a younger man, in order to accept a civil chiefship. While the duties of civil chiefs and war chiefs were clearly separated, in times of military crisis or when there was a panic about witchcraft the role of the war chief became more important and, for the duration of the emergency, war chiefs, with the support of younger men, might make decisions normally made by civil chiefs. As conditions returned to normal, civil chiefs regained their influence over the war chiefs, telling them when they could and could not wage war or seek out witches.

Only civil chiefs had seats on the national and confederacy councils. These met periodically and were responsible for maintaining order within the confederacy and peaceful relations with foreign peoples. War councils, which were held when needed to plan campaigns at the community, national, and confederacy levels, were attended by the war chiefs of the various clan segments. In Arontaen, the house of the leading war chief served as one meeting place for such councils. When greater security was desired, meetings were held at night in secret places in the forest. Sometimes the representatives of other nations at war with the Iroquois were invited to these meetings. In the late 1630s, the Jesuit missionaries were being asked to attend war councils as the representatives of the French.

Huron chiefs had no constitutional authority to coerce their followers or to force their will on anyone. Moreover, individual Huron were sensitive about their honor and intolerant of external constraints, and friends and relatives would rally to the support of someone who believed himself insulted by a chief. Overbearing behavior by a chief might, therefore, encourage a violent reaction and lead to conflicts within or between lineages. In the long run, chiefs who behaved arrogantly or foolishly tended to alienate support and would be deposed by their own lineages. The ideal Huron chief was a wise and brave man who understood his followers and won their support by means of his generosity, persuasiveness, and balanced judgement.

The enforcement of a chief's decision depended upon his securing the backing of public opinion and bringing this to bear against refractory individuals. The support that a skillful chief could muster in this fashion was quite considerable. The Jesuits recount that on one occasion when a young man struck a well-respected chief, the whole village rushed to the chief's aid and were restrained only with great difficulty from killing the young man on the spot. This reaction also reflected the commonly held belief that young men were irresponsible and had to be kept in line for the benefit of the community. By acquiring a good reputation, a chief was able to influence decision making to a considerable degree. To maintain such influence, he had to remain unstintingly generous and avoid any public display of arrogance or bad temper. Nor could he hope to retain public respect if he insulted or belittled anyone.

Many men who were neither civil chiefs nor war chiefs acquire a reputation for bravery, sagacity, or generosity which served to enhance their influence in the community. In later life, the opinions of these men came to carry considerable weight in the affairs of their village or people. While these prestigious individuals were known collectively as the Old Men, the more outstanding among them were called chiefs. The possibility of being recognized as an outstanding individual, even if no clan office was available, was a great encouragement to men to excel in subsistence activities, trade, and war.

CRITICAL THINKING QUESTIONS

1. Define the basic organization of the Huron confederacy. Why does Trigger argue that this structure did not disrupt the essentially egalitarian nature of Huron society?
2. In general, what were the primary duties and functions of the chief?
3. Discuss the office of the "civil chief." What were his duties, how was he selected, and what personal characteristics was he expected to possess?
4. How was the investiture of a new chief celebrated?
5. What were the limitations of a chief's powers?
6. Who were the "Old Men," and how did they achieve that status?

War, Factionalism, and the State in Afghanistan

Nazif M. Shahrani

Abstract Since September 11, 2001, the explanations offered to account for the rise of a foreign-led terrorist network on Afghan soil have variously focused on the political vacuum opened up by the Soviet withdrawal from Afghanistan in February 1989, interference by foreign powers in Afghanistan's internal affairs, the failure of Afghanistan to produce a "strong state" because of ethnic factionalism, and an internal moral incoherence inherent to Afghan culture. I argue that none of these explanations is entirely satisfactory in itself. To understand the situation in Afghanistan, we must recognize that its political and military chaos is not an isolated or unique phenomenon, and at the same time acknowledge the particular social and political dynamics of Afghanistan's history that have set the parameters for current events. I show that communal conflicts in Afghanistan are part of a much wider affliction common to many postcolonial states and multinational societies, and that Afghanistan's current situation can only be understood by focusing on its failed attempts at nation-state building within the broader geopolitical circumstance of foreign manipulation and proxy wars that have given rise to particular forms of ethnic division. [Keywords: Afghanistan, nation-building, ethnic factionalism, warfare, the State]

AFTER SEPTEMBER 11, 2001

Following the tragic attacks in New York City, Washington, D.C., and Pennsylvania on September 11, 2001, people in the United States, shocked and in disbelief, wondered who had committed such acts and why. When U.S. government authorities cautiously revealed the identities of the alleged perpetrators to be members of the al-Qaeda terrorist network, believed to be led by the Saudi Arabian national Osama bin Laden, with headquarters in Taliban-held Afghanistan, everyone wanted to know the facts about the Taliban: Where did they come from? What internal and external forces created and supported them? What brand of Islam were they brandishing? What was the relationship between the al-Qaeda terrorists and the Taliban regime in Afghanistan?

Those of us concerned with the long-term study of the more than two-decades-long conflict in Afghanistan were not at all surprised by the links between the alleged perpetrators of these horrors on U.S. soil and those who had been waging terrorist wars for the previous five years against a large segment of the Muslim peoples of Afghanistan. Indeed, we were appalled by the lack of international concern prior to September 11 for the plight of the victims of Taliban and al-Qaeda terrorist wars in many parts of Afghanistan (see Maley 1998; Rashid 2000; and Shahrani 1998, 2000a, 2000b). Contrary to the assumptions of the advocates of the "clashes of civilizations" thesis that would blame all of Afghan "culture" for what had happened, we knew that the inhabitants of the western, central, and northern parts of Muslim Afghanistan who did not belong to the ethnic-linguistic and sectarian community of the Taliban, as well as all Afghan women and girls, had themselves been the targets of a systematic and sustained terror campaign in the name of Islam by the extremist Taliban movement and their international terrorist allies since 1995.

Although the answers to even the most basic questions about the Taliban were largely unknown

Source: Reproduced by permission of the American Anthropological Association from *American Anthropologist*, Vol. 104, Issue 3, pp. 715–722 (2002). Not for sale or further reproduction.

before September 11, it was not long before even more complicated ones were raised: Why and how did Afghanistan become the safe heaven for al Qaeda and other terrorist groups? What explained the meteoric rise of the Taliban as an extremist Muslim militia movement in post-Soviet Afghanistan? Why and how did the mujahideen fighters in Afghanistan fail so miserably to form a workable national governance structure after successfully fighting the former Soviet occupation forces and their puppet communist regimes? How had the long-established, ideologically organized mujahideen parties lost their political significance, giving way to intense intercommunal proxy wars fought by coalitions of tribal, regional, and ethno-linguistic-sectarian forces, financed and managed by foreign powers? What in the history of Afghanistan and its political culture provided the space for the rise of such an extremely harsh and violent militant movement at the dawn of the 21st century? Was this an expected manifestation of recognizable historical patterns in the country? or was it an aberration and a product of novel circumstances of post-jihad Afghanistan?

FROM HOLY WAR TO HOLY TERROR

One way to begin to answer some of these questions is to focus on the transition in Afghanistan from military successes following the Soviet withdrawal to political disasters, or as Olivier Roy has put it, "From Holy War to Civil War" (1995). The explanations offered have focused on the role of outside forces especially following the Soviet withdrawal from Afghanistan in 1989; the effects of meddling by outside powers (both governmental and nongovernmental) in a fragile multinational state; and the presence of deeply contradictory moral codes within the Afghan political culture.

International security experts, Zalmay Khalilzad and Daniel Byman,[1] provide an example of the first type of explanation. They assert that,

As the United States departed [after the withdrawal of Soviet Red Army from Afghanistan], a vicious civil war spread throughout the country. Once the Soviet-backed regime fell, war, anarchy and fragmentation followed. The conflict became increasingly one of ethnic and sectarian groups, particularly Pashtuns, Tajiks, Uzbeks, and the Shiah Hazaras. . . . The war also became a proxy war between Iran and Pakistan, with each power backing different factions. [Khalilzad and Byman 2000:67; also see Khalilzad et al. 1999][2]

The role of outside powers and foreign forces in the factional wars of the post-jihad period (1992 to the present) is undeniable and fully documented (Maley 1998; Rashid 2000).

Afghan leaders also look to external factors for an explanation for Afghanistan's current crisis (with, I hasten to say, considerable justification). They blame foreign conspiracies against Afghanistan for the country's internal political chaos. This explanation suggests that foreign powers (governments both near and far and, more recently, multinational corporations such as Unocal of California, Delta Oil of Saudi Arabia, and Bridas of Argentina) have tried to undermine the gains of a militarily successful jihad and Islamic revolution, and have interfered directly in the country's internal affairs in order to further their own policy goals in the region by financing and managing proxy wars.

Other international relations and regional security experts (e.g., Goodson 2001; Rubin 1995) explain the chaos in Afghanistan by invoking the notion of a "weak/failed state syndrome." According to Goodson, for example, Afghanistan

is an extremely weak state, almost the archetypal one, made all the weaker by . . . years of war. [It] . . . is the axle on which several regions swivel [especially the relatively weak post-Soviet Central Asian Muslim states]. [It] . . . also borders on or is influenced by several [competing] regional powers [some of them with nuclear capabilities such as Russia, China, India, and Pakistan, as well as Iran, Saudi Arabia, and Turkey]. Finally, Afghanistan has been the on-again, off-again recipient of superpower and international attention and manipulation, which has contributed to its weakening. [2001:12]

For Goodson, states that have failed to build strong centralized government with capabilities "to penetrate society, regulate social relationships, extract resources, and appropriate or use resources" are weak states that pose serious threats to the international order in the new millennium (Migdal 1988:4, in Goodson 2001:11). Certain unchanging "political, social, economic, demographic, and even geographic" (Goodson 2001:11) factors in such societies are implicated in hampering attempts to build strong and stable centralized state institutions. In Afghanistan, one such factor is said to be the existence of many quarrelsome ethnic, tribal, and religious-sectarian communities that occupy rough mountainous terrain, jealously guarding their communal autonomy. These fragmentary constituencies of a weak state are allegedly prone to resorting to violence for resolving interpersonal and intercommunal problems.[3] They are also thought to be susceptible to manipulations by meddling outside powers, which may account for the ultimate failure of the weak Afghan state.

A final, and more novel, explanation for the predicament of the peoples of Afghanistan is offered by David Edwards (1996). He suggests a cultural thesis in which Afghanistan's political chaos is seen to derive "less from divisions between ethnic and religious-sectarian groups or from the ambitions of particular individuals than they do from the moral incoherence of Afghanistan itself" (1996:3). According to Edwards, this moral incoherence is the product of the conjunction of three contradictory and incompatible moral systems or codes that undergird Afghan political culture: the ultraindividualistic codes of honor (nang), the universalist moral system of Islam, and the codes of monarchical state rule.

None of these explanations is entirely satisfactory in itself. To understand the current situation in Afghanistan, we must at once recognize that its political and military chaos is not an isolated or unique phenomenon, and at the same time acknowledge the particular social and political dynamics of Afghanistan's history that have set the parameters for current events. This involves recognizing that internal communal conflicts in Afghanistan are part of a much wider affliction common to many postcolonial (and now post-Soviet) states and multinational societies, especially smaller and poorer ones, which have found themselves in a geostrategic location within the post-Soviet, unipolar New World Order. Thus, Afghanistan's current, complicated situation can only be understood by focusing on its failed attempts at nation-state building within the broader geopolitical circumstance of foreign manipulation and proxy wars that have given rise to particular forms of ethnic factionalism.

NATION-STATE BUILDING AND SOCIAL FRAGMENTATION

The failure of Afghan governments to achieve their goal of building a strong, sovereign, centralized, and unified nation-state is generally justified and explained by government officials and researchers alike by pointing to intrinsic factors such as the conflictual and fragmentary character of Afghan society. The country's difficult topography, ethnolinguistic and religious-sectarian cleavages, and tribal loyalties are all cited as contributing factors. From this perspective, the problems of state building are safely severed from the larger economic and political context of which they are a part, and Afghan citizens themselves are blamed for their troubles.

The geophysical characteristics of Afghanistan and the sociocultural and social structural heterogeneity of Afghan society have played some part in affecting the processes of state building in the country. However, the transformations of existing sociocultural pluralism into articulated forms of social structural fragmentation along ethnic, religious-sectarian, regional, and tribal parameters, I argue here, can be understood as calculated responses to the imposition of an utterly inappropriate model of a "modern" nation-state governance structure with its discriminatory policies and practices in Afghanistan. As we will see, it was the incessantly centralizing state policies and practices of internal colonialism, generally aided and abetted by old colonialist powers, which produced a cumulatively negative impact on state-building efforts in Afghanistan.

SOCIAL IDENTITY AND GOVERNANCE

Ethnicity and kinship, which are expressed linguistically through the same terms, *qawm* (people, tribe, community), *wulus* (nation, tribe, relatives), and *tyfah* (clan, tribe, group), represent the same or similar ideological frameworks in

Afghanistan. Together with Islam, they provide the most fundamental bases for individuals and collective identities and loyalties, and they are the most persistent and pervasive potential bases for the organization of social formations, for the mobilization of social action, and for the regulation of social interaction among individuals and between social groups. As generalized social organizational principles, Islam, ethnicity, and kinship have been equally available to individuals and collectivities in Afghan society at large, as well as to those who have controlled the central government powers. They have been applied and manipulated not only to further common or similar collective national goals, but also to pursue separate, often divergent, and sometimes conflicting and contradictory aims by individuals, groups, and state institutions (for further details see Shahrani 1986, 1998).

Ethnic, kinship, and religious ideologies, like other social organizational principles, are filled with internal ambiguities, contradictions, limitations, and conflicts. Therefore, the use of these principles by individuals, organized pluralities and governments for instrumental purposes has often resulted in unforeseen consequences. However, social organizational principles, whether based on ethnicity, kinship, religion, or any other sources of social identity, are not in themselves causal in the actual organization of social relations. Rather, individuals, organized social pluralities, and governments apply such principles according to the specific political, economic, and historical contexts in which they find themselves. It is within the context of the operations of real economic and political forces, both internal and external to the particular society, that the value of particular ethnic, kinship, or religious identities, loyalties, and ideologies, and their efficacy in organizing social relations, mobilizing for a cause, as well as their relation to the state, can be studied. It is also within the changing historical contexts of the political economy of both the state and society that the nature of relations between the ongoing formation and reformation of ethnic, tribal, and religious-sectarian groupings in the country, and the formation and transformation of the government power structures at the center, can be examined and understood (so see Shahrani 1986, 1998, 2000a, 2000b).

The relationship of social identity to changing power relations and attempts at state building in

Afghanistan must therefore be examined in relationship to its structure of governance and its political ecology—that is, the relationships of Afghanistan's political economy and political culture to its broader national and regional history. First, it is necessary to identify the major sociocultural principles that provide cultural ideas and norms for conceptualizing and ordering identities and informing politics of difference between social groupings that articulate the relations of domination, as well as resistance, between social groups and communities, as I have done elsewhere (see Shahrani 1998, 2000a, 2000b). Second, it is essential to assess the history of the modern state in Afghanistan and its relationship to its heterogeneous communities of citizens during the last one hundred years as I do below, focusing on the period of Mohammadzai/Durrani dynastic rule preceding Soviet intervention, the decade of the jihad struggle against communism and Soviet occupation (see also Roy 1990; Shahrani and Canfield 1984), and the ongoing post communist and post-jihad struggle for control of state power.

HETEROGENEOUS COMMUNITIES AND THE STATE

At first glance, the problems in Afghanistan might seem to have begun with the communist coup in 1978, which ignited the war that has continued for 24 years. That was not, however, the beginning of the problem, which actually extends back to the creation of the first modern state under the name "Afghanistan" more than a century ago. The foundation of the modern state of Afghanistan was laid when Britain invaded Afghanistan from the Indian subcontinent in 1879 for the second time in 40 years. The British could not adequately control the country because of a prolonged, bloody civil war underway over royal succession. Britain had lost many fighters during its wars of conquest and was faced with stiff resistance by many warring groups headed by competing princelings of the Muhammadzai/Durrani ruling clan of the Pashtun tribes, groups that had been fighting each other for the Kabul throne for some time. The British picked Abdur Rahman, one of the princelings, and pronounced him "King of the Afghans." They provided him with weapons and money to be used to create a buffer state between czarist Russia and British India.

The borders of Afghanistan—drawn by Britain and czarist Russia during the onset of this "Great Game" in Central Asia in the closing decades of the 19th century—were gerrymandered to split members of ethnic groups between or among different neighboring states. Along the northern frontiers, for example, the peoples of Turkistan, the Turkic- and Tajik-speaking Muslim Central Asians such as the Uzbek, Turkmen, Kazak, Kirghiz, and Tajiks, were divided. A large area of southern Turkistan between the Hindu Kush mountains and Amu Darya (Oxus River) was included within the borders of the new buffer state of Afghanistan, which existed until 1967 when the government in Kabul eliminated the province of Turkistan by means of an administrative "reform," replacing it with a number of newly named smaller provinces: Balkh, Jawzjan, Samangan, and Faryab. This politically motivated administrative fiat by the Pashtun-dominated Afghan government in the 1960s paralleled Joseph Stalin's policy of National Delimitation. In 1924 Turkistan was replaced with five language-based Central Asian Soviet Socialist Republics: Uzbekistan, Turkmenistan, Kazakstan, Kyrgyzstan, and Tajikistan. Further east in western China, Sharqi Turkistan—a large territory occupied by the Turkic-speaking Muslim Uyghur, Kazak, and Kirghiz peoples—became officially known in China as Xinjiang province. Thus, as a result of the creation and re-creation of national frontiers that began with the drawing of boundaries of Afghanistan in the 1880s, the larger identity and territorial reality of Turkistan was wiped clean from the face of the world map.

On the western frontier, the Farsiwan, a Persian-speaking people who speak the same dialect as people in eastern Iran, were located on both sides of the Iran-Afghanistan borders. The area to the south and southeast populated by the Baluch population was divided among three countries: Afghanistan, Iran, and British India (now Pakistan). The Pashtun/Pathans (the Afghans) were divided by the Durand Line on the eastern borders, leaving most of the Pashtun/Pathans on the British-India side, which, after the partition, became part of Pakistan. The Durand Line, Afghanistan's eastern frontiers with Pakistan, was drawn by the British to effectively divide the Pashtun between two separate states. The predominantly Mongol-looking, Persian-speaking, Shi'i Hazara became the only large community that was contained wholly within the boundaries of Afghanistan because of their location in the central highlands around Bamyan.

The demarcation of these borders as part of the Great Game by Britain, during the reign of Emir Abdur Rahman (1880–1901), laid the foundation for the troubled status of Afghanistan as a modern nation-state. Backed by Britain, Emir Abdur Rahman terrorized the people within these freshly marked borders. He and his Muhammadzai/Durrani Pashtun clan hailed from Kandahar, the recent spiritual headquarters of the Taliban, as well as the home of Hamid Karzai, the leader of the current U.S.-installed Interim Administration in Afghanistan. The Pashtun in this southwestern area of Afghanistan belong to different tribes than those living further east along the borders with Pakistan. After decimating the leadership of the eastern Ghilzai Pashtun tribes whom he did not trust, Emir Abdur Rahman moved against the Hazaras in the center of the country. The Hazaras resisted Abdur Rahman's conquest (as they also recently opposed the Taliban invasions) of their territory and, as a result, were subjected to extremely harsh punishments: entire villages were massacred, people were skinned alive, and women and children were enslaved. A particularly gruesome form of torture perpetrated against the Hazara people was to form a rim of dough around the shaven heads of men so that boiling oil could be poured on them to fry their brains. Stories of such atrocities remain a permanent part of public memories in this area of the country and are still in circulation (see Mousavi 1997).

Emir Abdur Rahman employed violence and torture in his rampages of conquest and subjugation of all of the peoples within his designated domain. In the east, where the inhabitants were not Muslims (Kafiristan), he forcibly converted them and renamed the area Nooristan (Land of Light). The same brutalities were used in subjugating Uzbek, Turkmen, Tajik, and other ethnic communities in the northern region. Throughout the entire country during the 21 years of his reign, people were brutally terrorized into submission. Emir Abdur Rahman created a relatively strong centralized state through the use of such tactics, by advocating a conservative and xenophobic interpretation of Islamic ideology, and by the liberal use of foreign money and weapons. Indeed, Emir Abdur Rahman—nick-named by his British colonial masters, the "Iron Emir" for his cruel two-decade-long rule—laid the foundation for an ill-suited centralized state structure that lasted for most of the 20th century.

The Iron Emir was intensely suspicious of his citizens, especially of those Pashtun who did not belong to his own clan or tribe and the non-Pash-tun groups in the center and northern regions of the country. In order to insure his sovereignty over the non-Pashtun peoples in the north and central regions of the country, Emir Abdur Rahman mobilized large groups of Durrani Pashtun nomads from the south to occupy large areas of pastureland in central Afghanistan belonging to Hazaras (see Ferdinand 1962; Kakar 1979; Mousavi 2000). He also resettled tens of thousands of Pashtun tribes-men from the south in the strategic parts of Afghan Turkistan along the borders with Central Asian Khanates under czarist Russian control (Tapper 1973). By doing so, he laid the ground for the enforcement of century-long policies that were nothing but a crude form of internal colonialism run by the ruling clique in Afghanistan.

This system of governance lasted until the 1960s when a very small window of opportunity for democratic experimentation opened up as a result of constitutional changes (1964–73). It was during this brief period that some freedom of the press and rudimentary forms of political activity were allowed. Under pressures from the former U.S.S.R., the government did not object to the formation of Afghanistan's Communist Party (Khalq, in 1965), although it strongly opposed the Islamist youth movements. By 1973, King Zahir Shah (r. 1933–73) was overthrown by his own paternal cousin and brother-in-law, prince Muhammad Daoud, with help from the leftist military officers belonging to the Parcham faction of the Communist Party. Five years later, in 1978, the communists killed Muhammad Daoud and massacred his entire family. They also installed a communist regime and, in 1979, faced with overwhelming popular resistance, they "invited" the Soviets to invade the country, beginning Afghanistan's 24-year-long war.

Long-simmering communal tensions rose to the surface after the collapse of the autocratic monarchic state and were further aggravated because of the prolonged proxy wars, leading to the creation of the Taliban and their regime's brutal policies of ethnic cleansing directed against the Hazara, Uzbek, Farsiwan, and Tajik populations in western, central, and northern Afghanistan. The intercommunal wars that had spiraled out of control since the mujahideen military victory in April 1992 are in fact the virulent manifestations of the century-long policies of internal colonialism carried out by Pashtun-dominated governments, supported in large measures by decades of Cold War politics in the region.

During the anti-Soviet and anti-Communist struggles of 1978–92, communities everywhere across Afghanistan organized themselves militarily to defend their own territories. They also created civilian structures at the local level to provide basic health and educational services with the help of international NGOs, as well as for the administration of justice. By 1989, with financial and military help from the United States and some Muslim countries, Afghans serving as the foot soldiers of this proxy war managed to defeat the Red Army, forcing the Soviets to withdraw their troops from Afghanistan in April 1989. But the communist regime they left behind in Kabul lingered until 1992. In the meantime, Pakistan and Iran encouraged their respective client Afghan political parties to fight not only the communist regime and the Soviets but also amongst themselves. The ethnic dimension of Afghan conflict was purposefully heightened and manipulated by Afghanistan's neighbors: Pakistan, the former Soviet Union, and Iran.

The United States reportedly had invested some three billion dollars in the anti-Soviet war and then, after the Soviet defeat and troop withdrawal in 1989, simply abandoned Afghanistan. When America walked away, it left behind a country that was shattered economically, politically, and in every other conceivable sense, and left to the mercy of its quarrelsome neighbors. In 1992, when the communist regime in Kabul finally fell, Pakistan quickly cobbled together a so-called broad-based government of the mujahideen in which the only party they did not favor, the one headed by a non-Pashtun, Burhanuddin Rabbani, managed to take control of Kabul. Feeling slighted by the "usurpation" of power by the non-Pashtun groups from the rightful Pashtun rulers, Pakistan urged Hekmatyar, the leader of Hizb-i Islami (Islamic party), to take control of the capital from the Tajiks militarily, resulting in the bombardment of Kabul for two years and in unimaginable crimes between 1992 and 1994. The resistance against Hekmatyar's onslaught in Kabul was fierce given the Shia Hazaras' powerful presence in some major areas of the city. The Uzbek forces of Abdur Rashid Dustom that had played a critical role in the collapse of the communist regime and mujahideen takeover of Kabul by the Tajik forces of Ahmad Shah Massoud, all fought together initially to resist Hekmatyar. Alliances of forces shifted repeatedly and the interethnic factional fighting in and around Kabul grew worse. Lacking any alternative vision of governance, the leading contenders in these struggles envisioned, if successful, the same system of government dating back to Abdur Rahman: a centralized state in which the ruling faction could impose itself on the rest of the unwilling communities in the country with help from their close kinsmen and friends and support by a foreign sponsor.

Two years of warfare by Gulbuddin Hekmatyar against Kabul could not secure the prize that his Pakistani sponsors wished for him to win. And, at that point, the country had, more or less, been divided into five or six different semi-independent regions. In the western region, the Persian-speaking Farsiwan communities had created an alliance under Ismail Khan with the city of Herat as its center. Ismail Khan had disarmed its own population, enforced a legal system, and began to reopen schools. General Abdul Rashid Dostam, who is vilified as a Northern Alliance warlord by his Pakistani detractors in the media, in fact, had managed to unify several provinces in northwestern region, where he had also brought peace and order. In the area under his control, centered around the city of Mazar-i Sharif and predominantly inhabited by Uzbeks, the conditions for the local population improved: They had local autonomy and thriving commercial ties with the newly independent Central Asian republics. Schools and universities functioned and radio, television, and print media enjoyed considerable freedom and support. The northeastern parts of the country, together with mountain valleys just

north of Kabul such as Kohistan, Kohdaman, Panjsher, and Tagaw wa Nijraw, were ruled by the Shura-i Nazzar (Northern Council) under the command of the late Ahmad Shah Massoud. These areas were more or less peaceful. In the center, the Hazara Shias controlled their own territory and sectarian community with virtual autonomy. In the east, the Pashtuns had created a coalition of several provinces under Shura-i Mashreqi (Eastern Council), peacefully running their own affairs.

By late 1994, factional fighting was mostly limited to the national capitol, Kabul, and to Kandahar, a predominantly Pashtun tribal area where chaos reigned. Not surprisingly, in 1994 it was in Kandahar that Mullah Mohammed Omar emerged along with a group of ex-mujahideen fighters who challenged some of the most notorious of the local warlords. Initially, he succeeded in attracting considerable popular support in and around the city of Kandahar for bringing a semblance of order to that unruly city.

By 1995, a plan by a consortium of oil companies, including Unocal and Delta Oil of Saudi Arabia, was underway to build a natural gas pipeline through Afghanistan from Turkmenistan to the Pakistani seaports of Gwadar. Immediately, Pakistan saw the potential usefulness of the newly rising Pashtun force in Kandahar and adopted Mullah Omar's small movement, naming it "Taliban," the movement of seminary students. Pakistan offered them money, weapons, and logistical support and wanted them to secure a corridor for Pakistan so that Unocal and its partners could build the Turkmenistan-Pakistan oil/gas pipeline across western parts of Afghanistan. Early in 1995, the Taliban secured the allegiance of local Pashtun commanders, mostly through bribes, all across the southern and southeastern Pashtun belt approaching Kabul. Then in the autumn of 1995 they attacked the forces of Ismael Khan in western Afghanistan. Because the population of Herat had been disarmed by its own leaders, the area quickly fell to the Taliban and Ismael Khan took refuge in Iran. But the capture of Herat by Pakistani forces for the Taliban did not end the war. Emboldened by their easy victory, the Taliban and their Pakistani patrons proceeded to take the rest of the country by force, pursuing a policy of total war. During this period of Taliban conquest, large-scale massacres of civilians occurred as the peoples of northern and central Afghanistan defended their territories against the Taliban and their Pakistani allies. The defenders argued that when the war against the Soviet Union was fought, no Pashtun had come from any other part of Afghanistan to help liberate the territories inhabited by the Uzbeks, Tajiks, and Hazaras. These territories were defended by their local inhabitants who had liberated themselves from Soviet occupation forces and Afghan communists, even though non-Pashtun Afghans had joined their Pashtun compatriots in southern Afghanistan to liberate Pashtun areas. Non-Pashtun peoples of Afghanistan put up stiff resistance to the Pashtun army led by the Taliban, who were supported by the government of Pakistan, which planned to conquer their territories and resubjugate them to a form of internal colonialism.

In 1995, Osama bin Laden, who had initially come to Afghanistan in 1981 to fight in the jihad against the Soviet invaders, returned to Afghanistan. Enraged by the Gulf War, bin Laden became a vocal opponent of the U.S.-led coalition war within Saudi Arabia, organizing antiwar demonstrations resulting in his exile from Saudi Arabia to Sudan. In 1995, ISI, the Pakistani Intelligence Service, brokered a deal to move bin Laden and his entourage from Sudan to Pakistan and into Afghanistan, an act that laid the foundation for a Taliban–bin Laden alliance. Bin Laden financed the Taliban's war against their non-Pashtun enemies, with his al-Qaeda militants fighting alongside Taliban forces, and supported the training of other disgruntled Muslim militant groups from virtually anywhere around the world.

TERRORISM AND MODERN NATION-STATE: SOME CONCLUSIONS

There is no doubt that Afghanistan exemplified a weak and fragile modern nation-state prone to failure. When challenged by a leftist coup d'etat and later invaded by the former Soviet Union, the frail state apparatus collapsed and the country was turned into an arena for proxy wars, eventually becoming a safe heaven for global terrorism. The failure of Afghan governments to build a viable state structure was because of, in large part, the inappropriate model of the state adopted and implemented by its leadership at the end of the 19th century. The prospects for building an effective governance structure was further weakened by two additional factors: the inability of Afghan governments to find or create adequate, reliable, and renewable domestic sources of state revenue and the discriminatory and abusive policies and practices of its government leaders toward ethnic and tribal "minorities" during the last hundred years. More specifically, collapse of the Afghan state apparatus was not the function of an inherent aversion to central authority on the part of the people of Afghanistan because of the diversity of extant tribes and ethnic groups, or extreme individualism, as are often suggested. Indeed, I have argued here that the transformation of tribal structures and ethnic differences into social fragmented groups along ethnic, linguistic, and sectarian cleavages was the direct consequence of the policies of centralizing governments.

The art of governance and of state building in Afghanistan became immobilized and trapped within an inordinately "rigid framework of the problem and institution of sovereignty,"[4] rather than the development of the "governmentalization of the state," as Michel Foucault might put it (1991:98–104, emphasis added). As a result, an organic relationship between the state and its subjects/citizens based on their just and equitable treatment did not exist.

There is no need, however, to lament the failure and collapse of the old state structures in Afghanistan. A mechanical relationship between the state and its citizens based on an expanding, corrupt, and nepotistic bureaucracy must fail. Now that the Taliban have been dislodged, and the old inappropriate state structures shattered, what are the prospects for Afghanistan? They will be stronger if attention is focused on how a multiethnic society should be governed, rather than who should govern it. This is especially important to note given Partha Chatterjee's analysis suggesting that the political miseries in Afghanistan stem "not in our inability to think out new forms of the modern community [or identity] but in our surrender to the old forms of the modern state" (1993:11). A similar view has led Guehenno to suggest that instead of accepting the nation-state "as a political form that is self-evident, a kind of natural culmination of all societies" (1995:2), we must problematize and question the appropriateness and adequacy of the forms of postcolonial states,[5] critically examining them to determine whether such state structures are part of the problem in breeding communal violence, conflicts in multiethnic societies, and international terrorism. If the old forms of nation-state are shown to be part of the problem, we must ask why we continue to consider such institutional forms to be a part of the solution for alleviating the crises in Afghanistan.

Because the majority of ethnic groups in Afghanistan live in relatively compact communities in rural areas, to be successful a government structure must allow for local self-government. At the village, district, urban wards, and provincial levels, people must have the right either to elect or to hire their own community administrators, and, wherever feasible, adjacent provinces should be encouraged to create common regional administrative units. What is called for is a very different kind of governance structure than the old sovereignty-driven centralized system of misrule that has characterized the history of Afghanistan since 1880. Afghanistan needs to create a loosely structured federal government that is decentralized and adapted to the local and national conditions in post-Taliban Afghanistan (for more details, see Shahrani 1998, 2001a, 2001b, 2002).

The United States has the opportunity to set a new precedent for combating the conditions that give rise to terrorism worldwide by aiding in this effort. This daunting task can be accomplished by doing two things. First, now that the people of Afghanistan are freed from being terrorized by the Taliban and their global terrorist partners, they must be assisted in establishing an appropriate national governance structure that should not only facilitate the national reconstruction and reconciliation of their battered society but must also avoid returning to the utterly inappropriate previous system of centralized misrule. Second, the United States must take the lead in mobilizing sustained and long-term international reconstruction assistance for Afghanistan. By means of these integrated and coordinated international efforts in Afghanistan, the international community may be able to begin to address one of the root causes of global terrorism. It should be obvious that the strategies of waging war against global terrorism, no matter how militarily effective, will not solve Afghanistan's problems and will not solve our national security concerns here in the United States. The question remains: Is the United States leadership willing to conduct its foreign policy differently to find out what the outcome might be? Afghanistan can be a very important test case, if done right.

Notes

1. Zal (Zalmay) Khalilzad, an Afghan American, formerly working for the RAND Corporation, is currently a member of President George W. Bush's National Security team and the Special Envoy of the President for Afghanistan. His role as the principal architect of U.S. policies toward Afghanistan since September 11, 2001, cannot be underestimated.

2. Hence, these authors advocated for the return of the United States in the region and resumption of its presumed responsibilities to help bring peace. Not surprisingly, after the events of September 11, 2001, and the start of the war on terrorism campaign, the United States has returned to Afghanistan in full force.

3. One of the frequently cited facts introduced to prove the violent nature of Afghan society is that during the 20th century, seven out of 12 political leaders of the country met violent deaths (Habibullah I, Habibullah II, Nadir Shah, Daoud, Taraki, Amin, and Najibullah), while Amanullah, Zahir Shah, Rabbani, and Mullah Omar, four of the survivors, were violently deposed, and Karmal was sent into exile. This fact, however, tells more about the nature of political succession in the country and the violent nature of the Afghan state than it does about the peoples of Afghanistan.

4. Significantly, as Foucault points out, the goal of the sovereign was "not so much to increase the wealth of the country as to allow the ruler to accumulate wealth, build up his treasury and create an army with which he could carry out his policies" (1991:98).

5. A critical assessment of the old forms of the modern nation-state and their continued relevance as effective political institutions, especially in Asia, Africa, and Latin America, is necessary. This is particularly so in view of the fact that in Europe—the original birthplace of this "ephemeral political form"—the nation-state is losing much of its historic purpose in the face of increasing consolidation of such states within the European Union (see Chandhoke 1995; Guehenno 1995).

References Cited

Chandhoke, Neera. 1995. *The State and Civil Society: Explorations in Political Theory*. New Delhi: Sage Publications.

Chatterjee, Partha. 1993. *The Nation and Its Fragments: Colonial and Postcolonial Histories*. Princeton: Princeton University Press.

Edwards, David B. 1996. *Heroes of the Age: Moral Fault Lines on the Afghan Frontier.* Berkeley: University of California Press.

Ferdinand, Klaus. 1962. Nomad Expansion and Commerce in Central Afghanistan. *Folk* 4:123–159.

Foucault, Michel. 1991. *Governmentality. The Foucault Effect: Studies in Governmentality.* Graham Burchell, Collin Gordon, and Peter Miller, eds. pp. 87–104. Chicago: University of Chicago Press.

Goodson, Larry P. 2001. *Afghanistan's Endless War: State Failure, Regional Politics and the Rise of Taliban.* Seattle: University of Washington Press.

Guehenno, Jean-Marie. 1995. *The End of the Nation-State.* Minneapolis: University of Minnesota Press.

Kakar, Hasan. 1979. *Government and Society in Afghanistan: The Reign of Amrir 'Abd al-Rahman Khan.* Austin: University of Texas Press.

Khalilzad, Zalmay, and Daniel Byman. 2000. Afghanistan: the Consolidation of a Rogue State. *Washington Quarterly* 23(winter):1.

Khalilzad, Zalmay, Daniel Byman, Elie D. Krakowski, and Don Ritter. 1999. *U.S. Policy in Afghanistan: Challenges and Solutions.* Washington, DC: Afghanistan Foundation.

Maley, William. 1998. *Fundamentalism Reborn: Afghanistan and the Taliban.* London: C. Hurst and Company.

Mousavi, Sayed Askar. 1997. *The Hazaras of Afghanistan: An Historical, Cultural, Economic and Political Study.* New York: St. Martin's Press.

Rashid, Ahmed. 2000. *Taliban: Militant Islam, Oil and Fundamentalism in Central Asia.* New Haven, CT: Yale University Press.

———. 2002. *Jihad: The Rise of Militant Islam in Central Asia.* New Haven, CT: Yale University Press.

Roy, Olivier. 1990. *Islam and Resistance in Afghanistan.* 2nd edition. Cambridge: Cambridge University Press.

———. 1995. *Afghanistan: From Holy War to Civil War.* Princeton: Darwin Press.

Rubin, Barnett R. 1995. *The Fragmentation of Afghanistan: State Formation and Collapse in the International System.* New Haven, CT: Yale University Press.

Shahrani, Nazif M. 1986. State Building and Social Fragmentation in Afghanistan: A Historical Perspective. In *The State, Religion, and Ethnic Politics: Afghanistan, Iran, and Pakistan.* Ali Banuazizi and Myron Weiner, eds. pp. 23–74. Syracuse, NY: Syracuse University Press.

———. 1994. Honored Guest and Marginal Man: Long-Term Field Research and Predicaments of a Native Anthropologist. In *Others Knowing Others: Perspectives on Ethnographic Careers.* Don D. Fowler and Donald L. Hardesty, eds. pp. 15–67. Washington, DC: Smithsonian Institution Press.

———. 1998. The Future of the State and the Structure of Community Governance in Afghanistan. In *Fundamentalism Reborn? Afghanistan and the Taliban.* William Maley, ed. pp. 212–242. London: C. Hurst and Company.

———. 2000a. The Taliban Enigma: Person-Centred Politics and Extremism in Afghanistan. *ISIM Newsletter* 6:20–21.

———. 2000b. Resisting the Taliban and Talibanism in Afghanistan: Legacies of a Century of Internal Colonialism and Cold War Politics in a Buffer State. *Perceptions: Journal of International Affairs* 4:121–140.

———. 2001a. Not "Who?" but "How?": Governing Afghanistan after the Conflict. *Federations: What's New in Federalism Worldwide.* Special Issue on Afghanistan, October 2001. pp. 7–8. Ontario, Canada.

———. 2001b. Afghanistan Can Learn from Its Past. *New York Times,* October 14: A13.

———. 2002. *Afghanistan, the Taliban and Global Terror, Inc. The Kirghiz and Wakhi of Afghanistan: Adaptation to Closed Frontiers and War.* 2nd Edition. Seattle: University of Washington Press.

Shahrani, Nazif M., and Robert Canfield. 1984. *Revolutions and Rebellions in Afghanistan: Anthropological Perspectives.* Berkeley: Institute of International Studies, University of California, Berkeley, Research Series, 57.

Tapper, Nancy. 1973. The Advent of the Pushtun Maldars in Northwestern Afghanistan. *Bulletin of the School of Oriental and African Studies* 36(1):55–79.

CRITICAL THINKING QUESTIONS

1. The war and chaos in Afghanistan have been explained from a number of different perspectives. Discuss the major theories Shahrani examines, and give examples of the evidence cited for each theory.

2. Why does Shahrani believe the Western model of a "modern" nation-state is inappropriate for creating stability and national unity in Afghanistan?

3. How are ethnicity, kinship, and Islam interrelated in the creation of social identity for individuals and groups in Afghanistan?

4. How did the British creation of Afghanistan's modern borders in the nineteenth century lay the groundwork for the present chaos in the country? Give examples from the article.

5. What role did the intervention of outside countries, particularly Pakistan, play in the Taliban's rise to power?

6. How does Shahrani suggest that a stable national government could be created in Afghanistan?

Negotiated and Mediated Meanings: Ethnicity and Politics in Israeli Newspapers

Daniel Lefkowitz

Abstract   *In this article the author explores the ways in which the media articulate discursive structure and lived experience through an analysis of the coverage of the 1999 Israeli national elections in one Israeli newspaper. Recent changes in Israeli electoral law unleashed new social forces that granted major political influence to ethnic parties. The renewed salience of (Jewish) ethnicity clashes, however, with dominant discourses of national identity, according to which a unitary Israeli identity subsumes particularistic Jewish ethnicities, while silencing Palestinian identity. Such changes imply an important role for the Israeli media, which has traditionally marked identity difference through distinct regimes for the expression and control of affect. The author examines constructions of affect, and their inscription onto particular social identities, in Yediot Ahronot, Israel's widest-circulation daily. [Israel, elections, Shas, media, ideology]*

The increasing presence of broadcast and print media in our everyday lives compels students of discourse to develop correspondingly sophisticated methods for evaluating its impact. In particular, the packaging of information as "news" takes on ever greater significance as the world becomes increasingly global and interconnected (Friedman 1999; Appadurai 1990). In a trenchant series of publications the Dutch linguist Teun van Dijk (for example, 1991) has explored the role of news in perpetuating racism and prejudice. Summarizing findings for modern industrial societies, such as the U.S. and U.K., van Dijk writes:

> . . . analysis of . . . everyday talk shows that many people are not only increasingly

afraid of crime and violence, but explicitly associate this with minority group members, and refer to the media to substantiate their prejudices (1989: 220).

Van Dijk argues that the media plays a complex role in the production and reproduction of prejudice. When people refer to media images to "substantiate" the prejudices they express in everyday talk, they are completing a cycle, for van Dijk also argues that it is essentially the media that creates the link between minority ethnic groups and (here) crime in the first place. Van Dijk points out, for example, that while most Whites in Britain (or the U.S.) will feel this link, very few have actually experienced it. For such a notion to be shared by so many, it must have been spread by the media (1989: 200).

To fully understand how news affects individuals' experience and understanding of the physical, social, and moral world they live in, we must understand not just how the news is produced, but also how it is interpreted. Recent work in anthropology and linguistics has greatly improved our analysis of interpretation by showing that meaning is both contextual (cf. Goffman 1972; Durand and Goodwin 1992) and interactional (cf. Schegloff 1981).

Meaning is contextual in that language takes on specific reference only with respect to the context in which it is uttered (and interpreted). Words like "we" depend for their reference on who is speaking, just as core cultural concepts, like "nation," depend for their meaning on who is being spoken of. Meaning is interactional in the sense that parties to a conversation[1] may

---

Source: Reprinted with permission of *Anthropological Quarterly Journal*, The George Washington University.

bring to their interaction different ideas about what concepts mean—leading in some cases to misunderstanding, but in other (more interesting) cases to negotiations over meaning.

By providing an ethnography of interpretive practices, the articles in this issue help to explicate the phenomenon of communication by deconstructing the constituent notion of interpretation. In this article I argue that a full understanding of discourse requires an analysis of the ways that production and interpretation are interdependent. Such a position builds upon the theoretical work of such scholars as Charles Peirce, Mikhail Bakhtin, Roland Barthes, and Pierre Bourdieu to claim that meaning is an infinite and recursive chain of negotiations, in which various forms of mediation play a crucial role.

Studying the interpretation of news is therefore tantamount to studying the interpretation of an interpretation. Analysis of such recursive processes necessarily proceeds outward in all directions from a particular starting point. In actual conversations, for example, interlocutors deploy symbols they glean from public discourse (media). These images themselves stand in dialogic relationship to series of other, intertextually related images. Yet in conversation particular meanings may be emphasized. And these emphases are—through the abstract but very familiar processes we describe as "the market" and "opinion polls"—reincorporated into public (media) discourses.

In this article I examine how newspapers mediate discourses of identity in Israel. Specifically, I look at how newspaper coverage of an ethnic political party hegemonically reproduces ideologically dominant representations of identity. I begin, however, by showing how such mediation becomes a resource for negotiations of status and prestige in everyday conversation.

MEDIA IMAGES OF IDENTITY IN CONVERSATION

It was a slip-of-the-tongue. I was interviewing two Israeli women—whom I'll call Haya and Nurit—at Nurit's home.[2] The women were talking about their memories of childhood and about learning pop songs as kids. Then the conversation turned to the Eurovision Song Competition

that they—along with most Israelis—had watched on television a few months before.[3] Haya inadvertently referred to one of the singers as "Nurit Ben." She meant to say "Zehava Ben," the singer's actual name, but she substituted "Nurit," her friend's first name, thereby condensing the two identities. As Sigmund Freud has pointed out, slips-of-the-tongue may be less than innocent,[4] and in this case a rich interpretation presents itself.

Unpacking the meanings of Haya's slip-of-the-tongue requires some background on Israeli cultural politics. In the early 1990s Zehava Ben was one of most popular singers in Israel, selling more tapes, records, and CDs than almost any other performer. Her popularity, however, was sharply divided along lines of social identity. Ben's songs belong to the genre of Israeli pop music called *muzika mizrahit* (literally "oriental music"), which draws on Arab rhythms, melodies, and styles.[5] While *muzika muzrahit* was enormously popular among Mizrahim, or Jews whose families had come to Israel from Arab and Middle Eastern countries,[6] most Ashkenazim, or Jews of European heritage, actively disliked the style.

Musical tastes are part of an elaborate hierarchy of symbolic capital (cf. Bourdieu 1984) that represents and reinforces the social divisions in Israeli society. The three main social groups—Ashkenazi Jews, Mizrahi Jews, and Palestinian Arabs[7]—live along two simultaneous dimensions of social difference: the dimension of religion/nationality, and the dimension of socio-economic class. While Mizrahim share Jewish religious/national identity with Ashkenazim, they share (working-)class position with Palestinians. Mizrahim thus occupy an intermediate position between the unambiguously elite Ashkenazim and the clearly subaltern Palestinians.[8]

Returning to the interview, then, we can see that Haya's slip-of-the-tongue expressed indirectly what would have been awkward for her to express directly, namely that she sees Nurit as the "other" kind of Israeli. Indeed, the two women do come from diametrically opposed backgrounds. While Haya's parents left Poland to come to Palestine in the 1930s, Nurit's family came to Israel from Morocco in the 1950s—after Israel had already gained its independence.

While Haya grew up in the elite environment of a Kibbutz.[9] Nurit grew up in the poverty of immigrant slums. In their conversation Haya's slip-of-the-tongue shows that she sees her friend, Nurit, primarily as a Mizrahi woman—so much so that she subconsciously identifies her with the public-culture symbol of Mizrahi identity, the singer Zehava Ben. The conversation unfolded as a negotiation of identity, as each laid claim to core Israeliness for herself and semiotically challenged the Israeliness of her interlocutor. Within this negotiation Haya's deployment of a prominent and polyvocal media image asserts more about status, role, and identity than she can comfortably say.

IMAGES OF ETHNICITY IN THE PRESS

Haya's slip-of-the-tongue shows how public discourse crystallizes and transforms representations of Self and Other into images made available for deployment in everyday conversations. The slip reveals something about her interpretation both of media discourse and of her relationship with Nurit. Examination of the coverage of the Eurovision competition, however, reveals a great deal about interpretive practices of the media.

Zehava Ben's appearance in the 1992 Eurovision preliminary competition turned into a disaster. Going into the competition, Ben's mass popularity made her a likely favorite, but her song placed dead last among the twelve entries. The winning song was musically mainstream and ideologically Ashkenazi (as were most of the other entries).[10] Her proposal that a *muzika mizrahit* song represent Israel to the European community challenged dominant ideas about what constitutes Israeli selfhood—and was dramatically rejected.

Subsequently, newspaper coverage legitimized the original preference by embedding the image of the rejected Other (Ben and *muzika mizrahit*, for example) in a collage of rejected behaviors (emotionality and violence, for example). The next day Israel's largest newspaper, *Yediot Ahronot,*[11] covered Ben's appearance—and her shocking failure—in splashy detail. Celebratory images of the victorious singing group were juxtaposed against angry images of Ben. *Yediot's* coverage framed Zehava Ben as a poor loser, and emotion was a key signifier in this framing. Ben was pictured displaying great emotion by crying over her loss. She was quoted expressing great emotion by complaining of ethnic bias in the judging of the songs. And her supporters were shown gushing great emotion as they reacted with violent words and threats of violent actions.

This very emotionality challenges dominant notions of the ideal Israeli Self, which is characterized by emotions that are rational, controlled, and interior. The classic symbol for this image of the Israeli Self is the sabra, which refers literally to the fruit of the prickly-pear cactus, and metaphorically to native-born Israelis.[12] The metaphorical connection highlights the centrality of emotion: the sabra fruit—like the native/ideal Israeli—is said to be soft and sweet on the inside but rough and thorny on the outside.

Against this image of Self, cultural Others are constructed as violating the ideal of emotional control. Palestinians, for example, are prominently represented either as violent and irrationally emotional (typified by the image of the terrorist) or as sensual and familial (typified by the image of the harem). But emotion is also used to distinguish among Jewish Israelis. Israeli public culture thus represents the Mizrahi as an Arab-Jew, an internal Other, that mediates between the Arabness of Palestinians and the Israeliness of European Jews. Ella Shohat, for example, has argued that Israeli movies have tended to cast Mizrahim as primitive characters—violent, emotional and traditional (Shohat 1989). And in other work I have argued that newspapers reproduce this pattern by representing Jewish violence—such as rioting—as linked to Mizrahi, rather than Ashkenazi identity (Lefkowitz 1995).

Thus the televised Eurovision contest provided a set of highly condensed symbols for Israeli identity—affirming the Western-oriented, Ashkenazi Self (through its selection of the winning song), while dramatically rejecting a Middle-Eastern oriented, Mizrahi Other (through its rejection of Zehava Ben's song). Zehava Ben's failure became a dramatic representation both of cultural hegemony and of social alienation.[13]

ETHNICITY, POLITICS, AND THE PRESS IN ISRAEL

In this context the emergence—and meteoric rise to political power—of a Mizrahi political party, is of great interest. In what follows I will show how newspaper coverage of the Shas party reproduces stereotypical representations of the Mizrahi Other and legitimates dominant tropes of Israeli identity.

Emergence of Shas

The Shas political party[14] represents the Mizrahi ultra-orthodox Jewish community. It is remarkable neither because it is an ethnic party—many have emerged—nor because it is a religious' party—there have always been several. Rather, it is unprecedented in both regards because it has been so enormously successful.

In 1984 Rabbi Ovadia Yosef, a former Sephardi Chief Rabbi of Israel,[15] broke away from the Ashkenazi ultra-orthodox political establishment to form his own movement (Peled 1998). That year, running in their first elections, Shas won four seats (out of 120) in the Knesset, the Israeli parliament. Since then, Shas's representation in the Knesset has grown dramatically. In the most recent elections, in 1999, Shas garnered 17 seats, and Shas now constitutes a third major party. For decades Israel has had a two-party system, in which Labor[16] and Likud were the two large parties. Shas has thus significantly transformed the Israeli political system (at least temporarily) by shifting it to a three-party system.

The extraordinary strength of Shas has also completely changed the role of religious parties in Israeli politics. Orthodox religious movements have played an important role in Israeli politics since the very first Israeli elections in 1948. In earlier elections the religious party representation in parliament had been consistent but small, sharing 5–10% of the popular vote. Until recently the religious parties had been content to join any governing coalition, playing little role in the policy debates, but laying claim to religious matters, issues of family law, and (considerable) funding for religious institutions and schools. This pattern was already changing, however, in the early 1980s, when Ovadia Yosef

created Shas. The ultra-orthodox religious parties, headed by Agudat Israel, were becoming much more involved in a broader range of policy issues, developing a right-wing leaning. At the same time, the National Religious Party (NRP), a religious but non-orthodox party, was becoming closely tied to the settler movements in the West Bank and Gaza—and therefore even more tied to right-wing politics (cf. Cohen and Susser 2000). Thus when Yosef and the Mizrahi orthodox leadership broke away in 1984, they helped set in motion a major political realignment.

Yet it is important to view Shas in ethnic, as well as religious terms. Ethnic parties have emerged from time to time in Israeli political history, but none has approached the success and longevity of Shas. Palestinian (Israeli) political expression, for example, has long been channelled through the communist party, which was an Arab/Jewish party, while nationalist Arab parties have been repressed when they emerged in the past. Nor have Jewish ethnic parties fared well in Israeli elections, in large part because "major efforts at delegitimizing ethnic political organizations were undertaken by the dominant Ashkenazi institutions" (Peled 1998: 714). The success of Shas (as an ethnic party) parallels the success of Natan Sharansky's Russian immigrant party, Israel B'Aliya, and of Azmi Bishara's unprecedented run in 1999 as a Palestinian candidate for Israeli Prime Minister. The newfound acceptability and influence of Russian, Palestinian, and Mizrahi parties signifies a major change in Israeli political discourse.

Newspaper Coverage of Shas

Their newfound political power put Shas—and therefore Mizrahi identity also—in an intense media spotlight. This spotlight was enlarged by the important elections of 1999, but also by a series of four media crises that received special attention in the press. In April Arye Deri, Shas political leader and a cabinet minister, was convicted of accepting bribes; in June Shas held up formation of a new government (after the 1999 elections) by wrangling over cabinet positions; in August Shas delayed transportation of an electric power generator because it would violate the Jewish Sabbath; and in September Shas leadership struggles threatened to tear the party apart.

During each of these crises Shas made front-page, headline news, and each crisis was covered in excruciating detail. Since much of the coverage involved stories about crime and corruption (including a long-running investigation into improprieties in the handling of government funds for Shas schools), Shas was frequently presented in a negative light. A survey of the coverage in *Yediot Ahronot,* Israel's largest newspaper, however, shows more specifically that the coverage of Shas reproduced stereotypical images of Mizrahim as quintessentially Other, as criminal, violent, and emotional, and as poverty-stricken and backward.[17]

Yediot's coverage of the Deri verdict on April 16 visually constructs difference and opposition. This visual meta-narrative can be seen [in] the leftmost portion of a banner header [which spans] the top of the first of two two-page spreads devoted to the Deri story (that is, pages 2–3 of the issue).[18] The banner visually identifies the two-page spreads, linking the articles together into a coherent story. [There is] a picture of Deri on the left, and on the right a picture of one of the Supreme Court justices who delivered the guilty verdict. Next to Deri is the banner's title for the spread: "4 Years in Jail: The Verdict." Between Deri and the justice is an excerpt from the court's decision.[19]

The visual narrative of opposition is constructed in part through the juxtaposition of photographic images. As can be seen, the banner header shows Deri looking across toward the justice, and the justice's face is positioned so that she too seems to be looking toward Deri. The rest of the banner continues this pattern, as each of the three Supreme Court justices is pictured gazing across at Deri. At the right edge of the banner is a second picture of Deri, in which he is facing the same direction as the three judges—as if gazing back toward himself.[20] Immediately below this banner header, on the left side of the spread, is a much larger picture of Deri, in which he is gazing upwards, again facing the three judges. Deri is thus shown left, right, and below the three judges, framing their faces—and words.

The visual and spatial deployment of text also plays an important role in constructing this opposition. Four short excerpts from the judicial opinion are included in the banner header. Each excerpt appears in a large headline font, under quotation marks, beneath an underlined heading.

One excerpt is printed to the left of each judge's picture, and the fourth excerpt appears to the left of the (second) picture of Deri. The juxtaposition of the judges' pictures (with their names printed below their picture) with the quoted text creates the impression that the words are attributed to the individual judges. In fact, however, the texts are taken from the decision. This becomes clear from the fact that one such excerpt is placed next to the picture of Deri, the defendant.

The titles given to the excerpts augment the quotative effect of the visual juxtaposition: while the segments alongside the judges' pictures have the titles "The Seriousness of the Offense," "The Precedent," and "The Essence of the Bribery," the segment next to Deri himself bears the title "The Personal Responsibility." While the judges individually and collectively state the facts, Deri is made to "speak" about personal responsibility.

If the first spread in the April 16 issue visually constructs the notions of opposition, conflict, tension, and guilt, the second spread uses visual imagery to represent Shas adherents as emotional.[21] . . . Three large pictures show Shas supporters reacting to news of the verdict. All three pictures show orthodox religious Jewish men (identifiable from their head-coverings and beards), and all three pictures depict men in the act of extreme emotional display. In one picture a man appears to be crying, and in the other two pictures men are yelling—mouths wide open, eyes squinting with intensity. The vehemence of the latter men's silent screams leaps out from the page directly at the reader.

Much of the Shas coverage when not devoted to one of the four major crises, such as the Deri verdict, involved either the elections or controversies over government funding for Shas (religious) schools. In both cases, coverage of Shas represented Mizrahim in stereotypical ways by linking the news to poverty. In Israel, as in the U.S., explicit reference to ethnicity is rare—almost taboo—in many conversational and media genres, but implicit reference to identity through proxies is abundant.[22] In the early 1990s, for example, American media discourses indexed African-American identity through proxies such as crime and welfare moms (cf. Mendelberg 1997). Similarly, Israeli media have long indexed Mizrahi identity through proxy topics, such as poverty, educational failure, and development towns. The indexicality stems from the fact that Mizrahim earn less money and fewer academic degrees than do Ashkenazim, and that during the 1950s they were systematically settled in geographically marginal frontier settlements called "development towns" (Swirski 1989).[23]

Yediot's coverage of the 1999 election results, for example, link Shas' success to the issue of poverty. A May 21 article reads: "In 30 Settlements Shas is the Strongest Party."[24] The settlements listed are all development towns—well known to combine high proportions of Mizrahi residents and high poverty rates. What is interesting, though, is the apparent newsworthiness of this story: Shas garnered about 15 percent of the national vote, only 1–2 percentage points fewer than did Likud. Therefore, it should not be significantly more newsworthy for Shas to be the majority party in some localities than for Likud. Yet the newsworthiness of Shas' success in these settlements stands in sharp contrast to the lack of comparable stories about settlements where the other two large parties—either Likud or One Israel (that is, Labor)—were dominant.

Coverage in *Yediot Ahronot* of the long, simmering controversy over government funding for Shas schools also stereotypically represents Mizrahim as poverty-stricken. In July, 1999, reports surfaced of financial irregularities in a network of schools run by Shas.[25] From there the thread moved first to stories showing that Shas schools provide inferior education, and then to the poverty of families who send their children to Shas schools. In the July 23 issue, for example, articles focus on parents' reasons for electing to send their children to Shas religious schools, rather than to other (government) schools. The conclusion this thread reaches is poverty: parents claim that they are too poor to afford the costs of the public, state-run, secular schools. Such articles contest the potential interpretation that rapid growth in Shas school enrollments is due to the movement's principles, substituting the interpretation that parents send their children to Shas schools out of more pedestrian motivations.

Finally, throughout the summer and fall of 1999 newspaper coverage of issues related to religious observance facilitated a stereotypical representation of Shas as traditional, backward, and primitive. Specifically, the media focused a critical lens on the role that religious leaders (rabbis) play in Shas decision-making. Such coverage highlights Shas as a "religious" party, and inserts it into the virulent religious-secular struggle in Israel.

In early August, for example, the crisis over transporting an electric power-generating turbine broke out. Authorities suggested moving the turbine—so large and heavy that transporting it would stop traffic along a congested highway for hours—on a Saturday, the Jewish Sabbath, when few Israelis drive. The authorities aimed to minimize disruption to traffic and business, but Shas objected on the grounds that doing this work on a Saturday would violate the work prohibition on the Jewish Sabbath. Shas spokesmen presented the party as taking an unpopular and impractical stance on the basis of religious principle, but newspaper coverage subverted this representation by presenting Shas as hypocritical, corrupt, and backward. This discursive construction is achieved by representing Shas political leaders as controlled by behind-the-scenes (and unelected) religious leaders, by portraying the Rabbis as old and feeble, and by focusing on the pettiness of factional struggles within Shas.

Pictures of Shas leaders and activists are marked for religious identity because the figures themselves wear the hats, black suits, and full beards associated with Orthodox Jewish men. The proliferation of discourse about religion, however, can be seen in the prominence of the religious leaders, especially Rabbi Ovadia Yosef, who is usually identified as the "spiritual leader of the Shas movement." Articles that discuss Shas politics often focus on the apparent dependence of Shas politicians on their rabbinic sponsors. [F]or example, [in] a portion of the 1999 election coverage from the June 25 issue of *Yediot Ahronot*, [a]rticles discussing the election results are set off by the "Turbine Crisis" thread evolved into a "Shas Factionalism Crisis" thread. Articles repeatedly analyze the "Turbine" issue as an artificial conflict having little to do with religion, religious principles, or national welfare. Rather, the Israeli nation (and pursuit of commerce) is represented as hostage to whimsical and petty rivalries between ancient rabbis and their quisling politicians. [Another] banner headline there entitled "Revolution '99: On the Way to a Coalition . . ." is framed by large pictures of three very old rabbis with enormous white beards.

The image of Rabbi Yitzhak Kaduri (upper left) is especially striking, since he appears feeble, walking with a cane, and wearing a headcovering that recalls the Ottoman tarbush.[26] In other cases, articles about politics often are accompanied by pictures showing politicians visiting, or studying, praying, or conferring with these senior rabbis, example, shows part of the July 30 issue's coverage. Here the spread of articles is framed by the title "Earthquake in the Orthodox World," and we see large photographs of the two opposed rabbis, Yosef and Kaduri, facing each other over their long white beards.[27] The newspaper representation makes the conflict look petty, trivial, almost childish.

Ethnicity, Politics, and Discourses of Nation

Mainstream media representations of Shas recapitulate earlier tropes of Mizrahi identity, representing Shas politicians and supporters as emotional, violent, irrational, and primitive. At the time when Shas' electoral gains threatened to give Mizrahim real political power, media representations tended to subvert this possibility through discourses that repositioned Shas—and thereby Mizrahim—onto delegitimized images. The efficacy of these discourses to re-position Shas stems, I would argue, from its success in reconfiguring the religious/secular cleavage in Israeli Jewish society. The focus on Shas reinscribed religious orthodoxy onto Mizrahi, rather than Ashkenazi, identity.

The rise of Shas has dramatically shifted the anti-religious discourse to one focused on Mizrahi, rather than Ashkenazi, ultra-orthodox organizations and symbols. Israeli discourse has expressed discomfort with the growth in popularity (and influence) of Ashkenazi fundamentalism, because it conflicts with core Zionist and Western ideals. In the early 1990s Israeli newspapers tended to delegitimize leaders of the Ashkenazi ultra-orthodox parties. An old and feeble Ashkenazi rabbi would be shown on election day making a speech to direct his followers how to vote. And an especially corpulent ultra-orthodox Knesset member was often photographed from below, looking up, so that his belly was foreshortened and exaggerated, highlighting his absurd physical proportions.

The "sephardization" of Jewish fundamentalism, however, fits comfortably within broader Israeli nationalist discourses, which oppose the Western orientation of Israel to its Eastern geography, and which use the position of the Mizrahi "Arab-Jew" to mediate between the inherently Western Ashkenazi and the unalterably Eastern Arab (cf. Shohat 1989). For by telling the "Story of Shas" newspapers are reformulating the recent history of Israeli politics in general. The story of Shas resolves into a foil for the narrative of Israeli political and social progress.

In the early 1990s, the mainstream parties—Labor and Likud—switched to a "primary" system for electing its leadership. The new Israeli "primaries" were so clearly modeled on the American example that Israelis borrowed the English word "primaries" to describe it. The impact of this innovation was dramatic. The Labor party adopted a primary system in time for the 1992 elections, while the Likud continued its older method of choosing its leaders. Labor's primaries helped them project a positive image as a progressive and modern party. In sharp contrast, the Likud suffered through a particularly nasty leadership struggle, appearing backward, corrupt, and absurd in its internal factionalization and behind-the-scenes bargaining.[28] Following the victory of the Labor candidate, Yitzhak Rabin, in the 1992 elections, the Likud quickly followed suit, adopting a primary system in time for the next election.

Thus, current Shas politics, which are portrayed so negatively in the press, merely recall a political style that used to be mainstream. In the constant shifting of symbolic capital, dominant groups have re-defined the symbols, and the new terms are used to disparage newcomers to the political arena.

Notes

1. I am using the word "conversation" in an intentionally ambiguous way to mean both an actual talk interaction among individuals and a more abstract communication, similar to the Bakhtinian notion of "dialogue" (cf. Bakhtin 1981).
2. This interview took place in Haifa, Israel, on September 9, 1992.
3. The Eurovision Song Competition, or Eurovision, is an annual international television event simulcast throughout Europe (and Israel). Individual countries hold "preliminary" national contests to choose one song (and performing group) that represents the country in the subsequent Europe-wide

competition. The event enjoys extraordinary popularity in Israel, and both the "preliminary" and "final" competitions draw enormous television audiences. The text refers to the Israeli preliminary competition of March 28, 1992, and the European finals, which took place in Sweden, on May 9, 1992.

4. In *The Psychopathology of Everyday Life* Freud analyzes slips-of-the-tongue as (indirect) representations of thoughts that the speaker has repressed. To cite a typical example: In a therapy session with a female patient, Freud suspects that she is ashamed of her family, but she denies any such feelings. During therapy, however, while talking about her family, the patient inadvertently asserts that they all possessed Geiz, German for "greed," when she had meant to say Geist, which is German for "cleverness." The apparently accidental slip-of-the-tongue thus revealed to Freud the source of the patient's repressed shame (Freud 1960: 87).

5. For interesting analyses of music and social identity in Israel, see Horowitz 1999, Regev 1995, Halper et al. 1989, and Shiloah and Cohen 1983, inter alia.

6. The term *Mizrahi* (pl. *Mizrahim*) literally means "Eastern," or "Oriental." Its meaning overlaps with the older term, *Sephardi(m)*, but "Mizrahi" is the identity label that many Mizrahi scholars and activists themselves prefer.

7. In this article I use the term "Palestinian" (Arab) to refer to Palestinian Arab citizens of the State of Israel. This social group is often referred to in English-language scholarship on the Middle East as "Israeli Arabs," the translation of a Hebrew phrase that many Palestinian (Israeli) scholars and activists dislike.

8. While Mizrahim now constitute a plurality of Israelis, Ashkenazim still constitute the "majority" in social, political, and economic terms (cf. Kraus and Hodge 1990). This position of dominance stems at least in part from the history of Jewish (re)settlement in Palestine. Ashkenazi Jews began to emigrate to Palestine in significant numbers much earlier than did the bulk of Mizrahi Jews. At independence, in 1948, the vast majority of Israeli Jews were Ashkenazim, and they were well entrenched in positions of prestige and authority. Hundreds of thousands of Mizrahi Jews emigrated to Israel during the 1950s, but for the most part they were settled in peripheral communities and given working-class jobs (cf. Swirski 1989).

9. The kibbutz is a communal farm. Many of the early Jewish settlements in Palestine were of this successful and pioneering type, and kibbutzim continue to this day to provide a disproportionately high number of Israel's political and military leaders.

10. The ideological undercurrent in many of the more successful songs can be seen from the titles of two of them: Anat Atzmon sang a song called "HaTikvah," "The Hope," which is the name of Israel's national anthem. Ronen Boniker entered a song called "Yerushalem," which is a play-on-words, combining the Hebrew words for "Jerusalem," yerushalayim, and "complete," shalem. The meta-message thus relates to both the "final status" of Jerusalem at a time when negotiations with Palestinians were about to begin, and also to the "wholeness" of Israel in the wake of the 1991 Persian Gulf War.

11. *Yediot Ahronot* is an afternoon newspaper. The name means, roughly, "Late Tidings." My source for articles in *Yediot Ahronot* is the Hebrew-language American edition, *Yediot Ahronot International Edition*, which is transferred from Is-

rael by satellite for printing and distribution in the U.S. While I have not yet done a systematic comparison, it is my impression that the Israeli and American editions do not differ substantially in terms of article text. Advertisements, however, appear in English and are clearly tailored to an (Israeli-)American readership.

12. It should be pointed out that sabra refers most naturally to Jewish Israelis. It would be infelicitous to apply that metaphor to Palestinians, even to citizens born in Israel after 1948.

13. The subsequent Eurovision finals brought out an interesting irony. While the national competition in Israel saw hegemonic tastes enforced upon the musical representations of Self, several European countries were pluralizing their national musics. France, for example, was represented by a Caribbean group.

14. The name, Shas, is an acronym in Hebrew, meaning "Sephardi Torah Guardians."

15. Two Chief Rabbis are appointed in Israel—one to represent Ashkenazi communities, and the other to represent Sephardi communities.

16. The Labor party changed its name to One Israel for the 1999 elections.

17. This analysis is based on a sampling of the Friday editions of *Yediot Ahronot International Edition* from April 16 to October 15, 1999 (missing one issue). Israeli Friday editions are roughly equivalent to American Sunday editions, containing week-in-review and other special-feature sections. The sample included all articles from the front news section that mentioned Shas (or an identifiable member of Shas) either in the headline or the first paragraph of text. Newspapers are particularly important in Israel, where daily paper readership is among the highest in the world (Lavie 1992). There are three large national-circulation newspapers, of which two cater to a high-brow readership. Of the high-brow papers, *Ha'aretz* represents the left-wing politically, and *Ma'ariv* represents the right-wing (Caspi 1986). *Yediot*, on the other hand, is politically central (and unaligned) and is oriented toward a popular readership. *Yediot's* news coverage tends toward the spectacular, the scandalous, the racy, and the melodramatic. In the sample analyzed here, 25 of the 26 Friday issues contained at least one news story about Shas in the front section, and, in all, 44 stories were devoted to the party.

18. This icon text is different for the two spreads. The first spread is subtitled "The Verdict" and the second spread is subtitled "The Political Implications."

19. Note that Hebrew text is read right-to-left, and consequently the direction of reading a Hebrew newspaper is the reverse of what it is for an English newspaper.

20. In fact, it appears that the two images of Deri may derive from the same picture—one the mirror image of the other.

21. The second spread's banner header presents an interesting variation. The Deri verdict was announced in the midst of the 1999 Israeli Knesset election campaign, and the second banner replaces the judges' faces with the faces of four candidates for Prime Minister. In the second banner the national politicians confront Deri by gazing in his direction. Here, however, the visually parallel juxtaposition of gazes, faces, and words breaks down in an interesting way: the words appearing next to the face of each candidate are the candidate's words. It is also interesting to note that there were at the time five candidates in the race for Prime

Minister—the Palestinian candidate, Azmi Bishara, has been left out of this representation of nation.

22. In sharp contrast, explicit media reference to Arab or Palestinian identity is almost obligatory. Newspaper articles almost always identify an Arab individual as "Arab" no matter what role the person plays in the text.

23. The term "development town" is a translation of the Hebrew phrase *ayarat-pituax*.

24. Yediot Ahronot International Edition, 21 May 99, p. A8.

25. Israel has a complex system of public education, in which parents can choose between religious and secular (among other) schools. Various religious movements may petition for the right and funds to establish public schools.

26. Yediot Ahronot International Edition, 25 June 99, p. AS.

27. Yediot Ahronot International Edition, 30 July 99, p. AS.

28. The highly publicized and somewhat scandalous struggle over then-Foreign Minister David Levi's position in the party provides a good example. Levi was at that time Israel's most important Mizrahi politician.

References Cited

Appadurai, Arjun. 1990. Disjuncture and difference in the global cultural economy. *Public Culture* 2(2): 1–24.

Caspi, Dan. 1986. *Media decentralization: The case of Israel's local newspapers.* New Brunswick NJ: Transaction Books.

Bakhtin, Mikhail M. 1981. *The dialogic imagination: Four essays by M.M. Bakhtin,* ed. Michael Holquist. Trans. by Caryl Emerson and Michael Holquist. Austin: University of Texas.

Bourdieu, Pierre. 1984. *Distinction: A social critique of the judgement of taste.* Cambridge MA: Harvard University Press.

Cohen, Asher and Bernard Susser. 2000. *Israel and the politics of Jewish identity: The secular-religious impasse.* Baltimore MD: Johns Hopkins University Press..

van Dijk, Teun A. 1989. Mediating racism: The role of the media in the reproduction of racism. In *Language, power and ideology: Studies in political discourse,* ed. R. Wodak. Amsterdam: John Benjamins.

———— 1991. *Racism and the press.* London: Routledge.

Duranti, Alessandro and Charles Goodwin, eds. 1992. *Rethinking context: Language as an interactive phenomenon.* Cambridge: Cambridge University Press.

Freud, Sigmund. 1960 [1901]. *The psychopathology of everyday life,* ed. James Strachey. Transl. by Alan Tyson. New York: W. W. Norton & Company.

Friedman, Thomas. 1999. *The Lexus and the olive tree.* New York: Anchor.

Goffman, Erving. 1972. *The neglected situation. In Language and social context: Selected readings,* ed. P. Giglioli. Middlesex: Penguin Books.

Kraus, Vered, and Robert W. Hodge. 1990. *Promises in the Promised Land.* New York: Greenwood.

Halper, Jeff, Edwin Seroussi, and Pamela Squires-Kidron. 1989. Musica Mizrahit: Ethnicity and class culture in Israel. *Popular Music* 8(2): 131–141.

Horowitz, Amy. 1999. Israeli Mediterranean music: Straddling disputed territories. *Journal of American Folklore* 112(445): 450.

Lavie, Smadar. 1992. "Blow-ups in the borderzones: Third world Israeli authors' gropings for hotter." *New Formations* 18: 84–106.

Lefkowitz, Daniel. 1995. Constructing affective responses to ("nationalistic") violence in Israel. *Political and Legal Anthropology Review* 18(2): 105–117.

Mendelberg, Tali. 1997. Executing Hortons: Racial crime in the 1988 presidential campaign. *Public Opinion Quarterly* 61(1): 134–158.

Peled, Yoav. 1998. "Towards a redefinition of Jewish nationalism in Israel? The enigma of Shas." *Ethnic and Racial Studies* 21(4): 703–727.

Regev, Motti. 1995. Present absentee: Arab music in Israeli culture. *Public Culture* 7(2): 433–448.

Schegloff, Emanuel. 1981. Discourse as an interactional achievement: Some uses of "uh huh" and other things that come between sentences. In *Analyzing discourse: Text and talk,* ed. Deborah Tannen. Georgetown University Roundtable on Languages and Linguistics. Washington DC: Georgetown University Press.

Shiloah, Amnon and Erik Cohen. 1983. The dynamics of change in Jewish Oriental ethnic music in Israel. *Ethnomusicology* 27: 227–252.

Shohat, Ella. 1989. *Israeli cinema: East/West and the politics of representation.* Austin: University of Texas Press.

Swirski, Shlomo. 1989. *Israel: The Oriental majority.* London: Zed Books.

CRITICAL THINKING QUESTIONS

1. What are the major ethnic divisions in modern Israel? Describe and define the various traits assigned to each group by the media and society.

2. How are these groups symbolically represented by musical choices?

3. What is Lefkowitz's analysis of the role of the Israeli newspaper *Yediot's* coverage of the Zehava Ben incident in encoding the dominant ideas concerning Israeli national identity and the identity of the Mizrahit?

4. Shas is both an ethnic- and a religious-oriented political party. Discuss this dual orientation of the party and how it helps to form and maintain group identity.

5. How did the Israeli media use coverage of problems and issues that Shas was involved in to reinforce stereotypes and common perceptions of the Mizrahit?

Genesis of Suicide Terrorism

Scott Atran

Author's Abstract *Contemporary suicide terrorists from the Middle East are publicly deemed crazed cowards bent on senseless destruction who thrive in poverty and ignorance. Recent research indicates they have no appreciable psychopathology and are as educated and economically well-off as surrounding populations. A first line of defense is to get the communities from which suicide attackers stem to stop the attacks by learning how to minimize the receptivity of mostly ordinary people to recruiting organizations.*

According to the U.S. Department of State report Patterns of Global Terrorism 2001,[1] no single definition of terrorism is universally accepted; however, for purposes of statistical analysis and policymaking: "The term 'terrorism' means premeditated, politically motivated violence perpetrated against noncombatant targets by subnational groups or clandestine agents, usually intended to influence an audience." Of course, one side's "terrorists" may well be another side's "freedom fighters." For example, in this definition's sense, the Nazi occupiers of France tightly denounced the "subnational" and "clandestine" French Resistance fighters as terrorists. During the 1980s, the International Court of Justice used the U.S. Administration's own definition of terrorism to call for an end to U.S. support for "terrorism" on the part of Nicaraguan Contras opposing peace talks.

For the U.S. Congress, "'act of terrorism' means an activity that—(A) involves a violent act or an act dangerous to human life that is a violation of the criminal laws of the United States or any State, or that would be a criminal violation if committed within the jurisdiction of the United States or of any State; and (B) appears to be intended (i) to intimidate or coerce a civilian population; (ii) to influence the policy of a government by intimidation or coercion; or (iii) to affect the conduct of a government by assassination or kidnapping."[2] When suitable, the definition can be broadened to include states hostile to U.S. policy.

Apparently, two official definitions of terrorism have existed since the early 1980s: that used by the Department of State "for statistical and analytical purposes" and that used by Congress for criminal proceedings. Together, the definitions allow great flexibility in selective application of the concept of terrorism to fluctuating U.S. priorities. The special category of "State-sponsored terrorism" could be invoked to handle some issues,[3] but the highly selective and politically tendentious use of the label terrorism would continue all the same. Indeed, there appears to be no principled distinction between "terror" as defined by the U.S. Congress and "counterinsurgency" as allowed in U.S. armed forces manuals.[4]

Rather than attempt to produce a stipulative and all-encompassing definition of terrorism, this article restricts its focus to "suicide terrorism" characterized as follows: the targeted use of self-destructing humans against noncombatant—typically civilian—populations to effect political change. Although a suicide attack aims to physically destroy an initial target, its primary use is typically as a weapon of psychological warfare intended to affect a larger public audience. The primary target is not those actually killed or injured in the attack, but those made to witness it. The enemy's own information media amplify the attack's effects to the larger target population. Through indoctrination and training and under charismatic leaders, self-contained suicide cells canalize disparate religious or political sentiments of individuals into an emotionally bonded group of fictive kin who willfully commit to die spectacularly for one another and for what is perceived as the common good of alleviating the community's onerous political and social realities.

Source: From *Science* magazine Vol. 299, Issue 5612, pp. 1534–1539 (March 7, 2003). Reprinted with permission from AAAS.

RECENT HISTORY

Suicide attack is an ancient practice with a modern history. Its use by the Jewish sect of Zealots (sicari) in Roman-occupied Judea and by the Islamic Order of Assassins (hashashin) during the early Christian Crusades are legendary examples.[5] The concept of "terror" as systematic use of violence to attain political ends was first codified by Maximilien Robespierre during the French Revolution. He deemed it an "emanation of virtue" that delivers "prompt, severe, and inflexible" justice, as "a consequence of the general principle of democracy applied to our country's most pressing needs."[6] The Reign of Terror, during which the ruling Jacobin faction exterminated thousands of potential enemies, of whatever sex, age, or condition, lasted until Robespierre's fall (July 1794). Similar justification for state-sponsored terror was common to 20th-century revolutions, as in Russia (Lenin), Cambodia (Pol Pot), and Iran (Khomeini).

Whether subnational (e.g., Russian anarchists) or state-supported (e.g., Japanese kamikaze), suicide attack as a weapon of terror is usually chosen by weaker parties against materially stronger foes when fighting methods of lesser cost seem unlikely to succeed. Choice is often voluntary, but typically under conditions of group pressure and charismatic leadership. Thus, the kamikaze ("divine wind") first used in the battle of the Philippines (November 1944) were young, fairly well-educated pilots who understood that pursuing conventional warfare would likely end in defeat. When collectively asked by Adm. Takijiro Onishi to volunteer for "special attack" (tokkotai) "transcending life and death," all stepped forward, despite assurances that refusal would carry no shame or punishment. In the Battle of Okinawa (April 1945) some 2,000 kamikaze rammed fully fueled fighter planes into more than 300 ships, killing 5,000 Americans in the most costly naval battle in U.S. history. Because of such losses, there was support for using the atomic bomb to end World War II.[7]

The first major contemporary suicide terrorist attack in the Middle East was the December 1981 destruction of the Iraqi embassy in Beirut (27 dead, over 100 wounded). Its precise authors are still unknown, although it is likely that Ayatollah Khomeini approved its use by parties sponsored by Iranian intelligence. With the assassination of pro-Israeli Lebanese President Bashir Gemayel in September 1982, suicide bombing became a strategic political weapon. Under the pro-Iranian Lebanese Party of God (Hezbollah), this strategy soon achieved geopolitical effect with the October 1983 truck-bomb killing of nearly 300 American and French servicemen. America and France abandoned the multinational force policing Lebanon. By 1985, these attacks arguably led Israel to cede most of the gains made during its 1982 invasion of Lebanon.

In Israel-Palestine, suicide terrorism began in 1993, with attacks by Hezbollah-trained members of the Islamic Resistance Movement (Hamas) and Palestine Islamic Jihad (PIJ) aimed at derailing the Oslo Peace Accords.[8] As early as 1988, however, PIJ founder Fathi Shiqaqi established guidelines for "exceptional" martyrdom operations involving human bombs. He followed Hezbollah in stressing that God extols martyrdom but abhors suicide: "Allah may cause to be known those who believe and may make some of you martyrs, and Allah may purify those who believe and may utterly destroy the disbelievers;" however, "no one can die except by Allah's leave."[9,10]

The recent radicalization and networking through Al-Qaida of militant Islamic groups from North Africa, Arabia, and Central and Southeast Asia stems from the Soviet-Afghan War (1979–1989). With financial backing from the United States, members of these various groups were provided opportunities to pool and to unify doctrine, aims, training, equipment, and methods, including suicide attack. Through its multifaceted association with regional groups (by way of finance, personnel, and logistics), Al-Qaida aims to realize flexibly its global ambition of destroying Western dominance through local initiatives to expel Western influences.[11] According to Jane's Intelligence Review: "All the suicide terrorist groups have support infrastructures in Europe and North America."[12]

Calling the current wave of radical Islam "fundamentalism" (in the sense of "traditionalism") is misleading, approaching an oxymoron (supporting online text). Present-day radicals, whether Shi'ite (Iran, Hezbollah) or Sunni

(Taliban, Al-Qaida), are much closer in spirit and action to Europe's post-Renaissance Counter-Reformation than to any traditional aspect of Moslem history. The idea of a ruling ecclesiastical authority, a state or national council of clergy, and a religious police devoted to physically rooting out heretics and blasphemers has its clearest historical model in the Holy Inquisition. The idea that religion must struggle to assert control over politics is radically new to Islam.[13]

DUBIOUS PUBLIC PERCEPTIONS

Recent treatments of Homeland Security research concentrate on how to spend billions to protect sensitive installations from attack.[14,15] But this last line of defense is probably easiest to breach because of the multitude of vulnerable and likely targets (including discotheques, restaurants, and malls), the abundance of would-be attackers (needing little supervision once embarked on a mission), the relatively low costs of attack (hardware store ingredients, no escape needs), the difficulty of detection (little use of electronics), and the unlikelihood that attackers would divulge sensitive information (being unaware of connections beyond their operational cells). Exhortations to put duct tape on windows may assuage (or incite) fear, but will not prevent massive loss of life, and public realization of such paltry defense can undermine trust. Security agencies also attend to prior lines of defense, such as penetrating agent-handling networks of terrorist groups, with only intermittent success.

A first line of defense is to prevent people from becoming terrorists. Here, success appears doubtful should current government and media opinions about why people become human bombs translate into policy (see also supporting online text on contrary academic explanations). Suicide terrorists often are labeled crazed cowards bent on senseless destruction who thrive in the midst of poverty and ignorance. The obvious course becomes to hunt down terrorists while simultaneously transforming their supporting cultural and economic environment from despair to hope. What research there is, however, indicates that suicide terrorists have no appreciable psychopathology and are at least as educated and economically well off as their surrounding populations.

PSYCHOPATHOLOGY: A FUNDAMENTAL ATTRIBUTION ERROR

U.S. President George W. Bush initially branded 9/11 hijackers "evil cowards." For U.S. Senator John Warner, preemptive assaults on terrorists and those supporting terrorism are justified because: "Those who would commit suicide in their assaults on the free world are not rational and are not deterred by rational concepts."[16] In attempting to counter anti-Moslem sentiment, some groups advised their members to respond that "terrorists are extremist maniacs who don't represent Islam at all."[17]

Social psychologists have investigated the "fundamental attribution error," a tendency for people to explain behavior in terms of individual personality traits, even when significant situational factors in the larger society are at work. U.S. government and media characterizations of Middle East suicide bombers as craven homicidal lunatics may suffer from a fundamental attribution error: No instances of religious or political suicide terrorism stem from lone actions of cowering or unstable bombers.

Psychologist Stanley Milgram found that ordinary Americans also readily obey destructive orders under the right circumstances.[18] When told by a "teacher" to administer potentially life-threatening electric shocks to "learners" who fail to memorize word pairs, most comply. Even when subjects stressfully protest as victims plead and scream, use of extreme violence continues—not because of murderous tendencies but from a sense of obligation in situations of authority, no matter how trite. A legitimate hypothesis is that apparently extreme behaviors may be elicited and rendered commonplace by particular historical, political, social, and ideological contexts.

With suicide terrorism, the attributional problem is to understand why nonpathological individuals respond to novel situational factors in numbers sufficient for recruiting organizations to implement policies. In the Middle East, perceived contexts in which suicide bombers and supporters express themselves include a collective sense of historical injustice, political subservience, and social humiliation vis-à-vis global powers and allies, as well as countervailing religious hope (supporting online text on radical Islam's historical novelty). Addressing such perceptions does not entail accepting them as simple reality; however, ignoring the causes of these perceptions risks misidentifying causes and solutions for suicide bombing.

There is also evidence that people tend to believe that their behavior speaks for itself, that they see the world objectively, and that only other people are biased and misconstrue events.[19] Moreover, individuals tend to misperceive differences between group norms as more extreme than they really are. Resulting misunderstandings—encouraged by religious and ideological propaganda—lead antagonistic groups to interpret each other's views of events, such as terrorism/freedom-fighting, as wrong, radical, and/or irrational. Mutual demonization and warfare readily ensue. The problem is to stop this spiral from escalating in opposing camps.

POVERTY AND LACK OF EDUCATION ARE NOT RELIABLE FACTORS

Across our society, there is wide consensus that ridding society of poverty rids it of crime.[20] According to President Bush, "We fight poverty because hope is the answer to terror. . . . We will challenge the poverty and hopelessness and lack of education and failed governments that too often allow conditions that terrorists can seize."[21] At a gathering of Nobel Peace Prize laureates, South Africa's Desmond Tutu and South Korea's Kim Dae Jong opined, "at the bottom of terrorism is poverty"; Elie Wiesel and the Dalai Lama concluded, "education is the way to eliminate terrorism."[22]

Support for this comes from research pioneered by economist Gary Becker showing that property crimes are predicted by poverty and lack of education.[23] In his incentive-based model, criminals are rational individuals acting on self-interest. Individuals choose illegal activity if rewards exceed probability of detection and incarceration together with expected loss of income from legal activity ("opportunity costs"). Insofar as criminals lack skill and education, as in much blue-collar crime, opportunity costs may be minimal; so crime pays.

Such rational-choice theories based on economic opportunities do not reliably account for some types of violent crimes (domestic homicide, hate killings). These calculations make even less sense for suicide terrorism. Suicide terrorists generally are not lacking in legitimate life opportunities relative to their general population. As the Arab press emphasizes, if martyrs had nothing to lose, sacrifice would be senseless:[24] "He who commits suicide kills himself for his own benefit, he who commits martyrdom sacrifices himself for the sake of his religion and his nation. . . . The Mujahed is full of hope."[25]

Research by Krueger and Maleckova suggests that education may be uncorrelated, or even positively correlated, with supporting terrorism.[26] In a December 2001 poll of 1,357 West Bank and Gaza Palestinians 18 years of age or older, those having 12 or more years of schooling supported armed attacks by 68 points, those with up to 11 years of schooling by 63 points, and illiterates by 46 points. Only 40% of persons with advanced degrees supported dialogue with Israel versus 53% with college degrees and 60% with 9 years or less of schooling. In a comparison of Hezbollah militants who died in action with a random sample of Lebanese from the same age group and region, militants were less likely to come from poor homes and more likely to have had secondary-school education.

Nevertheless, relative loss of economic or social advantage by educated persons might encourage support for terrorism. In the period leading to the first Intifada (1982–1988), the number of Palestinian men with 12 years or more of schooling more than doubled; those with less schooling increased only 30%. This coincided with a sharp increase in unemployment for college graduates relative to high school graduates. Real daily wages of college graduates fell some 30%; wages for those with only secondary schooling held steady. Underemployment also seems to be a factor among those recruited to Al-Qaida and its allies from the Arabian peninsula.[27]

THE INSTITUTIONAL FACTOR: ORGANIZING FICTIVE KIN

Although humiliation and despair may help account for susceptibility to martyrdom in some situations, this is neither a complete explanation nor one applicable to other circumstances. Studies by psychologist Ariel Merari point to the importance of institutions in suicide terrorism.[28] His team interviewed 32 of 34 bomber families in Palestine/Israel (before 1998), surviving attackers, and captured recruiters. Suicide terrorists apparently span their population's normal distribution in terms of education, socioeconomic status, and personality type (introvert vs. extrovert). Mean age for bombers was early twenties. Almost all were unmarried and expressed religious belief before recruitment (but no more than did the general population).

Except for being young, unattached males, suicide bombers differ from members of violent racist organizations with whom they are often compared.[29] Overall, suicide terrorists exhibit no socially dysfunctional attributes (fatherless, friendless, or jobless) or suicidal symptoms. They do not vent fear of enemies or express "hopelessness" or a sense of "nothing to lose" for lack of life alternatives that would be consistent with economic rationality. Merari attributes primary responsibility for attacks to recruiting organizations, which enlist prospective candidates from this youthful and relatively unattached population. Charismatic trainers then intensely cultivate mutual commitment to die within small cells of three to six members. The final step before a martyrdom operation is a formal social contract, usually in the form of a video testament.

From 1996 to 1999 Nasra Hassan, a Pakistani relief worker, interviewed nearly 250 Palestinian recruiters and trainers, failed suicide bombers, and relatives of deceased bombers. Bombers were men aged 18 to 38: "None were uneducated, desperately poor, simple-minded, or depressed. . . . They all seemed to be entirely normal members of their families."[30] Yet "all were deeply religious," believing their actions "sanctioned by the divinely revealed religion of Islam." Leaders of sponsoring organizations complained, "Our biggest problem is the hordes of young men who beat on our doors."

Psychologist Brian Barber surveyed 900 Moslem adolescents during Gaza's first Intifada (1987–1993).[31] Results show high levels of participation in and victimization from violence. For males, 81% reported throwing stones, 66% suffered physical assault, and 63% were shot at (versus 51, 38, and 20% for females). Involvement in violence was not strongly correlated with depression or antisocial behavior. Adolescents most involved displayed strong individual pride and social cohesion. This was reflected in activities: for males, 87% delivered supplies to activists, 83% visited martyred families, and 71% tended the wounded (57, 46, and 37% for females). A follow-up during the second Intifada (2000–2002) indicates that those still unmarried act in ways considered personally more dangerous but socially more meaningful. Increasingly, many view martyr acts as most meaningful. By summer 2002, 70 to 80% of Palestinians endorsed martyr operations.[32]

Previously, recruiters scouted mosques, schools, and refugee camps for candidates deemed susceptible to intense religious indoctrination and logistical training. During the second Intifada, there has been a surfeit of volunteers and increasing involvement of secular organizations (allowing women). The frequency and violence of suicide attacks have escalated (more bombings since February 2002 than during 1993–2000); planning has been less painstaking. Despite these changes, there is little to indicate overall change in bomber profiles (mostly unmarried, average socioeconomic status, moderately religious).[28,29]

In contrast to Palestinians, surveys with a control group of Bosnian Moslem adolescents from the same time period reveal markedly weaker expressions of self-esteem, hope for the future, and prosocial behavior.[30] A key difference is that Palestinians routinely invoke religion to invest personal trauma with proactive social meaning that takes injury as a badge of honor. Bosnian Moslems typically report not considering religious affiliation a significant part of personal or collective identity until seemingly arbitrary violence forced awareness upon them.

Thus, a critical factor determining suicide terrorism behavior is arguably loyalty to intimate cohorts of peers, which recruiting organizations often promote through religious communion (supporting online text on religion's role).[34] Consider data on 39 recruits to Harkat al-Ansar, a Pakistani-based ally of Al-Qaida. All were unmarried males, most had studied the Quran. All believed that by sacrificing themselves they would help secure the future of their "family" of fictive kin: "Each [martyr] has a special place—among them are brothers, just as there are sons and those even more dear."[35] A Singapore Parliamentary report on 31 captured operatives from Jemaah Islamiyah and other Al-Qaida allies in Southeast Asia underscores the pattern: "These men were not ignorant, destitute or disenfranchised. All 31 had received secular education. . . . Like many of their counterparts in militant Islamic organizations in the region, they held normal, respectable jobs. . . . As a group, most of the detainees regarded religion as their most important personal value . . . secrecy over the true knowledge of jihad, helped create a sense of sharing and empowerment vis-à-vis others."[36]

Such sentiments characterize institutional manipulation of emotionally driven commitments that may have emerged under natural selection's influence to refine or override short-term rational calculations that would otherwise preclude achieving goals against long odds. Most typically, such emotionally driven commitments serve as survival mechanisms to inspire action in otherwise paralyzing circumstances, as when a weaker person convincingly menaces a stronger person into thinking twice before attempting to take advantage. In religiously inspired suicide terrorism, however, these emotions are purposely manipulated by organizational leaders, recruiters, and trainers to benefit the organization rather than the individual (supporting online text on religion).[37]

RATIONAL CHOICE IS THE SPONSOR'S PREROGATIVE, NOT THE AGENT'S

Little tangible benefit (in terms of rational-choice theories) accrues to the suicide bomber, certainly not enough to make the likely gain one of maximized "expected utility." Heightened social recognition occurs only after death, obviating personal material benefit. But for leaders who almost never consider killing themselves (despite declarations of readiness to die), material benefits more likely outweigh losses in martyrdom operations. Hassan cites one Palestinian official's prescription for a successful mission: "a willing young man . . . nails, gunpowder, a light switch and a short cable, mercury (readily obtainable

from thermometers), acetone. . . . The most expensive item is transportation to an Israeli town."[30] The total cost is about $150.

For the sponsoring organization, suicide bombers are expendable assets whose losses generate more assets by expanding public support and pools of potential recruits. Shortly after 9/11, an intelligence survey of educated Saudis (ages 25 to 41) concluded that 95% supported Al-Qaida.[37] In a December 2002 Pew Research Center survey on growing anti-Americanism, only 6% of Egyptians viewed America and its "War on Terror" favorably.[38] Money flows from those willing to let others die, easily off-setting operational costs (training, supporting personnel, safe houses, explosives and other arms, transportation, and communication). After a Jerusalem supermarket bombing by an 18-year-old Palestinian female, a Saudi telethon raised more than $100 million for "the Al-Quds Intifada."

Massive retaliation further increases people's sense of victimization and readiness to behave according to organizational doctrines and policies structured to take advantage of such feelings. In a poll of 1,179 West Bank and Gaza Palestinians in spring 2002, 66% said army operations increased their backing for suicide bombings.[39] By year's end, 73% of Lebanese Moslems considered suicide bombings justifiable.[38] This radicalization of opinion increases both demand and supply for martyrdom operations. A December 2002 UN report credited volunteers with swelling a reviving Al-Qaida in 40 countries.[40] The organization's influence in the larger society—most significantly its directing elites—increases in turn.

PRIORITIES FOR HOMELAND SECURITY

The last line of defense against suicide terrorism—preventing bombers from reaching targets—may be the most expensive and least likely to succeed. Random bag or body searches cannot be very effective against people willing to die, although this may provide some semblance of security and hence psychological defense against suicide terrorism's psychological warfare. A middle line of defense, penetrating and destroying recruiting organizations and isolating their leaders, may be successful in the near term, but even more resistant organizations could emerge instead. The first line of defense is to drastically reduce receptivity of potential recruits to recruiting organizations. But how?

It is important to know what probably will not work. Raising literacy rates may have no effect and could be counterproductive should greater literacy translate into greater exposure to terrorist propaganda (in Pakistan, literacy and dislike for the United States increased as the number of religious madrasa schools increased from 3,000 to 39,000 since 1978).[27,38] Lessening poverty may have no effect, and could be counterproductive if poverty reduction for the entire population amounted to a downward redistribution of wealth that left those initially better off with fewer opportunities than before. Ending occupation or reducing perceived humiliation may help, but not if the population believes this to be a victory inspired by terror (e.g., Israel's apparently forced withdrawal from Lebanon).

If suicide bombing is crucially (though not exclusively) an institution-level phenomenon, it may require finding the right mix of pressure and inducements to get the communities themselves to abandon support for institutions that recruit suicide attackers. One way is to so damage the community's social and political fabric that any support by the local population or authorities for sponsors of suicide attacks collapses, as happened regarding the kamikaze as a by-product of the nuclear destruction of Hiroshima and Nagasaki. In the present world, however, such a strategy would neither be morally justifiable nor practical to implement, given the dispersed and distributed organization of terrorist institutions among distantly separated populations that collectively number in the hundreds of millions. Likewise, retaliation in kind ("tit-for-tat") is not morally acceptable if allies are sought.[41] Even in more localized settings, such as the Israeli-Palestinian conflict, coercive policies alone may not achieve lasting relief from attack and can exacerbate the problem over time. On the inducement side, social psychology research indicates that people who identify with antagonistic groups use conflicting information from the other group to reinforce antagonism.[19] Thus, simply trying to persuade others from without by bombarding them with more self-serving information may only increase hostility.

Other research suggests that most people have more moderate views than what they consider their group norm to be. Inciting and empowering moderates from within to confront inadequacies and inconsistencies in their own knowledge (of others as evil), values (respect for life), and behavior (support for killing), and other members of their group[42] can produce emotional dissatisfaction leading to lasting change and influence on the part of these individuals.[43] Funding for civic education and debate may help, also interfaith confidence-building through intercommunity interaction initiatives (as Singapore's government proposes).[35] Ethnic profiling, isolation, and preemptive attack on potential (but not yet actual) supporters of terrorism probably will not help. Another strategy is for the United States and its allies to change behavior by directly addressing and lessening sentiments of grievance and humiliation, especially in Palestine (where images of daily violence have made it the global focus of Moslem attention).[44] For no evidence (historical or otherwise) indicates that support for suicide terrorism will evaporate without complicity in achieving at least some fundamental goals that suicide bombers and supporting communities share.

Of course, this does not mean negotiating overall goals, such as Al-Qaida's quest to replace the Western-inspired system of nation-states with a global caliphate, first in Moslem lands and then everywhere (see supporting online text for history and agenda of suicide-sponsoring groups). Unlike other groups, Al-Qaida publicizes no specific demands after martyr actions. As with an avenging army, it seeks no compromise. But most people who currently sympathize with it might.

Perhaps to stop the bombing we need research to understand which configurations of psychological and cultural relationships are luring and binding thousands, possibly millions, of mostly ordinary people into the terrorist organization's martyr-making web. Study is needed on how terrorist institutions form and on similarities and differences across organizational structures, recruiting practices, and populations recruited. Are there reliable differences between religious and secular groups, or between ideologically driven and grievance-driven terrorism? Interviews with surviving Hamas bombers and captured Al-Qaida operatives suggest that ideology and grievance are factors for both groups but relative weights and consequences may differ.

We also need to investigate any significant causal relations between our society's policies and actions and those of terrorist organizations and supporters. We may find that the global economic, political, and cultural agenda of our own society has a catalyzing role in moves to retreat from our world view (Taliban) or to create a global counterweight (Al-Qaida). Funding such research may be difficult. As with the somewhat tendentious and self-serving use of "terror" as a policy concept,[45,46] to reduce dissonance our governments and media may wish to ignore these relations as legitimate topics for inquiry into what terrorism is all about and why it exists.

This call for research may demand more patience than any administration could politically tolerate during times of crisis. In the long run, however, our society can ill afford to ignore either the consequences of its own actions or the causes behind the actions of others. Potential costs of such ignorance are terrible to contemplate. The comparatively minor expense of research into such consequences and causes could have inestimable benefit.

References and Notes

1. "Patterns of global terrorism" (U.S. Department of State, Washington, DC, May 2002); available at www.state.gov/s/ct/rls/pgtrpt/2001/. "The U.S. Government has employed this definition of terrorism for statistical and analytical purposes since 1983."

2. U.S. Code Congress. Admin. News, 98th Congress, 2nd Session, v. 2, par. 3077, 98 STAT. (19 October 1984).

3. Until 1983, official U.S. positions on "terror" followed the term's common meaning in use since the French Revolution, referring to state-sponsored terror. For example, under "sources relating to Operation Enduring Freedom and the struggle against terrorism," the U.S. Navy's Web guide on terrorism regularly links to Department of Defense articles on Iraq (www.history.navy.mil/library/guides/terrorism.htm).

4. The recent Guatemalan truth commission report singled out the U.S. Army School of the Americas (SOA), now at Fort Benning, Georgia, for counterinsurgency training that "had a significant bearing on human rights violations during the armed conflict." A 1998 human rights report released by the Guatemala Archdiocese Human Rights Office also linked SOA graduates in Guatemala's military intelligence (D-2, G-2) to a civilian-targeted campaign of kidnappings, torture, and murder that left tens of thousands dead. References available online through Network Solidarity with the People of Guatemala (NISGUA), "U.S. Army School of the Americas cited in Guatemalan Truth Commission Report," 17 July 2001; available at www.nisgua.org/articles/school_of_the_americas.htm.

5. B. Lewis, *The Assassins* (Basic, New York, 2002).

6. M. Robespierre, "Principes de morale politique," speech delivered to French National Convention, 5 February 1794; available at http://membres.lycos.fr/discours/1794.htm.

7. A. Axell, *Kamikaze* (Longman, New York, 2002).

8. A precipitating event was the exiling of 418 Palestinians suspected of affiliation with Hamas (18 December 1992), the first mass expulsion of Arabs from Palestine since 1948.

9. Quran, chapt. 3, verses 140–146.

10. Compare this statement with that of Hamas leader Abd Al-'Aziz Al-Rantisi, Al-Hayat (London-Beirut), 25 April 2002.

11. U.S. Department of Justice, Al Qaeda Training Manual, online release 7 December 2001; available at www.usdoj.gov/ag/trainingmanual.htm.

12. "Suicide terrorism: A global threat," *Jane's BioSecurity* (2002); available at www.janes.com/security/internationaL security/news/usscole/jir001020_1_n.shtml.

13. B. Lewis, *What Went Wrong* (Oxford Univ. Press, New York, 2002). The notion of a distinct religious authority, or clergy, was traditionally alien to Islam. The de facto modern clergy recognized by Islamic suicide attackers includes mullahs of Pakistan and Afghanistan, as well as the 19th-century administrative office of ayatollah in Iran and the former Ottoman office of State Attorney, or mufti (e.g., in Palestine, Syria, and Arabia). Many in this "clergy" also oppose suicide bombing.

14. D. Malakoff, *Science* 295, 254 (2002).

15. D. Chapin et al., *Science* 297, 1997 (2002).

16. D. Von Drehle, *Washington Post*, 7 October 2002, p. A1. Warner's example of "rational deterrence" was the Cold War doctrine MAD (mutually assured destruction). MAD's key premise was the apparently irrational threat of guaranteeing one's own destruction in order to destroy the enemy.

17. Unitarian Universalist Association of Congregations, "Confronting anti-Arab or anti-Muslim sentiments," 21 September 2002; available at www.uua.org/uuawo/issues/respond/confront.html.

18. S. Milgram, *Obedience to Authority* (Harper & Row, New York, 1974).

19. L. Ross, C. Stillinger, *Negotiation* J. 7, 389 (1991).

20. R. Clark, *Crime in America* (Simon & Schuster, New York, 1970).

21. White House news release, 22 March 2002; available at www.whitehouse.gov/news/releases/2002/03/20020322-1.html.

22. J. J. Jai, *Christian Science Monitor*, 10 December 2001, p. 7.

23. G. Becker, *Pol. Econ.* 76, 169 (1968).

24. "They are youth at the peak of their blooming, who at a certain moment decide to turn their bodies into body parts . . . flowers." Editorial, *Al-Risala* (Hamas weekly), 7 June 2001.

25. Sheikh Yussuf Al-Qaradhawi (a spiritual leader of the Muslim Brotherhood), Al-Ahram Al-Arabi (Cairo), 3 February 2001.

26. A. Krueger, J. Maleckova, NBER Working Paper no. w9074, National Bureau of Economic Research, Cambridge, MA, July 2002; available at http://papers.nber.org/papers/Wg074.

27. T. Friedman, *Longitudes and Attitudes* (Farrar, Strauss, Giroux, New York, 2002). Leaders of Al-Qaida's international cells are often middle-class, European-educated converts to radical Islam. Family histories indicate little religious fervor before emigration to a solitary existence in Europe and subsequent belonging to a local prayer group or mosque (available tapes preach a revolutionary end to daily, personal alienation through collective action to destroy perceived impediments to "restoring" Islam's values and dominance). As with other radical Islamic groups, ordinary cell operatives are often resident Middle East bachelors from middle-class families.

28. A. Merari, paper presented to Institute for Social Research seminar series, "The Psychology of Extremism," Univ. of Michigan, Ann Arbor, MI, 11 February 2002.

29. R. Ezekiel, *The Racist Mind* (Viking, New York, 1995).

30. N. Hassan, *The New Yorker*, 19 November 2001; available at www.newyorker.com/fact/content/7011119fa_FACT1.

31. B. Barber, *Heart and Stones* (Palgrave, New York, in press).

32. D. Brooks, *The Atlantic Monthly* 289 (6), 18 (June 2002); available at www.theatlanticmonthly.com/issues/g002/06/brooks.htm.

33. Unlike people willing to blow themselves up, for frontline soldiers in an apparently hopeless battle, there usually remains hope for survival [G. Airport, J. Gillespie, J. Young, J. Psychol. 2S, 3 (1948)]. The distance between no hope and some (however small) is infinite, which represents the ultimate measure of devotion that religions typically uphold as ideal. While commitment to die for non-kin cannot be rendered within standard theories of Expected Utility, there are moves theorists attempt, such as invoking "infinite utility." Using "infinite utility" to patch theories of rationality creates holes elsewhere in the system. Thus, expected utilities are usually weighted averages, which has scant sense when one term is infinite. The deeper point is that notions of maximization of anticipated benefits cannot account for such behaviors, and ad hoc moves to maintain rational utility at all costs result in a concept of rationality or utility doing little explanatory work. In sum, reliance on rational-choice theories may not be the best way to understand and try to stop suicide terrorism.

34. D. Rhode, A. Chivers, *New York Times*, 17 March 2002, p. A1.

35. "White Paper—The Jemaah Islamiyah Arrests," (Singapore Ministry of Home Affairs, Singapore, 9 January 2003); available at www2.mha.gov.sg, Recruitment and indoctrination into Jemaah Islamiyah are similar in other radical Islamic groups: "The first stage . . . involved religious classes organised for a general mass. . . . The second stage . . . involved identifying those who were captivated enough to find out more about the plight of Muslims in other regions. [JI spiritual leader] Ibrahim Maidan identified potential members from those who were curious enough to remain after classes to enquire further. He engaged those students' interest and compassion and finally invited those he deemed suitable to join JI. This recruitment process would usually take about 18 months. The few who were selected as members were made to feel a strong sense of exclusivity and self esteem . . . a strong sense of in-group superiority."

36. In much the same way, the pornography, fast food, or soft drink industries manipulate innate desires for naturally scarce commodities like sexual mates, fatty foods, and sugar to ends that reduce personal fitness but benefit the manipulating institution. E. S. Atran, *In Gods We Trust* (Oxford Univ. Press, New York, 2002)].

37. E. Sciolino, *New York Times*, 27 January 2002, p. Ag.

38. "What the world thinks in 2002: How global publics view: Their lives, their countries, the world, America" (Survey Rep., Pew Research Center, 4 December 2002); available at http://people-press.org/reports/display.php3?ReportID=165.

39. Reuters News Service, 11 June 2002; accessed at http://story.news.yahoo.com/news?tmpl=story&u=/nm/2002061l/wknm/mideast_palestini.

40. C. Lynch, *Washington Post*, 18 December 2002, p. A27.

41. R. Axelrod, W. Hamilton, *Science* 211, 1390 (1981).

42. M. Bazerman, M. Neale, *Negotiating Rationally* (Free Press, New York, 1991).

43. A. Eagly, S. Chaiken, *The Psychology of Attitudes* (Harcourt Brace, Fort Worth, TX, 1993).

44. One possibility is to offer and guarantee a clear resolution of "final status" acceptable to majorities of Israelis and Palestinians. Without clear resolution of final status before implementation of "confidence building" measures, with an understanding by all parties of what to expect in the end, it is likely that doubts about ultimate intentions will undermine any interim accord—as in every case since 1948. E. S. Atran, *Politics and Society* 18, 481 (1990).

45. N. Chomsky, *9-11* (Seven Stories Press, New York, 2001).

46. Thanks to D. Medin, N. Chomsky, R. Gonzalez, M. Bazerman, R. Nisbett, and reviewers.

CRITICAL THINKING QUESTIONS

1. Discuss the differences and similarities between formal governmental definitions of terrorism and Altran's definition of "suicide terrorism."

2. What is the history of suicide terrorism, and why is suicide terrorism generally chosen as a weapon of war?

3. Why does Altran say that calling modern radical Islam "fundamentalism" is misleading?

4. Why does Altran suggest that the American characterization of suicide bombers is incorrect and misguided?

5. What are the institutional factors at play that motivate communities to support and encourage such attacks?

6. What approaches does Altran suggest to help combat and alleviate the recruitment of suicide bombers?

Religion, Religious Specialists, and Religious Rituals

STATE OF THE ART: Religion

Since the beginning of recorded history, and very likely deep into the human prehistoric past, the human reaction toward interactions with the numinous has been both creative and practical. From its inception, anthropology has been fascinated with religious phenomena such as beliefs, attitudes, and practices pertaining to the supernatural. The religious domain was separated from the general domain of culture for the purpose of understanding through in-depth studies. Since then the field has found widespread ideas in various societies regarding the supernatural, and has noted variation in religious beliefs and practices. Despite the efforts at identifying universal themes, and cultivating theories for understanding such universal phenomena, anthropologists have struggled with the problem of articulating a "definition" of religion that would fit cross-culturally. The initial concern with definition ran concurrently with a search for the "psychic unity of humans," the "origins" of religion (Salamone 2006), and of religious change. From the mid-nineteenth century onwards the focus of inquiry was expanded to include religious "forms and practices" and the "social and cultural processes" that underlie them (Vokes 2007). Tylor's 1871 'Primitive Culture' sought the causes and effects of religious change, in all phases of human history. James Frazier's 1890s "The Golden Bough" became the prelude to a collection of numerous, descriptive accounts of religious diversity and change worldwide (Vokes 2007). Both Tylor and Frazier remained evolutionary in focus. But Frazier was the first to call attention to the phenomenon of 'revitalization' in a rather subtle, nonsignificant way.

Franz Boas anti-evolutionary perspective offered cultural relativism as its alternative model, focusing on the uniqueness and history of particular cultures. This approach set the stage for later studies of religion. The twentieth-century functionalist approaches of Malinowski and Radcliffe-Brown (see Section One—"State of the Art") were utilized in studies of religion. Earlier concerns with "origins" were abandoned but the 1950s continued to explore the phenomenon of religious change. Anthony Wallace's seminal contributions to "revitalization movements" was the main attempt to merge the concept with the theme of "culture and personality," the place of "the individual" in the socio-historical context, and how they are situated in the wider torrent of religious change (Harkin 2004; Vokes 2007). Among recurrent issues is how to define religion. Since Evans-Pritchard's (1965) refusal to define religion, many anthropologists including Peter Worsley (1968), Kass and Weisgraw (1999), Adams and Salome (2000), Glazier and Flowerday (2003), Hertz (2006) shy away from such an attempt (Salamone 2006) but offer working definitions. In addition, anthropologists are returning to old issues: unsuccessfully reattempting a universal theory of religion and reexamining old concepts. For instance, it was believed that religious phenomena could not be explained by science. The gap between religion and science seems to be closing as science had begun to find explanations for things in the natural world that were previously thought to reside in the realm of religion. Currently, the relationship between science and religion derives from how humans perceive, interpret, and react to their environment. Salamone (2006:159) notes that Bastide (2001), "contrary to much anthropological sentiment," concluded that "magic does not lead to science."

"It also does not lead to religion." "Magic freezes people in time and space." "Science moves them out of their time and space." Anthony Wallace (2003d) for his part sought to explicate the concept of revitalization which, he says consists of five basic stages ranging from "the advent of external stimulus and the introduction of stress" to "experimenting with bodily practices . . . involving intoxicants and new sexual practices," the "revitalization or renewal proper," and the emergence of a "new order" (Vokes 2007).

Anthropologists (Sections One and Two) are constantly devising new methodological approaches to guide ethnographic research and all culture-related research including religious studies. Results of fieldwork reveal that all cultures have their religious specialists, ranging from shamans to diviners to sorcerers, magicians, and many more. Religious syncretism, the combination of old and new religious practices, has been seen in many societies. Furthermore, some societies exhibit the practice of old religions in new guises (Rosman, Weisgraw & Rubel 2009; Scupin 2008). One influence on this pattern is colonialism, which reshaped indigenous religions in many parts of the world (Rosman & Rubel 2004; Scupin 2008).

During the past century, the field has seen a new convergence of religion and politics. In many areas of the world with serious economic hardships, there has been a greater move toward revitalization of cultural forms and institutions. The computer age is witnessing the onset of online religions on the Internet. This milieu has influenced large numbers of people, bringing masses from vast distances into a spiritual fellowship. The renewed interest in spiritual matters and the proliferation of new religious denominations and beliefs in many parts of the world are subjects of anthropological concern in fieldwork (Rosman & Rubel 2004). In the last few decades religious fundamentalism has been on the rise. Religious conflict has produced a climate of tension as religious organizations struggle to influence their nations and the world around them. Individuals see personal spiritual enrichment and proselytism as the means for achieving stability.

In the twenty-first century, devotion to Mary, the mother of Jesus, and her popularity have reemerged as a global phenomenon, locally configured, and incorporating many anti-Catholic doctrines and rituals. According to anthropologist Anna-Karina Hermkens (2007), although Christianity in New Guinea is "a burgeoning field of study," Marian devotion is an area neglected by this new focus. The study of the present global resurgence of Marian devotion is one of the tasks of anthropology. Anthropologists continue to look at the relationship between religion and other domains of sociocultural life such as art, gender, economics, kinship, language and other systems of communication, and socialization. Future research needs to pay greater attention to the effects of revitalization, conversion, evangelism, and all other forms of spirituality on the individual, society and the material world.

ABOUT THE ARTICLES

The articles presented here deal with some of the issues surrounding the reality of religion in the world today. They treat the emerging problems as they are encountered by modern-day anthropologists. The articles also deal with human systems of sacred belief.

The Singh article examines part-time religious practitioners called shamans. Although the article is not anthropological in origin, it presents a good concise overview of who shamans are, how they are called to their positions, and cultural beliefs regarding the spirit world and its relationships with humans and its impacts on human activities. An interesting facet of the article is Singh's relating shamanistic practices to some trends in modern mental health practices. The student should ask him- or herself if the more holistic practices of shamans are more conducive to mental health, and if some of those practices can be adapted for use in their culture.

Both the Jacobson article and Eidelman article focus on the relationship among religious beliefs, ritual behavior, and animals in two quite different religious traditions. Jacobson explores the Indian "reverence for cows" that, to Westerners, seems quite irrational. He explains how the cow provides immense economic benefits to Indian society and outlines behaviors Indians exhibit when dealing with cattle. Jacobson uses the story of Sidha Singh and people's reaction to the death of one of his calves as an ethnographic demonstration of this reverence.

Eidelman deals with a different approach to humans, animals, and their place in the sacred and secular world. The interrelationship of Jewish ritual classification of animals, their ritual preparation, and the influence of religious ideas on everyday behavior is the basis for this discussion of Jewish dietary law and its role in the self-identification of different Jewish sects.

Wilreker's article, an original offering written for this reader, takes a fresh look at a ritual form that anthropology has defined as the *Rite of Passage*. Found in every society, it comes in many forms and at different times of a person's or group's social existence, yet its structure is remarkably similar no matter what culture it occurs in or under what circumstances it is invoked. Wilreker looks at funerals as rites of passage, but from the perspective of American neo-pagans, a widely diverse religious movement that has gained greater traction in modern American society. In the end, despite differences in specifics of the ritual, it is the similarities of the American neo-pagan rituals to other funerary rites that is most striking.

The Rafferty article is offered last for good reason. Possession, possession states, and the concept of exorcism have existed for as long as there have been written religious records, and probably during the prehistoric period as well. Such beliefs connect all religious systems from shamanism to monotheism with a common thread: the potential for personal and intimate interaction by the individual with the supernatural world. Rafferty looks at both traditional religious and scientific explanations regarding the onset of possession states around the world and how those states reflect the experience and belief systems of individuals and cultures across the globe.

References

Adams, W. R., & Salamone, F. A. eds. *Anthropology and Theology: Gods, Icons, and God-Talk*. Lanham, MD:- University Press of America, 2000.

Bastide, R. *Social Origins of Religion*. Minneapolis: University of Minnesota Press, 2001.

Evans-Pritchard, E. E. *Theories of Primitive Religion*. Oxford: Oxford University Press, 1965.

Frazier, J. G. *The Golden Bough*, 1st ed. London: Macmillan, 1890.

Glazier, S. D., & Flowerday, C. A. *Selected Readings in the Anthropology of Religion: Theoretical and Methodological Essays*. Westport, CT: Praeger, 2003.

Harkin, M. E., ed. *Reassessing Revitalization Movements: Perspectives from North America and the Pacific Islands*. Lincoln: University of Nebraska Press, 2004.

Hermkens, A. "The Power of Mary in New Guinea." *Anthropology Today* 23, no. 2 (2007): 4–8.

Hertz, R. *Death and the Right Hand*. New York: Routledge 2006 [1960].

Klass, M., & Weisgrau, M. K. *Across the Boundaries of Belief: Contemporary Issues in the Anthropology of Religion*. Westport, CT: Westview Press, 1999.

Rosman, A., & Rubel, P. *The Tapestry of Culture: An Introduction to Cultural Anthropology*, 8th ed. New York: McGraw-Hill, 2004.

Rosman, A., Wiesgrau, M., & Rubel, P. *The Tapestry of Culture: An Introduction to Cultural Anthropology*, 10th ed. New York: Alta Mira Press, 2009.

Salamone, F. A. "In Search of Religion." *Reviews of Anthropology* 35 (2006): 155–167.

Scupin, R. *Cultural Anthropology*, 7th ed. Upper Saddle River, NJ: McGraw-Hill, 2008.

Tylor, E. B. *Primitive Culture: Researches into the Development of Mythology, Philosophy, Religion, Language, Art, and Custom*. London: Murray, 1871.

Vokes, R. "Rethinking the Anthropology of Religious Change: New Perspectives on Revitalization and Conversion Movements." *Reviews in Anthropology* 36 (2007): 311–333.

Wallace, A. F. C. Mazeway Resynthesis: A Biocultural Theory of Religious Inspiration. (2003d). *Revitalization and Mazeways: Essays on Culture Change*. Vol 1. Robert C. Grumet, ed. Lincoln: University of Nebraska, 2003.

Worsley, P. *The Trumpet Shall Sound: A study of "Cargo" Cults in Melanesia*. New York: Schocken, 1968.

For Further Research

Almost every great (and not so great) anthropologist has written about religion, and there are literally thousands of books, monographs, and articles a student could discover. A classic that influenced the anthropological study of religion is Emile Durkheim's *The Elementary Forms of the Religious Life* (1915, Allen & Unwin). One that has heavily influenced the senior editor's (Rafferty's) work is Bronislaw Malinowski's *Magic, Science, and Religion and Other Essays* (1948, The Free Press). Rather than cite numerous individual works, there are two overviews that will introduce the student to the broader field. *Magic, Witchcraft, and Religion: A Reader in the Anthropology of Religion* (8th ed., 2010, McGraw-Hill) by Pamela Morrow and James Myers reprints both classic and more recent articles, which allows the student to be exposed to older and more recent thinking in the field. Scupin's *Religion and Culture: An Anthropological Focus* (2nd ed., 2008, Pearson/Prentice Hall) presents a series of well-written chapters that deal with a broad spectrum of topics: anthropological perspectives, both modern and historic; specific topics such as myth, shamanism, and ritual, among numerous others; and anthropological appraisals of modern world religions. For additional information on researching the topics discussed in the "State of the Art" section, please visit *www.mysearchlab.com*.

Shamans, Healing, and Mental Health

Ashvind N. Singh

The term *shaman,* as it is used today, is derived from the Siberian Tungus word, *saman,* meaning a person who has direct experience of the mysteries of life and the universe. Shamans are people who are the repositories of specialized knowledge and sacred practices in a culture, passing this knowledge from generation to generation. They are born with or develop a special sensitivity about the nature of the world, the interconnectedness of all things, and the need to maintain a balance in the universe. As children, they often feel that they have a spiritual calling and must endure greater hardships than others in their culture, such as serious illness and personal injury. If they are able to overcome these hardships, they are apprenticed to a shaman or several shamans, who help them to develop their special skills so that they can continue the shamanic tradition. Among other things, fully trained shamans can compose special healing songs, cause him/herself to enter into a trance-like condition, travel after souls or seek lost objects, and diagnose and cure illness. Although shamans are usually male, both males and females can be shamans.

THE TRADITIONAL SHAMAN

A shaman is a person who traverses the boundary between the physical and spiritual worlds. The ability to travel between these worlds, and often in other states of consciousness, is what defines a shaman, and is believed to be the source of his strength and power. There are as many forms of shamanism as there are cultures in this world, each one with its own beliefs, practices, and rituals. In western cultures, the shaman is of the physical world only, and is commonly known as the medical doctor.

A Shaman's Apprentice

Shamans begin their life pre-ordained from an early age to be village healers. It is their calling, and it often comes by way of a dream, vision, or an illness. This calling can, and usually does, disrupt the person's life. Although in some societies being chosen as a shaman is seen as a misfortune, it is most often seen as a great blessing. When the child is old enough, he is sent to work with and become the apprentice of the current village shaman.

As an apprentice, the young child begins by learning which plants have medicinal properties and those which are harmful or toxic. Later, he will learn how to use the toxic plants for medicinal purposes as well. Although almost everyone in a village has some knowledge of plant species and their general properties, it is the shaman who is the expert. A rudimentary knowledge of medicinal plants is common among most villagers because of its survival value. For example, when villagers are out hunting and are bitten by insects, or brush up against toxic plants, they need to know enough about medicinal plants to be able to heal themselves, or at least to stabilize their condition until the local shaman can attend to them.

Through years of training and practice, a shaman's apprentice learns how to heal afflictions of the body and mind. He may begin by collecting different species of plants for his

Source: Reprinted wiith kind permission of Springer Science +Business Media from *Journal of Child and Family Studies,* Vol. 8, #2, June 1999. Copyright © 1999 Springer Science+Business Media, LLC.

teacher and learning how to combine them to heal specific ailments. He learns to treat not just the body or the mind, but both, because the body and mind are seen as different aspects of the same entity. In learning to treat the mind, the apprentice learns to call on spiritual guides who exist in the cosmic world. This requires intensive and closely supervised training, such as in Native American vision quests, for the apprentice to harness his spiritual powers. While these powers can also be used for non-healing purposes, the shaman teaches his apprentice how to use his physical and spiritual resources to heal the mind, body, and spirit. As the apprentice gains this knowledge, he realizes that spiritual power is gained by becoming one with all that exists and learning the intricate balance of nature.

Shaman Belief System and Healing

The healing power of the shamans is tied directly to their cultural belief in the spirits of the dead and in the living spirits of the world in which they live. The living spirits include those of everything that exists in the universe, not just those of humans and animals. Direct communication with these spirits provides the shaman with the knowledge and tools for healing. This type of healing process is based on the idea that everything in the universe is interconnected, without any fundamental parts. Thus, human beings are seen as being one with the universe, and in balance with nature.

The concept of oneness is so fundamental to the shaman belief system that diseases are not even considered to be an individual affliction, but a disruption in the balance of life. When there is imbalance, there is suffering and pain, either of the body or the mind, or both. The balance and harmony among physical and spiritual entities are considered especially important. For example, shamans in many cultures believe that the cause of many ailments can be traced to an imbalance or disharmony of specific spirits. In some cultures, for example, people believe that epilepsy is caused by a spirit who has become angry, and that the sprit conveys its displeasure by periodically draining the life force out of the individual, causing him to drop to the ground and shake uncontrollably. Because of the

shaman's understanding of the spirit world, he is able to work with the individual to appease the angry spirit, restore balance and harmony, and enable the individual to be healed.

In addition to medicinal plants and objects, spirituality is a cornerstone of the shamanic system. The concept of spirituality can have several meanings; however, within the aboriginal shaman system it usually refers to the life energy that flows among everything. When one aspect of this system is disrupted, it must be healed or great misfortune may fall on those who have caused the disruption. As everything is understood to be interconnected, each individual is considered a part of the collective spirit of the culture. Thus, if one person has an ailment, especially one dealing with the psyche, then not only is the problem within the individual but it also resides within the collective. For this reason, the healing of an individual may involve the whole family or an even wider network of people. In addition, rituals may be used that bring everyone together so that their collective life energies can be directed toward healing the individual.

Healing and Mental Health

Shamans flourish in holistic cultures. In these cultures, individuals value harmony with their environment, cooperation and cohesiveness above mastery of and control over the environment, and holistic over dualistic thinking. They value the relational context of their lives and find comfort in extended family relationships. Indeed, they place the well-being of their extended family above their own. This kind of understanding of one's place in the universe—as an integral part of all things rather than as a separate entity—lends itself to a healing model of health and mental health. The shamans believe that their role is to provide or restore balance in nature so that everything is in its place. When there is disharmony, there is pain and suffering. Thus, they see themselves as being instrumental in removing an individual's pain and suffering and facilitating wholeness.

Healing implies wholeness or a state of equilibrium. For the shaman, good physical and mental health implies not only that the individual is free from suffering, but also that the individual is in a larger state of equilibrium. That is, the individual is in a harmonious relationship with all things—with his biological, social, psychological, physical and cosmic environment. This implies that everything needs to be in balance for the human being to be whole, to be healed. Thus, for the shaman, healing requires much more than attention to the specific pain or suffering.

This model of healing is gaining some momentum in current western mental health practice. For example, recent emphasis by therapists on finding out how the individual view his mental illness, what it means to him, and what he thinks can be done to heal him suggest that the individual's world view or context is seen as a critical aspect of mental health treatment. After all, the individual cannot have harmony in his life if the mental health treatment being prescribed for him is not consistent with his world view. Like the shamans, who view healing as coming from within the individual and treatment from external sources, modern mental health professionals are acutely aware that long-term mental health gains can only be sustained by building on the individual's instrumental and spiritual strengths rather than by externally imposed treatments that focus solely on a disease or disorder.

Much of this thinking is evident in holistic treatment models, such as Person Centered Planning, which mandates that all treatment endeavors be centered around the individual's strengths. Person Centered Plans are developed not by one or two professionals but a much larger group of people who may have some role to play in enhancing the individual's quality of life, including but not limited to family members, friends, advocates, spiritual advisors, doctors, psychiatrists, nurses, psychologists, social workers, other therapists, teachers, vocational counselors, financial advisors, community providers, and so on. Having this kind of an extended treatment team enables the individual to draw upon the rich topography of resources that are available so that he can achieve and maintain a state of good mental health. These kinds of treatment plans provide the networking and linking to community resources that enable the individual to stay healthy, remain inextricably linked with his community, and maintain his state of equilibrium. After all, good mental health is not an absence of mental affliction but a joyous and harmonious relationship with oneself, one's community, and the universe.

CRITICAL THINKING QUESTIONS

1. Define the characteristics of a traditional shaman as discussed by Singh.
2. According to the author, how is the healing power of a shaman affected or determined by the cultural beliefs of his/her culture?
3. How are shamanistic healing and mental health related in a traditional society?
4. According to Singh, in what ways are "Person Centered Planning" and the shamanistic approach to healing similar to each other?

A Reverence for Cows

Doranne Jacobson

For millennia, cattle have supplied South Asians with milk, animal power, and dung for fertilizer and fuel. Tractors, petrochemicals, and nuclear power seem unlikely to dethrone these animals from their special place in Indian society.

"In America, what do they do to someone who murders a cow?" Some thirty years ago, as an anthropologist visiting the village of Nimkhera, in central India, I faced this loaded question. A local farmer, Sidha Singh, stood accused of murdering his calf. He had whacked it with a stick to drive it out of his granary, and it had died shortly thereafter. A council of village elders had convened to consider the case. Fortunately, my interrogator, an earnest Hindu youth, knew nothing of the flagrant U.S. trade in hamburgers and T-bone steaks. "Oh," I said, "in my country, murderers are sent to jail." My young friend nodded approvingly.

Thus I evaded discovery, but Sidha Singh did not. The council found him guilty of cow murder—*gao hatya*—a significant sin within Hinduism. They sentenced him to pay a substantial fine and host a banquet for all the villagers. Until he met these obligations, Sidha Singh and his family would be excluded from all local social events, and no parents would consider allowing their children to marry his. A man of modest means, he surely intended his valuable animal no harm, but his misfortune meant a lengthy period of religious and social purgatory, as well as severe economic strain for himself and his family.

The case of the murdered calf brought home to local youngsters the importance of treating their cattle well. Throughout India, Hindus revere these humped and dewlapped animals (*Bos indicus*, known to Westerners as zebu cattle) and refrain from harming them. People love their cattle, give them pet names, feed them special foods, adorn them for festivals, and worship them in rituals. The finest feasts include dishes made with milk and ghee (clarified butter), cooked over fires fueled by cakes of dried cow dung. For observant Hindus, eating beef is anathema, much as eating dog meat is to most Europeans and North Americans. However, by consuming a few drops of a mixture of the five products of the cow—milk, curd (yogurt), ghee, urine, and dung—ritual purity can be enhanced. And for rituals in the home, cow-dung paste is applied to a small area of the floor to purify a sacred space before the deities are invited to provide their blessings.

To Western observers, this reverence for cows may seem illogical. Why should McDonald's have to serve mutton burgers in India, when beef burgers sell by the billions elsewhere? Why are those scrawny creatures allowed to roam city streets and impede trucks, cars, and motorcycles? As milk producers, they can hardly compete with Wisconsin's hefty beasts. And think about all that beefsteak going to waste. Meanwhile, environmentalists ponder whether or not India's 200 million cattle—one-quarter of the world population—cause environmental degradation through overgrazing.

The place of the sacred cow in Indian culture and ecology has been intensely debated for decades among social scientists and animal husbandry experts. Some argue that Hindu practices regarding cattle are largely irrational and have led to excessive numbers of animals. Anthropologist Marvin Harris has strongly challenged this view, demonstrating that religious prohibitions against killing and eating cattle are of crucial material benefit in India. Such taboos, he points out, help preserve essential draft and milk animals, not only in times of plenty but also in times of famine (see *Cows, Pigs, Wars, and Witches: The Riddles of Culture*, Vintage Books, 1990).

Zebu cattle often appear scrawny, but these animals are extremely disease-resistant and hardy. In harsh conditions, they can survive on surprisingly little, including garbage and scrub vegetation. When fodder is more plentiful, they regain their robust condition, pulling the plows so necessary to feeding India's multitudes.

Cattle have been important to South Asians since prehistoric times. Humped cattle appear with other animals in hunting scenes on the walls of central Indian rock-shelters, probably painted in the Late Stone Age. Cattle bones at a few archaeological sites in Pakistan and central India suggest the keeping and possible domestication of cattle more than seven thousand years ago. The great Indus valley civilization (sometimes called the Harappan culture), which flourished from approximately 2600 to 1900 B.C. in an area now part of both India and Pakistan, depended heavily on domesticated animals—predominantly zebu cattle—as well as on wheat and barley. Indus valley farmers and traders yoked cattle to plows and carts and transported cargo in long caravans of pack oxen. Carved stone seals from that time prominently feature beautiful images of sacred bulls—precursors to today's widely found statues of Nandi, the bull ridden by the God Shiva.

The debate on the Indian cow remains lively. Recent research by anthropologist Carol Henderson and others suggests that Hindu attitudes and fluctuating cattle demographics reflect complex interactions between ideology, ecology, politics, population levels, and land usage rights (see "The Great Cow Explosion in Rajasthan" by Carol Henderson, in *Advances in Historical Ecology,* edited by William L. Balee; Columbia University Press, 1998). Today, as in past millennia, Indian cattle continue to provide milk, as well as cow dung for fertilizer and cooking fuel (in the form of the traditional dried cakes or, increasingly, as bio-gas generated from composted dung). Even in a nation that is building nuclear capability, cattle remain a crucial source of power for drawing plows and carts. And as the animals browse on crowded city streets, their ability to recycle garbage is phenomenal.

Although Hindu ideology is uncompromising, Indians are practical people. Cattle population figures vary according to local historical and ecological conditions, hinting at a quiet culling. Even as stray dogs in the United States somehow disappear, unwanted Indian cattle also vanish. Some are allowed to roam free until they die naturally, their meat consumed by dogs and vultures and their hides claimed by low-status Hindu leatherworkers. Other surplus cattle are sold to Muslim traders, who are not averse to slaughtering them. Some Indian Muslims and Christians and a few Hindus, Sikhs, and Parsis occasionally eat beef.

As India's population grows, more families need animals. At the same time, more tractors and trucks are being purchased by those who can afford them, and many farmers are giving up their bullocks. Pasture lands are shrinking as irrigated agriculture takes over previously uncultivated areas, making it harder to maintain large animals. In cities, too, the situation continues to evolve. To keep traffic flowing smoothly, cattle have been banished from the main streets of Mumbai (formerly Bombay). In New Delhi, home of politicians sensitive to conservative backlash, municipal cow catchers gently kidnap stray cattle from downtown areas to save them from traffic accidents and from killing themselves by eating plastic bags. The revered bovines are then delivered to a comfortable suburban refuge to have out their days.

Thirty years have passed since Sidha Singh was sentenced for cow murder. On a recent visit to his village of Nimkhera, I met Hindu farmers proud of their new prosperity, gained from Green Revolution crops, chemical fertilizers, and electric- or diesel-pump-powered irrigation. Several local farmers had purchased tractors with which to plow their fields, worked until recently by teams of oxen. The farmers informed me that they had increased profits by reducing the number of cattle they owned. In Nimkhera and other settlements throughout India, prosperous farmers and dairymen now increasingly favor water buffalo over zebu cattle as milk animals. Buffaloes do cost more to purchase and maintain, but they yield greater quantities of richer milk—and greater profits.

I learned that it took Sidha Singh nearly a decade to save up enough to pay his fine and feast hundreds of his neighbors. He had also succeeded in arranging proper marriages for his son and daughter. I noted that his cattle seemed healthy and that their horns sparkled with tinsel, remnants of their Diwali holiday decorations. But when Sidha Singh's name happened to come up in conversation with a group of women, one of them turned to me. "You remember him," she said. "He was the one who murdered his calf."

Doranne Jacobson ("A Reverence for Cows") has conducted research in India for the past thirty years. An anthropologist, writer, photographer, and lecturer, Jacobson, left, lives in Springfield, Illinois. She is the author-photographer of *India, Land of Dreams and Fantasy* (W. H. Smith, 1992) and coauthor, with Susan S. Wadley, of *Women in India: Two Perspectives* (South Asia Books, 4th ed., 1999). Lori Grinker, a New York City-based photographer with Contact Press Images, has traveled the Indian subcontinent to record the many ways cattle are celebrated and honored there. She collaborated with writer Diana Bletter on *The Invisible Thread: A Portrait of Jewish American Women* (The Jewish Publication Society, 1990). Grinker won the 1998 W. Eugene Smith Fellowship Grant for her project documenting veterans of war. Her previous work for *Natural History* includes stories on a blind women's orchestra in Cairo (November 1995) and on Jamaa el-Fna, the great public square in Marrakech (May 1996).

CRITICAL THINKING QUESTIONS

1. What was Sidha Singh convicted of by the Council of Village Elders? What were the circumstances behind the "crime"?
2. What impact did Sidha Singh's conviction have on his life and social standing in his village?
3. How is Indian reverence for cattle expressed in behavior and attitudes toward them?
4. What evidence is there for the antiquity of the importance of cattle in Indian culture?
5. Many Westerners see Indian cow reverence as largely irrational and ecologically unsound. What are the practical reasons that anthropologists like Marvin Harris discuss which make the cow important to the functioning of Indian society?

Be Holy for I Am Holy: Food, Politics, and the Teaching of Judaism[1]

Jay M. Eidelman

Abstract *Food is an important teaching tool in the study of religion because it is a common cross-cultural element. This essay examines the author's experience teaching a course on the place of food in Jewish ritual and culture. The essay then examines two historical incidents in which challenges to Jewish communal authority centered around the issue of kosher slaughter.*

INTRODUCTION

In a particularly funny vignette from the film *Hannah and her Sisters,* a neurotic Woody Allen, playing his standard nebbish, decides he wants to convert to Christianity and goes out for supplies. He returns with a large paper shopping bag and proceeds to remove a variety of "Christian" icons including a rosary, a photograph of Pope John Paul II, a loaf of "Wonderbread" and a jar of mayonnaise (Allen, 1986). The audience watching *Hannah and her Sisters* recognizes the humor in this scene because they understand that on some level Jews and non-Jews eat differently. This is true even in the case of non-observant Jews like the character portrayed by Woody Allen. This scene draws on several classics of Jewish humor most notably, Lenny Bruce's famous routine "Jewish and *Goyish*" (gentile) in which the world is divided into two camps. According to this taxonomy, all things hip and cosmopolitan are Jewish, while all things bland and staid are *goyish.* As Bruce points out, "evaporated milk is *goyish* even if the Jews invented it" (Bruce, 1981).

What is clear from both jokes is that food and eating are important to Jewish culture, but are they important to Jewish studies? Well, the answer is of course yes. More importantly, however, food provides a very useful teaching tool for introducing students of various backgrounds to Judaic studies. Since all people eat and food is both a requirement for survival and a source of pleasure, the study of Jewish food laws and traditions offers students a way to relate to the material on a very personal level. I discovered this about a year ago when I taught a course at Hobart & William Smith Colleges entitled "Kitchen Judaism: Food and Jewish Ritual."[2] I will briefly discuss my experience teaching that course and then I am going to narrow the focus and look at one particular aspect of Jewish foodways—the laws of kosher slaughter.

As the title implies, this course examined the place of ritual in Judaism through discussions of Jewish food customs from their biblical beginnings to modern times, special emphasis was paid to contemporary Jewish society. The course considered several topics including dietary laws, holiday observance, and a variety of rites-of-passage. Looking at Judaism's approach to dining and food traditions offered a relatively unexplored path to understanding Jewish social and religious development. The course assumed no prior knowledge of Jewish history, but students were required to have taken at least one Religious Studies course. Most of the students in the course were not Jewish, but many had taken other Judaic studies courses. In some cases students were quite knowledgeable about Jewish theology, but very few could connect this knowledge to issues of Jewish religious practice. By looking at the interaction of Jewish thought and practice and seeing how each influence the other, students were better able to understand the ongoing development of Judaism as a religious and

Source: Reprinted from *Journal of Ritual Studies* (2000), Department of Anthropology, University of Pittsburgh.

cultural system. For at its core traditional Judaism truly believes that you are what you eat, or perhaps more accurately, how you eat.[3]

In traditional Judaism all human action is ritualized through *halakhah*, "Jewish law." Actions are *asur* and *mutar*, "permitted and forbidden," *chayav* and *patur*, "obligated and not obligated," or *kadosh* and *hol*, "sacred and profane." Piety is not measured in terms of belief but in terms of ritual action. As Mary Douglas has demonstrated, this ordering of the universe prepares the individual and the community to receive God's holiness and to prosper (1996). Jewish beliefs are made concrete through daily, weekly, and yearly cycles of *mitsvot*, "commandments," actions like prayer, study, bathing and eating. Furthermore, as Susan Starr Sered has shown, this focus on action opens Judaism, a religion whose ritual life is dominated by males, to women, who, in their role as keepers of the household, sanctify their families through food preparation (1996). Men's prayer and study may be important but it is women's actions that create holiness in Jewish life.[4]

Indeed, understanding the centrality of *mitsvot* in Judaism, particularly commandments concerning food, explains a great deal about a great many things ranging from the basic differences between Judaism and Christianity to why the Passover *seder* continues to be the one Jewish observance that commands overwhelming popularity. If we turn now to the practice of kosher animal slaughter we can see how ritual issues can have a much broader impact.[5]

KOSHER SLAUGHTER

Central to the Jewish dietary laws are the prohibitions against mixing dairy and meat, but equally important are the laws indicating which animals are permissible as food and how they are to be prepared. Kosher slaughter or *shehita* refers to the method of dispatching animals for human consumption as developed by rabbinic Judaism. It prescribes the appropriate manner in which permitted animals must be killed and inspected to determine whether they are kosher or *nevelah-terefah*, "carrion." The laws concerning which animals are permitted are based on lists enumerated in Leviticus 11 and Deuteronomy 14. According to rabbinic interpretation of these lists, permitted animals include mammals that have cloven hooves and chew their cud, as well as chickens, turkeys, ducks, geese, pigeons, and pheasants according to some authorities. Fish with both fins and scales are also permitted, while reptiles and insects, with the exception of four types of locusts, are forbidden. *Shehita* is only required for mammals and poultry. This consists of a person skilled in the laws of slaughter and animal physiology cutting cleanly through the windpipe and esophagus in cattle and one of the two in fowl. To do this the *shochet* "slaughterer" used a special knife. The rationale behind *shehita* is the concept of *tsa'ar ba'alei hayim* or "prevention of cruelty to animals."[6] As Rabbi Moses Maimonides, the 12th century physician, philosopher, and sage, noted in his *Guide to the Perplexed*:

> The commandment concerning the killing of animals is necessary because the natural food of man consists of vegetables and the flesh of animals; the best meat is that of animals permitted to be used as food [in the Torah]. No doctor has any doubts of this. Since, therefore, the desire of procuring good food necessitates the slaying of animals, the law enjoins that the death of the animal should be easiest. We are not permitted to torment the animal by cutting the throat in a clumsy manner, by poleaxing, or by cutting off a limb whilst the animal is alive. (Maimonides 1956:3:48; Klein 1979:308)

Another suggestion concerning the purpose of *shehita* hints at a reluctance to allow the eating of meat altogether. In Genesis 1:29, God only provides vegetation for food: "Behold I have given you every herb bearing seed which is upon the face of all the earth, and every tree on which is fruit yielding seed; to you it shall be for food." But after the flood the list of permitted foods grows: "Every moving thing that lives shall be food for you; and just as I gave you the green plants I give you everything. Only, you shall not eat flesh with its life, that is its blood" (Genesis 9:3–5).

Prohibitions against consumption of blood— an animal's life force—are further elaborated in Deuteronomy 17:20 and Leviticus 17:13 where animal blood is connected to atonement sacrifices at the temple in Jerusalem. Blood from animals used specifically for food must be spilled on the ground and covered with dust. "The permission to eat meat was thus a compromise," notes 20th century scholar Rabbi Isaac Klein. The idea being that after the flood, once God concedes human carnality, the eating of meat "should, at least, be controlled by refraining from eating certain parts of the animal, especially the blood, and by special regulations governing the preparation of the meat" (Klein 1979:309). In other words, Israelite religion demanded that part of every animal dispatched for food be reserved as a sacrifice to God. Removing the blood also prevented the transgression of eating "flesh with its life."

Whatever their reasons, Jewish dietary restrictions and the rules of *shehita* have two immediate results. They provide a method of sanctification for God's people Israel as mentioned in Leviticus 11:44 "I am the Lord your God; sanctify yourselves and be holy; for I am holy." Adherence to the laws of *kashrut* defines the Jewish community, tying Jews to one another and deterring defection. In this sense control of the supervision of the dietary laws is essential to communal authority. It is not unusual, therefore, that challenges to that authority often involve challenges to *shehita*. I am going to present two such challenges: Hasidism—the 18th-century Jewish pietistic movement—and a 19th-century American incident I came across in my own research.

HASIDISM

Hasidism developed in mid 18th-century Poland around the mystic and healer Israel ben Eliezer *Ba'al Shem Tov* also known as the Besht. A *ba'al shem tov* (literally master of the good name) is a wonderworker or psychic healer and Israel ben Eliezer became the *ba'al shem tov* par excellence. The movement that developed around him had some of its roots in the 16th-century kabbalistic thought of Isaac Luria. Lurianic Kabbalah placed greater emphasis on individual action in the process of messianic redemption than previous kabbalistic schools. Another factor in the development of Hasidism was the contraction of power within the Polish Jewish community to a smaller number of individuals and families. It

was this combination of piety and perceived corruption that gave rise to the Hasidic movement which initially rejected traditional learning as the most profound expression of piety. Instead, Hasidism substituted personal devotion and intercession of charismatic leaders (the *tzaddik*) in their stead. In relation to *shehita*, Hasidim and their opponents literally came to blows over the method that should be followed.[7]

Between 1770 and 1790 great debate erupted over the Hasidic use of a brightly polished *shehita* knife. Rabbi Shneur Zalman of Liady (1747–1812) explained: "most *shohtim* 'slaughterers' at present employ a blunt and heavy knife. They are obliged to sharpen it much in order to eliminate every knick from the cutting edge. Even the most skilled *shohtim* do not obtain satisfactory results for it is difficult to produce a flawless edge on a dull knife. This decision of ours should not be taken to reflect upon the *kashrut* of meat slaughtered by those who use the heavier knife." The Jewish authorities resented this intrusion into what they saw as their exclusive domain and feared that the hasidic sect was being spread by hasidic *shohtim* and other minor officials. Worried about tax revenues gained through *shehita* and concerned about spreading transgression, the authorities countered Hasidic opinion with the judgement of Egyptian rabbi David Ibn Zimra (1479–1589) who warned against the use of a knife too thin to hold a sharp edge through a whole day. The Hasidim noted that they were aware of the opinion of Rabbi Ibn Zimra but preferred their blades nonetheless (both quoted in Berman 1941:78).

As a result of the refusal to comply, on the 20th of the Hebrew month *Sivan*, 1772, authorities in Vilna placed a ban of excommunication on Hasidic *shehita* that forbade Jews to eat meat slaughtered in the Hasidic manner. In at least one town the ban was extended. Anyone in the Jewish community of Zelve who ate meat slaughtered in Hasidic fashion would not be counted in a prayer quorum, transact business with other Jews, be lodged by them, marry with them, or be buried in Jewish cemeteries (Berman 1941:79).

Hasidic defiance was rightly seen as an effort to break communal authority. But it was the *herem* "ban" imposed by the authorities that divided Polish Jewish society into two antagonistic factions. In addition to sociopolitical factors, more recent scholarship has pointed to spiritual reasons for the new slaughter method. Namely, *gilgul,* "metempsychosis," or the transmigration of souls, especially those of sinners into animate and inanimate objects. Knives had to be especially sharp when dispatching an animal in order to avoid the possibility of hindering the *gilgul* of a human soul. If the blade were too dull the soul might suffer the "injury" of being reincarnated into another base form. If, on the other hand, the knife was keen enough to effect a perfect slaughter, then the soul had a chance to be redeemed (Wilensky 1991:256–257).

AMERICA

In North America things were very different. There were no rabbis here until the 1840s. Communal authority rested in the governing boards of synagogues. Each Jewish community in early 19th-century North America had one congregation that provided for all the ritual and spiritual needs of the Jews resident in that locale. In the wake of the American Revolution and the ratification of the Constitution, American synagogues went through a process of revising their system of governance in keeping with the new political ideology of the United States. Many positions in the synagogue that had once been appointed by the ruling board were now elected by the membership. Membership was also extended to a wider group of male residents (Eidelman, 1997:122–170).[8]

As for *shehita,* this was always a problem in early America since the butchers who supplied the meat were often Christians who sold both kosher and non-kosher products. There was always the temptation to affix seals certifying *kashrut* on non-kosher meat. In 1803, a New York butcher named Caleb Vandenberg was so accused and convicted. As a result, the City Common Council revoked his license. Vandenberg subsequently had help from the Congregation Shearith Israel—New York City's only synagogue at the time—getting his license reinstated. In that same year, a man named Jacob Abrahams was elected *shohet,* a position Congregation Shearith Israel always had trouble

filling because of the lack of qualified individuals. All went well until 1811 when serious allegations arose against Abrahams (de Sola Pool 1955:241).[9]

After denying complaints that he had not performed his duties properly, in July of 1811 Abrahams was accused by congregants Jacob Hart and Napthali Philips of various improprieties including eating food that was not kosher. Abrahams was brought before the congregation and confirmed by a majority of the 50 congregants who had gathered to hear the case. He was later reelected *shohet* with only one dissenting vote. This did not put an end to the disquiet surrounding him and the position of *shohet.* The congregation split into two factions, with Abrahams' supporters on one side, and the congregation's trustees and their supporters on the other. The *shohet's* once unanimous support eroded to the point that in 1813 his contract with Shearith Israel was not renewed. Abrahams then set himself up as an independent, thinking that the business provided him by his faction would yield an adequate income (de Sola Pool 1955:242).

Fearing that the loss of central control over *shehita* would result in impropriety, Congregation Shearith Israel appealed to the City of New York to uphold its authority as the sole licensor of kosher slaughterers. The City granted the request on February 1, 1813, but congregational records indicate that the opposing faction sought an injunction against the city ordinance on the grounds that it was "an encroachment on [their] religious rights and a restriction on those general privileges to which [they] were entitled." The opposition was accused by congregational authorities of being "wicked and irreligious" and of sullying the reputation of the Jewish community. On February 8th, the City Council met to hear both sides. The Council's vote split down the middle but the presiding officer broke the tie in favor of the Abrahams' faction. From that day forward Shearith Israel no longer had complete control over *shehita* in New York City (de Sola Pool, 1955:243–244).

Having gained the right to elect *shohtim* in Shearith Israel's 1805 constitution, Jacob Abrahams' supporters were not about to let congregational authorities curtail or abrogate this privilege through the use of the City Council. They also refused to accept the notion that the Congregation's collective rights outweighed their rights as individuals. Matters were made worse in 1824 when a split developed in the congregation and the offshoot synagogue hired their own *shohet*.[10]

What is interesting about these episodes—and perhaps what can serve as my conclusion—is that these controversies were as much political events as conflicts over ritual and theology. In our modern, secular society we tend to separate the religious from the practical so that most of us fail to recognize the important role religious traditions play in everyday life. We need only look around the globe to see the political ramifications of religious belief, but when we look closer to home we lose sight of the way religion influences us day-to-day. Focusing on food highlights the interplay between ideology and practice, and, in so doing, allows students to grasp the larger picture. Whether they were familiar with Jewish tradition or not, every student in my class was able to relate to the material because they could draw on their own experience. The unfamiliar was made familiar and simple curiosities became departure points for deeper study.

Dr. Jay M. Eidelman is an historian at the Museum of Jewish Heritage—A Living Memorial to the Holocaust in New York City. He is the curator most recently of Yiddish on Stage: Posters and Artifacts from the World of Yiddish Theater (with Ellen Smith) and France Divided: Impassioned Responses to the Dreyfus Scandal. Originally from Montreal, Canada, he taught at Hobart and William Smith Colleges before coming to the Museum.

Notes

1. I want to thank my colleagues in the Department of Religious Studies at Hobart and William Smith Colleges and the students who participated in the course "Kitchen Judaism: Food in Jewish Ritual" for their encouragement and insight. I also wish to thank my co-contributors Professors Mary MacDonald, James-Henry Holland, and Philip Arnold.
2. I taught at Hobart and William Smith Colleges during the 1997–1998 academic year.
3. The course took its name from the book *The Wonders of America: Reinventing Jewish Culture, 1880–1950* (Joselit, 1994). The class had 14 students, two of whom were Jewish. It met in the Colleges' guesthouse, which had kitchen facilities, and I was able to incorporate actual cooking sessions into the curriculum.
4. For a general discussion of *halakhah*, see "Halakha," *Encyclopaedia Judaica* (1972:7:1156–1166).
5. For discussions of the continuing importance of food in Jewish ethnic self-definition, see Joselit (1994:171–263).
6. For an overview of the Jewish dietary laws regarding *shehita*, see Klein (1979:302–378); "Shehita," *Encyclopaedia Judaica* (1972:14:1337–1344).

7. For a discussion of the origins of Hasidism, see Dinur (1991). On the Ba'al Shem Tov, see Rosman (1996). On Lurianic Kabbalah, see Scholem (1961:244–286). On ritual conflicts between Hasidim and their opponents, see Wilensky (1991).
8. For the early history of Jewish life in North America, see Marcus (1989).
9. Hyman Grinstein reports that Shearith Israel was already divided over other matters but he does not list any details (Grinstein, 1947:302).
10. On *kashrut* and communal authority in early New York City, see also Gastwirt (1974:21–25).

References

Allen, Woody. 1986. *Hannah and Her Sisters,* Orion Pictures.

Berman, Jeremiah J. 1941. *Shehitah: A Study in the Cultural and Social Life of the Jewish People,* New York: Bloch Publishing Co.

Bruce, Lenny. 1981. "Jewish and Goyish" in *The Big Book of Jewish Humor,* 60, New York: Harper and Row. William Novak & Moshe Waldoks (eds).

de Sola Pool, David & Tamar de Sola Pool. 1955. *An Old Faith in the New World: Portrait of Shearith Israel, 1654–1954,* New York: Columbia University Press.

Dinur, Benzion. 1991. "The Origins of Hasidism and Its Social and Messianic Foundations" reprinted in *Essential Papers in Hasidism,* 86–208, New York: New York University Press. Gershom D. Hundert (ed.).

Douglas, Mary. 1996. *Purity and Danger,* New York: Routledge.

Eidelman, Jay M. 1997. In the Wilds of America: The Early Republican Origins of American Judaism, 1790–1830, Ph.D. Diss., Yale University.

Encyclopaedia Judaica. 1972. Jerusalem: Keter Publishing Jerusalem, Ltd.

Gastwirt, Harold P. 1974. *Fraud, Corruption, and Holiness: The Controversy Over Supervision of Jewish Dietary Practice in New York City, 1881–1974,* Port Washington, NY: Kenikat Press National University Publications.

Grinstein, Hyman. 1947. *Rise of the Jewish Community of New York, 1654–1860,* Philadelphia: Jewish Publication Society of America.

Joselit, Jenna Weissman. 1994. *The Wonders of America: Reinventing Jewish Culture, 1880–1950,* New York: Hill and Wang.

Klein, Rabbi Isaac. 1979. *A Guide to Jewish Religious Practice,* New York: Jewish Theological Seminary of America.

Maimonides, Rabbi Moses. 1956. *The Guide for the Perplexed,* New York: Dover Publications. M. Friedlander (trans.).

Marcus, Jacob R. 1989. *United States Jewry, 1776–1985,* vol. 1, Detroit: Wayne State University Press.

Rosman, Murray Jay. 1996. *Founder of Hasidism: A Quest for the Historical Ba'al Shem Tov,* Berkeley: University of California Press.

Scholem, Gershom. 1961. *Major Trends in Jewish Mysticism,* New York: Schocken Books.

Sered, Susan Starr. 1996. *Women as Ritual Experts: The Religious Lives of Elderly Jewish Women in Jerusalem,* New York: Oxford University Press.

Wilensky, Mordecai L. 1991. "Hasidic-Mitnaggedic Polemics in the Jewish Communities of Eastern Europe: The Hostile Phase" in *Essential Papers in Hasidism,* 244–271, New York: New York University Press. Gershom D. Hundert (ed.).

CRITICAL THINKING QUESTIONS

1. How does Judaism use ritual to define and direct human life?
2. Where are the Jewish laws regarding permitted and nonpermitted animals found? What are some of these rules?
3. How are *shehita* (ritual slaughter) and the laws concerning permitted animals related?
4. What is Hasidism? How did disputes over *shehita* knives result in a break between Hasidism and Orthodox Jews in Poland?
5. How does this dispute, and a similar one in America, highlight the influence of religion on people's day-today lives?

The Funeral Rite of Passage: An American Neo-Pagan Example

Benjamin C. Wilreker

Although most Americans conceive of death as a precise point in time, death is actually a process without an objective beginning or end, culturally constrained through ritual at a variety of different points in time. Funerals are rites of passage bracketed by rites of death on one end and funeral and burial rituals on the other separated by a period of liminality. In this article I will look at Americans' increasing ability to choose the point of death and the decreasing significance of the period of liminality as a consequence of medical technology and the increasing professionalism of the funeral industry. This decrease in the period of liminality and resulting compression of the process of the funerary rite of passage restricts the social locations within which mourners may express their grief during this cycle. American Neo-Pagan funerary practices provide a counterpoint to the American Civil funeral and highlight an alternative rite of passage that responds to these changes which the American civil tradition has, in large part, not yet fully addressed.

THEORETICAL PERSPECTIVES ON DEATH

There is a striking lack of consistency in the funeral literature about what the various parts of the funeral ritual should be called. For the sake of clarity, I will use the following terms to describe the structure of the cycle: (1) *death ritual* refers to the bedside events when a person dies attended in a hospital, hospice, or at home; (2) *liminality* refers to events between the death ritual and funeral ritual; (3) *funeral ritual* refers to events in a funeral home or religious establishment leading up to disposal of the remains; (4) *burial ritual*

refers to the ritual disposal of human remains, and (5) *funeral cycle* refers to items 1–4 as a collective whole.

The first serious taxonomy of funeral ritual was written by the Sociologist Arnold van Gennep, in *Les rites de passage* (1908). Van Gennep sought to model the funeral rite of passage and describe the functions it served in society. In its most basic form a rite of passage contains five steps:

1. *The old social state.* The old social state is the publicly recognized identity of an individual prior to undergoing the rite of passage.
2. *Rite of separation.* The rite of separation is a collective ritual, at a discrete point in time, which removes an initiate from the old social state.
3. *Liminality.* Following the rite of separation, the individual undergoing the rite of passage, in theory, has no social identity; they are betwixt and between, neither a member of the social identity that they have left behind, nor part of the one that they will enter.
4. *Rite of incorporation.* The period of liminality is terminated by a rite of incorporation, at a discrete point of time, which incorporates the individual into his new social state.
5. *New social state.* The new social state is the new, publicly identifiable social identity that the person enters having resolved the rite of passage.

Current scholarship has developed a distinction between a rite of passage and a rite of intensification. A rite of passage is a community ritual used to change the identities of particular *individuals*. This is in contrast to "rites of intensification" that seek to change *collective identity* (Chapple and Coon; 1942). The rite of passage

Source: Used with permission by the author, Benjamin Wilreker, Anthropology Instructor, Dept. of Human Behavior, College of Southern Nevada.

functions to reintegrate people into a new identity with altered or completely new linkages of obligations and responsibilities, while the rite of intensification reinforces community solidarity within a liminal space. The funerary cycle simultaneously changes both the deceased's identity and the identities of particular survivors. Surviving wives become widows, surviving husbands become widowers, and the deceased transitions between "alive" and "dead." A funeral is has elements of a right of intensification as well; it helps the survivors as a collective to reaffirm the ties of family and community so that each individual's rite of passage leads them to strengthen and reorganize their identities to account for the absence of the deceased.

For Americans, death is the point where "culture" becomes "nature" where "I" becomes "it." The rite of passage functions to mediate this change in social identity for both the deceased and the living. Advanced medical technology, which can prolong the death process, demands a reevaluation of theoretical approaches to funerary ritual as a rite of passage. Previous work primarily discussed the role of the funeral ritual. The tacit assumption is that what comes before the funeral ritual (i.e., death) is so obvious and straightforward that it requires little elaboration. Research in the United States, (Sudnow 1967; Lock 2002) has clearly shown that the point of death—even in biological terms—is not nearly so cut and dried as previously assumed. Sudnow and Lock both reaffirm Van Gennep's conclusion that death is a process, with no objective beginning or end, constrained through ritual at a variety of locations. With the advent of modern medical technology, this process has been altered so that the process of separation has increased in importance at the expense of the period of liminality.

TECHNOLOGICAL IMPACT ON THE LOCUS AND PROCESS OF DEATH

The rise of life-saving technology raises questions about traditional assumptions of the point of death. Lock (2002), for example, describes three different loci of death: (1) *biological death*, when a human body ceases to function as an integrated unit; (2) *personal death*, when the higher brain exhibits no coordinated electrical activity; and (3) *social death*, when other people do not interact with an individual as if they were an agent. A century ago, prior to the advent of modern medicine, there was no effective means to distinguish between personal and biological death. Lock points out that modern medical technology has had the effect of decoupling death of the personality from death of the body. A person who has suffered personal death may be kept alive, in rare cases indefinitely, through medical intervention: A living corpse.

A biologically and personally living human is in a position to actively assert that they are either "living" or "dead." However, a person who is either personally or biologically dead may have the status of "living" or "dead" applied to them by others, regardless of the objective truth. The rise of modern medical technology has increased the likelihood of a person becoming socially dead while they remain biologically alive serving to blur the boundary between the traditional stages of separation and liminality.

AN EXAMPLE OF A FUNERAL RITUAL IN AN AMERICAN NEO-PAGAN COMMUNITY

American Neo-Paganism was founded in Britain in the 1930s and imported to America in the 1960s. The central beliefs of the movement include the recognition of the existence of many gods; the deification of the feminine and the natural world; an orientation towards reconstructing pre-Christian European beliefs; and a belief in and practice of ritual magic.

Although Neo-Paganism has been exported to the entire English-speaking world, the American branch of the movement is by far the largest, probably numbering over 200,000 individuals (Berger 1999). Nearly every "essential" theological tract written to a Neo-Pagan audience in the past twenty years has been written by an author living in the United States or Canada. Furthermore, all of the large-scale new sects within the movement, such as Unitarian Universalist Pagans (Berger 2003), Neo-Shamans (York 2003), Druidic and Norse Reconstructionists (Berger 2003), and Goddess Worshippers (Salomonsen 1997; Berger 2003), have been founded by Americans or outsiders transplanted to the United States, within the geographical confines of the United States, and situated within an American socio-political context. Both British history and globalization aside, contemporary Neo-Paganism is an American religion.

During the course of my research, I studied seven American Neo-Pagan churches, normally called *covens*. I will focus on a single coven, Mountain Moon Circle or MMC, located in Groen, Pennsylvania. MMC is a medium-sized eclectic Wiccan coven, with about 25 full members and a congregation of just over a hundred. A typical worship service draws about sixty people. As members of a new religious movement, American Neo-Pagans are for the first time dealing with death in their midst. I was present as an MMC member, Jack Bowman, lost his fight with cancer and passed into the Summerland. In the following pages I will provide an ethnographic example of how Jack's coven brothers and sisters used a rite of passage to mediate Jack's transition between "life" and "death."

A RITE OF SEPARATION: AN AMERICAN NEO-PAGAN DEATH RITUAL

On the afternoon of March 17th 2004, Jack was rushed to the hospital due to renal failure. Jack was located in the intensive care unit and "hooked up" as Jack's wife May put it, "to all these crazy machines." By the morning of March 18th, Jack was largely paralyzed. He was in the hospital bed on a ventilator, his eyes half-open because voluntary muscle control of his eyelids had failed. The children arrived as quickly as they were able. Coven members trickled in, and soon Jack and May's natal family members began to arrive, including Jack's elderly mother. By ten thirty, there were thirty people jammed into the little room. May describes the scene:

Well, he knew we were there. And I know he knew because he was hooked up to all these crazy machines. And every now and then, one of these machines would emit

this strange sound. . . . And I couldn't figure out why the heck this stupid thing was beeping because it didn't seem to have a regular pattern to it. . . . Finally, after a while a nurse came in to check on him, and I asked her what the machine was and what it's doing, and she said "that monitors his pulse rate." And I said, "how come that's making these random beepings?" And she said, "Oh, he's reacting to what's happening around him." And I said, "You're kidding. If I say something to him, that's what makes the beep?" And she says, "Yeah. He can understand what you're saying and his body is registering his awareness. . . . We were all around the bed, and then people just started pouring in, and pouring in. . . . And every person who came in, came over and held [Jack's] hand, and said, "It's me Jack, Natalie's here." "It's me Jack, Anne's here." "It's me, Jack." You know, everybody would come over and say their name and let him know that they were there for him. And he would beep.

This continuity of awareness is the common feature of Neo-Pagan responses to Jack's death. The Neo-Pagan survivors perceived that Jack was communicating to them that he remained a social agent; that he remained alive. They were not attending to witness a *death*, they were attending to witness a *departure*. Natalie said "I had a sense of him expanding—being *more* than confined to his body." The American civil identity suggests that the individual agent dies when death is pronounced; within the American Neo-Pagan view, the ego retains its agency, although the form that agency may take must be altered due to the fact of biological death.

Around eleven o'clock, based on the doctor's advice, May made the decision to remove life support. This decision was particularly hard on May because she had to actively choose to let Jack's body die. The American civil religion schema, which introduced a fear that Jack's ego would be irrevocably removed from the world of the living, was placed into direct conflict with the American Neo-Pagan schema which said Jack would continue to experience and interact with the world of the living. After the medical apparati had been removed, May returned to Jack's side, and took his hand:

> I finally accepted that he wasn't coming home. I let him go. I told him he didn't have to fight any more, and I was ok, we would be all right. And he couldn't talk, and he couldn't move . . . he had no muscular control at all. But I know he heard me because I saw a tear come down. And I told him to go dance with the Lady and go shake hands with the Lord and it was ok for him to go.

Once again, for May, the key feature was Jack's retention of agency, even to the end.

As Jack's family, friends, and Neo-Pagan community stood in vigil by his bedside, the Neo-Pagans contributed energy to his passage. Normally, energy is directed by pointing with one or both hands extended, with fingers either spread apart, palms outward; by extending both hands before the practitioner, palms outward, with thumbs and index fingers touching each other so as to form a triangle; by using an index finger or a ritual tool; or by making physical contact with the person to be given energy. May remembers seeing people with their fingers discretely extended in their laps, or forming a triangle. She said, "the place was swirling with energy." The purpose of committing all this energy was to facilitate Jack's transition; to give *him* the energy he needed to leave his body behind.

As Jack approached cardiopulmonary arrest, Jack's mother asked May if she could say the Lord's Prayer. Jack's mom was praying to *her God* for *Jack's reception and salvation* in Heaven, while the American Neo-Pagans around her were offering energy to *Jack* for *his journey* to the Summerland. This is a difference in kind, not quality. The American civil understanding is that the soul's final resting place is sequestered away from the living at the right hand of God, without direct agency. The American Neo-Pagan understands the soul to exist in a place identical to the choice of the ego and retaining agency. From the American Neo-Pagan perspective, Jack needed that energy in order that his soul would be able to fully experience, choose, and participate in its journey to the Summerland.

Jack's daughter Kussina, who sat on Jack's right as he lay in bed that morning, recalls that she felt bad that there was no pentacle visible in the room. She took off her Goddess necklace, which is surmounted by a pentacle, and clasped it between Jack's right hand and hers. She explains:

> I always wore it. I never took it off, because I needed some kind of strength. I needed Goddess to be with me all the time. I thought he deserved a pentacle somewhere, and he hadn't told my grandparents that he was Pagan, and he always wanted to, but he hadn't, and there was no pentacle in the room with him, so I took off my necklace and let him hold it. I thought he should have that, you know?

The attending physician noted Jack's death from renal failure at 11:35 a.m. on March 18th, 2004 at the age of 53.

As it was for Jack, in many cases the American Civil death ritual occurs when an expected death occurs in the hospital. First the family is notified of the impending death and travels to the hospital to await the physician's pronouncement of death. A discussion about organ donation may occur. As the chief mourner(s) the next of kin may be invited to make a decision to discontinue life support. A clergy member is often summoned. Prayers are said. The medical staff usually leaves the next-of-kin with the deceased as long as he or she wishes following the pronouncement of death. The spouse or parent is typically the last family member to leave the deceased's bedside. When the widow or next of kin has left the deceased's bedside to fill out the paperwork, the deceased has now also *socially* died and may be treated as such by hospital and funeral staff. This death ritual has been heavily impacted by changes in medical, communication, and transportation technology over the past half century. The end result of all this technology is that the death ritual is now heavily attended, where in the past it was not. The technology allowed May to *choose* the point of her husband's death. She waited to do so until the chief mourners had assembled, each having been notified by technological advances such as cell phones and the internet.

American Neo-Pagans specify a different social location for their dead than other participants in the American Civil Religion. In Jack's case, although both American Neo-Pagans and their American civil counterparts experienced the same death ritual, they interpreted the events of the rite of separation in systematically different ways. American civil participants experienced a "death;" physically and socially the deceased's ego had come to an end and was now journeying away from the world of men. American Neo-Pagan participants experienced an "expansion;" the deceased was "expanding" to become a part of this world, not traveling to another world. None the less, there is very strong social constraint to conform with the American civil death ritual to the greatest extent possible. Thus, the Neo-Pagan community has not developed a standard alternative ritual of death. Instead they have modified the conventional American civic ritual. Natalie, for example, describes Jack as "expanding." In essence, we see a multivocalic interpretation of death and the transition in the rite of incorporation that completes the rite of passage.

THE PERIOD OF LIMINALITY

Technology has significantly changed the rite of passage by shifting the duration and importance of segments of the process. Van Gennep noted that the traditional rite of separation was the least important and that of incorporation (burial) the most elaborate:

> "A study of the data . . . reveals that the rites of separation are few in number and very simple, while the transition rites have a duration and complexity sometimes so great that they must be granted a sort of autonomy. Furthermore, those funeral rites which incorporate the deceased into the world of the dead are most extensively elaborated and assigned the greatest importance." (Van Gennep 1908 [1960]: 146)

Now that technology gives the living much more control over the moment of death, the rite of separation is expanded elongating the grieving process.

The American civil funeral cycle is much shorter than the funeral cycles of some traditional societies. The formal process ends following the burial which may be as little as a week after the death of the deceased. There is strong social pressure for the bereaved to return to work within a given period of time. Employers normally allow three to five days of leave for bereavement, for example, and this bereavement leave is normally only offered to people who could conceivably fill the role of "chief mourner." In this very short period of time, there is a tremendous amount of work to be done by the next of kin. The deceased must be memorialized in a way consistent with his income, resources, and social capital. May was not only chief mourner of her husband; she was also hostess of a social event that included nearly a thousand people. Insurance companies had to be notified, and hospital bills paid. A funeral home had to be contracted. Distant friends and family had to be contacted, and bed and board had to be found for out of town guests. May had to select what her husband would wear at the service, and provide it to the funeral director. Memory boards had to be made. Certainly these activities are all *ritual activities.* However, they did not allow May time to grieve. The sale of labor in the urban marketplace has enforced an artificially short period of mourning. Furthermore, The professionalization of both the funeral and medical industries over the last century have had the effect of inserting a great deal of social obligation into a liminal period that would otherwise consist of reflection and mourning with immediate family, clergy, and close friends,

American Neo-Pagans have identified an alternate theology to explain the soul's repose during the period of liminality. For a Neo-Pagan, in the immediate period following death, the deceased's soul remains in the vicinity of the body, and then travels to contact important individuals in his or her life. Because there is no compulsory, formal theology in Neo-Paganism, there is little consistency between mourners concerning the location of the soul at any point of the process, or even the words that should be used to describe it. Most agree, however, that prior to the funeral ritual the soul is present in the world of people. The soul of the deceased during this liminal period may spontaneously contact the mourners directly and may be accessed through ritual means such as divination or channeling.

A RITE OF INCORPORATION—AN AMERICAN NEO-PAGAN FUNERAL

The funeral ritual portion of the funeral cycle serves two purposes: (1) incorporating the deceased into the afterlife, and (2) incorporating most mourners back into the world of the living. American Neo-Pagan funerals often occur in a funeral home. This seems to be the case because Neo-Pagans have few dedicated houses of worship, rather than as a consequence of theology. The participants normally take their seats in a circle. At a funeral home service there will be an altar in the center. At a graveside service, the open grave will be in the center. The celebrants sit in the circle with the mourners. The celebrants will begin the ritual by casting a sacred circle and calling quarters. A person tapped in advance will usually read a prepared eulogy. Members of the congregation will read eulogies, perform prayers, songs, or speak *ad lib* about the significance of their relationship with the deceased. The chief mourner may facilitate the service in conjunction with a clergy member or by himself, and usually addresses the community. There may be a cakes and wine ceremony similar to that in the Full Moon ceremony, a core ritual of Neo-Pagan worship. At the conclusion of the service, the clergy members will ritually close the circle.

Like most American dead, following autopsy, Jack's remains were handed over to the funeral director for transport to the funeral home and embalming. Jack was arterially embalmed, and placed on display as if he were sleeping, in a painted aluminum casket, wearing his best dark suit with a silk shirt and tie showing a scene from "starry night" that May had bought him on a recent trip to Paris. Over top of it all, he still wore the little herbal pouch that his friend Natalie made for him; she felt very touched that he was still wearing it. The casket lid was divided in two; the portion covering his feet was closed, while the portion covering his head and torso was open. His head was on a pillow, and the interior of the casket was lined with white satin.

Most funeral homes have large viewing rooms that can be subdivided and used simultaneously for smaller events. Because a large crowd was expected, Jack was set up in his casket in one of these rooms with the partition withdrawn. Most of the chairs had been folded up and leaned in stacks against the right hand wall (see Figure 1). The remaining chairs, about eighty, had been set in a large, oblong circle. More people than expected attended, and so more chairs were brought out in a series of second rows around the perimeter of the circle. Jack's casket was moved out and placed into the circle with the head facing to the left, towards English armchairs reserved for the chief mourners. The coven's altar was placed in the center of the circle. Jack had been dressed with his black ritual robe, and the cord that marked him as a member of the coven. His hands were folded across his unsheathed ritual dagger, as a knight with his sword on the tombs of a bygone age. Next to him was set out his hand-made wooden staff. When I asked May about how she decided to dress him, she was very explicit:

> Those were the tools that he made himself. He made his [dagger] and that was his magical tool, and his staff. He used that all the time. And he put hours and hours . . . of work into creating that staff and each part of that staff had meaning to him. Each one of the vines had meaning . . . the copper he . . . shod it with was used to conduct electricity and energy. And the wax that he used to polish it was a natural wax, it wasn't chemical. And the crystal that he put on top was held by a dragon's claw for power. And it was a . . . personal choice and he used that staff a lot. . . . It was the farewell ritual for him, and it was right for him to be in his ritual raiment. And to have his ritual tools with him. And for him to be part of the circle. Because when we made the circle, he was in it, he wasn't apart from the circle, he was a part of the circle.

Note that, in May's view, the deceased retains agency and thus is intentionally not sequestered from interaction. It was critically important that Jack continue to participate in the ritual community, and as such his remains were situated within the circle as if he were alive.

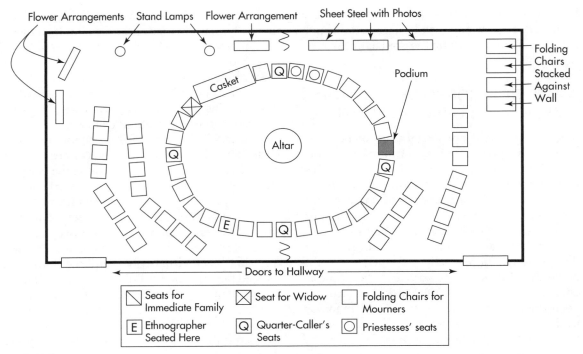

FIGURE 1

Alyssa and Sayward, clergy members and founding members of the coven, facilitated the service as priest and priestess at May's request. May says she had little to do with the arrangement of the service. She requested a favorite song, Bette Midler's (1989) *Wind Beneath My Wings*, and told the clergy members to come up with what they thought would be best. Neither clergy member had facilitated a funeral service in the past and Mountain Moon Circle does not have a standard liturgy to draw upon. The clergy members turned to other, outside organizations with which they were affiliated, in addition to a variety of internet Neo-Pagan resources, for guidance. Here we see a very important impact of technology on the process by which Neo-Pagans create ritual. Most Protestant denominations have well established mortuary theology to which any clergy member has easy access. Likewise the funeral industry specifies standards for the treatment of remains that are easily accessible to funeral professionals. Neo-Pagans, on the other hand, must actively create funeral ritual. Computer technology gives them access to information provided by far-flung Neo-Pagan communities in order to create a new ritual on short notice.

The service began when Jack's coven sister, Debbie, read a eulogy she had written. During this ritual, several reversals of pattern occurred that were intended to bring the practitioner partly into the underworld, where meeting the spirit of the dead would be possible. In a conventional Mountain Moon Circle circle building ritual, most ritual actions proceed clockwise around the circle. At Jack's funeral, the circle was created counterclockwise, or "widdershins." Following Debbie's introductory eulogy, the priestess identified herself by her religious name and identified herself as a member of the coven. She then took a moment to describe her social relationship to Jack. Having done so, she turned to the priest on her right, took her hand, and said: "Hand to hand and heart to heart, I build this circle of Jack." Alyssa, serving as priest, then repeated this process, identifying herself by her religious name, acknowledging her coven membership, and identifying her social relationship to Jack. She then turned to the congregant on her right, took her hand, and repeated: "Hand to hand and heart to heart I build this circle of Jack." This process continued around the circle, as people tearfully identified themselves: "I'm Jack's coven sister." "I'm Jack's coven brother." "I'm Jack's daughter." "I'm Jack's friend." One of the central features that stood out was the use of the present tense. Jack is alive, Jack is a part of the circle, and Jack is participating. Perhaps one of the most emotionally moving moments in this building of the circle occurred when it came May's turn to speak, and she grasped hands with Jack in the casket, completing the circle. By this time, many people present were openly crying.

After the participants cast the "circle of Jack," the priestess and priest misted each other lightly in turn with sage water in a plastic spray bottle, proceeding clockwise, beginning with the head. They then proceeded around the circle counterclockwise, spraying each congregant lightly, until they reached Jack's remains, which were thoroughly sprayed. This ritual was intended to banish negative energy of the funeral home and set the circle apart from the world of the living. The community now stood on the threshold of the world of the dead. Sayward acknowledged this process by saying to the assembled congregation "This is a place which is not a place in a time which is not a time halfway between the worlds of the Gods and of mortals."

Certain participants had been tapped in advanced to "call a quarter." Quarter callers were given a typed slip of paper with a four line poetic statement about Jack's life to read. In this case, the west quarter was the first to be called, the reverse of the usual pattern. On a cue from the priestess, the West-quarter caller turned to face the west. The congregation turned to face the same direction. Most of the congregation will assume a particular posture that they associate with this particular direction. After the quarter-caller had finished speaking, a celebrant rang a bell once. The South quarter was then called, followed by East and North. This is reverse of the usual pattern. As in the American civil tradition, the quarter callers were not members of the nuclear family. As a full member of the coven, had May requested it, she could have called a quarter, as could any of the family. She left this task to others; her grief was too great. The west is seen as the locus of sunset, the place where the deceased's ego enters the world of the dead, while the East is the locus of rebirth. For the American

Neo-Pagan, the world of the dead is a womb, a place of growth and rebirth. The "circle of Jack" transported the congregation to the threshold of that womb, where the kicking of the growing soul within could be felt.

The priest and priestess returned to the east side of the altar, facing west. In most services, a text evoking the energy of the goddess and god is written in advance of the ritual, although in practice the celebrants often leave the script and wing it during the ritual. The more experienced a member is, the more likely that they are to "intuit" the evocation of the goddess or god than to read it from the script. Both Sayward and Alyssa are senior clergy members, each with over a decade of experience. So neither wrote what would be said at this ritual, but rather intuited their evocations at the time of the ritual performance. Following the invocation of the goddess and god, the priestess and priest, respectively, delivered the "charge of the goddess" and the "charge of the god." During the charge of the goddess, the priestess enters a trance-like state and speaks with the voice of the goddess present in her body. When a celebrant performs this task, they usually do not remember what they have said. During her charge of the goddess, Sayward told the participants that dying was a rest of the soul, a means of forgetting. For her, Jack had *chosen* to leave his body behind, *chosen* to forget the physical world, and *chosen* to rest, and will eventually *choose* to be reborn.

Like most American Neo-Pagan services, the body of the funeral ritual was theoretically egalitarian and invited everyone present to participate. The clergy had tapped particular members of the coven in advance to perform readings and poems. In between each of these poems, Alyssa asked if anyone would like to share a memory of Jack. People spoke of their relationships with Jack—his idiosyncrasies, the gifts he gave, times spent together. Toward the end of the poems, May, flanked by her children, stood and addressed the community. She thanked everyone for being there, and for the outpouring of love from the community.

As people spoke, the clergy members stood near Jack, or walked slowly clockwise around the circle. Two to three people spoke between each poem reading. As such, the body of the ritual was long, extending for over two hours. No one with whom I spoke complained about the length of the service. Jack's son, Jack Jr., likewise felt that the time for open sharing by the community was preferable to a traditional service. He contrasted the funeral with a friend's father's Protestant funeral, which Jack described as "looking at the back of everybody's head." At the end of the open forum for grieving, the clergy members returned to the script for a sacramental sharing of food called the cakes and wine ceremony.

The closing of the ritual was short. The congregation stood and faced inward toward the altar. The priest and priestess returned to the center of the circle following the cakes and wine ceremony, and dismissed the god and goddess, returning the participants to the world of the living, and Jack to the world of the dead. The quarters were dismissed in the reverse of the order they were cast. As the quarter caller spoke the dismissal, the congregation faced the appropriate direction, and made an appropriate hand gesture.

Mountain Moon Circle full moon ritual uses a song entitled "The Circle is Open" to complete the circle. The standing congregation joins hands, raising their hands over their heads after the third time through the song. "The circle is open" is usually sung in an upbeat, energetic way, while this song was sung in a way that could only be described as a dirge. There were none of the usual chorus line kicks or arm swinging that normally occurs—there was no doubt that this event memorialized a traumatic passing.

BURIAL RITUAL IN AMERICA

Major Christian denominations specify earth burial the day of the funeral service. This serves the function of disposal of the mortal remains, and completes the formal funeral cycle. Most graveside services are short and include a clergy member, the funeral director, chief mourners, and helpers. The burial ritual is now considered less "essential" than it has been in the past, and is often omitted entirely, with the remains interred unceremoniously by paid specialists using mechanized equipment. One of the curious consequences of the very short American funeral cycle is that it is simply inadequate to allow grieving to occur. Although most people associated with the ritual are removed from the status

of "mourner" and returned to the status of "alive" at the conclusion of the civil funeral cycle, chief mourners retain the trappings of liminality for upwards of a year, long after they, in theory, have been reincorporated into the world of the living. For the American civil mourner, this is an issue to be directed to their therapist, clergy member, and supporting family friends—there is no further ritual, such as secondary burial, for a grieving American civil chief mourner to publicly walk away from their mourning status and conclude the funeral rite of passage. The American civil mourner is left waiting: Waiting to live, waiting to die, waiting for an absolution from guilt and grief that comes very slowly, and in private.

American Neo-Pagans usually cremate the remains of their dead. The American civil religion specifies that the deceased's remains are to be segregated from the world of the living. After the funeral ritual incorporates the soul of the deceased into the world of the dead, sequestered away from the living, the burial ritual incorporates the deceased's mortal remains into the world of the dead, sequestered off in delimited cemeteries far away from the living spaces of the survivors.

Like over half of Neo-Pagan funerals May retained Jack's ashes in her home, *not sequestered away from the living.* Jack's ashes were placed at the center of a large shrine on a buffet table in the family room. In order that chief mourners may grieve for a longer period, American Neo-Pagans change the location of the burial ritual. In the civil funeral, the burial occurs immediately following the funeral ritual, and is a part of the rite of incorporation. The Neo-Pagan burial ritual occurs several months after the death, and changed its focus to addressing the chief mourner's grieving process. Unless the deceased died in late September or October, a typical time for the burial is at a Samhain ritual, held near the end of October each year. Samhain is the Neo-Pagan religious New Year and day of the dead. Many Neo-Pagan groups hold large, public rituals at Samhain, and it is typical for a Neo-Pagan to attend three to five large scale rituals during the last two weeks of October. In some cases, as it was with Jack, a special burial service is held particularly for this purpose; in other cases, the chief mourners meet at a regularly scheduled ritual to negotiate this grieving process; the remains may or may not be buried at the same time.

THE NEW SOCIAL STATE: POST-MORTEM AGENCY

Following death, the mourners *impose upon the corpse* an identity that they have constructed in two parts, one based upon the *social roles* the deceased occupied in life, and the other based upon *how they interacted* with the deceased in life. When placed against the landscape of *theology*, these two elements determine the *general social identities* the deceased occupies in death, and the specific ways in which mourners may *relate to the deceased*. American civil and American Neo-Pagan mourners, during the funeral cycle, share similar interpretations of the deceased's socially identical roles *except theological understanding of the way the world works*. Religious affiliation informs the theological landscape against which people make *relational decisions*. Thus, American Neo-Pagans *relate* to their dead in radically different ways than most Americans.

The American civil religion, in keeping with its Protestant history, proceeds from a theological assumption that values actors according to their work potential (Fulton; 1976). American Neo-Pagan dead become one with the *natural world*, rather than being removed from it. The practitioner may relate with the deceased in any place of nature. The practitioner may relate by contributing *energy* to the deceased, as well as through ritual magic and divination. The Neo-Pagan dead are partners and may be petitioned for aid by practitioners when a need arises. These petitions take on a character of generalized reciprocity, much like those reported in a traditional society. Unlike the dead in traditional societies who are often powerful and capricious, I have never heard of a Neo-Pagan employing magic to hold off the vengeful ghost of an immediate ancestor. The assumption is that no dead person would have a reason to harm an immediate descendent.

Taken from the Neo-Pagan perspective, a Neo-Pagan ancestor is able to add his own voice to his identity by generating paranormal experiences that will be meaningful to his descendents. Neo-Pagans do not take anything that could possibly be paranormal to be paranormal. Likewise, of the subset of events that several people agree are of a paranormal character, only a very small few may be considered to constitute direct communication or intervention by a particular Neo-Pagan ancestor.

For an American Neo-Pagan certain social actors, particularly nuclear family members and close family friends, include the subjective experience of *direct post-mortem interaction* ("PMI") *with the deceased* within the post-mortem identity construction process. Invocation of contact with the deceased may occur at any time after death, but it is likely to be taken most seriously during the several months immediately following death. Any potential claim for contact is scrutinized by the chief mourners for consistency with the post-mortem identity that they have already created for the deceased. Elements that are seen as particularly important in scrutiny include: (1) A distant social relation gaining information about the deceased's life through independent, paranormal means that is known only to the chief mourners; (2) a striking coincidence consistent with the interests of the deceased; (3) paranormal behavior associated with an object owned by the deceased that is consistent with how the deceased might have utilized that object; or (4) a direct paranormal experience between the deceased and a chief mourner. May calls such coincidences *synchronicities*. They are among the core pieces of evidence considered by a Neo-Pagan in determining if a particular event constitutes post-mortem communication. Magic in action looks like luck. One of the core features that distinguishes between an accident and intentional communication is that the person relaying the communication must have no prior knowledge of the synchronicity.

Once confirmed by the chief mourners, a Neo-Pagan's direct interactions with the deceased become a point of authority by which that mourner may add their voice to the PMI construction process preferentially over the voices of others who lack direct access to the deceased. The mourner who had a confirmed post-mortem experience of the deceased gains some of the authority of a chief mourner, and is able to speak on behalf of the deceased. The story of a Neo-Pagan's interaction with a mourner is in turn told and retold among members of the community and becomes an integral part of the collective post-mortem relational identity of the deceased.

THE UNDISCOVERED COUNTRY

I would like to take a few moments to return to the principle themes of this article. All Americans, regardless of their religious affiliation, have been deeply impacted by changes in technology over the past fifty years. The greatest impact of technology on the American civil funeral cycle has been to decrease the importance of the period of liminality while increasing the significance of the rite of separation. Because the chief mourners can choose the point of death, death rites now can be community affairs, with dozens assembled to bid their loved ones farewell. Because of the decreasing importance of the period of liminality, the chief mourners seldom have time to mourn. A widow or widower has no structure to tell them when it is ok to start dating again, dispose of their spouse's effects, or do any of the other myriad of things that a survivor must do to move on with their life.

American Neo-Pagans have developed an alternative funeral cycle to accommodate these problems. By delaying burial until up to a year after death, the chief mourners may take their time to mourn, while having a clear, socially recognizable rite of incorporation in the form of the burial to return them to the world of the living. During this period, the ashes of the deceased are located on a shrine in the family home, providing a focal point for family grief. Likewise, by attributing agency to the deceased, the survivors can directly seek permission from their loved ones to move on.

In his famous "to be or not to be" speech, Hamlet refers to the afterlife as:

> The undiscover'd country, from whose bourn
> No traveler returns, puzzles the will,
> And makes us rather bear those ills we have
> Than fly to others that we know not of?
>
> *Hamlet,*
> III.i.78-81

In this speech, Shakespeare refers to many things—fear of the future, fear of death, the life and death of both people and communities—many of the same things that come to the minds of modern Americans when they consider their own mortality. Shakespeare views the undiscovered country to be a fixed location, shrouded from the eyes of men. Neo-Pagans understand the ancestors to guide their hands, until the living become ancestors themselves.

Works Cited

Adler, Margot. 1986. *Drawing Down The Moon.* Boston, MA: Beacon Press.

Barner-Barry, Carol. 2005. *Contemporary Paganism.* New York, NY: Palgrave Macmillan.

Bellah, Robert. 1970. *Beyond Belief.* New York, NY: Harper & Row.

Berger, Helen. 1999. A Community of Witches: Contemporary Neo-Paganism and Witchcraft in the United States. Columbia, SC: University of South Carolina Press.

Berger, Helen, Evan A. Leach and Leigh S. Shaffer. 2003. *Voices From the Pagan Census.* Columbia, SC: University of South Carolina Press.

Blain, Jenny, Douglas Ezzy, and Graham Harvey, eds. 2004. *Researching Paganisms.* Walnut Creek, CA: AltaMira Press.

Bloch, Maurice, and Jonathan Parry. 1982. *Death and the Regeneration of Life.* London: Cambridge University Press.

Ehrenreich, Barbara. 2001. *Nickel and Dimed: On (Not) Getting By in America.* New York, NY: Henry Holt and Company.

Fulton, Robert, ed. 1976. *Death and Identity.* Bowie, MD: Charles Press.

Hardman, Charlotte, and Graham Harvey. 1996. *Paganism Today.* London: Thorssons.

Harvey, Graham. 1997. *Contemporary Paganism: Listening People, Speaking Earth.* New York, NY: New York University Press.

Hertz, Robert. 1960. *Death and the Right Hand.* New York, NY: Free Press.

Huntington, Richard, and Peter Metcalf. 1979. *Celebrations of Death.* New York, NY: Cambridge University Press.

Lock, Margaret. 2002. *Twice Dead: Organ Transplant and the Reinvention of Death.* Berkeley, CA: University of California Press.

Luhrmann, T. M. 1989. Persuasions of the Witch's Craft: Ritual Magic in Contemporary England. Cambridge, MA: Harvard University Press.

Magliocco, Sabina. 2004. *Witching Culture: Folklore and Neo-Paganism in America.* Philadelphia, PA: University of Pennsylvania Press.

_____. 2001. *Neo-Pagan Sacred Art and Altars: Making Things Whole.* Jackson, MS: University Press of Mississippi.

Mitford, Jessica. 1963. *The American Way of Death.* New York, NY: Simon and Schuster.

O'Gaia, Ashleen. 2003. *In the Service of Life: A Wiccan Perspective on Death.* Sacramento, CA: Citadel Press.

Orion, Loretta. 1995. *Never Again the Burning Times.* Prospect Heights, IL: Waveland Press.

Pike, Sarah M. 2001. Earthly Bodies, Magical Selves: Contemporary Pagans and the Search for Community. Berkeley, CA: University of California Press.

Rountree, Kathryn. 2004. Embracing the Witch and the Goddess: Feminist Ritual Makers in New Zealand. New York, NY: Routledge.

Scarboro, Alan, Nancy Campbell, and Shirley Stave. 1994. *Living Witchcraft: A Contemporary American Coven.* Westport, CT: Praeger.

Solomonsen, Jone. 2002. *Enchanted Feminisim: The Reclaiming Witches of San Francisco.* New York, NY: Routledge.

Starhawk, M. Macha Nightmare, and the Reclaiming Collective. 1997. *The Pagan Book of Living and Dying.* New York, NY: HarperCollins.

Sudnow, David. 1967. *Passing On.* Englewood Cliffs, NJ: Prentice Hall.

van Gennep, Arnold. 1960 [1908]. *The Rites of Passage.* Michaela Vizedom and Mari Caffee, trans. Chicago: University of Chicago Press.

York, Michael. 2003. *Pagan Theology.* New York, NY: New York University Press.

_____. 1995. *The Emerging Network.* Lanham, MD: Rowan and Littlefield.

CRITICAL THINKING QUESTIONS

1. What is a rite of passage? What are the stages of a funeral rite of passage? What happens at each stage?

2. What function does the funeral rite of passage serve? Name two and explain.

3. Explain three ways that the American funeral cycle has changed as a consequence of changes in technology.

4. Why do Neo-Pagans feel that their dead retain agency?

5. The author notes that the death ritual he observed was *multivocalic*—meaning that the ritual was experienced as speaking with different voices to different people who were present at the same event. Watch a local newscast. How is a newscast a multivocalic event? How is it similar to, and different from, the multivocalic funeral cycle that the author describes?

Possession States across the World:
An Anthropological Approach

Kevin Rafferty

Religion has always been a subject of keen interest to anthropologists, particularly those of traditional peoples. A large percentage of research has been concerned with the phenomenon of trances and possession states, no more so than in the last three decades of the twentieth century. Popular culture has dealt with the issue for years, with movies such as *The Exorcist,* and the rash of imitators such as *The Omen, The Night Child, The Devil In Miss Jones* (an X-rated film), and others dealing with the phenomenon from a spectacular, entertaining point of view. However, a spate of books by anthropologists, theologians, and laymen have appeared, discussing possession from a biological, psychological, cultural, and theological/spiritual perspective. This literature appears to be divided between two main schools. On the one hand, there is the school composed of theologians and educated laymen interested in possession from a perspective of the western cultural tradition. They delve into the history of possession in the Western tradition, and how this state is seen and occurs in the present day.

On the other hand, there are anthropologists who tend to study the subject matter mainly in its non-Western setting. They examine and explain the utility of possession and possession cults from a utilitarian perspective—that is, the function of such cults, how possession states are induced, and other facets of the subject as applied to traditional peoples. Many seem reluctant to apply similar techniques and approaches to our Western tradition, acting almost as if this type of belief system was an embarrassment, a holdover from medieval times that is an interesting historical sidelight but with little utility to present-day Western concerns. The one significant exception to this rule

would be Michael Harner, who has emphasized that the existence of spirits had not been conclusively disproven by science and thus should not be ignored because he suggests that scientists would be basing their dismissal on "faith," a decidedly unscientific attitude (Hriskos 1999).

The fact remains that possession states and the correlating rites of exorcism exist today in the "modern" world. The major and minor sects of Christianity retain this belief as a viable tenet of belief, with well-defined concepts about possession states and the rituals whose function it is to treat such states. Modern science and anthropological reasoning has not driven the idea from the corpus of Western cosmology and thought. We would do well to heed Lewis's (1971: 28) advice in this matter: "the anthropologist's task is to discover what people believe in and relate their beliefs operationally to other aspects of their culture and society." He has neither the skills nor authority to pronounce upon the absolute "truth" about ecstatic manifestations in different cultures. That this is true is evidenced by a number of reports regarding possession and exorcism in North America and elsewhere in the western world in the last few years:

—"Woman Admits Guilt in Exorcism Death" (*The Globe and Mail*, 6/22/95)
—"French Villagers Summon Exorcist" (CNN, 10/22/98)
—"Vatican Issues First New Exorcism Ritual Since 1614" (CNN, 1/26/99)

Other examples are recounted (Ebon 1974, Martin 1976) mostly by clergy and laymen. Only a few anthropologists have discussed possession in Western civilization, foremost of which are

Source: "Possession States across the World: An Anthropological Approach," by Kevin Rafferty from *Faces of Anthropology: A Reader for the 21st Century* (2003, Pearson Custom Publishing).

Bourguignon (1976) and Zaretsky and Leone (1974). This short essay will correlate ideas, concepts, and information from the anthropological and non-anthropological perspectives in a non-exhaustive, cross-cultural comparison of these states around the world.

DEFINITIONS

Numerous definitions of possession/trance states are available. Winick (1970: 43) described possession as "an extranatural force that enters a worshiper of a deity so that he temporarily is the deity. It is the ultimate religious experience." He further defines possession in light of voluntary categories, institutionalized or semi-institutionalized forms in traditional societies where possession is seen as a desirable and even necessary adjunct to the worship of a deity.

Wallace (1959) and Walker (1972) stress the differences between possession and trance states from the perspective of individual cultures in which such phenomena occur. Wallace (1959: 59) defines trance and possession as "any native theory which explains any event of human behavior as being the result of the physical presence in the human body of an alien spirit which takes control of the host's executive functions, most frequently speech and control of the skeletal musculature." Refining Wallace, Walker (1972: 3) describes trance as "the scientific description of a psychological state in western terminology, whereas possession is the folk explanation, in more philosophical terms, for the same type of state." These will be the operative definitions throughout this article.

The important point is that such states occur only where native folk theory recognizes these states as a viable category of reality, that has meaning and relevance in the lives of the bearers of the culture, and not where the category is imposed on the data by outside observers (Walker 1972: 3). Douglas's (1966) discussion about purity rules has general relevance here, in that possession and trance states (like defilement) are not isolated events but occur only within the context of a systematic ordering of ideas about the world and the universe. This holds true whether one is discussing these states in a traditional society or within the Western cultural tradition.

In addition to a working definition, it must be realized that possession and trance states cover a variety of phenomena. In Western terms, possession is a serious psychological state, an "altered state of consciousness" that causes an individual to lose touch with everyday cultural reality and enter a culturally defined religious plane of existence. These "realities" serve as ideas, beliefs, and concepts that serve to define and interpret behavior (Bourguignon 1976: 7). A person's patterns of thought, speech, and behavior may undergo such marked changes that these changes are interpreted as the presence of a second personality inhabiting the body of the possessed. As a corollary, where similar behavior is interpreted as being the result of a psychosis or mental aberration, then it must be treated as such by the anthropologist.

Such belief systems and states have been studied by anthropologists in numerous traditional cultures, and this article discusses a number of cases (see Lewis 1971 for a general overview). Almost all Christian denominations have a belief in demonic possession and exorcism. The Roman Catholic Church has a well-defined belief system in possession (Roman Catholic Church 1994: 416–417, Sec. 1673) and a distinctive ritual, the *Rituale Romanum,* to drive out Satan and his demons. The Church of England has issued commission reports on the subject (Petitpierre 1972). The Greek Orthodox Church has a well-defined belief in this area (Mastrantonis 1990–1996), and most Protestant denominations also follow suit (Cogan n.d.).

In a discussion regarding the psychological aspects of possession, Wallace (1959) suggests that such beliefs are the folk explanations for three types of psychosomatic behavior:

1. Obsessive ideation and compulsive action.
2. Hysterical disassociation, including multiple personalities, somnambulism, and conversion hysteria.
3. Hallucinations, defined as pseudo perception without relevant stimulation of external or internal sensory perceptors, but with such subjective vividness equal to or greater than that aroused by such stimulation.

Bourguignon refers to these states as "altered states of consciousness" that share general characteristics that can be observed and studied. These characteristics include alterations in thinking, a disturbed time sense, loss of control, a change in body image, a change in emotional expression, changes in the meaning or significance of everyday events, a sense of the ineffable, feelings of rejuvenation, and hyper suggestibility (1973: 3). In most traditional societies, these states become institutionalized religious experiences and can be seen as a means of worship or contact with the supernatural world.

In regard to the Christian worldview, these same concepts can be applied. Possession by an evil spirit involves an "altered state of consciousness," alterations of personality and thought patterns, loss of control, changes in emotional expression and body image, and other accompanying symptoms (Martin 1976). Possession states are explicable cultural phenomena, even in the western context, as are the culturally acceptable rituals used to end such states of being.

ARCHAEOLOGICAL AND HISTORICAL BACKGROUND

There are numerous examples of archaeological, historical, and early anthropological ruminations on the subject of possession. The earliest written records, dating from approximately 6000 B.C. in Mesopotamia, already reveal a well-developed structure of thought regarding possession. This suggests that such beliefs must have existed for a significant length of time prior to the advent of writing. Surviving cuneiform tablets found in Mesopotamian cities describe a multitude of spirits waiting to attack unsuspecting humans to cause many types of illnesses through possession. There are numerous formulae of conjurations and exorcisms that were available (Oesterreich 1930: 147–148).

Egypt, Rome, and the Greek city-states left records concerning the belief in the reality of possession. Many records deal with involuntary possession states in which the individual was inhabited by a spirit without the host's consent (Dodds 1951). Also recognized were voluntary possession states employed by ecclesiastical religions used in ceremonies for divining the future. This form of possession was encouraged and controlled by priests or mediums whom the gods entered. The most famous example of this was the Oracle of Apollo at Delphi, Greece, where a medium would attempt to induce possession by Apollo to acquire knowledge about the future or the hidden present (Dodds 1951: 69–70).

The ancient Hebrews also had a belief in the possibility of spirit possession, which helped form the later Christian concepts about this subject. The only detailed discussion of such states in the Tanakh (Old Testament) is found in the Book of Samuel, where God sent an evil spirit to possess and plague King Saul (I Samuel 16:14). In the New Testament, later Jewish beliefs about such states become apparent. The Apostles who recorded the Gospels noted a number of incidents where Jesus of Nazareth acted as an exorcist to cure cases of possession. Such states could only have been recognized as such if this category of cultural reality was prevalent among the Jewish populations of first century A.D. Israel. The most famous exorcism performed by Jesus occurred at Cepharnum (Mark 1: 23–27). It should be noted that most of the biblical possessions seem to have been of the involuntary demonic sort where individuals were seized by spirits against their will requiring exorcisms to free the possessed. The exceptions happen when Jesus' followers were "filled" with the Holy Spirit as part of religious devotions and as a gift from Jesus.

The early and medieval Christian Church elaborated on these early ideas. One of the four minor orders of early clergy was that of the exorcist, a function gradually absorbed by regular clergy in the Middle Ages. The medieval mind saw the world as a battleground between God and Satan, Good and Evil, and possession was one of many weapons employed by Satan (Naumann 1974: 74–76). The Middle Ages saw many recorded cases of possession outbreaks, some involving a single person, but many others involving mass outbreaks of possession in convents (Lyons 1970: 96). Priests sent to deal with such incidents often became possession victims themselves (Oesterreich 1930), probably due to autosuggestion from a combination of contact with victims and the strength of the priest's own belief in demonic possession.

During the period of European expansion, evidence was uncovered regarding possession beliefs from all parts of the globe. The Chinese had well-developed tenets about possession and exorcism, and these can possibly be traced back in history nearly 2,700 years before the Christian era (Ebon 1974: 41–42). Similar reports cropped up regarding such beliefs among peoples under the control of the various European colonial empires, stirring an interest in such phenomena among early anthropologists.

One such anthropologist, E. B. Tylor, synthesized many such reports in his book *Primitive Culture* (1958). Employing ethnographic examples from around the world, he discussed the allied concepts of possession and exorcism as being logical adaptations of "primitive" man's animistic beliefs. He wrote of the ideas that many peoples had regarding a second personality inhabiting a person (1958: 219). There are numerous other early anthropological examples, many of which can be found in Zaretsky (1966).

Much of the early discussion on possession presented the state within the context of the larger cultural institutions of a specific culture an anthropologist was examining. The most recent research on the subject attempts to deal with possession as a multi-componential phenomenon that has cross-cultural similarities. This work tends to treat possession as a subject whose causes are many and varied, taking into consideration human experiences in the biological, psychological, and cultural realms. In addition, none of this work deals with the questions as to whether there is a spiritual reality to possession, whether spirits are "real" or not. They treat with visible behaviors that can be observed and measured, leaving the "reality problem" to theologians.

THE ATMOSPHERE OF BELIEF AND "NATIVE" THEORIES OF POSSESSION

In general, possession may consist of either voluntary or involuntary states. Voluntary possession is when a potential human host actively seeks possession by a god or a spirit to act as a medium or as an act of worship. Involuntary possession occurs spontaneously, without the willing consent or active participation of the afflicted individual. Both states have many of the same social, cultural, and psychobiological triggers, but the relative importance of these triggers vary between cultures and even between individuals of the same culture. Most of these factors play a role in possession states in both traditional and western societies.

Walker (1972) has undertaken a detailed discussion of these trigger factors. The first and primary factor is the necessity of a prevailing "atmosphere (or environment) of belief" surrounding the event, a well-developed belief that possession can truly occur. Possession must be a strongly accepted societal reality and be widespread in its belief (Walker 1972; Bourguignon 1976: 16–18). Without this belief, such psychosomatic activities as described by Wallace (1959: 59–60) are dismissed as mental aberrations or as the result of disease as defined by western medicine.

Haiti is a fine example of this, where the peasants believe not only in God but in a host of lesser spirits called *loa*. It is "known" that during religious celebrations *loa* can enter individuals and "ride them like horses," using the host to speak and dispense advice to believers (Metraux 1972: 120). Children regularly witness such ceremonies and are filled with such stories outside of the ceremonies and thus are steeped in the "atmosphere of belief necessary for a belief in the reality of possession. They expect that some day such states may occur to them, laying the groundwork for the entry into possession states later in their lives" (Bourguignon 1965; 1976: 16–18).

Christian sects also create similar atmospheres, due to the fact that there is a long tradition of belief in the possibility that spirits exist, both good and evil, that can possess an individual. Among Pentecostal or extreme fundamentalist groups that interpret the Bible literally, and among charismatic Catholics, there is a phenomenon known as *glossolalia* or "speaking in tongues" in which the Holy Spirit enters an individual and endows that person to speak and interpret totally unknown languages. Without such an unshakeable faith in the power of God through the Holy Spirit, there can be no glossolalia (Kildahl 1972: 60; Bourguignon 1976: 55–57).

Even demonic possession, seizure by spirits of evil, requires an intense belief system. Satan has been a prominent figure in Christian belief for centuries, becoming especially important in the late Middle Ages as a figure of ungovernable evil (Cohn 1970; Armstrong 1994). Many fundamentalist sects steep their believers in a "fire and brimstone" atmosphere about evil, and the Roman Catholic Church also expounds on the reality of Satan and his demonic minions (1994: 416–417, Sec. 1673). This leads to incidents such as that reported in Yakima, Washington, in 1976:

> The decomposed body of a 3 year old boy, David Weilbacher, was found in a fly infested room sealed with tape, a Yakima County Superior Court jury was told yesterday in the trial of his mother and four other adults charged with beating the boy to death because they believed he was possessed by the Devil. . . . David was beaten by adults for four months prior to his death because they believed he was inhabited by the Devil (*Newsday*, November 12, 1976).

In Germany in 1976 two Catholic exorcists were investigated for their role in the death of a girl during an exorcism. The girl had built her life around extreme religious devotion, covering the walls of her room with pictures of the saints and saying daily rosaries. The faith included a firm belief in Satan and the reality of his powers (*Time*, September 6, 1976), creating the necessary "atmosphere of belief" within which possession states can be expressed. This belief was probably reinforced by the exorcists' belief in the reality of the situation they viewed unfolding before them.

When the proper environment has been established, a number of different factors must be in place to trigger a possession state, and symptoms may vary from culture to culture. In many cases, the first possession may occur spontaneously without the human host seeking out the privilege. This is often heralded by a sickness that lingers or recurs. In many traditional societies, this is a sign that the afflicted individual is being selected by the spirit world to serve as a host or a medium. Eventually, with proper training, the selected can learn to control the onset of

such states under specified conditions, such as in religious ceremonies or rituals (Lewis 1971).

The "call" varies from culture to culture. Shamans in Siberia and Alaska, who have the ability to be possessed voluntarily, often exhibit their select status from an early age. Among the Vogul a future shaman usually exhibit a generally nervous condition or personality and is often seized by epileptic fits that are interpreted as meetings with a god or a spirit choosing the shaman as a vessel (Eliade 1964: 15). Among the Korekore of eastern Africa, future mediums are called via a series of extended illnesses that curing rituals do not alleviate. The ailing person is sent to a medium for extended observation and, if it persists, is determined that a spirit guardian is calling the afflicted to be its spokesman (Garbett 1969: 115).

In Christianity, the only certain determinant of possession, usually demonic in nature, is the expression of a full-blown possession state, with the accompanying physical, mental, and moral manifestations created by the possessing demon. Most theologians agree that by the time the victim (or anyone else) realizes what is happening, the possession is *well* underway and has actually commenced some years prior to its manifestation. Symptoms such as convulsions and shaking, multiple personalities, and psychokinetic phenomena are normal, but one Christian denomination, the Roman Catholic Church, insists that the victim undergo a battery of physical and psychological tests to rule out disease or mental illness as the cause of the symptoms. The life history of the patient also is investigated to see if incidents in the sufferer's past, suppressed by his or her mind, are responsible for the behavior (Nicola 1974: 29–32; Martin 1976: 11).

If these tests are negative, then spiritual criteria are applied as a final determinant. Most authorities agree that the following symptoms help define a true case of possession: revulsions to symbols and truths about religion; an inexplicable stench emanating from the possessed; freezing temperatures in the possessed's room; telepathic powers about purely religious and moral matters; a peculiarly unlined, completely smooth or stretched skin or an unusual distortion of the face; "possessed gravity" where the victim becomes physically immovable or those about him become weighted down by a suffocating pressure; levitation of the possessed with no visible means of support; violent smashing of furniture, opening and slamming of doors and windows untouched by human hands; superhuman strength; the eating of offal or other disgusting aberrations of normal human activities and bodily functions (Lewis 1971: 98–99; Ebon 1974: 94; Leek 1975: 90–92; Martin 1976: 13).

In both traditional societies and Christian sects, there are general culturally accepted patterns of events that occur during possession states. In traditional societies that practice shamanism, such states often begin with illnesses that linger and cannot be cured, leading to observation of the victim by a professional curer or medium. The afflicted is then taught the esoteric knowledge he/she requires to control such states and they are initiated into a possession cult. After this, the shaman or medium can bring on voluntary states of possession on demand or request. In cases of demonic possession in such societies, the seizure of the individual usually occurs quickly with the onset of a serious illness and then a full-blown possession experience. This is then followed by an exorcistic ritual to drive out the offending spirit.

In Christian sects, in cases of glossolalia or possession by the Holy Spirit, some patterns also occur. Such states usually occur within the throes of religious ritual and expectation, but no particular pattern of events seems to occur before or during such states. No particular sequence of thoughts needs to be followed, although there is an intense atmosphere of belief that exists, and there are no special bodily movements that are attached to the experience (Kildahl 1972: 5–6).

In cases of demonic possession, there appears to be a specific sequence of events, at least from the Roman Catholic perspective. Step one is the *Entry Point*, where the demon enters the victim upon their decision, however tenuous, to allow the demon to enter the body. Next comes a series of *Erroneous Judgments* in matters of faith and morality, influenced by the demon. This sets the stage for the *Voluntary Yielding of Control* to the demon because temporary advantages accrue to the possessed as a result of this yielding. Finally, there occurs the *State of Perfect Possession* where the demon is in total control of the individual's will

so that free will no longer exists (Martin 1976: 435–436).

The most important difference between possession states in traditional societies and Christian sects, especially Roman Catholicism, is the idea of choice or free will. In many traditional societies, the initial onset of possession states seems to be totally involuntary, even in individuals who later become practitioners of voluntary possession states. Among Siberian groups such as the Buryat and Altai, potential shamans have an obligation to accept initial possession and accept their calling as shamans. The spirit world will not allow them to refuse but persistently return until the future shaman submits (Eliade 1964: 18). Among the Sidamo of Ethiopia, a spirit induced illness can be cured only if the victim agrees to feed the spirit and accept it as his/her guardian spirit (Hamer and Hamer 1966: 397). In Suriname, a person's soul may resist possession and keep out an intrusive spirit, but the rebuffed spirit returns and creates serious illness until the unfortunate individual submits to the spirit (Herskovits 1966: 266).

Modern Christian theology holds that in demonic possession a demon can never force its way inside a person; some form of consent, conscious or subconscious, must be granted, and various temptations are used by the demon to achieve this goal. These temptations are adapted to the temper and circumstances of the victim and are unleashed at the extremes of the physical and emotional extremes of the human experience, such as extremes of poverty or prosperity, the pinnacle of joy or depths of despair, or other similar circumstances. It is here that the potential victim is most off-guard and vulnerable to attack. Once inside, the demon cannot force an individual to act in a certain way. It can only cajole, convince, frighten, bully, or lie to an individual into making a series of bad choices regarding faith and morality. This prepares the person to yield control and accept demonic possession (Buck 1974: 24–25).

In a traditional setting, the situation often affects the nature of the spirit entering an individual. In Haitian vodoun, only good spirits, the *loa*, may possess an individual. These spirits concern themselves with how people live their lives and dispense advice to believers through the medium to other believers. In other circumstances, such as possession of sick individuals by spirits of the dead, this state is feared and exorcistic rituals are required to save the person's life (Bourguignon 1976: 27).

Sometimes the spirits have a sexual identity as either male or female. In some societies, the victims are usually female and are possessed by female spirits, and victims are organized into cults to cure periodic attacks of possession. This usually happens in heavily male-dominated societies (Lewis 1971). Among the Gurage of Ethiopia, poor males regularly are afflicted by spirits that can be placated only by ceremonies where the victims are allowed to gorge themselves on food until the offending spirit is full and satisfied (Shack 1971).

Possession within Christian sects is also somewhat situationally dependent. The glossolaliast form is actively sought and usually occurs in the context of group prayer or ritual where the Holy Spirit descends on a believer with the assistance of a cult leader. The spirit has no real gender identity although it usually is symbolized as a dove. In cases of demonic possession, there appears to be no particular context that triggers such states, which usually occur over a long period of time. Demons are also usually sexless because although Satan often is depicted as a male, in reality it was originally an angel serving God, which is genderless. Also, it seems that diabolical possession is more prevalent in the West than the glossolaliast type, or at least it gets the most publicity and can strike both genders equally (Martin 1976; Ebon 1974).

An additional difference between traditional and Western concepts concerns the number of spiritual entities that can enter an individual. Most traditional societies believe that a large number of entities, both good and evil, can possess an individual. Christians usually only have a "choice" between the Holy Spirit and the Devil and its associated minions, which can be quite numerous (Ebon 1974: 133). In the earthly realm, the Devil's agents are numerous and theology asserts that God allows such entities to exist as tests of the believer's love in and trust of God. This moral dimension is a concept that appears to be missing in traditional cosmologies.

NONRELIGIOUS EXPLANATIONS OF POSSESSION STATES

In the West, a number of alternative explanations serve to deal with such possession states. Western medical culture suggests a number of biological and psychological triggers that can be used to explain seeming states of possession. As previously noted, an individual entering into or within a possession state exhibits markedly abnormal patterns of motor and mental activity. An excess of sensory stimulation is aimed at an individual within a religious context where glossolalial possession is the goal. Such sensory stimulation also can be created in situations where an individual's mental faculties are overwhelmed by psychological harassment, indoctrination similar to brain washing, or physical deprivation, often all at the same time (Walker 1972).

Some specific factors that can create sensory overload and hyper-stimulation include rhythmic drumming, dancing, and singing. Often public religious ceremonies such as those held in Haiti involve an intense mental involvement in the activities and emotional atmosphere of the occasion. Both participants in ceremonies and the onlooking crowds create an atmosphere of religious fervor and expectation that the arrival of the *loa* is imminent. Drums beating out several monotonous repetitive rhythms, strenuous dancing, and loud fervent singing leads to sensory overload within the potential spirit host, heightening the possibility that he or she will soon enter a possession trance and be the *cheval* (horse) of a *loa*. (Metraux 1972; Walker 1972; Bourguignon 1976).

As far as can be determined, modern cases of demonic possession in the West lack such a context. There are no drums and no rhythmic dancing or singing, although in some cases an atmosphere of expectation and heightened emotion can be created under certain conditions. Ebon (1974) reported a case in Europe where a young girl fell under the mental and religious domination of two people who claimed to be her "holy parents." This couple led a strict apocalyptic cult that expected a momentary end of the world and they brought this girl, her sisters, and her parents under their control. The girls were indoctrinated in the "divine education" of the cult, continually harangued about sin and Satan in brainwashing sessions that often lasted all day and night. The leaders became convinced that one of the girls, Bernadette, had made a pact with the Devil and was possessed by him. The fanatic attempts by the cult to exorcize Satan and the "evil within her" led ultimately to her death and the prosecution of cult members for murder (Ebon 1974: 168–176).

In this case, the constant haranguing and questioning, the lack of sleep from all night sessions leading to sensory deprivation and overstimulation, and a heightened mental state maintained by the cult probably led to the girls' "state of possession." The proper environment was created by the religious fervor of the "holy parents" and the cult members who created the atmosphere of belief for possession. Eventually, the girl succumbed to the pressure and admitted to being possessed.

In circumstances of glossolalia, people often participate in ecstatic ceremonies involving dramatic religious conversions, spiritual healing, group participation in ritual, singing and music, and often dancing, which creates hyperstimulation of believers. There is a group feeling of religious emotion and fervor, leading to heightened expectations of the Holy Spirit entering true believers (Kildahl 1972: 70; Bourguignon 1976: 55–56). This is similar to practices found in many traditional cultures.

Hypnosis and autosuggestion also usually play a role in these "altered states of consciousness." Hypnosis and hypnotic states can be triggered by a variety of external stimuli. In hypnosis, the first step is to detach the subject from his or her external and internal realities to create a new set of realities. In traditional societies, rhythmic drumming, dancing, singing, and other stimuli affect the neurological and physiological functions of the body to create a detachment from reality. Then an object of transference, often a spirit or deity, is used to create a new reality for the believer. In the West, a priest or a religious leader may act as this object of transference during a religious ceremony, such as a charismatic prayer meeting or an exorcism. The victim is on the verge of a possession state and the priest/practitioner may then devote all of his attention to the believer, staring intently into his eyes and

talking in an incessant, insistent monotone while demanding the entity to manifest itself. Crowds witnessing such ceremonies also can act as such objects of transference by their unspoken yet fervent belief in the reality of the possibility of possession. This all works to detach a potential host's mind from the present reality and create a new reality where possession may occur (Walker 1972: 27–28).

In glossolalia, the group leader may act as the hypnotist or transference object for his followers. He directs activities and rituals, leads the singing and prayers, and plants the suggestion among the faithful that the Holy Spirit is on the verge of entering the group. Research suggests that glossolaliasts are more submissive, dependent, and suggestible in the presence of authority figures who assist in the triggering of such states. The glossolaliast submits to the person who first introduced him or her to this realm of belief and who then acts as the object of transference to trigger the possession event (Kildahl 1972: 40, 50).

In more formal Christian cults, such as Catholicism, Anglicanism, and others, the priest-exorcist may unwittingly give the victim of diabolical possession the appropriate hypnotic suggestions that push the afflicted into their altered state of consciousness. To be effective, the exorcist must firmly believe that there is a Devil who can possess individuals and that this evil entity is within the person confronting the priest. This attitude can serve as a form of hypnotic suggestion to a person on the verge of an altered state of consciousness, locking the belief in the reality of his/her possession firmly within the mind of the believer. He serves as the necessary object of transference that completes the person's entry into the possession state (Ebon 1974: 22–23). The priest thus has unwittingly helped to make the enemy he fears most, Satan, a reality that he must then confront until one of them is defeated.

Such factors must also enter into such cases of demonic possession that occur within fundamentalist cults, such as the one that killed Bernadette. After "brainwashing" and the entry into the altered state of consciousness, the cult leader serves as an appropriate object of transference by the strength of the belief of the leader in

Satan and in his insistence that the person he is haranguing is truly possessed by the Devil.

A number of social and cultural factors must also be considered as causes in the onset of "possession states." The socialization process that creates the necessary atmosphere of belief is a necessary cause. In traditional societies where possession states are commonplace occurrences, children are raised to view this phenomenon as a normal factor in religious belief and are led to believe that such events can occur to them. The same may be said about Christian sects who have a strong belief in the reality of demonic possession and Satan's power. This lays the groundwork for future states of possession. If one is suddenly immersed in such an atmosphere of belief and is "brainwashed" into believing in this reality, as Bernadette was, this enhances the possession possibilities.

In Bali, socialization of children occurs in such a way as to encourage future states of possession. Walker (1972) suggests that Balinese culture fosters a personality structure that is susceptible to hypnotic suggestion or trance states. Children are taught nearly everything via the manipulation of their limbs by parents or teachers, not by verbal communication. The child must be "waxy limp" in the hands of an adult, with his consciousness almost in reserve. Walker suggests that this leads to a loose ego boundary, one that is fluid enough to be extended to include anything in the child's external environment, for early in life the child and teacher become extensions of one another's ego boundaries. These loose ego boundaries are a factor in inducing auto-hypnosis and possession states (Walker 1972: 61–63).

In many societies, certain social institutions may actually encourage and bring on possession states, either overtly in the case of possession cults, or covertly in that these institutions aim not to purposely bring on states of possession. In the latter case, possession serves as a means of aiding an individual to bypass or cope with societal pressures and demands.

In many traditional societies, possession cults play a major role in the life of the common people. These cults establish a dogma or doctrine that places spirit possession in a central role, and initiates true believers by training them in the proper manner of propitiating and controlling the spirit(s) that will occupy their bodies on occasion. In Haiti, a person experiences his first involuntary possession upon entering adolescence. Priests are consulted to identify the possessing spirit and then conduct rites of initiation into the cult associated with that spirit. This is a learning experience where the neophyte is taught the appropriate behavior to engage in when participating in the periodic rituals that bring on possession states as part of religious worship (Bourguignon 1976: 17). Similar cults exist in Bahia (Verger 1954), parts of Africa (Beattie and Middleton 1969), and on the Indian subcontinent (Jones 1976).

In some traditional societies, the social institutions and behaviors bring on possession states rather than specific cults oriented toward that end. These institutions and their associated belief structure may invite the state as a means of responding to the everyday pressures of social life. The custom of men among the Ethiopian Gurage is to restrict public food consumption to an absolute minimum, despite yearly crop yields that are plentiful. At night, though, wealthier males gorge themselves on hoarded food, thus avoiding sharing food with their kin and neighbors, which is considered a cultural obligation. The wealthy also conduct monthly ritual feasts that are socially acceptable outlets for hunger gratification (Shack 1971: 32–33).

Poor males have no such outlets because they lack food to both hoard and participate in the public feasts of the wealthy. Possession appears to be the socially acceptable manner to satisfy their hunger. A possessed male has curing rituals run for him, and if those fail, the "wizard" orders that an exorcistic ritual be run. A portion of the ritual requires the victim to eat until he is satiated, thereby satiating the occupying spirit. Such states can re-occur and necessitate the repetition of the exorcistic ritual (Shack 1971: 34–37). Thus two societal institutions, food deprivation and possession trances, interact so one alleviates the other.

Institutionalized male superiority also can be a trigger mechanism for possession or trance states among women as oblique "strategies of aggression" to be used against men. I discuss such events and their onset when I discuss the social value of possession states.

In the West, Pentecostal groups that encourage possession by the Holy Spirit are societal institutions that allow believers to cope with the everyday pressures of life. Personal pressures create a turn to glossolalia states: anxiety over a life crisis; feelings of worthlessness; a desire to regress to childhood and place yourself in the stronger, surer hands of group leaders or of the Holy Spirit; and a general low level of emotional stability (Kildahl 1972: 57–63). Groups such as Pentacostalists provide a reasonably complex integrated pattern of behavior to meet basic social needs and desires and to exert social control over their followers, including a ritual designed to deal with the pressures of everyday life (possession by the Holy Spirit) (Winick 1970: 287–288).

In the belief in Satan and his powers, other Christian denominations become institutions that can encourage the onset of possession, both glossolalial and demonic, that are most visibly manifest in possession states and exorcism rituals. The sincere belief in the Devil and his powers can goad individuals desirous of attention, such as the poor, women who feel victimized or oppressed (such as nuns in medieval times), those suffering from real or imagined social injustices, and the socially unimportant to become "possessed" and to undergo exorcisms in search of the attention and social affect they crave and need. The Roman Catholic Church may have been the unwitting creator of the epidemic of possession that swept Europe from the Dark Ages to the middle of the Renaissance that affected thousands, especially nuns in convents under strict male control and domination (Nicola 1974: 141–143).

In modern times, fundamentalist groups like those led by the previously mentioned "holy parents" have an extreme emphasis on strict biblical interpretation, the reality of Satan and demonic possession, a "fire and brimstone" approach to ideas of good and evil, and thus encourage, explicitly or tacitly, possession states. These institutions, though not formally structured and often of short duration, organize and control the lives and worlds of their followers and thus regulate their followers' lives and fulfill their need for structure and social affect. They help create a community that creates a social reality that includes rejection of the world as the "realm of Satan." They see themselves under siege by Satan and his minions and regard demonic possession states as attempts by the Devil to destroy the community of "true believers." The belief in an essentially evil world may actually encourage possession states as symbols of the reality of the "truth" of the belief system of the group.

POSSESSION AND THE INDIVIDUAL

Although patently obvious, the social circumstances and individual personality of the possessed are primary factors in the onset of possession states. The individual is at least partly responsible for the onset of such states due to his/her reactions to societal pressures and the strains of everyday life. In many traditional societies, the history and the institutions of possession cults can combine with the life circumstances of an individual to bring on altered states of consciousness. First occurrences of possession in Haiti are often the result of life circumstances that cause tension and stress to build up, such as a change in social status or responsibilities, or the death of a family member (Walker 1972: 81). Among Somali women, possession appears to be closely correlated with societal situations that create conflict, competition, rivalry, or tension within the family, especially in regard to members of their own gender. Somali are polygynous, allowing men to have more than one wife at a time, and often the first wife of a man feels that her status and competence as a wife is being threatened by her husband's desire to take a second wife. It may be that an attack of spirit possession is the senior wife's way of reaffirming her status and prestige: the cure for such attacks requires luxurious feminine gifts be presented to the victim to obviate the condition (Wilson 1967: 366, 370). Although not specifically studied, an assumption can be made that in monogamous marriages or marriages where the senior wife feels secure in her status that there are few or no cases of possession.

In Christian denominations, personal life crises or changes in social status may trigger possession states. Such circumstances among glossolaliasts have been recounted above. Freud

(1959; original 1923) analyzed a case of diaboli-cal possession in the seventeenth century and what he concluded in this case is still pertinent in examining current occurrences of demonic pos-session and their onset. In 1677, a painter named Christoph Haitzmann came to a priest for help in being released from a pact with the Devil he had made many years ago. He said that he bound himself to the Devil as a son for nine years, and promised himself totally to the Devil after his death. This "pact" was entered into shortly fol-lowing the death of Haitzmann's father, a period in which he sank into a deep melancholia and could not work. Freud suggested that "the train of thought motivating this pact seems to be as follows: owing to my father's death I am despon-dent and can no longer work; if I can but get a father substitute I shall be able to regain all that I have lost" (1959: 446). Freud concludes that the individual circumstances of Haitzmann and his reaction to them are what brought on the sup-posed pact with and possession by the Devil. Freud was analyzing this case from the twentieth century psychoanalytical perspective, but did not necessarily take into careful consideration the atmosphere of belief within the culture that could have influenced Haitzmann in his belief in the reality of this satanic pact he had entered into. However, this sort of analysis can very likely be fruitfully applied to most cases of pos-session in both the western world and traditional societies of the present time.

The individual is also quite important in determining how the possessing spirit will act and what sort of personality it will evidence. In most traditional societies, each spirit or deity has unique personality and behavioral charac-teristics that they exhibit. As with most social constructs, these characteristics are sufficiently flexible enough to permit variations according to the personality of the host body. The personality of the host appears to help determine the traits and speech patterns of the spirit, giving the af-flicted flexibility to express their hidden desires, tensions, or hatreds in a socially acceptable manner. Belo (1960: 1) suggests that the posses-sion trance sets into action "behavior springing from a deeper level of the personality." Yap (1960) argues that possession or trance states are problem-solving processes that result in the dramatization of a certain part of the ego or self, "that part being constituted by forced and urgent identification with another personality believed to be transcendent in nature. The nature of the possessing personality can be psy-chologically understood in the light of the sub-ject's own personality needs; his life situation, the personality characteristics . . . of the possess-ing agent; and the subject's cultural back-ground. . . ."(Yap 1960: 125).

It seems to be more difficult to apply this gen-eralization to practitioners of glossolalia or pos-session by the Holy Spirit. They believe in possession by one transcendent being who is part of a triune god, and not in possession by a myr-iad of individual spiritual entities or personali-ties. These people may develop more or less individualized patterns of glossolalia or motor responses, but little else to mark off their unique-ness. They act within a group setting where a group leader is there to conduct prayers and to usher in the possession state, but there is little variation, it appears, in personality manifesta-tions (Bourguignon 1976: 57).

In demonic possession in the West there appears to be an overall generalized behavioral pattern but in terms of personality there are any number of personalities and identities that can be expressed. Repressed fears and desires, resent-ments and frustrations can cause an individual to manifest all of their culture's outward symptoms of possession in order to draw attention to them-selves and their life circumstances. Lyons talks about just such circumstances when discussing the psychological causes of satanic possession in the Salem colony and elsewhere in America:

> The psychological affliction remained the same. Firstly it provided a means of throw-ing off authority for, once possessed, a man is no longer responsible for his actions, all of his actions being perpetrated by the demonic invader. Secondly it provided a method of projecting any doubts or guilt feelings held by the tormented person to the outside. Like schizophrenia, it enabled a man to split his own personality, attribut-ing those elements of his personality which he found undesirable or of which he was ashamed to someone on the outside; that

part of himself is externalized and takes the shape of the tormentor, the demon. Taking these facts into consideration, it is possible to conclude that possession would be most likely to occur in those areas where authority, manifested in overpowering social structure or system of values, was the greatest and the emotional safety valves the least (1970: 96).

This is especially true of fundamentalist Christian sects that can create such an overpowering system of values and controls with few safety valves save that of possession.

Bourguignon (1976: 53) attributes such attacks as being partially due to disassociated or split off parts of the personality that the conscious mind represses or disowns. Ebon (1974: 220) calls possession "a cry for help; call it a ritualized tantrum if you like. At any rate the patient calls attention to himself for a variety of social, emotional, or even economic reasons. He, or more frequently she, dramatizes a cry for help. . . ." The importance of the individual in possession manifestations cannot be overemphasized, for it is he or she who internalizes the cultural beliefs and expectations regarding this phenomenon, helps create or participates in the external conditioning necessary to trigger the onset of such states, and then displays the manifestations of this cultural belief and behavioral system within an appropriate context. Many of the reasons for these states are found deep within the individual mind, as conditioned and influenced by cultural belief systems.

THE SOCIAL VALUE OF POSSESSION

Such states of being provide a number of benefits to the society within which possession beliefs and possession states are found. One of the more mundane factors in traditional society is the entertainment factor derived from public displays of possession and exorcism rituals. Public ceremonialism relieves the day-to-day routine of life, which often is oppressively monotonous, often within the midst of grinding poverty. Possessed individuals and the public ceremonies performed to cure them provide a break from this routine and give people a chance to participate in

a dramatic, uplifting, religious activity and have fun at the same time. Spectators are entertained by the activities of the possessed individual, the priests or exorcists, and by the rituals used to bring such states of being to an end (Walker 1972: 97).

In the Middle Ages in Europe, exorcisms were often conducted in public, with crowds surrounding the principal actors in the drama, the priest-exorcist and the victim. The public spectacle concerning the struggle between good and evil, presented in such a concrete fashion, must have been of great interest to the local populace. Even today, in modified form, possession supplies public entertainment, albeit on the silver screen or the television screen. People still love to be frightened in a controlled safe setting, despite the general drop-off in belief in the reality of possession, as the success of such movies as *The Exorcist* and others of the genre can testify to.

Possession and possession cults also contribute to social solidarity and stability by focusing on areas of stress and strain in societal structure that threatens the status quo (Walker 1972: 101; see also Shapiro 1998 for Brazilian possession cults; Lewis 1986). Among the Watarto of Kenya, married women are often struck by possession states, called *saka*, which are characterized by compulsive body movements. This society is heavily male dominated, women have little structural power, and are almost totally dependent on men, first their fathers and later their husbands. They are barred from sharing in their father's estates, they cannot participate in trade or wage labor, and they have little effective say in how their lives are to be handled. This is particularly true when family funds are allocated for items considered to be prestigious or important (Harris 1971: 1050–1052). Women afflicted with *saka* exhibit an inordinate desire for material goods or experiences normally within the male domain; owning cattle, participating in wage labor, and other male activities. The cure for *saka* is to give women the goods they desire and/or to have them participate in a public curing dance. Harris suggests that this dance is a symbolic public presentation of societal conflicts between men and women. He states, "In this way, participating in ritual indicates agreement on the forms of social relationships . . . the *saka* attack allows a round-about acknowledgment of conflict, but in the saka dance the theme is peace, dignity, and festivity" (Harris 1971: 1064). The *saka* attacks and the public dance appear to reaffirm the status quo while allowing women the opportunity to publicly express their desires and frustrations.

In a smaller way, possession cults in the West perform similar duties, but not in a society-wide manner. They may serve to express frustration with society for a small segment of the population, the true believer, but mass movements seem to have usurped this function for most individuals in the West, particularly in the United States. Political parties, special interest groups, and single-cause groups serve the function of protesting the status quo in a public forum, allowing the disaffected a voice in the larger society.

Possession cults and their rituals focus on the group and its needs, define reality for the group, and provide the means by which this reality is to be dealt with (Walker 1972: 98). The cult enlists the aid of the supernatural world in solving group problems and meeting group needs. The gods or spirits can give advice on matters of importance and can give the group confidence that, in serious crises, the group has avenues and definite courses of action it can pursue to influence the outcome of events, mainly by turning to the supernatural for assistance. They are not helpless in the face of turbulent times and therefore can deal successfully with the world.

Some cults use possession states as a way to define the reality of their belief systems. By publicly displaying the presence of the possessed and the ability of the cult to assist the afflicted, such cults "prove" the reality of their cosmology by means not normally available. The Roman Catholic Church (1994) requires the afflicted individual to undergo a battery of physical and psychological tests to rule out medical causes to the behavior and activity of the victim of demonic possession. It then applies spiritual criteria as a final form or proof of the "reality" of the possession state. Then the efficacy of the *Rituale Romanum* in driving out the possessing entities corroborates the existence of God as defined by the Roman Catholic Church specifically, and Christianity in general. In this manner, the Roman Catholic Church "proves" the reality of its cosmological and theological structure of reality by employing both modern science and age-old spiritual practices. Both the possession state and the exorcism demonstrate that where medical science has failed to alleviate the condition, the power of Jesus Christ has provided the victim with relief and succor from the forces of evil. Such proof allows the church to be forward looking while still confirming the ancient truths taught for two millennia.

Glossolaliast cults also employ possession states in a similar manner. They become a group set apart from the everyday world and united by commonly experienced phenomenon. They generally suffer rejection, or at least suspicion, from larger mainstream Christian sects and society at large. This aids in increasing the cohesiveness of the association of these individuals (Kildahl 1972: 70). The existence of possession by the Holy Spirit supports the theological beliefs of the followers and leaders of such groups.

Such an occurrence must also buttress the solidarity of fundamentalist and/or millenarian groups with a belief in demonic possession. In the case of the unfortunate Bernadette recounted earlier, the "holy parents" of the "family" to which Bernadette belonged were convinced of the reality of her demonic possession and convinced Bernadette of this reality sufficiently enough to extract a "confession" from her. This must have enhanced the stature of the leaders and increased the faith of the followers, for ferreting out the Devil's handiwork would have been seen as proof of the special status of the leaders. This belief must have been so strong that the followers obeyed the orders of the leaders without hesitation or questioning, for it resulted in the death of the unfortunate Bernadette. I suspect that even the death may have seemed proper to the followers, as a confirmation of the terrible strength of the evil inhabiting the girl. The solidarity of the group was probably enhanced, at least temporarily, but at a terrible price.

CONCLUSION

When a cultural phenomenon of this magnitude, cross-cultural extent, and time depth is being examined, firm conclusions are difficult to come by.

The subject of possession and exorcism is a vast and difficult one, bringing into play psychological, biological, cultural, and theological viewpoints in an attempt to understand the whys and wherefores of this behavior.

There are both differences and similarities in the way possession states are viewed by different societies, and the various factors that trigger such states vary from culture to culture and person to person. One final point to be considered is this: Why has there been a marked reduction in incidents of possession in Western culture since their heyday in the Middle Ages? One answer is found in the nature of Western epistemological thinking. The culture of the West has become much more secularized and scientifically oriented in the last 300 to 400 years. We can concoct and examine numerous scientific explanations of phenomena that could once be explained only in terms of the cosmology of good and evil within the Western Judeo-Christian context. Religion, particularly the various denominations of Christianity, no longer dominates the thinking of the majority of people in the West in the same manner as it once did. Even the veracity of the basic tenets of Christianity are under attack by critics and researchers dealing with the origins and basic belief systems of this world religion. It is hard for many to believe that, in this "scientific" day and age, belief in the Devil and demonic possession still exists in our world.

Possession states are rare in the Western context because more adequate paradigms and explanations have been developed that explain the onset of possession states more completely and accurately than did previous "native" explanations about it. Seizures that were once the hallmark of this state can now be explained as epileptic fits or the results of Tourette's syndrome or Parkinson's disease. Manifestations of other personalities can be explained by resorting to a diagnosis of schizophrenia or other psychological causes (Allison 1998, n.d.). Even mainstream denominations such as the Catholic Church insist that medical or psychological causes be ruled out prior to even considering the alternative explanation of demonic possession (Mahoney n.d.).

Perhaps more importantly, Ebon (1974) has suggested that Western culture has developed its own, more subtle form of possession that has in part replaced the traditional form. They may not be as dramatic but are just as effective. He suggests that the potential of "mass man" to be possessed by an idea, to be a "true believer" in a cause and get caught up in a "we versus they" syndrome is perhaps the most pervasive form of possession active in today's world. It is certainly the form most acceptable to modern societies, and is even considered highly valuable and extremely desirable by those holding the reins of power (Ebon 1974: 233). Anyone who was present during the Cuban Missile Crisis of the 1960s, or lived through the "Cold War" until its demise in 1989 could testify to the existence of this phenomenon. The same could be suggested as partial explanations for the Gulf War, the "ethnic cleansing" in Bosnia and Kosovo, the gulags of the Soviet Union, or the Holocaust. Caught up in such situations, individuals do not have to take responsibility for their actions, only believe what the leaders tell them and follow orders, and all personal ethical and moral responsibility falls by the wayside. This is similar in a mass way to the abdication of personal responsibility within individual possession states, whether found in traditional societies or pockets of Western culture. In fact, suggests Ebon, if Satan does exist "a good case can be made that he hasn't really bothered possessing individuals for some time, finding a much more receptive vessel in mass man, whether in a lynch mob, a military or civilian crowd set upon massacre, the rioters, the self-degraders who by means of word, drug, or drum, turns into a thousand-footed super animal" (Ebon 1974: 233).

The discomforting question we must ask ourselves in the West is this: Are we that much different from our brethren in traditional societies? Have we traded individual possession states and personal encounters with the spirit world, particularly with evil entities, for mass possession and evil on an industrialized scale and in an impersonal form? And if the answer is yes, does this make us different only in form and not functioning of these states of being? If anthropology truly studies man in all times and in all places then these are questions we must face in order to do our jobs as students of humanity correctly.

References

———. 1949. *The Holy Bible.* Cleveland: World Publishing Company.

———. 1976. A Phenomenon of Fear. *Time,* Vol. 109, No. 34. September 6.

———. 1976. Exorcists on Trial in Death. *Newsday,* Vol. 37, No. 60.

———. 1995. Woman Admits Guilt in Exorcism Death. *The Globe and Mail,* June 22. http://wchat.on.ca/humanist/rlv03.htm

Allison, Ralph B.N.d. "If in Doubt, Cast It Out? The Evolution of a Belief System Regarding Possession and Exorcism." www.disassociation.com/index/unpublished/CastltOut.txt.

———. 1998. Multiple Personality Disorder, Disassociative Identity Disorder, and Internalized Imaginary Companions. *Hypnos* 25: 125–133.

Armstrong, Karen. 1994. *A History of God.* New York: Alfred A. Knopf.

Beattie, John, and John Middleton. 1969. *Spirit Mediumship and Society in Africa.* New York: Africana Publishing Company.

Belo, Jane. 1960. *Trance in Bali.* New York: Columbia University Press.

Bourguignon, Erika. 1965. "The Self, the Behavioral Environment, and the Theory of Spirit Possession." In *Context and Meaning in Cultural Anthropology,* edited by Melford E. Spiro, pp. 39–60. New York: The Free Press.

———. 1973. "A Framework for the Comparative Study of Altered States of Consciousness." In: *Religion, Altered States of Consciousness, and Social Change,* Erika Bourguignon, ed. pp. 1–30. Columbus: Ohio State University Press.

———. 1976. *Possession.* San Francisco: Chandler and Sharp Publishers, Incorporated.

Buck, Charles. 1974. "Exorcism and the Bible." In: *Exorcism Through the Ages,* St. Elmo Naumann, Jr., ed. pp. 21–30. New York: Philosophical Library.

Cohn, Norman. 1970. *The Pursuit of the Millennium.* New York: Oxford University Press.

CNN. 1998. French Villagers Summon Exorcist. CNN.com, October 22, 1998. www.CNN.Com/WORLD/europe/9810/22.france.devil.church

———. 1999. *Vatican Issues First New Exorcism Ritual Since 1614.* CNN.Com, January 26, 1999. www.CNN.comWORLD/europe/9901/26/exorcism/

Cogan, J. F.N.d. *Handbook About Demonic Possession for Human Service Workers.* www.gelservices.com/hs.html.

Dodds, E. R. 1951. *The Greeks and the Irrational.* Berkeley: The University of California Press.

Douglas, Mary. 1966. *Purity and Danger: An Analysis of Concepts of Pollution and Taboo.* Harmondsworth: Penguin Books.

Ebon, Martin. 1974. *The Devil's Bride.* New York: Harper and Row Publishers.

Eliade, Mercea. 1964. *Shamanism: Archaic Techniques of Ecstasy.* New York: Pantheon Books.

Freud, Sigmund. 1959. "A Neurosis of Demoniacal Possession in the Seventeenth Century." In: *Sigmund Freud: Collected Papers,* Vol. 4: 436–472. Edited by Ernest Jones. New York: Basic Books.

Garbett, G. Kingsly. 1969. "Spirit Mediums as Mediators in Valley Korekore Society." In: *Spirit Mediumship in Africa,* John Beattie and John Middleton, eds. pp. 104–127. New York: Africana Publishing Company.

Hamer, John, and Irene Hamer. 1966. "Spirit Possession and its Socio-Psychological Implications among the Sidamo of Southwest Ethiopia." *Ethnology* 5: 392–407.

Herskovits, Melville. 1966. *The New World Negro.* Bloomington: Indiana University Press.

Hriskos, C. 1999. "Review of Spirit Hypothesis Panel in the Society for the Anthropology of Consciousness Section." *Anthropology Newsletter* 40: 52.

Jones, Rex. 1976. "Spirit Possession and Society in Nepal." In: *Spirit Possession in the Nepal Himalayas,* John T. Hitchcock and Rex Jones, eds. pp. 1–11. Warminster: Axis and Philps Limited.

Kildahl, John P. 1972. *The Psychology of Speaking in Tongues.* New York: Harper and Row Publishers.

Leek, Sybil. 1975. *Driving Out Devils: An Exorcist's Handbook.* New York: G.P. Putnam's Sons.

Lewis, I. M. 1971. *Ecstatic Religions.* Baltimore: Penguin Books Incorporated.

———. 1986. "Religion." In: *Context: Cults and Charisma.* Cambridge: Cambridge University Press.

Lyons, Arthur. 1970. *The Second Coming: Satanism in America.* New York: Dodd, Mead, and Company.

Martin, Malachi. 1976. *Hostage to the Devil.* New York: Thomas Y. Crowell Company.

Mastrantonis, Reverend George. 1990–1996. "Exorcism. Greek Orthodox Diocese of America." www.goarch.org/access/orthodoxfaithexorcism.html.

Metraux, Alfred. 1972. *Voodoo in Haiti,* translated by Hugo Charteris. New York: Schocken Books.

Naumann Jr., St. Elmo. 1974. "Exorcism and Satanism in Medieval Germany." In: *Exorcism Through the Ages,* St. Elmo Naumann, Jr., ed. pp. 73–86. New York: Philosophical Library.

Nicola, Reverend John T. 1974. *Diabolical Possession and Exorcism.* Rockford: Tam Books and Publishers, Incorporated.

Oesterreich, T. K. 1930. *Possession, Demoniacal and Other, among Primitive Races, in Antiquity, The Middle Ages, and Modern Times.* New York: Richard R. Smith, Incorporated.

Petitpierre, Father Robert. 1972. *Exorcism: The Report of a Commission Convened by the Bishop of Exeter.* New York: Popular Library.

Roman Catholic Church. 1994. *Catechism of the Catholic Church.* Liguori: Liguori Publications.

Shack, William A. 1971. "Hunger, Anxiety, and Ritual: Deprivation and Spirit Possession among the Gurage of Ethiopia." *Man* 6: 30–43.

Shapiro, Dolores J. 1998. "Blood, Oil, Honey, and Water: Symbolism in Spirit Possession Sects in Northeastern Brazil." In: *Religion in Culture and Society,* John R. Bowen, ed. pp. 94–116. Needham Heights: Allyn & Bacon.

Tylor, E. B. 1958. *Religion in Primitive Culture: Part II of Primitive Culture.* New York: Harper and Brothers Publishers.

Verger, Pierre. 1954. Role Joue Par L'Etat d'Hebetude aux Cours de L'Initiation des Novices aux Cultes des Orisha et Vodun.*Bulletin de L'Institute Fondamental d'Afrique Noire.* Serie B, No. 16: 322–340.

Walker, Sheila. 1972. *Ceremonial Spirit Possession in Africa and Afro-America.* Leiden: E. J. Drill.

Wallace, A. F. C. 1959. "Cultural Determinants of Responses to Hallucinatory Experiences." *AMA Archives of General Psychiatry,* No. 1.

Wilson, Peter J. 1967. "Status Ambiguity and Spirit Possession." *Man* 2: 366–378.

Winick, Charles. 1970. *Dictionary of Anthropology.* New York: Philosophical Library.

Yap, P. M. 1960. "The Possession Syndrome: A Comparison of Hong Kong and French Findings." *Journal of Mental Science* 106 (44): 114–137.

Zaretsky, Irvin I. 1966. *Bibliography of Spirit Possession and Spirit Mediumship.* Evanston: Northwestern University Press.

Zaretsky, Irvin I., and Mark P. Leone. 1974. *Religious Movements in Contemporary America.* Princeton: Princeton University Press.

CRITICAL THINKING QUESTIONS

1. Define the differences between "native" theories of possession and Western explanations of the same phenomenon.
2. What is an altered state of consciousness, and what conditions can trigger such a state?
3. How can possession beliefs be used to enhance social solidarity and group cohesion?
4. What is the role of the individual within a society in the onset of possession states?
5. What is the Christian "native explanation" for possession states, and what form do these states take?
6. Consider and discuss your own attitudes toward possession states. Are such states real? Do you accept the Western scientific explanation? Define the reasons for your answer.

SECTION EIGHT

Symbolic Expression

STATE OF THE ART: Symbolic Expression

Symbolic expression is a much later focus of anthropological inquiry. About midway through the twentieth century, specialists began to see the study of symbols and their meaning in culture as an alternative to scientific modes of analysis in understanding human behavior. Anthropologists have found that the meaning of people's behavior varies from one culture to another, and that behavior is the result of, and is influenced by, particular symbols representing cultural ideas that can be analyzed by reading culture like a text. This scholarship has led to the study of symbols in culture, in which words, actions, and objects are deciphered for hidden meaning.

The recognition of symbols in social life goes back to before the beginnings of anthropology. Ideas for the foundations of anthropology, as it is known today, originated with several social thinkers, including Max Weber and Emile Durkheim. In the late nineteenth century, Max Weber introduced the subject of *verstehen,* or understanding, that is, the act of grasping the meanings people attach to their actions, to the study of society (Schaefer 2002). Durkheim's work on religious life found that religious beliefs carry symbolic and psychological meanings that should not be taken literally (Sidky 2004).

In the early 1900s anthropologist Franz Boas highlighted the *symbolic domain of culture* by construing culture as a system of symbols, meanings, and values. Despite the divergence in views between Boas and the evolutionary anthropologists at that time, the role of symbols in culture also gained recognition among evolutionists, especially Leslie White (a neo-evolutionist), who recognized that role and wrote about it in 1949. According to White, symbols are important and control how we perceive the universe and all its details (Sidky 2004).

The symbolic anthropology that emerged after White in the 1960s and 1970s focused *exclusively* on the symbolic domain of culture rather than all pertinent areas (Sidky 2004). While science operates on the basis of cause and effect, symbolic anthropology is concerned with people's interpretation of their own actions from the meanings derived from their own culture.

Two kinds of symbolic anthropology emerged and now coexist. One grew out of the British structural functionalist tradition and was spearheaded by Victor Turner and Mary Douglas, both of whom were influenced by the works of Emile Durkheim and the structural functionalism of Radcliffe-Brown. Radcliffe-Brown dealt with *structural institutions* in society, such as the social, political, and economic branches and how they serve to integrate the whole society. Turner's interest in the structural institutions of society eventually developed into a focus on the *social processes* surrounding those institutions, such as *conflict* typical of Max Gluckman's processual approach. Turner's major concern was the relationship between symbolic action and the social processes of society (Turner 1975). He was interested in deciphering the *hidden structural patterns* that lead to conflict. The hidden structural processes are the *social drama* that he refers to. His concept of social drama is a series of discordant situations by which conflict is made visible (Turner 1974; Sidky 2004).

Turner's symbolic method derives from his conception of ritual symbols as flowing from the meanings that feelings and emotions evoke in the participant (Sidky 2004), a legacy of Boasian influence. Among his methodologies is his threefold approach to the study of symbols: the exegetic, the operational, and the positional dimensions. The *exegetic* refers to the explanations that come from the participant in the ritual. The *operational* means that the anthropologist will merge the symbolic meaning with the form in which the participants use it. In the *positional* dimension, the symbolic anthropologist determines through his or her own interpretation how each symbol is related to other symbols to create meaning (Turner 1977; Sidky 2004). The positional dimension makes the anthropologist the sole interpreter of *uncomprehended* symbols, defined by Turner as symbols whose meanings are elusive to the members of the culture.

Another aspect of Turner's symbolism, *condensation,* is the process of loading symbols "with multiple and disparate meanings" that "can concurrently represent many ideas, relations between things, actions, interactions, and transactions" (Turner 1977:184; Sidky 2004:311).

Mary Douglas, following in Turner's footsteps, was interested in the significance of meaning in sociocultural life. She sought the universal patterns of symbolism and how they are interpreted. She views culture as a symbolic system that is superimposed upon nature for the purpose of order. To Douglas, culture is the symbolic means by which humans organize things in the world to fit into one "idea" or another. One example is the idea of pollution, which encompasses the things and behaviors a culture considers pollutants. Douglas, like Turner, believes that symbols can best be understood by looking at the larger structures of meaning in which they occur and which gives meaning to the symbols. Following Levi-Strauss, she posits *classification* on the basis of opposing categories of things in the world, and contrasts elements, such as defilement versus purity.

The second kind of symbolic anthropology, which developed in the United States, was spearheaded by David Schneider and Clifford Geertz (Sidky 2004). Geertz (1973) expanded American symbolic anthropology and differed from Turner by arguing that the meaning of symbols can be derived only from the native's point of view, and not from the anthropologist's interpretation of the culture. His concept of culture, which lies at the heart of this view, holds that culture is a system of signs and symbols and therefore must be read like a text—*thick description.* Thus, cultural symbols have layers of meaning which must be uncovered by delving deep into the ethnography of a group and during the translation of the ethnographic details that have been *fixed by writing* in the ethnographer's field notes. The Geertzian symbolic analysis employs, among others, the method of *parts* and *wholes.* The symbols in a culture (the parts) and their meanings are identified, and linked to the cultural whole. The whole gives meaning to the parts, and the parts in turn form the meaning of the whole.

Sherry Ortner, a contemporary of Clifford Geertz, adopted a different approach to the study of symbols. In her article, *On Key Symbols* (1973), Ortner introduced a mode of symbolic analysis that is suited for the study of *key* symbols of a culture—symbols that play a central role in the culture. She proposes two kinds of symbols, *summarizing* symbols versus *elaborating* symbols. The summarizing symbols are those that condense meaning, such as the U.S. flag, which embodies and unifies several symbols and their meanings. Turner's influence can be seen in the idea of condensation or summarizing of symbols. The second kind of symbols, the elaborating symbols, are those that encourage the expansion of signification to take in more and more referents.

Contemporary varieties of symbolic anthropology abound. The areas of research focus have increased. For example, anthropological studies of symbols have also looked at the link between expressions of symbols in all domains of social life. Social groups, social categories, gender relations, religious phenomena, economic behavior, and political affairs among others all carry meaning. For example, the burning of a U.S. flag by Iraqi militants may signal a challenge to U.S. global hegemony.

Anthropologists study the various metaphors for life in different societies. In doing so, they have found that ritual serves as a metaphoric expression for life. Gender meanings inform how a society is structured and reveal the power structure of the culture. Art objects in a culture carry meaning and are linked to the power structure of a society. The verbal arts are another insightful arena of anthropological study, in which the stories people tell in a culture are investigated. Myths, folktales, and legends contain symbols integral to a culture and often are symbolic expressions of historical and current trends of social life. Anthropologists have devised various theoretical approaches to the interpretation of myths and other forms of symbolic expression which reveal how cultural actors render their perceived world (Rosman & Rubel 2004). These themes constitute the current focus of anthropology in this millennium. Anthropologists continue to cover fresh ground by identifying symbols, such as new forms of political expression, that directly relate to current realities, and use them to understand and resolve emerging social problems.

ABOUT THE ARTICLES

The ability to create and use symbols to comprehend and explain the world is intrinsic to what makes us human. The articles in this section examine this human need to symbolically deal with the universe from several different perspectives. These articles illustrate the anthropological studies of symbols in the past and present that highlight the human ability to create and use symbols to comprehend and explain the world.

The Whitley article deals with rock art from the perspective of the role of such art in prehistoric societies. The interpretation of the functions and meaning of rock art has been a point of contention for archaeology and anthropology for almost as long as both fields have existed. Whitley suggests a novel approach to comprehending the origins and meaning of such art, based on a modern understanding of the workings of the human mind. Although it is expressed through culturally specific iconography, he argues that universal neuropsychological effects of induced trance states are the source of this artwork. Shamans express their inner consciousness through the medium of art, translating their individual experiences into cultural symbols that are easily understood by those who observe the artwork.

Juzhong and Kuen's article examines archaeological interpretations of music, an important symbolic system for humans. The recovery of many flutes during the excavation of the village of Jihua can raise a myriad of questions in the symbolic realm. These can include: Who made the flutes and why? What role did music play in the lives of the inhabitants of Jihua? Were there symbolic and sacred reasons why red-crane bone was selected for flute manufacture, and can these reasons be related to more recent Chinese mythological concepts involving cranes? Although speculative, these flutes may represent a thread of continuity between Neolithic Chinese culture and that of more recent centuries.

Frey deals with the oral arts, most likely the first symbolic art form of the human species. He looks at the tradition of storytelling among the Apśaalooke (Crow) Indians and its role in the maintenance of cultural identity. An important aspect of identity maintenance is the ability to enculturate the young with appropriate cultural beliefs and ideas. Frey argues that the recounting of traditional tales is an important method for transmitting such information, without which the Apśaalooke are not truly themselves.

Saris and Bartley examine modern visual arts, in this case mural painting, in its social setting among urban poor in Ireland. They explore the relationship between the social and economic conditions in Cherry Grove, an urban enclave in Dublin, and art as an expression of social reality. They ask how artwork either does or does not reflect the reality of the conditions that people living in this area face. Does it express the true situation, or does it present an idealized view of the world in order to deflect reality?

The final article deals with the symbolic connection among the dead, the living, and the land on which both depend. Traditional Hawaiian beliefs saw the bones (*na iwi*) of the dead as being sacred, imbued with a supernatural power (*mana*) that fed the living both spiritually and through the fertilization of food the living ingest. As such they symbolize the connection and continuity of generations of Hawaiians to their land. In his article, Ayau looks at what happens when another culture that lacks this idea of such interconnections disturbs the bones of the Hawaiians' ancestors. Ayau argues that there is a relationship between the disruption of the ancestors and the current economic and social conditions faced by modern ethnic Hawaiian populations. He contends that the physical loss of the dead is symbolic of the loss of the man–land relationship and cultural autonomy of native populations in Hawaii, which has resulted in spiritual loss and decay. Ayau then addresses the legal and social avenues of redress available to native Hawaiians and how these approaches can correct and reverse such losses.

References

Geertz, C. *The Interpretation of Cultures*. New York: Basic Books, 1973.

Ortner, S. "On Key Symbols." *American Anthropologist* 75 (1973): 1338–1346.

Rosman, A., & Rubel, P. *The Tapestry of Culture: An Introduction to Cultural Anthropology*, 8th ed. New York: McGraw-Hill, 2004.

Schaefer, R. T. *Sociology: A Brief Introduction*. New York: McGraw-Hill, 2002.

Sidky, H. *Perspectives on Cullture: A Critical Introduction to Theory in Cultural Anthropology*. Upper Saddle River, NJ: Pearson Education, Inc., 2004.

Turner. V. *Rerelation and Divination in Ndembu Ritual*. Ithaca, NY: Cornell University Press, 1975.

Turner, V. "Symbols in African Ritual." *In Symbolic Anthropology: A Reader in the Study of Symbols and Meaning*, J. Dolgin, D. Kemnitzer, and D. Schneider (eds.). New York: Columbia University Press, pp. 183–194, 1977.

For Further Research

Symbolic expression is often difficult to define, and harder to study, as it is often closely tied to the study of religion. There are many other facets to human symbolic expression as well. Three good general sources can be suggested. Victor Turner's *The Ritual Process: Structure and Anti-Structure* (1969, Aldine) is a densely written study of the interaction between symbols and rituals. It is a difficult read but well worth it to the student interested in symbolic human behavior. *Purity and Danger: An Analysis of Concepts of Pollution and Taboo* (1966, Praeger) by Mary Douglas examines how people use symbols to define themselves and erect barriers that differentiate between "we" and "they." Richard Anderson takes on visual and other forms of expression in his *Art in Small-Scale Societies* (1989, 2nd ed., Prentice-Hall), a small but informative introduction to the study of art by anthropologists.). For additional information on researching the topics discussed in the "State of the Art" section, please visit *www.mysearchlab.com*.

Reading the Minds of Rock Artists

David Whitley

Pictographs and petroglyphs are very different from potsherds and projectile points, the staples of traditional archaeological research. Painted (in the case of pictographs) or engraved (as petroglyphs), rock art adorns the faces of caves, cliffs, and boulders. Rock art isn't subject to the natural processes of stratigraphic burial that affect most aspects of the archaeological record. It's as visible on the landscape today as it was when first created hundreds and, in some cases, thousands of years ago. Yet its very visibility and accessibility have made rock art the ultimate archaeological tease: So easy to see and find, yet so hard to understand.

The enigma of American rock art is an old one. Decades before Thomas Jefferson's famous excavations of earthen mounds in Virginia, Cotton Mather (of Puritan fame) wrote about Dighton Rock, a Massachusetts petroglyph site, for the Royal Society of London, giving rock art research pride of place in the history of American archaeological reporting. However, Mather's view of petroglyphs—that they were a kind of proto-writing which would eventually succumb to linguistic analysis—was misguided. His efforts, along with those of subsequent researchers, did little to advance the interpretation of the art.

Proving that perseverance pays, a new generation of archaeologists is finally making headway in understanding rock art, nearly 300 years after Mather's initial report. Breakthroughs have come via an analysis of the ethnographic record (the published and unpublished studies of historically known American Indians conducted by anthropologists since the early part of this century), combined with a much less obvious method—the examination of human neuropsychology. This combination is shedding light on who made this art, why they made it, and what it symbolizes.

REOPENING THE RECORDS

Often the most profound discoveries aren't the hardest to find, but those longest overlooked. Nowhere is this truer than in rock art research. For generations, archaeologists ignored the ethnographic record in favor of striking out into the prehistoric unknown, with no real clue as to why people might have made rock art, or what it may have meant. There are a number of reasons why researchers ignored the ethnographic record, one of which is the fact that most archaeologists lack intensive training in ethnographic interpretation. In my own case, I disregarded ethnography for a simpler reason: When I began my research, all the published authorities claimed the ethnographic sources contained no useful information on rock art. To my detriment, I believed this bold traditional claim for many years.

My perspective changed in the mid-1980s. Inspired by the research of South African archaeologist David Lewis-Williams with San (Bushmen) rock art, some of my colleagues and I began systematically reexamining the ethnography of far-western North America. This region includes the art of California, the Great Basin, and the Columbia Plateau, or essentially the hunter-gatherer West, as opposed to the farming Puebloan Southwest. With Julie Francis, James Keyser, Larry Loendorf, and others, we've found that substantial ethnographic information exists on the making and meaning of rock art—information that confirms, in dramatic fashion, hypotheses that had been suggested but never proven. This information connects much far-western rock art with shamanism, the pervading religious system of hunter-gatherer Native America.

Although there were slightly different expressions of it, all shamanistic religions believed that humans may directly interact with

Source: Reprinted from *American Archaeology,* Fall 1997, by permission of the author.

the supernatural world by entering a trance. While in this state, the shaman could obtain supernatural power (often in the form of an animal spirit helper), or conduct supernatural undertakings, such as healing the sick, making rain, finding lost objects, or bewitching an enemy.

Anthropologist Alfred Kroeber was the first to suggest that rock art might be linked to shamanism in his 1925 *Handbook of the Indians of California.* Although archaeologists were aware of Kroeber's hypothesis, no firm evidence confirmed it. Indeed, the few widely recognized ethnographic passages about rock art seemed to indicate a fundamental lack of American Indian knowledge about this art. A good example of this belief involved many informants' claims that rock art was made by a "rock-" or "water baby." Archaeologists incorrectly equated "water baby" with traditional European tales of wood sprites and faeries, concluding as a result that the Indian informants knew nothing about rock art. Recent, more detailed studies of the ethnography show that rock- and water babies weren't inconsequential spirits. On the contrary, they were among the strongest spirit helpers of the shaman. As anthropologist Carobeth Laird notes in her book *Mirror and Pattern,* the actions of shamans and their spirit helpers were considered indistinguishable, so claiming that art was made by a water baby was a way of saying it was done by a shaman. This deception was necessary in order to avoid speaking the names of the dead.

The ethnographic record clearly indicates that many rock art motifs portray the visionary images of trance. American Indian informants of anthropologist Harold Driver claimed that rock art symbols are the "spirits" seen in a trance. In much of California and the Great Basin, shamans were the only individuals making rock art, while in southwestern California, the Columbia Plateau, and along the Colorado River, puberty initiates also made art.

Rock art sites, then, were vision-quest locales. In California's Southern Sierra Nevada, sites were called various names (in different languages and dialects) that translate as "shaman's spirit-helper place." Among the Numic of the Great Basin, a rock art site was known as a "house of supernatural power." The sites were portals into the supernatural, with the motifs themselves representing images of this sacred realm.

CONSERVING SACRED IMAGES

Rock art has long captivated the imagination of the American public. Kokopelli, the humpbacked flute player of the Southwest, is so renowned that a Las Vegas casino lounge now bears his name. Disney's *The Lion King* includes a scene featuring Rafikki (a monkey shaman) painting pictographs. Rock art has insinuated itself into our popular cultural awareness like no other aspect of the archaeological record, yet no other aspect of this record is so inherently fragile or so greatly imperiled.

The difficulties in conserving rock art sites are numerous: wind and rain erode unprotected art, livestock rub against rocks and scratch away the art; natural freeze-thaw cycles break off rock panels. But the bigger problem is irresponsible human visitation. As Jannie Loubser, a specialist in rock art site management with New South Associates, puts it: "People can destroy in an instant what has lasted for thousands of years." While most people are familiar with the negative effects of graffiti, they often don't realize that chalking the outlines of motifs, taking castings or rubbings, touching motifs—even trampling one's feet near a site (which allows dust to accumulate on and obscure the art)—all have immediate and long-term adverse consequences for rock art.

Recognizing rock art's importance, the Archaeological Conservancy has acquired two important California rock art sites (a number of the Conservancy's Southwestern sites also contain rock art components). The Rocky Hill site, near the town of Exeter, is an archaeological resource of world-class significance. It is the largest concentration of pictographs in California, containing more than two dozen paintings associated with a Late Prehistoric/Historic-period Wukchumni Yokuts village site.

The second site, Willis Wells, in the Mojave Desert outside of Barstow, is a good example of a "typical" desert petroglyph site. Situated near a spring, Willis Wells contains about 50 petroglyphs and adjacent habitation debris. While the

Conservancy's acquisition and management of these sites represent a key step in safeguarding California rock art, only time will tell whether we can preserve our rock art sites for posterity.

The Coso Range Example

The importance of shamanism to the understanding of rock art is well illustrated by the petroglyphs of the Coso Range in eastern California. The Cosos are a western extension of the Great Basin, occupied historically by Numic speakers (the Shoshone and Northern and Southern Paiute). The range contains between 75,000 and 100,000 petroglyphs, but no one really knows how many motifs are in this isolated and rugged region of basalt flows and volcanic domes. Regardless, it is undoubtedly the biggest concentration of rock art in North America. About half the petroglyphs at Coso sites depict bighorn sheep. Other identifiable motifs include humans, weapons, "medicine bags," and a smaller number of other animal species. Geometric forms of myriad shapes represent about one-quarter of the total.

Knowing that Great Basin petroglyphs were made by Numic shamans allows archaeologists to use their understanding of Numic shamanistic beliefs and practices as a guide to interpreting their art. The early research of anthropologist Isabel Kelly indicates that the bighorn was a specialized kind of spirit helper, one who imparted power to make rain. Certain locations were associated with specific kinds of supernatural power, and shamans sometimes traveled great distances to these spots to obtain desired types of potency. Given the predominance of bighorn petroglyphs, shamans obviously saw the Cosos as a source for rain-making power. Shamans often traveled from as far as northern Utah to the Cosos for their ritual activities.

Recently, scholars have tried to expand their understanding of rock art beyond historical cases to identify the human "universals" underlying the making of this art. One approach to the problem has involved the study of how the brain functions during trance. Since we know that rock art was made historically to portray the visions of trance, it follows that understanding the biological and mental effects of trance should give us additional insight.

"All human beings are *Homo sapiens sapiens* regardless of where they live," explains New Mexico State University's Larry Loendorf. "Neuropsychology gives us an anatomical opportunity to explore an area of human uniformity in culture." In other words, our reactions to trance are broadly similar, which means scientists can use the similarities as analytical guides to test our ethnographic interpretations against prehistoric rock art, or to study rock art regions with no ethnographic records.

Still, the question remains: Why did shamans create rock art? Although every culture throughout the world had different reasons for making the art, neuropsychology gives us one important clue. Laboratory studies have shown that, during a trance, chemical changes in the brain result in impaired short-term memory. Ethnographic accounts reflect this neuropsychological universal, with a number of informants recounting the great importance and difficulty attached to remembering the hallucinations the shamans experienced in the supernatural realm. By "fixing" visionary images on the landscape with hammerstone or paintbrush, shamans ensured their permanence as records of easily forgotten sacred experiences.

Neuropsychology also helps explain the frequent occurrence of geometric motifs found in much hunter-gatherer rock art. During a trance, our optical system commonly generates a series of mental images—light patterns known as entoptic ("within the eye") phenomena, including designs such as zigzags, meanders, grids, and spirals. (These entoptic patterns may also occur during a migraine headache, or after a blow to the head, or even if we stare at a bright light and then close our eyes and press on our eyelids.) Different cultures interpret these motifs in different ways, but neuropsychology tells us that geometric forms can be expected in rock art that portrays the mental imagery of trance.

Another insight from neuropsychology concerns the emotions of the prehistoric artists—a subject long assumed to be archaeologically unknowable. Abundant emotions are a common characteristic of trance and, although we usually think of trance as euphoric, clinical studies have shown that unpleasant emotions such as grief and rage are also typical. Ethnographic accounts confirm this by emphasizing the dangerous and frightening (rather than beneficent) nature of the supernatural. It was commonly stated that shamans were required to pass immense grizzly bear and rattlesnake spirits to enter the supernatural, or to fight off attacks by skeletons or ghosts—all events that are tied to unpleasant rather than ecstatic emotions.

As we now realize, far-western North American rock art is more than just quaint imagery, useful only for embellishing the covers of archaeological monographs or decorating T-shirts. Rather it is a valuable record of the American Indian's view of their sacred realm. It is also a glimpse inside the consciousness of the shaman, taking us beyond the technology of stone and ceramic artifacts, to examine the prehistoric mind responsible for making the archaeological record.

David S. Whitley is an archaeologist who lives in Fillmore, California.

CRITICAL THINKING QUESTIONS

1. Why did archaeologists ignore ethnographic data and research in their attempts to understand American Indian rock art?

2. To which aspect of American Indian culture does Whitley suggest rock art is related? According to Whitley, what evidence is there in the ethnographic record to support this contention?

3. What biological phenomenon does Whitley suggest the rock art designs are associated with, and why? How does this relate to the cultural institution Whitley says rock art represents?

4. A thought question: How may petroglyphs and pictographs reflect the worldview (cosmology) of American Indian groups?

The Magic Flutes

Zhang Juzhong and Lee Yun Kuen

Nine thousand years ago, Neolithic villagers in China played melodies on instruments fashioned from the hollow bones of birds.

Long ago in Jiahu village, an acclaimed musician passed away at the mature age of thirty-five. People who had appreciated his music flocked to the funeral ceremony. The musician's body was dressed in his finest clothing, and a turtle shell was tied to his right shoulder. In life he had often worn the shell: with a few pebbles placed inside, it rattled as he danced to his own music. One of the musician's two surviving sons, young men in their late teens, directed several helpers as they lowered the body into the rectangular earthen pit dug the day before. Then, kneeling in the grave, he separated the head from the torso with a stone ax, and carefully turned the head to face northwest—a customary treatment for special people of the time.

Leaning over the edge of the grave, the musician's other son then passed down the sixty or so offerings. His brother put the three-legged cooking pot, along with a jar and a vase containing provisions for the afterlife journey, near the head. Arrows and barbed harpoons were placed near the right leg; milling stones, awls, chisels, knives, and other offerings were set to the left of the body. Finally, the musician's two flutes, each crafted from the hollow wing bone of a red-crowned crane, were tucked on either side of his left leg. Then the son climbed out of the grave, and six or seven helpers started the backfilling with stone shovels.

We hope the reader will indulge the small license we have had to take in telling this tale. Our story is consistent with the abundant physical remains, but the burial took place long before history was written down. Yet, unlike most tales based on archaeological reconstruction, this one concludes with an episode that almost sweeps away the fog of the intervening centuries and brings the dead to life. In May 1987, more than 8,000 years after it had last been touched by human lips, one of the musician's two flutes was played again. The room was dead silent as Ning Baosheng, the flutist of the Central Orchestra of Chinese Music in Beijing, held the bone instrument at a forty-five-degree angle to his mouth. One by one, he tested the holes. The assembled archaeologists and musicians were amazed by the sound produced by a flute of such great antiquity. The tones seemed so familiar. In Europe, archaeologists have discovered the remains of even more ancient flutes, also fashioned from animal bone, but none in playable condition.

Jiahu is the name of a modern village in central China and, by extension, the name of the ancient flute-owner's village, or at least its archaeological remains. The setting is the upper valley of the Huai River, which flows east between the Huang He (Yellow River) to the north and the Chang Jiang (Yangtze River) to the south [see map on next page]. The site was discovered in 1961 by Zhu Zhi, an administrator of cultural resources, who plucked pottery shards and other material remains from the walls of wells and gullies. Archaeological excavation began in 1983, when the site was threatened by local development.

Chinese archaeologists cannot possibly excavate all sites threatened by development, but they consider Jiahu special. The artifacts collected even at the surface are as much as 9,000 years old, dating from the early Neolithic, or New Stone Age, when people first began to rely on domesticated crops and animals. Moreover, little was known about this stage of prehistory in this part of China. Six seasons of fieldwork, lasting between several weeks and several months each, were conducted between 1983 and 1987. A second round of excavations started in 2001 and is still under way.

At the outset, however, no one expected to find anything as exotic as a flute. Indeed, by the middle of the fourth season of excavation, in early May 1986, the archaeologists were beginning to feel bored, as the same arrowheads, harpoons, milling stones, spades, vessels, and other utilitarian artifacts surfaced over and over again.

Then one of us, Zhang, the director of the excavation, was approached by Yang Zhenwei, the field director, who was excavating a grave designated only by its field label: M78 (in the convention of Chinese archaeology, M designates a burial, because mu is the Chinese word for grave). Two bone tubes, each with seven small holes drilled on one side, lay within the collection of artifacts. Neither Yang nor Zhang dared utter a word about what was racing through their minds. Although the two artifacts bore a striking resemblance to a modern Chinese folk instrument—a kind of upright bamboo flute—nothing like that had ever been discovered in China from so early a time.

The finds were unprecedented but, as it turned out, not unique. Another flute was discovered in another grave the next day, and another in still another grave. Then they just kept coming. By the end of the first series of excavations, in June 1987, twenty-five specimens had been discovered. Seventeen were intact, or nearly so, six were broken or fragmented, and two were half-finished. All were made from the ulna—a wing bone—of the red-crowned crane. The naturally hollow bones were first cut to a length of between seven and ten inches, then smoothed at the ends, polished, and finally drilled on one side to make a row of between five and eight holes.

Among the flutes was M282:20, the twentieth object documented in grave M282, and the basis for the vignette at the beginning of our story. That flute was found in pristine condition and was the first to be tested. During more recent seasons of excavation, Zhang's team has uncovered still more flutes from the burials, bringing today's total to thirty-three. And more tests have been conducted on the playable flutes. Those instruments have now afforded some insight into the evolving musical knowledge and skills of people who lived millennia before the first written records of music. At the same time, we must admit that their motives for playing music and their "ear" for appropriate musical composition and sound are still steeped in mystery.

The musical cultures of the past, like the ones of today, did not exist in a vacuum. Jiahu's location was apparently quite favorable because Neolithic people occupied the site almost continuously from 9,000 years ago—near the dawn of agriculture in China—until 7,800 years ago. The archaeological work at the site to date has yielded fifty house foundations, 430 storage pits, eleven pottery kilns, 439 burials, and thousands of artifacts made of bone, pottery, stone, and other materials. The stratigraphy of the site shows that it was occupied again in historical times, beginning in the Han Dynasty (second century B.C. to second century A.D.), and continuously thereafter down to the present. The intervening time is still a blank, but so far only 5 percent of the site has been excavated; further work could well show additional periods of occupation.

One surprising discovery is that the villagers grew japonica rice, a short-grain subspecies. Many scholars have believed that rice cultivation began with the long-grain indica subspecies, a crop domesticated in the tropics and subtropics 6,000 years ago. The short-grain type arose—or so the thinking went—as the crop spread to the cooler, more northerly latitudes. The early appearance of japonica rice in the north, together with some equally early finds of both subspecies in the lower Chang Jiang valley, has complicated that picture.

Apart from cultivating rice, the Jiahu villagers hunted and fished, taking carp, crane, deer, hare, turtle, and other animals. They also collected a broad variety of wild herbs, wild vegetables such as acorns, water chestnuts, and broad beans, and possibly wild rice. And they possessed domesticated dogs and pigs.

Living conditions in an ancient community are reflected not only in the artifacts unearthed, but also in the inhabitants' skeletal remains. Factors such as diet, disease, and mechanical stress leave indelible marks on bones. Barbara Li Smith, a forensic archaeologist at Harvard University, examined the skeletons of 248 individuals recovered in the excavations. She concluded that the villagers enjoyed reasonably good health. The Jiahu life expectancy, or average age at death, was about forty years, longer than usual for Neolithic farmers. Bone lesions from infectious disease or parasitic infection are rare. Osteoarthritis, a sign of bone degeneration with age or of the mechanical stresses of repetitive motion, appears in 38 percent of the skeletons.

As for more serious health problems, more than two-thirds of the skeletons show signs of iron-deficiency anemia. The tip-off is the presence of spongy lesions in the skull: marrow in the skull, compensating for the anemia, expands to make additional red blood cells. Anemia may reflect infection, but people whose dietary staple is grain often have a high incidence of iron-deficiency anemia simply because grain is deficient in iron.

To learn more about the Jiahu diet, archaeologists examined the ancient pottery vessels. The vessels' contents had long since decayed away, but pottery is quite porous, and the hope was that residues trapped and preserved in the minute holes might be detectable with the right kinds of high-tech equipment. Patrick McGovern, a biomolecular archaeologist at the University of Pennsylvania Museum of Archaeology and Anthropology, analyzed potsherds of sixteen jars and vases. He extracted organic chemicals from thirteen of them, finding signs of rice, honey, and grape or hawthorn fruit.

McGovern concluded that many of the pottery jars and vases were used for fermenting and storing wine or beer. The ancient villagers not only fed themselves well, but also made alcoholic drinks from surplus grain. Besides being intoxicating, McGovern maintains, alcohol may have been healthful, because it kills many disease-causing microorganisms. The villagers also offered wine or beer to the dead, placing jars and vases in many of the graves.

The excavation at Jiahu uncovered the remains of 439 juveniles and adults, buried in pits, and 32 infants, buried in urns. Some pits contained just one individual, others as many as six. The multiple interments usually represented the reburial of skeletal remains from earlier burials, though in a few cases one new, or primary, interment was added. No one knows how the individuals buried together may have been related, but they were mixed in sex and varied in age.

In thirty-seven primary burials, the skull, mandible, or other bones of the extremities are missing from the skeleton; cut marks show that they were removed when the bone was fresh. Either the individual died of the cuts, or the parts were removed soon after death. In a dozen or so examples, such as the body of the musician in grave M282, body parts were severed, but the parts remained in the grave. We think that the various manipulations of the skeletons were reserved for important members of the society, simply because they involved more labor. Their purpose at Jiahu remains obscure, but in prehistoric Europe, some human bones seem to have been circulated among the graves and the living population, presumably because they were valued or venerated.

The flutes discovered so far all came from graves, usually graves that were fairly rich in burial goods. We and our colleagues have tested the tones of six flutes that are still playable. Those tests can tell us something about the musical scales that the instruments could have produced, and from the scales we can infer something about the complexity of possible melodies. In addition, the site was occupied in three distinct phases, from 9,000 until 8,600 years ago, from 8,600 until 8,200 years ago, and from 8,200 until 7,800 years ago. A comparison of flutes from those three periods can tell us whether the scales and possible melodies became more sophisticated with time.

A flute makes a sound because the player causes the column of air in its tube to vibrate. In a vertical flute, the customary way to set the air in motion is to rest the upper end of the tube against the lower lip and blow across the opening—much the way one makes an open bottle hum by blowing across its rim. The angle and strength of the player's breath affect both pitch and sound quality, but what mostly determines pitch is the length and volume of the column of vibrating air. When the instrument is more than a simple tube, such as a flute with finger holes, the player can manipulate the size of the air column by covering or uncovering the finger holes.

Skilled musicians can get complex sounds and a variety of pitches out of an instrument by only partly covering the holes or by opening and closing them according to relatively complex patterns (known as cross-fingering). Without knowing the playing techniques of the ancient musicians, though, we were limited to testing the pitches that could be made with simple fingering. We measured the frequency of each pitch with an electronic sound-analyzing instrument called a Stroboconn.

Only two flutes have been recovered from the earliest phase of settlement; both came from the grave of an adult male. One has five holes, and so it can produce six discrete pitches, one for each hole, plus the pitch produced by the entire length of the instrument, when all the holes are covered. In two cases, however, notes are repeated an octave apart, so the musical variety is somewhat restricted. If you try constructing a scale, you wind up, in a sense, with only four notes, separated by wide gaps. Nevertheless, even such a simple scale shows that the flute players sounded more than single notes, and if one assumes that Jiahu musicians used cross-fingering and other means to vary the pitch, they could have played fairly elaborate pieces of music.

The second flute from the earliest phase of settlement has six. This flute can play seven discrete pitches, but again, in two cases, notes are repeated an octave apart. Thus the flute gives ready access to a five-note scale—an intriguing discovery in itself, given that a pentatonic, or five-note, scale is the basis of Chinese folk music even today. The presence of a five- and a six-hole flute in the same grave indicates that different musical scales probably coexisted during this phase of settlement in Jiahu.

About two dozen flutes were unearthed from the second phase of Neolithic settlement. Fifteen of them were intact or could be reconstructed. One of those has only two holes, but the others all have seven. Three of the seven-hole flutes are still playable, including the two that were found in grave M282, the burial of our now-famous musician.

Those two flutes alone are quite revealing. One of them, as we noted earlier, is in pristine condition, and the other, though broken into three sections in antiquity, had been carefully repaired. The ancient repair involved drilling fourteen tiny holes along the breakage lines and then tying the sections together with string, traces of which are visible. Modern laboratory technicians re-repaired the flute with glue, and to everyone's satisfaction, its tones could still be tested.

Thanks to the additional hole, each flute can play eight pitches, and despite some differences, the range of pitches and the intervals between them are similar. Those similarities led us to propose that the repaired flute was made first, and was highly esteemed by its owner. After the breakage and repair, we think, it was used as a model to cut the second flute. A tiny hole just

above the bottom hole of the second flute is a telling clue. We believe it was a test hole, drilled in an effort to match the pitch of the repaired flute, but the pitch it gave proved too high. The bottom hole was therefore drilled a bit farther from the mouth, and perhaps the little hole was plugged up. During our pitch analysis, the small hole had to be closed for the flute to produce the "right" tone.

The latest Neolithic deposits yielded seven flutes. One of them, with eight holes, is still playable. By that time the flute makers and players had become much better experienced with the acoustic capabilities of their wind instruments. They knew that by adding more holes and structuring the pitch intervals closer together, they could increase the variety of melodic structures in their music. In addition, the flutes became more standardized in pitch, presumably so that compositions could be played in a more consistent musical scale, perhaps for ensemble playing.

More evidence for the tuning of Neolithic scales has turned up at Zhongshanzhai, a site about eighty miles northwest of Jiahu and contemporaneous with the third phase of Jiahu settlement. A six-inch section of a bone flute unearthed from Zhongshanzhai has ten holes, arranged in a staggered pattern along two parallel rows. The holes are so close to one another that there is no room for comfortable fingering. Tonal tests show that the intervals between adjacent pitches closely approximate the half step (the interval, for instance, between a white key and an adjacent black key on a piano). This flute was very likely a tuning instrument, rather than one used for performing.

Unfortunately, the actual tunes played by musicians so long ago are beyond the reach of our archaeological tools. And we may never know why there were so many flutes in Jiahu. Some archaeologists speculate that the flutes were related to shamanistic rituals. If that were the case, our counts of flutes and burials imply that there was one shaman for every twenty people in the community—an unusually high proportion of ritual specialists for a farming village.

We think the music played a less esoteric role. Certainly it was an important element of community life. Given the availability of alcoholic drinks, we like to think the people of Jiahu enjoyed festive times.

Another mystery is why the villagers of Jiahu selected the wing bones of the red-crowned crane to craft their flutes. In Chinese legend, the Yellow Emperor cut flutes from bamboo, and bamboo may also have been used to make flutes at Jiahu and other Neolithic sites. But bamboo does not normally survive burial for thousands of years, so we archaeologists can be grateful for the choice of bone.

Standing nearly five feet tall, possessing an eight-foot wingspan, and bedecked with snow-white plumage accented with black and red, the red-crowned crane is an inspiring bird. The dance ritual of the male and female during courtship and pair-bonding is one of the most entertaining spectacles in the world of birds. It is replete with bows, leaps, extensions of the wings, and other dramatic gestures. The couple also performs a duet of loud, ringing calls between dances. Music is often inspired by the animal world. Did the musicians of Jiahu intend to imitate the crane's calls in their music? If so, perhaps they sought a magical assist by making flutes out of the birds' very bones.

CRITICAL THINKING QUESTIONS

1. What was considered so significant about Jihua that it was selected for excavation?
2. What did Jihua reveal about Neolithic Chinese life in terms of subsistence, health, and other social factors?
3. What changes in flute construction and probable tonal qualities occurred between the time of the oldest and youngest Neolithic occupation of Jihua?
4. Music is an aspect of human symbolic behavior. Speculating a little, what symbolic purpose might music have had in both religious ritual and everyday life in Jihua?
5. The red-crowned crane is an important mythic symbol in China. After looking up information on the crane, why do you think that the musicians of Jihua concentrated on this bird for flute-making material? What special symbolism might have been at work in the selection of crane bone?

Re-telling One's Own: Storytelling among the Apsáalooke (Crow Indians)

Rodney Frey

Abstract   *The following article suggests the role oral literature and storytelling has in contributing to the learning and perpetuation of the cultural identity of the contemporary Apsáalooke (Crow Indians). The stories not only describe the world-view of the Apsáalooke, presenting it to the listeners, but given the manner language is understood and applied and the techniques of storytelling, they engage the listeners in a participation in the events and characters of the narrative. During the telling of a story, the world-view themes are thus experientially participated in by the listeners.*

INTRODUCTION

In 1974, while involved in an ethnographic project on the Crow Indian reservation in Montana, I became acquainted with the activities of the bilingual curriculum specialists. The federally sponsored bilingual programs at the Crow Agency, St. Xavier and Wyola public schools, were in their infancies, enthusiastic and eager to contribute to the educational process of Apsáalooke children. Several of the curriculum specialists were engaged in collecting biographical and historical materials relevant to the Apsáalooke, and after transcribing these materials into the Apsáalooke phonetic system, incorporating them into their specific programs. What seemed like an insignificant though somewhat curious fact at the time was brought to my attention. While the histories of the treaties and reservation, and the life-histories of prominent individuals of former times were acknowledged as obviously important, many Apsáalooke students as well as their parents preferred to have something else incorporated into the curriculum. What they really desired to hear were the stories of the creator-trickster figure, Old Man Coyote, and any of the other Apsáalooke legends, all of which were less frequently being heard on the reservation. This curious fact I have since come to realize has very significant implications.

My intent is to offer a few suggestions as to the vital and perhaps indispensable role that oral literature and storytelling have in helping maintain Apsáalooke cultural identity. In oral literature the basic world-view qualities that organize a people's conception of time, space, being, and causation, and the affective ethos that colors these qualities are presented to the listeners. In addition, intrinsic to the morphology of oral literature, of doing storytelling, are performative creativity and participatory dynamics, both significantly lacking in written literature and chronological history. When a story is being told it is being relived, participated in by those assembled. History unfolds anew, to be rewitnessed or witnessed as if for the first time. With this experiential dimension to storytelling and given the specific contents of the stories, definitions of and the ethics for the self, others, and world about emerge, and are merged with the listener. Thus, in the content, i.e., the adventures and misadventures of the characters, of oral literature and with the structural dimension in doing storytelling, the Old Man Coyote story helps spawn and perpetuate the cultural identity of the Apsáalooke.

In order to better appreciate the character of Apsáalooke oral literature as well as have a reference point for the discussion that follows, let me briefly sketch the story of Burnt Face. Still told today, the story of Burnt Face was also shared among the Apsáalooke of the buffalo days, as Robert Lowie has recorded (1918:152–156). Variations on its symbolic theme—orphaned status, questing for

Source: Reprinted from *Plains Anthropologist* 28(100): 129-135 (1983) by permission of the author.

aid, adoption by a spiritual patron, and personal transformation—are seen in other Apsáalooke stories, e.g., Bear White Child (Nabokov 1967:7–10) and The Dwarf's Ward (Lowie 1918:165–171). This latter story has also continued into the present and is still told by the Apsáalooke. Variants on the Burnt Face theme are also present in the oral literature of other Plains cultures, as in the instance of the Blackfoot, for example (Grinnell 1972:93–103; San Souci 1978; Wissler and Duvall 1909:61–66).

It is, of course, only in an oral presentation of the Burnt Face story that one can fully grasp the story's complete significance. What is lacking in this written account of the story, and by implication, lacking in all written literature, is that dimension to storytelling that much of the following discussion addresses. Not only will the participatory dimension be absent, but also deleted will be the embellishment, detail, and repetition inherent in Apsáalooke oral literature and in the idiosyncrasies of a particular storyteller. There is the additional concern involved in any translation of materials from one language to another, and in this instance, from an oral language tradition to a written. Let me offer but one example of the translation problem. As we are all aware, the English language utilizes three verb tense forms—past, present, and future—and, correspondingly, the temporal dimension is conceptualized as a linear continuum. Apsáalooke, on the other hand, utilizes principally only a nonfuture and future verb tense structure (G. Hubert Matthews 1974: personal communication). The English past and present verb forms are thus merged into the Apsáalooke nonfuture form. That which is of the past, events in history, are not linguistically easily discernible from those of the present. To say that Old Man Coyote had created the buffalo and molded the mountains is to say, using Apsáalooke verb forms, that Old Man Coyote is now creating the buffalo and molding the mountains. This is not to say that the Apsáalooke do not have a time depth, for there are phrases that designate past eras, for instance. But for the listener's participatory involvement in the story, this verb form function has considerable implications, which will be discussed later in this paper. For the concerns of a viable translation, the verb formation illustrates but one of the potential problems that must be considered.

BURNT FACE

A young boy is running through camp and stumbles into a fire pit, the hot coals burning the right side of his face. His parents comfort him, but the right side of his face is badly scarred. As the years pass, few see Burnt Face, except on those rare occasions when he emerges from his lodge, his face painted over.

One day Burnt Face tells his parents he is going to the hills to fast. His mother is reluctant at first but finally gives in. In the Big Horn Mountains, Burnt Face finds the bluff that allows him a view of the rising sun on the horizon. Without food or water, Burnt Face spends his time praying for help and arranging stones into a large medicine wheel.

After several days, a great wind comes out of the east. Fearful and with his pipe in his hands, Burnt Face remains, facing it. As it approaches, the force of the wind moves trees to one side. Burnt Face remains sitting. Just before the wind overtakes Burnt Face, it stops and a huge Eagle emerges.

"Why are you crying, my son?"

"Because I hate part of myself."

"I've taken pity on you. If you help me, I'll help you, my son."

Burnt Face gets on the back of the great Bird and they fly to a distant land. In the lodge of the Eagle, Burnt Face meets the children of the Bird.

"Why are you crying, my brother?"

"Because I hate part of myself. My face is so badly scarred."

"Make me a bow and set of arrows."

"Make me a ball."

With a kind heart, Burnt Face goes out and makes from the finest materials a bow and set of arrows, and a ball for the son and daughter of the Eagle.

"Why are you crying, my brother?"

"Because I hate part of myself."

The son of the Eagle goes over to one side of the lodge and pulls out a mirror, and holds it before Burnt Face. As the young man looks at himself, he sees his skin as that of a newborn child's. Tears come to Burnt Face's eyes.

"Because we have helped you, you must now help us, my son. There is a great monster—Long Otter—that comes out from the river and endangers my children. You must kill it."

Burnt Face waits beside the swift-moving waters, having heated four rocks red, as those that are used in a sweat. A stillness falls over the land; not a sound can be heard from bird or leaf, and a thick fog blinds the sight of Burnt Face. But soon the sun and birds return. Again sight and sound are lost and again they return. A third time the stillness and fog covers the land, but as quickly as it came, it quickly departs. Then the stillness returns a fourth time along with the thick fog. Burnt Face, fearful, waits. Out of the waters, something approaches that is large and without shape. Louder it gets. Then, just in front of Burnt Face, the sharp teeth of the wide open jaws of Long Otter can be clearly seen. Without hesitation, Burnt Face quickly flings each of the four heated rocks into the open mouth of the monster. Rolling this way, then that, Long Otter falls back into the river, never to be seen again.

"Because you have helped us, I will help you, my son."

The great Eagle gives Burnt Face the right to paint on his lodge the image of the great Bird, for the Eagle will now always be with Burnt Face, as a father is always with his son, guiding him. Burnt Face lives to such an age that when he moves, his skin tears.

DISCUSSION

There are numerous levels in which oral literature and storytelling can be appreciated. It perhaps goes without saying that a story like Burnt Face can entertain, offering a sense of adventure in a young man's quest and encounters with powerful and mysterious forces. Other stories, such as Old Man Coyote stories, can bring a smile, or a laugh, as an adventure, or more likely, a misadventure is related. For the Apśaalooke, stories are shared in a variety of social contexts. A good story told after the evening meal is a fine way to help complete a cold winter's day. While gathered around the fire heating the sweat rocks, time and the company one is with, become relaxed as stories are shared. In the midst of a rather tense conversation, a segment of some Old Man Coyote story is interjected, helping to ease the apprehension.

But there is much more to be learned from Apśaalooke oral literature. Within oral literature,

like the language system it is a part of, a world-view, a description of the conceptualized spatial, temporal, and causal order of the world about is offered. Set forth in the stories are patterns of relationship that help define the self, the collective, and the sacred, as is the affective tone, the ethos that colors the quality of these various relationships. In the instance of the Burnt Face narrative, natural phenomena are animated with volition, addressed with kinship terms, able to "adopt" human children, and a source of transformative power. The human, natural, and spiritual worlds are intimately linked, interdependent each with the other. Such stories represent symbolically a microcosm of the content and structure of the conceived world in its totality; the narrative is both an analogy of and an imagery for that world. For the listener, the story contributes to the visibility and concreteness of what ordinarily in invisible and vague.

In the instance of many of the Old Man Coyote narratives, while patterns of relationship are offered, they are patterns of reversal, of how not to define one's self and the world around. Should one define one's self in the image of Old Man Coyote, the narratives offer what consequences may await one's actions. Old Man Coyote is often characterized as an assertive, self-focused individual, attempting to dupe and take from others before getting duped himself. Inevitably the deception is turned against him, and Old Man Coyote is duped at his own game.

This notion of oral literature, as descriptive of the cultural conception of the world and helping to delineate the world, is vividly exemplified in the manner some Apśaalooke utilize Old Man Coyote stories. Before telling of some event or situation occurring in the present involving another or themselves, some Apśaalooke will preface it with an abbreviated or partial segment of some Old Man Coyote narrative of parallel theme. It is as if the adventures of the trickster not only happen to exemplify and clarify the event for the listener's sake, but that the event in the present is somehow a mirror image, a reflection of the original. The models of action set forth by Old Man Coyote or Burnt Face are analogous and applicable to the world and its events occurring in the present.

But there is something else that can be learned from Apśaalooke storytelling. Oral literature not only describes a reality, but in the act of telling a story the listener participates in that reality. In the manner that words are understood and used, and in the techniques of telling a story, the imagination of the Apsáalooke listener is engaged in the narrative to such an extent that the characters and events of the narrative are experientially encountered.

For the Apsáalooke, words not only serve as a vehicle for the exchange of ideas and knowledge of the world, but words also contribute to the creation of that world. When I first began my association with Apsáalooke one of the very first lessons I learned involved not saying "good-bye" upon departing from a visit with someone. Rather, one says, if speaking in Apsáalooke, *diiaẃakaawik*, or if in English and having the same meaning, "see you later." I was told that in saying "good-bye," "It is too final; you may not see them again." During this initial association I was involved in a tribally sponsored project, part of which focused on discerning Apsáalooke categories of disease and illness. After facing a significant amount of reluctance on the part of most Apsáalooke in discussing the subject of sickness, I was introduced to the term, *dasshússuua*. The expression literally means "breaking with the mouth." That which comes through the mouth—words—has the ability to break—alter—that which is in the world. People were reluctant to talk about disease, a disease a family member or they themselves may have had, for fear of causing in another or themselves the affliction in question. The words describing the state can in fact create that state. One should not say "good-bye."

As words possess this transformative power, a personal Indian name is particularly so endowed. In an elaborate ceremony involving an opened medicine bundle, sweat cedar smudging, sacred water, eagle feathers, and prayer, an Indian name is given to a small child. The name may be indicative of the kind of life desired for the child, a particular ability desired for him or her. A name may reflect the good deeds of another, a particular beneficial experience, and the desire that that experience and ability now be with the child. If used properly, respected, and never taken in vain, the name can help realize a sought after quality or a desired future. When the name is ceremonially given, there is often

voiced the concern that it "agrees with the child." If it does, the child will mature well and remain healthy. Should the name, the words of it, not agree with the child's disposition, the child may become "sickly and in need." A new name may then be requested. With the name, and the respect given it, e.g., not casually discussing it publicly, over the years its significance is made known and acknowledged. Personal achievements, an election to a tribal office, a hand-game win, success in Vietnam, being chosen as a princess for a pow wow, can be linked to the power of a person's Indian name. One can hear the expression, "I didn't do it on my own, but with the help of my name."

Spoken words are not only semantic means of communication, descriptive of a reality, but they are also animated with a power that can affect the context in which they are expressed. A song, a prayer, a dialogue, a vow are considered by the Apsáalooke as physically real, as active a force when publicly expressed as any behavioral action. The one who announces the good fortune of an individual at a giveaway or the blessing the veteran wishes to bestow on the Sun Dance most likely does so because he has a medicine bundle pertaining to the proper use of words in public. To misuse words is to desecrate them and possibly break with the mouth. When a vow is publicly made to sponsor an important event such as a Sun Dance, the words must be followed by action on the part of the sponsor or else action of a very different, nondesired sort may occur. The health to one's self or family is in possible jeopardy. This notion that words are endowed with power is shared among other Indian peoples as well. For example, Sam Gill (1977) has demonstrated the "performative force" of Navajo prayer acts. The semantic structure of prayer is that of a "person," specifically that of a Holy Person, Yei. For the Navajo, "prayer acts are active forces which can render effects on the world. In other words, the Navajo conception of prayer acts is one which emphasizes their pragmatic character" (Gill 1977:143). While a prayer, a song, or a word in the Apsáalooke context is not conceived of as an acting "person" or a deity, each is nevertheless understood as an acting agent. Words in whatever form they are expressed have a power, a force that can affect the environment they refer to.

With this acknowledged disposition toward words by the Apsáalooke, through the application of words one can imagine themselves, the world, and whatever scenario they desire, into being. For the Apsáalooke, the world of meaning and significance is fundamentally the culmination of their creative imagination of it. N. Scott Momaday, the Kiowa poet and scholar, puts forth this understanding most elegantly as he says:

> We are what we imagine. Our best destiny is to imagine, at least, completely, who and what, and *that* we are. The greatest tragedy that can befall us is to go unimagined (1969:103).

The words do not simply passively reflect the world, but as they are expressed, they mold and contribute to the definition and animation of the landscape one is traveling through.

Concerning oral literature, then, in the act of weaving the fibers of words into a story, the story is brought to life through the imagination of the listener. As the story of Burnt Face is being told, it is not simply entertaining or descriptive of a character and the world he is a part of, though it is both of these. But as the deeds of Burnt Face and the Eagle are portrayed in words, the words through the imagination of the listener create the portrayed deeds. In this life that now animates the story, the listener is not a passive recipient but an active participant in the haps and mishaps of Burnt Face or Old Man Coyote. One feels the burn of the hot coals or experiences the terror as the Long Otter approaches. A tear is shed as one becomes a newborn child again. The story is participated in experientially.

This participation in the story is enhanced all the more given the techniques and vehicles of expression utilized in storytelling. As a story unfolds the imagery of each scene is made more vivid as well as more immediate and personal as the storyteller embellishes the narrative. The plot of the story is seemingly lost in the maze of detail, sequence repetition, and addendums. Keep in mind the significance of storytelling is as much the revealing of a specific plot as it is the process of movement of the listener into the world of the story. Typical of this application of storytelling embellishment is the example of an

individual who wished to share the story of a European tour with his family. He had spent six months experiencing sights few in his family had dreamt. Early one evening with family gathered around, he began the story. However, by the early morning hours and with several fast asleep, those awake were still waiting to board the ship for Europe. Every detail of the journey to New York first had to be undergone, brought to life with the listeners.

An overt way in which Apsáalooke listeners participate in a story is by acknowledging their involvement aloud. When a story is being told it is the common practice for listeners to periodically say *ée,* the Apsáalooke word for yes. As the evening story continues into the late hours, when this form of participation ceases, indicative of all form of participation ceasing, the storyteller knows it is time to pause.

Not only are the stories linked to the participation of the listeners, but many stories are linked to the participation of the seasonal cycles. For example, many storytellers share Old Man Coyote stories only during the winter—from the first frost through to the first lightning. The long, winter evenings, when activities center around the warmth in the home, are an ideal setting for storytelling. Some hold that the telling of winter stories out of season is dangerous to the well-being of family and self. Seasonal stories are thus in part an extension and expression of the vitality and life of that which they are associated. Consequently, as many stories are nestled in the texture of a particular season and given the degree to which an individual is aware of and involved in the season, an individual's awareness of and involvement in the cyclical seasons heightens the degree of his or her involvement in the stories. As one feels the frostbitten wind as it blows across the field, one can hear the voice of Old Man Coyote close by.

Storytelling, as one form of oral dialogue, necessarily reflects the structural characteristics of the language system it is a part of. As I previously mentioned, the Apsáalooke language is divided into principally two verb tense forms, nonfuture and future. What in English would be past and present verb forms are combined in the nonfuture form. Consequently, an act or state of being of the past is not linguistically discernible from an act or state of being in the present. In relating the story of Burnt Face, to say that he sat on the mountain top and saw the Eagle is to say that Burnt Face is sitting on the mountain top and seeing the Eagle. The verbs sit (*aẁaackik*—he, she, it sit) and see (*ikaak*—he, she, it see) refer to both past and present action simultaneously. While the story might be prefaced with a phrase placing Burnt Face in another time era, for the listener undergoing the story the temporal distance is eliminated, and the listener has a sense of witnessing the unfolding of the events as they are occurring. You sit alongside Burnt Face as you both see the Eagle emerge from the wind. The effect for the listener is that he or she is brought into an immediacy with the surrounding events and with the character of Burnt Face and Old Man Coyote, the imageries of which become timeless and ever-present.

It is thus not only in the themes of the narratives but in the manner the narratives are told that the Apśaalooke actively participate in the world about them. The world-view themes in the oral literature refer to and describe an animated world full of life and meaning in which the Apśaalooke are intimately linked as participants. The Eagle is a father who can guide and aid an adopted son or daughter. In addition, given the Apśaalooke understanding and application of their language, and the techniques involved in storytelling, the oral literature not only describes the vitality of the world, but the listeners through their imagination participate in it as the narrative unfolds. One witnesses the tears of a boy as he stumbles into the hot coals and as an eagle holds up a mirror before him.

CONCLUSIONS

Barbara Myerhoff, in a recent article entitled *Telling One's Story*, discusses the vital role storytelling has for a group of immigrant Eastern European Jews. In the act of telling one's life-history, the elderly are able to integrate their lives into their cultural heritage, thus helping to make their life meaningful. "It is a process of *re-membering*, struggling toward self-knowledge and integration" (Myerhoff 1980:27). Storytelling for the Apśaalooke is not so much telling one's life-history as it is telling the stories that have molded one's life. Specifically, it is the re-telling of stories one has participated in that facilitates this integration. The Apśaalooke phrase for storytelling is *baaeechichiwaau*, literally meaning "re-telling one's own." Traditionally, stories were owned by individuals who had received them through purchase or as a gift from another, and who thus had the right to tell them. Storytelling was a matter of re-telling the stories one owned. This practice is no longer followed. But similar to the Jewish instance, Apśaalooke storytelling is a matter of re-membering.

The re-membering involves a return to and a reuniting with the original. Given the participatory dynamics of Apśaalooke storytelling, as the listener experiences the unfolding of the Burnt Face epic, not only is the story in its entirety, but each sequence, each adventure of it is encountered as if anew, for the first time. The excitement and anticipation is always alive in the listener. This was made clear to me in the re-membering an old woman would share with her husband. The woman had had a full and diversified life, very much an exemplary life others wished to know about. When guests would spend an afternoon or evening with her, she would share some aspect of her life, a story that was virtually unchanged in its content from the last time it was told. But each time she related an episode, an incident her husband must have heard countless times previously, instead of tiring of the story the old man would still be absorbed in it as if he had never before heard it. I would see grief and laughter in his responses, in his participation in and re-membering of the story. In the re-membering one can witness Old Man Coyote's creation of the world, witness it as it unfolds in the beginning.

The re-membering is not only of a temporal returning, but it also involves a spatial reuniting. Not only is the participation in a story an act of original experience, fresh and anew, but in the re-membering of the story, the members in the story are reunited. You not only witness the tears of Burnt Face and the Eagle emerge out of the wind, but the tears are your tears and the Eagle asks you why you are crying. It is your body that is molded from the earth and a life breath blown into it by Old Man Coyote. And you are Old Man Coyote. As the listener participates in the story, the listener's membership and being are reestablished, reaggregated in the fibers and essence of the story's imagery. And in being re-membered in the fibers and essence of the story, the listener becomes defined and integrated into the pathways of the cultural heritage that is Apśaalooke. In the re-membering of the listeners, oral literature and storytelling spawns and perpetuates a sense of cultural identity and purpose.

It is in this light that we should understand the yearnings of the Apśaalooke children. They are not simply wanting to be entertained by the stories of Old Man Coyote; they are seeking to participate in them and thus in their cultural identity in the most vital of manners. While the written histories and biographies are critical, they lack the performative creativity and participatory dynamics of oral literature. In the re-membering of the stories, not only does Burnt Face live to such an age that when he moves his skin tears, but so will the Apśaalooke people.

References Cited

Gill, Sam. 1977. Prayer as Person: The Performative Force in Navajo Prayer Acts. *History of Religions* 17:143–157.

Grinnell, George Bird. 1972. *Blackfoot Lodge Tales: The Story of a Prairie People.* Corner House, Williamstown, Massachusetts.

Lowie, Robert. 1918. Myths and Traditions of the Crow. *Anthropological Papers of the American Museum of Natural History* 25:1–304.

Momaday, N. Scott. 1975. The Man Made of Words. In *Literature of the American Indians: Views and Interpretations,* edited by Abraham Chapman. Meridian, New York.

Myerhoff, Barbara. 1980. Telling One's Story. *The Center Magazine* 8:22–40.

Nabokor, Peter. 1967. *Two Leggings: The Making of a Crow Warrior.* Thomas Y. Crowell, New York.

San Souci, Robert. 1978. *The Legend of Scarface: A Blackfeet Indian Tale.* Doubleday, Garden City, New York.

Wissler, Clark, and D. C. Duvall. 1909. Mythology of the Blackfoot Indians. *Anthropological Papers of the American Museum of Natural History* 2:3–163.

CRITICAL THINKING QUESTIONS

1. How does oral literature assist the Apśaalooke in acquiring and maintaining their cultural identity?
2. What symbolic themes does the story of Burnt Face share with other Apśaalooke tales?
3. What problems do presenting Apśaalooke oral literature in English present in terms of comprehension and proper transmission of ideas?
4. What purpose(s) does the author say that words play in the oral literature of the Apśaalooke?
5. What is "re-membering," and how does it affect Apśaalooke storytelling and life?

The Arts of Memory: Icon and Structural Violence in a Dublin "Underclass" Housing Estate

A. Jamie Saris and Brendan Bartley

This paper deals with the complex relationships between, and some of the everyday practices that go into, remembering and forgetting within a conflicted political field. The object of this analysis is a set of murals in an economically and socially marginal housing estate on the outskirts of Dublin, and some of the social activities that they either commemorate or pass over.[1] This analysis requires an "archaeology" of a sort, in the sense that both virtual and material layers have to be scraped away, not to reveal some deeper truth, but to outline the field of forces that create truth-effects within this context (Foucault 1973a, Rabinow 1996). If this process is conducted carefully with due regard for local knowledge, however, the rewards are high. An obscure wall in an unfashionable Dublin suburb that most people in the capital have never been to (and that many people would never want to visit), displays multiple and conflicting configurations of violence, resistance, community, ownership, even hope. To understand this wall, though, an entire local world needs to be outlined, and the connections between this local world and national and transnational forces need to be appreciated.[2] Perhaps appropriately, the analysis begins and ends with a defaced *tabula rasa*.

... Despite its surface changes and the new houses around it, locals still refer to this pile of bricks as "the Red Wall," and it still forms an important local landmark. This wall is in Gallanstown, Cherry Orchard, which is part of Ballyfermot, a western suburb of Dublin. Although only about five miles from the city center, it is worlds away from the new construction and "high street" capitalism which is currently remaking the Dublin built environment.

Its 5,500-strong population fits the demographic profile of a neighborhood in trouble.

It is a high-crime area, with low employment and high rates of illicit drug use, particularly heroin abuse among young people (Bartley and Saris 1999, Saris and Bartley 1999, 2000a, 2000b). If this community was situated in North America or parts of England, Scotland or Wales, it would most likely be labelled "underclass," with all the pejorative associations and political conflicts implied by this term (Wilson 1989, Bourgeois 1996, Dalrymple 2001 among many others). In turn, the area has a strained relationship with most official organs of the state: the schools, the Gardaí (police), and, perhaps most especially, Dublin Corporation (the organization responsible for social housing).

To make matters worse, Cherry Orchard has benefited only lately and slightly from the economic development known as the Celtic Tiger, the decade-long boom that has seen the Republic of Ireland change from one of the most economically marginal areas in Europe into one of its wealthiest member states (Breathnach 1998). This economic growth has been driven by neo-liberal macroeconomic policies, and it has the same shape as similar booms seen in other areas of the world: better-off segments of society have gained more in both relative and absolute terms than poorer ones. Indeed, during this period Cherry Orchard has had to deal with a set of severe social issues, in particular a growing youth drug (opiate) problem. While in the last couple of years some employment has slowly trickled down to this population, particularly to those who are willing to staff the lower echelons of the service industry such as office cleaning, many people in

Source: Reprinted from *Anthropology Today*, vol. 18, no. 4, (August 2002) by permission of Wiley-Blackwell.

Cherry Orchard are still losing socio-economic ground—most notably young, unskilled males.

As these problems have been developing, much of Irish society has also moved away from the notion that "We as a society have poor members" to the idea that "There are poor communities in our environment" (Saris and Bartley 2000a). In technical terms, Irish public policy towards poverty has been spatialized, looking to address the "social exclusion" of areas and populations in line with continental, especially French, models (Room 1995, Nolan, Whelan and Williams 1998). Less charitably, one could argue that this ecological model of poverty led to a sense that poverty and severe social problems now exist largely in national parks for the socially excluded, complete with socially designated rangers (such as specially trained police and social welfare officers) to maintain the boundaries of, and keep the peace in, these people preserves.

DRUGS, DEPRIVATION AND STRUCTURAL VIOLENCE

When Cherry Orchard intrudes on the Irish national consciousness at all, it is generally through the reporting of severe problems to be found therein. Perhaps the most spectacular demonstration of this tendency in recent years is the media coverage of the serious troubles in the area around Halloween 1995. At that time, the Gallanstown Housing Estate in Cherry Orchard erupted into a major civil disturbance which was described by the Gardaí at the time as an "organized riot." [In a] photo taken immediately after the riot, . . . some planning for (or at least expectation of) a conflict is in evidence on "the Red Wall." We can read clearly, several times over, the phrase "Let the games begin."

As with any important event, accounts attributing both the cause and the meaning of this disturbance vary considerably. The magnitude of the incident, though, is not in doubt. On Halloween night, several units of the Gardaí were lured into the area in hot pursuit of joyriders in stolen cars. They were then surrounded and driven off the street by crowds bearing rocks and petrol bombs. The Gards came back in force and were driven off the streets again. Over the course of several hours, tens of people were injured, two children very seriously, and dozens of arrests were made. In addition, a number of Gardaí were severely traumatized by these events (we know of at least three early retirements connected to this incident). Indeed, the Halloween Riots are still viewed by the authorities as one of the most disturbing incidents of public unrest in the Republic of Ireland within living memory.

The background to these troubles is complex, and we can only outline it here. It is generally acknowledged, however, that the atmosphere in Cherry Orchard had been tense long before Halloween night of 1995. Drug dealing and joyriding had reached critical levels. In some parts of Cherry Orchard, especially around the Red Wall in Gallanstown, heroin was being dealt openly: indeed, people were being ferried to Red Wall from all over the city and from up the country to buy illegal substances.

One group of individuals, in particular, were pointed to locally as being centrally connected to a wide variety of criminal activities, especially drug dealing. They seemed better organized than most other groups, with an older set of men who had some criminal connections (some of them had done jail time). They also possessed strong local kin connections in a population that had only recently been moved into the area from all over the greater Dublin area. Around these men was a larger set of younger members with only loose affiliation to the group. Their leader was a charismatic figure in his own right: to this day, some find him very threatening, while others openly admire and respect him. This younger group enjoyed their local notoriety, styling themselves "The Red Wall Gang" after their favorite hanging-out spot. But however important "The Red Wall Gang" might have been in the area's, and indeed the nation's, drug problem, there is no doubt that by 1995 their eponymous pile of bricks had become one of the central nodes in a nationwide market for illegal substances.

Drugs were one aspect of a bigger problem, however. In our interactions, many residents articulated a feeling that they had been substantially abandoned by the state and the broader society, that Cherry Orchard had become the designated "skip" of Dublin Corporation, the last stop on the line before final eviction from the system. Garda interactions with the community became progressively more strained from the late 1980s, as police, largely from rural or more middle class backgrounds, began to conflate all activity in the area into "street culture" and "criminality." Thus, the local penchant for track suits, sovereign rings, and particular hairstyles became the uniform of the enemy and their civilian sympathizers. In short, the Gards believed themselves to be involved in a war that they were in the process of losing. As one policeman recalled the situation to us,

> [W]e made the mistake of allowing the minority to turn this into an enclave where "anything goes," the strongest survive, the weakest go down. Now, that is the perception that the criminal element had. [O]nce they got into their stride [pause], the stakes were increased as time went on. Until people said "this is a no-go area."

The section of the Gardaí that was most committed to a warfare model of policing saw the riot as a providential opportunity to develop more heavy-handed tactics. Some police, for example, "leaked" to the media that the Halloween "attack" had resulted directly from a misguided community policing initiative. They claimed that this initiative had been infiltrated by criminals for the purpose of gathering information about policing policies, organization and activities, information that was then used by the ringleaders of the local gangs orchestrating the rioting.

Specifically, these Gards pointed to a group of local youths with criminal records, known as WHAD (We Have A Dream, a title borrowed and adapted, of course, from the Martin Luther King speech), some of whom had a peripheral association with the Red Wall Gang. WHAD is a grass-roots initiative founded in 1988 to provide at-risk youth with some structure to help them avoid getting further into trouble. Hitherto, this group had been seen in a very positive light. In the event, the charge that they were some kind of criminal fifth column was subsequently described in another media report (*Irish Times* 1995) as "factually inaccurate and a misplaced criticism of local community groups." According to this report, as well as local historical memory, only one of the participants in WHAD was caught up in the Halloween Riots.

All accounts agree, however, that the Halloween Riot was a turning point for the whole of Cherry Orchard. The Gardaí decided that they could no longer afford to be as alienated from the community as they clearly were. Other state bodies were also prodded into embarrassed action to salvage a situation that seemed to have spun completely out of control. Dublin Corporation, for example, began proceedings to evict those tenants whom they (and many locals) saw as the most troublesome. At the same time, local activists were frightened into an uneasy alliance with state organizations, despite their severe reservations about many of these bodies. From early 1996 this alliance began to cast around for "a way to put the riots behind them." It was eventually decided that, to symbolize the new birth of the area, the dreary walls in and around the housing estates of Cherry Orchard, which had hitherto been little more than convenient graffiti canvases, were to be repainted by "the youth of the area." In the event, the "youth of the area" turned out to overlap substantially with the membership of WHAD.

At this point, events took another turn. In the spring of 1996, some months before the murals were painted, but following the advent of a much more intense, some would say harassing, police presence in the area, a sometime member of WHAD, Mark Hall—an enjoyable young man from all accounts, possessed of an infectious sense of humor and a God-given facility for hot-wiring cars—died tragically on the main western thoroughfare into and out of Dublin, at the wheel of a stolen vehicle. This seemingly garden-variety road accident had a profound and unexpected effect on Cherry Orchard's youth. Mr. Hall's funeral turned into a major community event, attracting hundreds of local youths, the majority of whom would scarcely have known him. As one of our consultants remembered things,

> The whole area, I mean, it was like a silence that came over them and you would just see gangs of them linking [with] one another— boys and girls, walking around. You wouldn't see one or two of them, just these massive gangs, and the silence that came over them. The girls were more inclined to be crying and the lads just walking around in groups—not doing anything, just being.

Within days of this incident, moreover, Mark's death had been radically refigured. Rather than a senseless death due an unfortunate combination of speed and bad luck, the story grew that Mark's car had been chased by the police, and that it was this hot pursuit that had forced him to accelerate to his doom. None of our local consultants were able to cite the source of this rumor, but they all agreed that it almost instantaneously became common knowledge among the more alienated youths of the area, many of whom would, again, scarcely have known Mark.

The first public pronouncement of this new "truth" was accomplished with paint. Within a couple of weeks of Mr Hall's funeral, the slogan "Mark Hall was killed by the Gardaí" went up prominently on the Red Wall. This simple declaration was almost immediately contradicted—again, with paint. Within a week, Mark's mother Dolores took matters into her own hands, personally effacing this revisionist version of events that she felt intruded on her family's private grief. As another consultant, a friend of hers, said,

> She had enough of the nonsense. Well I mean, she had a lot to deal with and the last thing she need was them using her son an excuse to have another riot.

This painting and repainting, however, once again brought the problem of the subject matter, as well as the authors, of the planned murals, to the forefront of many people's thinking. An effort was then made to displace WHAD from their position of preeminent mural designers and executors by the Red Wall Gang, who argued that they had the best claim to ownership of that particular wall at least. They put forward the case that the most appropriate subject matter for a painting on it was the regular discrimination and occasional incidents of outright violence that they felt they had experienced at the hands of the Gardaí. In short, they seemed to be saying that while Mark Hall might not actually have been killed by the Gardaí, he was the sort of person who could have been. Those connected to the Red Wall Gang (and some others), therefore, argued that their sense of being at the sharp end of state violence was the element of their experience that was most relevant for "community" representation.

Since it had no standing with (indeed was feared and disliked by) the middle-class professional-led community groups organizing the mural-painting, the Red Wall Gang was institutionally sidelined from the start. Its savvy leader, however, had one

play left in him. Rechristening himself and his colleagues as a community group, "Gallanstown Vision," they made a seemingly quixotic attempt to obtain official recognition and funding. In itself, this tactic says something about the ubiquity as well as the ideological and material preeminence of the Community Development movement in poor neighbourhoods in present-day Ireland (Saris and Bartley 2000b). However, this stroke of insight came too late to earn him a place at the mural-planning table. The community groups pressed ahead, figuring that they had won a struggle to get non-contentious, positive paintings on the walls of Cherry Orchard.

A SUBURBAN IDYLL?

Ironically, the most common theme of these non-contentious murals, painted by kids from the suburban underclass, appears to be idylls in rural Ireland, such as this one of a middle distance harvest scene. Others of these pictures have more politics in them than is immediately apparent.

. . . Only [one] large mural in Cherry Orchard was not subsequently seriously defaced. Tellingly, it is a picture of horses. Horses are important vehicles for both people and meanings in this area (Saris and Bartley 2000a). A few families in this area, for example, have a long tradition of horse ownership: indeed, as recently as the 1980s, horses were still used commercially to haul coal or milk. As the 1990s heroin wave grew in intensity, many local youths became interested in horse ownership, as one of the few positive aspects of living in Cherry Orchard. By the mid-1990s, however, legal moves were afoot to drastically curtail horse ownership in the greater Dublin area. Since the end of 1996, with the passing of very harsh legislation that effectively rendered every horse in the capital illegal, a "horse protest," including everything from raising media awareness of this issue to battering the enforcers of the new regulations, has been ongoing in this area, as well as other poor neighbourhoods in the Irish capital. In other research, our team has explored some of the ways that horses have been used by various local forces both to stake a claim to ownership of specific spaces and to contest the lack of respect and spoiled identity that they feel are projected upon them by "mainstream" society (Saris and Bartley 2000a). The painters of this mural, then, found a subject that not even the most alienated youth would have been inclined to deface.

This does not mean that the picture is non-contentious, however. Note that this is a picture of harness racing or trotters. This is a lesser-known and not a very respectable form of horse racing in Ireland. The sport was only introduced to the island about 30 years ago, and various attempts to bring it under the auspices of the better organized equine sports regulating agencies have not been successful. Most betting shops, moreover, will not take bets on these races as they are seen to be eminently fixable by the various interests that currently control the sport (horses substituted, papers forged, etc.), and consequently impossible to calculate rational odds on. "Respectable" racing fans moreover speak of "knackers" and "scumbags" being in this line of sport, suggesting that it is mostly Travelers and the "lower" orders (particularly the criminal elements thereof) who get involved.

Clearly, this mural says something about dynamics within Cherry Orchard as well as the area's experience of structural violence through a cultural appreciation, and the social position, of horses and related equine activities. However, an enormous amount of both recent and older local knowledge is required to make sense of what it is saying. The subsequent respect that it has been accorded is an indication of how well its authors judged the relationship between what they could say under the watchful eye of the community groups and their official sponsors and the long-term reception they could anticipate from the more alienated end of their audience.

Other murals fared very differently. While the harness-racing picture seemed to strike a chord of universal acceptance, the Red Wall was to continue its existence as a site of conflict and debate, a veritable argument conducted in paint. The scene that went up here is perhaps the most interesting of the murals that were painted in 1996. It is so full of rural kitsch that one is tempted to read it ironically: indeed, even if it were cleaned up *Bórd Fáilte*[3] would be slow to use it even for the American market. It is full of what Vico might call "dead" metonyms of Irish tradition, stressing tranquil rural landscapes, timeless icons and traditional music and entertainment.

Moving from right to left, a crudely painted serene older man plays a *bódhran* against a backdrop of a profoundly peaceful countryside. Further left, crudely drawn but still comely maidens dance in the shadow of what looks suspiciously like Crough Patrick, Ireland's holy mountain overlooking Clew Bay in Mayo, some 150 miles away. Finally, the figures are framed on the other side by more peaceful countryside.[4] The contrast between such a vision and what had been the major drugs distribution point for the greater Dublin area, not to mention the epicentre of the most severe urban rioting in the Republic of Ireland in this generation mere months before, is so striking that one scarcely knows where to begin to analyze it.

Obviously, fate has been harder on this painting, but what was depicted stayed pretty stable from about the end of 1996 until the end of 1999, when Dublin Corporation decided that a blank wall was needed in the area. There are three obvious defacements that deserve special mention, however. First, and probably least interesting, are some fires that were started in the middle of the picture. Two of these were clearly deliberately set, seemingly to have rendered the activities of the comely maidens something of a toss-up between step-dancing and fire-fighting. The second and third defacements are far more interesting: they are the splash of red in the upper right hand corner of the work and the obvious lettering. The two are closely connected, but only if you know the history of this pile of bricks.

. . . [T]he upper right-hand corner of the piece has been painted red. Clearly, this modification was added with some care: a white undercoat was laid, and then a red overcoat was applied. No local needed to be told what this patch of red meant: it indexed the Red Wall underneath the painting, and hence the Red Wall Gang. To drive home the point, someone also drew in red (again) the words "Garda" and "WHAD" in crossword fashion, followed by "out now." WHAD, it seems, gets the stick from both sides.

I want to draw particular attention to the technique of this remembering. It is a layer of paint that "portrays" the layer below, consequently rendering its substrate visible. As in a *memento mori*, an artistic device is used to make visible otherwise unseen depths that are then constructed as more real than the surface phenomenon. At this level, at least, the Red Wall Gang got the last word—if only for a while. While not directly represented, the structural violence and actual assault that they claimed to have experienced at the hands of the Gardaí, or at least the debate about these issues, was shown to be just under the surface of things.

A NEW STABILITY?

The relative stability of this multi-authored production belies the conflict in the area during the second half of the 1990s between the various internal divisions within Cherry Orchard and different forces from outside the area. An important focus of this conflict has been the relentless pressure on horse ownership in this area by a new, privately contracted enforcement arm of Dublin Corporation (now rechristened Dublin City Council), alongside the continuing expansion of a severe youth heroin problem. From a high of more than 150 beasts at the beginning of our research in 1997, we estimated that fewer than 40 horses remained in the area in 2000 when our work terminated (Saris and Bartley 2000a). During this period, Cherry Orchard's drugs problem worsened.

Local response to this state of affairs has taken two forms. First, in common with nearly every other socially excluded neighborhood in the greater Dublin area, an equine center was completed in 2000 in Cherry Orchard. From the beginning it was intended to house a mere 30 "high-quality" horses, so many local lads understandably developed a strong suspicion that they were being set up to lose a game of musical stable-places. Elements of the Red Wall Gang have been the main organizers of protests against this state of affairs, to date with little effect, although they have attracted some media attention to the situation (*Irish Times* 1997, Dooley 1998). Meanwhile, Corporation seizures of horses continued unabated, while the wasteland that once provided cover for everything from drug dealing to informal horse shows has been "developed" by the Corporation at a breakneck pace. In the final act of the seeming normalization of this suburb, a grey wall (slightly defaced) now stands in front of what looks like profoundly uninteresting tract housing.

CONCLUSION

If we learn anything from Foucault (1973a, 1973b, 1975, 1979), it is that power is productive: it is productive of subjectivities, of resistance, even of reality itself. With respect to the themes of this paper, we can identify at least two emerging strands manifesting different relationships between violence, icon, and memory in relation to the sorts of issues arising in places like Cherry Orchard.

The first of these strands is the wholesale aestheticization of aspects of the lives of those subject to structural violence in Ireland. This trend probably finds its current acme in the work of the one-time fashion photographer Perry Ogden. In his beautifully photographed coffee-table book, poor kids and their horses (freshly purchased at Dublin Smithfield's Horse Fair and now likely to be seized within the month by those enforcing the recent draconian anti-horse legislation) are materially cleaned up and symbolically airbrushed of any qualities that might make a middle-class viewer squeamish, from stray dirt in the horse's mane to track marks on children's arms.

The cover of this work is a study of horse and boy staring through their local context to share a moment with a viewer. The presumed authenticity and purity of the boy's relationship to his horse is suggested by his seeming unconcern for his surroundings (which are, in the event, conveniently covered by a white sheet) and his obvious ease with the animal. Such romantic depictions of the "urban horse" have blossomed at the precise historical moment when it has become state policy to remove horses from the capital.

The second strand can be traced by literally going back to the drawing-board, that is, by looking at some of wall painting extant in Cherry Orchard.... [M]y favorite, discernible until mid-2000, [was] the temporary hoarding surrounding the recently completed Eastern Health Board Resource Centre. Many local people believed that this building was really a treatment centre for junkies, yet another problem directed resource in this community, less a service and more an index of how much trouble the neighborhood was in.

In this work, there is no escape from either the problems or the context of Cherry Orchard. A chip van, the only service industry besides drugs that is locally available, stands in the background of a figure with a syringe. The syringe is held neither in its medical/drug injecting position nor in its threatening/mugging posture, but is clearly available for either purpose. The body of the figure (and note that the gender of the user is difficult to judge, reflecting the recent social development that young women are becoming involved in opiate use at ever-increasing levels—see Saris and Bartley (1999) is marred by physical violence (facial scars) as well as by track marks along both arms—portals between the inside and outside that show the paths of a little temporary ecstasy at the price of local stigmatization, profound medical risks, and almost inevitable criminal sanctions. The instrument that does the scarring, the hypodermic needle and syringe, is both the privileged channel between the inside and outside of the body and an important means of drawing the life blood of the global economy, money, into local worlds from the outside environment. Robberies at syringe-point became a daily occurrence in Dublin's city center in the 1990s, and they continue at present. Such crimes do not only threaten, materially and symbolically, the injection of dirt and contagion into the respectable body politic; they also draw into local markets the money that sustains and reproduces a local dystopia.

Far from placing the figure at a remove from the rest of the mundane world, such as the circulation of commodities, the artist emblazons the figure holding the syringe with both "Nike" and "USA": the first one of the most successful exemplars, and the second the symbolic and material epicenter, of the global market. This technique condenses several social realities. Drug dealers in the area, like their counterparts in the United States, for example, often use expensive, comfortable sports clothing to indicate their vocation and their success. US designer sports labels, manufactured by near slave labor in the third world, are preferred over all others. The relative bagginess of the garment is convenient for concealing either gear (heroin), cash or weapons, and when new, its price is well known: thus local assessment of success is easy to make. No sportswear manufacturer or retailer is unaware of this fact; indeed, some market goods precisely for this audience (see e.g., Fleischer 1995). Never slow to take up a trend, marketers on both sides of the Atlantic have also placed the Nike "swoosh" on gaudy jewellery, such as sovereign rings and pendants (a favourite item of many people involved in the drug trade in this area). Like a tenner bag of gear or a vial of crack cocaine, such products are meant to supply a transient high that soon wears off and has to be replicated. Thus, what Jello Biafra insightfully calls the Nike swooshstika indexes and underwrites not merely the misery in the sweatshops of quasi-fascist US-allied regimes like Indonesia, but a wider world of capital and commodities that elevates some to opulence while ruthlessly confining others to misery.

Clearly, the "classicized" body of Perry Ogden (sec Stallybrass and White 1986) cuts off any interpretation that places us and the boy in the same frame, while the dystopic carnivalesque body drawn on the hoarding in front of a state building which the locals believed would eventually be directed towards "their" drug problem absolutely requires it. The first depiction removes the boy and his horse from the here-and-now, the white sheet and a little preparation effacing the unpleasantness of a global system that, willingly or not, we share with this young man. Potentially, however, it is the same boy, or his best mate, or, increasingly, his girlfriend, that holds the syringe. She/he shares our products, but not our means; she/he shares our passion for self-construction through a repetition of commodity consumption, but in a way that we would rather not know about. The figure reminds us that what we buy either politically or economically at the beginning of the new millennium does not come cheap. Our solution to date has been to suppress this sense of structural cracking just beneath the surface of everyday life. Like Dublin Corporation, we paint things over and hope for the best.

Notes

1. Urban Studies in Ireland has largely been the preserve of sociology or small reports by activist researchers (e.g. Fahy 1999). For statistical and policy background on poverty in Ireland, see Nolan, Whelan, and Williams 1998. Two volumes, *Memories of the present: Irish sociological chronicles*, Vols. 1 and 2 (Peillon and Slater 1998, 2000), contain some recent research in urban settings in Ireland. See also Curtin, Donnan, Wilson 1993 and Donnan and McFarlane 1989 for some anthropological perspectives from both sides of the border.

2. Our team worked in Cherry Orchard from the end of 1997 until the end of 2000. During this period, we developed contacts with a variety of residents and with professionals working in the area, both in formal state structures like the schools and police and in newer para-state institutions such as Area Partnerships and Task Forces. Two field researchers had daily contact in the community, examining everything from the rhythms of community life to the serious social problems found therein, but certain politically sensitive topics, such as the serious drugs problem (predominantly opiate

abuse) and the largely tense relationship between local people and the Gardaí, were worked on by the principal investigators (see Saris and Bartley *et al.* 1999, 2000a, 2000b).
3. The Irish Tourist Board.
4. Indeed, the picture clearly resonates with one of the more famous, if controversial, depictions of Ireland, that of Eamon DeValera's St. Patrick's Day Address of 1943:

> The Ireland which we dreamed of would be the home of a people who valued material wealth only as the basis of right living, of a people who were satisfied with frugal comfort and devoted their leisure to things of the spirit; a land whose countryside would be bright with cosy homesteads, whose fields and villages would be joyous with the sounds of industry, the romping of sturdy children, the contests of athletic youths, the laughter of comely maidens; whose firesides would be the forums of the wisdom of serene old men. [*Irish Press.* 18 March 1943:1]

In present-day Ireland, the St. Patrick's Day Address has been seized on by many commentators as the veritable nadir of an economically backward, culturally inward-looking, religiously and socially conservative state, out of which a modern society in Ireland is finally emerging (see Saris 2000).

References

Bartley, Brendan and A. Jamie Saris 1999. Social exclusion in Cherry Orchard: Another side of suburban Dublin. In MacLaren, Andrew and Killen, James (eds). *Dublin contemporaries: Trends and issues for the 21st century,* pp. 81–92. Dublin: Geographical Society of Ireland.

Breathnach, Proinseas 1998. Exploring the "Celtic Tiger" phenomenon: Causes and consequences of Ireland's economic miracle. *European Urban and Regional Studies* 5(4): 305–16.

Curtin, C., Donnan, Hastings and Wilson, Thomas 1993. *Irish urban cultures.* Belfast: Institute of Irish Studies. The Queen's University of Belfast.

Dalrymple, T. 2001. *Life at the bottom: The worldview that makes the underclass.* London: Ivan R. Dee.

Donnan, Hastings and McFarlane, Graham 1989. *The social anthropology of urban Ireland.* Aldershot and Brookfield: Avebury.

Dooley, Mark 1998. Horse owners march to highlight animal slaughter. *Irish Times,* 11 March: 8.

Fahy, Tony (ed.) 1999. *Social housing in Ireland: A study of success, failure, and lessons learned.* Dublin: Oak Tree Press.

Fleisher, Mark S. 1995. *Beggars and thieves: The lives of urban street criminals.* University of Wisconsin Press.

Foucault, Michel 1973a. *The archaeology of knowledge and the discourse on language.* New York: Pantheon Books.

_____ 1973b. *Madness and civilization.* New York: Vintage Books.

_____ 1975. *Birth of the clinic.* New York: Vintage Books.

_____ 1979. *Discipline and punish.* New York: Vintage Books.

Irish Press 1943. 18 March: 1.

Irish Times 1995. Social Affairs correspondent. 7 November: 7.

_____ 1997 Horse owners protest against new Act. 12 October: 12.

Nolan, B. et al 1998. *Where are the poor households? The spatial distribution of poverty and deprivation in Ireland.* Dublin: Oak Tree Press.

Peillon, Michel and Slater, Eamonn (eds) 2000. *Memories of the present: Irish sociological chronicles,* Volume 2. Dublin: Institute for Public Administration.

Rabinow, Paul 1996. *Essays on the anthropology of reason.* Princeton University Press.

Room, G. 1995. Poverty and social exclusion: The new European agenda for policy and research. In Room, G. (ed.) *Beyond the threshold.* Bristol: Policy Press.

Saris, A. Jamie 2000. Culture and history in the half-way house: Ethnography, tradition, and the rural middle class in the West of Ireland. *Journal of Historical Sociology.* 13(1): 10–36.

Saris, A. Jamie and Bartley, Brendan 1999. *Final Report: Life histories of drug users and drug use in the community in Ballyfermot and Cherry Orchard.* Dublin: Ballyfermot Area Partnership.

_____ 2000a. The culture of protest in West Dublin. In Peillon, Michel and Slater, Eamonn (eds) *Memories of the present: Irish sociological chronicles,* Volume 2, pp. 117–130. Dublin: Institute for Public Administration.

_____ 2000b. "Community development organizations and European social inclusion discourses as ethnographic problems." Paper presented at American Anthropological Association 98th Annual Meeting. San Francisco, USA.

Stallybrass, Peter and White, Allon 1986. *The politics and poetics of transgression.* London: Methuen.

CRITICAL THINKING QUESTIONS

1. Describe the economic and social conditions in Cherry Orchard.
2. What conditions contributed to the Halloween riots in Cherry Orchard?
3. What changes in the Gardaí and other state bodies occurred as a result of the riots?
4. Visual arts can reflect a number of different cultural viewpoints. What sort of artwork has been painted on the Red Wall, and what segment of Dublin or Irish society have they reflected?
5. What two trends do the authors suggest have emerged in the power relationships within Cherry Orchard? How do the murals they examine at the article's end reflect these trends?

Native Burials: Human Rights and Sacred Bones

Edward Halealoha Ayau

TRADITIONAL BELIEFS AND VALUES REGARDING THE ANCESTORS

Ola nā iwi (The bones live).
Said an elder who is well cared for by his family
or in praise of the relatives providing such care.
—*'Ōlelo No'eau (Hawaiian Proverb)*

Traditional Native Hawaiians believed *nā iwi* (the bones) to be the primary physical embodiment of a person. Following death, only *nā iwi* were considered sacred, for within the bones resided the person's *mana* (spiritual essence). *Mana* was greatly valued, and Native Hawaiians spent their lives maintaining and enhancing their *mana*. Thus, supreme care was accorded to *na iwi* following death. Ancestral bones were guarded, respected, venerated, and even deified. It was believed that the *'uhane* (spirit) of a person hovered near *nā iwi*. Desecration of *nā iwi* resulted in an insult to the *'uhane* and trauma and harm to living descendants.

In the Hawaiian language, the word *kanu* means to plant or to cultivate, and to bury, as with a deceased person. The burial of the deceased was considered a planting by traditional Native Hawaiians and was followed by physical and spiritual growth. The Hawaiian people believed they were nourished from foods fertilized by the bones of ancestors. According to Native Hawaiian belief, when *nā iwi* are planted in the bosom of Haumea, Earth Mother, they eventually become part of the *'āina* (land). Through this planting and decomposition, *nā iwi* impart the *mana* of the deceased to the *'āina,* and the *'āina* becomes imbued with spiritual essence and energy necessary to sustain it and the families. This planting serves to strengthen the ancestral foundation, by placing *nā iwi* where they belong.

Traditional Hawaiian belief maintains that it is the *kuleana* (responsibility) of the living to care for and to protect *'ohana* (family) burial sites and to pass on this knowledge and responsibility to the next generation. These practices assure that living Native Hawaiians will always provide perpetual care and protection to their ancestors, thereby maintaining the integrity of the family. Central to the physical and spiritual well being of Native Hawaiians is the inheritance of *mana* from their ancestral past. In turn, the *kûpuna* (ancestors) care for and protect the living, affirming the interdependent relationship between them and living descendants, where each cares for and protects the other. This relationship is best expressed by the traditional Hawaiian value of *løkahi*.

DISTURBANCE AND DESECRATION

When the first documented Europeans arrived at Kealakekua Bay on the island of Hawai'i in 1779, they showed little regard for the Hawaiian burials they encountered. However, in the years that followed, that lack of regard would escalate into wanton acts of desecration. During this period, radical social, economic, and political changes in Hawai'i had devastating consequences for Hawaiians. By 1832, less than fifty years following contact, the Native Hawaiian population collapsed, declining from 800,000 to 130,000. These drastic changes also resulted in Native Hawaiians being separated from their ancestral homelands, effectively interfering with their ability to protect *'ohana* burial sites. Over time, Hawaiians became alienated from cultural values and responsibilities, including the *kuleana* to care for *nā iwi kûpuna*.

The loss of cultural values had a severe and adverse impact on *nā iwi kûpuna*. Over the next

---

Source: Reprinted from *Cultural Survival Quarterly,* Spring 2000.

century, looting, archaeological collection, erosion, and construction resulted in the desecration and removal of thousands of ancestral Native Hawaiians. Many of these ancestral remains were shipped to institutions throughout the United States and Europe and studied in the name of science. In the last century, the burial sites of more than 5,000 *kūpuna* have been desecrated with their remains removed to museums around the world.

The continued separation of these ancestors resulted in the severe loss of *mana* (spiritual essence) from the land, the families, and the Hawaiian nation. The consequences of the separation of *nā iwi kūpuna* have been tangibly felt throughout this century. Native Hawaiians face the worst economic, social, health, housing, and political conditions. It is therefore imperative that efforts be undertaken toward healing the Hawaiian people. A fundamental means by which to heal both the living and those ancestral Hawaiians who await reunification with their homelands, is to bring them together, to *kanu* (bury, plant) the *iwi* and thus restore precious *mana* to the land and the families.

The largest disturbance and desecration of ancestral Native Hawaiian remains took place between 1915–1990, during which time the *iwi* of approximately 3,000 ancestral Native Hawaiians were systematically removed from the sand dunes of Møkapu Peninsula, located on the island of O'ahu. The majority of the ancestral remains were archaeologically disinterred through a joint excavation coordinated and conducted by the University of Hawai'i Department of Anthropology and the Bernice Pauahi Bishop Museum between the years 1938 through 1940. During this period, approximately 800 ancestral Native Hawaiians were disinterred.

Following the completion of the 1938–40 excavation, the United States condemned the Møkapu Peninsula to construction of a Marine Corps Base. During base construction, and throughout World War II, another estimated 250 ancestral Hawaiians were disturbed and removed from Møkapu. When all was said and done, archaeologists, bulldozers, and *maha'oi* people removed about 3,000 ancestors from their final resting places at the sand dunes known as Møkapu, Heleloa, and Ulupa'u. Due to the lack of notification by the Bishop Museum, University of Hawai'i, and U.S. Marines, most Native Hawaiians never knew about the burial disturbances at Møkapu. As of this writing, ancestral Native Hawaiian remains are still being disinterred and removed from Møkapu Peninsula. Sadly, the mass desecration does not stop at Møkapu.

In 1988, the remains of approximately 1,100 ancestral Native Hawaiians were archaeologically removed to make way for construction of the Ritz-Carlton Hotel on the island of Maui. The place known as Honokahua became the focal point for Native Hawaiians with respect to the legacy of burial site disturbance. This time, Hawaiians were keenly aware of what was taking place. However, a lack of legal protection limited their ability to prevent the desecration.

Following vociferous protests, the excavations were halted, and a settlement was reached wherein the hotel was relocated, the ancestral remains were ceremonially reinterred by Hui Alanui O Mākena, and the reburial site set aside in perpetuity. An important lesson from Honokahua was that legislation was needed in order to protect and to promote the cultural responsibility of Native Hawaiians to determine the proper treatment of ancestral burial sites. A second lesson was that Native Hawaiians needed to relearn cultural protocols relating to the care of ancestral remains. A Native Hawaiian Organization called Hui Mālama I Nā Kūpuna O Hawai'i Nei was born from the tragedy and enlightenment of Honokahua.

ESTABLISHMENT OF HUI MĀLAMA I NĀ KŪPUNA O HAWAI'I NEI

The primary goal of Hui Mālama is the care of ancestral Native Hawaiian remains through repatriation and reinterment and the protection of burial sites. Hui Mālama members have been trained in traditional protocols relating to the handling of ancestral remains and funerary objects. The Hui Mālama mission is to restore and maintain the ancestral foundation of Native Hawaiians by assisting families and communities to resume the responsibilities of care and protection of the ancestors, thus strengthening our sense of Hawaiian self-identity, and perpetuating our culture.

Hui Mālama members have been taught the importance of *pule* (prayer) through which we request the assistance of *ke Akua* (God) and *na kupūna* (the ancestors) to provide us the tools accessory to conduct our work:

E ho mai ka 'ike
Grant us knowledge

E ho mai ka ikaika
Grant us strength

E ho mai ka akamai
Grant us intelligence

E ho mai ka maopopo pono
Grant us righteous understanding

E ho mai ka 'ike papalua
Grant us visions, avenues of communication

E ho mai ka mana
Grant us spiritual energy

As the living, we have a *kuleana* (responsibility) to care for our *kūpuna*. In turn, the ancestors have a responsibility to care for and protect us on the spiritual side. Hence, there exists an inherent reliance and need for each other.

THE NATIONAL MUSEUM OF THE AMERICAN INDIAN ACT (1989) AND THE NATIVE AMERICAN GRAVES PROTECTION AND REPATRIATION ACT (1990)

In addition to the need for cultural training relating to the care of ancestral remains, the events at Mōkapu and Honokahua pointed to the need for legal protection of ancestral Hawaiian remains and burial sites at the federal and state levels. Fortunately, between 1988 and 1990 discussions were taking place within the halls of the U.S. Congress to enact two pieces of legislation that would help address the need for proper treatment of ancestral skeletal remains, funerary objects, sacred objects, and cultural patrimony of Native Americans defined to include Native Hawaiians.

In 1989, Congress passed the National Museum of the American Indian Act in order to address two important needs. The first need was to construct a national museum in Washington, D.C. to house the Heye Collection, the largest collection of Native American Indian cultural items. This museum would be a member institution of the Smithsonian. The second purpose was to require the Smithsonian to inventory, identify, and in response to a request by the appropriate tribe or Native Hawaiian organization, repatriate ancestral skeletal remains and funerary objects. The law named Hui Mālama and the Office of Hawaiian Affairs as Native Hawaiian Organizations authorized to repatriate.

On November 16, 1990, President Bush signed the measure into law, which became known as the Native American Graves Protection and Repatriation Act (NAGPRA). In general, the law established two deadlines by which federal agencies and any institution that receives federal funding must identify all objects and human remains that meet the definitions of cultural items established in the law. NAGPRA authorizes federally recognized Indian tribes, Hui Mālama, and the Office of Hawaiian Affairs to exercise their responsibility to their ancestors, their belongings, sacred objects, and cultural patrimony by repatriating them to the possession and control of the culture's living descendants.

REPATRIATION BY HUI MĀLAMA I NĀ KŪPUNA O HAWAI'I NEI

As a result of both cultural training and the authority of federal law, Hui Mālama has repatriated the remains of hundreds of ancestral Native Hawaiians.

Over the past nine years, Hui Mālama has completed repatriation projects involving the reburial of ancestral Hawaiian remains and funerary objects held in 26 institutions in Hawai'i, the continental United States, Switzerland, Canada, and Australia. In addition, Hui Mālama has assisted other Native Hawaiian Organizations to conduct repatriation. The number of *nā iwi kāpuna* (ancestral remains) repatriated total approximately 5,607 individuals.

Some of the notable repatriation efforts include: (1) the American Museum and the Field Museum of Natural History in June 1991; (2) the University of Pennsylvania Museum and the Smithsonian Museum of Natural History in August 1991; (3) Harvard and Yale Universities in March 1994; (4) Dartmouth College, Earlham

College Moore Museum, and the Los Angeles County Museum of Natural History in June 1995; and (5) dozens more museums since 1995. In November 1997, eight Hui Mālama members sailed 800 miles to repatriate and reinter nine ancestral Hawaiians to the remote islands of Nilloa and Necker. In 1999, Hui Mālama was one of 15 claimants that participated in the repatriation of approximately 3,000 ancestral Hawaiians from Møkapu, O'ahu.

These accomplishments stand as a testimonial to the revitalization of traditional cultural values, traditions, and practices. Moreover, the repatriations prepared Hui Mālama for the tasks and challenges ahead including efforts to repatriate and reinter *iwi kūpuna* now in institutions in London, England, Edinburgh, Scotland, St. Peterburg, Russia, and Dresden, Germany.

HAWAI'I REVISED STATUTES

At the state level, Hui Mālama advocated for passage of a law that would prevent the type of desecration that took place at Honokahua. Following spirited negotiations with large landowners who opposed the idea of allowing for the preservation in place of unmarked Hawaiian burial sites, Act 306 was enacted into law in May,

1990. This law restored Native Hawaiians to a position of decision-making authority over previously identified, unmarked Hawaiian burial sites over fifty years old. This was done by establishing five island burial councils for the island of Hawai'i, Maui/Lana'i, Molokai, O'ahu and Kaua'i/Ni'ihau. Moreover, the law requires the burial councils to have a member ratio of not less than two to one and not more than three to one in favor of Hawaiian representatives. Furthermore, when Hawaiian remains are inadvertently discovered, the burial councils have the right to make recommendations to the State Land Department relating to treatment. Finally, the law increased the penalty for violations by increasing the fines from $1,000 to $10,000 and making it a criminal misdemeanor to disturb a burial site.

CONCLUSION

As with many struggling Native societies, Hawaiians have persevered in their attempts to protect their families, resources, and rights. The return of ancestral skeletal remains back into the *'āina* (land) strengthens the ancestral foundation, nourishing the living with mana needed to restore self-determination, and assure cultural perpetuation. *Ola nā iwi*, the bones live.

CRITICAL THINKING QUESTIONS

1. How do Native Hawaiians view the relationship between ancestral bones (*nā iwi*), a person's spirit (*'uhane*), and families (*'ohana*)?
2. What types of activities have destroyed or disinterred thousands of the *nā iwi* of ancestral Hawaiians?
3. How have the Native American Graves Protection and Repatriation Act (NAGPRA) and the organization Hui Mālama contributed to the revival of ideas and behaviors in regard to traditional Hawaiian beliefs and culture?
4. A thought question: Archaeology is the science of reconstructing and studying the past through the excavation and analysis of the material and physical remains of past cultures. How do the aims and philosophy of archaeology conflict with traditional Native Hawaiian views on life and the past?

Globalization and Its Challenges

STATE OF THE ART: Globalization

The paradox of modern life is that we live in a world that is both expanding and shrinking at an amazing rate. Through the interconnections of trade, politics, and information technology (particularly the Internet), the horizons of every nation on the globe and of a good many people around the world have expanded. Ironically this very expansion has also shrunk the world via the instantaneous transmission of information and attitudes. Many of our traditional ways of viewing the world are no longer viable, as we congeal into a sort of "global village" where the marketplace, in which often radically different ideas interact, makes each of us painfully aware that we can no longer isolate ourselves from outside influences. This hybridization of ideas often acts synergistically, creating change at a more rapid pace than anyone could have previously imagined.

Anthropology started out by viewing cultures as static, unchanging enclaves. In the early part of the twentieth century, anthropological studies revealed that cultures formerly thought of as unchanging were undergoing changes. Since then anthropologists have always been interested in the ways cultures adapt to changing social, economic, and environmental circumstances. Whereas in the past, smaller traditional cultures were our laboratories of study, today the whole world is a vast test case of anthropological theories about culture change. Globalization means that cultures, often with radically different worldviews, regularly come into contact with one another. What impact will this increased and intensified pace of contact have on both individual cultures and on human life in general?

Even before the dawn of globalization, anthropology had begun to turn its attention to the effects of colonialism, which presented the strongest force of change. The changes succeeding colonialism were rural–urban migration, expansion of the economy as the formerly colonized nations became markets for Western economies, and mass communication in the new era of technological transfers (Rosman & Rubel 2004; Ember & Ember 2004).

Anthropology faced bigger changes in the mid-to-later part of the twentieth century and into this millennium. Transnationalism and forced migration have produced a population of refugees and other migrants who impact the host countries through cultural exchanges (Lewellen 2002). High-tech equipment and other products from developed economies are acquired by people in developing nations. Values and attitudes have been changing as different cultures meet (Spindler & Stockard 2006). Anthropology has been interested in the process by which indigenes adopt the values of the developed world, and the effects of the global market and the introduction of new products on people in developing nations. Similarly, the extent to which developed nations incorporate some aspect of customs from the less-developed societies is a matter of anthropological concern.

Anthropologists are confronted with the issues of resistance to globalization due to damage to the environment, labor conditions, and shifts in the dynamics of power (Rosman & Rubel 2004). The 1992 United Nations resolution to safeguard the rights of indigenous peoples (Rodrigues & Games 1998) was ignored by some nations. Ecotourism has prompted some nations to encroach upon some sacred sites and traditional lands for the purpose of economic development and tourist attraction spots as a source of revenue for the state. Some nations allow indigenous representatives in international meetings to respond to and to protest any form of violation of their rights (Bonvillain 2010). Some indigenous peoples continue to suffer displacement due to their nations' inability to properly harness globalization for the mutual benefit of both the state and the indigenous peoples. This and the responses of people to the impacts of globalization and the challenges of manufacturing new products and finding markets for them (Ember & Ember 2004), and how applicable and suitable the products are in the local environment, are ongoing areas of anthropological study.

ABOUT THE ARTICLES

The four articles in this section represent a cross-section of the potentials and problems involved in the globalization process. Pieterse provides a definitional and theoretical grounding for this section. He discusses and defines the concept of globalization and deals with the different perspectives on the movement between the "developed" and "developing" worlds regarding this phenomenon. He then highlights why this trend cannot be explained by the somewhat tired concepts of "neocolonialism" or "neo-imperialism" but is a completely different phenomenon that must be explained on its own terms.

Bergin deals with sport, a human activity that generates worldwide interest. Wherever Western culture goes, it brings its sports with it. Using the Maori as an example, he examines how sport can be used to both maintain and enhance cultural identity while at the same time facilitating cultural integration. The Maori adoption of Western sports, particularly rugby, is used as a mirror to examine how the Maori use sports to maintain their cultural distinctiveness while integrating into a larger Australian society. In a sense this is what certain sports, particularly football, do in American society. The reader should compare the role of sport in American society, discussed by Arens in Section Two, through the lens of the Maori adoption of rugby and other sports in Australian culture.

The article by Tsai, Lee, and Wang looks at globalization from a micro-perspective, that of the individuals whose lives are being swept up by the globalization phenomenon. By examining the lives of individuals, they bring to life the people behind the statistics. It serves as a humanistic reminder that real human beings are behind the statistics and that the detached clinical view fails to illuminate the impact of this massive trend on people's very ability to exist. Students reading this article may wish to look at ways the trends toward globalization are affecting them personally.

Finally the article by Bodley can be seen as a companion piece to that of Tsai, Lee, and Wang. Bodley takes a pessimistic look at the impacts of globalization on traditional societies. What Western culture defines as "progress" often turns out to be detrimental to peoples with no experience in dealing with Western ideas and economic realities. He highlights through ethnographic and historical examples the damage that can be wrought to such unwitting "victims of progress." In doing this he sounds a cautionary note that demonstrates that all "progress" is not always beneficial.

References

Bonvillain, N. *Cultural Anthropology*, 2nd ed. Upper Saddle River, NJ: Prentice Hall, 2010.

Ember, C., & Ember, M. *Cultural Anthropology*, 11th ed. Upper Saddle River, NJ: Pearson/Prentice Hall, 2004.

Lewellen, T. C. *The Anthropology of Globalization: Cultural Anthropology Enters the 21st Century*. London: Bergin & Garvey, 2002.

Rodrigues, E., & Games, J. "Anthropology and the Politics of Representation." *Economic and Political Weekly* 33, no. 42/43: 2709–2714, 1998.

Rosman, A., & Rubel, P. *The Tapestry of Culture: An Introduction to Cultural Anthropology*, 8th ed. New York: McGraw-Hill, 2004.

Spindler, J. Stockard, J. *Globalization and Change in Fifteen Cultures: Born in One World, Living in Another*. The Spindler Series. Eds. George Spindler & Janice Stockard. Florence, KY: Wadsworth, 2006.

For Further Research

There have been numerous books and articles written lately on the issue of globalization. Two historical treatises by Wallerstein—*The Modern World System: Capitalist Agriculture and the Origins of the European World-Economy in the Sixteenth Century* (1974, Academic Press) and *The Modern World System: II. Mercantilism and the Consolidation of the European World-Economy, 1600–1750* (1980, Academic Press)—set the stage for many subsequent analyses of globalization.

Most anthropological journals publish articles on the topic, but one that focuses heavily on the subject is Anthropological Quarterly. Solid books on the subject include Bodley's *Victims of Progress* (5th ed., 2008, Altamira Press) and Spindler and Stockard's reader *Globalization and Change in Fifteen Cultures: Born in One World, Living in Another* (2007, Thomson-Wadsworth). Scupin's *Cultural Anthropology: A Global Perspective* (7th ed., 2008, Pearson Prentice Hall) is a textbook that has specific chapters dedicated to globalization and incorporates this perspective in its chapter discussions. For additional information on researching the topics discussed in the "State of the Art" section, please visit *www.mysearchlab.com*.

Globalization North and South: Representations of Uneven Development and the Interaction of Modernities

Jan Nederveen Pieterse

A major feature of the global condition is the wide and glaring hiatus between wealth and poverty. One would like to say it's a feature of global experience, but for how many of us is it a matter of experience? Worlds of experience are segmented and representations across the fence are coded. Global poverty is routinized—"the poor will always be with you." Aid fatigue is periodically interrupted by emergencies that prompt selective media attention and out of the sky relief campaigns. Refugees are objects of charity, asylum seekers objects of scrutiny, illegal immigrants are criminalized along with drug traffickers and crime syndicates. Wealth and poverty are both relative and contextual, and according to the soap stories that make up the comfort zones of capitalism "the rich also suffer." Indeed they probably suffer a lot more than the poor do because their mishaps are being continuously aired. The steady succession of development fixes and failures is papered over by global economic management; poverty alleviation and development are being outmanoeuvred by the management of global growth, in the vague expectation that a rising tide will lift all boats.

While the buzzword is globalization, uneven development trails globalization like its shadow. Globalization is uneven among countries and regions, among regions within countries and among categories within regions. While globalization is often characterized as "truncated globalization" or "Triadization," concentrated in the triad of Western Europe, North America and Japan, its reach extends further. While the development gap between the advanced economies and newly industrialized economies has narrowed, the gap between these and most developing countries is widening. This reflects a partial reversal of an earlier trend of gradual integration of developing countries in the international division of labor. With regard to trade, international capital flows and foreign direct investment, there has been a marked downturn in participation in the world economy by developing countries since the beginning of the 1980s. In this context what is at issue are differences at multiple levels: material differences and technology gaps, measured in the familiar statistics of GNP per capita and human development; transnational economic regimes; power differentials relating to geopolitics, security and prestige; and differences in perceptions and images.

One of the features of collective reflection in media and social science today is the profound discrepancy between perspectives North and South.[1] On either side, representations are schematic and together they make up a stylized exchange of stereotypes and off-the-shelf knowledge. Since global inequality is a major part of the contemporary collective condition it would loom large in collective reflection, but does it? The buzzword is globalization but we inhabit a divided world, a cardboard world of stereotypes and caricatures. In media and social science there is a wide discrepancy between the worlds of experience of the world's majority who are poor and the world's privileged minority in the North. In the North, social science is taken or takes itself

Source: Jan Nederveen Pieterse, "Globalization North and South: Representations of Uneven Development and the Interaction of Modernities" from *Theory, Culture & Society*, vol. 17, no. 1, pp. 129-137 (2000). Reprinted by permission of SAGE.

to be at the forefront of collective understanding, while mostly it's too self-engrossed to take into account the experiences and perspectives of the world majority. Whether it concerns modernity, post-modernity or globalization, the social sciences tend to represent a narrow western or northern view. In the South, the engagement with northern perspectives is often out of context, out of touch with their historical context and with cultural variations. In the North, New Age scientists are foraging among mystical traditions in Asia and elsewhere on the basis of schemas and stereotypes, without much understanding of the actual variations in philosophy and practice. In the South, scholars seeking to negotiate modernity, scrutinize the European Enlightenment—Kant, Hegel, Habermas—without adequate understanding that rationalism was a programme, not a reality; that the Enlightenment also had a dark side; and that the Romantics were also part of the Enlightenment (Herder, Carlyle, Nietzsche). Lack of depth, lack of nuance, lack of experience and understanding on either side: the North–South hiatus in experience and reflection still creates the impression of our living in a cardboard world, making gestures to cut-outs rather than real figures. In a word, schematic understandings North and South, of the Enlightenment, modernity, capitalism, poverty, cultures. No wonder that the émigrés from the South in the North have been so influential in literature and social science, for they and not many others bridge the different worlds of experience.

North–South inequality runs very deep, *n'en déplaise* globalization and the "de-territorialization of poverty" (i.e. the rich in the South and the poor in the North). It relates profoundly to world images and perceptions of globalization that are held also among the middle class in the South (e.g. Gopal, 1998). Of course, the South is in the North and the North is in the South, and privilege and poverty are no longer neatly geographically divided. Yet the overall distinction between North and South, crude as it is, still makes sense. In demographic terms they are the minority world and the majority world. They are *worlds* because they make up complete life-worlds. The division does not simply run between middle class and underclass—as if globally these share

similar consumption patterns, lifestyles and values. In some respects, they do, but obviously class and status are not the only variables. Thus the middle class in the South shares many of the majority's economic, political and geopolitical frustrations and to some extent identifies with the nation, the region. The poor majority and the middle class in the South suffer domestic political incompetence and corruption, western double standards, superpower geopolitics and geo-economics, and share national and regional destinies.

In this reflection the focus is on differences in analyzing and representing global conditions between North and South, on different conditions (different modernities, different capitalisms) and on the articulations across different conditions. Existing analytics—such as dependency, imperialism, exclusion and conspiracy theories—are not adequate for dealing with these new relations. Thus, the economics of dependency overlooks reverse dependency, i.e. the dependency of de-industrializing regions in the North (Wales, Scotland, Brittany) on investors from Asia (South Korea, Taiwan). The analytic of boomerang effects—such as the debt boomerang (indebtedness in the South curtailing demand for products from the North)—is too blunt to monitor and capture the multiple links and their ramifications. Risk analysis and the globalization of risk can be a relevant instrument but needs greater fine-tuning to be effective.

Another account of contemporary globalization adopts the novel terminology of exclusion and refers to the *exclusion* of the majority of humanity—the majority in large parts of Africa, Asia and Latin America, who are excluded from life in the fast lane, from the "interlinked economies" of the "Triad zone." But exclusion is too crude a term to describe the actual situation.

The middle class in developing countries participates in the global circuits of advertising, brand-name consumerism and high-tech services, which, at another end of the circuitry, increasingly exclude the underclass in advanced economies. . . . The term exclusion ignores the many ways in which developing countries are *included* in global processes: they are subject to global financial discipline (as in structural adjustment and interest payments, resulting in net capital outflows) and part of global markets (resource flows, distribution networks, diaspora and niche markets), global ecology, international politics, global communications, science and technology, international development cooperation, transnational civil society, international migration, travel, and crime networks. For instance, the public health sector in many African countries is increasingly being internationalised. Thus, it would be more accurate to speak of *asymmetrical inclusion* or hierarchical integration. A classic term for this situation used to be "combined and uneven development," but now one of the differences is that the units are no longer nations. (Nederveen Pieterse. 1997: 80)

In the South if one is not participating in global market production or consumption one still partakes of ads, media and movies, developmental regimes (such as structural adjustment), economic, financial and political instability. Exclusion is too blunt a terminology if what is at issue is to examine the new uneven links that are developing in the framework of accelerated globalization.

Thus, people in the South are *within* the reach of global mass communications and advertising, within the reach of the message but not necessarily the action. This is how an Albanian émigré describes the impact of Italian TV on Albanians during the old days of seclusion:

> Step by step the entire advertising message is extracted from its (pragmatic) context . . . . The ultimate result is that ads are viewed as windows to an upper reality. This is the reality where people, and things, and behaviors, and actions are light, colorful, beautiful. People are almost always good looking, clean, and well dressed; they all smile and enjoy everything they do, and get extremely happy, even when confronted with a new toothbrush. . . . The repeated contact with mirages of a reality *beyond* the wall, not only created a diffuse desire, but also kept it alive for a sufficiently long time, so that desire could lose its initial property

of being a[n] . . . impulse for action, and become a *state of mind,* similar to profuse, disinterested love. (Vebhiu, 1999)

In Western Europe, at the other end of the TV set, viewers experience "long-distance suffering" and engage in schizophrenic behavior—making limited or vague gestures of solidarity, while finding shelter in the "chauvinism of prosperity" that is being sustained by institutions and media. Electoral politics in many advanced countries excludes "terrorists" and marginalizes welfare recipients and now this often extends to asylum seekers, refugees and "illegal migrants."

Globalization evokes much anger and anxiety in the South and tends to be experienced as yet another round of northern hegemony, another round of concentration of power and wealth. The common metaphor for globalization in the South, in the slipstream of 200 years of weary experience, is imperialism or neocolonialism revisited. Analytically this is mistaken: imperialism was territorial, state driven, centrally orchestrated and marked by a clear division between colonizer and colonized; and none of these features apply to contemporary globalization. Contemporary accelerated globalization is multidimensional, non-territorial, polycentric, and the lines of inclusion/exclusion are blurred and run between the middle classes and the poor North and South. Imperialism was multidimensional but ultimately driven by a single-minded intentionality. Unlike imperialism, globalization involves multiple intentionalities and crisscrossing projects on the part of many agents.

While the metaphor of imperialism does not apply and generates misleading analytics and politics, nevertheless the feeling itself that this is another round of hegemony is a political reality. What *is* common to both imperialism and globalization is the sense of powerlessness and frustration: only this time the dynamics of deprivation are different.

So are the current geopolitical circumstances. The world of the 1970s is no more. Then the momentum of decolonization was still in motion, the Nonaligned Movement was strong; the Eastern bloc provided a counter-balance and global alternative scenarios such as the New International Economic Order seemed to make sense.

TABLE 1 Differences Between Imperialism and Accelerated Globalization

Imperialism	Accelerated Globalization
State-centric, balance of power	Multiple actors and fields (technology, corporations, states, international institutions, civic organizations)
Primarily political	Multidimensional
Territorial	Non-territorial
Directed by metropoles	No central powerhouse; absence of a global hegemonic power
Clear division colonizer–colonized	Blurred division between inclusion/exclusion from "interlinked economies"

In the 1990s none of these conditions prevail. During the last 20 years globalization has coincided with a new period of hegemony of finance capital, in the wake of the recycling of petro-dollars and the ensuing debt crisis, resembling in some respects the turn-of-the-century epoch of Hilferding's finance capital. Open space is shrinking. De-linking as an option was overtaken by the new international division of labour in the 1970s and localism or building alternative enclaves has little future in the 1990s. This is why the "new protectionism" is a loser strategy. Countervailing power now is located in the diffuse realm of "global civil society," of civic organizations and NGOs, local and international.

Frustration fosters paranoia and conspiracy theories are a convenient shortcut. Lashing out against "Jewish financiers," as Prime Minister Mahathir Mohamed did, is not of much use. Much of the Middle East lives by a conspiracy theory centerd on Zionism in league with the United States on account of the Jewish American lobby (Pipes, 1996). In parts of Africa, the Caribbean and among African Americans, the lead conspiracy is white racism and its machinations. This is not to mention regional anxieties, such as India's worries about regional rivals in league with foreign powers (Pakistan and China supported by the US, and the Tamil Tigers supported by foreign elements) and Southeast Asian concerns about the decomposition of Indonesia.

These perspectives in the South are mirrored by conspiracy theories in the West—Jihad against McWorld, the clash of civilizations, or an Islamic-Confucian combine against "the West," the Islamic bomb. Saudi Arabia supports a girdle of conservative Islamic states (Sudan, Afghanistan, Pakistan) and movements. The "Afghanis" (trained by the CIA in the war in Afghanistan) are a destabilizing force in states in the Arab world. Smugglers of humans, illegal immigrants, criminal organizations, drug traders, terrorists threaten to erode and undermine the citadels of civilization. Conflicts in the South are trivialized as minor skirmishes in the periphery, or yield doomsday perspectives—either the end of history (Fukuyama) or the end of the world (Kaplan, 1996). The issue is not that these phenomena do not exist—where there's smoke there's fire. The issue is that of labelling, relative magnitudes and explanatory force.

THE INTERPLAY OF MODERNITIES AND CAPITALISMS

An alternative explanatory framework may run as follows. Ours is not a world of simple modernity or simple capitalism that exists in varieties of more or less, further or earlier, differentiated along a single-track path. That was the old panorama of evolutionism, progress, developmentalism, modernization, Westernization. Part of the problem is that the language of social science and politics invites the use of the singular—modernity rather than modernities, capitalism rather than capitalisms, industrialization rather than different types of industrialization. This generalizing language is in use across the political spectrum, right to left, and is inhospitable to nuanced political thinking.

It is tempting to conceive of modernity as a single historical sphere, to which there may be different roads but which is ultimately a singular experience. What matters in that case is only a before and after: pre- and post-modernity. Of course, within modernity differences run between early and advanced, high, radical, neo-modernity and at the edges of modernity there are variations as well—peripheral, failed, truncated and hybrid modernities, but these all refer back to more or less of a single modernity. On the other hand, from here it would be a small step to spatio-temporal variations—such as European, American, Japanese, Asian modernities, and variations within each of them (such as Northwest, Southern, Eastern, Central European variants). Another argument is to distinguish among different *sequences* in modernization processes, as is common in Asian analyses. Gradually the argument of different modernities is being accepted (e.g. Nederveen Pieterse, 1998).

A similar case can be made with respect to different capitalisms. There is recognition of multiple "cultures of capitalism" even among advanced industrialized countries (Hampdon-Turner and Trompenaars, 1993). There are different modes of regulation among different forms of national capitalism varying according to historical antecedents and cultures of capitalism—statist on the European continent, Manchester liberalism in Britain, free enterprise in pioneer America, statist in Japan. Concerning industrialization, distinctions run not merely between first- and late-comers but also between late late-comers and very late-comers to industrialization, or different generations of industrialization along with different stages of industrialization. East Asia belongs then to the fourth generation industrialization. "There are many rooms in capitalism's house" (Okita, 1993: 273).

Thus multiple modernities and capitalisms are each conditioned and articulated by historic and geographical circumstances and each take on a different character on account of different modes of fusion and articulation. Acknowledging the geographical and historical differentiations of modernity, capitalism, industrialism is one concern, analysing their relations is another. What is the relationship between difference and sameness, between the variations and the theme? This is not a world of different realms that are neatly separated—modern and pre-modern, North and South, etc. Besides the different modernities in Asia, the Middle East, Africa, the Americas and Europe, there is the *interaction* of modernities and capitalisms. Understanding this interplay is a major key to contemporary dynamics. "We live in a world in which competition is not only a feature of inter-firm relations, but of the relations between different capitalist economic systems" (Applebaum and Henderson, 1995: 3).

Post-Fordism, for example, brings together discussions on capitalism and industrialization, but is usually discussed as if it concerns dynamics in the advanced economies of the North only. But the actual options available and directions taken are likely to be more influenced by the *interactions* among different modes of capitalism than is indicated by merely examining varieties in the North, as if these represent the front end of capitalism (which is not tenable in view of the rise of Pacific Asia) and as if the front end would not be affected by the rear. Thus, "national variants of Fordism" include peripheral Fordism (Mexico, Brazil), hybrid Fordism (Japan) and "primitive Taylorization" (Southeast Asia) (Peck and Tickell, 1994: 286–7), and the question is, How are they related?

While post-Fordism and postmodernity are important analytics for understanding dynamics in the North, for a complete understanding we should consider the relations *between* post-Fordist economies, newly emerging markets and developing countries. The ramifications of the "East Asian Miracle" economies are a case in point. First, East Asian economies have been new investors in de-industrializing regions of the North and Eastern Europe, thus impacting on regional uneven development in the North. Second, labor standards in newly emerging markets (lower wages, longer working hours, less unionization) are affecting labor standards in multinational corporations in their operations North and South. Third, the rhetoric or perception of less government intervention in the newly emerging markets (while in several ways bogus) is being used to reinforce structural reform globally and government rollback in the North. Fourth, the financial crises in the newly emerging markets—the Tequila crisis, the Asian crisis, the Latin American crisis—have reverberated on markets North and South, and have led to serious consideration of the architecture of the international financial system from Wall Street and the US Treasury to the IMF. They have generated the notion of *contagion* as a successor to the Cold

War domino theory. In other words, links *between* economies in the North and the newly emerging markets are affecting developments North and South. This is unfolding at the level of material exchanges and economic and financial regulation and simultaneously at the level of rhetoric, discourse and imaging.

These diverse spaces are not simply stray parts and add-ons in a random arrangement but part of a structured, dynamic and self-reflexive configuration. Thus, according to Petrella (1996), the relevant distinction now does not run between "good" capitalism (social market, Rhineland) and "bad" capitalism (wild, casino), but between national and global capitalism. The articulation of different capitalisms and modernities is being processed and channelled through the nodes of global capitalism and global hegemony.

Imperial continuities—the British Empire succeeded by US hegemony—have shaped the global career of capitalism. Nesting in the interstices of empire and hegemony and carried on its waves, Anglo-American capitalism—that is, the least state regulated of all forms of capitalism—has become the leading and dominant form of global capitalism. Its economics, neo-classical economics, has become the norm of economic thought. By this logic, Keynesianism was an interlude that was only partially implemented. The Bretton Woods institutions have become de facto global spearpoints of Anglo-American capitalism. The Washington consensus, or what is left of it, still rules if only because of the absence of a coherent alternative. Because of the size and complexity of the United States as a large multinational state it is difficult for significant changes to pass through Congress. On issues of global significance—trade policy, financial regulation, environmental and labor standards—there is a stalemate so that by and large the conservative common denominator prevails. The structural stalemate in United States politics is being reproduced in global affairs, transmitted via the decomposing (post) Washington consensus and international institutions.

As part of global hegemony, differences are acknowledged but are being erased in the terms in which they are being acknowledged—as more or less of the same, early and late along the same course. Globalization has overtaken development or, more precisely, developmental globalism has become the successor to developmentalism; structural adjustment has become the successor to modernization—both refer to alignment in the global ranks, the subsumption of differences under a single standard set by the centre. Since the 1980s development policy has increasingly come to mean world market integration, through improvements of infrastructure, human resource development, structural adjustment, deregulation, good governance and transparency. If development was traditionally premised on the principle of a special status and treatment of developing countries, globalization means the end of development.

The buzzword is globalization and the key issue is uneven development. Contemporary accelerated globalization refers to a new distribution of power and comes in a new package together with informalization, informatization and flexibilization. The ramifications of North–South articulation range from security, migration, media representation to regional conflict, labour unrest and social movements. This is the backdrop to contemporary social unrest as well as to the growing need for global reform (Nederveen Pieterse, 2000, forthcoming).

Note

1. This reflection is inspired by many talks on globalization I have given in countries in the South—including Egypt, India, Indonesia, Pakistan, Senegal, Sri Lanka, Tunisia—and listening to reactions they evoked.

References

Applebaum, R. P. and J. Henderson (1995) "The Hinge of History: Turbulence and Transformation in the World Economy," *Competition and Change* 1(1): 1–12.

Gopal, Sarvepalli (1998) "Images of World Society: A Third World View," *Social Science Information Journal* 50(3): 375–80 (reprint of 1982).

Hampdon-Turner, C. and F. Trompenaars (1993) *Seven Cultures of Capitalism*. New York: Doubleday.

Kaplan, R. D. (1996) *The Ends of the Earth*. New York: Random House.

Nederveen Pieterse, J. (1997) "Globalization and Emancipation: From Local Empowerment to Global Reform," *New Political Economy* 2(1): 79–92.

Nederveen Pieterse, J. (1998) "Hybrid Modernities: Mélange Modernities in Asia," *Sociological Analysis* 1(3): 75–86.

Nederveen Pieterse, J. (ed.) (2000, forthcoming) *Global Futures: Shaping Globalization*. London: Zed.

Okita, Saburo (1993) "Many Paths to Development," pp. 272–81 in *The South Centre Facing the Challenge: Responses to the Report of the South Commission*. London: Zed.

Peck, J. and A. Tickell (1994) "Searching for a New Institutional Fix: the After-Fordist Crisis and the Global-Local Disorder," in A. Amin (ed.) *Post-Fordism*. Oxford: Blackwell.

Petrella, R. (1996) "Globalization and Internationalization: The Dynamics of the Emerging World Order," in R. Boyer and D. Drache (eds) *States against Markets: The Limits of Globalization*. London: Routledge.

Pipes, Daniel (1996) *The Hidden Hand: Middle East Fears of Conspiracy*. London: Macmillan.

Vebhiu, Ardian (1999) "Albanian Migration and Media," Amsterdam, unpublished paper.

Jan Nederveen Pieterse is at the University of Illinois Urbana Champaign. His books include White on Black: Images of Africa and Blacks in Western Popular Culture *(Yale University Press, 1992),* Empire and Emancipation *(Praeger, 1989), which received the 1990 J. C. Ruigrok Award of the Netherlands Society of Sciences, and* Development—Deconstructions/Reconstructions *(Sage, 2001).*

CRITICAL THINKING QUESTIONS

1. Globalization is a buzzword for worldwide development and the integration of national economies. What does the author say is one of the major features of this phenomenon, and how is it realized?

2. What are the differences and discrepancies between the views on globalization in the media and the social science institutions between the North and the South?

3. What does Pieterse mean by his statement that "asymmetrical inclusion" is a major feature of globalization?

4. What differences does the author see between the previous era of imperialism/colonialism and the contemporary phenomenon of globalization?

5. What ideas and beliefs are described as "convenient shortcuts" used in the South to explain "the hegemony of finance capital" around the globe?

6. What form of economic system has become dominant worldwide, and why?

Maori Sport and Cultural Identity in Australia

Paul Bergin

Sport is an important aspect of cultural identity for New Zealand Maori migrants living in Australia. Maori sporting endeavors, especially at festivals such as the Taki Toa Tournament in New South Wales, often reveal distinctive Maori features of cultural performance, in the rituals prior to a game, in the spirited manner with which a game is played, and in the whânau (large/extended family) spirit of belonging and celebration that is encouraged after a game.

However, notwithstanding the occasional Maori tournament or festival, Maori sporting participation in Australia is not restricted to an "ethnic ghetto." Widespread Maori involvement in sport has provided an important avenue for Maori migrants to mix socially with Aboriginal and other Australians in their local communities, and to gain acceptance, respect and, in some cases, economic advancement.

Many first-generation Maori migrants display a keen sense of a New Zealand rather than an Australian identity when it comes to trans-Tasman international sport. Transnational links are also important for Australian Maori who visit New Zealand with sporting teams and stay on various marae (tribal meeting places). The experience of "Maori culture" and hospitality offered by their New Zealand kinsfolk may have a significant influence upon the sporting visitors' subsequent development of Maori cultural identity.

Sport has become an important aspect of the cultural identity of Maori in Australia.[1] Some Australian Maori claim that their communities are more interested in sport than in "Maori culture" (referring to the traditional Maori performing arts and the learning of heritage features such as Maori song, dance and language).

However, while there is greater Maori participation in sporting activities than in cultural performance groups, sport cannot be divorced from culture. A significant feature of many Australian Maori sporting events are the traditional rituals of encounter, cultural performance and communal celebration. Maori sporting tournaments in Australia and sports visits to New Zealand provide an opportunity for some Maori to discover and experience their own cultural traditions. However. Maori involvement in sport provides a generally positive arena for closer association with other Australians and greater involvement in local communities.

SPORTING TOURNAMENTS: EXPRESSIONS OF MAORI CULTURAL IDENTITY

Among Australian Maori there are sporting tournaments that are enshrouded with Maori rituals of encounter and at which there are distinctly Maori ways of celebrating. Two main sporting festivals are held on an annual basis: the Taki Toa Challenge Shield Tournament and the Harry Bartlett Memorial Tournament. Sport also features at the major Maori cultural festivals that are held in Australia, notably the annual Sydney Maori Easter Festival and the biennial Australian Maori Festival. Other regular cultural festivals that also include Maori sporting events are the Melbourne Maori Festival and the Queensland Polynesian Festival.

The Taki Toa Tournament, which began in 1983, was the brainchild of Manu Sutherland and other New Zealanders playing rugby in Sydney.[2] The tournament follows an intense

Source: Reprinted from the *Australian Journal of Anthropology*, Vol. 13, No. 3 (2002).

"round robin" series of games in one day, similar to the sports competitions that have been popular at Maori field days in New Zealand. The Taki Toa shield is an impressive carving, standing one metre high, and was created by Manu's father, Henare Sutherland, to portray the new migration of Maori to Australia and the coming together of Maori and Australians. Although primarily Maori in their composition, the participating rugby and netball teams usually include a few Pakeha (New Zealanders of European ancestry) and Pacific Islanders, as well as the occasional Australian. Among the six regular competing teams are clubs from Sydney (Waverley, Matraville, South Sydney New Zealand, and Sydney Kiwis), the NSW Central Coast (North Lakes) and the Canberra region (Queanbeyan).

The second of the popular Maori sporting festivals in New South Wales is the Harry Bartlett Memorial Tournament. Dedicated to the memory of a young Maori killed in a motor-vehicle accident, the Harry Bartlett Memorial attracts teams from four regions of New South Wales (from Newcastle, the Central Coast, Sydney Kiwis, and Wollongong). As is the case with the Taki Toa Tournament the participating teams take turns to host the festival. The Harry Bartlett Memorial Tournament features a range of sporting activities over several days including snooker, darts, rugby, netball and golf. The tournament also includes some athletic events and a tug-o-war to occupy the children of participating adults.

The Taki Toa, the Harry Bartlett Memorial and other Maori sports tournaments value a distinctive Maori style of open rugby, which places an emphasis on running and passing (rather than kicking the ball). Maori spectators applaud the players who can beat opponents with clever footwork such as a side-step or a swerve, with swift and intricate passing movements such as the "scissors," the "double scissors," or the cut-out pass, or with feint of hand and a dummy pass. Some spectators also appreciate the players who crash their way through opposition defences as they take a direct course to the goal line, although this has traditionally been more a feature of Maori rugby league than rugby union. Consequently, brave tackling on the part of the defending side is also greatly admired.

Although both the Harry Bartlett Memorial and the Taki Toa Tournament have always had an emphasis on sporting competition rather than the Maori performing arts, they have taken on more formal cultural aspects in recent years. As these tournaments now commence with the traditional rituals of encounter, they could well be described as *hui* (gatherings according to Maori protocol; see Salmond 1975). In the absence of traditional *marae* or sacred tribal meeting places, the rituals of encounter have to take place in car parks, on sports fields or school grounds, in rugby club-rooms or civic halls. On some occasions, a formal *wero* (challenge) may commence the rituals, but the keening cry of the women's *karanga* (formal call of welcome) is always heard as the visiting teams move forward to be welcomed by the host club. Male elders then farewell the dead and greet the living, through the medium of *whaikorero* (formal oratory) in the Maori language. There are *waiata* (songs) after each speech, followed by the *hongi* (the pressing of noses) between hosts and visiting teams. A brief offering of *karakia* (prayers) then precedes an opening meal of welcome before the sporting events commence.

Pre-match *haka* (posture dance) from both teams have also become a feature of the festivals, especially prior to the final for the Taki Toa Shield. This contrasts with the first occasion that a final team unexpectedly introduced a pre-match *haka;* the other team was unprepared, took great offence and a meeting had to be called afterwards to resolve the hurt. Nowadays, any team that thinks it has a chance of getting to the finals had better be prepared for a convincing *haka*. It is not just a token cultural performance but a dramatic statement of group solidarity and determination to battle with any opposition.[3]

Although some Australian-born Maori have expressed enthusiasm for locally composed *haka* and songs that express the evolving and dynamic aspects of their new Australian environment, many prefer to learn traditional cultural items from New Zealand, clearly identifying their expression of Maori culture with their ancestral New Zealand homeland. The popularity of Maori sporting festivals was explained by Tumu,[4] a member of the Sydney Kiwis' rugby club, and a keen supporter of the Harry Bartlett Memorial Tournament:

> Maoris like to come together for sport because of their love of *whakataetae* [competition]. They take their sport very seriously when they do take the field. Also Maoris like coming together to tournaments or field days to be with other Maori and word gets round when people come back and tell their friends that they had a good time at such and such a place, and other people are attracted. People always hope that they might find someone that they are related to, so they come to a tournament, and just about always they'll meet someone to whom they can connect their *whakapapa* [family tree].

Many of those who attend Maori sporting festivals say that they enjoy the warm feelings of community and togetherness at such gatherings. One of the highlights of the weekend is when a *hangi* or huge communal meal that has been cooked in the ground for several hours is served on the Saturday evening. Rina, a young saleswoman from Sydney, was attending the Harry Bartlett Memorial at Newcastle (NSW). She described the tournament as an experience of *whanau* (extended family) and an experience of belonging:

> This *hui* [gathering] is great because all these guys over here don't realize they're experiencing Maori culture. They think it's all about doing action-songs and speaking the *reo* [Maori language] but it's not. It's all about being together and experiencing *whanau* [extended family]. There's no "aggro." We've just been eating together, drinking together and playing sport together. Look at what they've experienced together this weekend in terms of *whanau*, even if we only come together once a year. Everyone is accepted as belonging here, including Pakeha spouses.

There are also non-competitive Maori cultural performances on the Saturday evening of both these sporting tournaments which finally conclude with *poroporoaki* (farewell speeches), Maori *waiata* (songs) and some powerful *haka*.

RUGBY LEAGUE AND RUGBY UNION: MIXING WITH LOCAL AUSTRALIANS

Maori sportsmen have made an impact in Australia since 1884 when Maori players were represented in a New Zealand rugby union team that toured New South Wales (Hickie 1993: xiii). The New Zealand Maori team which toured England in 1888–1889 also played more than a dozen matches in Australia. Rugby union historian, Thomas Hickie (1983:26), suggests that a Maori tour was a promoter's dream as many of the spectators may have come out of curiosity as much as for the rugby. When a pioneering New Zealand Maori rugby league team landed in Sydney from the SS Moana in 1908, accompanied by four tribal elders wearing *piupiu* (flax skirts) and resplendent with the rare feathers of the native *huia* bird, they received a tumultuous local welcome, and were a favorite of the newspapers (Haynes 1996:151). Subsequent Maori league teams also made their mark on the field and were popular with Australian crowds. New Zealand Maori rugby union teams have also been invited to play top Australian sides, including the Warratahs (NSW) and the national Australian team, the Wallabies, on several occasions over the decades, and most recently in 2001.

As rugby league and rugby union are two of the main winter sporting codes in New South Wales, Queensland and the Australian Capital Territory, Maori participation in these sports has provided a generally positive area of involvement with many local communities. To some extent, this opportunity of close sporting contact with the dominant society replicates the New Zealand experience where rugby union has been a symbol of inclusiveness for Maori, Pakeha and Pacific Islanders. Journalist and rugby historian, Spiro Zavos, considers that rugby union, perhaps more than anything else, has fostered positive race relations in New Zealand (personal communication, Sydney, 12 August 1996; see also Zavos 1995:14–15; 1996a; 1996b). Another sports historian, John Haynes (1996:14) notes that from the earliest days of New Zealand rugby, the sport was seen as a positive area of social mixing and that All Black teams were respected for their combination of "fierce farmers and fleet-footed

Maoris." Michael King (1981:298) suggests that Maori participation in rugby union in New Zealand "fostered a sense of identity amongst Maoris, and on the football field Pakehas could see Maoris engage in an activity that they understood and appreciated."

The particular sporting experience of the New Zealand Maori migrant to Australia may be in contrast, however, with some migrant families from other countries who have felt that their passion for soccer has led to their being identified with the "ethnic ghetto."[5] In New South Wales, Queensland and the Australian Capital Territory, where rugby union and league are well established, many Maori prefer to play for local clubs rather than form exclusively Maori or Kiwi teams. This is partly because the local clubs are seen to offer a greater sense of permanence and reliability, and partly out of a desire to identify with the local scene. Maori support for some Australian sports' clubs has spawned some lighthearted new labels for the clubs concerned. Local Maori involvement in the Manly-Warringah rugby league club, for example, was such that I heard some people referring to the club as "Manly-Maoringah!"

In Victoria, South Australia, Tasmania, Western Australia, and the Northern Territory, where Australian Football League (AFL) has a much greater following, Maori and other New Zealanders have been among a minority of enthusiasts promoting rugby league and rugby union, and have become very much identified with the latter two codes. In both Victoria and Tasmania I heard interested Australians remark that "It was the Maoris who brought rugby league here." Some Melbourne rugby league clubs have had a strong Maori representation and image, such as the Kia Toa (Be Brave) club, until it was banned for fighting during the 1980s. Other clubs, such as St Kilda, have been basically Maori but have also included some Australian and other players. With the more recent development of the Melbourne Storm rugby league team, a number of Maori players have been prominent in the side. Few of the predominantly Maori clubs have their own club facilities for after-match functions. Instead they support particular hotels which provide sponsorship for their teams. The St Kilda Inn, for example, provided sponsorship for the St. Kilda rugby league team and used to be a popular meeting place for Melbourne Maori.

The Maori contribution to the developing sport of women's rugby in Australia has also been significant. In 1995, over half the Western Australian women's rugby team, including their captain, were Maori players. At one women's rugby tournament I attended in Perth, most of the coaches were Maori, including a *kaumatua* (elder) with a walking stick who stood on the sideline in an old *swandri* coat exhorting his team to greater efforts! The large Maori contribution to the teams was reflected in the aftermatch fare at the clubhouse, where local Maori served up a favourite Maori dish called "boilup," consisting of stewed pork bones, watercress and potatoes.

Some Maori women also play rugby league. Indeed, rugby league is, at times, a real family affair (see *Mana Tangata*, Hui-tanguru [February] 1993:25). Papa Koroheke, who followed in his father's footsteps as a league player, describes his family's passion for the game:

> A lot of our people play league because it's physical, hard and an open game, though when I play, I play my own game. League is really a family affair for me. I have four children and all my three boys play league in the under 7s, under 9s and under 11s. My wife has played but she hurt her leg. My daughter would like to play as well. My twin brother and I play together. He tries to play harder than me.

Rugby union and rugby league have clearly been the sports in which Maori have excelled in Australia's eastern states. In Melbourne, Hobart and Perth, however, I met young Maori who were playing Australian Football League (AFL) or Tasmanian Rules Football. They admired Wayne Schwass, a rare Maori star in AFL, who has played for South Warrnambool, North Melbourne, and Sydney Swans. It appears that some Maori families, especially those of "mixed race" parentage, have encouraged their sons to pursue the local sporting codes rather than stick to rugby union or league. Maryanne, a Melbourne mother, commented: "The boys played AFL because I thought it was important they played what their peers played. You've gotta fit in and mix with your peers and be part of the group.

You're more accepted. They were different anyhow because of their colour. Why make them more different?!"

SPIRITUAL AND CULTURAL FOUNDATIONS: TOUCH, NETBALL AND OTHER SPORTS

A lot of Maori also play touch (rugby) which is claimed to be one of the fastest growing sports in Australia. It is popular with both males and females. Some teams are mixed. Many Sydney Maori women who play netball in the winter, play touch in the summer. Touch is popular because little gear is required, the games are short, and with the small numbers in a side (seven, plus five substitutes allowed), it is easy for *whanau* and friends to organise their own teams. Furthermore, in many areas, the intensity of local competition is such that very little travelling is required.

Netball is a very popular sport for Maori women. It is also one of the most popular women's sports throughout Australia, and thus provides an important area of social contact between Maori women and other Australians. There are numerous netball teams with Maori or Kiwi appellations that reflect the cultural identity of the women who founded them. Although many of these teams are predominantly Maori they have not adopted an exclusive ethnic approach to team membership and have been happy to welcome Australian women into their ranks. The communal spirit within a lot of Maori netball clubs appeals not only to the Maori participants themselves but also to some Australians. Hiria, a Sydney artist and keen netballer, observed how young Australian women were attracted to her club:

> The European girls appreciated the communal side of our teams. Then there was the excellent food aspect and the Maori singing which was a major aspect of selling tickets to our fundraising. There would be a performance and the netballers would have to sing for their supper. You had to be involved! Our Aussie friends liked to join in. Some were the girlfriends of Aussie Maoris. It was *not* a question of "You're

white, you can't play for us." *Aroha* [warmth of love, compassion] was brought into it all.

The standard of coaching, the level of organisation and the communal spirit of some Maori netball teams have earned them respect from local netball associations. Nga Waka e Whitu (The Seven Canoes), a cultural and sporting club based at Tuggerah on the Central Coast (NSW), found that their approach to the game of netball had attracted a lot of interest from local people, as one of their *kaumatua* explained: "We have ten teams, mostly junior and mostly Aussie kids. Our Maori coaches over the years have been very good coaches, and parents and other kids see it. The end result is that each year they want to play for the Maori group . . . because of our attitudes."

It is clear that some Maori netball clubs try to instil particular Maori cultural values among their young team members. Huhana, the manager of Hui Mai (Come Together), a Sydney club, explained that her club was based on spiritual foundations which stressed symbolic links to the unity of the primal Maori parents, Papa-tu-a-nuku and Rangi-nui. Young club members were encouraged to reflect this unity in their attitudes on the court:

> We aim to develop attitudes of respect . . . Our kids have a lot of aggressiveness. We try to calm this down. We tell them to smile and say, *"Kia ora"* [May you be well], when the opposition gets angry . . . We're spiritually guided. Our kids understand this. Our name refers to the joining of Mother-Earth and Sky-Rangi who surrounds us. We have this design on our screen prints on our uniforms. [A priest] blessed them. Even among the Pakeha they seem to gather the spiritual sense of the club.

Softball, rather than cricket, has been another popular summer sport for Maori in Sydney. Some young Maori say that they prefer softball to cricket because a game of softball is much shorter, usually lasting less than two hours. Another popular sport for many Maori families is indoor basketball. Golf also attracts considerable interest, especially from an older group of Maori, some of whom take part in regional

Maori tournaments leading to the annual Australian Maori Golf Tournament.

PREJUDICE, SPORT AND EMPLOYMENT

Many Maori immigrants into Australia report that they have been well received by their new host society. In particular they note that their employers often comment favorably that they have a reputation as "hard workers." Other Maori state that they are well respected because of the bravery and commitment of Maori soldiers who have fought alongside Australian soldiers in various military campaigns over the decades. However, some Maori report cases of prejudice and discrimination against them. Many Maori immigrants state that they have had to contend with negative stereotyping, particularly the Bondi "urban myth" that suggests that New Zealand migrants (and Maori, in particular) congregate in this Sydney beachside suburb for a lazy time on the dole, at the expense of the Australian taxpayer. If there was ever any factual basis for this stereotype, there is certainly little basis for such an allegation today. Like other international visitors to Sydney, Maori people often include Bondi Beach on their tourist itinerary, but few Maori actually live or congregate in Bondi. Maori people reside in many different parts of metropolitan Sydney and have not formed enduring ethnic enclaves. Some indication of Maori dispersal throughout metropolitan Sydney is evident from the fact that I met with Maori from over 140 different suburbs during the course of my fieldwork in Sydney. Moreover, the vast majority of working-age Maori in Australia were in employment. Nevertheless the Bondi "urban myth" still persists.

More serious hostility towards Maori, especially in some rural areas, existed during the 1980s' shearers "wide comb" dispute, when New Zealand shearers (among whom Maori were prominent) faced the wrath of the Australian Workers Union and their supporters for not using the traditional "narrow comb" shears. By their use of the wide comb the Maori shearers were able to process more sheep per session than their Australian counterparts. They also allegedly breached union regulations by working longer hours. Although this made them popular with many farmers, the Maori workers faced intimidation and even violence from some of their opponents.

However, Maori involvement in sport has generally provided a more positive area of relations with the dominant society. Indeed, involvement in rugby union and rugby league has helped some Maori migrants settle into a new place and has provided useful avenues for finding employment in Australia. Miri, a young mother and homemaker who had migrated to Melbourne and then Perth, recalled how she and her husband were helped by membership of sporting clubs:

> When we moved to Melbourne we knew no one there. We were living in a little bed-sit, until we joined a rugby club and, next thing, different ones provided us with a TV, table and chairs, blankets and towels, and they'd even pick us up and take us to the rugby club because we had no car. If you have no money and no jobs, you'll find work through a rugby club after a few beers at the bar. Then when we moved to Perth my husband's first job was through the [rugby] league club!

Even before professional rugby union was introduced in the mid-1990s, some Australian clubs were offering accommodation and work to talented Maori players who were prepared to transfer from New Zealand. As rugby league has always been a professional sport, numerous talented Maori have pursued the game as a career in Australia.[6] During the mid-1990s' struggle for control of rugby league—between Superleague and the Australian Rugby League—Maori players signed contracts with Australian clubs worth millions of dollars in total (see "League's Great Money Trail." *Daily Telegraph Mirror,* 21 October 1995:150–51).

MAORI AND ABORIGINAL SPORTING RELATIONS

Sport has also provided an opportunity for closer association between Maori and Aboriginal people in the Northern Territory and other parts of Australia, especially through rugby union and league, and other sports such as netball and touch rugby. There are also a number of Maori coaches and managers who have worked closely with Aboriginal people in other sports. However, tensions may easily surface in rugby matches, and when predominantly Maori teams play Aboriginal sides there sometimes appears to be a racial edge to any "dust-ups" or heated incidents. The situation is not always helped by passionate comments from some supporters on the sidelines. On the field tension, however, is usually resolved over drinks at the after-match function.

A giant Aboriginal forward and president of a rugby club in the Northern Territory, who carries the nick-name "Big Bird," felt that his sport was a great way to deepen cultural understanding between Maori and Aboriginal youth. "Big Bird" had only one regret, "When I hear the young Aboriginal players singing Maori songs at after-match parties, it seems they know Maori better than their own Aboriginal languages!" Indeed, songs such as "Pokarekare Ana" and the *haka*, "Ka Mate, Ka Mate" (made famous by the All Blacks' rugby team) are familiar to Aboriginal sporting enthusiasts in many parts of Australia. Young Maori also speak of their friendship with Aboriginal children where they attend Australian schools together. Maori students mentioned, in particular, how they enjoyed participating with Aboriginal students in various school football and netball teams. Overall, sporting contact is seen as a largely positive area of Maori-Aboriginal relations.

YOUNG PEOPLE AND SPORT: MULTIPLE IDENTITIES

Although not all Maori children are interested in competitive sport, many are keen to participate in sports organized by schools or clubs. Some commentators have cited the clash of values seen in some migrant children to Australia, who find that their reverence for scholarship and aesthetic pursuits comes into sharp confrontation with Australian society's alleged demands that children concentrate primarily on outdoor sports and development of physical prowess (see, for example, Kern 1966:39). In the case of many Maori children, however, their interest in outdoor activities generally finds a ready welcome in Australia. Moreover, Maori families often express

delight with the sporting facilities and opportunities that Australia has provided for their children, as Rongomai, a Sydney mother, explained:

> Australia provides a huge amount of opportunity. The sporting facilities here are fantastic. The kids can come here and for a very reasonable amount of money, really, do any sport that you can imagine. Skiing might be a bit expensive but there is just about every sort of sport available in Australia. I mean it's a great climate for swimming, water polo, surfing and all those kinds of things.

The living rooms of Maori homes in Australia are often adorned with a variety of sporting trophies that have been won by family members. Multiple successes in rugby union and rugby league, netball and basketball, athletics, tennis, hockey, golf and snooker are all proudly displayed in a range of trophies across the lounge mantelpiece. Each of these sporting successes may also reflect a different context of identity for the individuals and families concerned.

The various sporting seasons are reflected in membership of different local clubs, each of which provides families with a unique sense of belonging. In Alice Springs, for example, Maori sportsmen might play for rugby union clubs in the summer and rugby league clubs in the winter, and for basketball and indoor cricket teams on different weekday evenings, while supporting other members of the family at netball during other times of the week. As Jeremy MacClancy (1996:3) suggests, "these sport-based identities are not necessarily exclusive . . . for people may have multiple identities either simultaneously, seasonally or consecutively."

NATIONAL SPORTING IDENTITIES: TRANS-TASMAN RIVALRY

Although Maori and other Australians generally mix well together through sport, international fixtures between Australia and New Zealand usually arouse a passionate sense of Kiwi identification on the part of Maori migrants to Australia. Even those first generation Maori migrants who have taken out Australian citizenship are likely to be loud in their support of New Zealand teams, especially in the Bledisloe Cup rugby competition between the All Blacks and the Wallabies. Maori and other New Zealand supporters will snap up tickets for these rugby internationals, providing tremendous local support when New Zealand plays in Australia. The ardent rivalry between the trans-Tasman neighbors is often portrayed in media advertising as though the two nations were about to go to war. In particular, images associated with the Maori as warrior are often portrayed as symbols of New Zealand's determination to challenge Australia. Maori cultural performances in front of Australian audiences are a feature of such trans-Tasman sporting battles.

Australian television commercials advertising coverage of Bledisloe Cup rugby union internationals have not only suggested a spirit of trans-Tasman conflict but have also run with the stereotype of the Maori warrior. Thus a Channel 7 advertisement in July 1996 featured images of the second world war, video footage of a New Zealand volcano erupting, and images of a Maori *haka* or war dance:

> Ninety-three years of ferocious competition . . . In times of war they were even prepared to die for one another [images of war], yet face to face, in times of peace, their friendship goes the way of Mount Ruapehu [images of this volcano erupting]. *"Ka mate, ka mate, ka ora, ka ora"* [images of a *haka*] . . . Translated, the *haka* goes, "It is life, it is life. It is death, it is death!" . . . Today another chapter in our short yet wondrous history: Australia and New Zealand. The tradition lives.[7]

Pnina Werbner's (1996) observations on sporting contests are relevant here. She suggests that sports "both objectify social divisions and nationalist sentiments and point to an alliance between contesters, a shared fanaticism." She also discerns an element of friendship and fun in the competing loyalties, and observes: "Sporting contests are, it would seem, like *moka* in Melanesia, a *substitute* for war, a domain of symbolic agonism, a token not of hatred and disloyalty but of friendly rivalry in the midst of peace" (Werbner

1996:104). Nevertheless, some Australians are infuriated by the level of New Zealand support evident at international rugby matches in Australia. The *Sydney Morning Herald* (3 April 1989) reported that Bob Dwyer, then coach of the Wallabies, was only half joking when he suggested that immigration laws should be changed to even up the crowds at home test matches: "The team is very pissed off at playing in front of vocal New Zealand supporters who want to adopt this country, but who maintain ties with their own country." Dwyer's complaints about New Zealand migrants echo views expressed in the United Kingdom by Norman Tebbitt, the Conservative Cabinet minister. Tebbitt complained that certain ethnic minorities had not passed the "cricket test," because when England played international fixtures against teams such as Pakistan and India, many people who claimed British nationality supported the Asian land of their families' origins (see Banks 1996:184; Werbner 1996:104).

Many Maori migrants identify passionately with New Zealand sporting sides in competition with Australia, and for this reason alone some were not prepared to contemplate applying for Australian citizenship, no matter how long they had lived in Australia. The issue of national sporting sides and citizenship can thus become a source for debate in a number of households, as Raina, a Sydney prison officer and grandmother, explained:

> I support New Zealand first and foremost. But I've thought about Australian citizenship. Why not? We will always be New Zealand Maori by birth but we should go along with the Aussies. Up until now I've thought of it as Kiwi betrayal, and that I'd lose my New Zealand citizenship. . . . There are four of us live here now. The boys are very anti-Australian and I say to them, "But you live in this country." Sport between us is like a mutual encounter between enemies. The rivalries are really on!

In some cases, Maori spouses take opposing sides over the question of Australian citizenship. Several Maori women stated that they wanted to become Australian citizens but had declined to do so because of their husbands' determined opposition to "disowning New Zealand" and the land of their ancestors. However, it is apparent that with the development of professional sport, the attitudes of some Maori males to identification as Australians may be changing. By the late 1990s, several New Zealand-born Maori migrants (Jeremy Paul, Glenn Panoho and Manuel Edmonds) were representing top Australian State sides and had been chosen to represent the Wallabies rugby union team. For the second and subsequent generations of Australian-Maori, self-identification as Australians may well become the norm. Some prominent young Australian-born Maori rugby league players, such as Tamana Tahu of the Newcastle Knights, have made it clear to New Zealand selectors that their national representative ambitions lie with the Kangaroos rather than with the Kiwis (*Evening Post*, 30 April 2001). Jai Taurima, the Queensland-born long-jumper who starred at the Sydney Olympic Games, has also stated his preference to represent Australia rather than New Zealand. Although immensely proud of his Maori heritage, Taurima has declared: "Obviously I have some feeling for New Zealand, but I'm an Australian through and through." (*Dominion*, 8 May 2001)

TRANSNATIONALISM: RECLAIMING MAORI CULTURAL HERITAGE

Sport has also proved to be a significant influence in the formation of cultural identity among Australian-Maori who visit New Zealand with sporting teams and stay at various *marae* (tribal meeting grounds). The experience of "Maori culture" and hospitality offered by their New Zealand kinsfolk may have a significant influence upon the sporting visitors' subsequent development of Maori cultural identity. Kere, a Sydney *kaumatua*, described how Australian-Maori sports enthusiasts sometimes feel ashamed for their lack of knowledge of the Maori language and are determined to reclaim their ancestral heritage:

You sometimes get [Maori] sports people in Australia who don't want to have anything to do with Maoris . . . who might accompany their children on a sports trip back to

New Zealand. Then they discover that one of the particular visits is to a *marae*. All of a sudden they realize, "Oh, I'm the senior Maori." Then they're requested to reply to the *mihis* [formal Maori speeches on the *marae*], and suddenly they're found wanting and they become very embarrassed. And then that's when they come back to us [elders in Australia] and they say, "Well, I've suddenly reached the point where I am the senior member of the group . . . wow, what do I do?"

In conclusion, it is clear that Australian-Maori involvement in sport is an important aspect of their cultural life. Maori sporting endeavors, especially at festivals such as the Taki Toa and Harry Bartlett Memorial in New South Wales, often reveal distinctive Maori features of cultural performance, in the rituals prior to a game, in the spirited manner with which a game is played, and in the *whanau* or extended family spirit of belonging and celebration that is encouraged after a game. One can also observe that there are particular ways in which Maori men and women approach their sport. Ideally, in rugby, for example, the players are encouraged to pursue a free-flowing, open style of game, with speed and vitality, imaginative moves, and with strength.

However, notwithstanding the occasional Maori tournament or festival, Maori sporting participation in Australia is not restricted to an "ethnic ghetto." Widespread Maori involvement in sport has provided an important avenue for Maori migrants to mix socially with Aboriginal and other Australians in their local communities, and to gain acceptance, respect and, in some cases, economic advancement. Although one can discern some distinctive expressions of Maori identity in Australian-Maori sport, Maori have tended to belong to a variety of local sports' clubs and teams such that one can speak of Maori individuals and families with multiple sporting identities. Although many first-generation Maori migrants to Australia display a keen sense of a New Zealand identity when it comes to trans-Tasman international sport, a change to an Australian identity is becoming apparent with the second-generation Australian-Maori. Nevertheless, transnational links are important for Australian Maori who visit

New Zealand with sporting teams and stay among New Zealand Maori relatives on various *marae* and in tribal meeting houses. The experience of "Maori culture" and hospitality offered by their New Zealand kinsfolk may have a significant influence upon the sporting visitors' subsequent development of their Maori cultural identity.

Notes

1. This paper is based on fieldwork conducted among Maori communities in Australia (between late 1994 and late 1996) and from subsequent research into Maori cultural identity in Australia. Analysis of the 1986 Australian Census revealed that there were nearly 27,000 people of New Zealand Maori descent in Australia (see Lowe 1990, 1992:97, 1993). The much-awaited return of the ethnic ancestry question in the 2001 Australian Census is likely to reveal a significant increase in the Maori descent group population in Australia.

2. Taki Toa is an abbreviation of Te Roopu Toa O Te Takitini Iwi Maori (The Brave Group of the Many Maori People. See Waverley Rugby Football and Sporting Club Inc. 1990).

3. Increasingly, Australian-Maori teams travelling to Maori tournaments in New Zealand have also felt the need to be well prepared for the performance of their *haka*, to prove that they have retained a sense of "*mana* Maori" or Maori pride and identity.

4. Where I have used first names alone to introduce statements recorded in interviews, they are pseudonyms to respect a person's privacy. In all instances where I have not sourced quotations, they are excerpts from fieldwork interviews in Australia. I am grateful to the many Australian-Maori people who participated in this research.

5. Mark Bosnich, the outstanding Aston Villa and Australian goal-keeper, told the *Observer* (1 February 1998: Sport 5) of his Australian upbringing: "My parents are Croatian, and it was always football, football, football in our house . . . Everywhere else in Sydney it was rugby, rugby, rugby. I took it up once but Mum stopped me . . ."

6. Several players with Maori ancestry have represented Australia at rugby league, including "Lord" Ted Goodwin, who was born in Sydney of a Maori mother; he played for the Kangaroos in 1972–73. Arthur Beetson, who was born of Aboriginal parents in Queensland, had a Maori grandfather, and represented Australia from 1966–1974 (see George 1988, and French n.d.).

7. As with rugby union, Australian television commercials, for rugby league matches involving New Zealand teams, have often centred on the combative aspects of the *haka*. Thus, in 1995–96, television commercials featured tattooed men from a Sydney Maori culture group, armed with *taiaha* (long, hand-held, wooden weapons) and performing dramatic *pukana* (facial gestures) close-up to the camera.

References

Banks, M. 1996. *Ethnicity: Anthropological Constructions.* London and New York: Routledge.

French, R. n.d. *Ray French's 100 Great League Players.* London: Queen Anne Press.

George, J. 1988. Big, strong and fast: Maori and Polynesians playing league in Sydney. *Te Iwi News,* 7 August.

Haynes, J. 1996. *From All Blacks to All Golds: New Zealand's Rugby League Pioneers.* Christchurch, NZ: Ryan and Haynes.

Hickie, T. V. 1983. *The Game for the Game Itself: The Development of Sub-District Rugby.* Sydney: Sydney Sub-District Rugby Union.

Hickie, T. V. 1993. *They Ran with the Ball: How Rugby Football Began in Australia.* Melbourne: Longman Cheshire.

Kern, K. K. L. 1966. Immigration and the integration process. In A. Stoller (ed.) *New Faces: Immigration and Family Life in Australia.* Melbourne: Cheshire.

King, M. 1981. Between two worlds. In W.H. Oliver with B.R. Williams (eds) *The Oxford History of New Zealand.* Wellington, NZ: Oxford University Press.

Lowe, J. 1990. *Nga Maori Ki Ahitereria: The Australian Maori Population.* Wellington, NZ: New Zealand Planning Council.

Lowe, J. 1992. "Maori in Australia": A comment on further research. *Population Review* 18 (1 and 2): 97–100.

Lowe, J. 1993. Maori in Australia. A statistical summary. In G. McCall and J. Connell (eds.) *A World Perspective on Pacific Islander Migration: Australia, New Zealand and the USA.* Pacific Studies Monograph No. 6. Kensington NSW: Centre for South Pacific Studies, The University of New South Wales, In association with the Bureau of Immigration Research.

MacClancy, J. 1996. Sport, identity and ethnicity. In J. MacClancy (ed.) *Sport, Identity and Ethnicity.* Oxford: Berg Publications.

Salmond, A. 1975. *Hui: A Study of Maori Ceremonial Gatherings.* Wellington, NZ: A. H. and A. W. Reed.

Zavos, S. 1995. *The Gold and the Black: The Rugby Battles for the Bledisloe Cup, New Zealand vs Australia 1903–94.* St Leonards, NSW: Allen and Unwin.

Zavos, S. 1996a. Always were warriors. *Sydney Morning Herald,* 6 July.

Zavos, S. 1996b. Indigenous rituals needed to profile a nation. *Sydney Morning Herald,* 8 August.

Waverley Rugby Football and Sporting Club Inc. 1990. *Waverley Rugby Football and Sporting Club Inc. Presents: Taki Toa Shield Challenge 1990* [Tournament Program].

Werbner, P. 1996. "Our blood is green": Cricket, identity and social empowerment among British Pakistanis. In J. MacClancy (ed.) *Sport, Identity and Ethnicity.* Oxford: Berg Publications.

Newspapers

Daily Telegraph Mirror, Sydney, NSW.
Dominion, Wellington, NZ.
Evening Post, Wellington, NZ.
Mana Tangata, Wanganui, NZ.
Observer, London, UK.
Sydney Morning Herald.
Te Iwi News, NZ.

CRITICAL THINKING QUESTIONS

1. What are the differences between Maori-style rugby and that normally played in Australia? What does the Maori style emphasize?
2. What Maori rituals often accompany Maori sporting tournaments?
3. How have rugby and other sports provided an avenue for integration into larger Australian society?
4. Why is "netball" popular with both Maori and European-descended Australian women?
5. How do international competitions between Australia and New Zealand both intensify national and cultural divisions while, at the same time, provide a common point of identification for fans and participants?

The Personal Consequences of Globalization in Taiwan[1]

Yung-mei Tsai, Mei-lin Lee, and Temu Wang

Accelerated globalization in Taiwan has affected the work, jobs, and lives of people since the 1970s. Examples reported here are from in-depth interviews with eight principal income earners selected from a sample of 1,000 households during 2000. Among them were more losers than winners. Those hardest hit were people whose work or business was in the informal, traditional economic sectors. (Globalization, Taiwan, personal economic consequences)

This article describes how internal economic growth and external globalization forces have jointly affected the lives of ordinary people in Taiwan. Toward the end of the last millennium, Taiwan faced domestic political and economic turbulence. The major economic problems centered on the outflow of capital and industries, mostly to mainland China. The total amount of Taiwan's FDI (Foreign Direct Investment) in China in 2004 ($3.18 billion) was far less than that of South Korea, Japan, and the U.S. (US-China Business Council 2004), but a perception of a massive exodus of capital and industry to China shook consumer and investor confidence. The Taiwan Stock Market Index dropped to nearly half of its valuation in one year in 2001, from 7847 to 4907, although it has since recovered to a high of 6842 in 2006 (Taiwan Stock Exchange). Unstable political conditions involving the transfer of power from the ruling party, the Kuomintang (KMT), to an opposition party added to a heightened sense of anxiety. All these conditions are part of the context of rapid globalization affecting Taiwan.

As a nation with scarce natural resources, the Taiwanese economy depends a great deal on international trade. The labor-intensive textile industries that brought foreign currency into Taiwan in the 1970s and 1980s was followed in the 1990s by capital-intensive electronics industries. These export industries were highly successful (Derber 2003) but also brought problems for subsequent development. Success in economic development created a rising standard of living. At the same time, labor costs concomitantly increased for four successive decades. The increasing cost of labor put many employers at a disadvantage in the world market for their products. One consequence of the political liberalization in the late 1980s was an increasing demand for a safer and cleaner environment. Today, the Taiwanese government's standards for environmental protection are said to be higher than those of China, Korea, and Japan (*Liberty Times on the Net*). To meet government environmental safety regulations, industries, especially those whose products involve the use of chemicals that generate toxic waste, face additional operating costs. The affluence brought about by economic development also created a generation of young people who are disinclined to work as hard as their parents. Population growth has accelerated urban and suburban development. Land for development thereby becomes increasingly scarce, and the demand for limited land increases the cost of building factories and office space. Last but not least, increasing demands for energy for homes and industry escalate production costs, especially with industries that use large amounts of energy. These problems are primarily domestic.

Other problems are external or supranational in origin, and are best considered under the general concept of globalization. Unfortunately, globalization has become a very popular academic term in recent years, which has resulted in vagueness and imprecision. In this article it refers to an

Source: Ethnology, Vol. 45, No. 4 (Fall 2006), p. 275–285. Copyright by the University of Pittsburgh.

accelerated process in recent years (Polanyi 1957, Mittelman 2000). During the past two decades, globalization's rapid development increased with computer-mediated communication technology, which made the "digitalization of economy" possible (Tapscott 1996). Rapid globalization has also increased with the establishment of regional and international express transports, such as Federal Express and United Parcel Service. These technologies made the global spatial restructuring of labor and production a reality, and generated a new and intense competition (Castells 2000 [1996], Sassen 1999, Mittelman 2000). This restructuring has created widespread dislocations, but it also has helped open new opportunities for many previously impoverished regions of the world and, as in Taiwan, raised the standard of living for many.

As Taiwan's economy became a part of the globalization process, its industries had to compete ever more intensely with those elsewhere in the world. Taiwanese industrialists increasingly had to wrestle with the cost of domestic labor, environmental safety and health constraints, workforce attitudes, increased energy needs, and escalating land values, all of which prompted them to relocate their factories and invest capital in foreign countries for cheaper labor, lower environmental costs, more docile workers, and cheaper energy sources. Workers whose factories were relocated lost their jobs.

The observations reported here are part of a two-year study on income and occupational dynamics of the principal income earners of 1,000 randomly selected households from Chia-yi City and Chia-yi County in southwest Taiwan. Chia-yi County is one of the most heterogeneous and also one of the most impoverished counties in Taiwan. This article presents the results of in-depth interviews with eight respondents. The results of the survey, currently still going on, will be reported elsewhere.

The three authors conducted interviews during the summer of 2000 with respondents chosen to cover the occupational categories of employers, employees of private industries, the self-employed, and those who worked in the public sector. They were selected after a preliminary analysis of the data determined them to be representative of the categories. In their 40s and 50s, these middle-age respondents are well suited for the research as they had much work experience, were years away

from retirement, and were assumed to be concerned about their future.

TAIWANESE LIVES

The Oyster Fisherman

Mr. Tsai, in his early 50s, was a middleman in the oyster business and had been an oyster fisherman all his life. His father, grandfather, and great-grandfather were all in the oyster business, either as wholesalers, middlemen, or fishermen. Oyster fishing is the most important industry in Tung-shih village, on the coast of Chia-yi County. Piles of oyster shells abound around the village. The young, elderly, and many women work next to the oyster piles, stringing shells on long plastic lines. Oyster fishermen plant these on the shallow ocean bed for young oysters to occupy.

Mr. Tsai retired recently because oyster fishing had sharply declined following the establishment of a petrochemical plant in a nearby town several years ago. The villagers believe that chemicals discharged from this plant polluted the coastal waters and diminished marine life there. Inviting the petrochemical plant to locate there was part of an effort of many country commissioners to attract businesses and capital investment to the area. Only three oyster fishing businesses remain in the village, and Mr. Tsai's wife strings oyster shells for one of them to make little money. Mr. Tsai explained that oysters are still consumed locally but production and competition have become global in scope.

> We are not producing enough oysters from our sea today. We imported more than half of what we sold from New Zealand. Restaurants in Taiwan are still buying from us because we have been doing that for many years. We know each other and can trust each other. But things may change. They may buy directly from New Zealand companies in the future.

Mr. Tsai said that the government is trading the fishermen's livelihood for chemical plants, and mentioned that several formerly prosperous fishing villages on Taiwan's west coast are in deep trouble. He dreads the time when another petrochemical facility under construction at a nearby village is completed and starts operating, as this will cause the entire area's marine life to vanish. Since many of the villagers know no other trade, they will be forced to buy oysters from other countries. China has become one of the major oyster exporters for Taiwanese customers. The problem of doing business with China, Mr. Tsai said, is that Taiwan does not have direct trade relations with China, so oysters from China must be imported through a third country. This increases costs, and sometimes an entire shipment can be ruined due to transport delay. Furthermore, Taiwan cannot compete with China because China is much bigger, and has fewer legal restrictions. The fishermen there use artificial techniques to produce more and larger oysters.

Tung-shih village oyster fishermen know no other way of making a living. Their life and work in the oyster business is hard but they manage. Mr. Tsai wants the Taiwan government to help the villagers produce more of their own oysters and to open direct trade between Taiwan and China. He and many of his cohorts never went to school, but they are aware of what is happening to them. They do not know the term globalization, but they do know that with modern transportation technologies, oysters can be produced almost anywhere in the world. They also know that the petrochemical plants employing neighboring villagers are taking away their livelihood and their future.

A Textile Factory Foreman

A foreman in a textile factory in Yi-tzu village, Mr. Ong had worked for this factory for the past 20 years. He looks forward to retiring in five years, when he will be eligible for a pension. But he fears that some of his fellow workers, many of them in their seventeenth or eighteenth year working for the factory, would lose their eligibility for a pension if the factory were soon to close. Mr. Ong said that the boss is a very nice person who moved to Taiwan from Shanghai in 1949, after the Communist Revolution, but that he could be forced to close the plant. The wages in Taiwan are getting too high for him to compete with other countries. In a hedge against the future, the boss recently returned to China to set up several textile plants there. The labor cost in China is about one-tenth that of Taiwan (*Liberty Times on the Net*). Mr. Ong did not blame his boss for considering closing the

plant. Instead, he blamed the labor laws that require workers to be employed by the same company for 25 years in order to receive pension benefits. Mr. Ong does not know what his co-workers would do without pensions. They are his friends and neighbors, and some are his relatives.

The plight of Mr. Ong and the villagers who work in the textile factory is a consequence of Taiwan's industrial dynamics during the past four decades. Labor-intensive jobs, as in this factory, were the major factor from the 1960s to the early 1980s which helped Taiwan become one of the "four little dragons" in Asia. In the last two decades, however, Taiwan has changed from a labor-intensive to a capital-intensive and technology-intensive economy (Change and Tsai 2002). It is only a matter of time before the factory where Mr. Ong works will close and more than 200 of its workers dismissed without a pension. The entire village will be affected.

At one time textile industries in Taiwan were producing 10 percent of the national GDP (*Liberty Times on the Net*), but a few years ago they began to experience a sharp downturn. The competition from Southeast Asian nations and China, all with much lower labor costs, was a major factor. Taiwanese textile industries cannot compete with countries such as Japan in producing upscale products. The owners of textile plants in Taiwan realize that to compete in the manufacturing of garments sold in Wal-Mart and K-Mart, they need to bring in cheap labor from other countries such as Indonesia. They must also raise the productivity of their workers, improve management skills, automate their production processes, and have government assistance with long-term, low-interest loans and a change in labor policies (*Liberty Times on the Net*). If the Taiwan government makes these changes, what will happen to people like Mr. Ong and his fellow workers? But if the changes do not occur and the factory moves to China, as Mr. Ong thinks it will, what will become of the people who do not know the term globalization but certainly know its implications?

A Flower Farmer

Mr. Chang has a small plot of land on the fringe of Chia-yi City. There he built a two-story house for his parents after his father retired and took ownership of the family farm, growing flowers. It is a small business with little capital. He works long hours, and when the flowers are ready he must harvest them within three days. His business has become increasingly uncertain since the florists in Taipei began to import flowers from elsewhere around the world. Mr. Chang regrets that his floral farm will have to end when he retires. Eventually, he will sell his land and it will be transformed by developers into apartment complexes or small high-tech factories. It saddens him to be the last in his family's business. None of his children would consider a career doing physical labor. However, Mr. Chang takes pride in his children being well educated and having professions.

Like his father and grandfather, Mr. Chang learned horticulture by working alongside his parents. They worked hard but earned enough for a decent living. Things changed when shipping flowers around the world could be done expeditiously and inexpensively, and the floral industry became global. Using the Internet, many of Mr. Chang's clients buy products where the prices are lowest, invest their money where it will generate the highest returns, and make rational economic changes at the first sign of advantage or trouble. Mr. Chang would not have believed, years ago, that one day he would be competing with floral farmers in the Netherlands. Yet, Mr. Chang is more fortunate than other self-employed persons because he has some land where he can grow produce. Other respondents in the survey must rely solely on their labor to make a living.

The Seamstress and Her Husband

Mrs. Chen's small tailor shop for custom-made clothes lies hidden amid hundreds of other small shops and food stalls selling traditional dishes. These shops and stalls fill the narrow streets branching away from the avenues of high-rise buildings, modern businesses, and condominiums in Chia-yi City. The contrast is stark. Street vendors in Taiwan began as immigrants from China over three hundred years ago. Most of them, like Mrs. Chen and petty farmers like Mr. Chang, have been doing small-scale trade in traditional economy that persists. But changes are on the horizon. The future can be seen on the main streets, where department stores sell merchandise from all over the world and restaurants

serve international cuisine. The latter include a McDonald's, where the children of newly affluent parents insist on being taken.

Despite its size, Mrs. Chen said she had run a successful shop for many years based on a group of faithful clients. This encouraged Mr. Chen to quit his high-tech sales job and join his wife as a self-taught designer, even though he had been making good money. He changed jobs because he did not want the stress that came with his former work, which required traveling and being away from his wife, family, neighbors, and friends. He wanted a life with a genuine sense of friendship and community. Mr. and Mrs. Chen love their work and are much happier being able to spend more time together. Business has dropped in the last few years. Customers still come, but a lot less frequently, and while they used to order a half-dozen dresses, now they order one or two. The Chens are sure the business will survive because their customers are their friends. Their business is personal, flexible, and client-oriented, and every transaction is a renewal and a strengthening of friendship.

Traditional tailor shops are being threatened by the mega-department stores featuring international designers' clothing. Despite the pressure of such global forces, it appears that local traditional commerce will survive for as long as people continue their previous way of life. But that may not last long. It is clear that as the new generation grows up with exposure to the world through television with its hundreds of channels from all over the world, the niches for traditional businesses will dry up.[2]

The Chens' business is hampered by the status symbols that come with renowned designer labels that have entered Taiwan. In response, Mrs. Chen tries to keep up with changing fashions by reading clothing design magazines from abroad. But status-conscious affluent clients want to wear Ann Taylor designer clothes regardless of the price, and the masses purchase their clothing made in China from the street vendors or the discount chain-stores that have sprung up in the suburbs. This "McDonaldization of society" (Ritzer 2000) is killing traditional businesses in Taiwan. The Chens, hard working and in their early 40s, are aware of how globalization affects their business and consequently their lives. As the government envisions a future

Taiwan based on high-tech industries and high finance, workers in the traditional economic sector and small-business people whose pension is their personal savings will have a hard time surviving.

An Animal-Feed Wholesaler

A wholesaler of animal feed, Mr. Tsai of Chia-yi City hopes someday to establish his business in China. Hindering this plan and making his business difficult is the problem of direct transportation between Taiwan and China. He now uses Hong Kong, Vietnam, and even Thailand as transfer points for his shipments, which creates additional costs and risks. Mr. Tsai's business had been dwindling because farmers requiring feed moved to China or Southeast Asian countries, or simply folded. Ranching and animal husbandry are labor-intensive, high-risk, low-margin businesses. They also require large parcels of land. In Taiwan, where land is scarce and expensive, husbandry faces a dead end. It is cheaper to import higher quality beef from Australia and pork from China or Vietnam. Mr. Tsai's only realistic option is to establish his business in China or Vietnam. But small investors like him, whose businesses are low-tech, are not important to China, which is more interested in high-tech industries and capital-intensive investments, or those who will establish factories with expansive infrastructure.

Thus the government is promoting high-tech development and high finance for Taiwan's future. On an island that has relatively few natural resources, and a constantly threatening China across the Formosa Strait, development of human capital is the alternative the Taiwanese government has chosen. This strategy raises the question of what will become of those with traditional economic pursuits, who may be marginalized as irrelevant and excluded from the rewards of a high-finance economy (Beck 2000b, Castells 2000 [1996], Burawoy et al. 2000).[3]

An Auto Repair Shop Owner

Mr. Kang and four of his brothers followed their father in the automotive repair business. After finishing his military service at age 21, Mr. Kang went to Taipei to learn computerized wheel-balancing techniques from his father's friend. Today he owns a wheel-balancing and tire repair shop located at a busy provincial highway. The shop also sells new tires from all over the world. With only several employees, the shop is small, but business is good. It is one of the few garages in Chia-yi City that uses computerized wheel-balancing machines and mechanized tire-repair procedures. Mr. Kang is a member of an automotive business association that provides information on new equipment, business opportunities, and world news of the automotive business.

The shop services commercial vehicles, mostly trucks and buses, but also autos from car dealerships. Mr. Kang's customers, especially drivers of large vehicles, prefer his service because his shop does jobs much faster than those still using manual procedures. He said time running on the road is critical for bus and truck owners, and added that his competitors must mechanize and computerize their operations or go out of business. About 90 percent of his customers are regulars. A lot of his trade is from car dealerships because, as land is expensive, dealerships are small and each is likely to have only one or two franchises. This is not enough to generate a volume of business sufficient to warrant having an expensive wheel-balancing machine and a qualified technician.

Mr. Kang said that without his wife's help he could not have been successful. She cares for the home and does his books in the office. The business, as he said, is highly competitive and requires keeping the shop open on Sundays and responding quickly to those needing emergency service. The business is thriving in part because in Taiwan today, ownership of an automobile is no longer a luxury but a necessity as well as a status symbol. Although his business is technologically modern, it is run in a traditional way; e.g., employees eat lunch together in the shop and are treated like family members, with the owner as a father figure (Redding 1993). All the technicians are either friends or the children of friends. It is unlikely that Mr. Kang's only son, in graduate school studying electrical engineering, will take over the business.

An Auto-Parts Shop Owner

A devoted Buddhist and family man, Mr. Lin has had a small auto-parts shop for 20 years. He and his wife believe that his wife's miraculous recovery from a coma was Buddha's blessing for all the good deeds they have done for their customers and their neighbors. Mr. Lin studies Buddhist teachings every day. His philosophy, he says, is to satisfy his customers' needs and not to make a large profit. His shop and home are typical of small businesses in Taiwan where the shop is on the first floor and the second floor is a residence. The shop's inventory consists of thousands of parts and Mr. Lin knows exactly where each is. His wife helped him run the business before she was hospitalized for an extended time. His daughter, after graduating college, decided to stay home to help in the shop. The family hopes that she might soon attract a young man, marry, and that the husband could, as a family member, help run the business. When asked if another auto-parts store located near his shop might be a threat to his business, Mr. Lin replied, "not at all." He thinks that it will bring more business to both of them, and believes that as long as he works hard, serves his customers well, and is not greedy, he will survive.

The shop is typical of the general way of doing business in Taiwan. It is based on trust, familiarity, and personal social networks. It is doubtful that this traditional way of doing business, especially in the auto-parts trade which is changing almost daily, will remain viable in the face of the more efficient, impersonal, mass-consumption ways of the international chain stores, such as Wal-Mart.

A Fruit Farmer

After completing his military service Mr. Kuo took over the family farm. Following Chinese tradition as the eldest son, Mr. Kuo felt obliged to maintain the farm. It was not large enough to support more than one family, so his younger siblings left to find work in various cities in Taiwan. One went to China to start his own business. Mr. Kuo and his neighbors harvest their crops at different times and help each other harvest by bartering and exchanging work hours. They do not make precise calculations about these exchanges because they are friends and do whatever is needed for each other.

Mr. Kuo is doing well. His large, modern brick house of two stories is adjacent to his warehouse.

When the crops are harvested with help from neighbors and temporary workers, most of them village women, they are brought to the warehouse, packaged by machine, and trucked away. Some of Mr. Kuo's orange trees come from foreign countries, primarily the U.S. Most of his crop is exported, but some goes to restaurants in Taiwan. All sales are through middlemen. The Farmers Association provides information about improved technologies and world market conditions. They advise on what, and how much to plant. Despite this help, every year is a gamble. Some crops do well in the market and others do not, but overall risks and rewards even out. Mr. Kuo's farm, though small by Western standards, is relatively large in Taiwan. Its size allows him to plant different types of oranges to reduce the risk of uncertain market conditions.

This farming village is located in the foothills, away from highways, factories, and petrochemical plants. It is near the forest and surrounded by fruit and tea farms. However, even with its relative isolation, the village feels the effects of globalization. It competes with citrus farmers in Florida, Texas, Australia, New Zealand, and elsewhere. Its livelihood depends on markets in Singapore, Hong Kong, and Southeast Asian countries. For the moment, it appears to be in good shape.

CONCLUSION

Taiwan, along with China, recently joined the World Trade Organization, and for many businessmen like Mr. Tsai, who is trying to establish a feed business in China, this is a welcome change. To politicians whose mission is to make Taiwan globally visible, it is a major achievement. Those in the high technology fields and those in the import–export businesses have benefitted from globalization, but for many in the more traditional economic sectors, globalization has reduced their income or terminated their livelihood (cf. Aristide 2000, Friedman 2000). Many of our respondents perceive the economy as poor in recent years and cannot understand why the news media portray Taiwan's economy as healthy. The examples in this article for whom globalization has been detrimental include the unemployed tailor, the workers in the textile factory who may lose their pensions, Mr. and Mrs. Chen, the custom-tailor store owners, and the entire oyster fishing village of Tung-shih.

The effects of globalization for Taiwan are a mixed blessing. On the one hand, Taiwan has changed to a high-tech, capital-intensive economy to be competitive in regional and international markets. More than half its high school graduates enter college, and the number of graduate schools in all fields is increasing rapidly. On the other hand, there are those who were too late to enter college and be trained for the knowledge economy of the 21st century. Polarization and income inequality are part of the cost of this rapid transformation.

Notes

1. An earlier version of this paper was presented at the American Sociological Association 99th Annual Meeting in Anaheim, California, August 18–21, 2001. This paper is part of a research project funded by the Chiang Ching-Kuo Foundation for International Scholarly Exchange and the National Science Council of the Republic of China in Taiwan. We wish to thank Dr. Phil Dennis of Texas Tech University for his very helpful comments and editorial assistance.
2. Dunkin' Donuts, recently established in Taipei, is doing a thriving business, and Japan's Mister Donut has been in Taiwan since 2004.
3. An unemployed tailor, not the Mr. Chen depicted previously, provides an ominous answers to this question. He had been doing alterations but there is no need for this line of work anymore. The mass-produced clothing, mainly from China, Indonesia, and even Costa Rica, destroyed his business. Mr. Chen had to sell his house and is living on the proceeds of the sale. He gets some help and handouts from neighbors, especially from Mr. Tsai from time to time. He said that he has been eating rice with salty water. In his 40s,

he is too old to get a new skill, and has all but given up looking for work.

Bibliography

Aristide, J-B., and L. Flynn (ed.). 2000. *Eyes of the Heart: Seeking a Path for the Poor in the Age of Globalization.* Common Courage Press.

Beck, U. 2000a. *What is Globalization?* Trans. P. Camiller. Polity Press.

_____. 2000b. *The Brave New World of Work.* Polity Press.

Burawoy, M., et al. 2000. *Global Ethnography, Forces, Connections, and Imaginations in a Postmodern World.* University of California Press.

Castells, M. 2000 (1996). The Rise of the Network Society. The Information Age: Economy, Society, and Culture, Vol. 1. Blackwell Publishing.

Chang, Y., and Y. Tsai. 2002. The Impacts of Information Age on Urban Development and Transformation in Taiwan. *American Journal of Chinese Studies* 9:179–201.

Derber, C. 2003. *People before Profit: The new Globalization in an Age of Terror, Big Money, and Economic Crisis.* Picador.

Friedman, T. L. 2000. *The Lexus and the Oliver Tree: Understanding Globalization.* Anchor Books.

Lee, M., Y. Tsai, and T. Wang. 2000. *Market, Industries, Firms, Occupational Dynamics, and Earnings: A Case Study from Taiwan.* Paper presented at the annual meeting of the Eastern Sociological Society.

Liberty Times on the Net. 2000. Special Series on Taiwanese Industries I, II, and III. October. http://www.libertytimes.com.tw/.

Mittelman, J. H. 2000. *The Globalization Syndrome: Transformation and Resistance.* Princeton University Press.

Polanyi, K. 1957. *The Great Transformation: The Political and Economic Origins of Our Times.* Beacon Press.

Redding, S. G. 1993. *The Spirit of Chinese Capitalism.* Walter de Gruyter.

Ritzer, G. 2000. *The McDonaldization of Society.* Pine Forge.

Sassen, S. 1999. *Globalization and Its Discontents: Essays on the New Mobility of People and Money.* New Press.

Taiwan Stock Exchange. http://www.tse.com.tw/en/.

Tapscott, D. 1996. *The Digital Economy.* McGraw-Hill.

US-China Business Council. 2004. http://www.uschina.org/statistics/fdi_cumulative.html.

CRITICAL THINKING QUESTIONS

1. How did the economy and industries of Taiwan adapt to the lack of resources on the island to become successful in the international economy?
2. Based on the article and other information, define what is meant by globalization. How has this process impacted, on a national scale, the economy and industries of Taiwan?
3. Traditional businesses in Taiwan are struggling. What are the characteristics inherent in some of these businesses, like tailoring and auto repair/parts shops, that may help them survive?
4. Based on the article and data from the news and other sources, compare the impact of globalization on businesses in both Taiwan and the United States.
5. As globalization impacts Taiwan, what do you think might be the ultimate fate of many people in traditional jobs or trades?

The Price of Progress

John Bodley

Until recently, government planners have always considered economic development and progress beneficial goals that all societies should want to strive toward. The social advantages of progress—as defined in terms of increased incomes, higher standards of living, greater security, and better health—are thought to be positive, *universal* goods, to be obtained at any price. Although one may argue that tribal peoples must sacrifice their traditional cultures to obtain these benefits, government planners generally feel that this is a small price to pay for such obvious advantages.

Evidence demonstrates that autonomous tribal peoples have not *chosen* progress to enjoy its advantages, but that governments have *pushed* progress upon them to obtain tribal resources, not primarily to share with the tribal peoples the benefits of progress. It has also been shown that the price of forcing progress on unwilling recipients has involved the deaths of millions of tribal people, as well as their loss of land, political sovereignty, and the right to follow their own lifestyle. This chapter does not attempt to further summarize that aspect of the cost of progress, but instead analyzes the specific effects of the participation of tribal peoples in the world-market economy. In direct opposition to the usual interpretation, it is argued here that the benefits of progress are often both illusory and detrimental to tribal peoples when they have not been allowed to control their own resources and define their relationship to the market economy.

PROGRESS AND THE QUALITY OF LIFE

One of the primary difficulties in assessing the benefits of progress and economic development for any culture is that of establishing a meaningful measure of both benefit and detriment. It is widely recognized that *standard of living,* which is the most frequently used measure of progress, is an intrinsically ethnocentric concept relying heavily upon indicators that lack universal cultural relevance. Such factors as GNP, per capita income, capital formation, employment rates, literacy, formal education, consumption of manufactured goods, number of doctors and hospital beds per thousand persons, and the amount of money spent on government welfare and health programs may be irrelevant measures of actual *quality* of life for autonomous or even semiautonomous tribal cultures. In its 1954 report, the Trust Territory government indicated that since the Micronesian population was still largely satisfying its own needs within a cashless subsistence economy, "Money income is not a significant measure of living standards, production, or well-being in this area" (TTR, 1955:44). Unfortunately, within a short time the government began to rely on an enumeration of certain imported goods as indicators of a higher standard of living in the islands, even though many tradition-oriented islanders felt that these new goods symbolized a lowering of the quality of life.

A more useful measure of the benefits of progress might be based on a formula for evaluating cultures devised by Goldschmidt (1952:135). According to these less-ethnocentric criteria, the important question to ask is: Does progress or economic development increase or decrease a given culture's ability to satisfy the physical and psychological needs of its population, or its stability? This question is a far more direct measure of quality of life than are the standard economic correlates of development, and it is universally relevant. Specific indication of this *standard* of living could be found for any society in the nutritional

Source: VICTIMS OF PROGRESS by John Bodley. Copyright © 1990 by John H. Bodley. Reproduced with permission of John H. Bodley via Copyright Clearance Center.

369

status and general physical and mental health of its population, the incidence of crime and delinquency, the demographic structure, family stability, and the society's relationship to its natural resource base. A society with high rates of malnutrition and crime, and one degrading its natural environment to the extent of threatening its continued existence, might be described as at a lower standard of living than is another society where these problems did not exist.

Careful examination of the data, which compare, on these specific points, the former condition of self-sufficient tribal peoples with their condition following their incorporation into the world-market economy, leads to the conclusion that their standard of living is *lowered,* not raised, by economic progress—and often to a dramatic degree. This is perhaps the most outstanding and inescapable fact to emerge from the years of research that anthropologists have devoted to the study of culture change and modernization. Despite the best intentions of those who have promoted change and improvement, all too often the results have been poverty, longer working hours, and much greater physical exertion, poor health, social disorder, discontent, discrimination, overpopulation, and environmental deterioration—combined with the destruction of the traditional culture.

DISEASES OF DEVELOPMENT

Perhaps it would be useful for public health specialists to start talking about a new category of diseases. . . . Such diseases could be called the "diseases of development" and would consist of those pathological conditions which are based on the usually unanticipated consequences of the implementation of development schemes [Hughes & Hunter, 1972:93].

Economic development increases the disease rate of affected peoples in at least three ways. First, to the extent that development is successful, it makes developed populations suddenly become vulnerable to all of the diseases suffered almost exclusively by "advanced" peoples. Among these are diabetes, obesity, hypertension,

and a variety of circulatory problems. Second, development disturbs traditional environmental balances and may dramatically increase certain bacterial and parasite diseases. Finally, when development goals prove unattainable, an assortment of poverty diseases may appear in association with the crowded conditions of urban slums and the general breakdown in traditional socioeconomic systems.

Outstanding examples of the first situation can be seen in the Pacific, where some of the most successfully developed native peoples are found. In Micronesia, where development has progressed more rapidly than perhaps anywhere else, between 1958 and 1972 the population doubled, but the number of patients treated for heart disease in the local hospitals nearly tripled, mental disorder increased eightfold, and by 1972 hypertension and nutritional deficiencies began to make significant appearances for the first time (TTR, 1959, 1973, statistical tables).

Although some critics argue that the Micronesian figures simply represent better health monitoring due to economic progress, rigorously controlled data from Polynesia show a similar trend. The progressive acquisition of modern degenerative diseases was documented by an eight-member team of New Zealand medical specialists, anthropologists, and nutritionists, whose research was funded by the Medical Research Council of New Zealand and the World Health Organization. These researchers investigated the health status of a genetically related population at various points along a continuum of increasing cash income, modernizing diet, and urbanization. The extremes on this acculturation continuum were represented by the relatively traditional Pukapukans of the Cook Islands and the essentially Europeanized New Zealand Maori, while the busily developing Rarotongans, also of the Cook Islands, occupied the intermediate position. In 1971, after eight years of work, the team's preliminary findings were summarized by Dr. Ian Prior, cardiologist and leader of the research, as follows:

We are beginning to observe that the more an islander takes on the ways of the West, the more prone he is to succumb to our degenerative diseases. In fact, it does not seem too much to say our evidence now shows that the farther the Pacific natives move from the quiet, care-free life of their ancestors, the closer they come to gout, diabetes, atherosclerosis, obesity, and hypertension [Prior, 1971:2].

In Pukapuka, where progress was limited by the island's small size and its isolated location some 480 kilometers from the nearest port, the annual per capita income was only about thirty-six dollars and the economy remained essentially at a subsistence level. Resources were limited and the area was visited by trading ships only three or four times a year; thus, there was little opportunity for intensive economic development. Predictably, the population of Pukapuka was characterized by relatively low levels of imported sugar and salt intake, and a presumably related low level of heart disease, high blood pressure, and diabetes. In Rarotonga, where economic success was introducing town life, imported food, and motorcycles, sugar and salt intakes nearly tripled, high blood pressure increased approximately ninefold, diabetes two to threefold, and heart disease doubled for men and more than quadrupled for women, while the number of grossly obese women increased more than tenfold. Among the New Zealand Maori, sugar intake was nearly eight times that of the Pukapukans, gout in men was nearly double its rate on Pukapuka, and diabetes in men was more than fivefold higher, while heart disease in women had increased more than sixfold. The Maori were, in fact, dying of "European" diseases at a greater rate than was the average New Zealand European.

Government development policies designed to bring about changes in local hydrology, vegetation, and settlement patterns and to increase population mobility, and even programs aimed at reducing certain diseases, have frequently led to dramatic increases in disease rates because of the unforeseen effects of disturbing the preexisting order. Hughes and Hunter (1972) published an excellent survey of cases in which development led directly to increased disease rates in Africa. They concluded that hasty development intervention in relatively balanced local cultures and environments resulted in "a drastic deterioration in the social and economic conditions of life."

Traditional populations in general have presumably learned to live with the endemic-pathogens of their environments, and in some cases they have evolved genetic adaptations to specific diseases, such as the sickle-cell trait, which provided an immunity to malaria. Unfortunately, however, out-side intervention has entirely changed this picture. In the late 1960s, sleeping sickness suddenly increased in many areas of Africa and even spread to areas where it did not formerly occur, due to the building of new roads and migratory labor, both of which caused increased population movement. Large-scale relocation schemes, such as the Zande Scheme, had disastrous results when natives were moved from their traditional disease-free refuges into infected areas. Dams and irrigation developments inadvertently created ideal conditions for the rapid proliferation of snails carrying schistosomiasis (a liver fluke disease), and major epidemics suddenly occurred in areas where this disease had never before been a problem. DDT spraying programs have been temporarily successful in controlling malaria, but there is often a rebound effect that increases the problem when spraying is discontinued, and the malarial mosquitoes are continually evolving resistant strains.

Urbanization is one of the prime measures of development, but it is a mixed blessing for most former tribal peoples. Urban health standards are abysmally poor and generally worse than in rural areas for the detribalized individuals who have crowded into the towns and cities throughout Africa, Asia, and Latin America seeking wage employment out of new economic necessity. Infectious diseases related to crowding and poor sanitation are rampant in urban centers, while greatly increased stress and poor nutrition aggravate a variety of other health problems. Malnutrition and other diet-related conditions are, in fact, one of the characteristic hazards of progress faced by tribal peoples and are discussed in the following sections.

THE HAZARDS OF DIETARY CHANGE

The traditional diets of tribal peoples are admirably adapted to their nutritional needs and available food resources. Even though these diets may seem bizarre, absurd, and unpalatable to outsiders, they are unlikely to be improved by drastic modifications. Given the delicate balances and complexities involved in any subsistence system, change always involves risks, but for tribal people the effects of dietary change have been catastrophic.

Under normal conditions, food habits are remarkably resistant to change, and indeed people are unlikely to abandon their traditional diets voluntarily in favor of dependence on difficult-to-obtain exotic imports. In some cases it is true that imported foods may be identified with powerful outsiders and are therefore sought as symbols of greater prestige. This may lead to such absurdities as Amazonian Indians choosing to consume imported canned tunafish when abundant high-quality fish is available in their own rivers. Another example of this situation occurs in tribes where mothers prefer to feed their infants expensive and nutritionally inadequate canned milk from unsanitary, but *high-status*, baby bottles. The high status of these items is often promoted by clever traders and clever advertising campaigns.

Aside from these apparently voluntary changes, it appears that more often dietary changes are forced upon unwilling tribal peoples by circumstances beyond their control. In some areas, new food crops have been introduced by government decree, or as a consequence of forced relocation or other policies designed to end hunting, pastoralism, or shifting cultivation. Food habits have also been modified by massive disruption of the natural environment by outsiders—as when sheepherders transformed the Australian Aborigine's foraging territory or when European invaders destroyed the bison herds that were the primary element in the Plains Indians' subsistence patterns. Perhaps the most frequent cause of diet change occurs when formerly self-sufficient peoples find that wage labor, cash cropping, and other economic development activities that feed tribal resources into the world-market economy must inevitably divert time and energy away from the production of subsistence foods. Many developing peoples suddenly discover that, like it or not, they are unable to secure traditional foods and must spend their newly acquired cash on costly, and often nutritionally inferior, manufactured foods.

Overall, the available data seem to indicate that the dietary changes that are linked to involvement in the world-market economy have tended to *lower* rather than raise the nutritional levels of the affected tribal peoples. Specifically, the vitamin, mineral, and protein components of their diets are often drastically reduced and replaced by enormous increases in starch and carbohydrates, often in the form of white flour and refined sugar.

Any deterioration in the quality of a given population's diet is almost certain to be reflected in an increase in deficiency diseases and a general decline in health status. Indeed, as tribal peoples have shifted to a diet based on imported manufactured or processed foods, there has been a dramatic rise in malnutrition, a massive increase in dental problems, and a variety of other nutrition-related disorders. Nutritional physiology is so complex that even well-meaning dietary changes have had tragic consequences. In many areas of Southeast Asia, government-sponsored protein supplementation programs supplying milk to protein-deficient populations caused unexpected health problems and increased mortality. Officials failed to anticipate that in cultures where adults do not normally drink milk, the enzymes needed to digest it are no longer produced and milk *intolerance* results (Davis & Bolin, 1972). In Brazil, a similar milk distribution program caused an epidemic of permanent blindness by aggravating a preexisting vitamin A deficiency (Bunce, 1972).

TEETH AND PROGRESS

There is nothing new in the observation that savages, or peoples living under primitive conditions, have, in general excellent teeth. . . . Nor is it news that most civilized populations possess wretched teeth which begin to decay almost before they have erupted completely, and that dental caries is likely to be accompanied by periodontal disease with further reaching complications [Hooton, 1945:xviii].

Anthropologists have long recognized that undisturbed tribal peoples are often in excellent physical condition. And it has often been noted specifically that dental caries and the other dental abnormalities that plague industrialized societies are absent or rare among tribal peoples who have retained their traditional diets. The fact that tribal food habits may contribute to the development of sound teeth, whereas modernized diets may do just the opposite, was illustrated as long ago as 1894 in an article in the *Journal of the Royal Anthropological Institute* that described the results of a comparison between the teeth of ten Sioux Indians and a comparable group of Londoners (Smith, 1894: 109–116). The Indians were examined when they came to London as members of Buffalo Bill's Wild West Show and were found to be completely free of caries and in possession of all their teeth, even though half of the group were over thirty-nine years of age. Londoners' teeth were conspicuous for both their caries and their steady reduction in number with advancing age. The difference was attributed primarily to the wear and polishing caused by the traditional Indian diet of coarse food and the fact that they chewed their food longer, encouraged by the absence of tableware.

One of the most remarkable studies of the dental conditions of tribal peoples and the impact of dietary change was conducted in the 1930s by Weston Price (1945), an American dentist who was interested in determining what caused normal, healthy teeth. Between 1931 and 1936, Price systematically explored tribal areas throughout the world to locate and examine the most isolated peoples who were still living on traditional foods. His fieldwork covered Alaska, the Canadian Yukon, Hudson Bay, Vancouver Island, Florida, the Andes, the Amazon, Samoa, Tahiti, New Zealand, Australia, New Caledonia, Fiji, the Torres Strait, East Africa, and the Nile. The study demonstrated both the superior quality of aboriginal dentition and the devastation that occurs as modern diets are adopted. In nearly every area where traditional foods were still being eaten, Price found perfect teeth with normal dental arches and virtually no decay, whereas caries and abnormalities increased steadily as new diets were adopted. In many cases the change was sudden and striking. Among Eskimo groups subsisting entirely on traditional food he found caries totally absent, whereas in groups eating a considerable quantity of store-bought food approximately 20 percent of their teeth were decayed. The figure rose to more than 30 percent with Eskimo groups subsisting almost exclusively on purchased or government-supplied food, and reached an incredible 48 percent among the Vancouver Island Indians. Unfortunately for many of these people, modern dental treatment did not accompany the new food, and their suffering was appalling. The loss of teeth was, of course, bad enough in itself, and it certainly undermined the population's resistance to many new diseases, including tuberculosis. But new foods were also accompanied by crowded, misplaced teeth, gum diseases, distortion of the face, and pinching of the nasal cavity. Abnormalities in the dental arch appeared in the new generation following the change in diet, while caries appeared almost immediately even in adults.

Price reported that in many areas the affected peoples were conscious of their own physical deterioration. At a mission school in Africa, the principal asked him to explain to the native school children why they were not physically as strong as children who had had no contact with schools. On an island in the Torres Strait the natives knew exactly what was causing their problems and resisted—almost to the point of bloodshed—government efforts to establish a store that would make imported food available. The government prevailed, however, and Price was able to establish a relationship between the length of time the government store had been established and the increasing incidences of caries among a population that showed an almost 100 percent immunity to them before the store had been opened.

In New Zealand, the Maori, who in their aboriginal state are often considered to have been among the healthiest, most perfectly developed of peoples, were found to have "advanced" the furthest. According to Price:

> Their modernization was demonstrated not only by the high incidence of dental caries but also by the fact 90 percent of the adults and 100 percent of the children had abnormalities of the dental arches [Price, 1945:206].

MALNUTRITION

Malnutrition, particularly in the form of protein deficiency, has become a critical problem for tribal peoples who must adopt new economic patterns. Population pressures, cash cropping, and government programs all have tended to encourage the replacement of traditional crops and other food sources that were rich in protein with substitutes high in calories but low in protein. In Africa, for example, protein-rich staples such as millet and sorghum are being replaced systematically by high-yielding manioc and plantains, which have insignificant amounts of protein. The problem is increased for cash croppers and wage laborers whose earnings are too low and unpredictable to allow purchase of adequate amounts of protein. In some rural areas, agricultural laborers have been forced systematically to deprive nonproductive members (principally children) of their households of their minimal nutritional requirements to satisfy the need of the productive members. This process has been documented in northeastern Brazil following the introduction of large-scale sisal plantations (Gross & Underwood, 1971). In urban centers the difficulties of obtaining nutritionally adequate diets are even more serious for tribal immigrants, because costs are higher and poor-quality foods are more tempting.

One of the most tragic, and largely overlooked, aspects of chronic malnutrition is that it can lead to abnormally undersized brain development and apparently irreversible brain damage; it has been associated with various forms of mental impairment or retardation. Malnutrition has been linked clinically with mental retardation in both Africa and Latin America (see, for example, Mönckeberg, 1968), and this appears to be a worldwide phenomenon with serious implications (Montagu, 1972).

Optimistic supporters of progress will surely say that all of these new health problems are being over-stressed and that the introduction of hospitals, clinics, and the other modern health institutions will overcome or at least compensate for all of these difficulties. However, it appears that uncontrolled population growth and economic impoverishment probably will keep most of these benefits out of reach for many tribal peoples, and the intervention of modern medicine has at least partly contributed to the problem in the first place.

The generalization that civilization frequently has a broad negative impact on tribal health has found broad empirical support (see especially Kroeger & Barbira-Freedman [1982] on Amazonia; Reinhard [1976] on the Arctic; and Wirsing [1985] globally), but these conclusions have not gone unchallenged. Some critics argue that tribal health was often poor before modernization, and they point specifically to tribals' low life expectancy and high infant mortality rates. Demographic statistics on tribal populations are often problematic because precise data are scarce, but they do show a less favorable profile than that enjoyed by many industrial societies. However, it should be remembered that our present life expectancy is a recent phenomenon that has been very costly in terms of medical research and technological advances. Furthermore, the benefits of our health system are not enjoyed equally by all members of our society. High infant mortality could be viewed as a relatively inexpensive and egalitarian tribal public health program that offered the reasonable expectation of a healthy and productive life for those surviving to age fifteen.

Some critics also suggest that certain tribal populations, such as the New Guinea highlanders, were "stunted" by nutritional deficiencies created by tribal culture and are "improved" by "acculturation" and cash cropping (Dennett & Connell, 1988). Although this argument does suggest that the health question requires careful evaluation, it does not invalidate the empirical generalizations already established. Nutritional deficiencies undoubtedly occurred in densely populated zones in the central New Guinea highlands. However, the specific case cited above may not be widely representative of other tribal groups even in New Guinea, and it does not address the facts of outside intrusion or the inequities inherent in the contemporary development process.

ECOCIDE

"How is it," asked a herdsman . . . "how is it that these hills can no longer give pasture to my cattle? In my father's day they were green and cattle thrived there; today there is no grass and my cattle starve." As one looked one saw that what had once been a green hill had become a raw red rock [Jones, 1931].

Progress not only brings new threats to the health of tribal peoples, but it also imposes new strains on the ecosystems upon which they must depend for their ultimate survival. The introduction of new technology, increased consumption, lowered mortality, and the eradication of all traditional controls have combined to replace what for most tribal peoples was a relatively stable balance between population and natural resources, with a new system that is imbalanced. Economic development is forcing *ecocide* on peoples who were once careful stewards of their resources. There is already a trend toward widespread environmental deterioration in tribal areas, involving resource depletion, erosion, plant and animal extinction, and a disturbing series of other previously unforeseen changes.

After the initial depopulation suffered by most tribal peoples during their engulfment by frontiers of national expansion, most tribal populations began to experience rapid growth. Authorities generally attribute this growth to the introduction of modern medicine and new health measures and the termination of intertribal warfare, which lowered mortality rates, as well as to new technology, which increased food production. Certainly all of these factors played a part, but merely lowering mortality rates would not have produced the rapid population growth that most tribal areas have experienced if traditional birth-spacing mechanisms had not been eliminated at the same time. Regardless of which factors were most important, it is clear that all of the natural and cultural checks on population growth have suddenly been pushed aside by culture change, while tribal lands have been steadily reduced and consumption levels have risen. In many tribal areas, environmental deterioration due to overuse of resources has set in, and in other areas such deterioration is imminent as resources continue to dwindle relative to the expanding population and increased use. Of course, population expansion by tribal peoples may have positive political consequences,

because where tribals can retain or regain their status as local majorities they may be in a more favorable position to defend their resources against intruders.

Swidden systems and pastoralism, both highly successful economic systems under traditional conditions, have proven particularly vulnerable to increased population pressures and outside efforts to raise productivity beyond its natural limits. Research in Amazonia demonstrates that population pressures and related resource depletion can be created indirectly by official policies that restrict swidden peoples to smaller territories. Resource depletion itself can then become a powerful means of forcing tribal people into participating in the world-market economy—thus leading to further resource depletion. For example, Bodley and Benson (1979) showed how the Shipibo Indians in Peru were forced to further deplete their forest resources by cash cropping in the forest area to replace the resources that had been destroyed earlier by the intensive cash cropping necessitated by the narrow confines of their reserve. In this case, a certain species of palm trees that had provided critical housing materials were destroyed by forest clearing and had to be replaced by costly purchased materials. Research by Gross and others (1979) showed similar processes at work among four tribal groups in central Brazil and demonstrated that the degree of market involvement increases directly with increases in resource depletion.

The settling of nomadic herders and the removal of prior controls on herd size have often led to serious overgrazing and erosion problems where these had not previously occurred. There are indications that the desertification problem in the Sahel region of Africa was aggravated by programs designed to settle nomads. The first sign of imbalance in a swidden system appears when the planting cycles are shortened to the point that garden plots are reused before sufficient forest regrowth can occur. If reclearing and planting continue in the same area, the natural pattern of forest succession may be disturbed irreversibly and the soil can be impaired permanently. An extensive tract of tropical rain forest in the lower Amazon of Brazil was reduced to a semiarid desert in just fifty years through such a process (Ackermann, 1964). The soils in the

Azande area are also now seriously threatened with laterization and other problems as a result of the government-promoted cotton development scheme (McNeil, 1972).

The dangers of overdevelopment and the vulnerability of local resource systems have long been recognized by both anthropologists and tribal peoples themselves, but the pressures for change have been overwhelming. In 1948 the Maya villagers of Chan Kom complained to Redfield (1962) about the shortening of their swidden cycles, which they correctly attributed to increasing population pressures. Redfield told them, however, that they had no choice but to go "forward with technology" (Redfield, 1962:178). In Assam, swidden cycles were shortened from an average of twelve years to only two or three within just twenty years, and anthropologists warned that the limits of swiddening would soon be reached (Burling, 1963:311–312). In the Pacific, anthropologists warned of population pressures on limited resources as early as the 1930s (Keesing, 1941:64–65). These warnings seemed fully justified, considering the fact that the crowded Tikopians were prompted by population pressures on their tiny island to suggest that infanticide be legalized. The warnings have been dramatically reinforced since then by the doubling of Micronesia's population in just the fourteen years between 1958 and 1972, from 70,600 to 114,615, while consumption levels have soared. By 1985 Micronesia's population had reached 162,321.

The environmental hazards of economic development and rapid population growth have become generally recognized only since worldwide concerns over environmental issues began in the early 1970s. Unfortunately, there is as yet little indication that the leaders of the now-developing nations are sufficiently concerned with environmental limitations. On the contrary governments are forcing tribal peoples into a self-reinforcing spiral of population growth and intensified resource exploitation, which may be stopped only by environmental disaster or the total impoverishment of the tribals.

The reality of ecocide certainly focuses attention on the fundamental contrasts between tribal and industrial systems in their use of natural resources. In many respects the entire "victims of progress" issue hinges on natural resources, who controls them, and how they are managed. Tribal peoples are victimized because they control resources that outsiders demand. The resources exist because tribals managed them conservatively. However, as with the issue of the health consequences of detribalization, some anthropologists minimize the adaptive achievements of tribal groups and seem unwilling to concede that ecocide might be a consequence of cultural change. Critics attack an exaggerated "noble savage" image of tribals living in perfect harmony with nature and having no visible impact on their surroundings. They then show that tribals do in fact modify the environment, and they conclude that there is no significant difference between how tribals and industrial societies treat their environments. For example, Charles Wagley declared that Brazilian Indians such as the Tapirape

> are not "natural men." They have human vices just as we do. . . . They do not live "in tune" with nature any more than I do; in fact, they can often be as destructive of their environment, within their limitations, as some civilized men. The Tapirape are not innocent or childlike in any way [Wagley, 1977:302].

Anthropologist Terry Rambo demonstrated that the Semang of the Malaysian rain forests have measurable impact on their environment. In his monograph *Primitive Polluters*, Rambo (1985) reported that the Semang live in smoke-filled houses. They sneeze and spread germs, breathe, and thus emit carbon dioxide. They clear small gardens, contributing "particulate matter" to the air and disturbing the local climate because cleared areas proved measurably warmer and drier than the shady forest. Rambo concluded that his research "demonstrated the essential functional similarity of the environmental interactions of primitive and civilized societies" (1985:78) in contrast to a "noble savage" view (Bodley, 1983) which, according to Rambo (1985:2), mistakenly "claims that traditional peoples almost always live in essential harmony with their environment."

This is surely a false issue. To stress, as I do, that tribals tend to manage their resources for sustained yield within relatively self-sufficient subsistence economies is not to make them either innocent children or natural men. Nor is it to deny that tribals "disrupt" their environment and may never be in absolute "balance" with nature.

The ecocide issue is perhaps most dramatically illustrated by two sets of satellite photos taken over the Brazilian rain forests of Rôndonia (Allard & McIntyre, 1988:780–781). Photos taken in 1973, when Rôndonia was still a tribal domain, show virtually unbroken rain forest. The 1987 satellite photos, taken after just fifteen years of highway construction and "development" by outsiders, show more than 20 percent of the forest destroyed. The surviving Indians were being concentrated by FUNAI (Brazil's national Indian foundation) into what would soon become mere islands of forest in a ravaged landscape. It is irrelevant to quibble about whether tribals are noble, childlike, or innocent, or about the precise meaning of balance with nature, carrying capacity, or adaptation, to recognize that for the past 200 years rapid environmental deterioration on an unprecedented global scale has followed the wresting of control of vast areas of the world from tribal groups by resource-hungry industrial societies.

DEPRIVATION AND DISCRIMINATION

> Contact with European culture has given them a knowledge of great wealth, opportunity and privilege, but only very limited avenues by which to acquire these things [Crocombe, 1968].

Unwittingly, tribal peoples have had the burden of perpetual relative deprivation thrust upon them by acceptance either by themselves or by the governments administering them—of the standards of socioeconomic progress set for them by industrial civilizations. By comparison with the material wealth of industrial societies, tribal societies become, by definition, impoverished. They are then forced to transform their cultures and work to achieve what many economists now acknowledge to be unattainable goals. Even though in many cases the modest GNP goals set by development planners for the

developing nations during the "development decade" of the 1960s were often met, the results were hardly noticeable for most of the tribal people involved. Population growth, environmental limitations, inequitable distribution of wealth, and the continued rapid growth of the industrialized nations have all meant that both the absolute and the relative gap between the rich and poor in the world is steadily widening. The prospect that tribal peoples will actually be able to attain the levels of resource consumption to which they are being encouraged to aspire is remote indeed except for those few groups who have retained effective control over strategic mineral resources.

Tribal peoples feel deprivation not only when the economic goals they have been encouraged to seek fail to materialize, but also when they discover that they are powerless, second-class citizens who are discriminated against and exploited by the dominant society. At the same time, they are denied the satisfactions of their traditional cultures, because these have been sacrificed in the process of modernization. Under the impact of major economic change family life is disrupted, traditional social controls are often lost and many indicators of social anomie such as alcoholism, crime, delinquency, suicide, emotional disorders, and despair may increase. The inevitable frustration resulting from this continual deprivation finds expression in the cargo cults, revitalization movements, and a variety of other political and religious movements that have been widespread among tribal people following their disruption by industrial civilization.

References

Ackermann, F. L. 1964. *Geologia e Fisiografia da Região Bragantina, Estado do Pará.* Manaus, Brazil: Conselho Nacional de Pesquisas, Instituto Nacional de Pesquisas da Amazônia.

Allard, William Albert, and Loren McIntyre. 1988. Rôndonia's Settlers Invade Brazil's Imperiled Rain Forest. *National Geographic* 174(6):772–799.

Bodley, John H. 1983. The World Bank Tribal Policy: Criticisms and Recommendations. *Congressional Record*, Serial no. 98–37, pp. 515–521. (Reprinted in Bodley, 1988.)

Bodley, John H., and Foley C. Benson. 1979. Cultural Ecology of Amazonian Palms. *Reports of Investigations*, no. 56. Pullman: Laboratory of Anthropology, Washington State University.

Bunce, George E. 1972. Aggravation of Vitamin A Deficiency Following Distribution of Non-Fortified Skim Milk: An Example of Nutrient Interaction. In *The Careless Technology: Ecology and International Development,* ed. M. T. Farvar and John P. Milton, pp. 53–60. Garden City, N.Y.: Natural History Press.

Burling, Robbins. 1963. *Rengsanggri: Family and Kinship in a Garo Village.* Philadelphia: University of Pennsylvania Press.

Crocombe, Ron. 1968. Bougainville!: Copper, R. R. A. and Secessionism. *New Guinea* 3(3):39–49.

Davis, A. E., and T. D. Bolin. 1972. Lactose Intolerance in Southeast Asia. In *The Careless Technology: Ecology and International Development,* ed. M. T. Farvar and John P. Milton, pp. 61–68. Garden City, N.Y.: Natural History Press.

Dennett, Glenn, and John Connell. 1988. Acculturation and Health in the Highlands of Papua New Guinea. *Current Anthropology* 29(2):273–299.

Goldschmidt, Walter R. 1952. The Interrelations Between Cultural Factors and Acquisition of New Technical Skills. In *The Progress of Underdeveloped Areas,* ed. Bert F. Hoselitz, pp. 135–151. Chicago: University of Chicago Press.

Gross, Daniel R., and Barbara A. Underwood. 1971. Technological Change and Caloric Costs: Sisal Agriculture. *American Anthropologist* 73(3):725–740.

Gross, Daniel R., et al. 1979. Ecology and Acculturation Among Native Peoples of Central Brazil. *Science* 206(4422): 1043–1050.

Hooton, Earnest A. 1945. Introduction. In *Nutrition and Physical Degeneration: A Comparison of Primitive and Modern Diets and Their Effects* by Weston A. Price. Redlands, Calif.: The author.

Hughes, Charles C., and John M. Hunter. 1972. The Role of Technological Development in Promoting Disease in Africa. In *The Careless Technology: Ecology and International Development,* ed. M. T. Farvar and John P. Milton, pp. 69–101. Garden City, N.Y.: Natural History Press.

Jones, J. D. Rheinallt. 1934. Economic Condition of the Urban Native. In *Western Civilization and the Natives of South Africa,* ed. I. Schapera, pp. 159–192. London: George Routledge and Sons.

Keesing, Felix M. 1941. *The South Seas in the Modern World.* Institute of Pacific Relations International Research Series. New York: John Day.

Kroeger, Axel, and Françoise Barbira-Freedman. 1982. *Culture Change and Health: The Case of South American Rain-forest Indians/* Frankfurt am Main: Verlag Peter Lang. (Reprinted in Bodley, 1988:221–236).

McNeil, Mary 1972. Lateritic Soils in Distinct Tropical Environments: Southern Sudan and Brazil. In *The Careless Technology: Ecology and International Development,* ed. M. T. Farvar and John P. Milton, pp. 591–608. Garden City, N.Y.: Natural History Press.

Mönckeberg, F. 1968. Mental Retardation From Malnutrition. *Journal of the American Medical Association* 206: 30–31.

Montagu, Ashley. 1972. Sociogenic Brain Damage. *American Anthropologist* 74(5):1045–1061.

Price, Weston Andrew. 1945. *Nutrition and Physical Degeneration: A Comparison of Primitive and Modern Diets and Their Effects.* Redlands, Calif.: The author.

Prior, Ian A. M. 1971. The Price of Civilization. *Nutrition Today* 6(4):2–11.

Rambo, A. Terry. 1985. *Primitive Polluters: Semang Impact on the Malaysian Tropical Rain Forest Ecosystem.* Anthropological Papers no. 76, Museum of Anthropology, University of Michigan.

Redfield, Robert. 1962. *A Village That Chose Progress: Chan Kom Revisited.* Chicago: University of Chicago Press, Phoenix Books.

Reinhard, K. R. 1976. Resource Exploitation and the Health of Western Arctic Man. In *Circumpolar Health: Proceedings of the Third International Symposium, Yellowknife, Northwest Territories,* ed. Roy J. Shephard and S. Itoh, pp. 617–627. Toronto: University of Toronto Press. (Reprinted in Bodley, 1988.)

Smith, Wilberforce. 1894. The Teeth of Ten Sioux Indians. *Journal of the Royal Anthropological Institute* 24:109–116.

TTR: *See under* United States.

United States, Department of State. 1955. *Seventh Annual Report to the United Nations on the Administration of the Trust Territory of the Pacific Islands* (July 1, 1953, to June 30, 1954).

————. 1959. *Eleventh Annual Report to the United Nations on the Administration of the Trust Territory of the Pacific Islands* (July 1, 1957, to June 30, 1958).

————. 1973. *Twenty-Fifth Annual Report to the United Nations on the Administration of the Trust Territory of the Pacific Islands* (July 1, 1971, to June 30, 1972).

Wagley, C. 1977. *Welcome of Tears: The Tapirape Indians of Central Brazil.* New York: Oxford University Press.

Wirsing, R. 1985. The Health of Traditional Societies and the Effects of Acculturation. *Current Anthropology* 26:303–322.

CRITICAL THINKING QUESTIONS

1. How do Western cultures define the word *progress*?

2. How do Western and traditional cultures compare in terms of quality of life, and how do you define this quality?

3. What diseases has Bodley defined as "diseases of development"? How have they come about, and how have they impacted traditional societies?

4. What are the ecological impacts of development and Westernization on traditional societies?

5. What additional social ills has contact with Western society brought to traditional peoples?

Solving Human Problems: Applied Anthropology in Focus

STATE OF THE ART: Applied Anthropology

Anthropologists in general have been concerned with the impact of social problems that affect the world—famine, diseases, environmental disasters, wars, violence, and other forms of human oppression. Unlike Ivory Tower anthropologists who hold the view that anthropologists should avoid practical matters and work in academic settings as teachers, or conduct basic research "to discover knowledge for its own sake" (Podolefsky 2008:77), applied anthropologists engage in applied research by working in social, rather than academic, settings, where they use anthropological knowledge—sociocultural data, theories, methods, and perspectives—to examine problems that have "direct practical outcome" (Podolefsky 2008:77). They take part in and/or evaluate programs targeted at improving the lives and conditions of people and provide results that are used to create or change social policies. Their work involves assembling relevant knowledge, developing plans, implementing programs, monitoring the operation, and assessing the impacts of specific program plans on the target population. They assume that the root causes of problems can be discovered as a means of mastering their solution (Ember & Ember 2007). To get a better understanding of human problems, they conduct research into cultural ideas and practices of a given society and other possible contributing factors. They work for government and donor agencies, and sometimes are hired by the target population itself.

Applied anthropology "encompasses all of anthropology" (Lenkeit 2007:13), including facets of physical anthropology—for example, forensic anthropology, which uses anthropological theories and knowledge to solve crimes—and medical anthropology, which employs biological and social factors in understanding the healing practices of cultures. Applied anthropologists look at cultural illnesses and their healing processes, and the healing agencies within the culture. Problems such as malnutrition, depression, AIDS, and the sociocultural factors surrounding health and disease are among the subjects of ongoing study (Ember & Ember 2007).

Applied anthropologists continue to deal with ethical issues that arise from the prospects of specific programs benefitting or hampering the native populations they are intended to help. They are sensitive to the effects of change on a given population. They work within parameters to ensure balance between the perceived needs of the agents of change and the recipients of such change (Ember & Ember 2007; Kingsolver 2008). They abide by a written code of ethics.

The development of applied anthropology is tied to the history of the discipline. The term *applied anthropology* was in use as early as 1906 when academic departments of anthropology began to appear. A major goal of the anthropology department of Oxford University in England "was to set up a kind of 'applied training program' to meet the empire's need" (Rylko-Bauer, Singer, &

Van Willigen 2006:179) to facilitate the process of colonial expansion. The British "made extensive use" (Rylko-Bauer, Singer, & Van Willigen 2006:180) of it in public policy. This led to increased interest in *ethnology* as policy makers sought descriptive research reports on cultural groups. According to McGee and Warms (2004:186) the role of the applied anthropologist became increasingly problematic. Anthropologists "frequently campaigned for natives' rights" but "generally believed in the legitimacy of colonial authority."

The need for more applied work grew during the Great Depression and intensified during World War II. Applied anthropologists were used to monitor Japanese–American relocation camps (Wax 1971). As members of the Committee on Food Habits, applied anthropologists worked to improve nutritional standards for malnourished citizens during the difficult war years. They were employed by the U.S. Office of Straegic Services (OSS—milliary intelligence), the predecessor to the Central Intelligence Agency (CIA). In their contradictory roles—both minimizing the suffering of inmates at relocation camps and participating in military propaganda to benefit the war effort—applied anthropologists were subjected to severe criticisms (Rylko-Bauer, Singer, & Van Willigen 2006; Kingsolver 2008).

The end of World War II, the *Era of Diverted Gaze*, signalled a shift in power relationships between anthropologists and indigenous peoples. Even before former colonies gained independence, indigenous peoples had begun challenging all forms of foreign authority including the representational authority of the anthropologist (Rylko-Bauer, Singer, & Van Willigen 2006). This served as a prelude to the *Post Modern Era,* which recognized the creativity and power of the individual, and asked for the inclusion of native people's perspectives and voices in ethnography. This *crisis of representation* resulted in a *reflexive cultural critique* within anthropology. Anthropologists began looking inward and loosening their grip on traditional practices of ethnography, by emphasizing the benefits of adopting cultural relativism (respect for and equal validity of all cultures). They began to pay attention to the harsh realities of social life—oppression, inequality, racism, and other social ills—of the people they studied. The result was an *Era of Action and Advocacy,* which led to *action anthropology* (Tax 1958), *human rights activism* (Doughty 1987:148), and the relinquishment of power to local communities, as exemplified by the Vicos Project in Peru. In the 1950s, with local self-sufficiency as its goal, the Cornell University-Peru Project leased a hacienda (agricultural estate) for a five-year period for use by landless peasants. It was an experimental grassroots development program designed to empower indigenous peoples who were given control of the means of production. Andean peasants controlled land use and allocation, including decision making about their circumstances (Dobyns 1966; Dobyns, Doughty, & Lasswell 1973; Thurner 1993; Hess 1995).

Later anthropologists engaged in more introspection by revisiting critiques and assessing previous stances. The result was increased *advocacy,* promoting and fighting for the rights of indigenous peoples, a complete deviation from the negative aspects of anthropology's early history. This called for a commitment to *action* that required *collaborative research* and *cultural brokerage* (the latter serving in the role of negotiator and interpreter between two cultures or between indigenous peoples and policy makers). Collaborative research, among other things, required the involvement of local peoples in some applied projects (i.e., archaeological excavations) whether they had the expertise or not. The goal is to promote *public anthropology* and "reclaim applied anthropology" (Rodriguez & Games 1998) to make it more tangible and relevant to everyday life. Thus contemporary applied anthropology is much different from that of the past. "The UN declaration of 1992 as the year of 'indigenous peoples'" (Rodriguez & Games 1998) has transformed the previously divergent agendas of nations and applied anthropologists into one of mutual interest—the optimal well-being of indigenous peoples. The challenge of the twenty-first century lies in the "trickling down" of development and on the equitable distribution of resources to benefit the rural poor in Third World countries. The long-term realization of these goals requires increased reliance on the professional expertise of applied anthropologists.

ABOUT THE ARTICLES

Sections Nine and Ten are interrelated in a number of ways. The impact of globalization varies from culture to culture. Some cultures adapt easily to changes while others suffer from problems inherent in dealing with alien economic systems and worldviews. Only one thing is certain: Change is inevitable, and it often brings problems in its wake. While Section Nine discusses the phenomenon of globalization and a number of inherent problems globalization causes, the articles in Section Ten deal with ways anthropologists can use their knowledge and skills to help deal with these problems.

The first three articles—by Downing and Downing-Garcia, Moles, and Terkildsen and Pickering—are interrelated. All deal with development projects and the problems they often inadvertently bring to traditional peoples in their wake. The articles contrast Plan A strategies (unequivocal resistance or support) with Plan B strategies (cooperation and collaboration) in three cases. They then define good Plan B strategies that appear to have a reasonable chance of achieving planned development while not seriously disrupting the lives of the very peoples the projects are intended to benefit.

The Bales article discusses the great "dirty little secret" of modern life. Despite increasing global economic integration and development, slavery as an institution still exists in different forms in many parts of the world. Bales defines the institution from an economic standpoint and illuminates the conditions that create slavery. He then identifies ways that the cycle of slavery can be broken by freeing both slave and slave master from the economic and psychological fetters that hold them together in mutual bondage.

La Lone's and Kerber's articles deal with a familiar topic to anthropologists and archaeologists: heritage preservation. When change occurs, older ways of life are usually abandoned and the knowledge and understanding of the older ways are lost. Using Appalachian coal mining lifestyles as an example, La Lone demonstrates ways in which anthropologists and local communities can come together to preserve knowledge about previous ways of life for future generations. Kerber demonstrates a growing trend in archaeology, the increased cooperation between the archaeological community and Native American peoples whose past the archaeological profession studies. Kerber demonstrates that relationships between the two groups can be mutually beneficial, rather than antagonistic, and can assist Native American societies in passing on their endangered cultural heritages to their youth.

References

Dobyns, H. F. "The Struggle for Land Use in Peru: The Hacienda Vicos Case." *Ethnohistory* 13, nos. 3/4 (1966).

Dobyns, H. F., Doughty P. L., & Lasswell, H. D. "Peasants, Power, and Social Change: Vicos as a Model." *Journal of Latin American Studies* 5, no.1 (May 1973): 175–176.

Doughty, P. L. Against the Odds: Collaboration and Development at Vicos. In *Collaborative Research and Social Change: Applied Anthropology in Action*, Donald D. Stull and Jean J. Schensul (eds.). Boulder, CO: Westview Press, pp. 129–157, 1987.

Ember, C., & Ember, M. *Cultural Anthropology*, 11th ed. Upper Saddle River, NJ: Pearson/Prentice Hall, 2007.

Hess, D. J. *Science and Technology in a Multicultural World: The Cultural Politics of Facts and Artifacts.* New York: Columbia University Press, 1995.

Kingsolver, A. Thinking and Acting Ethically in Anthropology. In *Thinking Anthropologically: A Practical Guide for Students*, 2nd ed. Philip Carl Salzman and Patricia C. Rice (eds). Upper Saddle River, NJ: Prentice Hall, 2008.

McGee, R. J., & Warms, R. L. *Anthropological Theory: An Introductory History*, 3rd ed. New York: McGraw-Hill, 2004.

Podolefsky, A. Applying Anthropological Knowledge. In *Thinking Anthropologically: A Practical Guide for Students*, 2nd ed. Philip Carl Salzman and Patricia R. Rice (eds.). Upper Saddle River, NJ: Prentice Hall, 2008.

Rodriguez, E., & Games, J. "Anthropology and the Politics of Representation." In *Economic and Political Weekly* 33, nos. 42/43 (1992): 2709–2714.

Rylko-Bauer, B., Singer, M., & Van Willigen, J. "Reclaiming Applied Anthropology: Its Past, Present, and Future." *American Anthropologist* 108, no. 1 (2006): 178–190.

Tax, S. "The Fox Project." *Human Organization* 17 (1958): 17–19.

Thurner, M. "Peasant Politics and Andean Haciendas in the Transition to Capitalism: An Ethnographic History." *Latin American Research Review* 28, no. 3 (1993): 41–82.

Wax, M., *Doing Fieldwork: Warnings and Advice*. Chicago: University of Chicago Press, 1971.

For Further Research

Employing anthropological knowledge to help solve human problems is generally considered to be the domain of applied anthropology. *Cultural Survival Quarterly* journal focuses not only on the impacts of globalization but on strategies that can be used to help indigenous peoples survive the impact of this process. Another journal in this vein is *Practicing Anthropology*. Additional introductory references include Erve Chambers's *Applied Anthropology: A Practical Guide* (1985, Prentice-Hall); Alexander Ervin's *Applied Anthropology: Tools and Perspectives for Contemporary Practice* (1999, Allyn & Bacon); and a textbook with an applied perspective in its title, Gary Ferraro and Susan Andeatta's *Cultural Anthropology An Applied Perspective* (8th ed., 2010, Wadsworth Cengage Learning). For additional information on researching the topics discussed in the "State of the Art" section, please visit *www.mysearchlab.com*.

Plan B: What Is Going to Happen to My People?

Theodore E. Downing and Carmen Garcia-Downing

Be it for profit, energy, development, or because of a desire to help Indian peoples, outsiders continue dreaming up projects to develop Indian lands. Here in Arizona, thousands of Phoenix commuters zoom down the new 101 Freeway. On one side, they see the Salt River Indian Reservation's agricultural land, casinos, and modest Bureau of Indian Affairs (BIA) houses. On the other, they see expensive Scottsdale luxury homes and malls. Here and in comparable places around the world, entrepreneurs are convinced that indigenous peoples are not properly developing their resources. The Salt River Indians, like their sisters and brothers on other lands, are perpetually pelted by project proposals. We have worked with indigenous development issues on several continents, and whether projects are accepted or rejected, we have heard one question echo in many tongues: "What is going to happen to my people?"

The struggle for cultural survival is not simply one of resistance. Indigenous people find that some projects improve their quality of life and strengthen their capacity for cultural survival. Other projects do not. In most cases, however, it is not easy to determine a project's impact on cultural survival.

PLAN A & PLAN B

Let's call either unequivocal resistance to or support for a project "Plan A." As strange as it may seem, the "just say no" and "just say yes" strategies have a lot in common. Both attract outside supporters whose primary interests may not include the cultural survival of the affected peoples. To win a battle in what, for them, is a much larger war, advocates on either side of the issue are likely to understate or misunderstand the project's potential impacts—both positive and negative. Project promoters and their allies recruit mercenaries, who come as consultants, researchers, surveyors, government bureaucrats, and—the modern day equivalent of Imperial Stormtroopers—lawyers. Indigenous peoples sometimes pick up a few volunteers or advocates—often with agendas distinct from their own.

Rest assured that as the proponents and opponents of a project argue over their Plan As, someone, somewhere, is preparing "Plan B" as an alternative to resistance and confrontation. Plan B is what happens after support for or resistance against the project withers. The controversial project along the Alto Bio Bio River in southern Chile offers a poignant example (see www.irn.org/programs/biobio).

A PROJECT BATTLEFIELD

In 1995, we were swept into a clash between environmentalists and *Empresa Nacional De Electricidad S.A.* (ENDESA), South America's largest power company, over whether a series of dams should be built on Pehuenche lands. The construction site of the first dam (Pangue) resembled a battlefield: as dynamite blew the sides off sacred mountains, armies of workmen marched into tunnels and convoys of heavy machinery wheeled down new penetration roads into what had been one of Chile's more isolated areas. Company sociologists and lawyers roamed Pehuenche lands, collecting signatures—signing Indian people up as members of a newly formed, company-controlled, indigenous development foundation—and handing out gifts.

Source: Reprinted from *Cultural Survival Quarterly*, Fall 2001.

In April 2001, we returned to the now-quiet battlefield. The Pangue Dam was operational, generating power for non-Indians throughout Chile. Lakeview homes and a resort for the wealthy occupied lands on which the Pehuenche once grazed their animals. The former president of the company-controlled indigenous development foundation relaxed in his palatial villa on the shoreline of the Pangue Lake. In the nearby Pehuenche community of Pitril, kerosene lamps still lit Pehuenche houses. Media cameras were turned off; microphones packed. Protest signs had long ago been used as kindling. A leading environmental warrior was camped out in a nearby town, writing about his experiences. A few mercenaries and indigenous supporters had moved further upstream to combat the construction of Ralco, a second dam. International concern had shifted to battlefields in other lands.

And the Pehuenche? Their economic and social structure is now in turmoil. Promised project-related benefits—primarily unskilled construction jobs—have almost disappeared. Traditional leaders have been undercut or deeply scarred in skirmish after skirmish. Factionalism has fractured kinship bonds. Women play an important role in early childhood acculturation. A Chilean sociologist reports that all single Pehuenche women who were of childbearing age at the project's outset had children fathered by the company's and its subcontractors' workers and managers. Given that the Pehuenche number only about 4,000, this is a significant cultural impact.

The company's vision of the Pehuenche's future—*its* Plan B—is unfolding. ENDESA has begun a resettlement of Pehuenche who are in the way of the second dam at Ralco. People are being forcefully relocated and divided into three groups. One is being moved to lands high in the snowcapped Andes, along the Chilean-Argentine border. Another is being transferred to privately held farmsteads in the valley, about two hours away when the roads are passable. The valley has a dearth of grazing lands and no viable communal resources; even firewood for the harsh winters is unavailable. A third group of relatives—brothers and sisters—is being left behind. During the winter, up to seven meters of snow may prevent communication between the displacees. The company's Plan B was prepared by company consultants working in city offices. Refusing to recognize Pehuenche culture, the resettlement was negotiated with the government and with individual Pehuenche. The Pehuenche were not consulted or permitted to make decisions as a cultural group. They never formulated their own Plan B. Regrettably, those claiming to be friends of the Pehuenche exhausted their efforts on Plan A. Both friend and foe seemed convinced that the Pehuenche were too incapable, ignorant, poor, or uneducated to develop their own vision. Indigenous peoples in the United States will recognize their own situation in this story. Many Indian reservations in the United States are the product of the U.S. War Department's Plan B.

COMPONENTS OF A GOOD INDIGENOUS PEOPLE'S PLAN B

A people's chances for cultural survival increase when they develop their own Plan B to deal with a proposed project. Plan B may be developed concurrently with Plan A. A good Plan B should have at least eight components. It begins with a careful economic and legal examination of the project itself. Second, an assessment is made of the project's particular risks and benefits. Third, specific actions are budgeted to mitigate each identified risk. Concurrently and fourth, the plan determines how the project fits within the people's cultural vision. Building on this foundation, the group may decide to take several additional steps. Fifth, institutional and financial arrangements are proposed to assure that the people share in the project's benefits. Sixth, arrangements are made to focus these benefits on a common group endeavor and/or distribute them within the group. The seventh component entails establishing strategies for negotiating with the project promoters, financiers, and other key stakeholders identified in the project assessment. The negotiations focus on benefit-sharing arrangements over and above risk mitigation. Within the indigenous group, arrangements are worked out for the distribution of benefits. Eighth, the negotiated arrangements with project promoters and other affected stakeholders are formalized in legally binding instruments.

Properly done, a good Plan B offers answers to the all-important question: "If this particular project is approved, rejected, or modified, what will happen to my people?"

1. TURNING A PROJECT INSIDE-OUT

The inside-out project analysis, as we like to call it, is the first step in preparing Plan B. It begins with questions: Whose money is being risked? Who are the investors? What obligations and policies—especially social and environmental policies—must the promoters and financiers follow? When will the project start and finish? What is the anticipated sequence of outside manpower being brought into the area? What government permissions and permits are necessary? What jobs and training are being reserved for the people? What loopholes in national legislation and regulations might be exploited by those negotiating in bad faith?

Just as fires need fuel, projects need financing. A project is more likely to be cancelled because it is unprofitable than because of political resistance. Project promoters rarely use their own money. Instead, they struggle to convince potential investors, including banks, that their project will yield better returns on investment with less risk. Projects are usually financed by multiple investors. Groups of investors known as syndicates pool their resources to finance projects.

An interesting financial twist works in favor of indigenous peoples. Members of a syndicate generally have distinct environmental and social policies. To maintain the integrity of the investment group and keep the project moving forward, the syndicate—as a group—is restricted by the most stringent policy of any one of its members. (This may turn out to be a minority shareholder.) The failure to adhere to any lender's policy may force that lender to pull out of the project. A lender's withdrawal from the project may in turn raise doubts within the financial community about its viability. No financing, no project. For this reason, individual institutional investors' policies on indigenous peoples are very important (see links at www.policykiosk.com). A people's Plan B is

strengthened by paying close attention to the environmental and social requirements of project investors—especially those with the most stringent policies.

The inside-out analysis also identifies the promoters' assumptions (often unstated) about the contributions that the people are expected to make to the project. These contributions sometimes go far beyond simple agreement about payments for the cost of extracted or disturbed resources. Assumptions may include predetermined local labor costs, assumed access rights, uncompensated demands on the indigenous group's leadership, and no-fee waste disposal and dumping.

Normally, for example, our university has aimed at having productive relationships with the 21 sovereign tribes in Arizona. Many years ago, one of our hotshot research administrators proposed an agricultural development plan to the San Carlos Apache. Project promoters sang the praises of a new oil-seed crop and its potential to boost the tribe's economic development. The San Carlos Apaches agreed to contribute land and labor to the experiment. Hidden within this project's economic analysis, however, was the unrealistic assumption that the Apache would be willing to perform seasonal, backbreaking work for minimum wage. Knowing that this arrangement was probably unacceptable to the Apache, university economists tested the option of implementation in a Third World country. The Apache were not aware that the technology being developed on their reservation was destined for another group. Once the Apache saw what was happening, they terminated their participation. A good inside-out analysis would have detected this flawed assumption and either saved Apache and university time or forced more reasonable terms for the Apache.

An inside-out analysis also probes deeply into non-disclosed arrangements. To protect their money, investors and lending institutions make legally binding agreements with project developers. These agreements should be disclosed to the people before an investment decision is made. Especially pertinent are any cost/profit-sharing arrangements with indigenous peoples. In 1992, the International Finance Corporation (IFC) and ENDESA signed a secret investment agreement that specified the company's financial and institutional obligations to the Pehuenche. The agreement included requirements that ENDESA share a fixed percentage of its net profits from the Pangue Dam's hydroelectric power with the Pehuenche. Neither the Pehuenche nor the Chilean government were party to the negotiations or the agreement. The company negotiated to channel benefit-sharing payments through a company-controlled development foundation. The Pehuenche were unaware that the company's ostensibly charitable assistance was actually interested, obligatory, and manipulative. It was used to improve public relations with Pehuenche living on land needed for ENDESA's second dam, Ralco. The IFC and ENDESA subjected the agreement to the legal jurisdiction of New York, effectively shielding it from Chilean eyes. Despite three or four charges of human rights violations, including two filed inside the World Bank by a long-time consultant, the investment agreement has remained secret for almost a decade. The IFC and the company argue that disclosure of their loan agreement may divulge trade secrets to competitors. We have responded that for a company and an investor to have a secret agreement about the future of an ethnic group or tribal people not only violates the group's human rights, but also undermines the sovereignty of the government under which the group lives. And it *is* possible to limit disclosure: all necessary confidential business agreements can be kept secret while environmental and social agreements are made transparent and public.

How would the Pehuenche have reacted had they known that decades of future profits from the Pangue Dam were required to be channeled for their benefit? Would this have encouraged a Pehuenche Plan B? The lesson here is to routinely request that promoters and lenders provide a legally binding assurance that they have not entered into undisclosed agreements about the future of the indigenous group to be affected by the project they are financing.

Investors and bankers also routinely conduct due diligence studies on proposed investments. The studies telegraph to a potential investor the strengths and weaknesses of a proposed project, its profitability, and its financial requirements.

On large investments, these studies' costs may run into the hundreds of thousands of dollars. When investors approach indigenous peoples as potential partners in a venture, it is reasonable for the people to conduct their own due diligence analysis. A California banker offered a helpful suggestion: the indigenous people should ask project promoters to put down a non-refundable performance deposit—a measure of their faith in their own project—to hire an independent third party to review the proposed project's business plans and financing. A review may suggest that the project is not economically feasible and that its further consideration would be a waste of time. Or, should the project appear feasible and Plan B be activated, this information would prove valuable to both parties for future negotiations.

2. ASSESSING RISKS

Large projects are routinely protected by risk-management, risk-financing, and risk-sharing arrangements. Insurance policies and bonds, for example, are used to protect investors. In contrast, indigenous populations are seldom protected against project risks. Relative to total project monetary costs, their potential losses are minute. But relative to what they have, the losses may be substantial. Depending on the scale and type of project, they may risk not only their limited capital, but also their cultural survival.

The risk assessment component of Plan B aims to determine the degree to which indigenous peoples are beneficiaries or victims of a proposed project. Projects may pose a wide variety of risks. In a widely used model, the World Bank identified eight "impoverishment risks" associated with projects that cause development-induced displacement (The World Bank, 1994). These risks include landlessness, homelessness, unemployment, loss of access to communal resources, food insecurity, health risks, marginalization, and social disarticulation (Cernea, 2000). Subsequent work added political destablization and the loss of civil and human rights to the list (Downing, 1998; www.displacement.net). The Bank's risk model offers a reasonable framework for evaluating the risks associated with investment projects' impacts on indigenous peoples in general, not simply those involving displacement. A project may be assessed in terms of its likelihood of increasing or decreasing homelessness, improving or undermining health, increasing or decreasing food security, etc. This multidimensional risk model intentionally covers different types of risks that cannot be consolidated, forcing a broader, qualitative and quantitative assessment of a project's anticipated impact.

The risk assessment component of Plan B changes dialogue and negotiations between the people, the project promoters, and the investors. A project promoter will not likely reject a risk assessment's result; the assessment clarifies the project's full cost, and someone, somewhere, must pay. Should the promoters fail to budget for identified project risks, they are overtly transferring project costs to the indigenous group or to the government. The assessment may then lay the groundwork for future legal action. The possibility—even remote—of legal action injects an undesirable financial uncertainty and an unspecified liability into the project's financial equations. A more likely reaction to a risk assessment is for promoters to open up negotiations and focus on identifying risks, their costs, and actions that might be taken to avoid or mitigate these risks.

3. MITIGATING RISKS

In risk assessment, methodological disagreements are likely to surface. Project promoters want their bottom lines to look good. A common technique to realize this goal is externalizing costs. Promoters are quick to dismiss as "indirect" those costs they feel are not related to the project. Indirect, in this case, means "it's not our fault, so we don't have to pay." In this manner, ENDESA dismissed as an unrelated, "indirect cost" between $3 million and $18 million in deforestation that followed the entry of their new road into Pehuenche territory. (ENDESA's development foundation, in contrast, provided less than half a million in company-controlled assistance over four years.) Here is the test to determine whether an impact is direct or indirect: a cost that would not have occurred if the project were not built is a project cost.

A mitigation and avoidance plan should accompany each specific risk identified in the assessment. A matrix should be prepared, listing each identified risk, segments of the population that are at disproportionately greater risk, mitigation efforts to be taken, anticipated costs, a time line, planned institutional arrangements, and monitoring methods to assure successful risk mitigation. Returning to the Pehuenche, the failure to protect Pehuenche women from the more than 4,000 mostly male workers and to provide for these single mothers was a specific, foreseeable impoverishment risk identified years before the project's outset. ENDESA did take measures to protect young Pehuenche women from the workers and management, but these proved trivial and ineffective. A Plan B matrix would specify steps to be taken if risk mitigation failed. An equitable solution, in this case, might have been for the company to arrange for an insurance company to provide for child support, health insurance, and the education of children born to deadbeat workmen, subcontractors, and managers.

As the risk assessment and mitigation proceed, project promoters become more aware of their actions' complex impact on the indigenous community. Frustrated, promoters will probably attempt to short-circuit the mitigation/avoidance plan with cash payments. Plan B provides the people with a realistic appraisal so that they may carefully evaluate their options when cash payments are offered.

4. SUBORDINATING ECONOMIC TO CULTURAL VISIONS

The next step is to determine whether or not project risks, benefits, and mitigation plans can be reconciled with the indigenous community's cultural vision. A cultural vision addresses the critical questions about the great mysteries of life: Where do we come from? Where are we? Who are we? Why are they here? Where are we going? How do we stay in balance with our environment? Different peoples have distinct pathways to unique cultural visions. A successful Plan B links the specifics of a proposed project to a specific cultural vision, and requires subordination of the promoters' economic visions to the people's cultural visions. A cultural vision is not an economic plan, but an economic plan may be an important part of a cultural vision.

Determining how a project will strengthen and/or weaken a cultural vision requires people's best facilitators and wise people, and, occasionally, technical assistants. Fortunately, numerous sisters and brothers and non-Indian facilitators have developed innovative, inclusive, participatory methods to move the process along. The Mountain Institute, among others, is using techniques that facilitate dreaming and turning cultural visions into on-the-ground actions (see Brewer Lama, *CSQ* 23:2).

As part of our evaluation of ENDESA's indigenous development foundation, we trained seven Pehuenche in evaluation and focus group methodologies that were adapted for working with heavily illiterate groups (see www.ted-downing.com). Our team met with different Pehuenche bands in a tent we erected. We encouraged group discussions of possible alternatives for investing windfalls should the Pehuenche gain control of their share of the project's profits. Three alternatives were drawn on slips of paper pinned to three pockets of a handmade apron. Each Pehuenche then privately expressed his preference by distributing five marbles in the pockets. After a lengthy discussion, the Pehuenche decided to vote on the alternatives of long-term, medium-term, and short-term distributions. Long-term investments included options like scholarships for their children. All were pleased when a small girl reached into the short-term pocket and found no marbles. The medium-term pocket likewise proved nearly empty. The group was delighted to realize that they shared a common concern for their long-term future. They had begun to craft their cultural vision of how the project might fit within their common hopes and goals.

Financiers and promoters should distance themselves from the process a group uses to form its cultural vision. Most are ill-equipped to lead the cultural visioning process and have a conflict of interest. As a condition for a loan, for example, the Pangue Dam's financier required the borrower, ENDESA, to create a foundation to study and preserve Pehuenche culture. Rather than listening to the Pehuenche's own visions, non-Indian staff formulated their own cultural vision for the Pehuenche. They contracted an expert—an anthropological consultant who completed his work with no participatory analysis or fieldwork with the Pehuenche. He reported that Pehuenche culture was destined to be homogenized into mainstream, Chilean culture, and advised that the company's cultural programs facilitate this inevitable transition. The foundation's final cultural promotion program included a few Pehuenche parents to be school monitors, the purchase of food and tobacco for Pehuenche ceremonies, a small museum to display Pehuenche artifacts to visiting non-Indians, and cultural horizon trips for Indian children to learn about Chilean cultural heritage. Their attempts were further skewed by religion. Company employees were of a common religious background and were extremely concerned, if not fixated, on reversing the damage caused by another group's evangelical work among the Pehuenche.

For several years, the *CSQ* has been reporting on events, plans, and organizations where indigenous peoples are using Plan Bs to take control of their own destinies. Indigenous peoples' policies define how external opportunities should fit within their cultural visioning. These policies should not be confused with general declarations of indigenous rights. Rather, they offer specific guidance to outsiders and remind a people how projects should and should not be worked out. An excellent example comes from the Kuna General Congress (CGK) in Panama. They recently reported on their 1996 Statute on Tourism (see Snow, *CSQ* 24:4), in which they defined their terms of interaction with outsiders and gained a measure of control over the burgeoning tourist industry. This new statute encourages project promoters from an entire sector to mold their proposals within the Kuna's crystallized cultural vision.

5. ARRANGING BENEFIT-SHARING

Sharing in a project's benefits means that compensation is received over and above payments for resources contributed to the endeavor, local wages, and payments for project-inflicted damages. This clarification is necessary because project owners and financiers often mistakenly view their risk mitigation costs, payment for damages, and locally generated project employment as a benefit being paid to the people. If a project promoter's Lexus slammed into another car on the freeway, would he dare argue that the damages paid to the injured party were benefits? The cost of rebuilding a displaced person's house does not constitute benefit-sharing.

The benefit-sharing component of Plan B specifies how the people are to receive project benefits. It determines how benefits are to be calculated, what benefits are to be shared, how payments are to be made, who makes and receives them, how long they are to be made, and the amount to be paid. Everything is on the table when it comes to determining benefits, including access rights, discounted products (electrical energy in the case of a power plant, for example), and—most important of all—money. Although benefits may involve monetary and nonmonetary arrangements, restoration of or additions to productive resources take priority. Templates for the preparation of Plan B may be found in tens of thousands of arrangements and agreements on how companies and governments will share benefits. (Unfortunately, these templates are scattered. Hopefully, some organization or foundation will establish a consultation library of sample agreements.)

Plan B forces agreement on benefit-sharing issues before a project gets underway. A great deal of mistrust surrounds this issue. Project promoters and financiers fear that benefit-sharing arrangements won't "stick." Payments might be mismanaged or misappropriated by corruption, especially when governments intervene in their distribution among the people. Segments of the indigenous community might later claim that they were not party to the agreement and demand additional payments. Some promoters are also concerned about equity. Benefits may not reach those who are actually harmed, or traditionally disenfranchised groups within an indigenous community. These groups might then question the legitimacy of the benefit-sharing arrangement. Project promoters are also bewildered by the great diversity of social organizations among indigenous groups. They sometimes forget that "indigenous" is a blanket term tossed around by outsiders over sovereign, distinct peoples. Such confusion makes it difficult for promoters to identify and negotiate benefit-sharing arrangements and to determine who is the group's

authorized authority. Mistrust may likewise occur within the affected group.

6. DISTRIBUTING BENEFITS

Defining institutional arrangements for the distribution of project benefits within an indigenous group is a delicate matter. Conflicts over the distribution of benefits may pose a greater threat to cultural survival than does the project itself. Pre-project factionalism may be exacerbated as money is poured, like salt, onto old wounds. People, indigenous or not, sometimes fight most bitterly over anticipated windfalls that never materialize. A good Plan B defines the way that benefits are to be distributed before a project begins. As Maximillan C. Forte recently reported about the Santa Rosa Carib community (*CSQ* 22:4), failure to define this arrangement ahead of time may stifle investment in shared dreams.

Following negotiation and agreement on the form of benefits, benefit-sharing arrangements must be firmly controlled and prepared by the affected people. The IFC and ENDESA were either unable or unwilling to decipher the Pehuenche's political organization. The Pehuenche are divided into multiple bands with consensual leaders who have limited traditional authority. Rather than negotiating benefit-sharing arrangements consistent with the group's socio-political organization, the company unilaterally named three leaders to a company-controlled foundation board. Four other company-named, non-Indian members of the board had veto power over Pehuenche board members. As a result, the Pehuenche were unable to fold project benefits into a Pehuenche cultural vision.

Plan B may consider several options for the internal distribution of project benefits, including moving funds through traditional indigenous political organizations or development foundations, fortifying or adding to common resources, and setting up trust accounts. In some cases, these organizations fall outside indigenous control. In Abuja, Nigeria, for example, NGOs and Shaman Pharmaceuticals, Inc. helped launch the Fund for Integrated Rural Development and Traditional Medicine (FIRD-TM) to channel the benefits of many contributors into multiple communities (see Moran, *CSQ* 24:4).

The FIRD-TM's independent board included not only indigenous peoples, but also leaders of traditional healers' associations, government officials, representatives of village councils, and technical advisors.

Each people must determine which methods fit best within their needs and cultural vision. Given the diversity of indigenous organizations, a great variety of ways are emerging to distribute benefits. Some tribes in Arizona have prudently invested their casino revenues in long-term ventures such as scholarships, land purchases, infrastructure improvements, and provisioning of social services (clinics, nursing homes) intended to strengthen their cultural and economic capacity. Some have also opted to channel part of their revenues into short-term, individual per capita payouts. Most distribution arrangements permit, with the group's consent, midstream adjustments to match changing tribal needs. The worst possible solution, however, is to surrender sovereignty and let the project promoter determine the distribution of benefits. Doing so plunges an outsider deep into internal tribal politics and may undermine a perfectly good investment option.

7. NEGOTIATING

Armed with an understanding of the project's financing, risks, and benefits, and with a knowledge of how the project might fit within their cultural vision, the people have the option of continuing with Plan A or negotiating Plan B. The negotiation agenda emerges from preparatory work on Plan B: the multiple risks identified, actions that might avoid or mitigate these risks, corrective actions to be taken when mitigation proves unsuccessful, payment for damages, procedures to make certain the people exercise informed consent, benefit-sharing arrangements, project scheduling, assumptions about the people's participation, and so on. Benefit distribution arrangements may or may not be part of these negotiations. Specifying which issues are non-negotiable is also useful. As each item on the agenda is brought forth, the cultural vision—folded into Plan B—provides guidance on when to harden and soften negotiating positions.

But who is authorized to negotiate? This is a critical question. Project promoters and their financiers prefer to deal with one person or with someone they designate as a spokesman. An important first step is to establish that the people—not the project promoter—decide who sits on the tribe's side of the table. It is sometimes effective to explain that unless indigenous people define who is present at a negotiation, the deal might "not stick." Equally important is the issue of transparency. Indigenous people are increasingly videotaping and tape-recording negotiations, not simply to confirm offers and counter-offers, but also to protect their own credibility with their people—confirming what they, as representatives, did and did not say.

As institutional arrangements are made, all parties must avoid the temptation to transfer responsibility for solving an unresolved issue to a third party. A company and people, for example, may agree to make the government responsible for environmental cleanups or impoverishment resulting from the project. At the Zimapan and Aguamilpas Dam, for example, the Mexican Federal Electricity Commission (CFE) was quick to assign the responsibility for cleaning up unresolved loose ends on a resettlement to ineffective, under-financed state governments. And in the negotiations between the IFC and ENDESA, both were willing to assign mitigation of risks to the Chilean government. The result in both cases was an unsatisfactory, illusory agreement. If third parties are being assigned responsibilities for mitigation or payment of costs, they must be party to the negotiations and consent to their role.

8. DRAWING UP AGREEMENTS

Negotiations must move beyond verbal understanding to produce concrete, legally binding agreements. Agreements may take on a wide range of forms, some of which are being reported in the *CSQ*. The Native Community of Infierno's Keieway Association's Participatory Agreement in Peru is noteworthy (see Stronza, *CSQ* 23:2). The community entered into full partnership with a private eco-tourism company that would ultimately transfer ownership to the community.

Given the legacy of the broken agreements, project promoters and indigenous peoples are justifiably wary of this phase of Plan B. In Third World countries, the judiciary may have a history of rulings against the people. This issue might be resolved through creative use of jurisdiction for the agreement. Consider the tactics of ENDESA and the IFC, for instance. Neither side appears to have trusted the other in Chilean courts, so they agreed to place their agreement under the jurisdiction of a willing judiciary external to their country—in this case, New York. The option of setting the jurisdiction for enforcement of an agreement outside the local system might be explored as a way to improve the chances of an acceptable Plan B. Multilateral financiers should also stand ready to underwrite the costs of Plan B preparation and independent legal representation for indigenous peoples.

Agreements contain standardized, contractual elements: cross-cutting commitments, financial and institutional arrangements, payment and performance schedules, and mechanisms for dispute resolution. Agreements, however, are also reflecting distinct indigenous concerns, including a focus on benefit-sharing arrangements, long-term commitments, providing for the group's children, training and technical assistance, shared ownership, future autonomous management, local employment, a minimal cultural and environmental footprint of the project, and provisions for waste disposal. Future issues of the *CSQ* will review specific options for different contractual elements.

VARYING CAPACITIES

Plan B preparations require time and money. The capacity of tribal groups to prepare a participatory Plan B varies greatly. The Pehuenche have only a handful of tribal members with secondary school education. Outspent by millions of dollars, they have jousted with one of the largest power companies in the world for more than 10 years. They still do not have tribal legal representation. Other tribes have the capacity to prepare Plan B's with minimal external technical assistance.

We feel that project promoters demonstrate good will and confidence in the proposed project when they are willing to underwrite some or all of the costs of Plan B. Alternatively, organizations active in Plan A should be willing to stand behind their commitment and pay some of the costs. This cost sharing must be undertaken without obligation on the part of the people. Because the promoter's access to capital may collapse as other opportunities come forward, project time lines are brutally short. Consequently, a people may be pushed to make decisions within a timeframe too brief for consensual agreements. Pressures to speed up the process should be folded back on the promoters. If they are in a hurry, then they should know that accelerating the schedule accelerates the costs of Plan B.

IMPACTS OF A GOOD PLAN B

At this point, it should be evident that a good Plan B is a plan for cultural survival, not a plan for surrender. A viable Plan B may be more important than a good Plan A. A willingness to prepare a Plan B indicates confidence and a desire to move beyond unequivocal support of or resistance to a project. The increasing number of reports in the *CSQ* of indigenous peoples throughout the world who are preparing their Plan B's is encouraging. A good plan does not end factionalism, but focuses discussions away from exhausting arguments and onto very specific topics. Plan B builds respect by redefining the project owners' and financiers' relationships with the people. The act of taking control—producing and ultimately implementing their Plan B—is a significant step toward self-determination. Plan B will alter project financing and economics, making clear the differences between payment for damages, risk mitigation, and benefit-sharing arrangements. And, most important of all, by laying out a project's full social and economic dimensions, a good Plan B influences whether or not Plan A ever takes place.

Carmen Garcia-Downing (cgarciad@ahsc.arizona.edu), a Zapotec Indian, is on the faculty at the University of Arizona School of Public Health and an indigenous affairs specialist for the World Health Organization's Border Health Collaborating Center in Tucson. Her husband, Ted Downing (downing@u.arizona.edu), was raised by George Downing, his full-blood Cherokee stepfather. He is on the Advisory Board of Cultural Survival and is the research professor of social development at the University of Arizona. Ted and Carmen have worked as a team for many years and in many countries, specializing in training local indigenous peoples in computer skills, advocacy, evaluation, and research skills. This article emerges from an ongoing cooperative project with a team from the Universidad de Concepción on monitoring involuntary resettlement in the Alto Bio Bio, sponsored by the Chilean National Fund for Development of Science and Technology (FONDCYT); Claudio Gonzales Parra, and Alejandro Diaz Mujica, principal investigators.

Acknowledgments

The authors are grateful to Yuri Downing, Jerry Moles, and Scott Robinson for their constructive suggestions on earlier drafts.

References and Further Reading

Cernea, M. & McDowell, C., Eds. (2000). *Risks and Reconstruction: Experiences of Resettlers and Refugees.* Washington: The World Bank.

Downing, T. & Restrepo, I. (1980). New Technology and Dry Land Agriculture. *Culture and Agriculture 7*, pp. 1–7. See also www.ted-downing.com.

Downing, T. (1996). Mitigating Social Impoverishment when People are Involuntarily Displaced. In *Understanding Impoverishment: The Consequences of Development-Induced Displacement.* McDowell, C., Ed. Oxford and Providence, RI: Berghahn Press. See also www.ted-downing.com.

The World Bank. (1994). Resettlement and Development: The Bankwide Review of Projects Involving Involuntary Resettlement, 1986–1993. Environment Department Paper No. 32. Washington: The World Bank.

Tradition: Cultural Solutions to Human Needs

Jerry Moles

The ecological sciences are discovering that the natural and cultural realms are not only more complicated than we think, but more complicated than we *can* think. Yet development specialists, pressured by their employers to make progress, have not paid attention to this lesson. They continue to devise plans and projects that reflect value systems incompatible with the values of local cultures in significant and subtle ways. (Goulet, 1980) It's not surprising that many well-intended development projects have unintended and often devastating consequences for local communities. A series of demonstrations in Sri Lanka shows that with an in-depth understanding of local systems and an appreciation of cultural values, projects can be designed that serve community needs without disrupting the social and cultural fabric. Solutions, it turns out, are not just technological, agronomic, silvicultural, or economic, but rather entail a holistic approach to people's life-spaces.

Sri Lanka is an ancient land with a written history stretching back more than 2,400 years. Long before the contemporary notion of nation-states, the island once called Serendib was ruled by tribal leaders and then by both Singalese and Tamil monarchs. Roughly the size of Costa Rica or the state of West Virginia in the United States, the island had three colonial masters—the Portuguese, Dutch, and British—before gaining its independence in 1949. While the Portuguese and Dutch were primarily interested in the extraction of tropical commodities, the British wanted more. They envisioned a tropical version of their government and economy, with English as the language of the bureaucracy and international trade.

The island is home to four ethnic groups: the predominately Buddhist Singalese, the predominately Hindu Tamils, the Tamil-speaking Muslims, and the indigenous Veddas. The history of conflict, cooperation, and coalitions among the former three is long; each struggled to gain increasing control over resources and the allocation of benefits. The British seized control of the educational system, producing people to serve their administrative needs. Promising youths from all three major ethnic groups were sent to England for advanced training in law, medicine, agriculture, warfare, and management. After more than 100 years of British colonial domination, many of the leaders poised to assume power at independence were predisposed to continue the lead of the colonial masters in establishing an export-oriented economy and a parliamentary system with a prime minister directing government services.

A SOCIAL SOLUTION TO INCREASED RICE PRODUCTION

The rush to follow the lead of the colonists did not go unnoticed or unquestioned. Ananda Coomaraswamy (1947), Sri Lankan philosopher and art historian, commented, "We who call art 'significant,' knowing not of what, are also proud to 'progress,' we know not whither." The leadership began to adopt technologies without understanding their long-term environmental, economic, social, or cultural consequences.

In the early 1960s, Upali Senanayake, son of the patriot who led the struggle against British domination, asked why the importation of foodstuffs and national debt were increasing. Unable to gain satisfactory answers from British-trained scientists and government administrators, he

Source: Reprinted from *Cultural Survival Quarterly*, Fall 2001.

returned to the village to practice traditional agriculture and focused on rice, the primary staple. His solution turned out to be social rather than agricultural. While he found that he could plow and plant his fields, he could not control the weeds that diminished yields. Traditionally, the village priests declared a holiday when the time came to weed the paddy. Yet under British administration, the European calendar determined the school year and the labor of the young was no longer available to cultivators. Returning to the traditional solution of putting the children in the fields required the cooperation of the Ministry of Education and of other ministries responsible for agricultural programs.

Mr. Senanayake, in the face of a leadership dedicated to the modernization of agriculture, appealed to then Prime Minister Dudley Senanayake, a cousin, to allow children to be absent from school to weed the paddy. After directing such an aggressive campaign that he suffered a mild heart attack, Mr. Upali Senanayake was rewarded with permission to organize the relevant government ministries and farming villages. Over 640,000 school children entered the paddy fields accompanied by village musicians and removed the weeds. The results were remarkable. Rice production increased by five bushels per acre and continued for four years. Yet political opposition put an end to the program (Moles & Melvani; Moles, 1984) because Mr. Senanayake's organization of 640,000 future voters made him a threat to aspiring politicians. Yields dropped five bushels in the subsequent season.

A TRUST DEDICATED TO ALTERNATIVE VISIONS OF THE FUTURE

While dismayed that the weeding campaign couldn't continue, the demonstrated success of traditional practices emboldened Mr. Senanayake to establish the National Heritage Trust of Sri Lanka as a nongovernmental organization (NGO). Arguing that the people have lost the right of self-determination in selecting their future, he envisioned the Trust as an educational medium, a "mirror reflecting back to the people

their history and culture." The Trust's role was to provide the broader community with a way of comparing their current means with alternatives proposed by those promoting different forestry and agricultural technologies. What is known to serve the people is that which has served them in the past. Accepting the unknown and untried is stepping into mystery, and in terms of food supply and environmental health, mystery may come at an unacceptable cost.

A SOCIAL SOLUTION TO INCREASED IRRIGATION WATER

The Trust was offered as a solution to increased agricultural productivity and as an alternative to blind acceptance of or opposition to colonial practices. The Trust was Plan B (see Downing and Downing-Garcia, [in this text]). Aware that the new technologies substituted capital for both labor and land, Mr. Senanayake argued that labor was not the limiting factor in production. Turning Western economic analysis on its head, he drew on traditional agriculture in Asia that demonstrated incremental increases in production with increased application of labor.

Government ears were closed to his pleas, so he turned to his traditional Singalese community to create yet another demonstration of the value of traditional practice. With the assistance of the Buddhist clergy, he organized 50,000 farmers to desilt the tanks—earthern reservoirs—that had filled because the British stopped the traditional *rajakaria*, the organization of thousands of men for public works, including the maintenance of the irrigation systems. As a result of the desilting, adequate water for two harvests per year was available and farmers experienced increases in rice yields of 100 to 400 percent. (Moles & Melvani, 1984)

According to Mr. Senanayake, what it meant to be Singalese was expressed in the traditional agricultural practices, the Buddhist temples that served to organize public works within the communities, and in the villagers themselves. Again, despite the successful demonstration, opposition to the campaign to desilt the reservoirs brought it to an end.

IMPROVING PERFORMANCE OF TRADITIONAL MANAGEMENT

In the late 1970s, Mr. Upali Senanayake's son, Ranil, returned to the island with a doctorate in systems ecology to explore in greater depth the ecological wisdom of traditional agricultural knowledge. He could see—as could traditional cultivators—the cultural and environmental costs of changes in management practices. The British had "modernized" the upland region by planting first coffee and then tea at the expense of most native montane forests and with the result of massive changes in resource availability and damage to the landscape's productive capacity. After attaining independence, and with an ever-increasing population, many of those in leadership positions proclaimed the need to modernize or perish. Agricultural leaders, trained first in the United Kingdom and later in Western Europe, North America, and Australia, looked to the outside for answers rather than looking at the strengths and weaknesses of the existing land management system. And yet these proponents of change offered only generic solutions. Armed with an environmentally and culturally destructive approach, they asked one-dimensional questions and found one-dimensional solutions. In response to the need for wood for cooking, the drying of tea, and the making of bricks and tiles, for example; thousands of acres were planted with exotic trees (both eucalyptus and pinus species), replacing the native forests and untold numbers of native species as habitats disappeared. Forest fires became endemic, soil loss was horrendous, and the plant material used for food, oil, fiber, and medicines became unavailable. Again, there was a traditional alternative: the forest gardens on the hills alongside the paddy fields provided food, fodder, fiber, fuel, oil, and raw material for medicines. The traditional economy that served as the backbone of the Singalese culture—and, with it, local control over life's circumstances—was being lost.

The traditional forest gardens provide many of the same environmental services as do the native forests, building soil, improving water quality, and protecting native biodiversity. Ranil Senanayake and I founded the NeoSynthesis Research Centre (NSRC) in 1982 as an NGO to (1) use contemporary ecological sciences to evaluate traditional practices and the alternatives proposed by government, international, and bilateral agencies, and (2) establish on-the-ground experiments in sustainable land management. From the perspective proposed by Downing and Downing-Garcia in this [text], NSRC is an incubator of environmentally sustainable Plan Bs.

The forest gardens were seemingly sustainable, having existed for more than two thousand years. A 14-acre abandoned tea estate was purchased to serve as an experimental station to explore the proposition of improving the gardens' productive and economic benefits. The goal was not to change traditional practices or challenge cultural forms, but rather to improve the performance of practices already understood. The focus was on intensifying the production of the forest gardens by selecting planting materials based on yields, changing the gardens' species compositions to increase incomes, improving the processing of existing crops, introducing new crops compatible with the ecology of the gardens and cultural practices, and composting to provide additional nutrients. Rather than changing technologies, requiring new tools, and changing cultural practices, the villagers managed their gardens as they had in the past.

The NSRC first provided the planting materials to improve the gardens' performance, and when demand outstripped supply, solutions were found within the villages as Buddhist temples turned over their grounds to produce planting materials and local entrepreneurs established small nurseries to serve local needs. In a two-year period, 101,795 plants were produced in nine participating villages.

Beyond the financial returns, there were environmental rewards. At the moment the population of an increasingly crowded island nation approached 19 million—five million more than in Australia—the plight of native species was dire and the rate of decline in biodiversity indexes increasing. By expanding the forest gardens to areas where the primary forest had been removed and turned into tea estates and pasture, habitats were established for rare and endangered creatures. Through educational programs, the NSRC staff shared their knowledge of the native flora and fauna and of how specific species could be protected at minimal cost to villagers. Clubs were set up in local schools and students volunteered to follow specific species, describing their habitats and recording their movements. Local environmental organizations shared their knowledge, research skills, and teaching capacities to assist in the effort.

Such a "back to the future" approach to forestry and agricultural improvement was not without its detractors, who had accepted the "modern" as inherently "better" than the traditional, yet villagers responded by the thousands. Happy that the approach fit within traditional village resource management and cultural practices and did not require additional indebtedness to participate, they visited the research center to see with their own eyes the transformation of the abandoned tea estate and the goods being produced there. Many offered their own lands for experimentation. At one point, an extension office near the experimental station was closed because the heavy demand for information and planting materials could not be met. With a limited budget, the NSRC had no means to expand services at that time. Nonetheless, the program's influence continued to reach farmers across the island. Other NGOs asked to have their staff trained to serve as village level extension agents, government funds were allocated to replicate the establishment of nurseries on temple grounds, and information on the program's success was incorporated into training programs for government-supported extension agents. Bilateral funding agencies financed parts of the experimental and extension programs and an international NGO served as a broker with the U.S. Agency for International Development to continue a multiple-year experiment in six agro-eco zones with careful documentation of village responses.

Villagers' increasing incomes also enhance their ability to maintain traditional cultural practices. As is the case in many agricultural communities, Sri Lankan cultivators are often at the mercy of middle-persons, processors, and distributors in setting farm-gate prices. To increase incomes and gain recognition and position in the domestic and international marketplace, and to give consumers the opportunity to "vote" on the value of the NSRC effort through their purchases, an innovative certification program has been established, entitled "Forest Garden Products." These products are created according to specifications based on the traditional practices of indigenous forest gardeners. Inspectors from an independent certification NGO are responsible for overseeing the program. The program's produce meets international organic standards and its production technology fulfills its goals of erosion control, maintenance of a forest structure, and habitat maintenance for local species. As a consequence, the villagers receive an income premium for their participation in the program. Forest Garden Products are now sold in North America, Western Europe, Japan, and Australia.

THE SPREAD OF BENEFICIAL PLAN Bs

As word spread of the NSRC's success, indigenous groups, peasant communities, and environmental groups have requested technical information. At present, efforts following the NSRC's lead are under way to protect traditional cultures, native species, and community economies in the Philippines, Zimbabwe, Canada, the United States, Mexico, Costa Rica, Ecuador, and Peru. This approach to forest gardens is called analog forestry; forest gardens are analogous to, or mimic, the environmental structure and function in native climax forests (Senanayake & Jack, 1998).

Other people, once or still dependent on forest products and facing the destruction of their forests, found the approach of improving existing systems and protecting both ecological and cultural heritages worthwhile. As noted by numerous indigenous peoples from around the world (see Senanayake, 1999), culture and environment are a seamless whole. An understanding of our surroundings and ways of dealing with other species is part of how we understand ourselves and our neighbors. Change within cultural and biological systems is a part of a continual process of adaptation in a dynamic universe, and both systems must be protected to survive.

The question for forest gardeners in Sri Lanka was whether they could preserve the way of life their ancestors had maintained for more than 2,000 years in the face of a growing population and increased pressures from the outside to adopt exotic technologies. Their solution ultimately came from the self-determination of thousands of villagers who decided that the protection and improvement of the forest gardens makes sense given their identity and present circumstances. As long as the forest gardens and paddy fields remain, a major element of Singalese culture continues.

Survival as a community and as a people entails having the right of self-determination. A Plan B that makes sense to local communities, requires minimal investment or indebtedness, and fits into current understandings and practices has a high likelihood of being adopted. The lesson to be drawn from these experiments is that culture and agriculture are indivisible. Traditional wisdom and knowledge—building on thousands of years of trial and error—are embedded in the carefully programmed relationship between people and nature.

Jerry A. Moles (jmoles@mac.com), an applied social scientist, serves as a co-chairman of the management committee of the NeoSynthesis Research Centre, and works with the New River Land Trust and the Blue Ridge Forest Cooperative. He has taught university, designed a plan for the future of California redwoods, and, on behalf of the California Resources Agency, mediated the dispute between the timber industry and the environmental community over the implementation of the Endangered Species Act (spotted owl) in seven counties in north-western California. He has assisted in establishing an organic industry in Sri Lanka, has served as a founding board member of the Watershed Research and Training Center in Hayfork, California, has assisted in designing eco-tourism programs in Costa Rica and West Virginia, and manages 230 acres of forestland in southwestern Virginia.

References and Further Reading

Coomaraswamy, A. K. (1947). *Am I My Brother's Keeper?* New York: John Day Company.

Goulet, D. A. (1980). Development Experts: The One-Eyed Giants. *World Development* 8 (7/8), pp. 481–489.

Moles, J. A. & Melvani, K. (1984). Future of Agriculture in Sri Lanka—A Clash of Values: Buddhism vs. Western Materialism. In *Agriculture, Change, and Human Values: Proceedings of a Multidisciplinary Conference.* Gainesville, Florida: Humanities and Agriculture Program, University of Florida.

Moles, J. A. & Riker, J. V. (1984). Hope, Ideas, and Our Only Alternative—Ourselves and Our Value: National Heritage and the Future of Sri Lanka Agriculture. In *Agricultural Sustainability in a Changing World Order.* Douglass, G. K., Ed. Boulder, Colorado: Westview Press.

Senanayake, R. F. (1999). Voices of the Earth. In *Cultural and Spiritual Values of Biodiversity.* Posey, D.A., Ed. Nairobi, Kenya: United Nations Environmental Programme.

Senanayake, R. F., & Jack, J. (1998). *Analogue Forestry: An Introduction.* Melbourne, Australia: Monash University Publications in Geography, Number 49. Department of Geography and Environmental Science.

The Lakota Fund: Local Institutions & Access to Credit

Monica Terkildsen and Kathleen Pickering

Access to credit has consistently been identified as one of the key elements necessary to increase economic capital and stimulate economic development, on or off Indian reservations. World Bank economists claim that the problem of gaining access to credit is an important determinant in low-income areas' participation in the economic growth of a country (Binswanger & Deininger, 1997; Mushinski, 1999). Indigenous communities often lack the collateral necessary to secure bank loans. They also commonly lack social or personal ties with bankers or investors. Financial institutions are typically associated with the settler communities that historically appropriated indigenous lands and resources. Indigenous poverty is also perpetuated by institutions at the local level that are controlled by the descendents of colonists and settlers and reflect historically constructed class, race, and culture divides (Ward, 1998). Alternative, indigenous-controlled institutions are needed to provide both economic capital and social linkages for historically excluded communities.

THE RESERVATION CONTEXT

The Pine Ridge Indian Reservation, established in 1889, is home to the Oglala Sioux Tribe. Located in a remote region of southwestern South Dakota, the Reservation is as big as the state of Connecticut and has a population of 11,000 to 35,000 residents.[1]

The Reservation presents a special challenge to economic development because development depends on effective access to and investment of several forms of capital, including financial capital, human capital, and social capital. The Reservation encompasses the county with the highest level of poverty in the last two United States Decennial Censuses. (Pickering, 2000) Low-income households do not have sufficient assets for collateral or sufficient assets to finance business projects.

High poverty rates also tend to be associated with low levels of education, which undercut the critical element of human capital needed for business development—the value found in people's knowledge and skills. In the 1990 Census, 55.8 percent of American Indians from the Pine Ridge Reservation had high school diplomas or higher, and 32.3 percent had some college or higher. In the U.S. population, 75 percent had high school diplomas or higher, and 45 percent had some college or higher.

Unemployment and underemployment are major concerns on the Reservation. Those with higher household and per capita incomes tend to be people with full-time employment, especially tribal or federal government jobs. Unemployment rates for the Reservation are deplorable. In 1999, the Bureau of Indian Affairs (BIA) reported 73 percent unemployment on the Reservation, although some speculate that unemployment is even higher. Since few people are able to locate full-time, year-round positions, they must piece together short-term or part-time jobs, making underemployment common. (Pickering, 2000) As a result, interest in starting small businesses to create jobs for unused and underutilized local people is growing.

FORMAL BANKING INSTITUTIONS

There is no bank on the vast Pine Ridge Reservation; most residents must travel to towns bordering the Reservation—between 40 and 180 miles

Source: Reprinted from *Cultural Survival Quarterly,* Fall 2001.

round trip—to take care of their banking needs. Lakota access to formal credit is dependent on institutions controlled by non-Indians in Reservation border towns. Yet these towns have a long history of racial tension and hostility toward Indians. Many Reservation residents feel oppressed by racial and cultural discrimination in border town banks. Said one Lakota businessman, "... the bank wouldn't give me a loan because I'm an Indian." Without local banking relationships, individual access to formal credit for economic development on the Reservation is severely limited. Some consumer loans are available when items purchased with them—such as cars or trailers—can serve as collateral, or when regularly deposited checks are used to secure small cash advances. But given Reservation poverty and the history of federal government housing programs dominating the housing market, potential Lakota commercial borrowers are less likely to have significant assets—like mortgages and privately owned houses—with which to secure loans with traditional banking institutions.

To the extent that credit is available, it is significantly easier to obtain for consumption purposes than for business purposes. (Pickering & Mushinski, 2001) And when capital is accessed for consumption loans it is removed from the Reservation to border town stores and enterprises and does not generate additional income and jobs within the Reservation. Lakota business people often express frustration with the limited level of communication they are able to establish with formal banks, even those they have accounts with. Small business owners running convenience stores, tourist operations, consulting businesses, or small-scale agricultural enterprises consistently express the need for additional credit.

THE LAKOTA FUND

To offset these barriers, the Lakota Fund was established in 1986 as a project of the First Nations Financial Project. A Lakota-controlled financial institution in the village of Kyle on the Reservation, it was established with an initial loan fund of $400,000 from the Ford Foundation. Its purpose was to make loans available for Lakota micro-entrepreneurs and small business

people. The Lakota Fund has provided varying levels of credit through several different programs over the years (Mushinski & Pickering, 1996; Pickering & Mushinski, 2001). Circle Banking was a form of peer group lending that provided loans of between $100 and $1000 to individuals willing to accept the obligation to repay loans for other members of their circle. The Lakota Fund is currently providing this same range of small loans to individuals with standard or alternative forms of collateral, like beadwork or family heirlooms. It has also provided individual loans of between $1,000 and $25,000 for small businesses with collateral. The Fund requires that a series of training courses be attended before any individual is eligible for a loan. The training curriculum, entitled *"Tokatakiya Iciskanpo:* Prepare for the Future," includes sessions on nation-building and capital, personal goals and skills, marketing, budgeting, bookkeeping, financial statements, human resources, and family dynamics.

BENEFITS OF LOCAL INSTITUTIONS

In contrast to border town banks, the Lakota Fund, an indigenous Plan B (see Downing and Downing-Garcia, this [text]), is a community development financial institution functioning inside the social capital networks of the Reservation. It is able to use local information unavailable to or unsolicited by banks. Through better access to information about local residents and lower costs of monitoring its local borrowers, the Lakota Fund is able to reduce some of the problems associated with off-Reservation banks. It could use local knowledge of applicants, for example, to extend credit to business people who had isolated and unrepresentative problems with their credit history. As one small business participant explained:

> I couldn't get a bank loan because of bankruptcy over our ranch, and that was because the bankers lied across the table. At the Lakota Fund, they're willing to help out and to sit down and listen to you, and not be afraid. Just because we had to file bankruptcy on the ranch, that didn't shut

my business career off. Indian people can go and get a loan without feeling that they are discriminated against. At Lakota Fund, they understand; they know our way of life.

As a result, residents consider the Lakota Fund to be the only source of business credit on the Reservation. To date, the Fund has offered technical assistance to 2,525 individuals and provided $1.9 million in loans. Among microenterprise loans, approximately 80 percent of the borrowers have been women, and approximately 30 percent of the larger business loans have been extended to women. The Lakota Fund currently has a 10 percent default rate across all loan programs. It was instrumental in getting a debt collection code enacted by the tribal council to improve the performance of the tribal court system in responding to commercial cases.

The Lakota Fund has been particularly effective in tailoring its assessment of collateral resources to the social, legal, and cultural context of the Reservation. Collateral requirements can have a notable impact on household access to credit in low-income areas. (Swaminathan, 1991) Such wealth-biased access to credit is even more insidious because it may restrict low-wealth households from participating in a country's economic development, producing unbalanced growth. (Binswanger & Deininger, 1997; Carter et al., 1994) Substantial numbers of both Lakota Fund microentrepreneurs and small business people reported having insufficient collateral to seek a bank loan for their business. (Pickering & Mushinski, 2001)

The Lakota Fund also has a better understanding of the unique legal conditions on the Reservation that create obstacles for Lakota business people attempting to marshal their assets for finance capital. The nature of land ownership for Reservation residents, for example, has a direct impact on access to credit. In general, land is a desirable form of collateral (Swaminathan, 1991). Most Lakota landowners, however, own allotted land that is held in trust by the federal government, and may have an undivided interest in land held by multiple heirs. While banks are, in theory, willing to consider trust land as collateral for loans, the reality is that the bureaucratic

delays and uncertainties associated with using trust land as collateral and with foreclosing on it make it an undesirable option. (Shepherd, 1997) In contrast to border town banks, the Lakota Fund is willing to consider trust land as collateral without requiring borrowers to go through the lengthy bureaucratic process of taking the land out of trust. It combines confidence in borrowers' ability to repay with knowledge of federal and tribal land policies and procedures should a default take place.

Also important to Reservation residents is the atmosphere at the Lakota Fund. As one resident noted, "They didn't look down on us like the banks did. . . ." The discrimination and racial tension associated with border town banks were not mentioned by borrowers discussing the Lakota Fund. As one Lakota Fund participant recalled, "It was people you can talk to and they were more willing to help. You didn't feel threatened by going and talking to them about what you wanted to do. It was just easier because I'm Native American and some of the workers are too. It was easy to converse there rather than go to the local bank. I wouldn't even try going [to the bank] up here." Having Lakota Fund personnel who speak the Lakota language was mentioned as another advantage over banks.

The Lakota Fund's provision of training in preparation for obtaining a loan uses social capital to expand the community's human capital. In effect, the Lakota Fund is focusing on increasing human capital along with its injection into the local economy of financial capital. The recipients of small business loans from the Lakota Fund described many ways in which this type of advice is valuable in saving money and avoiding business pitfalls. Other participants discussed the hands-on technical assistance provided by the Lakota Fund.

Through its increasing participation in the social networks of Lakota businesses, the Lakota Fund is developing important organizational integrity. The Fund is providing coherence, competence, and capacity with which to supplement economic development on the Reservation. It is able to bypass the border town banks and create macro-level synergies by tapping previously unused social relationships. Over the years, the Lakota Fund has attracted socially responsible investors for their lending capital from such major U.S. cities as Boston and San Francisco, who are willing to accept up to a 3 percent return for an investment of at least one year.

Like other Plan Bs around the world, the Lakota Fund for Native Americans on the Pine Ridge Reservation has helped an indigenous people cope with the results of a long history of prejudice and surmount obstacles to economic and cultural survival.

Monica Terkildsen is a loan officer for The Lakota Fund. She can be reached at olntbic@qwtc.net. Kathleen Pickering is associate professor in the department of anthropology at Colorado State University. She can be reached at Kathleen.Pickering@colostate.edu.

Acknowledgments

The authors would like to thank the participants in Lakota Fund programs and the Lakota Fund staff for their help in providing information for this article.

Notes

1. The current Reservation population count is uncertain, in large part, because estimates are based on the results of the 1990 U.S. Census, which seriously undercounted the population at 11,006 American Indian residents. The late 1990s saw an influx of people to the Reservation because of the imposition of welfare reform and the perception that regulations governing TANF (Temporary Assistance to Needy Families) are less stringent on the Reservation. The Oglala Sioux Tribe estimates the current population at 35,000.

References and Further Reading

Aoki, A. & Chatman, D. (1997, April). *An Economic Development Policy for the Oglala Nation.* Harvard Project on American Indian Economic Development.

Binswanger, H. & Deininger, L. (1997). Explaining Agricultural and Agrarian Policies in Developing Countries. *Journal of Economic Literature* XXXV:4, pp. 1958–2005.

Carter, M., Barham, B., Boucher, S. & Zegarra, E. (1994). *Closing the Financial Efficiency Gap: The Role and Design of Cooperative Financial Intermediaries in Low Income Countries.* Unpublished: University of Wisconsin–Madison.

Drabenstott, M. (1999, Spring). Rethinking Rural America's Financial Markets. *Forum for Applied Research and Public Policy* 14:1, pp. 96–100.

Mushinski, D. W. (1999). An Analysis of Offer Functions of Banks and Credit Unions in Guatemala. *Journal of Development Studies* 36:2, pp. 87–111.

Mushinski, D. W. & Pickering, K. (2001). *Credit Access for Indian-Owned Small Businesses—The Overlooked Need.* Unpublished Manuscript.

Mushinski, D. W. & Pickering, K. (1996). Micro-enterprise Credit in Indian Country. *Research in Human Capital and Development* 10, pp. 147–169.

Pickering, K. (2000). *Lakota Culture, World Economy.* Lincoln: University of Nebraska Press.

Pickering, K. & Mushinski, D. (2001). Cultural Aspects of Credit Institutions: Transplanting the Grameen Bank Credit Group Structure to the Pine Ridge Indian Reservation. *Journal of Economic Issues* 26, pp. 2.

Shepherd, D. (1997, October). The Native American Housing Market. *The Journal of Lending and Credit Risk Management* 80:2, pp. 36–39.

Swaminathan, M. (1991). Segmentation, Collateral Undervaluation, and the Rate of Interest in Agrarian Credit Markets: Some Evidence from Two Villages in South India. *Cambridge Journal of Economics* 146:2, pp. 161–178.

Ward, C. (1998). The Importance of Context in Explaining Human Capital Formation and Labor Force Participation on American Indians in Rosebud County, Montana. *Rural Sociology* 63:3, pp. 451–480.

CRITICAL THINKING QUESTIONS

The three previous articles discuss development projects and their impacts on traditional peoples. Both Plan A's and Plan B's approach to development are defined and discussed.

1. What do Plan A advocates, those either for or against a project, have in common with one another?
2. Why do so many well-intentioned development projects often have unintended and disastrous consequences? Select an example of such a project from one of the articles; briefly discuss its intended goals and its actual results.
3. What do Downing and Garcia-Downing identify as the eight components of a good Plan B?
4. What role do information and community relationships play in aboriginal communities? How can these roles be effectively employed to disseminate new information from the outside world throughout indigenous communities?

The Social Psychology
of Modern Slavery

Kevin Bales

For Meera, the revolution began with a single rupee. When a social worker came across Meera's unmapped village in the hills of Uttar Pradesh in India three years ago, he found that the entire population was in hereditary debt bondage. It could have been in the time of their grandfathers or great-grandfathers—few in the village could remember—but at some point in their past, the families had pledged themselves to unpaid labor in return for loans of money. The debt passed down through the generations. Children as young as five years old worked in quarry pits, making sand by crushing stones with hammers. Dust, flying rock chips and heavy loads had left many villagers with silicosis and injured eyes or backs.

Calling together some of the women, the social worker proposed a radical plan. If groups of 10 women agreed to set aside a single rupee a week from the tiny sums the moneylenders gave them to buy rice, he would provide seed money and keep the funds safe. Meera and nine others formed the first group. The rupees slowly mounted up. After three months, the group had enough to pay off the loan against which Meera was bonded. She began earning money for her work, which greatly increased the amount she could contribute to the group. In another two months, another woman was freed; the following month, a third came out of bondage.

At that point, the other members, seeing that freedom was possible, simply renounced their debts and declared themselves free. The moneylenders quickly moved against them, threatening them and driving them from the quarries. But the women were able to find jobs in other quarries. New groups followed their example. The social worker has taken me to the village twice, and on my second visit, all its inhabitants were free and all their children in school.

Less than 100 kilometers away, the land turns flat and fertile. Debt bondage is common there, too. When I met Baldev in 1997, he was plowing. His master called him "my *halvaha*," meaning "my bonded plowman." Two years later I met Baldev again and learned that because of a windfall from a relative, he had freed himself from debt. But he had not freed himself from bondage. He told me:

> After my wife received this money, we paid off our debt and were free to do whatever we wanted. But I was worried all the time—what if one of the children got sick? What if our crop failed? What if the government wanted some money? Since we no longer belonged to the landlord, we didn't get food every day as before. Finally, I went to the landlord and asked him to take me back. I didn't have to borrow any money, but he agreed to let me be his *halvaha* again. Now I don't worry so much; I know what to do.

Lacking any preparation for freedom, Baldev re-enrolled in slavery. Without financial or emotional support, his accidental emancipation didn't last. Although he may not bequeath any debt to his children, his family is visibly worse off than unbonded villagers in the same region.

To many people, it comes as a surprise that debt bondage and other forms of slavery persist into the 21st century. Every country, after all, has made it illegal to own and exercise total control over another human being. And yet there are people like Baldev who remain enslaved—by my estimate, which is based on a compilation of reports from governments and nongovernmental organizations, perhaps 27 million of them around the world. If slaveholders no longer own slaves in a legal sense, how can they still exercise so much control that freed slaves sometimes deliver themselves back into bondage? This is just one of the puzzles that make slavery the greatest challenge faced by the social sciences today.

Despite being among the oldest and most persistent forms of human relationships, found in most societies at one time or another, slavery is little understood. Although historians have built up a sizable literature on antebellum American slavery, other types have barely been studied. It is as if our understanding of all arachnids were based on clues left by a single species of extinct spider. In our present state of ignorance, we have little hope of truly eradicating slavery, of making sure that Meera, rather than Baldev, becomes the model.

THE NEW SLAVERY

Researchers do know that slavery is both evolving and increasing in raw numbers. Like spiders, it permeates our world, typically hidden in the dark spaces of the economy. Over the past few years, journalists and activists have documented numerous examples. Human trafficking—the involuntary smuggling of people between countries, often by organized crime—has become a huge concern, especially in Europe and Southeast Asia. Many people, lured by economic opportunities, pay smugglers to slip them across borders but then find themselves sold to sweatshops, brothels or domestic service to pay for their passage; others are kidnapped and smuggled against their will. In certain areas, notably Brazil and West Africa, laborers have been enticed into signing contracts and then taken to remote plantations and prevented from leaving. In parts of South Asia and North Africa, slavery is a millennia-old tradition that has never truly ended.

The plight of these people has drawn the attention of governments and organizations as diverse as the Vatican, the United Nations, the International Organization for Migration, and Amnesty International. Two years ago the U.S. government established a central coordinating office to deal with human trafficking. Academic researchers are beginning to conduct intensive studies. The anecdotal and journalistic approach is slowly transforming into the more rigorous inquiry of social science. For example, Urs Peter Ruf of the University of Bielefeld in Germany has documented the evolution of master–slave relations in modern Mauritania. Louise Brown of the University of Birmingham in England has studied women forced into prostitution in Asia. David Kyle of the University of California at Davis and Rey Koslowski of Rutgers University have explored human smuggling. I have posited a theory of global slavery and tested it through case studies in five countries.

A common question is why these practices should be called slavery rather than just another form of superexploitation. The answer is simple. Throughout history, slavery has meant a loss of free will and choice backed up by violence, sometimes exercised by the slaveholder, sometimes by elements of the state. That is exactly what other researchers and I have observed. Granted, workers at the bottom of the economic ladder have few options to begin with, but at some point on the continuum of exploitation, even those options are lost. These workers are unable to walk away.

Human suffering comes in various guises, yet slavery has a distinctive horror that is evident to those of us who have seen it in the flesh. Even when it does not involve beating or other physical torture, it brings about a psychological degradation that often renders victims unable to function in the outside world. "I've worked in prisons and with cases of domestic violence," says Sydney Lytton, an American psychiatrist who has counseled freed slaves. "This is worse."

Although each of the manifestations of slavery has unique local characteristics, one of the aims of social scientists is to understand their universal features, so that therapies developed in one place can be applied elsewhere. Foremost among these commonalities is the basic economic equation. In 1850 an agricultural slave cost $1,500 in Alabama (around $30,000 in today's dollars). The equivalent laborer can be had for around $100 today. That payment might be made as part of a "loan" or as a "fee" to a trafficker. A young woman in Southeast Asia or eastern Europe might be sold several times, through a series of brokers and pimps, before she ends up in a brothel.

One should not read too much into these specific dollar amounts, because what the slaveholder purchases is somewhat different in each case. The basic point is that forced labor represents a much smaller percentage of business expenses than it used to. It took 20 years of labor for an antebellum American slave to repay his or her purchase price and maintenance costs; today it takes two years for a bonded laborer in South Asia to do the same. This fall in price has altered not only the profitability of slavery but also the relationship between a slave and master. The expensive slave of the past was a protected investment; today's slave is a cheap and disposable input to low-level production. The slaveholder has little incentive to provide health care or to take care of slaves who are past their prime.

Several trends could account for this shift. The world's population has tripled since World War II, producing a glut of potential slaves. Meanwhile the economic transformation of the developing world has, whatever its benefits, included the loss of community and social safety nets, matched by the erection of vast shantytowns. But the vulnerability of large numbers of people does not make them slaves; for that, you need violence. The key factor in the persistence of slavery is the weak rule of law in many regions. Widespread corruption of government and police allows violence to be used with impunity even when slavery is nominally illegal.

FREE YOUR MIND INSTEAD

A second commonality among different forms of slavery is the psychological manipulation they all involve. The widely held conception of a slave is someone in chains who would escape if given half a chance or who simply does not know better. But Meera's and Baldev's stories, among numerous others, suggest that this view is naive. In my experience, slaves often know that their enslavement is illegal. Force, violence and psychological coercion have convinced them to accept it. When slaves begin to accept their role and identify with their master, constant physical bondage becomes unnecessary. They come to perceive their situation not as a deliberate action

taken to harm them in particular but as part of the normal, if regrettable, scheme of things.

One young woman I met in northeastern Thailand, Siri, has a typical story. A woman approached her parents, offered to find their 14-year-old daughter a job, and advanced them 50,000 baht (at the time, about $2,000) against her future income. The broker transferred Siri to a low-end brothel for twice that sum. When she tried to escape, her debt was doubled again. She was told to repay it, as well as a monthly rent of 30,000 baht, from her earnings of 100 baht per customer.

Siri had little idea what it meant to be a prostitute. Her initiation took the form of assault and rape. Shattered, the teenager had to find a way to carry on with life. In the world in which she lived, there were only those with total power and those with no power. Reward and punishment came from a single source, the pimp. Young women in Siri's position often find building a relationship with the pimp to be a good survival strategy. Although pimps are thugs, they do not rely solely on violence. They are adept at fostering insecurity and dependence.

Cultural norms have prepared these young women for control and compliance. A girl will be told how her parents will suffer if she does not cooperate and work hard, how the debt is on her shoulders and must be repaid. Thai sex roles are clearly defined, and women are expected to be retiring, nonassertive and obedient—as the women are repeatedly reminded. The pimps also cite religion. The young women are encouraged to believe that they must have committed terrible sins in a past life to deserve their enslavement and abuse. They are urged to accept this karmic debt, to come to terms with it and to reconcile themselves to their fate.

To live in slavery, the young women often redefine their bondage as a duty or a job or a form of penance. To accept their role and the pimp's, they must try to diminish their view of themselves as victims who have been wronged. They must begin to see their enslavement from the point of view of the slaveholder. At the time of my visit, the women in Siri's brothel were at various stages in this process of submission. Some were even allowed to visit their families during holidays, for they always came back.

A similar psychology operates in a different form of slavery, one that involves domestic servants that African and Asian diplomats and business executives have brought with them to Europe and North America. As an employee of the Committee against Modern Slavery, Cristina Talens worked for several years to free and rehabilitate domestic slaves who had been brought to Paris. She told me that liberating the body was much easier than freeing the mind:

In spite of the violence, and the living and working conditions, people in slavery have their own mental integrity and their own mechanisms for surviving. Some may actually like different aspects of their life, perhaps the security or their understanding of the order of things. When you disrupt this order, suddenly everything is confused. Some of the women who were freed have attempted suicide. It is easy to assume that this happened because of the abuse they had lived through. But for some of these women, slavery had been the major psychological building block in their lives. When that was destroyed, the meaning of their life was like a bit of paper crushed up and thrown away. They were told: "No, this is not the way it is supposed to be. Start all over again." It was as though their life had no meaning.

PLAUSIBLE DENIABILITY

The psychology of the slave is mirrored by that of the slaveholder. Slavery is not a simple matter of one person holding another by force; it is an insidious mutual dependence that is remarkably difficult for slaveholder as well as slave to break out of. Branding the slaveholder as pure evil may in some way comfort us, but maintaining that definition becomes difficult when one meets actual slave masters.

Almost all the slaveholders I have met and interviewed in Pakistan, India, Brazil, and Mauritania were family men who thought of themselves simply as businessmen. Pillars of the local community, they were well rewarded financially, well integrated socially, and well connected legally and politically. Their slaveholding was not seen as a social handicap except, possibly, by

"outsiders" who, they felt, misunderstood the local customs of business and labor.

How is it that such nice men do such bad things? A government official in Baldev's district who held bonded workers was frank about his slaveholding:

Of course I have bonded laborers: I'm a landlord. I keep them and their families, and they work for me. When they aren't in the fields, I have them doing the household work washing clothes, cooking, cleaning, making repairs, everything. After all, they are from the Kohl caste; that's what they do, work for Vaisyas like me. I give them food and a little land to work. They've also borrowed money, so I have to make sure that they stay on my land till it is paid back. They will work on my farm till it is all paid back. I don't care how old they get; you can't just give money away!

After all, there is nothing wrong in keeping bonded labor. They benefit from the system, and so do I. Even if agriculture is completely mechanized, I'll still keep my bonded laborers. You see, the way we do it, I am like a father to these workers. It is a father-son relationship; I protect them and guide them. Of course, sometimes I have to discipline them as well, just as a father would.

Other slaveholders also have told me that their slaves are like their children, that they need close control and care. They make the argument of tradition: because the practice has been going on for so long, it must be the natural order of things. For others, it is a simple question of priorities: they say that enslaving people is unfortunate but that their own family's welfare depends on it. Often slaveholders have interposed many layers of management between themselves and the slaves. They purposely deny themselves the knowledge of what they are doing and thus the responsibility for it.

FORTY ACRES AND A MULE

All this points to the need for a highly developed system of rehabilitation for freed slaves and slaveholders alike. Physical freedom is not enough. When slaves were emancipated in the

U.S. in 1865, the government enacted no such rehabilitation. General William Tecumseh Sherman's promise to give each former slave "forty acres and a mule" never materialized. The result was four million people dumped into a shattered economy without resources and with few legal protections. It can be argued that America is still suffering from this liberation without rehabilitation.

Human-rights worker Vivek Pandit of the Vidhayak Sansad organization in India has been liberating bonded laborers for more than 20 years. He is adamant that real liberation takes place in the mind, that physical freedom isn't enough—as was the case with Baldev. Conversely, mental freedom can bring about physical freedom—as it did for Meera.

Pandit's organization has devised a program of education that prepares former bonded laborers for a life of freedom. They are taught basic science to promote their curiosity and attention to detail; role-playing to stimulate problem solving; and games to develop strategic thinking and teamwork. This training comes after a challenging public dialogue in which the laborer recounts and renounces his or her bondage. The renunciation is recorded and read out in the village. "When the ex-slave has fixed his thumbprint to this public document," Pandit says, "they can't go back."

Several models of liberation and rehabilitation are currently being field-tested. The experience of these programs suggests that a combination of economic support, counseling and education can lead to stable, sustainable freedom. This kind of work is still in its early stages, though. No systematic evaluations of these programs have been carried out. No social scientist has explored a master–slave relationship in depth.

Slave economics are another puzzle. How can would-be liberators crack the dark economy and trace the slave-made products to our homes? Why are such large numbers of people being trafficked across continents, how many of these people really are enslaved, and why are these flows apparently increasing? What is the impact of this workforce on national economies? What are the links among the traffic in people, drugs and guns?

Studying bondage can be socially and politically controversial. Researchers in the field face numerous ethical dilemmas, and clarity and objectivity are all the more difficult to achieve when individuals and governments seek to conceal what they are doing. If there is good news, it is the growing recognition of the problem. The plight of enslaved child workers has drawn significantly increased funding, and new partnerships between antislavery organizations and industries that use slave-made commodities provide an innovative model for abolition. But if our figures are correct, only a small fraction of slaves are reached and freed every year. Our ignorance of their hidden world is vast.

Kevin Bales is a professor of sociology at the University of Surrey Roehampton in London. He is a trustee of Anti-Slavery International and a consultant to the United Nations Global Program on Trafficking of Human Beings, to the Economic Community of West African States, and to the U.S., British, Irish, Norwegian and Nepali governments. Bales began studying slavery in the early 1990s, when few Westerners realized it still existed. Unable to secure funding for his research, he took on a commercial research project and devoted the profits to travel. The outcome—his book Disposable People—*was nominated for the Pulitzer Prize in 2000. His work won the Premio Viareggio for services to humanity in 2000, and a television documentary based on it (shown on HBO and on Britain's Channel 4) won a Peabody Award in 2000.*

More to Explore

The Small Hands of Slavery: Bonded Child Labor in India. Human Rights Watch, 1996. Available at hrw.org/reports/1996/India3.htm

Crime and Servitude: An Exposé of the Traffic in Women for Prostitution from the Newly Independent States. Gillian Caldwell, Steven Galster and Nadia Steinzor. Global Survival Network, November 1997. Available at www.globalsurvival.net/femaletrade/9711russia.html

Disposable People: New Slavery in the Global Economy. Kevin Bales. University of California Press, 1999.

International Trafficking in Women to the United States: A Contemporary Manifestation of Slavery and Organized Crime. Amy O'Neill Richard. Center for the Study of Intelligence, Central Intelligence Agency, November 1999. Available at usinfo.state.gov/topical/global/traffic/report/homepage.htm

Sex Slaves: The Trafficking of Women in Asia. Louise Brown. Virago, 2000.

Ending Slavery: Hierarchy, Dependency and Gender in Central Mauritania. Urs Peter Ruf. Transcript Verlag, 2001.

Global Human Smuggling: Comparative Perspectives. Edited by David Kyle and Rey Koslowski. Johns Hopkins University Press, 2001.

Antislavery Web sites: www.freetheslaves.net, www.antislavery.org

CRITICAL THINKING QUESTIONS

1. What is "debt bondage," and how can it be considered a form of slavery?
2. How widespread is debt bondage and other forms of slavery in the modern world?
3. Why should such practices be defined as slavery rather than an extreme form of economic exploitation?
4. How can the psychological states of both slaves and slaveholders be seen as states of mutual interdependence?
5. What sorts of programs does the article suggest are necessary for both slaves and slaveholders to be rehabilitated after the elimination of slavery?
6. Based on information in the article, in which two areas of the world is slavery, as defined, most prevalent? Why do you think these areas are more prone to this institution than other areas of the world?

Putting Anthropology to Work to Preserve Appalachian Heritage

Mary B. La Lone

> Now it was a hard life, but it was a way of life. If we had a problem in the coal days, it was everybody's problem.
>
> Oakley Lilly in Mary La Lone, *Appalachian Coal Mining Memories*, 1997.

Former coal miner Oakley Lilly is describing a way of life, now long past in his area of Appalachian Virginia—a life of hard work, strong family survival strategies, and channels of community reciprocity that helped mining families make it through hard times. Coal mining was the main economy throughout much of the Appalachian Mountains. Men worked underground, blasting the coal out with dynamite and hauling it to the surface in coal cars, first using mule-power and later with electrical hoists. At home, wives and children worked equally hard, gardening, raising animals, and developing ingenious contributions to the household economy.

While modern forms of coal mining continue in many areas of contemporary Appalachia, other areas such as the New River Valley in Virginia have seen mining cease as a way of life. In the New River Valley, mining went into decline between the 1930s and 1950s, and the last of the small "truck" mines had closed by the early 1970s. As time passes, former miners and their families grow older and the potential increases for losing the first-hand knowledge of the mining way of life in this area. The New River Valley is rapidly being transformed as new highway systems, housing subdivisions, and mega-shopping centers cover the landscape where mines and mining communities once flourished. Few physical traces of the mines and mining communities now remain to remind today's younger population of their cultural heritage. But a series of cultural heritage partnerships joining anthropologists, a grassroots community group, and local government have rescued this area's nearly-forgotten knowledge of mining heritage and are putting it to use for community education and planning.

This article describes university-community-regional efforts to preserve the mining heritage in this part of Appalachia. In a series of heritage preservation projects over the past five years, Radford University undergraduate students have had an opportunity to apply their anthropology, working with the community in an effort to reclaim the past in ways that will help it live on. The "New River Valley Coal Mining Heritage Project" enabled students in my Economic Anthropology and Practicum classes to assist the region by documenting elders' memories of the coal mining past in book form through an oral history project that ran from 1995 to 1998. The second project, the "Coal Mining Heritage Park Project," has enabled students in my Applied Anthropology and Practicum classes, and follow-up internships, to put the knowledge to work to design and develop plans for a Coal Mining Heritage Park that will commemorate the mining heritage as a community focal point on the landscape.

ORAL HISTORY RESCUE WORK

Knowledge of the New River Valley's mining heritage was in danger of fading away in 1994. Then, stirred into action by a series of investigative newspaper articles by reporter Robert Freis in the *Roanoke Times,* a group of former miners and their families banded together to form a grassroots heritage group known as the Coal Mining

Source: Reprinted from *Practicing Anthropology,* Spring 2001.

Heritage Association of Montgomery County (Virginia). With heartfelt efforts and pooled resources, the group built a memorial monument to miners who had lost their lives in the region's mines and established an annual Coal Miner's Day memorial celebration.

As an anthropologist at Radford University, in the New River Valley, I witnessed the group's activities and recognized the need to lend anthropological assistance in the form of an oral history project designed to document and preserve knowledge of the mining heritage. Few written records have survived to document the area's mining. The bulk of knowledge about mining life existed in the minds of aging members of the mining families who, ranging in age from their late 50s up, were beginning to pass away without their memories being recorded. I also recognized the potentials that a collaborative university-community project would offer as an experiential training ground for anthropology students. I believe strongly in experiential education and try to develop hands-on training experiences for many of my classes. This project provided students with an experiential component to their Economic Anthropology classes, enabling them to practice the skills of anthropological interviewing and learn from Appalachian natives about mining household economic strategies, while making contributions to a systematic documentation project of great value to regional heritage preservation.

The university-community partnership became the foundation of the "New River Valley Coal Mining Heritage Project." The project started with modest intentions as a semester-long class project for my Fall 1995 Economic Anthropology class. Mining Association members Jimmie Price and Robert Freis worked with me to develop the structure of the first class project, a structure that we later repeated in successive classes. We started the semester with a series of orientation sessions designed both to familiarize the students with the region's mining history and to build rapport between the academic research team and the members of the mining association. To overcome any town-gown anxieties, we designed the orientation period to include numerous face-to-face opportunities for the local residents to get to know the students

before we began the interviewing (such as mine site tours and pot-luck orientation dinners). The orientation period was followed by interviewing, transcription, and analysis on mining household strategies. The mining association helped make initial contacts for the interviews, while the academic research team was responsible for conducting and taping the interviews, then transcribing tapes and doing content analysis as class activities. My role, as project director and professor, was to design the project scope and interview questions, teach the methodology and link it to the economic anthropology literature, guide the interviewing and transcription processes, and edit and compile the research team's final work into book format.

Although originally designed as a single-semester project, it developed into a three-year endeavor, involving three successive class research teams, and resulting in two volumes of oral histories. The Radford University Foundation provided funding and the Coal Mining Heritage Association (CMHA) gave valuable in-kind support for the research efforts. The urgency of collecting the interviews in this heritage preservation effort was the clear motivation to mining association members and students alike. As the first set of interview transcripts emerged, I recognized the quality of the data and felt it was far too important to end up in an archive where few people would view it. At this point, for me, the project took on a serious applied focus. I wanted to find a way that the interviews could be made readily available for use in Appalachian heritage education, so I approached a regional publisher about the possibilities of compiling a book of mining oral histories. Pocahontas Press joined the heritage preservation efforts, launching the project into an unexpected and exciting new dimension. A second team of students worked with me in 1996 to collect additional interviews and expand the ethnographic analysis. In 1997, we published *Appalachian Coal Mining Memories,* a collection of oral history interviews that documents mining life in the voices of the Appalachian people, along with the academics' ethnographic description of mining life. Even as this first volume was coming out, we realized that many elderly miners still needed interviewing, so another class research team took up the challenge. We continued the interviewing process in 1998 and produced a sequal volume of oral histories entitled *Coal Mining Lives*.

The two volumes of oral histories together contain sixty-one interviews in which forty-three men and thirty women describe their lives as coal miners, miners' wives, and miners' children. They describe the labor and dangers of mining underground, and also portray the pride that miners developed in their work. They tell about the contributions of wives and children, and the livelihood strategies in which family members engaged in a wide variety of additional activities to supplement the mining income. They tell about the role of kin, community, and religion in providing social support and economic safety nets for families that fell on hard times.

Anthropology was put to work in a three-year oral history project that documented these first-hand memories at a critical time, before the elders with this knowledge passed away. In an applied effort, the project produced the interviews in book format so the data can be passed to future generations, educating them about the Appalachian mining heritage. It also taught students about the reciprocal relations involved in fieldwork projects, as reflected in this quote from student Alicia Gallant: "The residents of the community gave their time and stories to us, and we, in turn, are giving back to them, by preserving their cultural heritage. It really struck me to see the effect our work is having on the people of the community."

HERITAGE PARK PLANNING

The oral history project, by itself, represents a remarkable collaborative effort between the academics and community to rescue cultural heritage data. It also laid the groundwork for a second project that takes heritage preservation to an even greater level of commitment, the establishment of a mining cultural heritage park. The first project set the stage for the second by 1) creating a renaissance of interest in the mining heritage in the schools, the community, and at the county government level; 2) generating a body of oral history data that could be used in developing signage and other forms of heritage park education; and 3) establishing strong rapport between the anthropologist and community that served as the foundation for spinning the first project into a second, applied anthropology project.

Mining was in decline in this part of Appalachia by the 1950s and ceased altogether in the early 1970s. Now, only the foundations of industrial buildings and houses mark the sites of once-active mines. This is the landscape seen today at the former Merrimac Mine, a mine made famous because its coal was used to power the ironclad Merrimac in its Civil War sea battle against the Monitor. In the 1990s, a rails-to-trails project turned the old Huckleberry Railroad line that ran through the Merrimac Mine site into a modern recreational trail named the Huckleberry Trail. As hikers and bikers pass along the Huckleberry Trail, all they can see are brambles and weeds covering the foundations of the large structure known as the tipple, where coal was once sorted into different sizes and dumped down into railroad cars waiting below.

As an anthropologist actively involved in retrieving the mining heritage, I felt it such a shame that trail users passing through Merrimac had no clue that a coal mine once operated there. They could not know of the site's history or the extent of the mining operation, which included an industrial complex, company-run store and hotel, and housing for the mining families. They were unaware of the site's cultural significance and of the lifestyle of mining families that lived in a dynamic mining community on the nearby hillside known as Bunker Hill. With the oral history project winding to a close, I turned my attention toward solving this problem at Merrimac by making it the focus of a class project for my Fall 1999 Applied Anthropology class.

The Merrimac project presented an excellent opportunity for me to put my background in museum studies, and my interests in living history museums and heritage tourism, to work to guide students in developing possibilities and plans for a coal mining heritage park. In spring 1999, I began laying the groundwork for the "Coal Mining Heritage Park Project" by establishing the university-community-regional partnership that would be the project's foundation. I am a strong advocate for taking a "partnership approach" toward work in the community, establishing mutually-beneficial relationships between regional groups and myself as the foundation for the experiential teaching projects used in my classes. The community partners share in designing the project orientation sessions, participate as teachers to instruct and guide the student research team, and see concrete results in the form of some tangible product which the class produces to aid the community group's efforts (such as a volume of oral histories or a consulting report).

In this case, the university–community rapport had already been established through the oral history collaboration. I approached Mining Association members Robert Freis and Fred Lawson with the project idea. They, in turn, helped extend the partnership to the county government by setting up a meeting for me with the director of county planning, Joe Powers. When the Huckleberry Trail was under construction, Montgomery County had purchased the property containing the Merrimac Mine site with the idea that it might be developed someday for recreational use. The property encompasses a little more than thirty acres lying on both sides of the trail. After some initial explanation about what applied anthropology is, and what it could offer (compared to the more familiar work of architects or engineers), the county planning office joined wholeheartedly in the partnership to support the class project. I then extended it into a four-way partnership by enlisting the support and assistance of the state archaeologist in the Roanoke Regional Preservation Office, Tom Klatka. In April 1999, we all met at Merrimac to walk the site and make plans for the Fall 1999 Applied Anthropology class. As the project got under way, the Radford University Foundation, the Montgomery County Planning Office, the CMHA, and the Merrimac church contributed funding and numerous support services to enhance the teaching/research activities (ranging from assistance with map-making to providing refreshments for community planning meetings).

The class assumed the role of an applied anthropology consulting firm and was charged with tackling a real-life assignment. Our team's challenge was to design a place/space for the community that would be used both for community recreation and cultural heritage education. The county planning office set the scope,

informing us that the focus should be on designing a park directed toward regional uses and needs. As one planner told me, we needed to "avoid using the 'T' word" in our final report, meaning that the county was primarily interested in serving the region rather than creating a park to attract tourists from outside. Contemplating a proposal for its first heritage park was a big step for the county since its previous parks were primarily recreation-based. To convince the county to take the leap from baseball fields to creating a heritage-based park became the motivation for the research team, inspiring us to complete the research and writing of a comprehensive consulting report within the course of a fifteen-week semester.

The project started with a series of orientation sessions for the research team. This included class visits and tours of the Merrimac Mine site in which former Merrimac miners, county planners, and the State Archaeologist oriented the research team to the layout and history of the site and the planning considerations. Next, we followed with a research stage that started with a visit to a heritage park located in our region of Virginia, Explore Park in Roanoke. This provided the team with visual examples of park layout and facilities, and the ways that signage, outdoor exhibits, and reconstructed buildings can be used for historic interpretation. Rich Loveland, curator of interpretive history, guided our tour and instructed the team on issues that need to be considered when planning heritage parks. Back in the classroom, reading assignments included the mining oral histories along with literature on heritage preservation and tourism, park planning and, of course, methodology and models from applied anthropology.

The community-oriented approach of applied anthropology guided our research methodology. For the park to be used and embraced by the community, it is critical that community members and potential park users have an active role in voicing ideas, desires, concerns, and solutions for park development. I directed the team's efforts to plan and design the park "for" and "with" the community, providing multiple opportunities for community input and involvement in the planning process. As part of the research, we developed a survey that was mailed to residents in the area, asking what types of activities and amenities they would like to see at the park. We also organized two community meetings, held at the Merrimac community center, for the purpose of gaining people's input and participation in developing the park plans. Mining families and community residents told us what they wanted to see in the park, and brainstormed ideas with the research team for heritage exhibits, nature education, and park facilities.

I was surprised, and pleased, at the degree to which the project became a magnet for community participation. In addition to mining association members, school teachers, senior citizen groups, railroad buffs, residents living near the proposed park, and a wide variety of Huckleberry Trail user groups became involved in the community meetings and offered further input, serving as "resource people" who worked with the research team. We soon realized that we were truly acting in the applied anthropology role of "liaisons" between the community and the county government. The actions of the anthropological research team brought community members and county planners together at the public meetings to collaboratively discuss ideas for the park. People wanted the park to focus on two educational themes, mining heritage education and environmental education. They also wanted the park to include a community recreation area, a place where families could picnic, hold reunions, and come together on summer evenings to enjoy music and storytelling. The ideas and concerns expressed to us by mining families and community participants were incorporated into our planning.

In addition, our focus on cultural heritage preservation strongly influenced the way we approached park planning. A central concern in developing the park design was in preserving the site's archaeological integrity. Many of the clues that document Merrimac's past lie on or just below the surface of the land. Our team's goal was to design the park so that today's citizens can enjoy the space and learn about the history, without development that unnecessarily disturbs the archaeological integrity. Our recommendations for the location of trails and park structures are designed to use previous road beds and sections of the property where mine cleanup operations

have already disturbed the land, rather than areas where the archaeological record needs preserving. We worked to strike a good balance between public use and protection of the site.

As the final step, we prepared a 136-page consulting report, *Coal Mining Heritage Park: Study, Plans, and Recommendations.* The first part of the report presents our overall design for the park and our recommendations on how to phase-in the park's development. The report then goes into greater detail on specific aspects of the park plan. One chapter presents recommendations for mining heritage education through signage, a self-guided walking tour around the mine site, outdoor interpretive exhibits, a replicated miner's house, a mining museum and visitors center, and heritage-based educational activities such as archaeology schools for community participants to foster public awareness of site and heritage preservation. Another chapter develops ideas for community recreation and a system of low-impact trails within the park. It details a plan for a community recreation area on one side of the park that will include picnic shelters, a playground constructed with a mining theme, and an open-air pavilion for staging community events. A third chapter discusses facilities and conveniences that will make the park user-friendly, including restrooms, drinking fountains, trail benches, parking, security, and accessibility for disabled and elderly visitors. A fourth chapter inventories the park's microenvironments and develops ideas for nature-based signage and education, including a recommendation for a nature education center housed along the Huckleberry Railroad line in an old railroad caboose.

This project, like the oral history project before it, evolved from a single semester project into a succession of teaching/research activities. Some students went on the following semester to take a Practicum in Anthropology class, jointly taught by county planner Meghan Dorsett and myself. In that class, anthropology students worked closely with the county planning office to develop selected aspects of the park plan to greater heights, and they learned grant-writing skills by actually writing a number of grants to fund those parts of the park. Three students, Melissa Lamb, Daliah Macon, and Matthew

Schrag, then continued their involvement through internships in the county planning and regional preservation offices.

Impressed by the plan and recommendations presented in our consulting report, Montgomery County decided to create the Coal Mining Heritage Park at Merrimac. The park that began as an idea in spring 1999 became a reality a year and a half later, with its dedication ceremony held on September 9, 2000. Plans now move forward for development of the trails, community recreation area, heritage signage, nature education, and mining museum, and to involve future Applied Anthropology classes in stages of the actual park development.

CONCLUSION

Throughout the oral history and anthro-planning projects carried out over a five-year period, anthropological skills and knowledge were put to work to help an Appalachian area reclaim and preserve its coal mining heritage. Academics joined forces with the community and the regional government to form collaborative partnerships, which provided experiential training for anthropology students while making tangible contributions to regional heritage preservation.

Anthropology classes provided the structure for research team efforts that enabled large amounts of data collection and investigative work to take place in a relatively short period of time—critical because of the urgency involved in recording the oral histories and then developing plans for a regional heritage park. It is doubtful that any one group—the researchers, the community, or the regional government—would have successfully carried out these projects acting alone; the collaborations gave the projects great momentum and ensured their success. Because of these efforts, knowledge of the coal mining way of life, once in danger of disappearing in this rapidly changing area, will be available so that future generations can study and contemplate its contributions to Appalachian cultural history.

Mary La Lone is a professor of anthropology at Radford University in Virginia. She received her Ph.D. from UCLA in 1985. Her research and teaching specialities are in historical, economic, and applied anthropology. Her work on the Appalachian projects described here includes Appalachian Coal Mining Memories (1997, Pocahontas Press), Coal Mining Lives (1998), and Coal Mining Heritage Park: Study Plan, and Recommendations (2000). Descriptions of her other teaching/research projects are available on her web site <http://radford.edu~mlalone/> http://radford.edu~mlalone. Dr. La Lone may be contacted at Radford University, Department of Sociology and Anthropology, Box 6948, Radford, VA 24142; (540)831-5397; e-mail: <mlalone@radford.edu>.

CRITICAL THINKING QUESTIONS

1. What values formed the core of Appalachian coal mining life?
2. What benefits did the Appalachian Coal Mining Project have for both the local community and the anthropology students who participated in the project?
3. How did the oral history projects lay the groundwork for the creation of a mining cultural heritage park?
4. How did the heritage park project become a magnet for community involvement?
5. A thought question: The Appalachian coal miners represent a vanished way of life. Why should we, in the modern world, care about understanding and preserving knowledge about this lifestyle?

Community-Based Archaeology in Central New York: Workshops Involving Native American Youth

Jordan E. Kerber

Beginning in 1995, Colgate University has offered seven two-week summer workshops in archaeology to members of the Oneida (Iroquois) Indian Nation of New York Youth Work/Learn Program. These workshops, directed by Jordan Kerber and funded by the Oneida Indian Nation, Colgate University, and the John Ben Snow Foundation, have provided more than one hundred Oneida teenagers with hands-on experiences in the limited excavation and laboratory processing of prehistoric and historic Native American remains in central New York State. This article also discusses the various challenges and benefits of involving a Native American descendant community in archaeological research.

Over the past several years, archaeologists and Native Americans have increasingly worked together in the common pursuit of learning about the past.[1] Many, if not most, of these cooperative opportunities have come in the wake of federal legislation, such as the National Historic Preservation Act of 1966 (and its most recent amendment) and the Native American Graves Protection and Repatriation Act of 1990, which requires consultation with Native American groups in specific circumstances. Other collaborative ventures between archaeologists and Native Americans are not mandated by law. This article discusses one such voluntary program of community-based archaeology involving Native American youth of central New York state.

Beginning in 1995, Colgate University, located in Hamilton, New York, has offered annually a two-week summary workshop in archaeology to members of the Oneida (Iroquois) India Nation of New York. These workshops, which total seven so far, have been directed by the author with assistance from numerous Colgate students and recent alumni, as well as other individuals. The workshops have provided more than 100 Iroquois teenagers with direct archaeological and laboratory experience in learning about their ancestors and other Native Americans who once occupied the region.

The goals of the workshop are threefold: (1) to strengthen the relationship between Colgate University and neighboring Native American groups by bringing together members of both communities in important educational opportunities, (2) to provide a hands-on experience in archaeology for Native American youth that involves the limited excavation and laboratory processing of prehistoric and historic Native American remains in central New York; and (3) to identify, manage, and protect significant archaeological resources located in the region.

I chose the Oneida Indian Nation as the target group for this workshop because it is geographically the closest Native American community to the university's campus. The initial design of the workshop was discussed in 1994 with a few members and employees of the Oneida Indian Nation with whom I had previously developed an informal relationship. After receiving a favorable response, it was suggested that members that members of the Nation's existing Youth Work/Learn Program be the sole participants in the workshop if funding were obtained.

Source: "Community Based Archaeology in Central New York: Workshops Involving Native American Youth" by Jordan E. Kerber from *The Public Historian*, Vol. 25, No. 1 (Winter 2003), pp. 83-90. Copyright © 2003 The Regents of the University of California and the National Council on Public History. Reprinted by permission.

The Youth Work/Learn Program employs Oneida Nation teens in a variety of activities over the summer months.

Teenagers were deliberately selected as the audience for the workshops, since there is a growing concern today among many Native American communities that the young are "losing touch" with their heritage. It was hoped (perhaps naively or romantically, in retrospect) that finding objects used in the daily lives of their ancestors, especially on tribal land, would help to "connect" the youth to their historic roots. For some participants, this may not be the case. But for several, I believe the workshops functioned this way, even though the students appeared to be teenagers first and Native Americans second, listening to rap music and wearing the latest style clothing during the excavation. Many may not realize the positive effect of the program for years to come.

Each workshop was organized in two five-day sessions during July and August. In some workshops, the same group participated in both sessions: other workshops involved two separate groups per session. The number of teenage participants in a session ranged between five and fifteen. The focus of each workshop was on the limited archaeological excavation of one or two sites and the laboratory processing of the recovered remains. The logistics consisted of an orientation on the first day of a session, followed by three days of archaeological fieldwork (weather permitting). The session concluded with a day of laboratory work (i.e., cleaning artifacts) at Colgate University and group discussion of the findings and their significance. For each workshop, two or three individuals with previous archaeological experience assisted me in the field and lab. Most of these assistants were Colgate undergraduates or recent alumni, some of whom have gone on to graduate school in anthropology and employment in contract archaeology.

In the orientation session, participants were introduced to key concepts in archaeology. Like the general public, most of the students have had no previous experience in the field and think that archaeology involves the study of dinosaurs. In order to familiarize the participants with the various types of artifacts that they may find in the excavation, actual archaeological remains were used in the orientation. Also in the orientation, I made it clear that we would not intentionally or knowingly excavate human burials or human skeletal remains. If any were to be accidentally discovered during our fieldwork, the excavation would stop and I would contact the Oneida Indian Nation for direction. This arrangement has been critical, and is specified in each workshop proposal submitted to the Oneida Indian Nation's Men's Council and Clan Mothers. I believe it has allowed me the opportunity to offer this program to the Oneida in the first place, which in turn has created a solid foundation of mutual trust and respect. Often relations between archeologists and Native Americans are strained, largely due to the excavation and analysis of Native American skeletal remains.[2] As for any human skeletal remains accidentally discovered in the workshops, only isolated teeth and a few disarticulated bones from nonburial contexts were found at two sites. In both situations, excavation of the sample units containing the human skeletal material was stopped, as instructed by the Oneida, but the dig continued elsewhere at the two sites.

For the first three summers, 1995–1997, the workshops were funded by the John Ben Snow Foundation and Colgate University. We focused on three prehistoric sites at which I had been conducting archaeological research with Colgate students in field methods classes. These sites, located in vicinity of the campus on private property (not Oneida territory), dated to between about 4,000 and 1,000 years ago and consisted primarily of stone tools and chipping debris. The artifacts recovered and cleaned by the participants of these three workshops were kept in the archaeology laboratory at the university. This was done so that Colgate students in my field methods classes in the semester following each workshop could catalog, analyze, interpret, and report on these remains, as the excavation by the class continued the work of the previous workshop. After the funding ended in 1997, I planned to continue this program due to its success. In 1998, I submitted a proposal to the Oneida Indian Nation Men's Council and Clan Mothers requesting Nation funding of the 1998 summer workshop on Nation territory. Further, I specified that all recovered artifacts from Nation territory would be curated at the Oneida's Shako:wi Cultural Center following their cataloging, analysis, and reporting at Colgate. Some of the objects have also been subsequently displayed at this cultural center. I decided to change the location of the workshop to sites on Nation territory (as close as 15 miles north of Colgate) not because the sites around Colgate that we had excavated were unimportant or unproductive, but rather that known sites on Nation territory were more recent. Many of these sites date to between the seventeenth and eighteenth centuries and were settled by Oneida people, indeed the direct ancestors of the workshop participants. I thought that finding artifacts from these Oneida sites would provide the spark to ignite the interest and curiosity of Oneida teens in their heritage. Apparently it worked for one workshop participant, who commented, "It was interesting to learn about what archaeologists do, but the best thing was holding the materials used by my ancestors. I learned more about my culture and our past."[3] Similarly, in the words of a Youth Work/Learn Program staff member and school teacher, "You can't get a better history class than this. The kids are learning more than they'd ever learn in public school."[4]

The Oneida funded my 1998 proposal. Beginning in 1999 and continuing through 2002, they have provided most of the funding for these workshops; Colgate has contributed a portion of the funds over the past four summers. Between 1999 and 2001, the workshops have been held at the Dungey site in Stockbridge, New York. This site dates to about the 1660s–70s and was occupied by Oneida people who lived in longhouses and practiced hunting, fishing, gathering, and horticulture. Although the site has been heavily "worked" by artifact collectors and avocational archaeologists over the past fifty years or so, we have recovered more than 4,000 historic remains from more than one hundred test units. The majority of the objects are Euroamerican in origin and represent trade goods (e.g., shell and glass trade beads, clay smoking pipe fragments, cassock buttons, and metal objects). Other remains are of Native American manufacture (e.g., stone tools and chipping debris, pottery, charcoal, animal bone, and a charred maize kernel). Analysis and interpretation of the recovered cultural materials is ongoing and is not

discussed here. To date, I have co-edited four unpublished reports, completed by Colgate students in my field methods classes, of the research conducted at Oneida sites between 1998 and 2002.

From all accounts, the workshops have been a success, and their goals have been met. The mutual respect and trust among all those associated with this program at Colgate University and the Oneida Indian Nation is extremely high. As stated by a member of the Nation's Men's Council and Clan Mothers:

> Everyone has studied our people, but not with cultural sensitivity. We revere those who have gone before us. We have our oral tradition, but to be able to provide our children with an actual hands-on experience with our past, that is invaluable.[5]

Another positive sign occurred when the Oneida asked that the 2000 workshop at the Dungey site include testing an adjacent area prior to the Nation's planned removal of two small structures, in order to avoid affecting any important archaeological remains that might exist at that location.

Especially over the past few summers, there has been a considerable amount of favorable local, regional, and national media coverage by newspapers (including the *Christian Science Monitor*) and television and radio stations (including programs on the local PBS affiliate and an interview on National Public Radio). Not only has this publicity been mutually beneficial for Colgate and the Oneida, but it has helped to increase public awareness about archaeology, the Iroquois people, and the benefits of involving a Native American descendant community in archaeological work. In addition, it also has provided an opportunity for some of the Oneida youth to articulate and reflect in a rather profound way what the experience has meant to them. According to one participant:

> I see this as an opening to many other things, not just archaeology. This is an opportunity that kids shouldn't overlook. It opens the door to religion and other issues around us. People need to get involved in our culture. We have lost a lot of people. . . . This makes me think about history and what's happened right here in

Stockbridge, Munnsville, and Oneida. I think about how our people were separated when these lands were settled, and I dream about us (Oneidas) uniting again one day. When I'm out here, I can dream and think. When I find a bead, that is special to me . . . I still bead . . . when I find a bead, I feel good, and I feel a connection with my ancestors . . . and I feel hope for our future. I dream of my people coming together again.[6]

The workshop participants need not become archaeologists for this program to be successful.

Jordan Kerber received his Ph.D. in anthropology from Brown University, and is currently an associate professor of anthropology, chair of the department of Sociology and Anthropology, and curator of collections, Longyear Museum of Anthropology, at Colgate University. He has conducted extensive research at Native American sites in the northeastern United States for more than twenty years. He has been involved in numerous projects in public archaeology, most recently collaborating with the Oneida Indian Nation in central New York to offer educational workshops in archaeology.

Acknowledgments

A version of this article was presented in 2001 at the 100th annual meeting of the American Anthropological Association in Washington, D.C. I wish to thank the Oneida Indian Nation Men's Council and Clan Mothers, particularly Richard Lynch, Brian Patterson, and Dale Rood, for permitting this archaeological workshop to occur since 1995 and for providing funding since 1998. I am also grateful for the support of Randy Phillips, Director of the Youth Work/Learn Program, and Dr. Anthony Wonderley, Oneida Indian Nation Historian. I am indebted to Colgate University and the John Ben Snow Foundation for their financial support of this project. Finally, I extend heartfelt gratitude to the more than one hundred participants in the workshops over the past seven years, as well as to Dixie Henry and all the other archaeological assistants who provided invaluable help.

Notes

1. See Kurt E. Dongoske, Mark Aldenderfer, and Karen Doehner (Eds.), *Working Together: Native Americans and Archaeologists* (Washington, D.C.: Society for American Archaeology, 2000); Anthony L. Klesert and Alan S. Downer (Eds.) *Preservation on the Reservation: Native Americans, Native American Lands, and Archaeology* (Navajo Nation Papers in Anthropology No.26, Window Rock, Ariz., 1990); George P. Nicholas and Thomas D. Andrews (Eds.), *At a Crossroads: Archaeology and First Peoples in Canada* (Publication No. 24, Department of Archaeology, Simon Fraser University, Burnaby, British Columbia: Archaeology Press, 1997); and Nina Swidler, Kurt E. Dongoske, Roger Anyon, and Alan S. Downer (Eds.), *Native American and Archaeologists: Stepping Stones to Common Ground* (Walnut Creek, Calif.: AltaMira Press, 1997).
2. See Tamara L. Bray (Ed.), *The Future of the Past: Archaeologists, Native Americans, and Repatriation* (New York: Garland Publishing, 2001); and Andrew Guilford, review of *Who Owns the Past?*, produced by Independent Producers Services for the Southern Resources Center, 2000, in *The Public Historian*, 24, no. 2 (Spring 2002): 138–40.
3. Jena Malone and Stephen Hanks, "What I Did on My Summer Vacation," *Dig: The Archaeology Magazine for Kids* (December/January 1999/2000): 23.
4. Christina McCarroll, "Oneida Teens Unearth Layers of their History," *Christian Science Monitor*, 14 August 2001.
5. Michelle Cronin, "Local Archaeological Dig Continues to Unearth Artifacts," *Oneida Daily Dispatch*, 1 August 2001.
6. Ibid.

CRITICAL THINKING QUESTIONS

1. What were the goals of the Colgate University summer workshops in archaeology?
2. Why were teenagers from the Oneida Indian Nation selected as the target audience for the workshops?
3. Why did Kerber change the location of sites that he was working on to ones situated on the territory of the Oneida Indian Nation?
4. What have been the benefits of the workshops for both the youth and larger community of the Oneida Indian Nation?